Lipman Kunstadt

Diary From Hell in Transnistria 1942–1944

This publication was generously supported by
Herbert Kunstadt, the son of Lipman Kunstadt z"l.

Lipman Kunstadt

DIARY FROM HELL IN TRANSNISTRIA 1942–1944

Translated from the Yiddish by Rebecca Wolpe
Edited by Sarah Rosen and Dalia Ofer

יד ושם
YAD VASHEM
THE WORLD HOLOCAUST REMEMBRANCE CENTER

THE INTERNATIONAL INSTITUTE FOR HOLOCAUST RESEARCH

Lipman Kunstadt

Traybt men yidn ibern Dniyester
Togbuch funem Transnistrishen gehenem

Language and Production Editor: Dania Valdez

P.O.B. 3477, Jerusalem 9103401, Israel
publications.marketing@yadvashem.org.il
First published in Hebrew by Yad Vashem, 2020

ISBN 978-965-308-666-1

Typesetting: Hava Salzman
Printed in Israel by Ayalon Amit and Raffi Ltd.

CONTENTS

Foreword

Diary from Hell in Transnistria

During the three days between *Hoshayne Rabbe*, October 12, 1941, and *Simches Toyre*,[1] October 14, 1941, the Jews of Rădăuţi,[2] a city in Southern Bukovina, Romania, were shoved into cattle wagons and deported by train to Transnistria. They knew only that they were being taken to Transnistria, nothing more. The future, unknown and threatening, evoked feelings of fear and anguish. Lipman Kunstadt and ten members of his family were among the Jews deported on October 14, 1941, the third day of the deportation. The long train took them to the first transit station, Atachi.

After spending several grueling and fearful days in Atachi, the deportees, including Lipman Kunstadt and his family, crossed the Dniester River on rafts and arrived in the city of Moghilev, which had been destroyed during the German–Romanian occupation. There they encountered masses of deportees from their hometown and from other parts of

---

1 Jewish holidays and months in the diary are in Yiddish transliteration. Hoshana Rabba is the seventh day of Sukkot, and Shemini Atzeret and Simhat Torah are the eighth day in Israel, and the eighth and ninth days respectively outside of Israel.

2 The city of Rădăuţi, founded in the fifteenth century, is located in the county of Suceava in Southern Bukovina, Romania. Before the outbreak of World War II, there were approximately 5,600 Jews in the city, constituting around a third of the town's population. Zionist parties, the Bund, and Agudath Yisrael were all active in the town. In the summer of 1940, when Romania joined the war against the Soviet Union as an ally of Nazi Germany, thousands of Jews were expelled from the surrounding villages and brought to Rădăuţi. In October 1941, the 9,169 Jews living in the city's ghetto were deported to ghettos and camps in Transnistria, and the great majority of them perished. At the end of the war, and following the rise of the Communist regime in Romania, the assets of the Jews in the city were nationalized, and most of the Jews who survived the war did not return to the city.

Bessarabia and Bukovina. They were housed in dilapidated buildings under deplorable conditions in the deadly cold. Starving and exhausted, they searched for a way to escape the suffering and to find shelter.

The Kunstadt family, together with the other deportees from their city, searched frantically for an alternative destination. A few days later, with the help of Siegfried Jagendorf,[3] who was related to Kunstadt's wife, they left Moghilev for the small town of Dzhurin (Djurin),[4] traveling in a truck that had been rented from the local German headquarters. At that time,

---

3 Siegfried Jagendorf was an electro-mechanical engineer who served as head of the Moghilev Central Council (the ghetto council) for most of its existence, which was in operation from November 18, 1941, until the liberation of Transnistria by the Soviets on March 6, 1944. See Shraga Yeshurun, "Hahitargenut Ha'atzmit Shel Yehudei Bukovina Begeto Moghilev" (Hebrew) (master's thesis, Haifa University, 1979), pp. 50–51.

4 The town of Dzhurin, in the county of Moghilev, is located about 45 kilometers northeast of the city of Moghilev and around 25 kilometers south of the town of Shargorod. The houses of Dzhurin were built on the slopes of two hills, which are divided by a stream. The Jews lived on the eastern slope, which later became the ghetto. The local Ukrainians lived on the western slope, on the other side of the river. At the end of the nineteenth century, around 1,600 Jews lived in Dzhurin. According to the census conducted there in 1926, there were 1,470 Jews in the town, accounting for 24.3 percent of the general population. Before the outbreak of the war, the Jewish population in the village numbered 2,000 persons, who lived in a separate quarter on the slope of the hill, as previously noted. The Jews in Dzhurin, as in the other shtetlach/villages/small towns in Transnistria, endured difficult economic circumstances and many lived in great poverty. Most were employed in the local sugar plant, while some worked in the Jewish agricultural cooperative. There was a synagogue and a Bet Hamidrash (a combination of a synagogue where Jews prayed and place of study of the Talmud), and a small cemetery in Dzhurin. The leader of the Jewish community was Rabbi Herşel Karalnic, who was respected by the entire population. The local committee in Dzhurin took care of all matters concerning burial and kosher food, and served as a link between the Jews and the Soviet authorities. On July 22, 1941, the Germans occupied Dzhurin. Only around 1,000 Jews of the 2,000 who lived there before the war remained. These were mainly the elderly, the sick, women, and children, since all the men of recruitment age throughout Transnistria had been conscripted into the Red Army upon the outbreak of the war. In the fall of 1941, a Romanian gendarmerie headquarters was established in the village. The Jews remaining in Dzhurin were forced to wear the yellow star and their movement in the streets was restricted. The local sugar plant, which constituted the main source of income for most of the local Jews, was bombed and partially destroyed, leaving the Jews without a source of income. Testimonies indicate that prior to the occupation of Dzhurin by the German and Romanian armies, Ukrainians from the surrounding area raided the town, robbing and plundering the houses. After the occupation, the Ukrainians collaborated with the German occupiers. The Dzhurin ghetto was an open ghetto, without a wall or fence; the Jews were forbidden to leave its borders. See Theodore Lavi, ed. in chief, *Pinkas Hakehilot*: *Rumania* (Hebrew), vol. 1 (Jerusalem: Yad Vashem, 1969), p. 421.

the Jewish population of Dzhurin was comprised of Ukrainian Jews who had survived the German–Romanian offensive and of deportees from Bessarabia and Bukovina. Although Dzhurin was considered reasonably preferable to the difficulties and uncertainties that they experienced in Moghilev, the new arrivals were astonished by the reality and the difficult living conditions that they discovered there. Kunstadt and his relatives remained in Dzhurin for the remainder of the war years, returning to Romania in the summer of 1944, a few months after the Soviet army liberated the area from German–Romanian occupation.

The Kunstadt family spent more than two years in Dzhurin. For about two years—from April 1942 until May 1944—Kunstadt wrote detailed entries in his diary almost daily, relating what happened to him and his relatives, as well as to the tens of thousands of deportees sent to Transnistria during the war.

Who was Lipman Kunstadt?

Eliezer Lipman Kunstadt was born on July 22, 1901, in the city of Rădăuţi in Southern Bukovina, Romania, and died in 1978 in the U.S. His father, Yitzhak Kunstadt, who served as rabbi of Rădăuţi from 1883 until 1909, was well known for his public activism in the local Jewish community.[5]

Kunstadt senior, who was known as a Talmud scholar and a highly eloquent speaker, had a strong affinity to Zionism. Together with Dr. Natan Birnbaum,[6] he established the Zionist association Ahavat Zion in

---

5 Israel Margalit-Postilnik, *Radauts*: *Kehila Yehudit Betzemihata Uvisheki'ata* (Hebrew) (Tel Aviv: Irgun Yotzei Radauts Bukovina Be'Yisrael, 1990), p. 36. For further discussion of the Jewish communal organization and the religious leadership in Rădăuţi, see ibid., pp. 28–46.

6 Nathan Birnbaum (1864–1937), a Jewish thinker, was initially a Zionist who then became a Yiddishist and eventually returned to religious life and was elected to serve as the secretary of the Orthodox Jewish political party Agudath Yisrael. Birnbaum formalized the terms Zionism and *Ostjuden* (Eastern Jews). The phrase "Eastern European Jews" or "Jews of the East" (from the German *Ostjuden*) was established during the nineteenth century in the German Empire and in the western provinces of the Austro–Hungarian Empire with the aim of distinguishing the integrated Jews in Central Europe from those in the East.

Romania, which he headed for a decade. His son, Lipman Kunstadt, was an educated man and a journalist by profession. From 1921 until 1941, he served as the general secretary of the Jewish community in Rădăuţi. He translated books from nine languages and published newspaper articles in German and Romanian about current affairs and topics related to Jewish culture,[7] as well as feuilletons. He married Roza Merling in 1927, and their daughter Iza was born in 1928, followed three years later by their son, Herbert (Bertl). Roza, who was from Rădăuţi, was born into a wealthy family who had very close ties with members of Kunstadt's extended family.

Kunstadt maintained a traditionally observant home. He attended synagogue on the Sabbath and on holidays, and observed the rules of kashrut and religious customs in his home. In addition to receiving a Jewish education, his children received a general education until they were forced to leave the public school in 1940. Kunstadt was well versed in traditional and modern Jewish literature, and was fluent in Hebrew and Yiddish, but he and his family spoke German at home. Kunstadt, who was active in the Zionist movement, as previously indicated, considered realizing his dream of living in *Eretz Israel.* His sister, Rivka, made aliya in the mid-1930s, but she found life too difficult there and returned to Romania about a year before the outbreak of World War II. Kunstadt was well respected in the Jewish community and was praised for the assistance that he provided to the refugees from Bessarabia, who arrived in Rădăuţi following the onset of the Russian occupation and the outbreak of the war between Germany and the Soviet Union.

Kunstadt, who was forty years old when he was deported to Transnistria, arrived in the Dzhurin ghetto on October 29, 1941. Due to his connections with Siegfried Jagendorf, who was very influential in Moghilev, where he played various roles in the ghetto, Kunstadt was appointed secretary of the Jewish Council. For two years, Kunstadt documented his life and the lives of his family members in a diary, which he wrote in Yiddish, interspersed with quotes from Jewish sources.

---

7 Lipman Kunstadt wrote for a Romanian newspaper, *Timpul* (The Time), and a German language paper, *Allgemeine Zeitung* (General News). Both newspapers were for the Jewish public.

The manuscript comprises five notebooks of 100 densely-written pages each. Following liberation, Kunstadt returned to Romania. He managed to take the diary with him and to preserve it in his home for many years. Kunstadt reread the diary from time to time, and he even edited the text and added information, usually making sure to mark the additions by inserting, "Added later," "Added in 1943," and even "Added in 1948," after he returned to Romania. He also added some comments and further information when he reread his diary later in Israel.

Kunstadt remained in Romania after the liberation and made aliya in 1960 with his family—his wife, his daughter, Iza and her husband, and their children. Before leaving for Israel, Kunstadt entrusted his diary to an acquaintance, fearing that it would be taken from him during the customs inspection that those leaving Romania were forced to undergo. In 1967, his son, Herbert, who had immigrated to the U.S. in 1961, visited Romania as an American citizen. Herbert approached the friend to whom his father had entrusted the diary and asked for the diary, intending to return it to his father. He requested the assistance of the Israeli Embassy to take the diary out of Romania, but his request was refused. Herbert therefore decided to risk smuggling the diary out of the country himself and was successful. On his way back to the U.S., Herbert visited his family in Israel, carrying the diary in his bag. Thus, in 1967, the original manuscript was returned to its author, Lipman Kunstadt, who was then living in Akko (Acre) with his daughter.

Following the death of his wife, Kunstadt joined his son in the U.S., taking the diary with him. His son relates that his father was eager to publish the diary and approached YIVO in this regard. Seeking to submit to YIVO a well-ordered manuscript, Kunstadt made a handwritten copy of the entire diary. It is not known whether he gave YIVO both manuscripts, the original written in Dzhurin and the copy, or only one of them. However, sadly, there is no copy of the manuscript in the YIVO archives.[8]

According to his son, the staff at YIVO decided not to publish the manuscript. Kunstadt's sister, Rivka, who was visiting the U.S. at the time, took the diary with her when she returned to Israel, promising to

8 Herbert Kunstadt interview by Dalia Ofer, November 7, 2016, New York.

make sure it that it would be published. Rivka kept her word: upon her return to Israel, she saw to it that a typewritten copy of the manuscript was produced and that 300 bound copies were printed and self-published, without any indication of the year of publication. Kunstadt was able to read the printed text before he died in 1978.

The fate of the original manuscript that was written in Transnistria and of the copy that Kunstadt handwrote in America remains unknown. Herbert Kunstadt and the editors of this publication sought to find the original manuscript in YIVO but without success. Kunstadt's granddaughter in Nahariya is not in possession of it and, likewise, there is no copy of the original manuscript in the Yad Vashem Archive. It seems that after the death of Rivka, Kunstadt's sister's family members disposed of the contents of her home, and the manuscript, which had already been printed and distributed, was thrown out inadvertently. However, bound, typewritten copies of the diary are preserved in various archives and libraries in Israel, as well as in the Yad Vashem Archive. This copy, which appears to have been the last version written by Kunstadt, is the source of this English translation.

As previously noted, Kunstadt himself reread the diary, editing it and adding comments. He noted on April 4, 1944, after liberation by the Soviets and before his return to Romania: "Since idleness enervates my soul, I have begun to draft a German–Russian dictionary, [writing] from time to time...Apart from this, I am reviewing my memories, erasing and writing about things that I have not mentioned."[9] It seems that he had intentionally left out the recollections, which he later added, because he feared that that the diary would fall into the hands of the Romanian authorities, or the heads of the Jewish Council in Dzhurin, which could have endangered him and his family.[10] Kunstadt usually noted, "Added in the year..." wherever he added additional text later; for example, he added an entire paragraph to the entry of May 30, 1942, describing the fate of his friend the hazan

9 The ellipses in the quotes in this Foreword indicate the omission of words by the editors, while the ellipses in the diary were written by Kunstadt and appear here as they do in the typewritten copy of the manuscript in Yiddish.

10 Nevertheless, his son recalls that he read sections from the diary aloud to family members, which they enjoyed. Presumably, he carefully selected which passages to read aloud to them.

(cantor) Moshe Solomon and his family, who moved to Israel in 1951, which he indicated with the heading, "Added in 1969 in Akko—Israel."[11]

The fact that we do not have access to the original diary created several challenges when preparing this publication. The typewritten copy contains typos and quite a few sentence fragments, and we made every effort to decipher the ambiguous passages. It was usually possible to understand the gist of the content based on the context, although in a number of cases we were forced to admit defeat and to note that the passages are unclear.

In the entry of December 21, 1943, Kunstadt noted in parentheses that it was "Written in Hebrew, as a *sgule*,"[12] yet this entry was written in Yiddish. In a few other entries, he simply noted "in the Holy Tongue" or "written in Hebrew." Did Kunstadt translate these entries back into Yiddish but leave the notes in order to remain faithful to the original diary before giving the manuscript to YIVO? If so, why did he not indicate this when he edited the diary, as he noted later additions to the text?

On November 23, 1943, Kunstadt added an entry entitled "Added after liberation in April 1944," in which he wrote, "The date at the beginning of the following entries is not written in numbers but in words. I feared that the notebooks would fall into non-Jewish hands and therefore sought to efface the appearance of a diary." The date of the next entry is indeed written out in words—"Twenty-Fourth of November, [Nineteen] Forty-Three"—but the dates of all the entries thereafter are written in numerals. Did Kunstadt forget about his decision in the fervor of his writing and write the dates in the following entries as he had written throughout the diary?

In the entry of April 9, 1943, the day that the tombstone was placed on his mother's grave, Kunstadt related that he had composed a poem entitled "At My Mother's Grave," which he intended to read at the unveiling ceremony on the 7th of Nisan 5703 (April 12, 1943), adding in parentheses, "This poem appears on the title page of this volume of memories." However, this poem does not appear on the title page

11 Similar comments that were added later appear throughout the diary.

12 Kunstadt uses the term *sgule* (*segula* in Hebrew) in the sense of a blessing, charm, or amulet to bring good fortune or ward off evil.

of the typed copy of the diary. Did the poem appear on the title page of the original diary but was omitted by whomever typed it? Since the original diary has not been found, this question, as well as others, remains unanswered.

The fact that the vowel points were omitted in the Yiddish in the typed diary posed a further challenge, in particular when trying to spell the names of many of the people and the places mentioned in the diary. Vocalization is an integral part of Yiddish; without it we cannot know whether the letter *Pey* is pronounced like a p or an f, or if the letter *Aleph* should be pronounced ah or oh. We have made every effort to decipher the names correctly, but it is possible that some of the unfamiliar names, including some unknown places mentioned by Kunstadt, may have been written incorrectly.

However, these challenges do not detract in any way from the importance of this diary, which is published here for the first time in an annotated edition. Dalia Ofer first became acquainted with the diary at the library of the Hebrew University of Jerusalem in the 1980s. It made a profound impression on her and served as a valuable guide in her research on Transnistria. While writing her PhD dissertation about the ghettos in the Moghilev district of Transnistria, Sarah Rosen discovered the diary in which she found a treasure trove of information that helped her understand daily life in the ghettos and the conduct of the leadership there.

Lipman Kunstadt's diary, *Diary from Hell in Transnistria*, provides authentic and detailed documentation of the Holocaust in Transnistria as experienced by the Jews of Bukovina, Bessarabia, and the Dorohoi district in northern Moldova. The diary focuses on one specific ghetto and is of great importance in microhistorical research. However, such microhistorical research has implications for other ghettos in northern Transnistria and sheds light on the social and political problems, the relations between various population groups, and the issue of Jewish leadership in the region in general.

Before reading Kunstadt's diary, it behooves us to embark on a short journey through interwar Romania for an understanding of the political and geographical diversity of the country. We will provide a brief overview of the events of World War II in Bessarabia, Bukovina, and Southern Ukraine, beginning with the German campaign to occupy the Soviet Union, and we will examine the fate of the deportees and the local Jews under the rule of the Germans, Romanians, and nationalist Ukrainian collaborators.

The intrinsic Jewish facets depicted in the diary are complex and varied. The Jewish population concentrated in the ghettos and camps of Transnistria was not comprised of one single bloc. The cultural and historical roots of the local Jews, who had lived in the area for generations, differed from those of the Jews deported from the northern periphery of Romania (Bessarabia, Bukovina, and the Dorohoi district). This diverse Jewish population—local Jews and exiled Jews who had been uprooted from their homes and deported to this foreign geographic landscape—had to work together in order to survive.

In our survey, we will briefly sketch the history of the Jews of Romania on the eve of the outbreak of World War II; describe the area of Transnistria and the fate of the Jews therein; compare Kunstadt's diary with Holocaust diaries, in general, and with the diaries that were written in Transnistria that have remained and are in our possession, in particular; and analyze the unique features of this diary.

Romanian Policy toward the Jews in Romania

The peace agreements made at the end of World War I altered the borders of Romania, which affected the many national and religious minorities within the country's territory, among them Germans, Hungarians, Ruthenians, and Jews. From a political and national perspective, these territorial gains created problems of identity and identification among the various minority groups, and the regime subsequently implemented a policy of maximum Romanization in the fields of education, governance, and culture. The Jewish population in Romania, the third largest in Europe, after the Soviet Union and Poland, was completely isolated from the other Jewish communities, and was also diverse and divided, both linguistically and culturally. Following the inclusion of the Jews from Bukovina, which prior to World War I had been under the rule of the Austro–Hungarian Empire, and of the Jews from

Bessarabia, which had been part of the Russian Empire, the Jews of the Regat,[13] a traditionally Romanian-speaking population, no longer constituted the majority of Romanian Jewry. The Romanian authorities treated all the minorities with suspicion, including the Jews who also were subjected to antisemitism, which was firmly rooted in Romanian religious and folk traditions.[14]

In the 1930s, Romania suffered from political instability, and the influence of the extreme nationalist parties intensified among the educated public and the bourgeoisie. Romania, which in the 1920s had considered itself part of the French, liberal, political tradition, increasingly gravitated toward nationalist regimes, among them Fascist Italy and Nazi Germany. The growing nationalism and the close ties that various Romanian military and student groups developed with the Nazi Party in Germany led to a significant rise in antisemitism, incitement against the Jews, and the implementation of anti-Jewish policy.

With the rise of the extreme right-wing parties to power at the end of the 1930s, and particularly under the leadership of the right-wing politicians Octavian Goga and Alexandru Constantin Cuza, anti-Jewish policy intensified. Although the Goga–Cuza government lasted only forty-four days—December 29, 1937–February 10, 1938—it succeeded in implementing some of its plans against the Jews. The most severe step was the law passed on January 22, 1938, which required a review of the citizenship of the Jews and resulted in depriving around a quarter of a million Jews from the areas of Bessarabia and Bukovina—approximately a third of all Romanian Jewry—of their citizenship.[15]

In February 1938, following the growth of the extremist right-wing groups and the Iron Guard, an extreme fascist group headed by Corneliu Zelea Codreanu, and Nazi Germany's massive interference, King Karol

---

13 In the context of this diary, the Regat, which means kingdom, refers to the Old Kingdom of Romania or the Vechiul Regat.

14 Jean Ancel, *The History of the Holocaust in Romania* (Lincoln and Jerusalem: University of Nebraska Press and Yad Vashem, Jerusalem, 2011), pp. 7–9; Elie Wiesel, *Final Report of the International Commission on the Holocaust in Romania* (Iaši: Poliron, 2005), pp. 54–55; Leon Volovici, *Nationalist Ideology and Antisemitism*: *The Case of Romanian Intellectuals in the 1930s* (Oxford: Pergamon Press, 1991).

15 Ancel, *The History of the Holocaust in Romania*, pp. 25–38.

declared himself the sole ruler of Romania. He suspended the existing democratic constitution, authorized a new constitution, and established a dictatorial regime under his leadership.

However, with the outbreak of the war, Romania's internal and international situation began to deteriorate. After Nazi Germany signed agreements with the Soviet Union in June 1940, the Soviets invaded Bessarabia and Northern Bukovina, and the Romanians were forced to relinquish their control of these areas. Moreover, in the summer of 1940, following the second Vienna Diktat, or Second Vienna Award,[16] northern Transylvania was awarded to the Hungarian regime and the lands of southern Dobruja were granted to Bulgaria. These blows further strengthened the right-wing parties in Romania and led to the fall of King Karol's regime. In September 1940, King Karol abdicated, and a nationalist government was established under the leadership of Ion Antonescu and the Iron Guard.

Antonescu's government sought to ensure law and order, and to embark on a radical process of strengthening Romanian national identity among the entire population. Venomous criticism was leveled at the Jews of Bessarabia and Northern Bukovina, claiming that they supported the Soviets, that they had inflicted damage on the Romanian army as it retreated, and that their behavior was detrimental to the state and to the honor of the Romanian military. The government began to decree a series of economic edicts against the Jews, seeking to drive them out of various economic sectors in order to Romanize the economy. As a result, many Jews were deprived of their livelihood. The trend of excluding Jews from cultural life, particularly from the press, also intensified, and the citizenship of increasing numbers of Jews was revoked.[17]

The situation of the Romanian Jews dramatically deteriorated during this period. Members of the Iron Guard at all levels of the government

---

16 This distinction was bestowed on August 30, 1940, by Nazi Germany and Fascist Italy as an arbitration award in the dispute between Romania and Hungary.

17 Ibid., pp. 34–38; Radu Ioanid, *Toledot Hayehudim BeRomania*: *Hashoah* (Hebrew), vol. 4 (Tel Aviv: Tel Aviv University, 2002), pp. 29–40; Benjamin Lya, Florin Alexandru, and Ciuciu Anca, *Cum A Fost Posibil? Evrei din România în Holocaustului* (Bucharest: Editura Institutul Naţional pentru Studierea Holocaustului din România "Elie Wiesel," 2007), pp. 60–68.

embarked on a campaign to terrorize the Jewish public in order to forcibly seize their property, especially the shops, businesses, and factories. Due to the terror that the Iron Guard perpetrated against the Jews, chaos soon ensued in the many sectors of the economy and industry. Antonescu refused to accept his colleagues' conduct, and demanded law and order. He determined that it was necessary to dispossess the Jews gradually, to prepare those who would take their place, and to avoid shaking the nation's economy. A new legal phrase was soon coined, "ethnic Romanians," which served to drive the Jews gradually out of all fields of activity and business. Professional organizations, for example, hastened to expel Jewish members from their ranks even before the special laws were enacted. In addition, members of the Iron Guard and their supporters frequently engaged in looting to enrich themselves.[18]

The decisive turning point in the situation of the Jews occurred when the Romanian government decided to join Germany in the war against the Soviet Union in June 1941. The alliance that the Romanian government concluded with the Nazi regime prior to Operation Barbarossa and the liberation of Bessarabia and Bukovina from Soviet control provided Antonescu and his government with an opportunity to rid Romania of Jews, first and foremost those in Bessarabia, Bukovina, and the Dorohoi district. Moreover, Antonescu hoped that this pact would return northern Transylvania to Romania.

The plan drawn up by Antonescu and his government entailed two phases: in the first stage, the northern tracts of Romania, Bessarabia, Bukovina, and the Dorohoi district in northern Moldova, parts of which had been annexed by the Soviet Union in June 1940, were to be cleansed. Orders given by Mihai Antonescu to the praetors—the heads of the districts nominated by the government—was to "cleanse the land," meaning the immediate destruction of the Jews in rural areas, the concentration of the Jews living in cities in ghettos, and the arrest of activists and persons who had held office under Soviet rule.[19] In the second stage, which was never carried out despite careful planning, the Romanian authorities intended

18 Stefan Gristian Ionescu, *Jewish Resistance to "Romanianization," 1940–44* (London: Palgrave Macmillan, 2015), pp. 34–110.

19 Ancel, *The History of the Holocaust in Romania*, pp. 457–467.

to deport the Jews of the Regat to the extermination camp of Belzec. This plan was shelved following developments in the war.[20]

The Fate of the Jews in Bessarabia, Bukovina, and the Dorohoi District

The status and economic situation of the Jews in Bessarabia began to deteriorate under the Goga–Cuza government, as previously noted. In June 1940, the Soviet Union annexed the region, pursuant to the Molotov–Ribbentrop Pact[21] and, consequently, the Jews of Bessarabia hoped that the new regime would ease their suffering. However, their hopes were quickly dashed.[22] During the year of Soviet rule, 1940–1941, the entire population suffered, particularly the Jews. The Jewish communities endured economic hardship as the Soviet regime nationalized the property of the bourgeois and middle-class Jews, impoverishing them. Owners of factories and large and small businesses alike were categorized as bourgeois, and the new Russian identity papers that were issued to them were stamped with the number 11, which referred to a clause that limited their freedom of movement, their right to change their place of residence, and their social status. The identity papers of rich Jews and Zionists were stamped with the number 39, which identified them as bourgeois, or as

---

20 Ibid., pp. 470–475, 477–488.

21 On August 23, 1939, the German foreign minister, Joachim von Ribbentrop, and his Soviet counterpart, Viacheslav Molotov, met in Moscow and signed the Treaty of Non-Aggression between Germany and the Union of Soviet Socialist Republics, which is commonly known as the Ribbentrop–Molotov Pact. According to this treaty, neither side would attack the other, nor assist a third party to launch an attack. It also stipulated that any disagreements between the two sides would be resolved in a friendly manner. A secret appendix, which was included in the treaty, divided Europe into German and Soviet spheres of influence "in the case of political–territorial changes" in the states of Eastern Europe, meaning Poland, the Baltic states, and Finland. The appendix also established the future border between the two countries following the planned division of Poland. The treaty was signed around one week before the outbreak of World War II and constituted the basis for the division of Poland between Germany and the USSR. It had been in effect for less than two years when, on June 22, 1941, the Germans unilaterally terminated it with their invasion of the Soviet Union.

22 Lavi, *Pinkas Hakehilot*: *Rumania*, vol. 2, p. 294.

suspect of hostile political activity and thus designated for deportation, and many were quickly arrested and deported to Siberia.[23]

The Soviets abolished traditional Jewish social institutions, banned the existence of political and religious cadres, and quashed all communal organization. The Jewish leaders were exiled to Russia and Siberia, and Zionist activity as well as the activities of Zionist youth movements were forbidden. The Jews were left without leadership and without a supportive community framework upon which they could rely for legal aid, assistance for the needy, and, as we will see further, recourse to manage contacts with the Romanian occupier in order to prepare the Jews for deportation.[24] This also applied to the Jews of Northern Bukovina. This region, as far as the Siret River, which includes the city of Cernăuţi, was annexed to the Soviet Union, as previously mentioned.[25]

When the war broke out in the summer of 1941, the Jewish community in Bessarabia was confounded and shocked by the statements that they heard on Radio Bucharest concerning a holy war against the Jews. Two weeks after the outbreak of the war, the Soviet authorities permitted the population to move eastward and accordingly opened the Dniester crossings. However, many Jews debated whether to embark on a journey to the unknown or to remain in their homes, hoping to be spared the worst. Jews who chose to flee to the areas under Soviet control encountered heavy German bombings and many were killed. Others were murdered

---

23 Dov Levin, *Tekufa Besograyim, 1939–1941*: *Temurot Behayei Hayehudim Be'ezorim Shesuphu LeVrit HaMo'atzot Bitehilat Milhemet Ha'olam Hasheniya* (Hebrew) (Jerusalem: The Hebrew University of Jerusalem and Ghetto Fighters' House, 1989), p. 75; Hayim Breiman, "Beitar BeNovoselitza," in Shalom Dorner, ed., *Novoselitza* (Hebrew) (Tel Aviv: Irgun Yotzei Novoselitza Be'Yisrael, 1983), p. 188.

24 Shlomo Shitnovitzer, "Kenisat HaRusim LeKhutin," in Shitnovitzer, ed., *Sefer Kehilat Hutin* (*Bessarabia*) (Hebrew) (Tel Aviv: Hotza'at Irgun Yotzei Hutin [Bessarabia] Be'Yisrael, 1974,) pp. 84–85.

25 Avigdor Shachan, *Burning Ice*: *The Ghettos of Transnistria* (Boulder: East European Monographs, 1996), pp. 23–28. Alex Druckman described in his testimony the terrible economic situation and the exile of his family to Siberia; see Alex Druckman testimony, Yad Vashem Archives (YVA), O.3/12085. Avraham Korn related that his father's farm and lands were confiscated; see Avraham Korn testimony, YVA, O.3/12272. Avraham Iwanir depicted the family's property, which was confiscated, and the family's fear of being exiled to Siberia, as were other prosperous households; see Avraham Iwanir testimony, YVA, O.3/12649.

by greedy peasants when they were seeking lodging, and some were caught on the roads by the occupying armies and brutally murdered. Few managed to reach the towns in northern Transnistria and to find refuge in the homes of local Jews.[26]

The cooperation between the Romanian and Germany militaries led to the swift occupation of Bessarabia and Northern Bukovina, which were returned to Romanian rule.[27] The German army was accompanied by the Einsatzgruppen death squads that were tasked with murdering the Jews throughout the Soviet Union. During the invasion, the Jews in these regions were ruthlessly slaughtered, spurred by Ion Antonescu and Mihai Antonescu,[28] who called "for the coldblooded annihilation of the Communists, the Bolsheviks, and the Jewish provocateurs, and the cleansing of the land…driving all the Jews out of the villages."[29]

Jean Ancel divides the murders into two stages: the spontaneous stage and the organized stage.[30] In the first stage, the spontaneous phase, which took place during the first weeks of the occupation, June–mid-July 1941, the murders were mainly committed by peasants and bands of local people who were incited by the Romanian propaganda against the Jews. When the Romanian and German armies entered these areas, special units of the Romanian army carried out the murder, deportation, and concentration of the Jews with the assistance of the German Einsatzgruppen. At the same time, the commanders of the Romanian army constantly prompted the local peasants to participate in the murders and looting.[31]

---

26 Lavi, *Pinkas Hakehilot*: *Rumania*, vol. 2, pp. 307–310. There are no figures regarding the number of those who fled to Russia and the number of Jews caught by the invading armies.

27 Concerning the stages of the occupation, see Jean Ancel, "The Romanian Way of Solving the "Jewish Problem" in Bessarabia and Bukovina, June–July 1941," *Yad Vashem Studies*, 19 (1988), pp. 187–232.

28 Matatias Carp, *Cartea neagră*: *Suferintele Evreilor din Romania, 1940–1944*, vol. 3 (Bucharest: n.p., 1947), pp. 91, 92.

29 Ibid., vol. 3, pp. 76–78, 91–92.

30 Jean Ancel, *Toledot Hashoah*: *Romania* (Hebrew), vol. 1 (Jerusalem: Yad Vashem, 2002) pp. 545–546.

31 Solonari Vladimir, "Patterns of Violence: The Local Population and the Mass Murder of Jews in Bessarabia and Northern Bukovina, July–August 1941," *Kritika*: *Explorations in Russian History*, 8:4 (2007), p. 755. See, for example, the testimony of Rabbi Shmelke

When the German and Romanian armies entered the area during the month of July, they concentrated the Jews in public buildings and brutalized them: the Jews were beaten; women, young women, and girls were raped in front of their menfolk, and afterwards they were shot on the edges of the village or in forests, and their homes were plundered. The Jews' neighbors participated in these acts of slaughter. It is difficult to determine the exact number of people murdered, although according to a report by the International Commission for the Study of the Holocaust of Romanian Jewry,[32] in the months of June, July, and the first half of August, 45,000–60,000 Jews were murdered. Those Jews who were not murdered were cruelly deported by the Romanian gendarmes, who took them on death marches to temporary ghettos and concentration camps, such as Edineţi, Secureni, and Chişinău, without prior organization or orderly planning.[33] At the beginning of August 1941, convoys of Jews were "forced" out of Soroca and Hotin, and driven beyond the Dniester River to German-controlled Ukraine. Because the Germans were still not prepared to receive large groups of people, the deportees were returned to temporary camps in Romania.[34]

On September 15, 1941, the deportees began to cross the border crossings into Transnistria. These were the remnants of the families who had perished from hunger or cold, or had been murdered by the Romanian gendarmes. They arrived at the border after enduring deportations and atrocities on death marches that had begun on June 21, 1941. These deportees were left virtually destitute and were drained, body and soul.

Drechner, a native of Berhomet, who was living in Staneşti during the reoccupation by the Romanians in 1941. In his testimony, he describes the acts of murder in Staneşti in Northern Bukovina; see Shmelke Drechner testimony, YVA, O.3/1443; David Keisch testimony, YVA, O.3/13166. Concerning the murder of the Jews by Ukrainian mobs in Ispas and Bănila in Northern Bukovina and in other places with Jewish populations, see Dov Shai, ed., *Sho'at Yehudei Tzefon Bukovina: Hakehilot Vehurbanan, Retzah Veheli'at Hayehudim Begeta'ot, Tza'adot Hamavet LeTransnistriya, Yuli–October 1941* (Hebrew) (Tel Aviv: The World Organization of Bukovinian Jewry, 1982), pp. 70–71. Concerning the slaughter in Novoselitsa, Bessarabia, see Zipora Galai testimony, YVA, O.3/13035. Concerning the slaughter of the Jews of Secureni, see Israel Frikman testimony, YVA, O.3/11180.

32 Wiesel, *Final Report of the International Commission on the Holocaust in Romania*.

33 Carp, *Cartea neagră*, vol. 3, p. 55.

34 Ibid., pp. 96–98.

In September and October 1941, the second stage of the deportations and slaughter began. This stage too was characterized by merciless death marches: those who had survived the destruction of the temporary ghettos and camps in Bessarabia—Edineţi, Secureni, and Chişinău—were taken to Transnistria.

The Organized Deportations of the Jews of Southern Bukovina and Part of the Jewish Population of Cernăuţi[35]

Although the Jews in Southern Bukovina had remained under Romanian control, this did not improve their fortune. They lived in a constant state of apprehension during the year 1940–1941, after receiving news of the persecutions of the Jews in the Dorohoi district and other parts of Romania.[36] Many men were taken away for forced labor, their children were expelled from schools,[37] and high school students were not allowed to take their matriculation exams. The Romanian administration limited the activities of the Jews in industry, confiscated their businesses, and prevented them from leasing agricultural lands and, consequently, the income level of the Jews dropped considerably. Antisemitism intensified, and Jews could no longer walk safely in the streets of their towns,

---

35 With the fervent intervention of the mayor, Dr. Traian Popovici, and due to his refusal to obey the order to murder the Jews, for which he was recognized as Righteous Among the Nations by Yad Vashem, around 19,000 Jews were allowed to remain in the city. This was justified by the argument that they were useful elements. Authorizations to remain in the city were referred to as "Popovici permits"; see ibid., pp. 158–182.

36 Group testimony, ghetto of Murafa, YVA, O.3/9669; group testimony, ghettos of Moghilev, Shargorod, and Dzhurin, YVA, O.3/10547.

37 On October 14, 1940, the minister of education, Prof. Traian Brăileanu, published a law forbidding Jewish students to study in Romanian educational institutions, and Jewish teachers to teach in Romanian schools. Romanian teachers were also forbidden from teaching in Jewish schools; see YVA, O.11/7; see also Hannah Meller-Faust, *Me'ever Lenahar*: *Pirkei Zihronot MiTransnistriya* (Hebrew) (Tel Aviv: Ghetto Fighters' House and Hakibbutz Hame'uhad, 1985), pp. 64–69. Meller-Faust describes the dismissal of beloved and esteemed teachers from their jobs in schools, followed by the expulsion of the students within days; see also Iehuda Tenenhaus testimony, YVA, O.3/7748; Kurt Shternshus testimony, YVA, O.3/9370.

because the members of the Iron Guard would frequently assault them.[38] Furthermore, during that year, the Jews from many villages were evicted from their homes and sent to large towns, such as Suceava and Vatra Dornei.[39] In addition to the persecution of the Jews noted above, 1940–1941 was a year of dread and apprehension prompted by the rumors of the events unfolding in Bessarabia and Northern Bukovina.

On October 4, 1941, the Romanian general military headquarters began to implement Antonescu's order to deport all the Jews from Southern Bukovina within ten days.[40] Within four or five days, October 10–14, 1941, around 21,000 Jews from Southern Bukovina[41] were deported to Transnistria, together with approximately 30,000 Jews from Cernăuţi.[42] With little advance notice, sometimes only a few hours, the deportees were required to transfer all their property to the National Bank of Romania—their homes, silver and gold objects, gems, money, jewelry, and anything else of value. They were able to exchange some of their money for the Reichskreditkassenschein (RKKS), a parallel, German-imposed currency

---

38 Meller-Faust, *Me'ever Lenahar*, pp. 46–63; Iehuda Tenenhaus testimony, YVA, O.3/7748; Kurt Shternshus testimony, YVA, O.3/9370; group testimony, ghettos of Moghilev, Shargorod, and Dzhurin, YVA, O.3/10547.

39 The Jews from the villages of Solca, Fratauţi, Vatra Candreni, Iacobeni, Brodina, Vicov, and others were deported to large towns; see Gusta-Zehava Shtern testimony, YVA, O.3/11021; Silva Hernik testimony, YVA, O.3/13178; Miriam Savion testimony, YVA, O.3/11435; Eliezer Perl testimony, YVA, O.3/ 10875; Tzvia Facht interview by Sarah Rosen, January 31, 2013, Haifa; Aviva Avrech interview by Sarah Rosen, August, 2013, Kiryat Bialik.

40 Carp, *Cartea neagră*, vol. 3, p. 143.

41 Beginning on October 9, 1941, the Jews of Suceava were deported over the course of three days. On the first day, October 9, 1941, the Jews of Burdujeni and Iţcani were also deported. On the following day, October 10, 1941, an additional group of the Jews of Suceava were deported with the Jews of Gura Humorului, in addition to a group of Jews from Vatra Dornei and the surrounding area. On the third day of the deportations, October 11, 1941, the remaining Jews of Suceava who had not been deported in the first two days were deported. During all three days of the deportations, Jews from Rădăuţi and the surrounding villages and Câmpulung were also deported. On October 13, 1941, the last Jews of Rădăuţi and Câmpulung were deported. On October 14, 1941, Southern Bukovina was declared "*Judenrein*" (cleansed of Jews). See Ancel, *The History of the Holocaust in Romania,* pp. 288–297.

42 Ancel notes that 21,229 Jews were deported from their homes in Southern Bukovina in 1941. He presents demographic statistics concerning the region and describes the deportations from the entire region according to areas and various cities in the region; see ibid., pp. 290–297.

that was used in Transnistria and other occupied territories.[43] Some deportees from Southern Bukovina were able to prepare themselves on the eve of the deportation: they hid clothes, valuables, and money among their utensils and thus succeeded in taking them to Transnistria.

The deportation to Transnistria was agonizing and humiliating. The deportees were taken in cattle wagons, packed fifty persons to a wagon. Many were in shock due to the sudden transition from their "orderly" lives to the cruelty, violence, and chaos of the deportation. All were mistreated by the peasants, soldiers, and Romanian gendarmes. They spent long days, sometimes even weeks, in the areas surrounding the bridges at Atachi and Yampol, in cold and rainy weather, without a real roof over their heads, waiting to cross the Dniester. Many could not bear the suffering and died; many others were murdered, and some lost their minds. However, due to the preparations made in advance of the deportation and the communal organization active in Southern Bukovina, the situation of the deportees from Bukovina who arrived in Transnistria was far better than that of the deportees from Bessarabia, who had arrived there before them. Many managed to keep their families intact. Likewise, the communal leaders maintained contact with the deportees, passing on information and managing to procure some relief measures and means of transportation by resorting to bribes and connections with Romanian military figures. In the first stage, many of the deportees from Bukovina were sent to Moghilev and some remained there. Others were sent to other ghettos in the Moghilev district.[44] All these factors helped in the first stages of acclimatization to life in the various ghettos and contributed significantly to the chances of survival among this group of deportees.

---

43 Carp, *Cartea neagră*, vol. 3, pp. 144–145.

44 Not all the deportees from Southern Bukovina arrived in the Moghilev district. Some of them were taken by train to Mărculeşti and from there they continued on foot to the other side of the Bug River. Many did not survive, and their bodies were left at the sides of the road, eaten by birds of prey and other animals; others were concentrated in cowsheds and pigsties at the edges of kolkhozes; yet others arrived in Bershad, Obodovka, and other ghettos and camps in the Balta district. These included some deportees from Cernăuţi, Rădăuţi and the surrounding villages in Southern Bukovina.

According to data that had not been disclosed until relatively recently, by the end of 1941, 167,712 Jews had been deported to Transnistria: 61,249 from Northern Bukovina (Cernăuţi, Storojineţ, and Hotin districts); 21,229 Jews (Câmpulung, Suceava, and Rădăuţi districts) from Southern Bukovina; 75,867 Jews from Bessarabia (55,867 plus 20,000 from the "hasty deportations," including 12,000 of the 35,867 returned to the Vertujeni camp[45]); and 9,367 Jews from the Dorohoi district. In the spring and summer of 1942, another 4,290 Jews were deported from Bessarabia and 231 Jews from Bukovina.[46]

The Fate of the Jews from the Dorohoi District

The persecution of the Jews in the Dorohoi district began when a pogrom broke out on July 1, 1940, before the signing of the alliance between Romania and Nazi Germany. Their suffering further intensified when the Romanians joined the war against the Soviet Union, although the entire region was part of the Regat, having been annexed to Southern Bukovina rather than passing to Soviet rule. On June 19, 1941, the authorities began expelling the Jews from the villages between the Siret and Prut rivers, following the instructions that Antonescu had issued the day before.[47]

The government confiscated the property of the Jews during the deportation, and further acts of plunder were committed by officials, soldiers, policemen, and local residents.[48] The deportees went on foot or were taken in cattle wagons: men between the ages of eighteen and sixty were taken to the Tărgu Jiu camp,[49] and women and

45 When the Jews from Bessarabia were deported, they were concentrated in transit camps; one of them was on the outskirts of the village of Vertujeni.

46 Ancel, *The History of the Holocaust in Romania*, p. 541.

47 Ibid., p. 510.

48 Natan Kraft testimony, YVA, O.3/111148; Leoni Tziyoni interview by Sarah Rosen, October 27, 2013, Kiryat Motzkin.

49 The Tărgu Jiu camp was established near to the town of Tărgu Jiu in the Oltenia district in southeast Romania, according to an order issued by Ion Antonescu on February 12, 1942. It was intended for the imprisonment and isolation of political prisoners, where they

children were sent to the Calafat camp.[50] After three months in these camps and following the intervention of the Jewish leaders in Bucharest, who were obligated to secure war loans totaling 10 billion lei, the Jews were released from the camps and their families were reunited in the town of Dorohoi. In total, 6,534 Jews were taken to the town of Dorohoi.[51] They were concentrated in two Jewish schools and a synagogue, where they remained under terrible conditions.[52]

All the Jews in the Dorohoi district were ordered to wear the yellow badge. They were forbidden to leave their homes from 8 P.M. to 7 A.M., and most were deported to the town of Dorohoi. They were not allowed to leave the city, even for emergency medical attention.[53] From November 5, 1941, to December 3, 1941, 9,367 Jews were deported to Transnistria—not before all their possessions had been plundered. Some of these Jews managed to remain in Moghilev, but many others met their deaths as they were dragged on marches through Transnistria.

To sum up, the ability of all the deportees to organize themselves in the first months was significantly affected by the political events that occurred before the deportation, the locations from which the Jews had been deported, the timing of the deportations, and the means of transport of the groups—on foot or by train—and, thus, the personal effects that they could take with them. The very existence of some kind of organization and the form it assumed often determined whether or

---

performed forced labor. From June 1941, around 200 refugees from Poland, Slovakia, and Hungary were imprisoned in the camp, as well as approximately 7,000 Jewish men from the Dorohoi, Vaslui, and Iaşi regions, including fourteen rabbis and leaders of Romanian Jewry. The conditions in the camp were extremely difficult. Its prisoners were forced to pave roads, lay railroad tracks, quarry stone, and deforest and prepare the land for agriculture, without any consideration of their health conditions. Any prisoner who was unable to perform the hard labor was punished severely with lashes and other forms of corporal punishment. See Lavi, *Pinkas Hakehilot*: *Rumania*, vol. 1, p. 184; Jacob Geller, *Ha'amida Haruhanit Shel Yehudei Romania Betukufat Hashoah, 1940–1944* (Hebrew) (Lod: Orot Yahdut HaMaghreb, 2003).

50 Carp, *Cartea neagră*, vol. 3, p. 75.

51 Ancel, *The History of the Holocaust in Romania*, pp. 298–305.

52 Shulamit Grinberg testimony, YVA, O.3/13430; Mita Barko testimony, YVA, O.3/6029.

53 Lavi, *Pinkas Hakehilot*: *Rumania*, vol. 1, p. 108.

not the Jews would be able to survive and somehow manage in the harsh reality of the ghettos in northern Transnistria.

Transnistria

Transnistria is a tract of land in the southwestern part of Ukraine, around 40,000 square kilometers in size, which stretches from the Dniester River in the west to the Bug River in the east, and to the city of Odessa on the banks of the Black Sea in the south. This area, which was occupied by the Germans and the Romanians in a joint operation in the summer–autumn of 1941, was transferred to Romanian control under the Tighina Agreement, concluded on August 30, 1941, in return for Romania's participation in the war against the Soviet Union. Hitler named this tract of land Transnistria, which means "beyond the Dniester" (Nistru, in Romanian).

Upon the outbreak of the fighting, the population of Transnistria numbered around 2.5 million. Ukrainians accounted for half of the population and the other half comprised three other large minorities: around 700,000 Russians; approximately 331,000 Jews; and about 290,000 Romanians. In addition, there was a minority of 125,000 German locals, who had established agricultural settlements, mainly in the southern part of Transnistria and on the banks of the Bug River. There were also Armenians, Roma, Bulgarians, Lithuanians, and Greeks. Until June 1941, the area belonged to the Soviet Union; it returned to Soviet control after the reoccupation by the Red Army in the spring of 1944.[54]

According to the census of 1939, 200,961 Jews—more than half of the Jews in Transnistria—lived in Odessa, the largest city in that part of Ukraine. The Jews accounted for around 30 percent of the city's population of over 600,000 residents. However, in the first months of the war, the number rose by tens of thousands due to an influx of refugees from the area around Odessa and southern Bessarabia.[55] The Jews in this Ukrainian tract of land lived in small towns, primarily in the

54 Shachan, *Burning Ice,* pp.151–154.

55 Ancel, *The History of the Holocaust in Romania*, p. 314.

northern and central parts. They mainly resided in towns in which the entire population or the majority was Jewish, such as Krasnoye, Olgopol, Krivoye Ozero, Bershad, Shargorod, Kopaygorod, and more.[56] The non-Jewish Ukrainian population lived in small villages in which most of the inhabitants worked in agriculture.

The agreement signed at Tighina permitted the presence of German units in the territory and established the boundaries of cooperation between the Germans and the Romanians in the area. During the war, the Germans continued to maintain logistical and administrative units in Transnistria. German headquarters were established by railroad junctions in order to coordinate the transfer of military units, equipment, and supplies to the front and to guard them. Likewise, German headquarters were established in a number of cities in Transnistria, such as Moghilev, Bershad, and Balta, and they were responsible for guarding the military facilities and managing the German labor camps in the region.[57] A number of German military units were placed at the disposal of Organization Todt, which built bridges and roads, for example in the Trikhaty camp on the bank of the Bug River. Paragraph 7 of the Tighina Agreement concerns the fate of the Jews in the camps and ghettos in Transnistria.[58] Although Transnistria was never annexed to Romania, Prof. Gheorghe Alexianu was appointed as governor on behalf of the Romanian authorities. The legal currencies in Transnistria were the RKKS and the Romanian lei.

Together with the German and Romanian armies, members of Einsatzgruppe D arrived in Transnistria. Alongside the soldiers of the German 11th Army, which included four Einsatzgruppen units—10a, 10b, 11a, and 11b—and the Romanian 3rd Army, they conducted the first wave of mass murders of the local Jews. Likewise, the units of ethnic Germans known as Vomi,[59] which in 1941 were integrated into the SS,

56 Ibid., p. 315.

57 These work camps were established in order to build new bridges over the Dniester and the Bug, and to renovate the existing bridges that had been damaged by the bombings during the war.

58 Jean Ancel, "Masa'ot Haretzah Hahamoni Shel HaRomanim BeTransnistriya, 1941–1942" (Hebrew), *Bishevil Hazikaron*, 38 (2002), p. 23.

59 Volksdeutesche Mittelstelle; see Shachan, *Burning Ice*, pp. 161–165. The Vomi, which was established in 1926, trained the German minorities outside the Reich to act in

participated in the slaughter, as did members of the Ukrainian militia and the Romanian gendarmes. Not all the local Jews were killed in the first wave, due to the scope of the undertaking and the expanse of the area, and because the Einsatzgruppen units continued to advance into the Soviet Union with the German army.

The assault on the Jewish population outside Odessa, which numbered 100,000 Jews, was swift and brutal. The Jews did not manage to flee and did not have time to prepare or to hide. Most were murdered, but some succeeded in escaping with the retreating Soviet army. The murder of these Jews was part of the "Final Solution." They were shot in pits—the system used by the units tasked with this job in the occupied Soviet territories. After the first wave of violence and murder, the Jews were marked and isolated, their property was seized, and they were imprisoned in ghettos. Order No. 23, which was issued on November 11, 1941, established the status of the Jews and their concentration in settlements (ghettos or colonies),[60] and instructed that Jewish Councils be appointed and that their leaders, who were to be chosen by the regional governors, be responsible for fulfilling the orders issued by the government. This sequence of events is similar to the model that the Nazis implemented in the areas of the Soviet Union, although the role played by the police and the Romanian army in instigating the murder of Jews in Transnistria and in the missions was defining.[61]

The Jews of Odessa suffered a different fate. Odessa was conquered by the Romanians after a siege that lasted about two months, August 5, 1941–October 15, 1941. Around half of the city's Jews fled with the

---

accordance with the needs of the Nazi state. In 1941, it was incorporated into the SS and became one of its departments. In December 1941, the commando units of the Vomi, with the help of the Ukrainian militia and the Romanian gendarmes, murdered 70,000 Jews in the Golta region. Most of these Jews were from southern Transnistria. Some had escaped the slaughter in Odessa, and some had fled or had been deported from Bessarabia and Bukovina to the area after the German–Romanian occupation.

60 The Romanians called the ghettos "colonies." The concept of colony is synonymous with the ghetto. Many Holocaust survivors indeed used the term colony. Kunstadt uses the terms colony, for the most part, as well as shtetl, village, camp, and ghetto interchangeably, to refer to what was in fact a ghetto.

61 Dalia Ofer, "Hashoah BeTransnistriya: Mikre Yotze Dofen Shel Hashmadat Am" (Hebrew), *Mesu'a*, 24 (April 1996), p. 26.

Soviet army, although approximately 80,000 to 90,000 Jews remained. Left without leadership, they were confused and completely at the mercy of the occupiers, who saw them, as well as all the local Jews, as Jewish Bolsheviks to be persecuted. In the first four days of the occupation, more than 10,000 Jews were murdered, and on October 23, 1941, 20,000 Jews were deported to the village of Dalnik, where they were murdered a few days later. From October 25 until November 3, the remaining Jews, around 40,000, were concentrated in a ghetto that was established in Slobodka, a suburb close to Odessa, where they endured terrible poverty and illness. They were subsequently deported to camps in the Golta region. The Romanian army, under the command of the Romanian colonel Mihail Ion Lisievici, participated in the murder of the Jews in Odessa and in the entire area, alongside the German Einsatzkommando 11b, units of Romanian gendarmes, and the nationalist Ukrainian militia.[62]

In southern Transnistria, an area that Jean Ancel refers to as "the kingdom of death," Jewish deportees, together with the remainder of Odessa's Jewish population, were concentrated in camps under inhuman conditions. Following the outbreak of the typhus plague, the Romanian authorities decided that it was necessary to murder the Jews in these camps to curb the spread of the plague. In six months, November 1941–April 1942, more than 110,000 Jews were slaughtered in compliance with this order.[63]

The Ghettos in Northern Transnistria

The lot of the Jews who arrived in the northern part of Transnistria was different. According to the official statistical data, between September 15, 1941, and January 1942, 55,913 Jews who had been deported from Northern and Southern Bukovina, Bessarabia, and the Dorohoi district passed

---

62 Ancel, *The History of the Holocaust in Romania*, pp. 353–365; Shachan, *Burning Ice*, p. 166.

63 Ancel, *The History of the Holocaust in Romania*, pp. 334–352.

through the city of Moghilev.[64] Order No. 23, which was mentioned above, ordered their concentration in ghettos in the region. Although the authorities did not intend to permit Jews to settle in Moghilev, around 8,500 remained there.[65]

Together with the local Jews, the deportees were concentrated in closed ghettos in Dzhurin, Murafa, Bershad, Shargorod, and Kopaygorod, or in small villages, such as, Nemerche, Tropova, Popovtsy, Luchinets, Derebchin, and more. All were placed under a curfew and all were required to wear a Star of David on their clothes. Although the Ukrainian Jews had an obvious advantage over the deportees, being familiar with the physical and human landscape and fluent in the local language, their situation was no better. In economic terms, their situation was even worse, because Ukraine had suffered years of hunger and economic distress as a result of the Five-Year Plan, which began in 1929.[66] They now found themselves unable to communicate with the Romanian administration and to bargain with the officials, because they did not speak German and Romanian and, thus, were dependent on the deportees' connections with the authorities.

With the arrival of the deported Jews from Bukovina, the economic situation of the Ukrainian Jews deteriorated further. Prices increased and, although some continued to work in those workshops that had not been destroyed, their financial situation was appalling. So too the overcrowding in their homes worsened as they took in deportees. Although renting rooms to deportees sometimes provided an alternative source of income for local Jews, not all the local Jews asked for payment, and many of the deportees had no way of paying rent. In the ghetto, which was managed by deportees from Bukovina, the local Jews were of inferior status. The Romanian authorities, who saw these Jews as Bolsheviks, showed no

---

64 Ibid., pp. 329–332.

65 Letter from Siegfried Jagendorf to the mayor of Moghilev, December 15, 1941, YVA, P.9/6; see also Yeshurun, "Hahitarganut Ha'atzmit Shel Yehudei Bukovina Begeto Moghilev," p. 7.

66 Concerning Ukraine during the period of the Five-Year Plans, especially the first Five-Year Plan, 1929–1934, see Timothy Snyder, *Bloodlands*: *Europe Between Hitler and Stalin* (London: Vintage Books, 2011), pp. 29–119.

interest in protecting them.[67] They were the first to be included on the lists of candidates for deportation that were drawn up by the ghetto leadership.

Nevertheless, the local Jews and the deportees, mainly craftsmen, such as tailors, painters, shoemakers, tanners, carpenters, and blacksmiths, had trade relations with the farmers who needed these services.[68] There was a shortage of almost everything, including clothes, shoes, household utensils, and more, and thus a barter trade began to blossom among the Jewish deportees, the local Jews, and the peasants, who could provide food in exchange.[69]

Holocaust Diaries

Kunstadt's diary pertains to a central genre of Holocaust literature—the diary. According to scholars, diaries are of particular importance, because they were written as the events unfolded, or in close proximity to them. Diaristic writing was common and widespread in European society in the nineteenth and twentieth centuries, and while diaristic literature was considered inferior in literary terms and was often associated with women, it was an important literary genre among enlightened literate groups.[70] Thus wrote the Jewish historian Berl Mark in his introduction to the diary of the Warsaw teacher Chaim Aron Kaplan:

---

67 Dalia Ofer, "Life in the Ghettos of Transnistria," *Yad Vashem Studies*, 25 (1996), pp. 229–274.

68 Ya'akov Meltzer, *Hamasa Shel Yanko* (Hebrew) (Kibbutz Daliya: "Ma'arehet," 1999), p. 92; Yeti Bertfeld, *Yeti*: *Yoman Ahava BeTransnistriya* (Hebrew) (Tel Aviv: Akad, 1998), p. 54; Meller-Faust, *Me'ever Lenahar*, p. 100.

69 Israel and Jetti Elenbogen interview by Sarah Rosen, January 18, 2004, Haifa; Ada and Yitzhak Noy interview by Sarah Rosen, January 25, 2004, Kiryat Tivon; Jetti Elenbogen testimony, YVA, O.3/9539; Israel Elenbogen testimony, YVA, O.3/10940; Hayim Noy testimony, YVA, O.3/10637; and Ada Noy testimony, YVA, O.3/10912.

70 Paul C. Rosenblatt, *Bitter, Bitter Tears*: *Nineteenth Century Diarists and Twentieth Century Grief Theories* (Minneapolis: University of Minnesota Press, 1983); Wendy Lower, *The Diary of Samuel Golfard and the Holocaust in Galicia* (Lanham: AltaMira Press in association with USHMM, 2011); Philippe Lejeune, *On Diary* (Honolulu: Published for the Biographical Research Center by the University of Hawaii Press, 2009).

> A diary is first and foremost what was written at the time of the events themselves…a chunk of living reality, not only in terms of its material but also with regard to the writer's perspective, [the diary] is a clear documentation of the time. The obvious sign of the boundary is the personal moment, and this distinguishes between a chronicle and a diary. A chronicle imparts the events and happenings of a certain time on a day to day basis. A chronicle contains facts, sometimes also the writer's interpretation, sometimes it is written beautifully and with great insight…on other occasions it can be dry and of a purely informative nature…it is natural that a diary contains elements of the personal, emotional, intimate, more or less. The diary is a place for the writer to pour out his soul.[71]

Some diaries include surveys of past events and reflect the author's perspective, even if only partially. We find this, for example, in the diary by Calel Perechodnik, who wrote most of his diary in hiding and describes therein the events prior to his arrival at his hideout,[72] and also in Kunstadt's diary, in which the author depicts the deportations and the initial period of acclimatization in Dzhurin, dating to around half a year before he began keeping a diary. Yet a diary that is written at the time of the events also presents the author's understanding and his personal interpretation of the unfolding events, and even responds to a significant degree to his spiritual needs. Amos Goldberg discusses this at length in his study of diary writing in the period of the Holocaust.

> The diary…is, nevertheless, a kind of ongoing story in the first person, which presents all the identity-creating characteristics of the life story and autobiography….This capacity of the diary may explain, in part, the prevalence of first-person writing during the Holocaust. In such a turbulent time, when all the components of identity are radically undermined, when the

---

71 Chaim Aron Kaplan, *Megilat Yisorin*: *Yoman Geto Varsha, 1 September 1939–4 Be'August 1942* (Hebrew) (Tel Aviv: Am Oved, 1966), pp. 20–28.

72 Calel Perechodnik, *Am I a Murderer? Testament of a Jewish Ghetto Policeman* (Boulder: Westview Press, 1996).

> concepts of yesterday can no longer explain what is happening today and are unable to offer hope for tomorrow, people find it hard to understand themselves and the world, to establish order and find meaning. At such a time, diary writing may help writers preserve a shred of their identity and afford a modicum of cohesion to the world into which they have been thrust. The diary weaves fine narrative threads between the fragments of the protagonist's disintegrating world.[73]

Alexandra Garbarini emphasizes in her book the importance of Holocaust diaries.[74] At the same time, she claims that diaries do not reflect the entire range of experiences and incidents that the Jews underwent during the war, and not even the entire spectrum of encounters and incidents that the writers themselves experienced. However, they shed light on the author's efforts to give meaning to the events and experiences.

Although diaries bring to the fore the personal aspect, they provide a great deal of information about the writer's surroundings, and the entire range of developments and events. Diaries that were kept by activists in Jewish organizations, or by people with a deep social consciousness, describe in great detail the general public and the environment. For example, the diary of Chaim Aron Kaplan[75] and Emmanuel Ringelblum's journal entries,[76] which were written in chronological order by date, mainly describe events of import to the general public and only sometimes mention personal events. Kunstadt's diary, which was written over a lengthy period, is representative of both types. It contains a great deal of personal elements and also devotes significant sections to general public affairs in the Dzhurin ghetto. He also describes the Romanian authorities

---

73 Amos Goldberg, *Trauma in the First Person*: *Diary Writing During the Holocaust* (Bloomington: Indiana University Press, 2017), p. 36.

74 Alexandra Garbarini, *Numbered Days*: *Diaries and the Holocaust* (New Haven and London: Yale University Press, 2006), p. xiii.

75 For an English translation, see Chaim Aron Kaplan, *Scroll of Agony*: *The Warsaw Diary of Chaim A. Kaplan*, ed. and tr. by Abraham I. Katsh (Bloomington: Indiana University Press, 1999).

76 For an English translation, see Emmanuel Ringelblum, *Notes From the Warsaw Ghetto*: *The Journal of Emmanuel Ringelblum* (San Francisco: Pickle Partners Publishing, 2015).

and even neighboring ghettos, such as Shargorod and Moghilev, as we will discuss further.

Few diaries from Transnistria have reached us. Some of the diaries that survived were written by young men and women in various ghettos and were published many years later. The diary of Miriam Korber, a seventeen-year-old young woman who was deported from Rădăuţi, Southern Bukovina, in the autumn of 1941, and was in the Dzhurin ghetto, was published only in 1995. She recorded the events that occurred in the ghetto almost every day, providing the reader with a description of daily life in the ghetto, while focusing on herself, her family members, and her friends.[77] A similar portrait is found also in the diary of Mordechai Kopshtein, from Câmpulung, Southern Bukovina, who arrived with his family in the Shargorod ghetto. Kopshtein described in detail his family and the difficulties that they faced when his father found himself unable to provide for the household following the deportation.[78] These diaries reflect the perspective of young people, and while they contain many insights regarding the difficulties faced by adults, they focus on the problems of young people and lack a broader and more mature perspective.

A few diaries that were kept by adults in Transnistria have survived and have been published. They focus for the most part on family life and their fate. An outstanding example is the diary of Cerna Bercovici, who was deported from Câmpulung in the autumn of 1941 and arrived, together with the rest of her family, in the Shargorod ghetto. She often detailed the daily difficulties of life in the ghetto, in particular the mass mortality due to the typhus epidemic.[79] In addition to the diaries, memoirs regarding Transnistria have also been published, although they are beyond the boundaries of our discussion here.[80]

---

77 Miriam Korber Bercovici, *Jurnal din Ghetou: Dzhurin Transnistria, 1941–1943* (Bucharest: Kriterion, 1995).

78 Sections of his diary have been published in Shmaya Avni, ed., *Sefer Zikaron Lekehilat Yehudei Kimpulong–Bukovina Vehaseviva* (Hebrew), vol. 1 (Tel Aviv: Irgun Yotzei Kimpulong–Bukovina Vehaseviva, 2003), pp. 228–258.

79 Cerna Bercovici and Willy Bercovici, *Hashashnu Pen Nitpogeg*: *Yoman Transnistriya*: *Zihronot Mehatzava HaBriti* (Hebrew) (Jerusalem: Yad Vashem, 2016).

80 Memoirs written in later years were published decades after the Holocaust. For example, see the book by Yosef Govrin, who was thirteen when he was deported to Transnistria, in which he describes daily life in the Moghilev ghetto, Yosef Govrin, *Betzel Ha'ovdan*:

There are likewise diaries that have never been published. For example, Zvi Weinberg, who was deported from Suceava and arrived with his family in the ghetto of Murafa, depicted in his diary the days prior to the deportation and the organization in preparation for it, the deportation itself, and daily life in Murafa, with all its difficulties. He also described the demographic tapestry created in the Murafa ghetto upon the arrival of the deportees, and the relations between the Jewish population in the ghetto and the leadership, which was comprised of deportees from Southern Bukovina.[81]

Kunstadt's Diary

Kunstadt's diary is comprised of five notebooks written in Yiddish in the first person. Since he began keeping a diary in April 1942, Kunstadt wrote in it almost every day, sometimes even two or three times a day. Although writing by nature is a tool to organize thoughts and events, Kunstadt's writing contains many associative elements, as well as rich and varied depictions of events from different perspectives.

The reader of Kunstadt's diary encounters the journalist's perspective in the depictions of the daily routine and the management of life in the ghetto. Many entries concern the ghetto leadership and the leadership of other ghettos in northern Transnistria. Kunstadt discusses the Romanian authorities, the personnel changes among those in command in the ghetto, and the Romanian police. He often mentions the constant threat of deportation to labor camps, the forced labor in the region, and the difficult conditions that the workers experienced. He likewise depicts the repeated demands to reduce the number of residents in Dzhurin,

---

Zihronot Al Transnistriya Ve'al Haha'apala Le'Eretz Yisrael (Hebrew) (Tel Aviv: Ghetto Fighters' House, 1999); the book by Herman Shulman, who was fifteen years old when he was deported and who later wrote about daily life in the Bershad ghetto, Herman Shulman, *Hesed Shel Emet: Edut Megeta'ot Hamavet Shel Transnistriya* (Hebrew) (Jerusalem: Yad Vashem, 2010); and the book by David Keisch, who was a ten-year-old boy at the time of the deportation and who published his memories from Transnistria in 2007, David Keisch, *Mota Shel Shtika* (Hebrew) (Tel Aviv: self-published, 2007).

81 Zvi Weinberg, "Yoman: Oktober 1941–Mai 1944" (Hebrew), an unpublished manuscript given to Sarah Rosen by Zvi Weinberg's son.

demands that meant deportation to camps on the banks of the Bug, from which almost no one returned. He describes occurrences in other ghettos, mainly comparing them with Dzhurin, which was considered "a model colony." On more than one occasion, Kunstadt reports news of the war and its developments, discusses the Nazi leaders and their worldviews, and clarifies his attitude about the Romanian government's policy.

The diary also sheds light on Kunstadt's character: a man with a developed social consciousness, who grieves and laments the relations among the residents of the ghetto. His anguish at the interpersonal relations and the social ties that developed among the deportees themselves, and the difficult relationship between the deportees and the local Jewish population with whom they shared their homes and their daily life, is evident.

Kunstadt was involved in the cultural life in Dzhurin. Together with friends, he endeavored to organize cultural evenings that expressed the longing to escape from the gray and onerous daily life. These efforts also reflect a practical approach—the evenings of readings of stories by Sholem Aleichem or performances by the co-organizer, the hazan Solomon, were intended not only to lift the spirits of the ghetto residents but also to yield some profit for the organizers.

The diary also offers a personal perspective regarding Kunstadt and his nuclear and extended family. This aspect of the writing is replete with emotions, the difficulties Kunstadt himself faced, and how he dealt both emotionally and physically with the reality of being uprooted and forced into the ghetto. On more than one occasion, he also expresses his thoughts on human nature, the significance of memory, and his role as a documenter. These various perspectives are not organized in any particular order—sometimes many appear in one single entry, sometimes one aspect is more prominent than the others, and sometimes only one perspective is presented in an entry, depending on the writer's mood that day. On days that Kunstadt was troubled by current events, he wrote more than one entry.

The language that he uses is sometimes suited to the various perspectives and the levels of detail of the narrative. His impressive command of language and extensive use of images, of spoken folk language, and of the sayings and proverbs that were part of the fabric of Bukovinian Yiddish,[82] as well as his remarkable knowledge of Jewish sources, and of both Hebrew and general literature, are evident throughout the diary.

Analysis of the Diary

In this section we will endeavor to highlight a number of central elements in the style and content of Kunstadt's diary. The first entry, dated April 11, 1942, constitutes a kind of personal declaration, spiced with a pinch of irony and perhaps even a certain degree of self-pity.

> I am beginning to write a diary—an odd, strange, and exceptional diary. It will be, if it merits survival, no less aberrant and bizarre than my present life (if you could call this life ...) and the lives of nearly 250,000 dispossessed and homeless people, who have now been wandering around the decimated shtetls and villages between the Dniester and the Bug for more than six months.

However, the remainder of the entry is permeated with sarcasm, as Kunstadt contemplates the fate of the "holy" pages of his diary, which were likely to be used for something that requires a "blessing," meaning toilet paper in the muddy bog of Dzhurin: "I cannot find words for "toilet" in the Dzhurin dictionary." These few lines reflect both Kunstadt's sharp, sarcastic style, which is like a recurring scarlet thread throughout the entire diary, and the depressing situation of the deportees who found themselves in the primitive small town of Dzhurin, where they lacked even the most basic commodities. These contemplations led him to the depressing conclusion that "it would have been no less preferable for the Angel of Death to have taken pity a few months earlier on the wretched Jews who fell like scythed hay along the roads of Bessarabia and Ukraine."

---

82 This Yiddish dialect was unique to Romanian Jews and differs from the Yiddish spoken by Jews in Poland and Lithuania.

Ostensibly, this opening statement declares his intention to write, yet it also questions this very intention due to concerns about the future threat to the fate of the diary. That same day, after a break of a few hours, at 3 P.M., while still at work in the office of the ghetto council, Kunstadt again took up his pen. The instinct to write, which he refers to as "the evil inclination," returned and seized him. His journalistic instinct again awakened, as it had in the city of Rădăuţi. As such, he endeavored to write in an organized manner, not in a chaotic or associative way as he had done when writing his first lines, trying to document events before the memory of them could become hazy and be forgotten.

> I was bothered by the thought that I have not yet written down a single letter regarding the turbulent experiences that have assaulted me and my relatives over the last six months…I have been longing to pour out the terrible memories on paper as quickly as possible, before the details become blurred and vague in my mind.

The first day of writing in his diary concludes with thoughts about human nature and the significance of memory.

> I wonder how quickly the intense impressions dissipate like clouds and lose their distinct features. Life here seems unreal, the people around me no more than dreamlike shadows, and all the fearful events but a nightmare, a phantasm—we will wake up very slowly from the dream, sigh deeply, spit three times, and quickly say, [banish] "all demons and spirits!"

These two entries from the first day reflect several features of the diary, alluding to the process of writing and its aim, and also to the author as a reporter who is involved, agitated, despairing, hopeful, and contemplative of human nature. For Kunstadt, writing was not only documentation. In emotional terms, it was a means to vent his anger, sorrow, and impotence. "Nevertheless, today I have been reconciled with my pen because of some news that jolted me so severely that I must try to calm my rattled nerves by dipping my pen in ink." Likewise, writing was also a source of comfort.

> And yet, I was grief stricken when I discovered the terrible end of my relatives, people with whom I had grown up and with whom I was in contact until the deportation. I will never see them again, and they too will never see me again. Hence, I seek comfort in the silent pages of this notebook and pour out my anguished heart. These pages listen and do not interrupt my words.

However, it seems that the desire to document and to preserve the memory for future generations was Kunstadt's main motivation for writing the diary. This is reinforced by his son, who related in his testimony that his father would sometimes read to them from the diary. Kunstadt thus conveyed to his family the importance of the diary for the family, and the fact that he read it aloud to them reflects the desire to shape his children's memory. Kunstadt felt that it was his duty to document the events, yet at the same time, he feared that his writing did not respond adequately to this need, that perhaps he did not have enough time, breathing space, or the perspective that such writing requires—this is a recurring conflict that appears in other entries. On August 26, 1942, after a few months of writing, during which he had filled dozens of pages, he writes,

> At first it seemed to me that this diary would write itself, because sensations literally roll around underfoot here, begging for mercy, just to be lifted up and preserved for future generations. Every Jew in this region has his own story, and he is the hero of a stirring tragedy that surpasses the imagination of Sophocles. However, it seems that every moment in Transnistria is so charged that it requires so much time and such a broad perspective that does not allow it to be squeezed into a few meager lines of a diary, recorded hastily, standing tensely on one foot. It may even be a sin to break the bloody chronicle of Transnistria into small change. The brutal and devastating material deserves a different approach.
>
> Therefore, I decided to stop writing the diary and to destroy the pages that make me angry and resentful, which I had written. I eventually overcame the despair and listened to the counterargument within me, which claimed: a miracle

> may occur and your fragmentary writings will be the only remaining memory of Transnistria, and when it will fall into the hands of someone who is more gifted than you, that person will make it more digestible, as is fitting.

Kunstadt also mulled over writing from a personal, private angle and writing from a general, public perspective, eventually concluding that the two are complementary. The entry dated April 27, 1942, is entirely devoted to this issue, to this internal debate.

> Since I began writing this diary, a difficult question has been bothering me. I keep asking myself: Should I note only general events and experiences, as in a chronicle, or perhaps also details about myself and my relatives, as in a book? It's just a question. After all, no one is forcing me to write, and anyone who is a good friend would surely try to dissuade me, using harsh words, from engaging in such a dangerous activity that could end badly. Should these pages fall into the wrong hands, God forbid, I may as well recite the *Videh* together with my family. Indeed, I am not accountable to anyone…However, the opposing argument sneaks in, claiming: What if a miracle occurs and this diary is salvaged and is found by someone who wants to know what the faded pages say about the Transnistrian tragedy? Although it is quite possible that someone will toss the memories with disdain and say: What a Transnistrian diary! It is full of drivel about himself, which interests me like last year's snow, instead of telling about the collective, about the general suffering of the masses.
>
> …I will truly strive to present both sides: the crux regarding the collective, but without forgetting my own sorrows.

However, he continues to mull over the proper way to write the diary. On April 11, 1943, after a full year of writing in the diary, Kunstadt celebrates a birthday and takes stock, which entails mixed feelings of satisfaction and despair.

> Today this diary celebrates a milestone: it is one year old. Its pages describe memories and events as experienced around me and within me—not all of them and not always in full detail. For the most part, I have found myself in a state of despair, observing everything with contempt, and mostly diverting myself with a chronicle while the roof burns over my head. It is possible that the few memories that I have saved from oblivion are of no real value due to their thoroughly subjective nature. I have devoted too much space to myself, as if I were more than a grain of sand in a desert. The fact that I have not refrained from judging people and situations according to their behavior toward me, for better or for worse, is also certainly a serious flaw. However, I have a bit of an excuse: this diary clearly bears a personal imprint, and I do not pretend to produce an academic chronicle. I do not intend to enter the realm of a future historian, were he to appear, and to demonstrate a measure of objectivity about the disaster of Transnistria.

Indeed, daily life, with its difficulties and its small gratifications, sometimes absorbed most of Kunstadt's emotional energy: the worries about how to procure food, how to obtain wood for heating in the harsh Ukrainian winter, and how to preserve clothing, especially shoes, which wore out quickly in the long months of deep mud and endless snow.

Kunstadt worked in the community building, which housed the Jewish Council, close to the heads of the council. He heard their discussions, was aware of the challenges and problems that they faced, and he did not hesitate to criticize the council members. According to Kunstadt, they took care of their own, even though they were supposed to be public leaders, and they were responsible for many of the injustices that occurred in the ghetto. Despite being in constant fear of dismissal from his position, he criticizes the behavior of the council without restraint in his diary. He portrays the council's policies and its leaders' priorities. He describes how the new demographic fabric created social layering that placed the exiles from Southern Bukovina at the top of the hierarchy, the Jews of Bessarabia below them, and the local Ukrainian Jews, whom he pitied, at the very bottom. In his pictorial language, Kunstadt compassionately describes the weak groups in the ghetto, the starving, destitute Jews, including the deportees from Bessarabia and Northern Bukovina, and the local Ukrainian Jews. He calls the former, half-cynically and half-angrily, "non-kosher" "*kapporres* chickens"[83] over whose heads the slaughterer's knife was waving. These Jews, he notes, were the first to be sent away from the ghettos.

> The Romanian overlords in Shargorod explained to him that Dzhurin is filled with too many Yids and that the overcrowding can be, God forbid, detrimental to people's health. Indeed, because of this rightful claim, the high-level officials came to the conclusion that the blood of the Jewish community must be shed and a significant portion must be deported to the camps by the Bug, or handed over to the Germans on the other side of the river….It seems that the Ukrainian and Bessarabian Jews, and also the "non-kosher" Jews from Northern Bukovina, will be the *kapporres* chickens.

The Ukrainian Jews—the additional group of even lower status—had fled from the camps on the other side of the Bug and had sought refuge in the ghetto, where they went into hiding. Kunstadt refers to these Jews as "the most non-kosher of the non-kosher," which in his cynical language makes it clear to the reader that they were deprived of any right whatsoever to exist.

> Among the people in hiding, quite a few are the most non-kosher of the non-kosher. They are not Romanian Jews, in general, but the few remaining remnants of the decimated Jewish communities in Ukraine, where German and Romanian murderers have slaughtered almost all the Jews.

Kunstadt criticizes the economic system that developed in the ghetto and the relations with the Romanian authorities, the use of bribes, and the

83 *Kapparot* in Hebrew, which means atonement, but in the sense of ransom, is a pre-Yom Kippur ritual in which the sins of a Jew are symbolically transferred to a chicken that is slaughtered or sold for charity.

various ways in which a minority of "influential people in the ghetto," whom he refers to as "the newly wealthy," established themselves in their new surroundings without any consideration for the suffering of the wretched poor among the deportees from Bessarabia and the local Ukrainian Jews. The newly wealthy, he claims, were unscrupulous and lacked any sense of social responsibility, and the leaders of the council usually backed them and apparently even feared them. Thus, the disparity between the weak segments of the population levels and those of means continued to grow—the weak were not only singled out by the hunger and sickness that accosted them but also by the greater likelihood of deportation to work camps and forced labor. Those in authority and the affluent managed to avoid the deportations that often determined whether a person would live or die.

Kunstadt also explains the relations between the deportees and the Ukrainian non-Jews. He distinguishes between two groups of Ukrainians: nationalist Ukrainians and rural peasants. Among the Ukrainian nationalists were members of the Ukrainian militias who cooperated with the occupying authorities. The mass murders of Jews throughout Transnistria during the Romanian–German invasion led to an outbreak of antisemitic sentiments that were common among Ukrainians. The latter participated in the slaughter of the Jews, which was carried out by the Romanian army and the gendarmes, as well as in the plundering of the property of those murdered or deported. The cooperation between the nationalist Ukrainian groups, who opposed the Soviet authorities, and the Germans and Romanians in harming the Jews is a known phenomenon, particularly in the first period of the ghettos' existence, until the Jewish police was established.

Kunstadt describes how members of the Ukrainian militia helped the gendarmes drive the Jews out of their homes for forced labor. Many members of the militia served as guards in the forced labor camps and treated the Jewish forced laborers with cruelty and brutality. On August 17, 1943, Kunstadt wrote, "We found out that more than thirty forced laborers had fled from the peat-pits in Tulchin, and apparently the gendarmes or the Ukrainian militia killed all of them."

Members of the Ukrainian militias, in full cooperation with the Romanian gendarmes, prevented Ukrainian farmers from bringing their goods to the market. In other cases, members of the Ukrainian militia would raid the marketplace on a rampage, indiscriminately beating anyone there, whether Jew or peasant, and together with the Romanian gendarmes would turn over the farmers' stalls and trample their produce. Kunstadt describes such an incident in his diary.

> The decree concerning the starvation of the camp is already in force today. The authorities have not only forbidden the farmers to bring flour, potatoes, and bread to the market…but also beans, peas, grits, and cattle…
>
> Peasants who had not yet known about the decree arrived at dawn in the market with all the best products—wagons loaded with flour, fresh produce, potatoes, and all kinds of provisions…
>
> The jubilation had not lasted for more than a quarter of an hour when the gendarmes suddenly savagely stormed in, whips in hand, and pillaged all the goods, even the "kosher" [legal] foods such as butter and poultry.

Kunstadt paints in his diary a complex picture of the Jews' relations with the rural peasants, simple, downtrodden people, who barely eked out a living from their agricultural labor. He was aware that they too suffered at the hands of the German occupiers and the Romanian authorities, who treated them with extreme cruelty and confiscated their produce.

> There are two obvious reasons for the lack of goods at the market. First, the Romanian occupation authorities steal fresh produce, livestock, dairy products, and all kinds of food from the farmers, leaving them only what is necessary to survive, unless a farmer hides part of his harvest at the risk of his life.

They in turn exploit the Jews and do not hesitate to plunder and fleece them.

> The peasants from the surroundings have discovered that really good deals are to be had literally in the streets, and many non-Jewish women are going up the hill to snatch up Jewish property at bargain prices. Clothes, shoes, bedding, tables,

> chairs, and all kinds of household goods are being discarded all around the hovels....The cunning peasants immediately see that the Jews are desperate for cash and bargain ten times before they show a whit of a mark and milk them dry.

Yet they also treat them humanely, perhaps due to feelings of brotherhood toward their fellow victims, sometimes betraying them at the same time.

> It often happens that non-Jewish women take pity on the fugitives and give them a piece of bread, while their husbands slip away to hand the "criminals" over to the gendarmes. There are also cases of kindheartedness among a few Ukrainians, and they provide food and clothes, and even hide someone in an attic for a while.

The villagers also passed on the news to the ghetto residents, for example, regarding the fate of the Jews in other places. On April 28, 1942, Kunstadt relates the news of the slaughter in Vinnitsa, in which SS men shot Jews into pits: "The peasants who conveyed the bitter news to Dzhurin recounted that the earth over the graves continued to heave for quite some time."

Descriptions of Kunstadt's extended and nuclear family account for a significant part of the diary. Kunstadt felt responsible for his family—his wife, son, and daughter—and was constantly worried about providing for them, leading him to cling to a job that disgusted him. He also feared infection with the Rickettsia bacteria that causes typhus—an illness that killed many Jews in the ghetto. He worried about his wife's family, his father-in-law, Şmuel Merling, a widower, and his sister-in-law, Rachel, but mainly for his mother and sister. He deeply admired and loved his mother, who had been widowed at an early age and had raised her children with great dedication. He saw her as a brave, independent woman who was infinitely devoted to her children. He describes his mother's devotion to his sister when the latter caught typhus and was hospitalized. "It torments me to see Mother shrinking more and more each day, barely able to stand on her feet, as a result of running to the hospital daily and standing for hours in front of the closed window." As his sister's condition deteriorated, his elderly mother continued to visit the hospital every day.

> Rivka is still burning with fever and does not recognize anyone. I have not been able to persuade Mother to limit her trips to the hospital and to stop standing for hours in front of the shuttered windows…but Mother is stubborn and is not willing to even listen. She drags herself with a walking stick to the hospital and is really wearing herself out.

His sister, Rivka, eventually recovered, but then his mother fell ill. Rivka devotedly cared for her, but his mother passed away. This death was a severe blow for Kunstadt to bear, and he found it difficult to find any comfort after her death. He entitled the second notebook of the diary "My Mother's Death."

Kunstadt recounts in his diary that he used to go to the market to buy food or wood for heating on the days that the farmers brought their goods. It is clear that he was responsible for providing for the family, while his wife cooked and prepared the meals under the difficult conditions of living in one room that served all purposes. A model of the family that emerges from the diary is characterized by gender relations that reflect the prevailing reality, not only in traditional Jewish society. Kunstadt was the breadwinner and decision maker who acted as a link between the external sphere and the family domain. The diary does not mention his wife's activities, or her relations with the extended family. Kunstadt talks mostly about her frail health and her heart condition. Yet at least one entry, written at a fateful moment, reveals their common concerns and the warm relations between the members of both the nuclear and the extended family, and their mutual feelings as well as Kunstadt's character.

On May 7, 1942, at 6 P.M., a rumor spread through the ghetto that all craftsmen and professionals in the camps in Transnistria were to be deported, which immediately prompted diverse opinions. The optimists thought that the craftsmen would be sent back to their old homes in Romania, where they were needed, while the pessimists believed that they would be sent to other camps, meaning the separation of families. People debated whether to register as practicing a profession or not.

> The news confounded and plagued me, as well as my household. Speaking about professions, I can register myself as an expert book printer, bookkeeper, translator, typist,

> graphologist, clerk....my wife, Roza, and my sister, Rivka, are certified nurses, who once had the pleasure of taking a course given by the Red Cross—may we not need it. Not to mention my sister-in-law, Rachel—she is certainly the cream of the crop—a doctor of chemistry! In short, there are plenty of trades but few blessings among us, and no one who can give me any advice: to register or not?
>
> When I told my family the news, they began to dance with joy. Roza and the children were bursting with happiness. It seems to them, poor things, that already tomorrow at dawn we will turn the wagon around to go back home, and the seven months of hell will vanish like a bad dream. My eleven-year-old daughter, Iza, a very sensitive soul, will not leave me alone and demands that I describe in great detail how we will travel home. What should I answer this child? How can I ruin this bright dream...
>
> Rachel burst into tears of great joy and ran swift as an arrow to tell her elderly father, my father-in-law, Șmuel Merling, the news. She wholly believes that for the sake of justice they will send all of us home quickly. A doctor's diploma is apparently no protection against naive delusions.

Kunstadt himself continued to wrestle with this the following day. "Oy, what should we do? My mind is about to explode, and there is no answer." The wavering continued, and in the entry of May 8, 1942, he writes,

> Rachel was fervently in favor of registering at first, and today someone put a bug in her ear, and she began to waver. That someone is her old father, to whom she is attached with a fanatic love. So, she is afraid that they will tear her away from her father.

And what about Kunstadt himself?

> I myself had a difficult afternoon, racked by the question of "yes" or "no," which is really driving me crazy....Roza proposes that I also register her—as a seamstress. My naive

> wife claims that if they send both of us somewhere, the authorities will agree in the name of justice not to tear the children away from their parents.

The debate persisted through May 9, 1942.

> I did not close my eyes all night, and feverishly tossed and turned around the fateful words "yes" or "no"...
>
> I did not allow my sister Rivka to register as a seamstress, because it would be a tragedy to tear her away from our elderly and frail mother.

On May 10, the decision was finally made. "Neither I nor anyone in my family registered and the matter is settled. The lists are already in Shargorod."

In the ghetto, Kunstadt, an intellectual and a scholar who had been active in the literary field and associated with writers and men of letters, found himself in a reality that pushed cultural activities to the farthest margins. The concerns of physical existence, obtaining food and wood for heating, personal safety, the need for clothes and especially shoes, all demanded most of his emotional energy and creativity. Yet despite this, the diary reflects Kunstadt's spiritual and intellectual world, and the breadth of his knowledge. He quotes from Jewish sources, from the Bible, Talmud, and Mishnah to the Kabbalah, Midrash, and Aggadah, from modern Hebrew and Yiddish literature, including Bialik, Sholem Aleichem, and Y. L. Peretz, and from general literature, ranging from Greek tragedies to Oscar Wilde and Shakespeare. He read in several languages and mentions his joy, for example, when he found a copy of Sholem Aleichem in Russian, and discusses the quality of the translation.

> I have just finished reading—no, devouring—Shalom Aleichem's novel, which I had previously only heard about: *Blondzendike Shtern*...However, I was not fated to fully rejoice because the stars did not speak to me in S.A.'s [Shalom Aleichem's] iridescent language, but rather in Russian. The truth is that the translation is quite good, a kind of Yiddishized

> Russian, which suits it but, nevertheless, without homey, Jewish charm.

Kunstadt describes his efforts to provide the wider public with a little culture. Together with his friend, the hazan Moshe Solomon, he organized evenings of entertainment, including the performance of cantorial pieces, accompanied by an accordion and readings of literature, as well as songs based on texts written by Kunstadt himself and set to music by Solomon's musician wife. On May 30, 1942, he describes a ditty that he wrote, which was influenced by the style of life in Dzhurin.

> This ditty, half mockery and more than half an imprecating joke, has only documentary value and no literary worth whatsoever. It even merited a fitting tune, composed by the *hazen* from Rădăuţi, Moshe Solomon...together with his wife, Linka, a distinguished musician who plays a number of instruments...Moshe Solomon, a creative composer of cantorial music and a rare musical talent, sang this ditty twice at the "Literary Enterprise" during *Hanuke* 1941 in Dzhurin. The crowd applauded him enthusiastically.

The first of three shows that he organized took place on *Hanuke* 1941, only months after arriving in Dzhurin.

> I will perhaps some other time elaborate on this project, which Solomon and I organized under strange conditions in a vacant barn somewhere. This "hall" was decorated with three lamps...the two female impresarios stood by the door—Roza and Linka—and collected payment: two potatoes or two cuttings of wood for an adult, three for a couple, and only one for a child...
>
> We did not manage to organize more than three performances, although we earned quite a handsome sum: my share of the income from the last performance was 18 large potatoes, no less than 40 medium sized potatoes, and 20 decent pieces of wood. Therefore, life was supposed to be beautiful, but then the council decided to settle three families...in our

> "concert hall." So, the muses were silenced. It seems that the "lords" slyly outwitted us, because we did not sing "*May Yofes*" to them.

At all the other performances in which he was an undercover partner, works that he had penned, humoresques, rhyming prose, and poems were read. Some are included in the diary. Kunstadt emphasizes that his intention was not to achieve a high poetic level but rather documentary writing. This is reinforced by the fact that he entrusted the literary, documentary notebook that he had edited in December 1941 to one of his friends who returned to Romania in 1942. As far as we know, this notebook has not been found.

On October 24, 1943, the orphanage in Dzhurin was inaugurated. Kunstadt describes the dedication ceremony.

> The Rădăuţi *hazen*, Moshe Solomon, sang "*Mizmor Shir Hanukes Habayis*," accompanied by an accordion ([played by] Grafer) and a fiddle ([played by] M. Farizer). The colony chief delivered a sermon in German, followed by the rabbi of Dzhurin, Rabbi Herşel Karalnic, the rabbi of Siret, Rabbi Baruch Hager, and the second-in-command, Moshe Katz, who spoke in Yiddish. People wiped their eyes with handkerchiefs during the sermons....I too took part in the program and read a poem that I had written in honor of the gala. I will include the text below, not, God forbid, because of its "literary value" (by no means! ...) but rather as a historical document.

Four months later, on February 15, 1944, a *Tu B'Shevat* celebration was held at the orphanage. In his description of the ceremony, Kunstadt expresses his social sensitivity and compassion for the weak.

> Today, the 21st of Shevat, a late *Tu B'Shevat* celebration was held at the orphanage, which was to serve as a farewell party at the same time, because we are waiting for the repatriation order of the orphans at any moment....The program included Yiddish folk songs, sung by a children's choir (directed by the

> *hazen* from Rădăuţi, Moshe Solomon); dance and rhythmic gymnastics; a dramatization of David Frishman's novel [*Shelosha She'ahalnu*:] *Tithadesh*"…
>
> We had to be tougher than iron to swallow the tears of joy upon seeing the miracle that had befallen the sixty children, who had been abandoned on the Ukrainian plains. They now look like other children, clothed and shod, their cheeks have the color of the living, and their eyes beam with happiness and childish mischievousness.

To summarize Kunstadt's cultural activity in the ghetto, we present his comments on a poem entitled "March Song of the Transnistrian Slaves," which he composed after "hearing the lamentations of the slaves returning from Tulchin, Trikhaty, and Varvorovka," that had a strong impact on him. The stanzas reflect a shred of the tragedies and deaths that occurred in the hell known as work camps.

> It is clear to me that the poem has little literary worth; perhaps only the poetic value of an onion peel. Nevertheless, I will preserve this modest memory of the catastrophes, because of the documentary spark that burns therein. Perhaps I am making a small contribution to the construction of the chronicle of Transnistria, which will be published sooner or later, provided that there will still be Jews left to assume this task…
>
> By the way, allow me to note an important fact here. In Transnistria, poets are as prevalent as mushrooms after the rain….According to the old axiom, the muses are silent when the cannons thunder, but in the mad times in which we live, everything is upside down, so why should the muses hold their tongues?

Hereafter

Three years after the outbreak of World War II, on September 1, 1942, Kunstadt wrote an entry that contains a historical, philosophical analysis characteristic of many of his diary entries. This entry was written at the height of the difficult days in Transnistria, before the lives of the deportees were eased somewhat by the aid sent from Romania and the change in the Romanian government's policy toward Nazi Germany. In our opinion, when reading these words, deep emotions are evoked that not only concern the past but also have significance for the reality of the reader's life, both in Israel and all over the world.

> The younger generation, who until then had not yet known the taste of war, did not understand the meaning of the menace now upon us as did we, the war veterans, who had lived through World War I in 1914–1918. It was clear to us, the veterans of war, that in the beginning it is greeted with cheerful cries and hopeful prophecies that foretell that within a few weeks the dove of peace will return and hover over God's beautiful little world again, but gradually the Angel of Death settles in and establishes himself as landlord for many years….
>
> Thus, it pleased God to establish the world order ever since He created Cain and Abel, and, apparently, thus it will continue to proceed as long as His beautiful little world continues to exist. There has never been a lack of justifications for mass slaughters: whether carried out in honor of God, or in honor of God's appointed kings and counts, or to defend the sanctity of the fatherland, or to uphold the sublime teachings of Karl Marx, or to save the world from those teachings—the Angel of Death is always just…
>
> This bloodthirsty madness has been raging for three full years, and millions of human beings have already been slaughtered, first and foremost the Jews. The demon who rules over the non-kosher people, the "writers and thinkers," has undertaken to annihilate all the Jews, old and young, as far as his *Stukas* and armored vehicles can reach…if some

extraordinary miracle does not occur quickly, of the 7 million Jews in Europe, no remnant whatsoever will remain.

The madness of World War II will certainly come to an end as well. They will sign peace treaties and delude themselves, whoever survives until then, that there must be no more war—there will not be. Diplomats will lay out plans for eternal peace, writers will flood the bookshop windows with pacifist musings and will brandish Isaiah's empty prophecy, "and they will beat their swords into plowshares." They will show films with real images of massacres in the movie theaters, and everyone will be revolted by the heinous, mutual slaughter of human beings. At the same time, the seeds of the next war will slowly ripen in the depths of the depraved human soul once more. Both sides will find an excuse at the opportune time, and the wedding will begin once again from the beginning, with more guests and with more abundant fare.

Acknowledgements

We would like to thank everyone who helped to make the publication of this diary possible.

Special thanks go to Herbert Kunstadt, who supported the publication and answered our questions in two extensive interviews concerning his family life in Transnistria, the return to Romania, and the fate of the lost manuscript. The information that he shared with us significantly expanded our understanding of the lives of Kunstadt's nuclear and extended family. He described in detail his mother's encounters with the local peasants, when she bartered various household items for food, and also told us about the family's daily routine and the lessons that his father and mother organized for him and his sister. They were taught core subjects, such as math and composition, and his father educated him in biblical texts in preparation for his Bar Mitzvah, while his mother taught the children French. He also described meetings with the extended family, visits to friends, and card games that are almost never mentioned in the diary, which he remembers with great fondness. Herbert Kunstadt joined us in our efforts, albeit without success, to find the manuscript in YIVO. As such, we thank him from the bottom of our hearts. We also wish to thank Lipman Kunstadt's granddaughter, Shuli Sadler, who shared with us what she knew about the family in a telephone interview and gave us a photograph of her grandfather.

Thank you to Rebecca Wolpe, who masterfully translated the manuscript from Yiddish to English; the Yad Vashem Publications Department, which decided to publish this diary; and the dedicated language and production editor, Dania Valdez, who toiled tirelessly in her efforts to discover the meaning of difficult terms, compared translations of various phrases, and spared no effort in bringing this important diary to the highest possible level. We are infinitely grateful to her for her professionalism and great effort.

Last but not least to the artist Shlomo Schwartz, a Holocaust survivor from Transnistria, who generously allowed us to use one of his drawings on the cover of this diary.

On April 13, 1945, upon returning to Rădăuţi after the difficult years of exile, Kunstadt wrote in his diary,

> And thus I conclude my painful memories of the "Deportation of the Jews beyond the Dniester ...," which I have been able to preserve at great risk and to bring to a safe shore. If I merit seeing the publication and distribution of these memories in the Diaspora of Israel, it will be the happiest day of my life.

Although Kunstadt did not live to see his diary published and distributed, we have done our best to fulfill his will and to publish the typed copy of his diary for the benefit of coming generations, so that they will never forget.

Sarah Rosen and Dalia Ofer
July 2022

Lipman Kunstadt (1901–1978).
Courtesy of the Kunstadt family.

Introduction[1]

Written on Six Fateful Calendar Sheets by the Minister of History Himself

Following the criminal 1939 agreement between the Soviet Union and Nazi Germany, which is naively and hypocritically called the "Molotov–Ribbentrop Pact," the two demon kings, Hitler and Stalin, may their names be blotted out, divided up the stolen patrimony of Poland, the Baltic states, and parts of Romania and Finland.

June 27, 1940

On that Thursday, the beginning of the dark times, a large number of Red Army troops burst into Romania with tanks, airplanes, cannons, and weapons galore, overwhelming and "liberating" the northern part of Bukovina, which includes the capital, Cernăuţi; the towns of Storojineţ, Vijniţa, Sadagura, Zastavna, Coţmeni, Ciudei, Baia, Noua-Suliţă, Bănila, and Seletin; and hundreds of rural villages. The "liberators" first stopped by the Siret River, which cuts Bukovina in half.[2] At that time,

---

1 Written after the war.

2 The Soviets annexed Bessarabia and the northern part of Bukovina as far as the Siret River, including the city of Cernăuţi. This was justified as rectifying an "injustice" committed in 1919, when Bessarabia was dissevered from the Soviet Union. As compensation, the Soviet Union demanded Northern Bukovina, whose population was for the most part Ukrainian, and whose history and culture were anchored in the historical past of the Ukrainian nation. The town of Seletin, which is located in southern Ukraine, close to the border with Romania, was part of the Austro–Hungarian Empire before World War I. During the interwar period, it was part of Romania.

approximately 100,000 Jews lived in Northern Bukovina—60,000 in Cernăuţi itself, which constituted the cultural center of Jewish Romania.[3]

The same bitter fate was inscribed on that fateful Thursday for the region of Bessarabia, which is separated from the Regat [Old Kingdom of Romania] by the Prut River. There were around 300,000 Jews in Bessarabia at the time. It was a flourishing community that was deeply rooted in its homeland for many generations. It had a high cultural level and, in particular, a strong Jewish consciousness, a national connection to Judaism and to our two languages—Hebrew and Yiddish—and a colorful and manifold spiritual character. The 800-year-old Jewish settlement of hundreds of thousands of Jews was the crown jewel of Greater Romania.[4]

---

3 According to the census conducted in 1930, the population of Bukovina numbered 853,009 persons: 379,691 Romanians; 248,567 Ukrainians; 92,492 Jews; and 75,533 Germans. According to the same census, the population in Bessarabia numbered 2,864,402, among them 1,610,757 Romanians; 314,211 Ukrainians; 351,912 Russians; and 204,858 Jews. Only the dominant ethnic groups in Bukovina and in Bessarabia are included in these figures. See Irina Livezeanu, *Cultural Politics in Greater Romania*: *Regionalism, Nation Building & Ethnic Struggle 1918–1930* (Ithaca and London: Cornell University Press, 1995), pp. 53, 92.

4 The lives of the entire population and, in particular, the Jews, was adversely affected during the year of Soviet rule, 1940–1941. The Russian regime confiscated the property of the members of the Jewish bourgeois and the middle class, impoverishing them, and consequently the Jewish communities suffered severe economic hardship. The Soviet authorities, who considered the owners of factories and businesses, large and small alike, bourgeois, issued to them new ID cards that were stamped with the number 11, indicating the clause that limited their freedom of movement and their right to change their residence. This number was also used in Russian-occupied areas of Poland; see Lea Prais, *Be'arafel Hanedudim*: *Asufat Eduyot Shel Plitim Yehudim Me'archiyon Oneg Shabbat, 1939–1943* (Hebrew) (Jerusalem: Yad Vashem, 2015), p. 17. The ID cards of the wealthy Jews and Zionists were stamped with the number 39, which marked them for deportation as bourgeois or as being involved in hostile political activities. Many were promptly arrested and deported to Siberia. The communities themselves lost most of their organizational features: the Soviets closed down cultural institutions and banned political and religious frameworks. The Jewish leaders were deported to Russia and Siberia, putting an end to communal organization, and Zionist activity was prohibited, as were the activities of Zionist youth movements. Following the collapse of the communal structure, the Jews were left without leadership or any supportive communal framework that could extend aid to the needy and provide legal assistance, as well as organize the population of the Jews, who would be deported to Transnistria in the future. See Dov Levin, *Tekufa Besograyim, 1939–1941*: *Temurot Behayei Hayehudim Be'ezorim Shesufhu LeVrit Hamo'atzot Bitehilat Milhemet Ha'olam Hasheniya* (Hebrew) (Jerusalem: The Hebrew University of Jerusalem and Ghetto Fighters' House, 1989), p. 75; Hayim Breiman, "Beitar BeNovoselitza," in Shalom Dorner, ed., *Novoselitza* (Hebrew) (Tel Aviv: Irgun

The Romanian military did not dare to oppose the Red giant and fled like poisoned mice from the occupied provinces to the Regat and Southern Bukovina. There the savage soldiers and their antisemitic commanders vented all their rage against the Jewish settlements. Rivers of Jewish blood flowed in Southern Bukovina and northern Moldavia.[5] Of the 250,000 Jews who were driven across the Bug and the Dniester, 50,000 extremely frail, gaunt skeletons, afflicted with all types of grave diseases, naked and barefoot, their spirits oppressed and broken, lived to see deliverance, without any strength to rejoice in the miracle of the exodus from Transnistria.

Yotzei Novoselitza Be'Yisrael, 1983), p. 188; Shlomo Shitnovitzer, ed., *Sefer Kehilat Hutin* (*Bessarabia*) (Hebrew) (Tel Aviv: Hotza'at Irgun Yotzei Hutin [Bessarabia] Be'Yisrael, 1974), pp. 84–85. During the period of Soviet rule in Northern Bukovina (1940–1941), the Jews in this region suffered the same fate as their brothers in Bessarabia.

5 This refers to the Dorohoi district in the northern Moldavia, Romania.

Jews waiting to cross the Dniester River.
Photo Collection, YVA, 90D07.

Jews waiting to cross the Dniester River.
Photo Collection, YVA, 90E06.

Jews crossing the Dniester River.
Photo Collection, YVA, 90E03.

Jews crossing the Dniester River.
Photo Collection, YVA, 90D08.

Notebook One

The Deportation of the Jews across the Dniester River

Dzhurin, April 11, 1942, 10 A.M.

I am beginning to write a diary—an odd, strange, and unusual diary. It will be, if it merits survival, no less aberrant and bizarre than my present life (if you could call this life ...) and the lives of nearly 250,000 dispossessed and homeless people who have now been wandering around the decimated shtetls and villages between the Dniester and the Bug for more than six months,[1] and who dream of the good fortune that was once theirs, which is so very, very distant.

It is very doubtful that this diary will unfold and reflect at the very least an inkling of the most painful and tragic period of my life, which began on *Simches Toyre* 5702 (October 14, 1941)[2] and will certainly one day come to an end—one way or another, as bad luck would have it. Whether I will have the desire to take my pen in hand and write anything on the pages of this notebook some other day is all the more dubious. It is very likely that tomorrow I, or someone around me, will use this paper on which I have written for something that requires a blessing,[3] and will not be aware of the "sanctity" of the diary ... not, God forbid, as an act of

---

1 From the summer of 1941 until the end of that year, 188,712 Jews were deported to Transnistria: 82,478 Jews from Bukovina; 96,867 from Bessarabia; and 9,367 from Dorohoi. An additional wave of deportations occurred in the spring and summer of 1942, during which 4,290 Jews were deported from Bessarabia and another 231 from Bukovina. See Jean Ancel, *Toledot Hashoah*: *Romania*, vol. 2 (Hebrew) (Jerusalem: Yad Vashem, 2002), pp. 1358–1360.

2 The Jews were deported from Rădăuţi, Kunstadt's hometown, over the course of three days, October 12–14, 1941. During the first two days of the deportations, on the last day of the Jewish holiday of Sukkot and on the following day, Shemini Atzeret, around 7,000 Jews were taken on freight trains to the town of Mărculeşti in Bessarabia. From there they continued on foot through the wilderness of Ukraine–Transnistria between the Dniester River and the Bug River, through rain and mud, in cold and frost, without any protection or cover. Of the deportees on these transports, 80–90 percent were killed. There were around 3,000 Jews on the last transport, which departed on October 14, 1941, Simhat Torah. They too were taken in freight trains to the crossing of the Dniester at Atachi, Bessarabia, opposite the city of Moghilev in Transnistria. Some of these deportees were dispersed among the ghettos in the area. So it was that Kunstadt arrived in the shtetl of Dzhurin. See Israel Margalit-Postilnik, *Radauts*: *Kehila Yehudit Betzemihata Uvisheki'ata* (Hebrew) (Tel Aviv: Irgun Yotzei Radauts Bukovina Be'Yisrael, 1990), pp. 144–145.

3 Meaning that the pages would be used as toilet paper; after relieving oneself, a Jew is required to say a blessing.

spite or indifference to these new "literary treasures" but because paper in Transnistria is something that everyone needs—to roll cigarettes and for somewhat more important purposes … and, you can imagine, it is at a premium. Therefore, the value of the paper is determined by its size.

Every morning during the first weeks of exile in Transnistria, I felt the stabbing of a needle in my heart upon seeing for what odious purpose the people used pages torn out of sacred books, eternal books, among the crumbling ruins in the muddy bogs where human needs led me (I cannot find words for "toilet" in the Dzhurin dictionary …). These crumpled and defiled pages that rolled in the filth and trash reminded me of the tortured and trampled victims who wasted away in the throes of death along the banks of the Dniester, in the thick mud of Atachi[4] and Mărculeşti[5] in Bessarabia.

While in the act [of relieving myself], I considered how much easier it surely would have been if the demeaned and defiled pages had in their youth—before they were uprooted from their respectable yellow cabinets with the clear glass panes—been burned in a fire and transformed into a pile of white ash. Moreover, I think that it would have been no less preferable for the Angel of Death to have taken pity a few months earlier on the wretched Jews who fell like scythed hay along the roads of Bessarabia and Ukraine, where they rotted in some ditch, or were eaten by dogs and birds of prey. However, talking about justice and equality today, when even absolute madmen do not mention such old nonsense, is tantamount to suddenly disturbing the eternal sleep of the dead …

---

4 This refers to the Romanian village of Atachi, in Bessarabia, on the western bank of the Dniester. Beginning on September 15, 1941, the village served as the northernmost crossing point on the Dniester River (Nistru in Romanian) through which the Jews were deported from Bessarabia and Bukovina to Transnistria. Additional crossing points on the Dniester for the deportation of the Jews from north to south were the Soroca–Yampol crossing point, the Rezina–Râbniţa crossing point, the Tighina–Tiraspol crossing point, and the Olâneşti–Yasca crossing point.

5 Mărculeşti is a village in Bessarabia, near the bank of the Dniester and the Bâlţi-Soldanesti railway line, around 45 kilometers from the regional capital, Soroca. The first residents settled in Mărculeşti in 1837. There were 2,319 Jews living in the city in 1930, constituting 87.7 percent of the population. After the outbreak of the war, convoys of Jews who had been expelled from Bessarabia, Bukovina, and the city of Cernăuţi arrived in Mărculeşti.

It seems that my pen has fulfilled its duty by writing these opening remarks. There is much for it to write, but I must make a living by doing my wretched work.[6] In such a blessed place as Dzhurin, a daily loaf of bread to feed four people is no trivial matter.

[April 11, 1942] The Same Day, 3 P.M.

The evil inclination once again has a hold over me and is dragging me to my desk. I thought that I had overcome the ink-thirsty evil inclination more than four years ago, when Hitler's loyal disciples in Romania had seized power at the end of 1937 and had begun a series of raging persecutions against Jewish newspapers, writers, and journalists.[7] Then, in those fateful December days, not only were all the Jewish newspapers in the country closed but also the entire democratic press in various languages, first and foremost, the two most widely-circulated Romanian daily papers, *Dimineaţa* (Morning) and *Adevărul* (Truth), which had a circulation of 500,000 copies. They followed a liberal line, and had a significant number of Jewish workers and distinguished columnists among their editorship. I was also associated with the "non-kosher"[8] press in Cernăuţi and Bucharest, and suddenly I was out of business.[9]

---

6 Kunstadt was appointed secretary of the council in the Dzhurin ghetto as a result of his connections with the engineer Siegfried (Sami) Jagendorf and also because of his public activities in his hometown of Rădăuţi, where he served as secretary of the Jewish community committee and worked as a journalist prior to the deportation. This position guaranteed him and the rest of his family—his wife and two children—basic sustenance, something that was not inconsequential in Transnistria. For information about Jagendorf, see the April 23, 1942 entry.

7 At the end of 1937, the Goga–Cuza government, which was led by Goga Octavian and Alexandru Cuza and espoused an openly antisemitic agenda, came to power. The government ordered the closure of democratic newspapers, and passed laws and published orders removing Jews from government posts, the administration, and so forth. The most extreme step was the law of January 22, 1938, which ordered a reexamination of the Jews' citizenship. Following the introduction of this law, one third of the Jewish citizens lost their civil rights.

8 Kunstadt uses the terms kosher and non-kosher in a broad sense to mean legal and illegal, authorized and unauthorized, acceptable and unacceptable, fit for labor or unfit for labor, and also noncommunist and communist.

9 The great majority of Jewish newspapers that were published in Romania closed after

End of story. I was left with nothing. It was a miracle that I did not pay a higher price for my terrible transgressions. I then bade my pen farewell, thinking this parting was final. Not so! A few hours have hardly passed since the introduction was born, and I am drawn to the pen as I was before.

First of all, allow me to reveal the secret of how a Jew like me ekes out a living in this local paradise and supports, alas, a wife and two children. In all the camps in Transnistria, the Romanian authorities have appointed so-called councils to direct the internal affairs of the deportees. The council constitutes a Jewish government of sorts, with its own institutions—soup kitchens, hospitals, schools, orphanages, and, of course, the Jewish militia,[10] which wielded the power of enforcement. Every council is led by a "colony chief" who is accountable to the Romanian occupying authorities.[11] Due to my experience in community matters—until the deportation I was the secretary general of the large community in

---

1938. Some of them survived until 1940. The last edition of the newspaper *Curierul israelit* (Israelite Courier) appeared in November 1940. A number of editions of the newspapers *Ecoul evreiesc* (Jewish Echo) and *Cuvantul evreiesc* (Jewish Word) appeared in 1941. During the war years, 1941–1944, the newspaper *Gazeta evreiasca* (Jewish Paper) was published by the Jewish Center established by Ion Antonescu's government. This newspaper was under the supervision of the Romanian censor.

10 A distinction must be made between the Jewish police and the Ukrainian militia. While the Ukrainian militia would enter the ghettos with the aim of persecuting the Jews, to injure and to kill them, and to steal their property, the Jewish police were appointed to maintain order in the ghettos and to seize the Jews for forced labor. Kunstadt frequently referred to the Jewish police as the Jewish militia to express his contempt for those who had abused their authority in their treatment of the Jews and for their cooperation with the Romanian government. This cooperation was especially manifest when it was necessary to evict Jews from their homes for forced labor.

11 At the order of the Romanian authorities and under Order No. 23, issued on November 11, 1941, and in light of the need for internal Jewish organization, Jewish councils (known as the Judenrat in Eastern Europe) were established in the ghettos. The Jewish council in the Dzhurin ghetto was established in the spring of 1942. Its chairman was Dr. Max Rosenstrauch. Although Kunstadt refers to Rosenstrauch primarily as colony chief, but also head of the ghetto, of the camp, or the council—all refer to the same function. Rosenstrauch was a well-known lawyer who was deported from the town of Suceava, called Shotz by the Jews, in Southern Bukovina. Moshe Katz, a known merchant from Rădăuţi, was appointed as his deputy. Rabbi Baruch Hager from Siret and the local rabbi, Herşel Karalnic, were the first to help the deportees who arrived in Dzhurin and succeeded, with the help of monetary donations, in establishing a soup kitchen that fed approximately 300 needy persons.

Rădăuţi—and with a touch of ancestral privilege, I managed to obtain work on the council as the secretary, and not, God forbid, for the sake of the next world but for a loaf of bread every morning. This wage saves us from dying of hunger and also protects us from being sent to a German forced labor camp. In the meanwhile, the council functionaries and the supervisors of the "colony" are being well taken care of.[12]

Today, while sitting in the council office at my desk, which is off to the side, I heard the daily heated arguments among a group of council members—six deportees, apart from the colony chief, Dr. Max Rosenstrauch from Suceava (Bukovina).[13] There is no lack of problems: typhus, the soup kitchen, roadwork, and the rest of the painful trifles that compromise the agenda. I listen with only one ear while scribbling with my pen, because my thoughts wander elsewhere, to my latest creation, which currently comprises only four pages. I was bothered by the thought that I had not yet written down a single letter regarding the turbulent experiences that have assaulted me and my relatives over the last six months, hurling us into an abyss of bizarre nightmares, daily

12 The council was required to provide quotas of Jews for forced labor in camps located on the Bug, such as Nikolayev, Trikhaty, etc. The Jews could exempt themselves from forced labor by paying a ransom.

13 Suceava was the capital city of Moldavia from 1348 to 1565. At the end of 1918, following World War I and after 144 years under Austro–Hungarian rule, Bukovina passed to Romanian control, becoming part of "Greater Romania." In the summer of 1940, the Red Army entered Bukovina and Bessarabia, and the Romanian army retreated without resistance, although Suceava remained under Romanian rule. However, the Jews of Suceava also endured antisemitic persecutions. In 1940, the authorities imposed many harsh decrees on the Jewish population as part of the policy intended to oppress, humiliate, and also impoverish the Jews. The Jews were forbidden to sell tobacco and schnapps, on which the government had a monopoly. This edict was intended to deprive thousands of Jews of their livelihood. In July 1941, thousands of Jews were expelled from the shtetls and villages in the region, and thousands of destitute Jewish refugees arrived in Suceava, where they found refuge in the homes of Jews and in synagogues. The community saw to their welfare. The persecution reached a peak when all the Jews were deported to Transnistria between October 9–11, 1941. Before their departure, the Jews were required to deposit all of their possessions in the hands of representatives of the international bank in exchange for amounts that bore no relation to the real value of their belongings. The Jews of Suceava arrived in cattle cars at the Atachi border crossing and from there they crossed the Dniester in rafts to the city of Moghilev in Transnistria in southwest Ukraine. For more information, see Benzion Fuchs, ed., *Sefer Yehudei Sutsheva* (*Shotz*) *Ukehilot Haseviva* (Hebrew) (Tel Aviv: Teper Publishing, 2007), vols. 1–2, and Lavi, *Pinkas Hakehilot*: *Rumania*, vol. 2, pp. 473–477.

hazards, and constant fear. I thought that if I would succeed in gathering not just a little of the mountains of material that emerges in every corner between the Dniester and the Bug, this diary would burgeon into a well of frozen tears, profound despair, and dashed hopes. I have been longing to pour out the terrible memories on paper as quickly as possible, before the details become blurred and vague in my mind. I wonder how quickly the intense impressions in these places dissipate like clouds and lose their distinct features. Life here seems unreal, the people around me no more than dreamlike shadows, and all the fearful events but a bad dream, a phantasm—we will wake up very slowly from this nightmare, sigh deeply, spit three times, and quickly say, [banish] "all demons and spirits!"

April 23, 1942

Twelve days have already passed since I wrote the previous lines. It is not because the source of the events has dried up, God forbid, that my pen has rested for so long. In fact, in the strange nightmare that we call the Transnistrian exile, every moment is engulfed with news and all kinds of calamities that shock the soul and make it difficult to breathe. The reason for the pause was completely different. The flaming compulsion that urged me to write the first pages was replaced by an abysmal pessimism, nearly black despair. Stupid questions began to torment my mind: for what and for when? Even if I indeed manage to draft an outline for a chronicle of the Dzhurin camp and, at the same time, pour out my feelings in watery ink on the simple paper of a notebook worth a kopeck, then what? Will I be granted time [in the future] to read the memoirs from the hell of Transnistria and serenely recall the suffering that we endured? Will at least some of my relatives be granted such a privilege? This is all so unnecessary, so worthless, so senseless. Nevertheless, today I have been reconciled with my pen because of some news that jolted me so severely that I must try to calm my rattled nerves by dipping my pen in ink.

[April 23, 1942] The Same Day, One Hour Later

I interrupted my words before, because I did not have the strength to hold the pen any longer. My fingers trembled and my heart pounded, as if it was about to explode. Now I feel a little better and will make every effort to continue.

The council delegates who had left for Moghilev eight days ago, at great personal risk, succeeded in returning, *in a guter sho.*[14] They had set out on the journey intent on establishing contact with the [Moghilev] Central Council,[15] which is headed by the engineer Sami Jagendorf,[16] to obtain some relief for the close to 4,000 homeless people in Dzhurin.[17] They achieved very little, because the functionaries in Moghilev have

---

14 The Yiddish expression, *in a guter sho, be sha'a tova* in Hebrew, which literally means "at a good hour," is said upon hearing welcome news and to express best wishes for success. Kunstadt often uses this expression ironically.

15 The Moghilev ghetto served as the main regional ghetto, and all the other ghettos, such as Shargorod, Murafa, Dzhurin, Kopaygorod, were affiliated with it. The leadership of the Moghilev ghetto wielded great influence over all the ghettos in the region and was responsible for the distribution of aid (money, clothing, work tools, glassware, etc.) that arrived from various sources in Romania. The council in the Moghilev ghetto was known to also have clout in appointments to the councils in the other ghettos in the region.

16 Siegfried (Sami) Jagendorf (1885–1970) was born in the town of Zviniace, Northern Bukovina. He received both a traditional Jewish orthodox education and a general, Austro–Hungarian education. Jagendorf studied in Vienna, where he became a certified engineer. During World War I, he served as a lieutenant in the Austro–Hungarian army and was awarded a medal by Emperor Franz Josef. Jagendorf arrived in Rădăuţi only in 1938, after fleeing Nazi terror in Austria. On the eve of the deportation, Jagendorf suggested to the local municipal authorities in Rădăuţi that they should exploit the Jewish workforce to develop industry and crafts in the city and, in this way, he was able to prevent the deportation of the Jews to labor camps in distant places and the separation of families. He also organized the deportation of the Jews of Rădăuţi and, consequently, the deportees came to see him as their leader. In a group interview, survivors from the Moghilev ghetto described Jagendorf as a man of impressive appearance who commanded respect. Despite the fact that he spent the first days in the Moghilev ghetto in a destroyed movie theater, together with the remainder of the deportees, under terrible conditions, he insisted on shaving daily, changed his shirt, and wore a clean and neatly ironed suit, leather gloves, and fine leather shoes. At the end of the war, Jagendorf and his wife immigrated to the U.S., and joined his daughter, who was already living there. See Siegfried Jagendorf, *Jagendorf's Foundry: A Memoir of the Romanian Holocaust, 1941–1944* (New York: Harper Collins, 1991), pp. 172–180.

17 The statistical registry of the Romanian gendarmerie of September 1, 1943, indicates that there were 381 Jews from Bessarabia and 2,490 Jews from Bukovina in the Dzhurin ghetto. See Carp, *Cartea neagră*, vol. 3, pp. 440–441.

enough people to take care of—about 10,000 refugees[18] from Bukovina, Bessarabia, and northern Moldova.[19] Unable to bring back bags full of cash, the delegates instead brought a bundle of news, each item worse than the last.

They say that all of Moghilev is nothing more than one enormous cemetery. In the last few months, approximately 6,000 deported Jews have died there from hunger, cold, typhus, and other illnesses, and the end is not in sight.[20] Entire families have been decimated. Thousands of widows and orphans wander the streets, if they have enough strength to drag themselves from their "apartments"—stables, ruins, cellars, and attics. There is not a single family without victims, not to mention those afflicted with typhus.[21]

The delegates take from their briefcases sheets of papers containing dense lists of the names of the martyrs and begin to read the memorial pages bearing the names of Jews from Rădăuţi, from Suceava, from Gura Humorului[22]—the names of the young and the old, of women and

---

18 The statistical registry of the Romanian gendarmerie of September 1, 1943, indicates that there were 348 deportees from Bessarabia and 12,836 from Bukovina in the Moghilev ghetto; see ibid., pp. 440–441.

19 Meaning the Dorohoi district.

20 Approximately 3,400 Jews died of typhus, cold, and starvation between the winter of 1941 and the summer of 1942. See Ancel, *Toledot Hashoah*: *Romania*, vol. 2, p. 1058. Ancel claims that although it is possible to estimate the number of Romanian Jews who died in the large ghettos and camps in Transnistria between the winter of 1941 and the summer of 1942, it is impossible to determine the exact number of those who died of typhus, because no distinction is made in the registry between deaths caused by typhus and the many caused by cold, hunger, and other diseases. Likewise, it is difficult to estimate the number of Jews who were sent from these ghettos to kolkhozes and sovkhozes, and died there.

21 There were apparently sick persons in almost every home. The ill and the healthy lay together on the floor in terrible overcrowded conditions and in temperatures of 40 degrees below zero (Celsius). The sight of dozens and hundreds of corpses piled up on the carts sent to collect them became a routine affair. See, for example, passages from the diary of Cerna Bercovici in Avni, *Sefer Zikaron Lekehilat Yehudei Kimpulung–Bukovina Vehaseviva*, vol. 1, p. 223; Batsheva Akerman testimony, YVA, O.3/VT/11356. See also the description of the magnitude of deaths in Yosef Govrin, *Betzel Ha'avadon*: *Zihronot al Transnistriya Ve'al Haha'apela Le'Eretz Israel* (Hebrew) (Kibbutz Lohamei Hageta'ot and Jerusalem: Ghetto Fighters' House, Yad Vashem, and Hamerkaz Leheker Yahadut Romania, The Hebrew University of Jerusalem, 1999), p. 46.

22 The town Gura Humorului is located in Southern Bukovina in the Câmpulung region. The town was established in 1774 at the estuary where the Humor River flows into the

men, who barely half a year before, when they were healthy, strong, and hopeful, were driven out of their homes by the Romanian gendarmes. Upon arriving in Transnistria, where they were promised a new life and work, the door of hell opened before them.[23] At every moment, they hoped for "deliverance" (which in Transnistrian meant going home), and they indeed were granted deliverance, but of another kind: in a mass grave in the Moghilev cemetery.

In the old country, the gates of heaven opened when a corpse was found in the shtetl. How was it possible? Everyone, child and adult, wailed—what a catastrophe! The deceased was barely sixty-five years old, or perhaps seventy, and was just about to really start living ... now we are numbed by the news of the death of hundreds of friends, acquaintances, or fellow townspeople. Six months in Transnistria have completed the job. He or she is no longer with us—so what! The pessimists take comfort in the thought that it is good that he is rid of all his troubles. The optimists, those who remain, are silent and think the same.

And yet I was grief-stricken when I discovered the terrible end of my relatives, people with whom I had grown up and with whom I was in contact until the deportation. I will never see them again, and they too will never see me again. Hence, I seek comfort in the silent pages of this notebook and pour out my anguished heart. These pages listen and do not interrupt my words.

Moldova River, explaining the origin of its name. The first Jews settled there in 1835. The Jewish population was comprised of craftsmen, laborers, and merchants. In the fall of 1940, Jewish students were excluded from state run schools. On October 10, 1941, all the Jews of Gura Humorului, a total of 2,772 persons, were deported in cattle cars to Transnistria. They arrived at the border crossing in Atachi, Bessarabia, and from there crossed the Dniester on rafts to the eastern bank, to Moghilev; see Shraga Yeshurun, ed., *Gura Humora: A Small Town in Southern Bukovina* (Hadera: Association of Former Residents of Gura Humora and Environs, 1997).

23 It appears that the Romanian authorities spread rumors among the Jews in the Cernăuţi ghetto that they were to be resettled in Transnistria, where they would receive agricultural plots that they could cultivate. The residents of the ghetto included many Jews who had been deported from the villages around Cernăuţi in the summer of 1941 and who had previously worked in agriculture, and the idea of receiving agricultural plots appealed to them. They were the first to volunteer for the deportation trains in order "to get the best land." See Herman Shulman, *Hesed Shel Emet: Edut Migeta'ot Hamavet Shel Transnistriya* (Hebrew) (Jerusalem: Yad Vashem, 2009).

[April 23, 1942] One Hour Later

In Moghilev, there was not enough time to deal with each cadaver separately and, therefore, they introduced an American custom—the assembly line. Wagons laden with corpses hurry through the streets to the Jewish cemetery, twenty or even more on a wagon, depending on the load of "goods" (if the transport is full of children, it is more economical …). The wagon owner stops there only for a few minutes—as long as it takes to empty the transport into a mass grave. After disposing of the "goods," he rushes back to the camp to bring a new load to the same grave, which is not yet full to the brim and is waiting for the guests. Only in the evening hours do they quickly cover the grave, because the gravediggers are pressed for time: at night, they must prepare another dwelling for new tenants. A shroud? What for? Who needs a coffin, or a tombstone! Jews living in Transnistria are nameless creatures. Like cats and dogs, they carry no documents and are not registered anywhere.[24] During the crossing of the Dniester, Romanian gendarmes not only confiscated all the deportees' cash and valuable objects, but they also took all their papers and documents. Who has the audacity today to suggest that the dead should be granted a name on a tombstone! …

I want to place at least a small monument for one of the Moghilev victims, my dearly beloved friend Dr. Max Gabor from my hometown of Rădăuţi (Bukovina). He, a dedicated doctor, devotedly saved dozens of sick people infected with the murderous Rickettsia bacteria (the medical term used by doctors for the executioner that causes typhus), and paid with his own young life—at the age of forty-five—for his supreme courage. Burning with a hellish fever, he struggled with the invisible, infernal bacterium for a few days until he surrendered his noble soul.[25]

---

24 Many Jews did not survive the grievous living conditions in the ghettos during the winter of 1941–1942, and typhus, in particular, claimed many victims. The gravediggers were unable to gather all the dead, and it was impossible to bury them during this particularly harsh winter, because the ground was frozen. Temperatures dropped as low as 40 degrees below zero and lower (Celsius). There were also not enough places to bury the numerous bodies. Consequently, in the spring, when the temperature rose and the ground began to thaw, the dead were buried in a mass grave. It should be noted that a few Jews who had the means buried their dead in individual graves.

25 Max Gabor, a well-known general physician from Rădăuţi, was deported together with

During my almost twenty-year relationship with Dr. Gabor, he was not only my family doctor, but also like a member of my household and one of my closest friends. As secretary of the Jewish community, I would often refer impoverished patients to him and would ask him to treat them. When he saw such a patient in his waiting room, he would usher him into his office, before the other patients and without charging him a cent, God forbid. If a patient was weak, Dr. Gabor would make a house call, walking through the muddy alleys of Jewish poverty by day or by night. He would also not charge any fees for these "home visits." In fact, he sometimes distributed the necessary medicines for free, even though he was not a wealthy man. How can one make money this way? He earned his livelihood by treating patients who did not require the assistance of the community.

During the month of the deportation—October 1941—about half of the Jews deported from Bukovina and Bessarabia were rounded up in Atachi, on the bank of the Dniester, the site of the main *Umschlagplatz* in Romania.[26] The "*Umschlagplatz* No. 2" was in Mărculešti,[27] about 200 kilometers away. I too, along with the members of my household, ended up in Atachi, where we suffered for ten gloomy days (October 16–October 25, 1941). Dr. Gabor "lived" with his family in our neighborhood. His "apartment" was no more luxurious than mine: a crumbling, rickety dwelling, without a roof, and no doors or windows. The cold rain poured down on the wretched walls and on the people, who were wrapped up in all kinds of covers. I did not recognize Dr. Gabor when I saw him in Atachi, even though we had only parted a week before. The elegant and neat young man, who was always dressed impeccably, like a nobleman, looked like one of the riffraff in Atachi, his clothes covered in filth, his trousers rolled up to the knee, his hat crushed, his shirt dirty. He had a

---

his wife and two sons, Jack and Kurt, to Transnistria. Dr. Gabor lived in the Moghilev ghetto, where he worked as a doctor. He died of typhus in the winter of 1942.

26 This refers to the northern most border crossing, Atachi, through which 55,913 deportees from Southern Bukovina, Northern Bukovina, and Bessarabia passed. See Ancel, *Toledot Hashoah*: *Romania*, vol. 2, p. 798.

27 A total of 35,276 Jews from Bessarabia, Southern Bukovina, and Northern Bukovina passed through the border crossing at Mărculeşti.

dazed look on his face. By the way, he did not recognize me either—a sign that my appearance was no less neglected than his.

To the extent that it was possible to rejoice in Atachi, alas, we were happy to meet, and each of us poured out all his sorrows and the details of the infernal journey.

A few days later, we met again in Moghilev, in the ruined university building, where there were hundreds of deportees, fifty or sixty on each floor, crammed in the hallways and the bathrooms. The university constituted the first "hostel" on the other side of the Dniester, until they chased us to our doom in Transnistria. Everyone was soaked from the pouring rain (the roof of the building was like a sieve as a result of the bombing during the occupation). Our teeth chattered in the cold, and a mortal fear oppressed our souls. We knew that we were destined for deportation at any moment, to trudge to the Bug and look death in the eyes.[28] These death marches meant collapsing on the side of the roads somewhere in a ditch, particularly elderly people, women, and children—a fate that had already struck thousands of victims in that accursed autumn. Dr. Gabor did not manage to stay in the same hall with me, but we spent those days together. The authorities eventually remembered me, and my family and I were sent to the paradise of Dzhurin on October 29, 1941, fortunately not on foot. Dr. Gabor, however, remained in Moghilev, and we parted like people who knew that this was their final farewell …

---

28 The Romanian authorities did not intend for the deported Jews to remain in the city of Moghilev. Rather it was to serve as a transfer point. Therefore, the Romanian gendarmes concentrated the Jews in abandoned Russian barracks or other public buildings, such as military academies, a structure referred to by the deportees as a casino, and another called a movie theater. Testimonies describe the terrible conditions in these locations. Thousands were crammed into dirty, partially destroyed halls, without windows and doors. The people lay one next to the other amidst a stench and smell of death. Every day the Romanians took away groups of deported Jews, forcing them to continue their march on the roads of Transnistria. The fortunate ones who could afford to pay a bribe rented trucks from the Germans at the headquarters in Moghilev, or wagons from local Ukrainians to make their way to the ghettos in the Moghilev region, such as Shargorod, Murafa, Dzhurin, Kopaygorod, etc. Thus Kunstadt and his family arrived in Dzhurin on October 29, 1941, fifteen days after they were expelled from their home in Rădăuţi. See Batsheva Akerman testimony, YVA, O.3/VT/11356; Chaya Klinghoffer testimony, YVA, O.3/VT/7337; Yitzhak Yalon testimony, YVA, O.3/1238.

April 27, 1942

Since I began writing this diary, a difficult question has been bothering me. I keep asking myself: Should I note only general events and experiences, as in a chronicle, or perhaps also details about myself and my relatives as in a book? It's just a question. After all, no one is forcing me to write, and anyone who is a good friend would surely try, using harsh words, to dissuade me from engaging in such a dangerous activity that could end badly. Should these pages fall into the wrong hands, God forbid, I may as well recite the *Videh*[29] together with my family. Indeed, I am not accountable to anyone. The pen is mine, the notebook is mine, the poor lamp[30] by whose flickering light I write is mine, so I can act according to my heart's desire. However, the opposing argument sneaks in, claiming: What if a miracle occurs and this diary is salvaged and is found by someone who wants to know what the faded pages say about the Transnistrian tragedy? Although it is quite possible that the same person will toss the memoirs with disdain and say: Some Transnistrian diary! It is full of drivel about [the diarist] himself, which interests me like last year's snow, instead of telling about the collective, about the general suffering of the masses.

Indeed, a reasonable argument, yet am I not also a member of the collective, however insignificant, and besides, do my feelings and distress not reflect the feelings and distress of the masses? Do all flesh and blood not possess the same nervous system and the same psychological complexes, although with some variations? Therefore, when writing about myself, everything that the deportees felt, thought, and suffered may be inferred. I will truly strive to present both sides: the crux regarding the collective, but without forgetting my own sorrows. I hope that I will succeed in making this compromise!

---

29 Jewish deathbed confessional prayer.

30 *Kantsil* are wicks that burn in oil. Jews in ghettos placed a little oil and a wick in a potato after removing some of the inner part.

[April 27, 1942] Three Hours Later

At night, on the hard boards of the wooden bunk, I lie for hours on end with my eyes closed. It seems to me that I am sitting in a movie theater, watching a ghastly horror movie directed by a demonic sadist. The scenes change every moment, one more dreadful than the next, while wild music drones and grates, piercing my ears and tearing my taut nerves to pieces.

In truth, there is a no more suitable setting for the hellish film of Transnistria than Ukraine, where every patch of land has been soaked with rivers of Jewish blood over generations, and the air has been poisoned with the cries and howls of tortured and tormented martyrs since the times of Bohdan Chmielnicki.[31] Even [small] shtetls, like Dzhurin, include a section for martyrs in their small cemeteries—about forty local Jews, shot by Petliura's bands in the 1920s.[32] Ukraine, a stronghold of the murder of Jews, strives to retain its place of honor in the annals of Jewish martyrdom ...

---

31 Bohdan Chmielnicki (1595–1675) led the 1648 uprising of the Cossacks and peasants against the Polish–Lithuanian Commonwealth. In the course of the uprising, they carried out terrible pogroms against the Jews, known as the 1648–1649 massacres, which claimed numerous victims. See Mordechai Eliav, "Kiddush Hashem Begezeirot Tah-Tat" (Hebrew), https://www.daat.ac.il/he-il/kitveyet/mahanayim/eliav-tah-tat.htm (accessed June 13, 2022).

32 Symon Vasylyovych Petliura (1879–1926), born in Poltava, eastern Ukraine, was a Ukrainian politician. He was involved in the establishment of the Social Democratic Party of Ukraine and was the last president of the independent republic of Ukraine, the Ukrainian political entity established during the Russian Civil War, which was conquered by the Russian army shortly afterwards. Petliura is regarded as a national hero in Ukraine, but among the Jewish people, he is remembered as an oppressor: his soldiers carried out pogroms that claimed the lives of tens of thousands of Jews. The Ukrainians committed horrors and carried out riots in the city of Lvov during the Holocaust, which were also called "the days of Petliura." See Yitzhak Oren, "Shalom Schwarzbard" (Hebrew), https://www.daat.ac.il/he-il/kitveyet/mahanayim/oren-shvarzbard.htm (accessed June 13, 2022).

[April 27, 1942] 10 P.M

This afternoon in the council room, I heard news that for me and my family is a flashing ray of light penetrating the dark clouds. If this news is not false, I will be spared the danger of hunger for the time being.

In short, the delegates who just returned from Moghilev told the functionaries of the Moghilev Central Council that I work as the community secretary in return for a loaf of bread each day. The president of the Moghilev Central Council, the engineer Sami Jagendorf—who, by the way, comes from my town and is a distant relative of my wife—has clout there [Moghilev], and he pledged to grant me a monthly supplement of 60 marks provided that the Dzhurin council will contribute 40 marks. I really cannot believe that I will receive 100 marks in cash every month—an amount that will suffice not only for a couple of potatoes, but also for a few pieces of wood and a handful of sugar. People will envy me, the new Rothschild ...

By the way, concerning the engineer Jagendorf, it is worth noting more than just a few lines in some margin of a notebook. He saved more than 10,000 Jews in Moghilev from deportation by foot to the German camps on the other side of the Bug, and not only obtained permission for them to remain in Moghilev but also to work there. While masses of persecuted Jews continued to pour into Moghilev in October 1941 and, from there, were deported to their doom in Ukraine, the engineer Jagendorf, himself a deportee, managed to enter the holy of holies of the Romanian commander of the city to propose an incredible plan to him: to renew the operation of the large iron foundry, which was demolished during the battles, on condition that only deported Jews would work there. The overlord[33] liked the plan and also laid down a condition: the factory had to begin manufacturing products within two months. With empty pockets and no outside help, the engineer Jagendorf managed to work magic on the foundry, making something out of nothing, even before two months had passed. He demonstrated the organizational talents of a real genius in strange and wretched

33 Kunstadt often uses the Yiddish word *paritz*, meaning a non-Jew who rules over the Jews, throughout his diary, which is translated as overlord in most instances.

conditions, and with people who, for the most part, had never done manual labor—former merchants, officials, or people who worked at odd jobs. The foundry now works for the government by every possible means, day and night, manufacturing all kinds of iron products that are needed for the war. Engineer Jagendorf, the director and father of the factory, is expanding it and bringing in more Jewish laborers. He runs a Jewish regime with an iron hand and has instituted a kind of military discipline, with harsh punishments for the least crime. He does indeed play the role of the dictator, and people fear him like they fear the devil. Otherwise, he could not accomplish his fantastic plan, which has saved thousands of people from death.[34] An interesting fact is that throughout his entire life, the engineer Jagendorf was disconnected from Judaism, and was absorbed entirely in his professional work and

34 Turnatoria, the factory founded at the initiative of the engineer Jagendorf, was a lifesaving endeavor. Turnatoria employed 300 deportees. Jagendorf discerned the inherent potential of productive work. He understood that it offered the Jews the opportunity to make a living from their own labor and that it could save them from further deportation convoys. The work in Turnatoria promised an income, although miniscule, and food. There were more people seeking jobs than there were positions, and Jagendorf wrote in his memoirs that workers were selected with the utmost punctiliousness: only those with professions suited to the task were accepted. Many among the deportees wanted to work in Turnatoria, because the work there, which was less harsh than the forced labor that was imposed on the Jews, promised the workers and their families immunity from deportation. Furthermore, in comparison to other places of forced labor, the relations in the workplace were humane, since the overseers were Jews. More workers managed to obtain work in Turnatoria over time through the system of "a friend brings a friend," because they knew one of the workers or one of the overseers. For more information, see Yitzhak Yalon testimony, YVA, O.3/1238; Yalon related that his father was able to find employment at Turnatoria, as did other friends, through his acquaintance with Jonas Kessler from Vatra Dornei. See also the group testimonies of the ghettos of Moghilev, Shargorod, and Dzhurin, YVA, O.3/VT/10547; Naftali Avneri testimony, YVA, O.3/VT/607. Avneri, a deportee from Rădăuţi, relates that he obtained a position at Turnatoria through his acquaintance with and connections to Jagendorf; see Yitzhak Yalon, ed., *Sefer Hazikaron Shel Yehudei Vatra Dornei Vehaseviva, Bukovina–Romania* (Hebrew), vol. 1 (Tel Aviv: Amutat Yotzei Vatra Dornei Vehaseviva, 2001), p. 327. Concerning forced labor and how the councils tackled this, and on Turnatoria, see Sarah Rosen, "Tzibur Veyahid: Hitargenut Umishpaha, Hayeihem Shel Hayehudim Begeta'ot Tzefon Transnistriya" (Moghilev, Shargorod, Dzhurin, Murafa, and Bershad) 1941–1944" (Hebrew) (PhD dissertation, The Hebrew University of Jerusalem, 2013), pp. 168–178; Jagendorf, *Jagendorf's Foundry*. A workshop was later established at Turnatoria to train youth in various professions, including mechanics, electrics, metal work, and more.

his friendships with prominent non-Jewish figures. However, when he was ferried across the Dniester and stood face to face with the tragedy of the deportees, the Jewish embers within him flared up. Dr. Herzl had a similar experience. The match that ignited the Jewish flame had to be dipped in Jewish blood, apparently.

[April 27, 1942] One Hour Later

I can't sleep—because of both the bedbugs and my nerves that say "no"—so once again I pour out my heart [in my diary]. The good news is indeed as sweet as honey but at the same time as bitter as bile. I now will have to beg my bosses to grant me the supplement of 40 marks. I don't mind swallowing this bitter pill as much as I fear that the council members will crush my dream and throw me down the stairs. Most of all, I fear the colony chief, Dr. Max Rosenstrauch—an old man from Suceava—who is evil and not very intelligent. He has only one reply ready when people ask him for a favor: What do you think? That they sent you here to enjoy yourselves, to have a good time? They sent you to die, to die. Do you or do you not understand …

April 28, 1942, 6 A.M.

In Transnistria, the Angel of Death works nonstop and annihilates entire families with one thrust of his sword. He has no time to choose and must hurry. He is very busy now. He carries the whole world on his shoulders, and it is high season in the East and the West. The entire land is one great front that is waiting for the slaughterer's knife, on land, at sea, and in the air, and in the midst of all this, a few million Jews from Europe force their way in and even want to dance in a circle—the odious nature of the Jews. Well, so the one with a thousand eyes[35] is doing the Chosen People a favor, and quickly, very quickly, at full speed.

---

35 A byname of the Angel of Death; see Y. L. Peretz, "Nit farmishpet," in Peretz, *Ale verk*, vol. 3 (Yiddish) (New York: Cyco, 1947), pp. 421–431.

The formidable task was accomplished a few days ago in the city of Vinnitsa, on the other side of the Bug, around 100 kilometers from Dzhurin. There the Germans are the masters, because the Bug is the eastern border of Transnistria. Before the war, about 60,000 Jews lived in Vinnitsa. During the occupation, their population was reduced to 5,000. The battered Red Army evacuated some of the remaining Jews to Asia. Most were killed by German bullets, or met other kinds of strange deaths. Now the Germans have also found a solution for the wretched remaining remnant and have "koshered" Vinnitsa—"*Judenrein*,"[36] as they say in their language. Last Monday, the slaughter was carried out with German precision.[37] During the "*Aktia*," the SS murderers drove the few [remaining] Jews, everyone, to a field outside the city, and ordered the men to dig two long pits. Then they forced the entire group to stand alongside the pits, and a few bursts of gunfire solved the "Jewish problem" of Vinnitsa forever. Dirt covered the perforated and bloodied bodies, including of those who were not fortunate enough to have died instantly.

The peasants who conveyed the bitter news to Dzhurin recounted that the earth over the graves continued to heave for quite some time. The information spread throughout the camp and caused a panic. Some thought: why would Dzhurin be more privileged than Vinnitsa? The panic subsided after only a few hours, and the daily routine was immediately

---

36 Cleansed of Jews.

37 Vinnitsa is a city in the Vinnitsa region of Ukraine. Jews lived there since the sixteenth century. Before World War II, the city had 92,868 residents, including 25,000 Jews, who constituted about a fourth of the population. Around 17,500 of the city's Jews succeeded in escaping eastward upon the outbreak of the war. The Germans entered the city on July 19 and found around 7,500 Jews there. A few days later, hundreds of young people were gathered and led to the Jewish cemetery, where they were murdered. The remainder were concentrated in the ghetto that was established in the city in Voenny Gorodok (military neighborhood). At the end of September 1941, a selection was conducted during which about 5,000 skilled workers and their families were set apart. The rest, the elderly, the women, and the children, were murdered. An additional *Aktion*, in which some of the Jewish skilled workers and their family members were murdered, was carried out in August 1942. Those who remained were transferred to labor camps, and few of them survived. Vinnitsa was liberated by the Red Army on March 20, 1944. See Israel Gutman, ed., *Entziklopediya Shel Hashoah*, vol. 2 (Hebrew) (Jerusalem: Yad Vashem and Sifriat Poalim, 1990), pp. 414–415.

resumed.[38] Hearts hardened, and the "writers and thinkers" froze, Goethe, Beethoven, Lessing, and … Hitler.

[April 28, 1942] 6 P.M.

A few Jews who risked their lives to flee from the camps in the district of Balta (Transnistria) have arrived. They relate horrible details concerning the 10,000 Jews from Bukovina and Bessarabia who were unable to cross the Dniester near Atachi during the expulsion, as all of us in the district of Moghilev had. They dragged these Jews to Mărculeşti, the "*Umschlagplatz* No. 2," and from there through "the parting of the Dniester"—the death march through marshlands, as cold rain poured down and stormy winds struck their faces, while the gendarmes tore out their souls, and the victims fell like flies. Nevertheless, whoever was able to endure the torture wandered to the city of Bershad and to the surrounding places—Obodovka, Yampol, Shumilovka, Zabocritch, Tsibulevka, and so on.[39]

In Transnistria, regardless of what our ears hear, our hair no longer stands on end, and thus the *Lagernikes* [camp inmates] listened stone-faced to the details of the Mărculeşti tragedy. The Romanian authorities transported the deportees by train—ninety or more persons crammed into cattle cars, packed like sardines. There they thrust them out of the cattle cars into an open field and immediately shoved them toward the Dniester. Thus began the death march. Their feet sank deep into the thick,

38 The peasants conveyed the news about the fate of the Jews in ghettos. Indeed, during the first period of their stay in Transnistria, the deportees were cut off from the outside world and had no reliable sources of information. This situation was fertile ground for the rumors that spread among the Jewish populations in the ghettos. The well-known phenomenon of rumors was characteristic of all the ghettos in the Nazi-occupied territories among people under siege who were in distressful situations and isolated from reliable sources of information. See Amos Goldberg, "Rumor Culture among Warsaw Jews under Nazi Occupation: A World of Catastrophe Reenchanted," *Jewish Social Studies*, 21:3 (2016) pp. 91–125.

39 Hundreds, even thousands, of Jews were held at these locations in pigsties, cowsheds, and stables on the outskirts of villages or kolkhozes—in filth, without food or drink. The Jews were not allowed to leave these makeshift prisons. In such conditions, typhus spread, claiming dozens of victims every day.

black mud of Ukraine. They could only pull out their feet from the mud with great effort, and already after a few kilometers not one shoe still had a sole.[40]

After lugging what remained of their meager possessions with their last ounce of strength onto the train to Mărculešti, they abandoned them on the bank of the Dniester and set out on foot from the other side of the Dniester, taking only as many packages and rucksacks that their bent backs could carry.[41] Parents with small children did not carry any packages, because their hands were occupied with the babies. Some of the children who devotedly supported an old, weak father or mother could not take another step and collapsed under the weight.

The death march continued for two weeks, stretching out like an evil snake. The deportees walked from morning until late in the evening without rest. The soldiers brutally murdered anyone who strayed one step too far from the convoy, beating them to death with the butts of their rifles. People had only one choice: to fall down and remain lying on the wet, cold ground. It no longer mattered to anyone, and the convoy proceeded as if nothing happened. The nights were spent in open fields, and anyone who did not have anything to spread under himself lay on the bare earth. At dawn, the soldiers prodded them on. Not everyone who had been among the crowd the day before remained. Many corpses, mostly of children, the elderly, and the weak, lay spread out in the fields. There was no talk whatsoever about burying the dead. The Ukrainian peasants from the surroundings prospered. Every morning, groups of non-Jews scattered through the fields next to the main road to strip the dead bodies and collected the booty—clothes, shoes, and discarded objects.

Over the course of a few weeks, the naked bodies of men, women, and children who fell during the death march were strewn on the sides of the

---

40 The soil of upper Podolia, later known as Transnistria, is black and heavy. In October and November 1941, strong rains fell, transforming the terrain into marsh and deep mud.

41 The railway line that took the Jews from Southern Bukovina, including the city of Cernăuţi, came to an end in a field next to Mărculeşti. There was no functioning railway line from Mărculeşti to the crossing of the Dniester at Soroca, and from there between the eastern side of the Dniester and the Bug. Therefore the deportees were forced to make their way on foot to Obodovka, Shumilovka, Zhabokrich, Bershad, and more—a distance of about 100 kilometers.

road from Yampol to Bershad. Dogs and birds picked at the dead bodies until the end of November 1941, when the winter took pity and covered them with a clear, white sheet of soft snow, burying them temporarily, until spring …

For the "fortunate ones" who in spite of everything reached the new "homes," a new series of calamities began. They were confined in ruined hovels, without even straw to spread out underneath them on the frozen ground, without a splinter of wood to warm their frozen limbs, without food, without a doctor, without medicines. Indeed, typhus quickly began to rage—the Angel of Death in neglected and dirty camps—and people dropped like flies.[42] No one even looked at the sick, and they themselves, emaciated skeletons wrapped in stinking rags and covered with lice, stubbornly refused to take anything into their mouths, turning their faces to the wall and waiting for the slaughtering knife of the assassin with a thousand eyes.

Approximately less than one third of the nearly 90,000 persons who had the misfortune of being thrust into the convoys from Mărculeşti continue to suffer as their number dwindles. I must stop because my hands are beginning to tremble. Oy, sentimental hands are so troublesome! …

[April 28, 1942] Two Hours Later

My fingers have regained their strength and now agree to hold the pen. Let us hurry, before they are overcome by madness again. This time I will indulge myself with what the film directors call "flashbacks" or, in our language, retrospection. I will not look back too far, only six-and-a-half months, to that dark *Sukkes* 5702 (October 1941), the week of the deportation of the Jews from Bukovina, which was the diabolical

---

42 Thus, for example, in Shumilovka or Kosharintsy, thousands of Jews were kept in a terrible state of overcrowding, without food, water, or medicine, in filth and the worst possible sanitary conditions. In these conditions, typhus quickly began to spread, claiming many victims. See Zipora Galai testimony, YVA, O.3/13035, in which she describes the conditions in the pigsty in Kosharintsy; Hannah Meller-Faust, *Me'ever Lanahar*: *Pirkei Zihronot MiTransnistriya* (Hebrew) (Tel Aviv: Ghetto Fighters' House and Hakibbutz Hame'uhad, 1958).

prologue to the "Transnistrian" tragedy. I do not know which scene is currently unfolding, or whether there will be any actors on the stage when the curtain falls.

This prologue began on the first day of *Sukkes* (October 6, 1941), when rumors spread in my hometown, Rădăuţi, imparting that the fate of the Jews of Southern Bukovina had been decided, and no ancestral privilege would help to save them from deportation to the desolation of Ukraine. The community immediately dispatched delegates to Bucharest with a respectable fortune in their briefcase to persuade the "high-level officials" to cancel the evil decree. However, the delegates encountered locked doors and deaf ears in Bucharest. The master key of bribery, which for generations had opened all the doors in Romania, was suddenly useless, because the German ambassador in Romania, Baron Manfred von Killinger, warned the puppet dictator Marshal Ion Antonescu in the harshest terms that he must not make a mockery of Himmler's [Hitler's] order. Antonescu did not object and took the first step against the Jews of Bukovina, whom he considered foreigners because, until the end of the World War I, they belonged to Austria, were imbued with Austrian culture, spoke German among themselves, for the most part, read German newspapers, and were far removed from Romanianism. He [Antonescu] persuaded the Nazi ambassador that the decree should be enacted gradually, town by town, and thus he was able to save "his" kosher Jews of the Regat, while the Jews of Bukovina and Bessarabia fell like *kapporres* chickens. Indeed, life for the Jews of the Regat was not exactly a bowl of cherries. Until the downfall of the Nazis (August 23, 1944), they wore yellow badges of shame, were seized for hard labor, and endured all kinds of persecutions and indignities. Nevertheless, they remained within the four walls [of Romania] and were not deported to Transnistria.

Consequently, the entire disaster struck the Jewish communities in Bukovina and Bessarabia, and not a single Jew remained.[43] As for

---

43 Antonescu perceived the collaboration and alliance between the Romanian government and Nazi Germany, when they invaded the Soviet Union in Operation Barbarossa in summer 1941, as an opportunity to dispose of Romania's Jews, in particular the Jews in Bessarabia, Bukovina, and Dorohoi. Moreover, Antonescu hoped that following this alliance, the area of northern Transylvania would be returned to him. In the first stage, in which the purification of Romania of its Jews began, the intention was to purify those

Cernăuţi, the capital of Bukovina, only 20,000 Jews were deported, while 40,000 people were saved, although they were confined in a ghetto.[44] This was one of the historical paradoxes: it was precisely the Jews from this city who had benefitted under the Red [Communist] non-kosher regime over the course of a year who were saved from the annihilation, for the most part, while the "kosher" Southern Bukovina Jews bore the brunt of it.[45]

While the delegates from the Rădăuţi community were still on the way [to Bucharest to nullify the deportation decree], the catastrophe was already raging in the cities of Suceava, Gura Humorului, Câmpulung,

---

same tracts of land that had been annexed by the Soviet Union in June 1940, a year before Operation Barbarossa. These were the northern parts of Romania: Bessarabia, Bukovina, northern Moldavia, and the Dorohoi district. The order to annihilate the Jewish residents was issued in a decree entitled "purification of the land." In the second stage, following the purification of the annexed territories, Antonescu intended to purify also the Regat of Jews. Manfred von Killinger, the German ambassador to Romania, representing the policy of the Reich Main Security Office, conducted negotiations with the Romanian deputy prime minister, Mihai Antonescu, in the summer of 1942, and under German pressure the two reached an agreement that beginning from September 10 or 12, 1942, all the Jews of Romania would be deported to the Belzec extermination camp in Poland. See Ancel, *Toledot Hashoah*: *Romania*, vol. 1, pp. 539–571; vol. 2, 1185–1189.

44 At the beginning of October 1941, a ghetto was established in Cernăuţi. All the Jews of the city were concentrated in a number of designated streets. From October 12, 1941, until November 1941, all the Jews were deported from the ghetto to Transnistria. With the decisive intervention of the mayor, Dr. Traian Popovici, and following his refusal to obey the command to murder the Jews—a step for which he was recognized by Yad Vashem as one of the Righteous Among the Nations—around 19,000 Jews were allowed to remain in the city, based on the claim that they were useful elements. The permits allowing Jews to remain in the city were known as "Popovici permits." An additional wave of deportations from Cernăuţi to Transnistria had taken place in the summer of 1942, during which the Jews carrying Popovici permits were deported as well. Following the two waves of deportation, about 15,000 Jews remained in the city. See Carp, *Cartea neagră*, vol. 3, pp. 158–182. For more information, see also Ancel, *Toledot Hashoah*: *Romania*, vol. 1, pp. 660–696; Lavi, *Pinkas Hakehilot*: *Rumania*, vol. 2, p. 507. Concerning the city of Cernăuţi, see Zvi Yavetz, *Tzernovitz Sheli*: *Makom Shehayu Bo Anashim Usefarim* (Hebrew) (Or Yehudah: Dvir, 2008). Sylvia Marko relates that Popovici himself gave her family a permit stating that her father was necessary to the economy of Cernăuţi, thus preventing their deportation to Transnistria. At the peak of the deportations, in the summer of 1942, Popovici hid her family members in his home; see Sylvia Marko testimony, YVA, O.3/VY/13197.

45 Southern Bukovina was not under Soviet rule in the years 1940–1941 and, therefore, its Jews had no connection to Communism. Thus Kunstadt refers to them as "kosher."

and Vatra Dornei. All the local Jews were crammed into cattle cars that transported them to the blessed land on the other side of the Dniester to begin "a new life" there. For some mysterious reason, the [Jews of the] city of Rădăuţi were the last to join the final, diabolical dance.[46]

On *Shabbes*, *Holemoyed Sukkes* (October 11, 1941), the prefect Ionescu, the governor of the Rădăuţi district, sent for the head of the Rădăuţi community Aizic Presner[47] and informed him that not a trace of the community of 10,000 Jews must be found in the city by *Simches Toyre* (October 14) at 8 A.M. Whoever dared to remain would be shot on the spot without a trial. Within half an hour, the gloomy news spread from one end of the city to the other. I dare not describe the panic that raged, because I would not be able to, even if I had the talent of Dante. His *Divine Comedy* is a refined paradise compared to the tragedy of the 10,000 Jews, which unfolded during three days of darkness that engulfed the Rădăuţi community—and to all that they endured on the days of "the time of our joy"[48]—*Hoshayne Rabbe*, *Shminatzeres*, and *Simches Toyre*.[49]

A commotion immediately erupted in the offices of the Jewish community because, by order of the authorities, 10,000 Jews would be deported in three transports—one transport each day—and the head of the community was responsible for preparing separate lists for every transport and for instructing the condemned to hurry to the train station, taking their meager possessions with them. The Romanian authorities

46 The town of Vatra Dornei in Southern Bukovina was primarily known as a summer vacation town due to its location on the slopes of the Carpathian Mountains. The town was also known for its fresh air that was beneficial to the health of the vacationists. The Jews in Vatra Dornei were transported to Transnistria on October 11, 1941. See Maraglit-Postilnik, *Radauts*: *Kehila Yehudit Betzemihata Uvisheki'ata*, pp. 143–145.

47 Aizic (Isidor) Presner, born in Rădăuţi on August 17, 1899, was the head of the community in Rădăuţi before World War II, and the owner of an ice factory and cooling house in Rădăuţi. See ibid., pp. 127, 143.

48 Sukkot, "the time of our joy," is the only holiday for which the Torah repeats three times the commandment to rejoice; see Deut. 16: 14–15; Lev. 33:40.

49 Within three days, all the Jews living in Rădăuţi were deported: the first transport left on Hoshana Rabba, October 12, 1941; the second on the following day, Shemini Atzeret, October 13, 1941; and the third transport on Simhat Torah, October 14, 1941. See Maraglit-Postilnik, *Radauts*: *Kehila Yehudit Betzemihata Uvisheki'ata*, p. 145.

sternly announced that they must take with them only basic necessities and by no means whatsoever should they take any Romanian currency, jewelry, or valuable objects—not to mention foreign currency and gold. Outside the government bank, thousands of people stood in line with bundles of currency in their hands and packages of jewelry, *Shabbes* candlesticks, silver cutlery, and spice boxes to deposit their fortunes as the overlord had ordered. The bank "exchanged" 50 lei for one ruble (the currency used in Transnistria), a tenth of its true value—and people could not take out more than 50 rubles. The bank clerks placed everything above that amount, uncounted, into their coffers, together with valuable objects, and without issuing any receipts to anyone.

That *Shabbes* afternoon, they were already sitting at the community building, drawing up the lists, which were actually death sentences for thousands of persons, as would become clear later. At the time, they did not know yet that at least 90 percent of the deportees on transports No. 1 and No. 2 [to Mărculeşti] and 50 percent of those on transport No. 3 [to Atachi] were condemned to death.

The first transport, which left on *Hoshayne Rabbe*, and the second, which departed the following day, on *Shminatzeres*, deported around 7,000 Jews to the shtetl of Mărculeşti (Bessarabia) on the bank of the Dniester.

The last transport, No. 3, carrying about 3,000 people, left Rădăuţi on *Simches Toyre* at dawn (October 14, 1941), and was more fortunate. My family and I (me, my mother, my sister, Rivka, my wife, Roza and the children, Iza and Bertl, my father-in-law, Şmuel Merling, my sister-in-law, Rachel, the married Elke with her husband, Moşe Sonenschein, and the child, Herş) were also among the "fortunate ones." Our train traveled for two days, transporting us to the ruined shtetl of Atachi, next to the Dniester, facing Moghilev-Podolsk. We traveled in cattle cars, eighty to ninety persons in each and, already on that journey, the first victims fell, those who could not endure the suffering and gave the finger to the Creator's "beautiful" world. In the adjacent cattle car, already on the first day of the journey, a fellow townsman David Eiferman, a respectable merchant in his fifties, resorted to such a trick. He sat down and fell over dead even before the train arrived in Cernăuţi. In Cernăuţi, I saw groups of Jews with yellow badges on their sleeves standing on the platform of the station. They apparently came to see relatives and acquaintances on the passing transport and to bid them farewell. The Romanian soldiers, who accompanied the transport, did not let anyone approach the cattle cars. However, they presented the Cernăuţi Jews with a holiday gift (after all, it was *Simches Toyre …*): the frozen bodies of the cunning Jews who had saved themselves from Transnistria just in time and will dwell forever in the holy land of Bukovina.

There were victims of another kind during the holiday journey to a "new life." A few women who did not actually fall down dead but rather were struck by a more severe calamity: they lost their minds, and burst into hysterical wailing and screaming—a fitting soundtrack for a horror movie. One of those unfortunate women was a fellow townswoman Glatter (I do not know her first name), a young, beautiful, thirty-year-old woman who, holding a baby in her arms, drowned out the other confused women with her heartrending cries, begging them to throw her off the careering train, because she was afraid to jump off herself. Failing to persuade anyone, she traveled to Atachi and arrived a few days later in Moghilev. By contrast, her mother-in-law, Mrs. Glatter, did not utter a sound in the cattle car, but upon reaching the banks of the Dniester, without giving it much thought, she stepped right into the river. She did not reach Transnistria …

In Atachi, Transnistria suddenly lost its charm also in the eyes of another fellow townsman of mine, the young optician Dr. Alfred Straminger, and of his elderly mother. Well, immediately upon crawling out of the cattle car, they both ingested a kind of powder [poison] that swiftly transported them to eternal deliverance. His wife refused to be the third in line, and now she is in exile in Moghilev. There were people in Atachi who envied the son and his mother, and there was talk: of course, only an optician could afford to do this …

[April 28, 1942] Two Hours Later

I took a breath to garner strength for another chapter of Lamentations. Yes, contrary to the cases that I described of those who had brought "deliverance" closer with their own hands, demonstrating a kind of negative bravery, according to some, or a weakness of character, according to others, I will now note a strange fact that was very striking during the three cursed holidays on the eve of the deportations from my hometown and then later, while wandering through the seven levels of the hell of the camps of Transnistria. The cases of suicide appear to be inversely proportional to the scope of the catastrophe. Precisely when there is good reason to sever the thread, the biological instinct to exist grows stronger, as if to inflame the urge to continue to live out of spite. This paradox is mainly evident during a mass calamity, according to the old saying: A shared sorrow is half a sorrow. Suicide corresponds with the need of the individual who cannot bear to see fortunate people around him.

For example, in my hometown during the three days of panic that was triggered by the deportation, there were only four persons who attempted suicide, and all but one succeeded. The first was a well-respected Jew, the owner of a kosher hotel, a seventy-year-old observant Jew, Zalman Rudich. His relatives found him on the morning of *Hoshayne Rabbe*, hanging in the attic of the hotel. On the evening of *Shminatzeres*, an entire family followed in his footsteps—the municipal government doctor Şlomo Weber, who poisoned himself together with both his daughters—Thea, a pharmacist, and Kozia, a doctor of philology. The elderly (eighty-year-old) physician, one of the most respected doctors in the city and a man of great culture, of unparalleled compassion and honesty, succeeded with only two-thirds of a flask of morphine. He and his younger daughter, Thea, never woke from their repose. By contrast, Kozia lay for a few days in a coma. Romanian gendarmes found her in the apartment a day after the last transport had been dispatched. Having no other choice, they took her to the local hospital where she remained for a few weeks. To avoid deportation to Transnistria, her only option was to convert [to Christianity]. (**Added in 1945**: She was granted true deliverance at home and returned to the Jewish faith directly following the liberation of Romania.—L. K.)

In the Dzhurin camp, where close to 4,000 deportees suffered bitter hardship, not a single person succeeded in committing suicide to date, although there was indeed an attempt. A fellow townsman, G. G., a respectable young man and the father of a child, hanged himself, but his neighbors took notice—it is difficult to hide in Dzhurin—and cut the rope. He was shaking as they lowered him. Whether they did him a favor remains to be seen.[50] Well, that's enough for today. If, first of all, the Romanian gendarmes and then His Beloved Name will grant me my life, then tomorrow will be another day …

April 29, 1942

We arrived in Atachi on Friday at dawn (October 17, 1941). The transport stopped far from the train station in an open field. An order was heard to empty the cattle cars within half an hour, and then the gendarmes chased the people to the shtetl of Atachi that had been destroyed during the battles a few months earlier. Obviously, there were no porters waiting to serve the dear guests, and we had to load our own luggage onto our shoulders, carrying as much as we had the strength to bear. Already from that moment, people began to lose the poor, meager possessions that they had succeeded in hauling there. Exhausted and battered from the horrendous journey, even strong, young men were not able to lug more than two suitcases at a time, let alone the women, the elderly, and the frail! The hands of mothers and fathers of young children were occupied with the infants, who cried heartrending cries, wailing at the top of their lungs. Soon, mountains of suitcases, rucksacks, bedding, and all kinds of rags were piled along both sides of the railroad track, cast aside by the newly arrived "guests," extending close to 1 kilometer—there were more than eighty cattle cars in the third transport.

The crowd scrambled for the "villas," occupying whatever ruins or hovels they could find. Not one building had a roof, doors, or windows. Nevertheless, the people were gratified just to have, if not a roof over their heads, then at least four walls around them that separated them from the Romanian soldiers. They knew then that the lodgings were not permanent, because Atachi was only a transit station from where they would soon be taken across the Dniester to the "promised land."

---

50 Some of the deportees evidently could not withstand the extreme distress and put an end to their lives. See Eva Gold, YVA, O.3/VT/8560; Carp, *Cartea neagră,* vol. 3, pp. 266, 268, 269; Ancel, *Toledot Hashoah*: *Romania,* vol. 2, p. 1019.

In the meanwhile, the stopover in Atachi lasted about two weeks, but the lucky ones were dispatched already after eight days. In Atachi, people fell like flies, mainly the frail and elderly, who lay dying in rows next to the Dniester until their souls left their bodies. They were then covered with the muddy earth, which was washed away by the seething river after a few days. Doctors made a vast fortune: relatives gave away their last shirt for an injection that would hasten the end of a dying relative. Indeed, some doctors hesitated, but others, with more mercy and ... zeal, put aside the Hippocratic oath, and they certainly should be congratulated, although they did not lose money in the business ...

My "apartment," a mud hovel, which was inhabited by ten other people, besides me and my family, was actually located right on the bank of the river. I witnessed scenes in which close relatives kissed the hands of the doctors and begged them to take the redemptive needle from their bags and put an end to the suffering of a dying grandmother or infant.

The eight days in Atachi, until October 25, 1941, were the most terrible during the trek on the route of agony so far. A cold, raging rain poured down unremittingly; soldiers ran around like demons between the ruins, pillaging and killing, mainly at night; and hunger raged. People gave away their last shirt to the peasants from the surrounding area for a loaf of bread or potatoes. The peasants would not accept money, only objects that were worth many times more than the value of the merchandise. I know of cases in which people "exchanged" a suit for a loaf of bread.

Crossing the Dniester meant being subjected to ancient, tsarist-style brutality. Soldiers foisted the people into narrow rafts and robbed them without mercy. They tore a watch from Roza's hand, which she had worn intentionally to appease the two-legged beasts and to save us from who knows what misfortune. Around the beginning of the week, we arrived in Moghilev and went to the university building, as previously mentioned.

A large portion of the deportees succeeded in hiding illegally in Moghilev[51] and later in the iron foundry that the engineer Jagendorf managed to establish. The majority, however, were sent further to various

51 The city of Moghilev was supposed to serve as a transfer point only, and the Jews were not permitted to stay there. See the monograph by Dr. Meir Teich in Carp, *Cartea neagră,* vol. 3, p. 260.

shtetls and villages in the Moghilev district—Shargorod,[52] Dzhurin, Kopaygorod,[53] Murafa,[54] Ivăşcăuţi,[55] and so on. Engineer Jagendorf was able to persuade the Romanian commander of the town to provide German trucks to drive the deportees to their new "homes" in exchange for a large amount of cash—obviously, only to those who proved that they could pay for the journey. Those whose pockets were empty were led on foot in a "convoy." A few thousand persons were destined to be dispatched to Kopaygorod[56]—German trucks did not drive them there.[57] That road that extends almost 50 kilometers did not claim any victims. People bribed the soldiers accompanying the convoy and, therefore, they did not drive them on mercilessly but rather allowed them to rest and treated the unfortunate ones decently. I should note that, in many cases, the engineer Jagendorf, who arranged the trip on the German trucks and who made the final decision regarding who would travel with whom, secured places for families of means on the condition that they would pay part of the cost for people who did not have the entire sum.

---

52 Shargorod, the administrative center of the region, is located around 37 kilometers east of the regional capital Moghilev.

53 Kopaygorod is a town in the region of Moghilev, 22 kilometers from Bar. See Lavi, *Pinkas Hakehilot*: *Rumania*, vol. 1, p. 501.

54 Murafa is a village in the district of Moghilev in Ukraine, in the region of Shargorod. See ibid., pp. 475–478; Fuchs, *Sefer Yehudei Sutsheva*, vol. 2, p. 333.

55 Ivăşcăuţi is a village in the Moghilev district, around 10 kilometers from the administrative center of Shargorod. Before the war, four to five Jewish families lived in this village; they found shelter with the village peasants during the occupation. In the fall of 1941, 2,000 deportees from Bessarabia and Bukovina arrived in the village. Following a typhus epidemic that broke out there, only 600 Jews survived. For more information, see Lavi, *Pinkas Hakehilot*: *Rumania*, vol. 1, pp. 397–398.

56 This refers to the Kopaygorod ghetto in the Moghilev district. Jews found in the Moghilev transit camp were referred to the Kopaygorod ghetto but were required to pay a ransom in exchange for permission to remain in the ghetto; see ibid.

57 The engineer Jagendorf and other private entrepreneurs managed to bribe the local praetor, Colonel Ion Bălianu, to drive the Jews in trucks to the ghettos of Shargorod, Murafa, Dzhurin, etc., for payment. See the Securitate Archive, Consiliul National pentru Studierea Archivelor Securitatii (CNSAS), P-8279, file 1, pp. 270–290.

[April 29, 1942] In the Evening

Once again, a "flashback" to my hometown of Rădăuţi. The date: the black *Shabbes* during *Holemoyed Sukkes*, when the community had to compose the lists for the three transports. The wheeler-dealers—suddenly dozens of new functionaries sprouted like mushrooms after the rain, people who had never been involved in communal affairs—sat down to feverishly write the lists, and there were not enough desks for the unexpected [number of] writers. They all had the same personal interest: to make sure that their own families, relatives, and friends were in the third, or at least the second, transport. It was clear to everyone that we were not invited to Transnistria to eat kreplach, so there was no reason to hurry. Although the decree was certain, they still hoped for a miracle—that the decree would be revoked, if not today then tomorrow, or even the day after tomorrow.[58] Indeed, the slaughterer's knife was poised over our necks and the entire group of Jews from Southern Bukovina, apart from Rădăuţi, were already prepared to be exiled in extremely overloaded cattle cars. Suceava, Gura Humorului, Câmpulung, and Vatra Dornei were already "*Judenrein,*" but Rădăuţi is indeed privileged! An indication of this is that the decree was issued in Rădăuţi a few days later.[59]

Aside from this, people deluded themselves that the miracle that had occurred in the shtetl a few months before would repeat itself. Then on Thursday, June 18, 1941, on a beautiful summer evening, four days before Hitler invaded the Soviet Union, the police suddenly announced to the

---

58 Although Kunstadt hints that it was impossible to prevent the edict of the deportation, they still hoped that the delegation to Bucharest, which had not yet returned, would succeed in canceling it. Therefore, they preferred to be included in the group of the third deportation, hoping that the delegation would return with good news by then. See Margalit-Postilnik, *Radauts*: *Kehila Yehudit Betzemihata Uvisheki'ata.*

59 The Jews of Suceava were deported within three days, beginning on October 9, 1941: on the first day, the Jews of Burdujeni and Iţcani were also deported; on the following day, October 10, 1941, an additional group of the Jews of Suceava was deported, together with the Jews of Gura Humorului and a group of Jews from Vatra Dornei and the surrounding area; on the third day, October 11, 1941, the remainder of the Jews from Suceava were deported. During these three days, the Jews of Rădăuţi and the surrounding villages, and of Câmpulung were deported. On October 14, 1941, the last Jews of Rădăuţi and Câmpulung were deported, and Southern Bukovina was *Judenrein*. See Ancel, *Toledot Hashoah*: *Romania*, vol. 1, pp. 701–702.

sound of drums passing through all the streets that the next day at dawn, at 6 A.M., all the Jews of Rădăuţi had to set out for the market with their bags to march from there to somewhere in exile. Transnistria had not yet been born and the Red flag was still raised on the other side of the Dniester. Had they announced that the world would be turned upside down the following morning, the panic certainly would not have been greater. Suddenly people began running through the streets like poisoned mice, knocking into one another and stumbling over their own feet, dragging suitcases and bundles. The Jewish shopkeepers distributed the merchandise in the shops to anyone who wanted it, but no one was interested. Within an hour, the city was transformed into a madhouse and every mouth uttered the same words: "Perhaps God will grant us a miracle after all!"

And the miracle did indeed take place at the last minute. At 9 P.M., a rumor that the decree had been revoked suddenly spread. It took only a few minutes for all the Jews to hear the glad tidings as they ran from house to house to convey the good news. People kissed each other in the streets, weeping for joy, and the entire Jewish community had a *Leyl Shimurim*.[60] Until today, no one knows who was the *meyletz yoysher*[61] who interceded on behalf of the Jews of Rădăuţi to issue an order in a telephone call from Bucharest that they not be displaced for the time being. The neighboring shtetl of Siret[62] was not so fortunate. All its 2,000 Jews, every one, were uprooted from their homes on Friday, June 19, 1941. First, they dragged them in cattle cars to Calafat and Craiova (the Regat), and then, two months later, to Rădăuţi, where they were condemned, together with the Jews of Rădăuţi, to set out for Transnistria.

Therefore, the dignitaries in Rădăuţi also waited for a miracle, like the one in June. The time was indeed ripe for a miracle; there was truly a need for one. After all, it was *Hoshayne Rabbe*, when the *kvitel*[63] was

60 *Leyl Shimurim* (night of vigil), from the root, *shamar*, has several meanings: to guard, to observe, to save. This term originally appears in Exodus 12:42: "That same night is the Lord's, one of vigil for all the children of Israel throughout the ages." Observant Jews are obligated to spend the first night of Passover studying all night.

61 White knight; advocate.

62 A city in the region of Suceava in Bukovina, halfway between Suceava and Cernăuţi.

63 Ashkenazi Jews greet each other on Hoshana Rabba with the blessing in Yiddish, "*A Gut Kvitel,*" which literally means "good note," because on this day the Creator supposedly

granted from above, a day that seemed to be permeated with secrets in the twenty-two synagogues and *bote midroshim*[64] that were filled with candlelight, *Yom Kipper* melodies, and expectations for a new, better, and brighter year. The synagogues were fully packed more than ever with men, women, and children. There were faces among the crowd that for a long time already had forgotten how to open the door of a holy place, and crying and wailing spread from one end of the city to the other, which must have pierced the seventy-seven heavens. Some lay their grievances before the Creator and pleaded with Him, as one would before an angry father who must forgive his child who implores him, writhing in anguish. Even those who had strayed from the faith hoped for something to occur during those fateful days that would save them from the looming peril—if not a miracle, then at least deliverance.

Regardless of the fact that it is forbidden to visit ancestral graves on a holiday, the cemetery was so crowded that there was no room. Wails from around the graves reached the heart of the heavens as people tried to obtain from the dead what they had not managed to attain from the living …

While the plaints rose and the rivers of tears continued to flow in the *bote midroshim* and the cemeteries, the functionaries at the community building were busy with the scratching of dozens of pens, writing down names in alphabetical order, declaring a verdict, here or there, on each line. So, it happened that these scribes, as well as all kinds of esteemed wheeler-dealers and people with sharp elbows, would remain until the last transport and would leave in the seventh *hakofe*.[65] Fate (Divine Providence, according to religious Jews) worked this time in such a way that whoever laughed now would eventually weep, and it was possible that the third transport in particular would be dragged to Mărculeşti, the gate to hell. No one knew where people would be thrown out, or which place was more dangerous.

---

delivers notes through emissaries with the judgement that can still be changed for the better until the verdict is signed at the end of the day.

64 A Jewish hall or school of study.

65 The joyous climax of Simhat Torah is the *hakafot* (singing and dancing with the Torah scrolls in a circle).

The community handed the lists to the prefect[66] in compliance with his order and, in the heat of the moment, he sent policemen and soldiers to each Jewish house to announce the good news. These messengers made it clear to them [the Jews] that if, after twelve hours, they would find a Jew in that same apartment, the culprit would be shot on the spot. No one considered testing whether the messengers were really telling the truth, and Jews began streaming to the train station, carrying their meager possessions on their shoulders as they hurried to grab a "good place" in the packed cattle cars. I will not attempt to describe the terrible panic, the wails, the chaos, and the dreadful scenes of those three days so as not to detract from the immensity of the catastrophe—the annihilation of an old, well-established, hallowed community of 10,000 Jews (together with the Jews of Siret).

The first two transports finally left on *Hoshayne Rabbe* and *Shminatzeres*, and the miracle remained hidden. Around 3,000 Jews were left for the *hakofes* of *Simches Toyre*, including me and my family. I did not force my way in, but I did make efforts to be registered for the third transport, not, God forbid, to mix in with the "large pot of potatoes,"[67] but because of the tried and tested rule that to get something good, you must hurry to snatch it before someone else does. I didn't think anyone would be interested in grabbing Transnistria …

So, it happened that on the evening of *Shminatzeres*, when Jews joyfully go to the *hakofes*, my family and I walked to the train station, trailing behind a cart belonging to a non-Jew (I rented it right in the midst of the parting of the Red Sea for an immense sum of money), which was loaded with the remainder of my belongings.

When we arrived at the station, the gates of hell opened before me. Thousands of Jews stormed the cattle cars and settled in the good places, hurling everything that they had brought with them inside. I could not fight the unruly people, but I finally managed to squeeze into a crowded cattle car with my family and with only a few packages in hand, while all my possessions and also those of my mother and my father-in-law

66 General Vasile Ionescu, the military commander of Bukovina; Ancel, *Toledot Hashoah: Romania*, vol. 1, p. 669.

67 This expression refers to the prominent figures and leaders.

were left behind, abandoned. What good would it do to protest? And to whom? The soldiers shoved everyone into the cattle cars mercilessly, prodding them, screaming, and not sparing them any blows with the butts of their rifles. Only in Transnistria did I realize that a few dozen families who could not find any place whatsoever in the cattle cars had remained behind on the platform. They actually won the biggest prize: the Romanian authorities, on their own initiative, specially arranged a fourth transport with several cattle cars, and they were able to travel in better conditions and to load their few meager possessions undamaged onto the cattle cars.

We spent the night between *Shminatzeres* and *Simches Toyre* in the cattle cars, still in our homeland. The first night in the graveyard is certainly easier for the deceased, because he lies in the grave and shows the world his middle finger. Only the next day at dawn did the transport of 3,000 persons begin to move toward Transnistria, the worst hell.

I lack the strength and the presence of mind to recount what took place during the three dark days of the transport of the "well-connected people." I will only mention one strange fact: the rabbi of Siret, Rabbi Baruch Hager, a son of the old Vijniţa rabbi, Rabbi Israel Hager,[68] of blessed memory, was in one of the cattle cars. Rabbi Hager and a group of Hasidim did not pay any attention to the diabolical surroundings and celebrated *Simches Toyre* to spite the enemy, calling everyone to the Torah (he was carrying a small, antique *Toyre* scroll with him). They held the *hakofes* standing in place, because it was impossible to dance in a circle seven times, as required, with about seventy people in that cattle car. Not only that, but Hasidic melodies mingled with the jarring cries

68 Rabbi Baruch Hager (1895–2 Heshvan, 5724 [October 19–20,1964]), known as "Makor Baruch" after the title of his book, was the son of Israel Hager, the Rebbe of the Vijniţa Hasidim, and the founder and first Rebbe of the Siret–Vijniţa Hasidim. He was the last rabbi of the town of Siret in Bukovina before the deportation of the Jewish residents to the Ukraine during the Holocaust. Rabbi Israel Hager with his two sons, Eliezer and Moshe, were among the first of those deported from Bukovina. On their arrival in Dzhurin, they arranged a soup kitchen for the benefit of the deportees from their town, Siret. In August 1947, he immigrated to the land of Israel and settled in Haifa. For more information see Aharon Sorski, "Dereh Hayav Shel Ha'admor R' Boruhel, z"l" (Hebrew), *Beit Ya'akov*, 165/166 (Tishrei 5724 [October 1964]) pp. 15–19.

and the heartrending wails that came from the other not-so-festive cattle cars. A demonic symphony composed by Ashmedai[69] himself …

The "lucky" transport arrived in Atachi at dawn three days later, on Friday (October 17, 1941). Who knows, perhaps those on the first transports deserved to be envied. Most of them had already died and no one had any power over them, while we, the "fortunate ones" in the Moghilev district, continuously yearned for yesterday, because every morning brought fresh decrees, new calamities, and mortal fear …

April 30, 1942

In a guter sho, I actually succeeded in swallowing my pride. Yesterday evening the council allotted me the pay of 40 marks per month, beginning in May.[70] Together with the 60 marks from the Moghilev Central Council, I will receive 100 marks in cash, and who will match that! Oh, my poor wealth! I will certainly not be able to buy a lamp like that of the rich—a bargain price for such an expensive item would be 50 [marks] … and my poor eyes will continue to be tormented by the light of a smoking oil lamp …

May 6, 1942

A series of distressing, gloomy days—both outside and within my soul—began, and I did not feel like even touching my pen when I came home late in the evening, exhausted and worn out from my work. Cold rain mixed with snow, turbulent winds, deep mud—this is the setting that nature adapted to match the last, sad week.

The mires of Dzhurin are a tormenting and agonizing plague, a sticky addition to the dark fate. Already when the door of the Dzhurin

69 In Jewish legend, Ashmedai is the king of demons.

70 Kunstadt received his wages from the treasury of the ghetto council. The money in the council's treasury derived from taxes imposed on people of means and owners of business, cooperatives, etc.

paradise opened before me on October 29, 1941, at 10 P.M., these mires were revealed to me in all their grace. As soon as I crawled out of the German truck, which hauled us to this godforsaken place, I became well acquainted with the mires of Dzhurin. It was a dark autumn evening, I slipped and fell face down, sprawled out in thick, ice cold, gray filth, which appeared to be bottomless. My black, fur, *Shabbes* coat, which I schlepped throughout the journey so that I would not lose it in the pandemonium, was in the blink of an eye covered with thick, sticky mud, and my shoes were packed with an unbearably heavy load of clay.

That is how Dzhurin saw me entering through its gate, loaded with packages and sloshing through the mud. It comforted me that a shared sorrow is half a sorrow, since I was not the only one in such fine form. This stubborn mud has continued to accumulate and spread until today in the month of May, except when it has had to succumb to a frost, poor thing, having no choice but to relent.

During the first days of exile in Dzhurin, when we still had some leftover food in the bags that we had lugged from home, I would not venture out of my cubbyhole to avoid sinking up to my knees in the black mud that clung to the sole like a demon and did not allow one to move one's feet.

However, I could not indulge myself like this for long. The local Jews could not understand why we—the "*Bukaviner bishenitzes*"[71] (in Russian: refugees, although this term does not apply to the actual situation, because we were forcibly driven out)—come here with complaints about their mud and voice only grievances. How can they claim that until today their fathers and grandfathers lived out their predestined years in the same mud, married, brought children into the world, went to celebrations and to funerals, and somehow were never annoyed by what stuck to their soles.

It's true that the Jews of Dzhurin all wear heavy, Russian, leather boots—men, women, and children alike. They gape in amazement at the sight of the *bishenitzes* from Bukovina whom they consider wealthy men yet do not even have high boots and drag themselves around, poor things, almost barefoot, given the questionable value of the poor boots on their feet. At first, we, the *bishenitzes* from Bukovina, also wondered why the

---

71 The local Ukrainian Jews called the refugees who came from Romania "*bishenitzes*."

Dzhurin Jews never tried at least to contend with the annoying mud and to make narrow paths alongside the houses, instead of relying entirely on Russian leather boots.

By the way, there are other reasons to be astonished in Dzhurin, precisely because of the things that, when compared with mud, make it explicitly … mud. For example, there is a question that every *bishenitz* from Bukovina asks himself at least once a day, provided that his stomach is in good condition: Why do the people of Dzhurin not know about that secluded place where even the emperor goes out alone? Are the Dzhurin Jews, one will ask, angels, who have no need for such a place? No, they are in fact the same flesh and blood as the strange Jews of Bukovina, but over the generations these strange creatures have found a way to cope, wherever and whenever necessary, as long as an evil eye, God forbid, does not see them in the act, in particular the eye of a militiaman … Well, then they actually see and feel [it] to the point of feeling weak—so what. So, they pay fines and their cries reach the heavens—the screams of the hosts who suspect the deportees of a repulsive act right outside their door, and the response of the deportees is to strike back in kind. Indeed, every morning, the ghetto is in turmoil for a while, the militia drag the criminals to the council, women shriek, and advocates hurry to persuade the Jewish council members to show mercy—until the panic subsides and the next day everything starts all over again.

That is how it has always been in Dzhurin, and certainly it will be so as long as it exists. The residents of Dzhurin claim they can do nothing today, because there is a dearth of timber—a material that at the present time is as easy to obtain as, for example, oranges, pepper, or … paper. This, however, is a lame excuse. Not long ago, when there was no lack of timber and no war raged, yet no one lifted a finger to equip his lodgings with such a secret place. This backwardness is not specific to Dzhurin but is manifest in all the places between the Dniester and the Bug. Fortunately, for the time being, I have no idea what the other side of the Bug looks like.

Take for example the grievous water problem. In the shtetl of Dzhurin, its 8,000 inhabitants—two-thirds Jews in the ghetto on the mountain and one-third Ukrainians in the valley, in the "*Zavad* [factory] quarter" (there was a big sugar factory there before the war)—are actually dying of thirst. There is only one well—an ancient pump in a swampy valley, which is extremely difficult to access throughout the year. In the muddy season, one literally sinks into the mire; in the winter, it is very dangerous to lug a full pail up the mountain—a distance of more than 1 kilometer—when the ground is slippery. A long line of people, with yokes [to carry buckets of water] and pails, stand next to the pump, sometimes waiting for hours to get a little water. There are always fights and cursing—that often come to blows—regarding who will be the first to get a bucket of water, and who will pay with his health, because of the appallingly rusty, crude pump from the days of Methuselah.

With God's help, when the pump breaks—which happens at least once a week—the shtetl is left without a drop of water. Then people find a way to draw from a filthy stream and, consequently, typhus has always been a member of the household in Dzhurin and has claimed many victims every year. Because of their backwardness, the inhabitants of Dzhurin have never thought that it might be worthwhile to dig a few more wells. When talking with them, you hear that only they are the truly "cultured" people, while those from Bukovina have never known the meaning of culture ...[72]

May 7, 1942

The sun is shining—a cold, freezing sun that is more characteristic around the time of *Hanuke*[73] than of *Lag B'Oymer.*[74] It seems that in

72 The new places in which the deportees arrived made a harsh impression on them, both because of the living conditions that were so different from those they had known and because of the immense cultural difference between them and the local Jews. It should be noted that the local Jews were influenced by the culture of their neighbors, the local villagers, who were also miserably poor. The impoverished appearance of the Dzhurin ghetto and the wretched surrounding conditions, as well as the poverty of the Ukrainian Jews, shocked the deportees from Bukovina. The infrastructure and houses were dilapidated, and the residents lived in terrible, even "primitive," conditions, in the language of the deportees. Due to the program of collectivization introduced by the Soviet authorities at the beginning of the 1930s, the residents of Dzhurin experienced a shortage of basic daily necessities.

73 The eight-day Jewish "festival of lights"commemorates the victory of the Jews against the Greeks in the second century BCE and the rededication of the Temple in Jerusalem.

74 The thirty-third day of the Omer, a period between Passover and Shavuot, is a minor

this region, the summer appears only at the end of June and does not last long. How indeed could a true spring and a long summer befit such dismal surroundings? Already over a week into May and there is no sign of a green blade of grass, or a blossom on a tree, of a buzzing May beetle, not to mention a fragrant flower. It seems that May in Transnistria is a kind of scourge, a worse version of Morris Rozenfeld's "*Yidisher Mai*."[75] Calendar pages that for generations have been imbued with romance and covered with a thousand days of grace—*Peysech*, *Sefires Ho'Oymer*, *Lag B'Oymer*, May 1—have been stripped of their colorful content and do not have the power to evoke more intense longing than do regular weekdays.

Lonely, sad, and monotonous days, weeks, months crawl by, and everything revolves around three vexing concerns: hunger, typhus, and the fear of tomorrow. As we survive another day, we feel as though a burden has been lifted from our heads, and we hope that soon we will be able to close our eyes and that our dreams will tear us out of this grim reality, and perhaps even carry us as far as our former homes that spewed us out. Perhaps we will be lucky enough to see in a dream the streets and buildings that we had ties to until the exile, so near and yet so far.

We wake up in the morning, broken from the hard, wooden bunk or the floor, where we tossed and turned during the long night, waging a war against the masses of small, loathsome creatures that are actually dying for a little Jewish blood—this is very onerous torture. Now another day dawns, bringing new misfortunes, sorrows, and worries with it.

Ever since I have been languishing in the torment of this camp, not one day has passed without events that rattle the soul and further darken the gloomy surroundings. Now the gendarmes have issued another decree, which pours bile into the bitterness; now prices suddenly have soared for no reason; now the farmers refuse, without reason, to accept marks, rubles, or lei at the market in return for food, produce, etc., having lost faith in the three currencies with which Transnistria is blessed; now one

---

holiday that commemorates the cessation of a plague among the disciples of Rabbi Akiva, that raged "because they did not act respectfully toward each other."

75 Kunstadt is apparently referring to the poem by the Yiddish poet Morris Rozenfeld (1862–1923); see Morris Rozenfeld, "Der ershter Mai," *Der yud* (Vienna–Kraków, January 1, 1899).

person or another is infected with typhus and is taken to the hospital; now a letter is smuggled in from another camp, bringing glad tidings and new memorials are organized in the names of fresh victims. Here comes someone from Moghilev—obviously, a council member, since a simple man of flesh and blood from the camp cannot move about, because of the risk of the death penalty.[76] He reports new decrees and new dangers, which are being prepared by the "high-level officials." Wild rumors spread, the devil knows from where, that soon we will all be driven further, everyone, to Bessarabia, over the Bug, then to Lublin, to the mountains of darkness, no longer to enjoy blessed Transnistria.[77]

It is true that there are sometimes bright days when a thin ray of sunshine pierces the black clouds briefly. Then rumors spread here and there that deliverance is approaching and the deportees will be sent home—if not all, then at least the well-connected people from Southern Bukovina or northern Moldavia. They never sampled the "non-kosher" Red regime in the years of the Soviet occupation and are, therefore, more kosher in the eyes of the Romanian authorities than both the Jews of Bukovina and Bessarabia with their poisoned souls. On such clear days, the power of imagination gets going very quickly and runs wild. Rumors spring up swiftly from moment to moment, and people whisper to each other the exact day of deliverance: the 10th of the month, the 15th, the 25th, and in the camp, there was "for the Jews" [light and joy].[78] Such days, however, have an odious tendancy of going wrong. Instead of loading their bundles and setting out for home, it is necessary to hide in panic in the attics and cellars, or to disappear completely in the empty fields so that the gendarmes will not catch you during the manhunt and

76 Anyone caught outside the boundaries of the ghettos or camps was liable to heavy punishments, which ranged from lashes to death by shooting. Members of the council who received permission from the praetor could move from place to place in the framework of their duties. See CNSAS, P-5678, pp. 5–36.

77 With these words Kunstadt reveals that rumors had reached him concerning the continued danger of deportations, and even concerning deportations to Poland.

78 "*Layehudim haytah orah vesimha vesason*" in Hebrew (the Jews enjoyed light, joy, and gladness), from Megillat Esther 8:16, which is read on the holiday of Purim that commemorates the story of the deliverance of the Jews in Persia.

send you to perform hard labor for the Germans on the other side of the Bug. It seems that the gendarmes themselves spread the false rumors about deliverance to facilitate carrying out the snatch-*Aktia*.

[May 7, 1942] 6 P.M.

Really, as if I were a prophet! Today too a ray of sun has broken through—let us hope that it will be for the best. In the shtetl, the praetor of the Shargorod district, Iosif Dindilegan,[79] unexpectedly appeared and drove straight to the council in his luxury car. Nothing like this has ever happened since the camp was established. The praetor is the head of the Romanian occupying authorities in the occupied regions. Dzhurin belongs to the Shargorod district, where Dindilegan, who is known to be an enemy of Israel, rules. The overlord immediately sent for the colony chief, Dr. Max Rosenstrauch, and argued with him for an hour in a separate room. When the overlord left, the big news spread quickly in the camp: by order from the Romanian headquarters, all the craftsmen and people with a profession in the "colonies" (that is, the camps!) in Transnistria will be deported. The council will receive the instructions already tomorrow.

The camp is agitated, like at a market, and everyone offers a different interpretation. Optimists believe that the craftsmen will be sent to their old homes in Romania, since the country desperately needs them, because of the war. In contrast, the pessimists claim that the craftsmen will indeed be sent away, but not to their homes, rather to other camps,

---

79 Iosif Dindilegan was born on July 6, 1906, in the small town of Ariniş in the district of Maramureş. He graduated from the Law Faculty in Cluj and was appointed as praetor of the Shargorod district. The headquarters of the district gendarmes was also located in the Shargorod ghetto (from an administrative perspective, the Shargorod district was part of to the Moghilev district). Dindilegan was appointed by the Romanian authorities in October 1941, two days before the first deportees arrived in Shargorod. Because Shargorod was a district capital, Dindilegan also served as the Romanian representative of the towns of Murafa and Dzhurin, also part of the Shargorod district. Dindilegan was extremely violent and saw himself as the "overlord of the lives and deaths of the Jews." He was tried in Bucharest and sentenced to imprisonment in 1945; he was released in 1956. See Carp, *Cartea neagră*, vol. 3, p. 264; CNSAS, I-329795, pp. 23–24.

perhaps even in Germany. The most pressing question is whether they will also send families together with their relatives to wherever luck or misfortune will take them? Otherwise, God forbid, this may have catastrophic implications: being separated from one's relatives forever and leaving wives and children abandoned in the camp, where they will starve to death. This fateful question arises in one's mind and no one can be consulted for advice. For the first time, our own fate and the fate of our families lie in our own hands. None of the leaders know who is or is not a craftsman, and each one must join the circle dance by himself. One person asks another for advice, and receives the same answer: "By all means, give me advice!" …

The news confounded and plagued me, as well as my household. Speaking about professions, I can register myself as an expert book printer, bookkeeper, translator, typist, graphologist, clerk. Obviously, any mention of my journalistic past would explicitly mean suicide. My wife, Roza, and my sister, Rivka, are certified nurses, who once had the pleasure of taking a course given by the Red Cross—may we not need it. Not to mention my sister-in-law, Rachel—she is certainly the cream of the crop—a doctor of chemistry! In short, there are plenty of trades but few blessings among us, and no one can give me any advice: to register or not?

When I told my family the news, they began to dance for joy. Roza and the children were bursting with happiness. It seems to them, poor things, that already tomorrow at dawn we will turn the wagon around to go back home, and the seven months of hell will vanish like a bad dream. My eleven-year-old daughter, Iza, a very sensitive soul, will not leave me alone and demands that I describe in great detail how we will travel home. What should I answer this child? How can I ruin this bright dream? For the time being, I see towering mountains before me, which we will have to climb, if it comes to that.

Rachel burst into tears of great joy and ran swift as an arrow to tell her elderly father, my father-in-law, Şmuel Merling, the news. She wholly believes that for the sake of justice they will send all of us home quickly. A doctor's diploma is apparently no protection against naive self-delusions …

May 8, 1942, 10 A.M.

The page has been turned. A special messenger from Shargorod brought the registration forms for craftsmen just now. The order is veiled in absolute secrecy and does not mention even a hint of what the government has in mind.[80] There are only thirty professions among the options. The colony chief himself, Dr. Max Rosenstrauch, will sit in all his glory to register the candidates this afternoon. He suspects everyone of deception and trusts no one, not even the council members. Tomorrow or, at the latest, the day after tomorrow, the completed forms will be sent back as the praetor commanded.

The form contains only three columns: name, profession, age. It does not ask about one's country of origin, or even about one's family. A somewhat strange sign, which troubles anyone whose mind is preoccupied with family concerns. Perhaps the authorities have devised a diabolical plan to tear families apart and to expedite the annihilation of the women, the children, and the weak? The camp is in a frenzy like a herd being attacked by a predator. The streets around the council [community] building teem with incensed and stunned people, buzzing like a beehive as people argue and wrangle vehemently, while others make prophecies and utter simplistic explanations, and yet no one knows whether to answer clearly, "yes" or "no."

Young men and women unencumbered by family run to the council to register and swear that they practice one or another of the required professions, although in truth their proficiency in these professions is like that of a goat at *slihes*.[81] No papers are demanded from anyone, and everyone is trusted in good faith. Who in Transnistria has papers? When crossing the Dniester, they confiscated everyone's papers and erased their names.[82] Thus a new life began, without a name, without a past, without memories, like a cat or a rat …

---

80 The registration was intended for forced labor in German camps beyond the Bug. Only a few of the forced laborers returned from there.

81 The liturgical poems recited as prayers of repentance and forgiveness on Jewish fast days and on the days preceding the High Holidays.

82 At the crossing points of the Dniester into Transnistria—the Atachi–Moghilev crossing and the Mărculești–Yampol crossing—the Jews were robbed of the valuables that they

[May 8, 1942] 11 A.M.

Of my seven lores, which I considered registering, only that of book printing is appropriate. They are not seeking any sophisticated workers nor compassionate nurses. In contrast, Rachel, the chemist, can register. In short, just because you can, does that mean you should? Will registering bring on a worse misfortune and endanger my wife and children? The opposing argument contends: you fool, if a tiny crack opens that allows you to escape from a dark prison, stop asking questions, there is no time to waste. Will you strike your breast in remorse when it is too late …

Oy, what should we do? My mind is about to explode, and there is no answer.

By the way, my professional skills in book printing are really not much. I once learned the trade for about a year in 1922, while preparing to immigrate to *Eretz Yisroel.* Yosef Kasvan, a friend of our family and a learned man—the son of Rabbi Avner, a scribe from Rimnik—took me into his printing shop, "taught me the entire Torah on one foot,"[83] and gave me a signed certificate that stated that I was an expert printer. I did not end up going to *Eretz Yisroel* at that time. I engaged in other crafts, which also involved paper and printer's ink but, ever since that distant time, my fingers have not approached leaden letters. If, God forbid, I would be put near a printing machine, it would end badly.

[May 8, 1942] 6 P.M.

Rachel was fervently in favor of registering at first, but today someone put a bug in her ear and she began to waver. That someone is her old father, to whom she is attached with a fanatic love. So she is afraid

---

had brought with them, such as money, gold jewelry, graduation certificates, etc. See Gil Kremer testimony, YVA, O.3/VT/9561. In his testimony, he relates that all the certificates pertaining to his father's medical studies were confiscated at the Atachi–Moghilev border crossing.

83 Kunstadt refers to an account in the Talmud of a potential convert who conditioned converting to Judaism on being able to be taught the entire Torah while standing on one foot to describe the brief instruction in book printing that he received; B. Shabbat 31a.

that they will tear her away from her father, who is weak and helpless, and cannot do without her. I discussed this with her at length, and she promised halfheartedly that tomorrow at dawn she would register. Time will tell who is right.

I myself had a difficult afternoon, racked by the question of "yes" or "no," which is really driving me crazy. In the meantime, only very few people who are married and have children have registered, due to the same fear, and I am a bundle of nerves. Roza proposes that I also register her—as a seamstress. My naive wife claims that if they send both of us somewhere, the authorities will agree in the name of justice not to tear the children away from their parents. In response, I tell her that today it is foolish to even use the word "justice"—a term which in good times had the value of an empty egg. Roza is also beginning to lose faith in justice, and neither of us knows what to do.

Only about seven months ago, I faced a similar dilemma upon arriving in Moghilev from the other side of the Dniester, on that "happy" *Shabbes* evening. Tossing and turning in the darkness in the ruined university building, I had to decide whether to go somewhere else, to some remote corner on a bumpy truck, or to hide in Moghilev, which, after all, is not a godforsaken hole beyond the mountains of darkness, and it is more or less centrally located. Trucks were constantly leaving for far-flung places, and there were rumors that whoever would not uproot himself in the course of a few days would be driven out on foot in convoys—in simple language, on death marches.[84] Well, I moved heaven and earth and, with the help of the engineer Jagendorf, I was able to be among the "fortunate ones" who traveled to Dzhurin on seven trucks on October 29, 1941, thanks to my ancestral privilege. Since I did not possess 36,000 lei, the price of the transport, Engineer Jagendorf ruled that I should only pay 10,000 lei—all the cash from Romania that I had managed to save. As was the custom

84 As was noted, the Romanian authorities did not intend to allow the Jews to remain in Moghilev. Every day the gendarmes violently expelled groups of Jews from the places of concentration in which they were being kept to lead them on marches to other locations in Transnistria. During these marches, the gendarmes accompanying the convoys treated the tired and exhausted deportees brutally, robbing them of any remaining property and shooting those who found it difficult to walk and lagged behind the convoy. See Carp, *Cartea neagră*, vol. 3, p. 141.

then, he imposed the payment of the remaining 26,000 lei on my fellow wealthy travelers, who had no choice but to agree.[85]

My haste at the time was perhaps an error. In Moghilev, I would certainly have come up with something and would not be suspended between heaven and earth as in godforsaken Dzhurin. Rather than eat my heart out because of my irreversible mistakes, I came up with a scheme: I became a fatalist and convinced myself that if something is ordained for someone, there is no use in fleeing. This belief has nothing to do with faith—it is a cure for the dangerous disease called weakness …

May 9, 1942, 7 A.M.

I did not close my eyes all night, and feverishly tossed and turned around the fateful words: "yes" or "no." In a few hours' time, the colony chief will sign the lists and send them immediately to Shargorod. My fate and that of my family may depend on those few hours. I say "may" because it is highly plausible that the registration is intended only to draw up a list of craftsmen in Transnistria just in case they will need them. (**Comment added in 1945**: And indeed this was the case. Those registered were not sent home but instead were gradually dispatched to hard labor in German camps on the other side of the Bug. Only a few returned from there.)

I did not allow my sister Rivka to register as a seamstress, because it would be a tragedy to tear her away from our elderly and frail mother.

May 10, 1942, Before Noon

Neither I nor anyone in my family registered and the matter is settled. The lists are already in Shargorod.

---

85 Some groups of deportees, in particular from Southern Bukovina, organized themselves around leaders from their hometowns. They hired trucks from the German and Romanian authorities, or wagons from local Ukrainians, and in this way managed to arrive in the towns in the region and inhabit them. This happened, for example, in Shargorod, Murafa, etc. The prefecture determined the "official" price of each truck: 125,000 lei. See Ancel, *Toledot Hashoah*: *Romania,* vol. 2, p. 803.

[May 10, 1942] 5 P.M.

Today, Sunday, it is the weekly market day in Dzhurin. Following an order from the governor of Transnistria, General [Gheorghe] Alexianu,[86] the peasants in the area must not stop tilling the land on weekdays so as not to harm the harvest that the state steals from them.[87] Only on Sundays are they allowed to bring their share of produce to the camps for trade. Sunday is the established market day in all the local regions. Every wanderer in the camp waits for Sunday like the coming of the messiah to furnish himself with food for the entire week. Slipping out of the camp to a village to buy something clearly means putting your life at risk.

Today an abundance of all the best [produce] is heaped up at the market, which the rich and full earth of Ukraine indeed has to offer. What emerges from it is that the ox costs a pittance but the pocket is empty! The cost of living is terribly high relative to the means of the paupers, as most of us can call ourselves. The prices continue to climb from Sunday to Sunday. Flour, the most important product, today stands at 30 rubles per pood,[88] three times more expensive than it was the previous month. Potatoes jumped to 8 marks per pood (both rubles and

---

86 Prof. Gheorghe Alexianu was appointed by the Romanian authorities as governor of Transnistria. Alexianu was a lawyer, a professor in the Faculty of Law at the University in Cernăuţi, an expert on administrative matters, and he was close to Mihai Antonescu. He was governor of Transnistria from August 19, 1941, to January 26, 1944. In 1946, he was tried in Bucharest for war crimes, convicted, and executed by a firing squad on June 1, 1946. See Alexander Dallin, *Odessa 1941–1944: A Case Study of Soviet Territory Under Foreign Rule* (Iaşi: Center for Romanian Studies, 1998), p. 76.

87 The Romanian government regarded Transnistria as a resource to be economically exploited for the benefit of the state treasury and as compensation for the population of Romania for the hardships of the war and the sacrifices it had made for Nazi Germany. The intention to exploit Transnistria economically is evident in the Tighina agreement, which was signed between Germany and Romania on August 30, 1941, and determined the division of authority and administration of the territory by the Romanians and the rights of the Germans therein. The agreement was also called the "Treaty Regarding the Security, Administration and Economic Exploitation of the Territory between the Dniester and the Bug (Transnistria) and between the Bug and the Dnieper (the Bug–Dnieper territory)." See Avigdor Shachan, *Bakefor Halohet: Begeta'ot Transnitriya* (Hebrew) (Tel Aviv: Ghetto Fighters' House and Hame'uhad, 1998), p. 135; Ancel, *Toledot Hashoah: Romania*, vol. 2, pp. 764–765.

88 A Russian unit of weight equal to about 36.11 pounds.

marks[89] are kosher currencies),[90] as opposed to 3 marks in March. Apart from eggs, whose high price is constant, food has become comparable to gold.

Hundreds of emaciated, starving creatures walk around the market, wearing tattered clothes and sometimes shirtless, looking with envy at the mountains of food and swallowing only their saliva. It is true that a few wealthy women and young people lug baskets filled with all the best—poods of butter, eggs, chickens, lard, honey, fruit, and whatever the heart desires—but they are only a small minority. Most of the deportees must be content with envying the rich, cursing the fathers of the wealthy, and swallowing their saliva.

I too walked around the market for a while, looking for bargains. I eventually managed to buy a half pood of potatoes, a dozen eggs, and a few handfuls of garlic. This must suffice for four people for an entire week. Not bad—dozens of greedy eyes watched even this purchase with envy …

Another brief addition: When I used the word "wealthy" above, I exaggerated a bit with regard to the meaning of this word in the old country. There are no millionaires who live in respectable villas and drive their own limousines among the deportees. However, in other camps in Transnistria (only in the Moghilev region), there are former rich people who risked their lives to smuggle great fortunes in cash—leis and even dollars—across the Dniester. Smugglers, who were in fact from among the upper crust,[91] "worked" in Atachi, near the Dniester, smuggling money, gold, and valuable objects across the river for the negligible fee: half for you and half for me. Whoever successfully took this risk lives in the camp like God in Odessa[92] and even indulges at night

---

89 The legal currency in Transnistria was the Reichskreditkassenschein (special German mark), RKKS.

90 One ruble was equal to approximately 6 lei.

91 A small group of deportees known as the nouveau riche served as agents who performed various functions, such as taking deportees on trucks or wagons to ghettos in the Moghilev district, or transferring funds from relatives in Romania to Transnistria—a service for which the agents charged a fee. The term "rich" should be understood in the context of the period and life in the ghettos and camps in Transnistria.

92 The Yiddish expression *vey god in Odes* denotes living a life of comfort and luxury. Hebrew writers who lived in Odessa toward the end of the nineteenth century adopted

in a game of poker, where one does not play for buttons … however, wealth does not provide any protection against typhus, or the bullets of the gendarmes.

May 12, 1942, 8 A.M.

I am facing a difficult problem that weighs heavily on my heart and I don't know what to do. There is a sharp conflict between duty and fairness, between justice and mercy. If I were my own boss and didn't have to worry about my meager loaf of bread, I would ask no questions and speak from my heart. However, how can I afford such luxuries in the hell of Dzhurin?

In short, the tale is short and not very pretty. One of the most important sources of community income comes from the taxes that the butchers pay on kosher meat. There are four Jewish butcher shops here—one belongs to a local butcher, and the owners of the others are butchers and former cattle merchants who were deported from Bukovina—really fine characters, pure as silk … These people are constantly trying to steal the taxes from the community wherever they can, even though they are loaded with money, since meat is the cheapest food, almost the price of wheat bread. Consequently, the community keeps a close eye on these people to make sure that they are not stealing.

The council tasked me with preventing any theft by the butchers and making sure that no *shoyhet*[93]—here there are more than a dozen, *ke'naynehore*[94]—slaughters an animal without a license, which must be signed by me. I must also weigh the slaughtered cattle immediately after it is slaughtered, because the tax is determined by weight. Since this job of mine is based on trust, I share it with a young man from

---

this phrase. Bialik, Ahad Ha'am, and many other Hebrew writers were active in Odessa, and many Hebrew-language journals were published there.

93 A person who is licensed to slaughter animals and poultry in accordance with Jewish laws.

94 This expression (*bli ayin hara* in Hebrew) is said to ward off the evil eye.

my hometown, Iankel Katz,[95] a brother of Moshe Katz, the second-in-command in the camp [that is, the deputy of Dr. Max Rosenstrauch,] who has more authority than the not too smart colony chief and is the real dictator.

My partner is fervent by nature, just the opposite of me who is "barely a Jew,"[96] and there are often sharp disputes with the butchers because of small transgressions that could be resolved without making a fuss so that the community would not suffer any damages. However, Iankel Katz claims that he is a man of unmerciful truth and of pure integrity, and I must bite my tongue. Otherwise, I will arouse the suspicion of my bosses for no reason, and it will end badly for me. I must remain silent when my partner claims that I show too much mercy and do not brandish the slaughterer's knife. Perhaps I am not suited to this work, which demands a heart of stone.

Something happened today at dawn, while I was lying on the hard, wooden bunk. A butcher arrived in a panic at my hut and shouted that in a certain butcher shop, that of a competitor, of course, they are selling stolen meat from a beast that was slaughtered without a slaughter permission slip from the community. How can this be permitted![97] By the way, such denunciations are part of the order of the day here, and not necessarily intended to protect the community funds …

Well, I throw on my clothes and run to Iankel Katz, and we hurry on our way to catch the thief together. In the denounced butcher shop, we find the object in question—a medium size beast, already cut into strips to eliminate any signs. At first, the butcher tried to lie but he eventually confessed. However, he refused to provide the name of the

---

95 Yaakov Katz, a native of Rădăuți, brother of Moshe Katz, deputy of Max Rosenstrauch, the head of the ghetto, was a well-known merchant in the city of Rădăuți. He was deported together with his wife, daughter, mother-in-law, and other family members from Rădăuți to the Dzhurin ghetto.

96 The non-Jews considered the Jews devious and cunning.

97 A cartel controlled the sale of meat in Dzhurin. This prevented the emergence of a black market and excessively high prices, while also ensuring that all meat sold was slaughtered according to halacha (Jewish law). Anyone caught selling non-kosher meat was threatened with punishment—imprisonment or the withdrawal of the license to sell meat.

corrupt *shoyhet*, whether out of pity or in order not to lose such a useful business partner …

We suspected A. G., a young *shoyhet*, from Vijniţa, who had already committed such an act and had received a fine. We went directly to the hovel where he lives with his large family cramped together in a dark cubbyhole. He was still lying on a wooden bunk, sleeping. When we arrived, his wife told us that her poor husband was tired, because he had had to get up early, when it was still dark, to go slaughter for a butcher … so everything is clear. Nevertheless, we woke up the sleeping *shoyhet*, who confessed. Indeed, that is certainly good—we could only wish our enemies such a [bad] year!

Now we, the two trustees, must take the trouble to go to the council and disclose everything. However, telling the truth means depriving the *shoyhet*, a father of three infants, a meager piece of bread. For such a crime, which he has just committed for the second time, they will take away his slaughtering knife without mercy. This means that the livelihood of an afflicted, homeless person and his family is in my hands, even though he has transgressed and deserves a fine. At the same time, if I remain silent, my family and I face the same danger. It is no longer a secret and will certainly reach the ears of the community members and, besides, I have a partner, who demands the absolute truth.

Eventually, calmly and with gentle words, I convinced Iankel Katz that we should first go to the home of his brother, the second-in-command, to discuss the entire incident, just the three of us, and at the same time dare to request mercy for the offender. Indeed, we immediately went there and treaded carefully before the second-in-command. However, he only made claims against us and asked why we were advocating on behalf of thieves against the common interests and contrary to our duty. He stood his ground and immediately summoned the council members to judge the transgressor. The trial took place straightaway and, unfortunately, I had to be the "crown witness." Did I have a choice?[98]

---

98 A court was established in the Dzhurin ghetto, which included some members of the council. It was headed by Rabbi Baruch Hager form Siret. The tribunal dealt mainly with financial matters and other minor offenses. The lawyer Dov Bernard (Bigo) Hart from Rădăuţi was the secretary of the court. Punishments took the form of fines and even imprisonment in the "cellar." The Jewish police was responsible for enforcing

[May 12, 1942] 1 P.M.

The trial is already over and everything went well, and not as I feared. The six "lords"[99] gathered together and sent for the *shoyhet*. At first, he tried to lie vehemently but quickly broke down in tears and begged for mercy. The council member Mentziu Rol, a fellow townsman of the *shoyhet*, innocently proposed inviting the rabbi of Siret, Rabbi Baruch Hager, a son of the *tzaddik*[100] of Vijniţa Rabbi Israel Hager, of blessed memory,[101] to the meeting because it could be a matter of Jewish law. The rabbi of Siret, a very interesting personality about whom I will speak at length another time, is a renown Torah genius with a sharp mind and an experienced diplomat and, therefore, no one opposed Rol's proposal. The rabbi promptly entered the community building and was seated at the head of the table. The rabbi was able to get the whole truth out of the accused *shoyhet* who had once been his student, reprimanding and scolding him as is fitting but not allowing the council to take the slaughterer's knife away from him. It turned out that the *shoyhet* did this work with the consent of the local rabbi, Rabbi Herşel Karalnic,[102] who

---

punishments. See Margalit-Postilnik, *Radauts*: *Kehila Yehudit Betzemihata Uvisheki'ata*, p. 171.

99 Kunstadt ironically used the Yiddish term "*pnei*" (face of), from "and he graced the face of the city"—to refer to the dignitaries, the ruling elite, and the members of the council, which is translated in his diary as "lords"; Bereshit Raba 79:6.

100 Righteous person.

101 Alongside the official leadership in Dzhurin, a secondary, rabbinical leadership was also active that exerted substantial influence on the Jewish public.

102 Rabbi Herşel Karalnic, the local rabbi, was a prominent figure in the secondary leadership of Dzhurin. The general Jewish population in the ghetto regarded Rabbi Karalnic as a respected leader and adjudicator of religious law, even before the arrival in Dzhurin of the deportees from Romania. The Soviets also respected him. Jews and Ukrainians alike would come to him for judgement and always accepted his rulings. Rabbi Karalnic did his utmost to help the deportees, and at his order they were welcomed into the homes of the local Jews, the synagogue, and the Bet Hamidrash. In the harsh winter of 1941–1942, when thousands of Jews froze to death on the roads of Transnistria, almost no Jews froze to death in Dzhurin. Rabbi Karalnic ordered that the houses be heated using the wooden furnishings of the synagogue, including the holy ark. With the donations that he succeeded in collecting (it is not known from where), he fed around thirty people daily. He even distributed his own clothes to the poor, while he and his wife made do with as little as they possibly could. With the power of his personality and charisma,

considers himself the *Mara D'atra*,[103] the only rabbi in town, even though there are six deported rabbis in the camp.

The dramatic trial concluded with the rabbi of Siret alone being charged with giving a ruling. "The doctor is a Jew" and certainly the rabbi of Siret will not take away a morsel of bread from the mouth of a Jewish patient, and it is quite possible that he will not even punish him.

Here is a mini-drama from Transnistria that had a "happy ending." I can say that today is my first happy day in Dzhurin, as if I myself had been saved from an evil misfortune. I saw on my partner's face that even he, the stubborn knight of truth and justice, derived some pleasure …

May 18, [1942] 1 P.M.

The summer has finally burst forth and disproved my harsh prophecy that dark Dzhurin means an eternal winter. As of about a week ago, the muddy and sad shtetl has really changed. There is no longer any sign of mud, and it is warm and full of light outside. The scent of blossoms and spring fills the streets and alleys (apart from the early morning hours, when other smells abound …), and we almost forget our dour fate for a while. Everyone has thrown off their winter rags. One encounters new faces in the streets that one does not recognize at first glance, because people are no longer wearing the same clothes that we are accustomed to seeing on them. People wrapped in sacks have disappeared from the landscape, not, God forbid, because people have suddenly become prosperous but rather because the summer allows them to walk around free as a bird with their upper bodies bare and without freezing.

---

he succeeded in preventing disasters among the Jews of Dzhurin more than once. For example, on July 17, 1942, when it became evident to the community council that the German authorities intended to expel the local Jews in order to reduce the number of Jews in the ghetto, Rabbi Herşel Karalnic began collecting funds to cancel the decree. See Margalit-Postilnik, *Radauts*: *Kehila Yehudit Betzemihata Uvisheki'ata*, pp. 171–172; Ancel, *Toledot Hashoah*: *Romania*, vol. 2, pp. 1147–1148.

103 *Mara D'atra*, which means local rabbinic authority in Aramaic, is the title of the local rabbi.

When we arrived in Dzhurin at the end of October 1941, it seemed to everyone that no one would be able to endure more than a month or two of such hardship. How would we manage to get a loaf of bread or a potato, a bundle of wood, or a flask of oil? How would we not freeze in the endless winter night, lying on the bare ground, covered with rags, or with ... nothing, in crumbling ruins with small windows covered with cardboard, and often without a stove? And yet, we have persevered and have lived to see the spring in Dzhurin. The terrible Ukrainian winter with its storms, blizzards, and intense cold has come to an end. Indeed, many victims fell in the Dzhurin camp from cold, hunger, epidemics, and exhaustion—but most of the deportees continue to breathe just barely, to suffer, and even, at times, to hope for deliverance.

This "happy" Dzhurin! Nevertheless, the comforting expression "just not worse" presses impatiently on the pen. In the regions of the Balta district, the Bershad district, and in Moghilev itself, the last winter claimed more than 100,000 Jews who were driven from their homes. They did not live to see the spring, as they indeed had feared.

Then we look in amazement at the miracles of nature and do not believe our own eyes. It turns out that even in Dzhurin, you can see green, sweet-smelling grasses and colorful blossoms on the trees. In the distance, across the river, outside the camp, we see peasants ploughing the fields, birds sing songs exactly as they once did in the old country, and non-Jewish men and women walk along the stream and sing sad, Ukrainian tunes—overall, it is spring in the countryside in all its glory. A spark of hope steals into our tormented souls, and we wait for the great miracle that will deliver us from exile in this place.

May 20, 1942, 6 A.M.

Sorrow and deprivation do not necessarily refine the character and suddenly make the victim nobler, better. As a matter of fact, it has been my lot to discover that as a person becomes increasingly immersed in suffering, he completely loses his virtues and his values of justice and mercy, and freely commits minor transgressions that previously would have shamed him. Obviously, this rule does not apply to everyone, but the virtuous individuals do not constitute the majority.

This sad fact is clearly evident in the Transnistrian exile, where honest, decent people who earned kosher livelihoods in the old country have become pinchers and pickpockets. Those who were functionaries and prominent figures until the deportation confiscated property from the unfortunate deportees already when they were being tossed about into the cattle cars to the Dniester. The transport had barely left the station on that black *Simches Toyre*, 5702 (October 14, 1941), when a gang of "lords" began operating feverishly, running like poisoned mice from cattle car to cattle car and imposing considerable taxes as a ransom on each family. They whispered in everyone's ears that they had to collect a few million lei immediately in order to then bribe the Romanian officials to try to ease the journey and to send them to "good places," to a real paradise.

The bewildered, dispossessed people, stupefied by the fearful blow and completely disoriented, grasping at straws, offered their benefactors their last lei, which they had risked their lives to save. The caretakers made empty promises, wrote down names on scraps of paper, defrauded people of their fortunes, and, in the end, showed them the middle finger.

Upon arriving in Atachi and after being driven out of the cattle cars, the unexpected functionaries immediately abandoned the thousands of people who were counting on them and vanished to the ends of the earth. They disappeared with all the loot, all together, somewhere far away from the ruined shtetl to a suburb on the top of a mountain, where apartments that had not been bombed and still stood intact were inhabited by Ukrainians, and haggled with the homeowners there. The price was no problem, since they did not lack cash. The mass of simple people, who had dreamed of ransoming themselves with their last lei while riding in the cattle cars, wandered among the crumbling ruins that lacked roofs, doors, and windows. The cold, autumn rain poured down pitilessly, no food was to be found, and the Romanian soldiers murdered and robbed [them] freely among those ruins. The people literally fell like flies, rotting on the wet soil on the banks of the Dniester.

At the same time, the gang of aristocrats, their purses bursting with the ransom money, hidden away in respectable, warm apartments and furnished with all the best, kept their distance from the masses to avoid the evil eye. They indeed initiated contact with the Romanian officers, but solely for their own benefit. Their only concern was to get their fortunes safely across the Dniester. The Romanian authorities prohibited transferring Romanian currency to the other side of the Dniester under threat of the death penalty.

A new *Aktia* was initiated by a different group of benefactors, some of whom had once belonged to the same elite. They promised to smuggle any amount across the Dniester for a small fee: half for me and half for you. These machers whispered in peoples' ears that they did this for the sake of the *mitzve*:[104] since their half will go completely into the pockets of the officers. Once again, they squeezed the last drop from the poor lemon and amassed a vast amount of Romanian money. After crossing the Dniester, some of the smugglers (there were also some honest people among them) showed their creditors the middle finger, claiming that the soldiers had stolen the fortune.[105] In the dour, chaotic world of Moghilev, there was nothing left to do but invite the criminals to the *Uneytane Toykef.*[106]

My family and I enjoyed the hell of Atachi for ten grim days—not exactly among the "aristocrats" but rather in the crumbling ruins. There we—my father-in-law and I—exchanged almost all of our few lei to rubles. When we arrived in the "blessed land," we had 10,000 lei and a handful of rubles, which lost their value completely within two weeks.

---

104 A commandment of Jewish law; a good deed.

105 The "benefactors" were entrepreneurs who understood how to exploit the situation and the distress of the deportees, were able to establish the necessary connections with members of the Romanian authorities, such as senior officials in the civil administration, and who also charged a fee for their services.

106 The piyut (religous poem) "*Unetane Tokef*" (we will ascribe holiness to this day) was composed by Rabbi Amnon of Magentza in the twelfth century and is said during the Musaf service, the additional morning service, on Rosh Hashana and on Yom Kippur. It describes the day of judgement during which God sits and decrees whether man will be punished or God will have mercy on him, whether he will be written in the book of life or death, and people's fear of this judgement. The oppressed in Moghilev had no choice but to leave the judgement in the hands of Heaven.

I was left stripped and totally destitute, without a leu and without any baggage just as I was on the day of my birth. Anyone who still has lei is a lucky man, because that currency retains its value.

[May 20, 1942] 2 P.M.

A hot summer day. I sit with my sleeves rolled up by the open window and breathe the air. In another hour, I must go to work, to scribble with my pen at the community building. It is so pleasant outside and so murky in my soul!

[May 20, 1942] 6 P.M.

A theft was discovered at the community soup kitchen, causing a sensation. This soup kitchen was set up in the month of December 1941, a few weeks after the arrival of the first transports of deported Jews in Dzhurin. The activists were faced with immeasurable difficulties. They strove to save hundreds of persons from death by starvation yet they constantly confronted greater obstacles. How can half a space be found for a kitchen in this ruined site where there is no room to toss a needle? Where can the necessary dishes and utensils be acquired, where can the food or wood be obtained? And above all, where can we come up with the cash to support such an important institution? Let us mention here a few activists in the council and those close to them who, to their credit, demonstrated true love of Israel, stubborn perseverance, and fervor until their hard work made it possible to manage to set up the soup kitchen, *in a mazeldike sho.*[107]

The leading activists were Rabbi Baruch Hager of Siret, Rabbi Herşel Karalnic of Dzhurin, Moshe Katz, Iehoşua Ungariş, Mentziu Rol, Bubi

107 *In a mazeldike sho*, which literally means "at a fortuitous hour, " like *in a guter sho*, is said upon hearing welcome news and expressing best wishes for success. Kunstadt sometimes uses this expression ironically.

Met,[108] David Buksbaum, and may those whom I omitted in error forgive me. Bubi Met from Gura Humorului altruistically runs the kitchen, and not for the sake of receiving a reward.

I am far from being a fervent follower of the "lords," and although they provide the slice of bread that I eat, I have undertaken to guard against flattery in these pages and to state the whole truth, which is usually bitter. I have kept my word until now and not flattered anyone. However, this should not prevent me from also speaking a sweet truth: the establishment of the soup kitchen under these terrible conditions is an immense accomplishment for the community leaders—the *mitzve* of saving lives daily is weighed against a mountain of transgressions and despicable deeds on a fearful balance of scales.

Until *Isre Hag Peysech*,[109] the soup kitchen distributed around 850 portions of food—half a liter of thick soup made from beans, groats, millet, and so on, for lunch, once a day. It certainly was not enough to satisfy the people's hunger, but it was enough to sustain the soul and to prevent people from dying of starvation. For a too large number of "customers" of the soup kitchen, this poor bowl of soup was their only meal in the course of an entire day. From the outset, the soup kitchen stood on shaky ground, and the council often arrived at the heart-wrenching decision to close the business. However, small miracles always occurred and meager funds were obtained from one day to the next, until they ran out. On *Isre Hag Peysech*, the doors of the soup kitchen were shut, because not enough food remained for even one meal. This surely would not have happened so soon, if the lords would have pushed more speculators and wealthy merchants against the wall and required them to pay taxes on their high gains. Similarly, the community's funds would not have dwindled so quickly had they spent less money on parties in honor of the Romanian overlords, but that is already another very grievous story.

---

108 Iehoşua Ungariş and Mentziu Rol, deportees from Rădăuţi, and Bubi Met, a deportee from Gura Humoruloi, established a soup kitchen that provided the needy with a bowl of soup every day.

109 A semi-holiday the day after the weeklong holiday.

That *Isre Hag*, when the emaciated skeletons with tin bowls in their shaking hands turned away hungry from the locked doors of the soup kitchen and backtracked, it was like *Tisha B'Av*[110] in the camp. A commotion erupted around the community building—wails and curses in every corner. Even the militia could not quiet the voices that reached the heart of the heavens. The "lords" realized that the kitchen could absolutely not remain shut, and badgered the wealthy men with force. This action was successful and, after a brief break, they once again lit a fire under both pots in the kitchen on May 15 [1942]. In order to minimize the costs, the community meticulously selected the recipients through a sieving process and accepted only 450 persons, the poorest of the poor—mainly the elderly, the weak, and children. The remaining 400 may in the meantime hang … padlocks on their own mouths!

May 21, 1942, 6 A.M.

Say what you will, I believe that there are periods of good fortune and periods of misfortune in a person's life in what they call "the rule of series." Roza laughs at me and firmly maintains that such "luck" does not exist outside the unhinged fantasies of people who have no hope, enthusiasm, or energy. I disagree, of course, demonstrating the opposite with signs and wonders, bringing real proof from my own biography, which is no secret to Roza. She has a ready excuse: coincidence.

I admit that I find no reasonable explanation for my fatalistic worldview, other than from Shakespeare's classic statement in Hamlet: "There are more things in heaven and earth…than are dreamt of in your philosophy."[111] Am I myself not that kind of passive person who waits for the fortuitous moment for deliverance to fall into his lap?

My life has always been divided, fluctuating between faith and indifference to religion, between periods of piety, according to Jewish

110 The 9th of Av is a day of fasting in commemoration of the destruction of the Temples and other catastrophes that befell the Jewish people throughout history on that day.

111 William Shakespeare, *Hamlet*, act I, sc. 5, ll. 919–920; see *Open Source Shakespeare*, https://www.opensourceshakespeare.org/views/plays/play_view.php?WorkID=hamlet&Scope=entire&pleasewait=1&msg=pl (accessed August 13, 2020).

law and faith, and periods of heretical behavior and an atheistic lifestyle. In the depths of my being, I have remained a believer in mysticism, even when I threw off my *tzitzis*[112] and allowed myself to indulge in all kinds of minor transgressions ... I strongly doubt that there is a lord of the manor high above the clouds, and in today's situation, I certainly do not swear by it in my *talis* and *tefilln*.[113] If He truly rules in the high heavens, if God is manifest in the world, then how can there be a God who is not merciful and compassionate, as is clearly written in small print? Nevertheless, it seems to me that the life of every individual is subject to the influence of supernatural powers that wield absolute control, acting at will and determining man's fate.

In the present period of my dark struggle, which began on the day of my deportation, I remain very far from religion. The brutal torrent of catastrophe and destruction has stunned my faith in God and in God's justice. I would only make a mockery of myself if I would don a *talis* and *tefilln* and praise God who has allowed—if He ever concerns himself with this matter—evil, two-legged beasts, who bear the "image of God," to turn His "Chosen People" into ash and dust, drowning them in blood and tears.

Most of the victims who have fallen were the Creator's pious and observant servants, who never hurt a fly or committed any transgression. In their great distress, they poured forth their hearts in fervent prayer, crying and wailing, waking the dead, and humbling themselves lower than dust in submission as servants before the "Beneficent Lord and Creator."

Rabbis, holy vessels, and simply zealous, faithful Jews, at first tried to offer justifications, as it were, muttering something about transgressions and iniquities that unleashed the wrath upon them, guilty and righteous alike. Little by little, these advocates realized that justifying the world's injustices will help like leeches on a dead man, and they began to waver. Some of them even began to go astray when the slaughterer's knife hung over their necks—they shaved their beards and side curls, ate non-kosher food in public in defiance, and

112 Tzitzit are fringes or tassles on the talit, a shawl with fringed corners worn by Jewish men during morning prayer; tzitzit also refers to a small talit.

113 Tefillin are phylacteries worn by Orthodox Jewish men during weekday morning prayers.

cried out, "there is neither law nor judge." We are aware of such cases. I will mention one single instance.

The rabbinical judge from Rădăuţi, Rabbi Azriel Kave, a Jew, a genius and a great sage, a *hazen*, and a master of the seven wisdoms, proficient in matters concerning God and man, was deported to the accursed camp of Kopaygorod in the district of Moghilev, where both he and his wife died at a young age from hunger, cold, and privation. The day before his death, he requested that a *minyen*[114] of Jews be sent to him so that he could recite the *Videh*. The Jews gathered and then he broke into the confessional prayer. However, he did not strike his chest over his heart in repentance, but rather enumerated the sins of the One in whom he had fervently believed all the days of his life. At the end, he exclaimed "Go call upon the Eternal, but upon Whom [are we calling]!" These were his final words.

For what have I poured out all this, namely, this philosophical introduction? To resist deluding myself that there has been a change for the better in my unfortunate situation after all. This week began with a triumph, so to speak—for the first time since the deportation, I earned more than 20 marks for some intellectual labor (a translation into Russian). The council paid me my first wages and, for the first time since the day that I began serving my employers in Dzhurin, they did not badger me for an entire week. In short, I interpret these signs as a good omen that signals the beginning of a new dawn …

And perhaps the reason for my optimism today is due to the atmosphere of *Shvu'es*[115] outdoors that sustains the living, whose oppressed spirits inhale a spark of renewed hope. In anticipation of imminent deliverance? Well, enough of speculations that lead to nothing! …

May 23, 1942

Yesterday, a true spring day radiated, as is indeed fitting for the first day of *Shvu'es* I went to bathe in the stream in the afternoon and was

114 Prayer quorum of ten male adults in Orthodox Jewry.

115 Shavuot is a holiday that commemorates the giving of the Torah at Mount Sinai.

happy to immediately wade in the water, take a swim, and lie in the sun as I did in the old country, after about two years. Last summer, even though I had not yet been uprooted from my own four cubits, the knife was already hanging over our necks and no one gave any thought to such nonsense as bathing in the Suceava, next to my hometown of Rădăuţi.

However, I did not take the overlords into account yesterday. I had only just taken off my clothes when Ukrainian militiamen from the factory quarter, where no Jews live, came running and drove off the crowd—a few dozen young people—who trampled the grass of the [...],[116] may the names of the wicked be blotted out—and our brothers, the children of Israel, fled like poisoned mice back to the stifling, stinking ruins where it's impossible to breathe.

Today it is cloudy and raining. There is mud in the alleys of Dzhurin again, but without its autumnal grace. Before noon, men and women went to participate in the *Yikzor*[117] —not so much to pray for the souls of their dead relatives, as much as to request favors from the dead and to pour out their tormented hearts in tears.

May 30, 1942, 2 P.M.

This diary has rightly earned the title Weekly Diary—a full week has passed since the last entry—a week filled with hot days, sweltering from the heat of the sun and from the Transnistrian hardships, one stranger than the next. I will try to give a brief account of what took place during this turbulent week, even though the recent events, the fear of death, and the joy of the Jews, so to speak, are no longer fresh in my mind and have faded a little.

I did not abandon these pages for an entire week due to laziness, God forbid, but because I was not able to find one free moment. From 5 A.M. until late at night, I was harnessed to the yoke of my work, taking a break of a few moments at 2 P.M. to swallow a spoonful of broth and then to

116 Illegible.

117 A special memorial service or prayer for the departed.

return to work. Coming home exhausted from work late at night, my taut nerves were at the point of bursting and my thoughts were disturbed by the calamities that I had heard about and witnessed all day long at the community building. I could not even imagine writing down what was on my mind. The turbulent waves subsided only today, and so I have picked up my pen.

The events began in the afternoon last *Shabbes*. The great overlord of Shargorod, Praetor Dindilegan, unexpectedly appeared in the camp. He is an evil worm, and people shake at the sight of him; killing a Jew is of less consequence to him than smoking a cigarette. (**Added in 1948**: a Romanian tribunal in Bucharest tried this oppressor as a war criminal after the war in 1947 and sentenced him to twenty-five years in prison for his good deeds in Transnistria). Since it was *Shabbes*, the community building was closed, so he sent a militiaman to summon the colony chief, Dr. Rosenstrauch, and informed him that he needed 400 men for labor to build a highway near Murafa and that the Dzhurin camp must provide these men. Therefore, he instructed the colony chief to dispatch a list of 400 men to him in Shargorod within a few days.[118]

Immediately upon learning about the decree—it took no more than a quarter of an hour—the camp was in an uproar. Every man was struck with fear that he would be the target of wrath and would be banished to the place of all the demons and spirits, who knows for how long, or if he would ever see his wife and children again. Let me explicitly note that this fear did not stem from the desire to be idle. Indeed, since the establishment of the camp, men are summoned every day to labor, to pave roads, and to do similar work, and it is certainly not very pleasant to toil under the supervision of the gendarmes from dawn until late in the evening without pay, at times on an empty stomach—whether it rains, a blizzard rages, or the frost burns and cracks. However, this labor does not cause anyone to panic. Yet, they still live in their homes, even if it is a cold, gloomy, stepmother of a home. So, no one asks any unnecessary

118 This refers to the road connecting Murafa and Yaroshenka, a village in the county of Shargorod. Jews from the ghettos of Murafa, Shargorod, and Dzhurin were forced to pave this road, which was intended to serve the forces of the German and Romanian armies.

questions and people stride to work with a shovel in hand, and a loaf of bread and a head of garlic in their bag.

Only a handful of the high-and-mighty, wealthy people can allow themselves to send a substitute who receives 2 or 3 marks for a day's work. There are enough volunteers to stand in for them, and it has become a kind of profession that saves several families from starvation. "Labor Minister" David Buksbaum,[119] a young man from Siret who rose to greatness because of his knowledge of the Ukrainian language, and because he is a smart, young man, registers all the candidates to work as substitutes and does the bookkeeping so that most of them will have an opportunity to earn a few marks paid by the rich two or three times a week. Obviously, whoever is in the good graces of this lord, makes a good profit.[120]

The council itself turns a blind eye and allows people to pay their way out [of forced labor] in this manner, because they do not want to quarrel with the wealthy from whom they collect a little money, or in order to assist some paupers so that they do not become a burden to the community.

However, this wisdom applies only to local work and not when it comes to dispatching people to who knows where for who knows how long. At first, the council was in sharp disagreement with the colony chief regarding who would go. The doctor (as he is called in the camp) insisted that all men between the ages of seventeen and fifty-five be registered so that there would be enough people. However, the council members argued that the obligation of forced labor in Romania only applied to men between the ages of eighteen and fifty and, after all, we were Romanian Jews in the past, albeit without a name and without any rights. Eventually

---

119 Buksbaum, a member of the council, was responsible for the consolidation of lists for forced labor.

120 It was a common practice in all the ghettos in Transnistria and in other areas of Nazi-occupied Eastern Europe for the people of means to release themselves from forced labor by paying a substitute to perform forced labor in their place. Regarding this phenomenon in the Shargorod ghetto, for example, see Meir Teich, "Haminhal Hayehudi Ha'otonomi Begeto Sa'argorod (Transnistriya)" (Hebrew), *Yad Vashem Studies*, 2 (1957/1958), pp. 203–235.

the doctor allowed himself to be persuaded. The "lords" explained to him that if this would not suffice, they would still have that option later.

On Sunday at dawn, the colony chief convened a committee of three doctors so that they could conduct a recruitment operation to sort the population, registering only healthy men without any real health issues. A series of detailed registrations began. Most of the men tried to dodge the draft and told the doctors that they suffered from all kinds of illnesses, which could not be detected without X-ray equipment and other complex machinery. The doctors of Dzhurin gave their expert opinion only with the aid of their stethoscope and a thermometer! So much for trusting anyone's word or oath!

A minority of the people were indeed broken, shattered, and exhausted, with heart disease, perforated lungs, frozen feet, blows to their entire body, without a drop of blood in their faces, and as yellow as a corpse—the result of the death marches and eight months of hunger, cold, filth, neglect, and fear. The colony chief sternly warned the doctors to be tough and show no compassion, to not let anyone fool them. Indeed, the committee of doctors did not make much use of the redeeming "unfit" tag, unless the person standing before them had a total and permanent disability ... or was a person with impressive ancestral privilege. The majority derived no benefit from the doctor being a Jew, and the president of the committee did not tire of repeating, "Give thanks to His Beloved Name that you are healthy!" Only about thirty sick men from among the "common" people were entitled to the mild diagnosis of "fit for work only here."

The committee completed its work, *in a guter sho*, on Monday afternoon and sat down to draw up the list. It included a total of 260 men. On Tuesday at dawn, a special messenger took the fateful list to the praetor and it seemed that we had completed the task.

There was a great commotion at the community building. Those who were registered moved heaven and earth to have their names erased up to the last moment. They cried, screamed, and threatened to denounce those who had safely escaped for one reason or another one. Advocates ran around, whispering in ears to put in a good word wherever necessary. The clamor of voices rose to the heart of the heavens, the wives of the condemned—with infants in their arms and clinging to their aprons—

threw themselves to the ground and fainted, but nothing worked. The colony chief carried out his mission and sent the list.

On Tuesday evening, Praetor Dindilegan arrived unexpectedly at the council [community] building in a murderous rage like a forest robber, fit to tear apart the colony chief. What is the meaning of this—he bellowed like a pig at slaughter—after expressly ordering you to provide me with a list of 400 men, the Yids have had the gall to mock me and send half this number. No one dared to open his mouth and to endanger his life. The colony chief turned as white as snow, trembling. The council members moved to the side, even though they are not accountable to the Romanian authorities regarding matters of labor, and the colony chief alone is responsible.

The praetor threatened that if they would not provide him with 400 persons, blood would flow in the camp. They could believe that he meant what he said, because he indeed specializes in killing Jews. Only a few weeks before, he had ordered the shooting of six Jews who had dared to set foot outside the boundary of the Shargorod camp. A person from my hometown was among those "criminals," Mordechai Leib Rauchbach, a brawny Jew, once a wealthy cattle merchant. These Jews had not gone out, God forbid, simply to take a stroll but to get a few potatoes from the peasants in the vicinity.[121]

After the overlord had departed, slamming the door without a word, the doctor and Moshe Katz decided to hand over their resignations to him—a decision that was never implemented. On Wednesday, they enthusiastically began to redo the list, together with the committee of doctors. This time, no one stood up to the colony chief when he ordered them to register all males, ages seventeen to fifty-five. This time, those who had been rejected were registered as kosher [fit].

By 11 A.M., the revised list of 400 names was ready to be sent. A militiaman went to look for a special messenger, a Ukrainian who could ride well, to leave immediately for Shargorod with the list, riding as fast as his nag would carry him. At that very moment, messengers from the

121 Most of the ghettos were open, but according to Order No. 23, which was issued on November 11, 1941, by the governor of Transnistria, Alexianu, it was strictly forbidden to leave the areas of the camps and ghettos. Anyone caught outside the ghetto was liable to punishments, ranging from lashes to being shot to death.

local gendarmes appeared—two Jewish militiamen on duty at the militia post in the factory quarter who were tasked with all kinds of errands—and informed the council of the news: they had just received a telephone call from Shargorod, informing them that there was no need to send the list. When they would require workers, they would notify the colony chief. This news spread quickly through the camp, causing happiness and rejoicing among the registered and their families. Alas, such is the joy of the Jews in Dzhurin, may we be spared …

So that the joy would not be complete, another messenger arrived unexpectedly at the council [community] building an hour later and brought a new decree. The praetor ordered all the Jews above the age of fourteen to wear an emblem of shame on the right side of their clothing: a black ribbon with a yellow Star of David embroidered on it, or attached to it. However, this spit in the face did not make any impression, first of all, because we are carrying the weight of much greater concerns on our shoulders and on our minds than any rag and, second, because the Star of David does not cause a sensation among the deported Jews, or among the permanent residents of Dzhurin. Immediately following the outbreak of the war against Russia in June 1941, such a decree was issued in all the towns of Bukovina, although it was quickly canceled in Southern Bukovina and remained in place only in Northern Bukovina, which was only recently "liberated" by the Romanian and German fascist armies.

When we arrived in Dzhurin at the end of October 1941, we saw that all the local Jews were wearing a filthy rag on their arms, which bore blurry marks of a Star of David. We, the newly arrived guests, did not adorn ourselves with such a rag and, when they saw the newcomers from Bukovina, the residents of Dzhurin cast off this decoration, and no one cared.

Meanwhile, today is *Shabbes* and no one is sporting a Star of David, apart from the colony chief, Dr. Rosenstrauch, He is one of the most strictly kosher of the strictly kosher, and he wants with all his heart to fulfill even a minor, non-Jewish order that could please the Romanian overlords. Therefore, since yesterday, he has been wearing this decoration with pride, indeed a badge of honor: from a mile away, the venerable Star of David shines as glaringly yellow as possible on his wide sleeve. There is nothing to understand, he says. If the authorities order him to wear such a decoration, he will do so, since it is not his business to argue. For the time being, he has not yet confronted the heretics who have not rushed to fulfill this order, but he can be trusted not to remain silent.

A group of jokers claim that this is a difficult religious question and that it is worthwhile to ask the rabbis for a ruling: what [is the point of a] judgment, if someone doesn't have a jacket and not even a shirt on his body—hundreds of people wander around like that here ... should he fulfill the obligation by attaching the jewel to his naked body? ...

[May 30, 1942] Two Hours Later

It should come as no surprise that I can allow myself to write on these pages in the middle of a bright day. While I am indeed busy with the community from dawn until late at night, I steal a free moment for myself, when instructed to swallow my pride and go to the front room, because the lords have secrets to transmit. Now is also a favorable time of sorts to jot down on a scrap of paper what bothers me—briefly, of course, to avert the evil eye—and then at night I write everything down in my notebook.

So, allow me to "immortalize" a strange incident that occurred in the camp last Thursday, which was literally like an episode taken from Sholem Aleichem's "Thousand and One Nights."[122]

That morning, it was business as usual "for the Jews" at the community building. There were fights and scandals, and even a sharp dispute between the colony chief and Bubi Met, the head of the soup kitchen, which almost came to blows. They literally threw chairs and files at each other's heads (it is lucky no one was hit ...) until a few council members forcibly separated the two roosters. In short, the Jewish regime proceeded in a civilized manner.

In the middle of the noise and commotion, a Jewish militiaman burst in and stammered out the news that a great calamity had just occurred. The gendarmes had captured an old couple, a Jew and Jewess from the Shargorod camp (Yosef and Maya Volach), who had set out on foot to

122 Sholem Aleichem, "Mayses fun toyznt eyn nakht," in Sholem Aleichem, *Ale verk*, vol 5:1 (New York: Forverts 1944), pp. 137–232.

Dzhurin to seek help from a relative and had tried to sneak in without a permit from the gendarmes. This is a very dreadful incident because, according to Order No. 23, issued by General Alexianu, the governor of Transnistria, the punishment for leaving a camp without authorization is death.

The council immediately began to take every measure to save the elderly couple. They sent a telegraph to the commander of the gendarmerie in Shargorod, *SS-Obersturmführer* Garama,[123] begging for mercy and promising him that they themselves would go to him to thank him personally. This guy doesn't need a detailed explanation … In addition, other advocates set out for the local gendarmerie and they too made promises, not necessarily for the sake of the world to come. This was not done only to save the lives of the two Jews but also to prevent a dangerous precedent of spilling Jewish blood in public. To date, no Jewish blood has been spilled in Dzhurin, even though the Angel of Death has raged enough using other methods. If this execution is allowed, it will whet the murderers' appetite and is liable to lead to many additional catastrophes in the camp.

The colony chief himself set off to place a phone call to the commander of the gendarmerie in Shargorod. He returned immediately and, for the first time, I saw tears in his eyes when he arrived like a storm and announced the news, "They have been saved!" After recovering his composure a little, he related how the overlord had assured him that he would order taking the guilty parties to Shargorod, where they would be tried. I will never forget that scene. The community building was packed with people who were very agitated, waiting tensely for a miracle, and suddenly this news arrived. Tears flowed from everyone's eyes and no one managed to utter a word. I realized then that even in the doctor's heart of stone, there is a Jewish spark that was lit at a time of great distress, which, it must be said, is to his credit. At times, one single good deed outweighs a full load of transgressions.

---

123 The Romanian gendarmerie post in Shargorod controlled the district of Shargorod. It was headed by *Oberlieutenant* Garama. This gendarmerie post was under the command of the gendarmerie legion in Moghilev. Garama received monthly bribes from the Jews in order to protect them from the nationalist Ukrainians.

The couple was taken back to the Dzhurin gendarmerie post and from there they were to go on foot to Shargorod. The people's only concern was that disaster would befall them [the couple], God forbid, while being escorted back to Shargorod. However, it quickly became apparent that we were mistaken: the danger was not lurking along the way but rather in Dzhurin itself. We learned that the gendarmes had indeed taken the elderly couple from the gendarmerie, but they had not set out on the road to Shargorod. Instead, they went through back roads that led to the Ukrainian cemetery on a hill outside Dzhurin. This means that these two persons only had a few more minutes left to live. It turned out that all the efforts to intervene were in vain. Happiness turned into despair, and wailing was heard from every direction, more than at a funeral.

A Jewish woman, who is among the few families who are permitted to live in the factory quarter outside the camp,[124] came running to the community building after having walked past the Ukrainian cemetery. She breathlessly related what she had just seen with her own eyes: an old man and an old woman were standing in the cemetery beside a newly dug grave, and two militiamen with rifles in their hands were barking at them in Romanian: "Strip naked!" The Jewish woman was too frightened to see what would happen next and ran to the council.

Before the terrified old woman managed to get to the end of her story, the door burst open and a gendarme stormed in, shouting: "The council member Moshe Katz must come to the cemetery immediately, and I will escort him." This order exploded like a bomb and it appeared to everyone that the murderers would not to be satisfied with two victims but rather wanted to snare the most central figure in the camp, because Katz indeed administered all matters in the camp.[125] Moshe Katz turned white as snow, abruptly arose from the bench, took leave of the crowd without a word, and went with the gendarme to the cemetery.

---

124 People of means from Southern Bukovina were permitted to live in the houses of Ukrainians in this quarter.

125 Moshe Katz, Rosenstrauch's deputy, was in fact responsible for managing internal affairs in the Dzhurin ghetto, because the members of the Moghilev council respected him, especially Jagendorf, and therefore also the Romanian authorities; see CNSAS, P-50679, p. 27.

All came running to the square in front of the council [community] building, even frail, elderly people and mothers carrying infants in their arms. It is true that the council members, in general, and Moshe Katz, in particular, were not dear to their hearts, and what the people wish for them behind their backs I wish for the enemies of Israel but, at that moment, tears were streaming from everyone's eyes as though their child was being led to slaughter. The panic reached its peak a quarter of an hour later when four shots were heard in the area of the cemetery. It was clear that a terrible calamity had occurred, because two shots would have sufficed for the elderly couple. Everyone knows that the Romanian gendarmes are adept at hitting a Jewish target … No one dared to sneak out of the camp to see, because that would have meant walking into the arms of the Angel of Death.

The crowd stood stunned, glued to the spot and then, through the window, we suddenly saw Moshe Katz running, out of breath, from the little hill where the cemetery lies. He burst into the community building straightaway. He did not have to speak—in any case, he could barely catch his breath—because his eyes imparted the news of a miracle. As soon as he regained his composure, he related the details to the crowd, but only what he was allowed to say. When he arrived at the cemetery, the two elderly people were indeed standing naked by an open grave, but the gendarmes with the rifles had not shot them yet. They were waiting for Moshe Katz so that he could witness the execution and warn the people in the camp of what to expect if they would transgress one of the ten commandments specified in "Order" No. 23. Moshe Katz did not provide an account of his conversation with the gendarmes, but allow me to reveal a secret to you—the talks were very expensive [costing a sum] that could have helped to continue to operate the soup kitchen for a while …

Once again, the planned tragedy ended as a tragicomedy. The gendarmes indeed fired four shots, because the commander informed them that they had to shoot, but whether or not they hit the target was their business. So, the bullets actually went astray somewhere between the branches of the willows and did not carry out their mission. In the camp, each shot was indeed like a blow of a hammer to the skull, and our blood froze in our veins, but this was a false alarm. The gendarmes stipulated one condition: the couple had to disappear somewhere because, if not, it would backfire on all the Jews. (**Added later**: so, they indeed hid in an attic for a few weeks until the matter was forgotten, and then they were registered as inhabitants of the Dzhurin camp and allocated two portions of green bean soup at the soup kitchen once a day).

The two persons who once again were saved from death by a miracle became dear to everyone's hearts, like close relatives, even though no one knew them. The man, as I later observed, was slightly mentally unstable, and the Jewess was a thin, wizened old woman who did not open her mouth—two poor people who would certainly not have evoked a sigh in Dzhurin if they had died of typhus in the hospital. (**Added in 1943**: thus, it was. The couple indeed died of typhus in the hospital shortly thereafter, both in the same week. Only the members of the *Hevra Kadishe*[126] attended [their funerals]. Another strange detail: It became known that the gendarmes had planned to lead the old people to the cemetery as an extortion device. Had it not been for the bribe, the two elderly people would not have come out of there alive.)

In honor of the miracle, council member Mentziu Rol invited the council members and other functionaries for a toast at his expense. The drinking continued until late at night and was very merry. Impassioned speeches about Jewish unity and love of Israel were delivered and, since the "lords" were somewhat tipsy, they hugged and kissed, swearing that henceforth there would be peace and harmony in the community building, and that they would treat everyone with kid gloves. They even asked the doctor to forgive them for the indignities that they had inflicted upon him. Bubi Met, the director of the soup kitchen, begged them to impose a fine on him to be paid to the kitchen for having attacked the doctor prior to the incident with the two old people.

Mentziu Rol was the most cheerful among them, even though it cost him a good deal of money in Dzhurin terms. Everyone dispersed late in the evening in a lighthearted mood, as following a miracle. The next day, Friday, it became evident that Rol indeed had reason to enjoy a moment of happiness, even though he himself could not have even dreamed of the

126 Literally, the "sacred society," this is a burial society.

momentous reason at the time. A quote from the Gemara[127] is in order now: "Though they themselves see nothing, their guardian angel sees it."[128] The commander of the gendarmerie in Shargorod unexpectedly called the Dzhurin gendarmerie to decree that Mentziu Rol and his family return to Romania, to his old home in Dornei.[129] Relatives there had managed to obtain his deliverance, and not for the sake of the next world …[130] The overlord informed him that a truck would come soon from Moghilev to take the Rol family to Romania. This was the first case of a little mouse sneaking out of Kafkaesque Dzhurin.

A real hoo-ha began in the camp, a series of farewells, *mazel tov* conveyed with a jealous heart and a smiling face, letters entrusted for delivery to the old country, and requests that he move heaven and earth when he arrive there in order to save the remaining remnant in Transnistria before it would be too late. By the way, Mentziu Rol, who was tough but also kind, liked to return favors and to lend a helping hand, and the people loved him for this reason.

That Friday, Rol once again became the key figure in the camp and he did not turn anyone away but lavished promises and even hinted that he had access to the overlords there—in fact, they were calling him back home. A spark of light glimmered in the thick darkness of the camp. Who knows if it was just an illusion that would later turn out to be glistening mud! … (**Added in 1943**: as soon as Rol left the camp, he forgot Transnistria, like a nightmare. It is as though he fell into the water and there was silence …)

Rol came to my cubbyhole to bid me farewell since we got along well. I did not give him any letters, nor did I ask him to act on my behalf in

127 The Talmud, the source from which the code of halacha (Jewish law) is derived, consists of the Mishna, the original written version of the oral law, and the Gemara, the record of the rabbinic discussions following the writing of the Mishna.

128 B. Sanhedrin 94a:2.

129 Jews from Vatra Dornei and surrounding villages in Southern Bukovina were deported to Transnistria on October 10, 1941.

130 Not for payment in the next world but rather for financial gain in this world. Very few were able to return from Transnistria to Romania during the entire period of the deportation, until the liberation in March 1944. These few people were able to do so, because of their connections with important figures in Romania and in exchange for large bribes for their release.

Romania. Instead, I gave him as a memento the text of a Yiddish ditty that I had written in December 1941, based on my impression of the new way of life in Dzhurin: exchanging possessions for food. It is called "*Meneien*" in Ukrainian.[131] The farmers then refused to sell anything for rubles. Most of the deportees did not have any other currency, so the people began to give away their last shirt for a bite of food, or for a plank of wood, which in truth amounted to only a small percentage of the value of their meager possessions.

This ditty, half mockery and more than half an imprecating joke, has only documentary value and no literary worth whatsoever. It even merited a fitting tune composed by the *hazen*[132] from Rădăuţi, Moshe Solomon, a good friend of mine from the old country. Solomon, my neighbor in exile, suffered terribly, together with his wife, Linka, a distinguished musician who played a number of instruments, and their talented five-year-old son, Arnold, who possessed a sweet little soprano voice and was all music and mischief ... Moshe Solomon, a creative composer of cantorial music and a rare musical talent, sang this ditty twice at the "Literary Enterprise" during *Hanuke* 1941 in Dzhurin. The crowd applauded him enthusiastically.

I will perhaps some other time elaborate on this project, which Solomon and I organized under strange conditions in a vacant barn somewhere. This "hall" was decorated with three lamps—one on an inverted herring barrel on the stage and two dangling from rotten walls through which the moon mercifully sent in a ray of light. The two female impresarios stood by the door—Roza and Linka—and collected payment: two potatoes or two cuttings of wood for an adult, three for a couple, and only one for a child. The wives of the two performers compassionately allowed a considerable number of people to enter free of charge—these were the poorest of the poor who were slowly dying in the poorhouse at the great synagogue. There were no marked seats, and people could stand wherever they wanted; in any case, there was nowhere to sit. Only Solomon and I shared the throne—a bin of sugar, which we found in an attic. While one

---

131 *Menyat'sya* is Russian for "to exchange." Such trade is known as bartering and is an accepted practice during periods of financial crisis, such as there was in Transnistria.

132 Synagogue official who leads the congregation in prayer.

of us stood and entertained the crowd—reading, reciting, or singing—the other sat and rested.

Material for the program was not lacking. Solomon knew a trove of Yiddish songs from memory, not to mention cantorial works. His grandfather, Hersh Leib Gottlieb, the "*Badhan*[133] of Sighet," had earned a reputation in his own right in the previous century in Eastern Europe for writing stinging, satirical songs, as well as well-known, poignant melodies.[134] Solomon had memorized the pearls of his grandfather's treasure and passed them on to the public. I read children's stories from a volume of Sholem Aleichem, the only book from my library that I had carried with me to Dzhurin. At each performance, Solomon incorporated one of the ditties about current affairs that I had written.

We did not manage to organize more than three performances, although we earned quite a handsome sum: my share of the income from the last performance included 18 large potatoes, no less than 40 medium sized potatoes, and 20 decent pieces of wood. Therefore, life was supposed to be beautiful, but then the council decided to settle three families—thirteen people all together—in our "concert hall." So, the muses were silenced. It seems that the "lords" slyly outwitted us, because we did not sing "*May Yofes*"[135] to them, and Solomon's songs—especially the songs of rebellion like the lines that I wrote—did not please the high-level officials. Here I present the stanzas from that ditty with a heartfelt request that the critics have mercy and not ruin my poetic future …

---

133 Jester.

134 Hersh Leib Gottlieb (1829—1930) was an entertainer and jester who lived in Sighet and achieved great fame in this town; see Menachem Keren-Kratz, "Hersh Leib Gotlib: Imperiya itona'it al ish ehad" (Hebrew), *Kesher*, 46 (2001), pp. 1–9.

135 "*Ma Yafit*" (How Yair), from Song of Songs, 7:7—"How fair and how pleasant art thou, O love, for delights!"—which is sung in the evening of the Sabbath, is used to refer to a display of sycophancy and humiliation before an overlord. The overlords used to force the Jews to sing this song before them and, since then, the Jews in Eastern Europe stopped singing this song on the evening of the Sabbath, and "*may yofes*" has become an idiomatic term for flattery.

Bartering

Everyone barters and everyone trades,
Exchange is the one word we hear.
Money is mud—the world newly remade,
Like it used to be yesteryear.

Refrain:
Please, brother, run quickly
There is no time to waste!
"I want to trade, what will you give me?"
At every door he asks in haste.

Yosel barters a shirt for bread,
Fayvush, his underwear,
Someone wants to trade the woman he wed
But he finds no buyers who dare.

(Refrain)

Matches are exchanged for tobacco
In a glass of sugar as pay.
For a flask of wine that he cannot forgo
The drunkard gives his socks away.

(Refrain)

One trades a hankie,
And another, a broken watch,
No longer a breath in his body,
Death he could not dodge.

(Refrain)

Everything may be bartered,
If you have wares to trade, well and good,
Your heart's desire may be garnered,
To live as people should.

(Refrain)

But if you have nothing, it's not so bad.
Just exchange a nice greeting.
Simply barter and trade and be glad.
Your worries are gone, they are fleeting.

(Refrain)

Oy, already I would exchange
All my worries and my woes
In bargaining I would not engage
Just to rid myself of those.

(Refrain)

Perhaps you will meet an avid man
Send him to me quickly!
He won't go away with empty hands,
On that he can rely completely!

(Refrain)

(Added in 1969 in Akko, Israel):

Moshe Solomon was released following the liberation of Transnistria in 1944, and he and his family moved to Israel in 1951. He became a renown composer of religious music and served as the *hazen* of the Great Synagogue of Kiryat Motzkin until 20 *Tammuz*, 5728 (July [16,] 1968), when a sudden heart attack snuffed out his song. The charming, mischievous Arnold, today called Avraham, completed degrees in Jerusalem in two fields (economics and [music] at the Academy of Music), and has earned a reputation on Israeli radio in the Department of Old Yiddish Music and Folklore. His sweet tenor is often heard on the radio.

[May 30, 1942] An Hour Later

The former head of the Rădăuţi community Dovid Wasserman, who endured a few tense days in Moghilev as a result of a bitter incident—the gendarmes had found letters from relatives sent to internees of Dzhurin in his possession—returned safe and sound today. He was saved from grievous danger.[136] A harsh judgment may be meted out to someone for such a "crime." Whoever is lucky ends up with a bullet in his skull on the spot. If luck is not on his side, then he will be sent over the Bug to a German labor camp, which is worse than death.[137] There is also a third category: women. Dovid Wasserman was a blatant example in that category, although they had to thoroughly grease the wheels of the carriage that bore the miracle ...[138]

---

136 Correspondence with family members in Romania and other locations in Transnistria was strictly forbidden. It was possible to maintain minimal communication via couriers—soldiers and officers serving in Transnistria who spent their vacations in their homeland, Romania. For a respectable payment, they passed on letters to relatives in Romania and brought back money and packages for the deportees. For copies of some of these letters, as well as of the order of Radu Lecca, April 17, 1943, which forbade direct correspondence between the deportees and their relatives in Romania that was not via the gendarmerie headquarters, see Lavi, *Pinkas Hakehilot*: *Rumania*, vol. 1, pp. 364–365. For the report of Fred Şaraga, following a visit to Transnistria between December 31, 1942–January 13, 1943, in which he asked the Romanian authorities in Transnistria to allow the transfer of letters between deportees and their relatives in Romania, as well as between deportees in various ghettos, see YVA, Romania collection, M.29/104.

137 The conditions in forced labor camps in the German territories were extremely harsh: punitive physical labor, harsh and humiliating treatment by the Germans, and miserable living conditions and a lack of food. Most of the deportees did not survive these conditions and many were executed when they were no longer fit for work.

138 It is not clear what this means. It may suggest that it was possible to place a man in the category of a woman through bribery, which afforded some degree of protection.

The person who was granted the miracle did not tire of relating all that he had seen and heard in Moghilev, the center of southern Transnistria. The deported Jews there regard the Dzhurin camp, which has made a name for itself as a "model colony," comparable to *Eretz Yisroel*, and are envious of the fortunate ones in Dzhurin.[139]

More than 10,000 Jews who have been uprooted from their homes are lying in Moghilev, 7 cubits deep in the ground. Every day brings new decrees, and they tremble at the prospect of another deportation. In the iron foundry, which the engineer Jagendorf set up literally out of nothing, arrangements were made for a few thousand people to do hard labor in return for a loaf of bread each day and the right to breathe the air of Moghilev and to receive blows from the Moghilev gendarmes. Those who are in some way connected to the foundry have received permission to settle in Moghilev for the time being. However, tragically, most of the deportees are not entitled to this privilege—in any case, the engineer Jagendorf stuffed too much cheese into the blintzes and, therefore, the lords had to cut some pieces off.

That is why the sword of the Angel of Death hovers over the heads of these miserable, precarious *luftmenschen*,[140] who were doomed to be chased on foot to the Bug, or even to the other side of the Bug, to German camps, where the SS executioners reign.

The calamity that we feared came to pass last week. One summer day, in the early hours of the morning, the gendarmes burst into the

---

139 The Dzhurin camp earned the nickname "model colony," partly because the death rate in the ghetto was among the lowest in the ghettos of Transnistria in general and in the Moghilev region in particular. During the entire period of the deportation, around 400 people died from typhus in Dzhurin—about 10 percent of the population. The conditions in the Dzhurin ghetto were "comfortable" compared with those in other ghettos where the Jews were not organized, were housed in pigsties, stables, and cowsheds on the outskirts of the kolkhozes, were forced to work in the kolkhozes, and were often sent to labor camps, where the work was extremely difficult and grueling. The Dzhurin ghetto was well organized, and there was a Jewish council that more or less managed the conditions there and operated a kitchen that provided 400 portions of soup daily to the needy. The mobilization of the doctors, nurses, and other volunteers at the hospital also significantly reduced the mortality rate from typhus, an epidemic that was raging throughout Transnistria at that time.

140 This refers to the deported Jews who were in Moghilev without authorization. *Luftmensch* is a Yiddish word that literally means "air person."

ghetto, dragged out about 4,000 persons, and chased them by foot approximately 30 kilometers to a wasteland. A camp was erected there, near the destroyed village of Skazinets, whose Ukrainian residents had long since fled. The camp is under the open sky, fenced in with barbed wire, and guarded by Romanian soldiers.[141]

The majority of the people in the Skazinets camp are Jews from Northern Bukovina or Bessarabia—the stepchildren among the deportees in Transnistria, because they bear the dangerous mark of Cain. About a year ago, under Russian occupation, life was sweet under the non-kosher regime of the hammer and sickle, and they certainly must have absorbed rebellious ideas. Therefore, the Romanian fascist regime looks upon them with pernicious hatred and would gladly get rid of them as quickly as possible.

At any rate, Jews from Southern Bukovina also ended up in Skazinets. They are in fact as kosher as well-inspected peas, but they are punished for either real or fabricated transgressions. If someone is caught stealing in the foundry, or if someone simply informs on someone to the boss—the engineer [Jagendorf] with the iron fist—then there is only one punishment: Skazinets. The engineer argues that he must run the factory according to the law to ensure discipline. Otherwise, the factory could lose its charm in the eyes of the Romanian overlords, and they will order the expulsion of the entire community to the Bug. He may be right ...

---

141 On May 19, 1942, 1,000 Jews were transferred from Cernăuţi to the camps of Skazinets and Pechora. At the request of Colonel Constantin Năsturaş, the governor of Moghilev, the deportation of another 3,000 Jews was authorized, and a total of 4,000 were deported. See Carp, *Cartea neagră*, vol. 3, pp. 272–273, 355, 361; Lavi, *Pinkas Hakehilot*: *Rumania*, vol. 1, p. 485. The camp of Skazinets was built on the remains of the barracks that were abandoned by the Soviets during their retreat in the face of Operation Barbarossa. The physical conditions in the camp were unbearably harsh. The camp was fenced in, and the deportees were forbidden to leave its boundaries. Most died of starvation, persistent cold, and typhus, and those who tried to leave the camp were shot dead. In the summer of 1943, the survivors were marched to camps on the eastern side of the Bug into the hands of the Germans, to the camp of Pechora, among others. See Ancel, *Toledot Hashoah*: *Romania*, vol. 2, p. 804. In her testimony, Keller Shternshuss relates how she, her mother, and her grandmother were deported from Moghilev to Skazinets. She describes in detail the terrible conditions in the camp, the severe hunger, and the deportation on foot to the eastern bank of the Bug and to Pechora. Pechora was a death camp, where thousands of Jews, who were deported directly to the camp or reached it via the ghettos in northern Transnistria, died of starvation. See Keller Shternschuss testimony, YVA, O.3/VT/9483.

The news that a couple from Rădăuţi, Kapel and Sheindel Kreizberger, had also fallen victim to the Skazinets calamity caused Roza and me considerable distress. Both—noble people of a kind nature and great generosity (the day before the deportation, they distributed all the merchandise from their large dry goods store to whomever wanted it, free of charge)—were welcome members of our household at our home for a number of years. For what fabricated transgression was such wrath unleashed against them? It is foolish to ask questions in Transnistria ...

[May 30, 1942] 8 P.M.

Disturbing reports, certainly not good news, have come from Moghilev. In the last few days, additional transports of approximately 8,000 deported Jews have arrived in the same paradise from camps in the Regat, mainly from the Târgu Jiu camp. Most are "political" prisoners who had been detained since the beginning of the war with the Soviet Union. Many died in those camps, and the rest were "liberated," that is, flung into a new hell, Transnistria.[142]

In Moghilev, people believe that soon all the Jews from Cernăuţi (nearly 40,000), as well as 15,000 Jews from Iaşi, may expect to travel to Transnistria. The old, established Jewish community of Iaşi sacrificed more than 10,000 victims on June 29, 1941, a few days after the beginning of the war, on "that Sunday," as the Romanians refer to it. At the time, a rumor that Jews had shot at Romanian soldiers from attics spread in Iaşi. A savage pogrom began to rage, killing around 6,000 Jewish persons who were victims of all kinds of strange deaths. In addition, Romanian soldiers and "Green Shirts" (hooligans who belonged to the bloodthirsty Nazi organization Garda de Fier)[143] seized close to 4,000 Jews in the streets

142 This refers not only to political deportees but mainly to Jews from Dorohoi, who were expelled from their homes on June 18, 1941. Antonescu ordered the eviction of all the Jews from the villages between the Siret River and the Prut River to the large towns, and the expulsion took place the following day, June 19, 1941. Men from the ages of nineteen and up were arrested and sent to the Tărgu Jiu camp.

143 Garda de Fier (Iron Guard) was an extreme, antisemitic, nationalist, fascist movement that was active in Romania from June 24, 1927, until the first stages of World War II.

or in their hideouts, including many women, elderly people, children, and babies, and drove them out to the train station. There two-legged beasts shoved the captives into cattle cars, ninety people or more in each, and locked the doors from the outside. The terrible journey on the historic "*trenul* [*sic*] *morții*"[144] (*toytentzug* [death trains] in simple Yiddish) then began, for five days and five nights nonstop. Not, God forbid, because the final stop, Podul Iloaei, was so far away—the distance was only 50 kilometers—but rather because the Romanian murderers had devised a "strange death" for the Yids, which was unparalleled in the long history of Jewish martyrdom. They ordered the train conductors to drive the fifty cattle cars at full speed there and back for five whole days, nonstop. The train conductors were replaced every six hours, but the passengers were always the same passengers. The number of Jews who were still alive diminished daily—until the evening of the fifth day. Only then, for the first time, the soldiers opened the doors and shouted jokingly, "*Domnilor poftiți afară*" (Gentlemen, [you] are invited to step out). However, no one set foot outside, since corpses are unable to crawl out of railroad cars.

During the death journey, 4,000 Jews suffocated in 40-degree [Celsius][145] heat, without a bit of air, without a drop of water, and without a bite of food. The iron walls of the cattle cars were white hot from the June sun, blazing like fire. Wailing rose from the speeding hell—that is what the peasants who stood close to the tracks and crossed themselves in terror recounted—but the locomotive continued to race by so as to drown out the terrible howls of the victims in their cemetery

---

The movement, whose original name was the Legiunea Arhanghelului Mihail (Archangel Michael Legion) was founded by Corneliu Zelea Codreanu. Its name was changed to Garda de Fier in 1929. This extremely radical and antidemocratic movement became popular among university and high school students, and its activities signaled a turning point in the history of the Jews in Romania and in all of Europe. Within a short time, it became a fascist movement with mystical Romanian nationalist characteristics based on Christianity, the sanctification of death, the clutch of the leader, and hatred of the Jews. The movement sought the elimination of the Jews from all strata of Romanian society, the negation of their citizenship rights, and, if possible, the "purification" of Romania of their presence, because the Garda de Fier considered the Jews responsible for the crises besetting Romanian society. On the development of antisemitism in Romania, see Ancel, *Toledot Hashoah: Romania*, vol. 1, pp. 7–31.

144 Death train in Romanian; plural form, *trenurile morții*.

145 One hundred four degrees Fahrenheit.

on wheels. What occurred inside the cattle cars will remain an eternal secret, since not one living soul left the death train. However, we actually know what happened thereafter in Podul Iloaei. The bodies, twisted in death spasms, were loaded on trucks—the terrible stench reached a mile away—and were dragged to a forest, where the 4,000 passengers finally found eternal rest in four long, mass graves. Tractors labored for two days to level the ground so that no traces would remain.[146]

A young friend of mine, the engineer Jack Goldshleger, who was murdered at the age of thirty-five, was among the martyrs of the death train. He was not only an intellectual with a noble soul, but also a dedicated Zionist from childhood and a devoted activist for the general good. He had settled in Iaşi only a few months before the catastrophe.

Apparently, the horrendous slaughter did not satisfy the Romanians, and they continued to try to devise ways to get rid of the remaining remanant from the "holy capital city" of Iaşi, the center and cradle of Romanian culture ... and of Yiddish theater, led by the father of Yiddish theater, Avrom Goldfadn.[147] At the time of the premiere of *Shulamit* in the historical Pomul Verde Garden,[148] could Goldfadn ever have imagined the fate that would one day befall the grandchildren of his "garden public"? ...

Such is the nature of our self-delusion about going home!

---

146 On the pogroms in Iaşi, see Jean Ancel, *Hakdama Leretzah*: *Pera'ot Yasi, 29 Yuni 1941* (Hebrew) (Jerusalem: Yad Vashem, 2003), pp. 149–174. Jean Ancel, *Prelude to Mass Murder*: *The Pogrom in Iaşi, Romania, June 29, 1941, and Thereafter* (Jerusalem: Yad Vashem, 2013).

147 Abraham Goldfadn, a native of the Ukraine (July 24, 1840–January 9, 1908), was a dramatist, poet, composer, theater director, actor in Yiddish and Hebrew theater, and the father of modern Jewish theater. In 1876, Goldfadn established a theater troupe that was considered the first professional theater troupe in the world to stage shows in Yiddish. Goldfadn, who arrived in Iaşi in 1876, was renown as a talented poet, and many of his poems were set to music and became popular songs, such as the song "*Rozshinkes mit mandlen*" (raisins and almonds).

148 Green Apple Garden.

June 5, 1942, 5 A.M.

Monday, June, 1, was one of the hardest days in the camp. Around 10 A.M., the praetor of Shargorod telephoned the Dzhurin gendarmerie, ordering the camp to dispatch 100 men by midday to the quarry stone in a village not far from here—Khomenki—for an unspecified period of time. The list of those men fit for work includes around 450 people, from the ages of seventeen to fifty-five. Many of those registered are indeed sick, and most are wearing rags, naked and barefoot.

Since they are currently content with 100 workers in Shargorod, the council allowed themselves to choose young, healthy people with small families. However, even though the "lords" were very careful not to make any mistakes when assembling the small crew, nevertheless, cries and screams were heard. Wives with babies in their arms and young children tugging at their aprons besieged the community building, pleading that they not be made widows. Some of those who were summoned took to their beds and suddenly became gravely ill. Advocates of various kinds came running to the doors on behalf of this one or that one. The influential sought to redeem themselves, offering hefty sums to substitutes. The 100 were finally gathered. The council distributed bread to the needy, Moshe Katz gave an impassioned sermon, and they set out on their way to work, accompanied by two gendarmes. The colony chief, who is overjoyed on such occasions when he can give orders and bluster, did not have the opportunity to do so, because he was in Moghilev at the time. It is better that way, because the "old man" would certainly have organized the affair in his own manner, which would have caused an uproar in the camp.

[June 5, 1942] 3 P.M.

In a guter, mazeldike sho! Since yesterday, we are once again blazoned with the token of shame in the camp—a yellow Star of David embroidered on a black cloth and attached to the left lapel. I also adorned myself with this decoration because, as Sholem Aleichem says, when the authorities issue an order, it must be obeyed, especially when under threat of being beaten up by the militia, as happened today before noon in the market.

This little decree did not surprise anyone. We constantly see the living dead wandering among the ruins of Dzhurin, reeking of the stench of a cemetery, or the scenes of the distribution of food at the soup kitchen: all this engraves a far deeper impression on the soul than a stupid rag, which does not hurt anyone. There is another reason for the indifference to the yellow Star of David: the Jews in the camp live segregated and isolated from the world. Indeed, there is no need to be ashamed …

A year ago, I wore the emblem of the "Chosen People" in my hometown of Rădăuţi for only a few days and was ashamed to go out in the streets.[149] Then I encountered Romanian overlords who knew me well, and some of them intentionally turned their faces to spare me the humiliation. There are also some, white ravens,[150] but just a few.

June 7, 1942

On Thursday, June 4, the praetor of Shargorod issued an order by telephone to dispatch about 100 workers to Khomenki by Friday morning.[151] In the blink of an eye, the camp was roused, seething even more than during the assembly of the first transport. The cream had already been skimmed off the top, and the wardens of hell in the Labor Office took off their kid gloves and adopted a strictly legal approach [to implement the order]. They no longer recoiled from registering fathers of children, or even the infirm, in order to arrive at the number 100. Although the praetor had explicitly ordered the convoy to leave early in the morning, the 100 men did not depart before 3 P.M., when they were flanked by sobbing wives and shrieking relatives. They had to threaten the use of the gendarmes to gather the 100 men and, nevertheless, some

149 The yellow badge was first instituted in schools in Rădăuţi. After the beginning of the 1941–1942 academic year, Jewish students were required to wear the yellow badge—a Star of David made of yellow cloth—on the sleeve of their clothes, which was distributed to the students in the school for 10 lei. See Margalit-Postilnik, *Radauts*: *Kehila Yehudit Betzemihata Uvisheki'ata*, pp. 141–142.

150 Meaning, rare, good individuals.

151 These workers were forced to pave the road between Murafa and Yaroshenka.

people hid. Those who hid were replaced by disabled persons and frail, elderly people.

This time no one wanted to deliver sermons and the "lords" moved off to the side to protect themselves from the enraged crowd who complained that quite a few well-connected people remained at home. Bread was in fact distributed to the "recruits," and the members of their families were even registered at the soup kitchen until those people would return.

June 10, 1942, 6 A.M.

On Monday, June 8, Dzhurin was honored with a third *hakofe*—to dispatch 100 men to work on the road near the shtetl of Murafa, around 11 kilometers from Dzhurin. The people in the Labor Office of the council, headed by "Labor Minister" David Buksbaum, were tasked with the preparation of this fateful list. This required great effort, because only the most pitiful remained in the camp, apart from a few close members of the inner circle of the lords and all those who work in the council institutions—the kitchen, hospital, militia, administration, etc.—in order not to destroy these institutions, which were already on shaky ground. I too was afforded this same protection, since I am the only community secretary, and I work from morning until late at night. As such, my face burns with shame when they dispatch people who are older and weaker than I am to [forced] labor. In my mind, a *meyletz yoysher* argues: so, what if you sacrifice yourself and leave your wife and children abandoned for the sake of the love of Israel, what good would that do? It would only mean that some well-connected person, or some speculator, will stay home; and someone else will grab your meager income. By the way, there does not seem to be a single lunatic in the camp who would be ready to sacrifice himself for me in this case …

In the third round, the "lords" required the help of the Jewish militia to assemble the crowd. Quite a few men disappeared somewhere in cellars, or in fields; others lay in bed and wrapped their heads with a towel. The wives of the ill suddenly burst into the council [community] building, bringing notes from doctors that listed patients with strange illnesses. One of those who had fallen ill was brought to the council [community] building by a militiaman in a wagon. The sick man was a stubborn Jew who managed to get his way.[152]

The convoy only set out from the camp close to midnight—a group of exhausted, depressed, broken creatures. Some of them could barely drag themselves on their feet, while the others were young, practically children, who were malnourished. Despite all the efforts and threats, it had not been possible to arrive at the sacrosanct number of 100, and only ninety-five people set out for Murafa, escorted by five gendarmes.

It is clear that the praetor has only just begun to dispatch workers from the camp and his appetite is growing. People are afraid that he will soon forgo the services of the council and will himself seize the people with the help of the gendarmes—then indeed there will be a real wedding[153] …

June 11, 1942, 6 A.M.

The cost of living is terribly high and is rising like yeast. One pood of flour costs 50 marks (half of my monthly salary …) and 1 pood of potatoes costs 15 marks. Not long ago, during *Peysech*, you could get these provisions for one-fifth of those prices. The peasants do not hurry to bring goods to the market, because their faith in the only legal Transnistrian currency, the German mark, has begun to weaken. Only the Romanian lei has not lost its appeal. If a farmer is still willing to accept marks, they must be first and foremost small notes of 2, 3, or 5 marks—provided that the bills look like they are fresh off the press—smooth, shiny, without any crease or flaw, God forbid. And even if a few marks happen to be rolling around in one's pocket, it is impossible to get rid of them, because they are generally "high denominations" of 20 or 50 marks.

---

152 The Jews in the ghettos feared forced labor and deportation to the various camps. They did everything in their power to avoid being sent to these camps. See, for example, the Yitzhak Yalon interview with Sarah Rosen, February 12, 2010, Beit Irgun Yotzei Bukovina in Tel Aviv; see also the group testimonies of the ghettos of Moghilev, Shargorod, and Dzhurin, YVA, O.3/VT/10547; Yaakov (Jacky) Pistiner interview by Sarah Rosen, January 17, 2008, Haifa; Shlomo Steinmetz interview by Sarah Rosen, January 17, 2010, Ramat Gan.

153 Kunstadt ironically refers to a wedding in his diary as a euphemistic expression that signifies the promise of trouble ahead.

As for their condition—may the year be [cursed] for the Germans like the special marks, the "marks of occupation," that they printed in honor of Transnistria on ordinary paper, which is destroyed and crumpled in an instant. A bill that is not torn and taped on the front and back with all kinds of bandages to conceal the damaged edges is a rare sight.

Alas, a new goldmine has been added to the sources of Jewish livelihoods in the camp: speculators exchange a bill of 50 marks for thirty-five oiled, shimmering, lower denomination notes and, for a bill of 20 marks, they display their generosity by giving 18 marks.

As a result of the terribly high prices, the shortages in the camp are increasingly acute, and hundreds of people are literally dying of hunger. The soup kitchen distributes 600 warm servings and thus saves 600 persons from death. However, this number must be doubled. On the other hand, the very existence of the kitchen is in danger, because the community income is meager and cannot meet the unusual expenses. Apart from this, the soup kitchen is not the only child of the community: there is a hospital; there are the 300 people who are sent to perform forced labor on the roads and the community must provide them with bread, according to the praetor's decree; then there's the beloved militia on the community's shoulders; and there is a worst affliction: so many Romanian leeches—both the local gendarmes and the great overlords in Shargorod, and sometimes even the tax extortionists from holy Moghilev, who suck out our bone marrow and whose appetite grows the more we give them.

At the same time, there is another problem that stems from the enormous difficulty of obtaining the necessary provisions for the kitchen (beans, millet, peas, oil, salt, wood, etc.). The farmers bring little produce to the market, and mobs of anxious people crowd around each peasant, snatching the few goods from their hands. How can the buyers from the kitchen fight the starving masses!

Following the dispatch of 300 men to work in Khomenki and Murafa, 300 families have been afflicted with hunger and misery. As difficult as life in the camp [Dzhurin] was, people somehow managed to adapt to the conditions and began to earn if only a little something. People risk their lives and sneak into the village to work for the farmers; they sell old rags and notions at the market; they work in the nearby forest (although outside the camp); they trade tobacco [homemade cigarettes], matches, buttons, sweets, and whatnot. They contritely stretch out a hand, and merciful Jews do not refuse—in short, our brothers, the children of Israel, are not forlorn of hope. Thus, a potato, a few beans, sometimes even an egg, a cup of cheese, and a handful of dried pears fall into one's hands, and everyone talks about the wonderful situation. Three hundred gold miners have been torn from their families now, and the members of their households have been left in dire straits. The alleys and the market are full of new hands asking for alms: [of] children who are trying to take the place of those who were sent away …

The alleys are deserted since the entire population of youth has disappeared. The few dozen young people who nevertheless have managed to remain at home are hiding in mouseholes. They do not show their faces in the streets for fear of the "good eye." …

[June 11, 1942] 2 P.M.

Summer is shining bright outside, reviving the soul, but it is not shining for me. I work from dawn until midnight, and if I manage to sneak outside for even a quarter of an hour, they immediately come looking for me everywhere. I used to indulge in bathing in the river in the past, but today I am bathing in perspiration. By the way, I have already completely lost any desire for such luxuries in Dzhurin. I have, God forbid, no complaints about my grueling work and guard it like a precious stone, hoping things will not get "worse."

Anyone who sees me is surprised that my face is green and yellow, without a drop of blood, although I too am a gold miner—a pittance, 100 [marks] in cash each month! I weighed myself on the scales in the soup kitchen and discovered that I weigh 15 kilos less than I did in the old country. Is it possible that some hidden illness is lodged within me, and only my face knows the secret? Oh well, I couldn't care less! …

June 12, 1942 (27th of *Sivan*, 5702)

I have made an exception and added the Jewish date to the secular one for a good reason. Today we are observing a painful *yortsayt*[154] and, hence, I am using the Hebrew calendar. Exactly one year ago, on the 27th of *Sivan*, Hitler pounced on the Soviet Union like an evil beast, and Romania became embroiled in the war. The destruction of the well-established Jewish population of Bukovina and Bessarabia swiftly ensued. *Vey, vey,*[155] how many tens of thousands of Jews have died since that Black Sunday (according to the non-Jewish calendar: June 22 1941)[156] and how many victims continue to fall today. All the Jewish communities of Bessarabia and Bukovina (apart from "lucky" Cernăuţi) were wiped out; a large portion of the Jewish residents were murdered on the spot, the victims of strange deaths, and the rest were sent to their doom in Transnistria. Masses died of starvation, cold, torture, and cruel beatings along the roads, and they were not even granted a Jewish burial. The miserable remaining remnant in the camps is slowly being obliterated, and the number continues to decline. People have already almost completely despaired of deliverance, seeing that the "good tidings" have come to nothing and have merely heralded more calamities.

Here is some good news, fresh from the oven, which the colony chief just brought from the neighboring camp of Murafa, after taking a wagon of bread for our laborers [from Dzhurin who are working] in that area. The doctor says that the Murafa camp (of approximately 3,000 deportees) is in a real uproar. They discovered that the engineer Jagendorf, the president of the Central Council in Moghilev, was summoned immediately to Bucharest, and indeed he flew directly there in a Romanian airplane. Jewish leaders in Murafa think that this is certainly a remarkable matter

---

154 *Yortsayt*, is the Yiddish word for Yahrzeit, the anniversary of the death of a parent or close relative.

155 *Oy vey* and *vey, vey* are shorter versions of the Yiddish expressions of dismay, frustration, or grief, *Oy vey ie z'mir* (woe is me).

156 Operation Barbarossa is the name of the German army's invasion of the USSR on June 22, 1941, that aimed to win the war before the winter arrived. The invasion was planned far in advance, and the Germans trained units of Ukrainian, Lithuanian, Latvian, and Belorussian nationalist and anti-Communist collaborators to participate in the fighting.

and a particularly positive development. Some even claim to know for sure that all the deportees from Southern Bukovina, the "kosher" part of the province where they never lived under the hammer and sickle, will be sent home. It is also clear to the prophets of Murafa that only the Jews from the districts of Suceava and Câmpulung will be granted this deliverance, while the Jews from the region of Rădăuţi, albeit also in Southern Bukovina, will remain in exile, poor things, because a third of the Rădăuţi district—the region of Seletin—was captured by the Bolsheviks in 1940, which made them abhorrently non-kosher. Will the kosher two-thirds pay the price for the sins of the Seletin region?[157] The people from Rădăuţi (who are a minority in Murafa, where the people from Suceava rule by force …) argue that the noble Romanians will not commit such an injustice against them and, most importantly, the engineer Jagendorf, the unofficial king of Moghilev who is himself from Rădăuţi, will certainly not allow such a ploy. Meanwhile, Murafa is seething, and the Jews from Suceava are fighting with those from Rădăuţi over an empty sack. The colony chief, himself from Suceava, complacently rubs his hands together.

Given my brilliant luck, it may indeed come to pass that Rădăuţi will be dishonored, since I myself am from Rădăuţi …

June 13, 1942, 1 P.M.

It never happened! I am not referring only to the engineer Jagendorf, who never left Moghilev. No one ever missed him in Bucharest and, furthermore, he never flew there, not even in a dream. All the "good tidings" that Mrs. "IPA" heaped upon them every Monday and Thursday also never was. "IPA" is a new name for all the liars and talebearers in the camps, the acronym for "*Idishe Platkes Agentur*" [Jewish gossip

157 The town of Seletin is in Northern Bukovina, close to the border with Romania. Before World War I, it was part of the Austro–Hungarian Empire. Between the wars, the town was part of Romania. The Jews of Seletin were deported to Rădăuți in the summer of 1940. From there, most of them were deported, along with the rest of the Jews, on trains to the crossing of the Dniester at Yampol. Some then marched from there to Bershad, and others were dispersed among the camps in the area.

agency]—all lies and untruths, from A to Z. Will they send us home [and] serve us cake, us, the kosher Jews from Southern Bukovina? This implausible news is actually reliable. They just now brought it from Shargorod, where the praetor rules and where people discover the truth more quickly than in Murafa. Jews from Rădăuţi no longer have to quarrel with the well-connected people of Suceava and everyone will, God willing, continue to suffer hard times together, 9 cubits deep in the same ground ...[158]

[June 13, 1942] One Hour Later

Troubles come in pairs in Transnistria. The news just arrived from Shargorod that Dzhurin may soon prepare for a fourth *hakofe*: to provide an additional 100 men for roadwork somewhere once again. Only despondent elderly and disabled people remain in the camp today—not to mention a group of fit, young people who have managed not to avoid the circle dance and, of course, their tricks will succeed even in the seventh *hakofe*.

The work reportedly will continue until late autumn. The Romanian authorities provide the workers with 180 grams of bread per day, and the council must send additional bread every two days so that the laborers will not collapse from the torment of the forced labor that lasts from dawn until sunset under the blazing sun. The community is struggling to fulfill its obligations to the 300 camp deportees, and the soup kitchen's existence is therefore in danger. The praetor does not care about the soup kitchen at all. It must certainly pain him that the Jews in Dzhurin are able to endure thanks to the soup kitchen and hospital.[159] The oppressor would have

158 Rumors were rampant in all ghettos due to the lack of reliable information among the Jews about world events, in particular during the first part of their stay in the ghettos. The rumors concerned developments on the front, what was happening outside ghettos, and daily life in the ghettos themselves. See Goldberg, "Rumor Culture among Warsaw Jews under Nazi Occupation," pp. 91–125.

159 Due to the mass morbidity and mortality from typhus, the ghetto councils in the Moghilev region understood that the battle against this plague was one of the most important and urgent tasks they faced. They founded hospitals and allocated isolation rooms for patients suffering from typhus or other infectious diseases. The hospital in Dzhurin was organized

preferred a duplication of what happened in Balta and Bershad, where the Yids did not linger for long but instead died swiftly in multitudes last winter.[160]

June 17, 1942, 6 A.M.

Governor General Alexianu published a decree expelling the remaining Jews from Moghilev—approximately 4,000 people. Around 2,000 people were already uprooted yesterday, and the remainder will meet their fate on Thursday. They are being chased on foot to the region of Tulchin, on the bank of the Bug, where they will dig peat, standing in water up to their knees.[161] This explicitly means annihilating the condemned. The Ukrainian Jews do not have any money at all and do not understand the language of the occupying authorities (Romanian or German) and, as a result of their past under the "non-kosher" [Communist] regime, the occupiers view them with much more hatred, suspicion, and disdain than

---

in an exemplary manner, thanks to the dedication of all the doctors and principally its first director, Dr. Moshe Greiff, and Dr. Efroim Şabat, who fell victim to the typhus epidemic, Dr. Gabriel Shtir, Dr. Frenckel, Dr. Rosenstrauch, and Dr. Klipper. Alongside the doctors, young people who had completed their high school studies worked with dedication as orderlies: Dov Katz, Bertl Hart, both from Rădăuţi, Emil Grabstein, Carl Rosenblatt, Sami Shapira, Poldi Ungariş, Bertl Neuman, and Burcshi Braun. Likewise, women volunteered as nurses, among them Mina Einhorn-Grabstein. See Margalit-Postilnik, *Radauts*: *Kehila Yehudit Betzemihata Uvisheki'ata*, pp. 168–169.

160 The conditions in Bershad were so harsh during the first winter of 1941 that thousands of the ghetto inhabitants died of hunger, cold, and typhus. According to Ancel, there were 4,000–5,000 Jews in Bershad before the war and, in addition to them, about 20,000 deportees were brought there from Romania. See Ancel, *Toledot Hashoah*: *Romania*, vol. 2, p. 1013. Regarding the statistical data from 1939, see Mordechai Altshuler, ed., *Destruction of the Jewish Population of the USSR, 1939* (Jerusalem: Center for Research and Documentation of the East European Jewry, The Hebrew University of Jerusalem, 1993). Only about 16,000 Jews remained in Bershad after the first winter of 1941–1942. See Ancel, *Toledot Hashoah*: *Romania*, vol. 2, p. 1017; Jean Ancel, ed., *Documents Concerning the Fate of Romanian Jewry during the Holocaust* (Jerusalem: Beate Klarsfeld Foundation, 1986), vol. 5, pp. 346–347; Carp, *Cartea neagră*, vol. 3, p. 279.

161 This refers to the peat mines where labor camps were established. The conditions in these camps were extremely harsh, both because of the living conditions and the punitive work, which was performed in knee-deep water in adverse weather.

they do the Romanian Jews. At the beginning of the war, all men from sixteen to fifty years of age were recruited by the Red Army and, when the Soviet Union was driven out of the Ukraine in July 1941, most of the Jews who still had the strength to travel fled deep into Russia and Asia. Those who remained in their homes were mainly women, young children, the weak, and the elderly. This group was doomed to dig peat; in other words, to dig their own graves.

In Tulchin, there are no camp–ghettos modeled after the "colonies" in the Moghilev district but rather barracks surrounded by barbed wire, where hunger and plagues rage ruthlessly. The Pechora death camp,[162] from where no one has yet to come out alive, is in the vicinity of Tulchin. At the beginning of the winter of 1942, there were approximately 6,000 people still there; about 1,000 remain there today. It seems that the occupiers will expel the Jews of Moghilev and will cast the "rubbish" into Pechora.

We know that in Atachi, which is next to the Dniester, transports of deported Jews are arriving continually. The "guests," some from Cernăuţi, report that after the great deportation of October 1941, approximately 40,000 Jews, who were ransomed by a tax called the "Popovici Authorizations," or who are simply hiding in the ghetto, remained in Cernăuţi. Now the Romanians intend to "clean up" the city and permit only 2,000 well-connected people to remain there. The rest will be sent across the Dniester.[163]

Also, rumor has it that the Jews of the Regat will soon contribute 40,000 persons to the paradise between the Dniester and the Bug—the upper crust "politicos" from the local camps, and those suspected of Communism whose names embellish the black lists of the Siguranţa.[164] It is doubtful whether the dictator Marshal Antonescu will succeed in saving "his Jews" from the Regat, as he pledged. A deportation like this means not only the annihilation of more than 250,000 Jews in the Regat, but also a catastrophe for the inhabitants of the camps in Transnistria. The

162 The Pechora camp was a death camp where thousands of Jews, who were deported directly to the camp or reached it via the ghettos in northern Transnistria, died of starvation.

163 This refers to the deportation of 4,000 Jews from Cernăuţi in summer 1942.

164 The Romanian secret police.

Romanian Jews continue to send money, clothes, food, and medicines to their relatives in Transnistria. In any case, at least some of the gifts arrive where they are needed and ease the hardship. Furthermore, some of the deportees have convinced themselves that the Jews in "free" Romania are not sitting idly by and are striving for the good of their deported brothers among the "high-level officials," although so far their efforts have been in vain ...

June 22, 1942

On *Shabbes*, several hundred Jews from the neighboring shtetl of Shargorod, at the center of the district, were driven out somewhere, to some remote villages, apparently to camps near the Bug. There are more than 4,000 Jews in the Shargorod camp (Jews from Suceava account for the majority) and it is run like a "Jewish regime"—a council headed by the colony chief, Dr. Meir Teich.[165] Fate struck the poorest of the poor, the living dead who roam around in crowded, neglected, and filthy neighborhoods, gaunt creatures reduced to skin and bones from hunger, cold, and suffering. It is unbelievable that not only have

---

165 Dr. Meir Teich was a lawyer and the head of the community of Suceava before the deportation to Transnistria. He organized groups of people from his town and led them in an organized fashion to Shargorod, together with Dr. Avraham Reicher, a medical doctor. Dr. Meir Teich, who served as head of the Shargorod ghetto council, describes Dr. Reicher's great contribution to the survival and salvation of the Jews in the ghetto in his article; see Meir Teich, "Haminhal Hayehudi Ha'otonomi Begeto Sa'argorod," pp. 203–235. However, contemporary diaries, memoirs written in the years after the events themselves, and testimonies given by survivors contain substantial criticism of how Dr. Teich and the council he directed behaved. One of the claims concerns discrimination on the grounds of origin. Teich's opponents claimed discrimination, in particular, preferential treatment of people from Suceava over deportees from other locations. Jacky Pistiner, who was deported from Câmpulung, said, "Dr. Teich, a man from Suceava, was the head of the community [Shargorod ghetto]. That is why people from Suceava were given preferential treatment over the others. Life was easier for the families of those who worked for the community than for all the others"; Yaakov (Jacky) Pistiner interview by Sarah Rosen, January 17, 2008, Haifa; See Avni, *Sefer Zikaron Lekehilat Yehudei Kimpulung–Bukovina Vehaseviva*, vol. 1, p. 287. Yehudit Ben Porat testified that Teich was a very difficult person who only helped those in his inner circle and deprived many of the food that they deserved, which meant death. See Yehudit Ben Porat testimony, YVA, O.3/42.

the local "lords" not made any effort to save these unfortunate people from a new expulsion—as evil tongues whisper—but what's worse, they have contributed to the expulsion of a gang of beggars who are fleecing the community. The Romanian overlords are capable of eradicating the Yids without any advice from foreigners, especially the enemy of the Jews, Praetor Dindilegan, the overlord of life and death in the Shargorod district.

Although the Shargorod camp considers itself superior to Dzhurin, the situation of the *Lagernikes* there is far worse than here. Last winter, more than 1,500 persons died of typhus and hunger in Shargorod; a third of all the deportees ended up in that paradise.

The Shargorod camp has gained a reputation as an antechamber to the cemetery for two reasons. The first reason is because of a kind of force majeure, and one can go complain to the Master of the Universe. The praetor Dindilegan resides there, where he rules like a ruthless despot over his Yids who tumble under his feet. The commander of the gendarmerie in the region also ensures that the measure of Jewish suffering will be greater [there] than anywhere else. Wherever a Jew sets foot, the Angel of Death jumps out at him with a rifle.

The second reason is precisely not ordained by heaven but it is a cause of shame and heartache. The leaders in Shargorod are not primarily concerned with saving the living dead, with waging a war against filth and lice—the faithful emissaries of typhus—with seeing to it that the deportees have a place to lay their heads, not to mention with encouraging broken spirits with a kind word or a friendly regard. Indeed, they have fulfilled the minimal obligation of a soup kitchen and a hospital, but they lack the true fervor and willingness to sacrifice themselves as required in such terrible circumstances. In contrast, they are too friendly with the enemy Dindilegan, ostensibly for the public good and, of course, to the community's detriment, and have cooperated in despicable actions at the expense of the community, and in other "achievements," which it is better not to mention. Rabbi Levi Itzhak of Berdichev[166] will certainly find some merit also in this behavior, but the

166 Rabbi Levi Isaac ben Meir of Berdichev (1740–1809), one of the great Hasidic rebbes, author of the book *Kedushat Levi*: *Al HaTorah Asher Hish'ir Beraha* (Hebrew) (New

common people of Shargorod have not reached such a level and suffer in silence. Speaking up signifies mortal danger …

Friday, June 26, 1942, *Parshat Hukat* [the *Shabbes* Biblical Portion]

Why have I suddenly added here *Parshat Hukat*? There is a reason for this. I am not, God forbid, suffering from a fever. Life is often vindicated by facts and mystical disasters that nurture superstitions. Thus, for example, there is a belief among pious Hasidic circles that the summer week that we read the Biblical portion *Hukat* is dangerous and often brings calamities upon the Jews. This belief is based on quotes from the Zohar and Kabbalistic works, and is also on *Targum Onkelos*,[167] which translates the words, "This is the statute of the law,"[168] into Aramaic as, "These are the decrees from the Torah." Indeed, for a few years now, all kinds of calamities have befallen Jewish communities in Europe during this fateful week.

The truth is that the remaining fifty-one weeks do not lag behind, God forbid, although *Targum Onkelos* does not overlook them, and they torture and kill our brothers, the children of Israel, everywhere throughout the year. It is like a rabbi's miracle, but vastly different. His promises to 999 barren women that they will bear children fail, but when the thousandth barren woman is blessed with a male child, the world goes wild. The moral of the story: Jewish catastrophes also occur during [the week of] *Parshat Hukat*.

York: S. Vaksman, 5706 [1946]). He was known by the moniker "Israel's defense attorney." Rabbi Levi Itzhak became famous as someone who found the good in every person, including sinners and criminals, as is described in many Hasidic tales. See Avraham Kahana, "R. Levi Yitzhak MiBerditshuv Ba'al *Kedushat Levi*," in *Sefer Hahasidut* (Hebrew) (Warsaw: Hatzfira, 1929), pp. 243–266.

167 *Targum Onkelos* is the Babylonian Aramaic translation of the Torah. For an English translation, see Israel Drazin, *Targum Onkelos to Numbers: An English Translation of the Text with Analysis and Commentary* (Hoboken: Ktav Publishing House, 1998).

168 Numbers 19:2.

What am I getting at? During this week of *Parshat Hukat*, wrath was poured in profusion upon the Diaspora in Transnistria and also on the Jewish community on the other side of the Dniester, in the old country. The 4,000 Ukrainian Jews of Moghilev who were recently deported have been roaming around already for eleven days in open fields in the surroundings of Tulchin and falling like flies. One young man risked his life to flee from there and managed to make his way to Dzhurin and to convey the good news.

In the camps of Vapnyarka[169] and Pechora, the Angel of Death will be idle very soon, because there will be no volunteers to receive the remedy of his sword. Jews from Cernăuţi are being deported continually to the Bug and also across the river to the German camps. There are rumors that the occupation authorities are preparing new decrees to accelerate the destruction of the remaining deportees. The air is fraught with worry and with voices reciting *Yizkor*.

That's the norm, so far. As for Dzhurin, here too the nature of *Parshat Hukat* has been revealed. In this case, the troubles began early Monday morning. A group of gendarmes with loaded rifles burst unexpectedly into the camp, led by the commander of the gendarmerie, *Feldwebel*[170] Floreanu—a murderer who boasts that he has killed more Jews than the number of hairs on his head. Like wild animals, they began to seize Jews for work, including the elderly and children, beating whomever they encountered with their rifle butts. A terrible panic broke out in the camp. Everyone fled to the fields or to the Jewish cemetery. Nothing like this had ever happened before in Dzhurin because, until now, the gendarmerie had only demanded workers from the council and had received exactly what they had requested. Nor had we experienced any pogroms at the hands of the gendarmes in the camp. It seems that the new commander intends to introduce a new custom according to his personal style.

The next morning brought another calamity. A band of senior Romanian officers appeared at the gendarmerie, where they spent an hour. When the overlords departed in their cars to return to Moghilev,

169 The camp of Vapnyarka in fact served as a forced labor camp for political prisoners and those suspected of being Communists. Jews from the Regat were also sent to this camp.

170 Noncommissioned officer.

the gendarmerie commander Floreanu announced to the colony chief that the distinguished guests had conveyed an evil decree: the Dzhurin *Lagernikes* were prohibited from going out in the streets, except between 6 A.M. and 9 A.M. The gendarmes will enforce this and will bestow a bullet upon anyone they meet in the streets outside of the three permitted hours. If this decree is not rescinded quickly, this signifies condemning 4,000 persons to death by starvation. The edict means: they can no longer appear at the market to sell an old garment, a pack of tobacco, or a box of matches; sneak into the village to work for the farmers; or extend their hands for alms. How will the living dead be able to go to the soup kitchen with bowls in their hands to receive a small serving of bean soup today? Until now, the gendarmes appeared in the camp only once in a blue moon, since the Jewish militia acted as their emissaries and brought them all kinds of good things at the community's expense. The murderers will prowl around the camp now, and we won't be able even to breathe.

In the meantime, today is already Friday, *in a guter sho*, and the decree is being enforced meticulously. Jewish militia carefully patrol the streets to ensure that at 9 A.M. they are as desolate as a cemetery, when indeed the gendarmes immediately rush in with whips in their hand at the hour. No one dares to stick the tip of his nose outside, and people even cover their windows with whatever they can for protection.

The soup is now distributed at the soup kitchen at dawn. For most of the recipients, this change means fasting for a full day, because they gulp down the small portion of food as soon as they get it, while standing, almost fainting, from hunger.

There is no such decree in force in the neighboring camps of Murafa and Shargorod, nor in the holy of holies, Moghilev. In other words, Dzhurin, the "model colony," received this distinction for being so exemplary.

June 27, 1942

It is a cool, refreshing summer day outside, but the soul is burdened with sorrow. The streets are empty and no living soul is to be seen outside. At exactly 9 A.M., everyone is driven out of the market, even the Ukrainians, and the crowd disperses like poisoned mice.

Today, *Shabbes*, the Master of the Universe also complied with the decree. Those in the small synagogues and the *minyonim* did not delay to promptly do what is required—not relying on the promise that "no harm comes to those who fulfill the commandments." The Rabbi of Siret, Rabbi Baruch Hager, even coined an expression: Fortunately for us, the gendarmes of Dzhurin are ignorant young men who know nothing about that promise …

Starting today, the decree has been eased a little: it is now permitted to be outside in the afternoon, 12 P.M–2 P.M., and in the evening, 4:30 P.M.–7:30 P.M. Does this news indicate that the decree will be annulled altogether?

June 29, 1942

Today the decree was rescinded. Thanks to whom? …

June 30, 1942

In the course of this week, the colony chief will leave for Moghilev, mainly to obtain the consent of the Central Council to renew the local council. All kinds of volunteers have shown up unexpectedly to grab a seat in the community building and they can hardly wait for the happy moment when they will be able to sacrifice themselves for the common good …

July 1, 1942

For now, the doctor's trip has been postponed until a later date, because he first had to travel quickly to Shargorod. A special emissary, Dr. Shapiro (himself a Jewish deportee from Suceava), brought a note from the Shargorod district to the community building yesterday afternoon that said: the boss of the Dzhurin camp must make sure to go immediately to Shargorod before it is too late.

This piece of paper, which is full of secrets, ignited everyone's imagination. The Jews are racking their brains to understand what is going on and the meaning of the words "before it is too late." One thing is clear to everyone: the colony chief has not been invited to eat dumplings and who knows what danger hangs over our heads. There are many prophecies, but who knows whom to believe!

Melancholy and fear envelope the camp like the familiar black cover on a bier in sharp contrast to the sunny and radiant outdoors, which should be the setting for another kind of life. Even people of deep faith believe that deliverance must come before the winter arrives, because no one will survive another winter in Transnistria.

We are slowly dying on a deserted island at the edge of the world, isolated from the seething, raging earth, where at every moment a shocking history is being created and a new world order, or indeed the destruction of creation, is being prepared. Only rarely does a Romanian newspaper find its way to us—the Jewish militia who serve as the gendarmes' messengers sometimes steal an old newspaper at the risk of their lives. The Russian rag *Odesskiye Novosti* [Odessa News], which the Germans print in Odessa, also occasionally turns up here. Obviously, not everyone manages to get his hands on the smuggled treasure, and yet it passes through dozens of hands, and people read it from front to back with bated breath no matter how outdated. Sometimes weeks go by between one issue and the next.

Seeking any hint of good news, the people not only read the newspaper but they also interpret it with a full commentary from MaHaRSHA [171] and keen pilpul. They also try to read between the lines things that never happened, hidden clues and winks that suit their own fervent wishes and feverish dreams. When they see only blank spaces—the sign of censorship—their minds start working immediately, as they attempt to speculate about the subject that the censor did not like.

---

171 MaHaRSHA—Morenu Harav Shmuel Eideles (Our Teacher Rabbi Samuel Eideles)—Rabbi Shmuel Eideles (1555–1631), was a famous rabbi and commentator on the Talmud, and a descendent of the Clonimus family, whose lineage can be traced back to King David.

In the meantime, Dzhurin is not, God forbid, left without any news between one newspaper and the next. On the contrary, absurd and strange phenomena arise overnight, which people whisper about secretly, because the walls have ears. Yesterday's rumors quickly give way to new statements from "the most reliable sources." Even those who, quite the opposite, by nature, don't like to buy a pig in a poke and are not easily fooled, gradually break down and do not refrain from spreading the simple lies and foolish stories while expressing astonishment: "What do you say about the nonsense that the masses are talking about! ..."

A lick of this opium momentarily brightens the dark fate and does not allow us to sink into abysmal despair. After all, we long for a happy ending and a good future! ...

[July 1, 1942] 2 P.M.

They spoke with the doctor this morning as he left for Shargorod, and asked that he make a phone call to apprise us of what is happening. In the meanwhile, we have heard nothing. At the community building, people are waiting for the news with their hearts pounding in mortal fear. The atmosphere is like that of *Tisha B'Av*, worse than on the days that we had to provide workers, because now all the Jews face the same danger, even those who sit by the eastern wall.[172]

Since bribery is a tried and tested remedy, the council is hurrying now, when everyone is so downcast, to spread out the fishnet and send out a call through the militia to the supposedly wealthy and powerful persons to ask them to dig deep into their pockets and donate a ransom in order to rescind the decree that hovers like a black cloud. Moshe Katz is working as hard as he can, using his glib tongue and eliciting many tears but little cash; it is easier to open hearts than pockets. Most of the well-to-do, whom Moshe Katz tries to persuade to donate [money], resorting to both threats and promises, come up with all kinds of excuses as to why they,

172 Kunstadt is referring to the prominent members of the community, according to the custom in many synagogues to seat the prominent members facing the direction of the Temple in Jerusalem.

poor things, cannot contribute. They solemnly swear that they themselves will be reduced to requiring soup from the soup kitchen in six months' time, because their resources will not last longer than that.

When the community completely fails to fulfill in its mission, they throw people into cellars, threaten to send them out to work, or to house poor families in the apartments of the affluent. The voices reach the heart of the heavens, and finally the wealthy man digs into his pocket and pulls out a few bills, although less than the required amount.

By the way, the affluent threaten in vain that they themselves will end up eating soup from the soup kitchen. What soup and what soup kitchen? The doors of the soup kitchen are again closed, and exactly at this moment in the midst of this trouble, 400 needy persons are cutting stone in some pit who knows where, and the members of their families are slowly dying of hunger. Some of the soup kitchen guests have begun to go from house to house, begging for a piece of bread and a potato, although many of them are not suited to this livelihood—either because their broken bodies can no longer bear it, or because they would rather die than beg for alms.

July 3, 1942

Welcome, guest! The doctor returned from Shargorod only last night. His first words upon crossing the threshold of the community building were, "I could not and was not allowed to impart over the telephone the good news that I will promptly reveal. The only telephone is in the building of the gendarmerie, and it is better that they not hear the good tidings too soon."

Barely regaining his composure, the doctor poured out a bundle of lamentations. In Shargorod, he negotiated with the non-Jewish overlords, the Jewish functionaries, and those close to the high-level officials, mainly the colony chief, Dr. Teich, and the regional physician, Dr. Shapiro, who have very close ties with the praetor and the commander of the gendarmerie. They informed him that evil decrees are about to be imposed on the camps in the Moghilev district and that Dzhurin will probably not retain its privileged status and will join the circle of dancers.

In general, they made it clear to him that an evil wind had begun to blow against the deported Jews—not to mention the "non-kosher" Ukrainian Jews. It is believed that the German ambassador in Bucharest, Baron Killinger, flew into a rage and angrily asked Marshal Antonescu why he ridicules the German authorities with respect to Transnistria. After everything that has happened, a significant number of Jews still live there, contrary to their agreement, and these subhumans continue to dwell in the Regat, as if it were their fathers' vineyards.

For a better understanding of the significance of the decree, which I will discuss below, I will briefly describe how the occupiers made the administrative arrangements regarding the deported Jews. The unpleasant word "camp" is not mentioned in the Romanian "ordinances" (orders) or in the Romanian press. The Jews have simply been "colonized" in "colonies," and only the towns in the districts of Moghilev, Balta, and Tiraspol[173] are not called "colonies," and certainly not camps. In truth, however, these places are camps with all the trappings, and leaving the enclosed area is punishable by death. The only advantage lies in the fact that, to this day, the Jews can settle wherever they find a ruined hovel, a stable, or a cellar ... in the shtetls and villages to which the Jews have been deported. The borders of the "colonies" are drawn on the gendarmes' maps but are not distinguished by any visible sign.

The government cabinet has now issued a decree stating that enclosed ghettos must be established wherever Jews reside in Transnistria. In Moghilev, where there are almost 12,000 Jews scattered throughout the entire city, the ghetto was created already a few days ago. At first, they crammed everyone into two streets. However, the engineer Jagendorf moved heaven and earth to convince the overlords that if workers from the foundry died, he would be forced to shut down the enterprise. The Romanian authorities accepted his argument, because they fear for the existence of the foundry as if it were a jewel, since they desperately need the products, which they receive for free. The prefect [Colonel] Mihail Iliescu therefore showed real "munificence" and opened a third street for Jews. Twenty or more Jews are crowded together in every home there.

---

173 A regional city on the Dniester River, facing the town of Tighina in Bessarabia. The city served as a Military Administrative Center under the command of the gendarmerie.

As for Dzhurin, most of the Jews live in the ghetto on the hill, where there are no Ukrainians. The second part of the city, the "factory quarter" by the main road between Vinnitsa and Moghilev, was at first closed to the Jews, but about 200 families later settled there—people of means under the protection of the gendarmerie who rented apartments in the houses of respectable Ukrainians. A ghetto surrounded by a barbed-wire fence means cramming these well-connected people into the ruined apartments on the hill, where people live in conditions of terrible overcrowding. Rumor has it—the "IPA" knows no rest … —that even in that ghetto on the hill, they will drive the Jews from the main street, confining them to the side streets and alleys. My mousehole, where four of us have been crowded together for over eight months, is on the uppermost floor of Iankel Axelrod's "palace," which is standing precariously on the main street itself, near the top of the hill. Knowing my luck, which is as bright as the new moon, the "IPA" will be right this time …

The report about the establishment of a ghetto, even according to the "IPA's" embellished version of it, however, is negligible[174] compared to the second piece of good news that the doctor brought from Shargorod. The Romanian overlords in Shargorod explained to him that Dzhurin is filled with too many Yids and that the overcrowding can be, God forbid, detrimental to people's health. Indeed, because of this rightful claim, the high-level officials concluded that the blood of the Jewish community must be shed, and a significant portion must be deported to the camps by the Bug, or handed over to the Germans on the other side of the river. They did not offer the colony chief any hints as to whose neck the knife is pressed against and who will decide who will leave. It seems that the Ukrainian and Bessarabian Jews, as well as the "non-kosher" Jews from Northern Bukovina, will be the *kapporres* chickens.

There is something despicable about the fact that the praetor ordered the colony chief, who is not the commander of all the Jews breathing the air of Dzhurin, to register them, writing only three details in the forms: name, age, and place of origin. These lists must be ready tomorrow. The

174 Kunstadt described the rumor as *Bitul B'shishim*, which refers to Jewish law regarding unintended mixture of kosher and non-kosher ingredients. Many Hebrew expressions, such as this one, became part of daily language, losing their "religious" aspect.

count has already begun and will be completed by evening. The doctor assigned this census-taking task to the twenty-four "group leaders." The camp is divided into twenty-four groups, each led by an elder who is very familiar with "his" families and is considered a member of every household.

[July 3, 1942] Evening

The colony chief is not as cruel as the evil tongues claim. Here, he did not reveal all his news from Shargorod at once, but rather spoon-fed us so that the community would not panic too much. An hour ago, he announced that the praetor had issued an evil decree in honor of the "model colony" of Dzhurin. Starting Sunday, the day of the weekly market, the peasants from the surrounding area will be forbidden to bring flour, bread, and potatoes—the most vital food products—to the market. If a peasant dares to disobey this order, the gendarmes will take the merchandise and pay the full legal price, which is a tenth of the real price. In simple Yiddish, this decree means that the *Lagernikes* have been condemned to death by starvation.

And for dessert—a fourth piece of news: the praetor demands another 100 men to do the work of building a road near Murafa. The doctor claims that he succeeded with great difficulty in reducing the number to only seventy. At the Labor Office, they have already begun to compose the list. What a group: the elderly, the frail, and even sixteen-year-old youths. The list will be sent to Shargorod tomorrow morning.

It is easy to imagine the panic that erupted in the camp when the people saw the black clouds approaching. The council members, in the meanwhile, are keeping the most dangerous decree—deportation—secret, but there are no secrets among the Jews. Everyone already knows where they will be taken, who will be taken, and when they will be taken. Go play games with our brothers, the children of Israel! …

For the most part, the local, Jewish residents of Dzhurin are in a tremendous uproar, because they apparently feel that the "non-kosher Bolsheviks" will be honored in the first *hakofe*. They have begun to distribute their meager household belongings for almost nothing, and are running to appeal to the council, moving heaven and earth and wailing that they are ready to give away their last shirt, if only they will be allowed to stay. The council members make every effort possible to calm them while trembling with fear for their lives. A dark cloud of tense melancholy hovers over the camp, just as on the eve of major events. There are also those who have nothing to lose and who long for a change, no matter what …

July 5, 1942

The decree concerning the starvation of the camp is already in force today. The authorities have not only forbidden the farmers to bring flour, potatoes, and bread to the market—as the doctor had announced—but also beans, dried peas, grits, and cattle. However, there is no ban on the provisions for the wealthy, for example milk, butter, cheese, eggs, chickens, fruit, honey, oil, and … watermelon seeds.

Peasants who had not yet known about the decree arrived at dawn at the market with all the best—wagons loaded with flour, fresh produce, potatoes, and all kinds of provisions. The market was replete once again, which befits the fat Ukrainian soil. Everyone thought that the high prices would go down a bit and that we would be able to breathe a little, because the farmers would lower the prices a little as a result of the newly arrived abundance.

The jubilation had not lasted more than a quarter of an hour when the gendarmes suddenly savagely stormed in, whips in hand, and pillaged all the goods, even the "kosher" [legal] foods, such as butter and poultry. Without taking payment or the maximum prices into consideration, pandemonium broke out in the blink of an eye in the market, as though a bomb had exploded there. Both the Jews and the Ukrainians began to run like poisoned mice, stumbling and falling over each other. As pots with milk products and baskets with eggs were overturned, yellow and white streams flowed through the square. Women lost baskets with money, men lost hats, yarmulkes, and walking sticks. Booths with all sorts of goods were torn apart by the turbulent wave of frightened people, and the miserable bits of poverty were scattered everywhere. This was accompanied by screeching, diabolical music; shrieking in every scale in Yiddish and Ukrainian; the wailing of young children; cries of distress from all the trampled creatures; the squawking of hens; and the blows of the gendarmes' whips on shoulders and heads. If this was not enough, one gendarme fired shots in the air.

Within a few minutes, the market was empty and looked like a cemetery. No, I'm wrong! The ground of a "holy site" is not covered with cream, cheese, smashed eggs, scattered millet and grits, trampled greens and fruits, broken pottery, crumpled hats, and yarmulkes. Everything was mixed together by diabolical cooks and made into porridge. It is clear that no peasant will show his face in the market any time soon. If a lunatic nevertheless risks his life, he will profit. In truth, the wealthy will somehow find a solution, but how many powerful people are already in the hot springs of Dzhurin! …

July 7, 1942, 6 A.M.

The sun has just begun to shine—splendid, great, content—and it announces a wonderful, beautiful, summer day. This glittering appearance does not at all match my low spirits. What new hardships will this bright day in July bring?

My forty-first birthday is approaching and the darkest year of my life until now is drawing to a close. If my family and I are still here among the living then perhaps this year has actually been a year of good fortune for me. How many rivers of Jewish blood have flowed during this year in Romania! How many thousands of deported Jews have died on death marches and in the calamities that befell them in Transnistria over the last twelve months! How many unfortunate Jews have already fallen today like flies on the other side of the Bug in the hells of Pechora, Tulchin, and Vapnyarka! So, it seems that it is forbidden to complain and, instead, we must continue to repeat the words of comfort: just not worse.

However, my stubborn heart refuses to wrestle with questions and conjectures, and does not allow me to catch my breath. As H. N. [Hayim Nahman] Bialik laments in his poem "City of Slaughter": The weather was sunny, the blossom burst, and the butcher's knife slaughtered [the slayer slew]. (I don't remember the Yiddish version, also written by the poet).[175] Indeed, the sun revives souls on a July day like today—that is my wish for all my loved ones—and nevertheless a blizzard of the month of *Shevat*[176] rages in my soul …

July 17, 1942, 2 P.M.

No more than ten days have passed since my last entry, and so much has happened in the camp in that time—ten days of darkness! What dramas have unfolded during those ten days of extreme panic, black despair and, at the same time, of shimmering hope and faith in miracles! How many strange scenes of human glory and of a readiness for self-sacrifice, as well as of the lowest depth of depravity, have unfolded in the last ten days!

While immersing myself wholly in retrospection to write the preceding lines, I was unexpectedly crushed by the harsh sense of the terrible humiliation that those who give me my bread had suddenly inflicted on me, because they themselves are suffering. I was actually trembling [with fear] that I would lose my meager morsels of bread. How insignificant and unimportant the entire matter now seems compared with the events that followed and are still underway!

The calamities began on Sunday, July 12 [1942]. A special messenger brought an order from Shargorod on behalf of Praetor Dindilegan, who summoned a number of leaders from the council to go to Shargorod immediately for some important news. The colony chief, accompanied by Moshe Katz, immediately made their way there. On Monday, they returned with alarming news. Of the almost 4,000 people in Dzhurin, the Romanian authorities will drive out at least half—either to camps or villages in the surrounding areas—we do not know yet. According to the praetor, there are too many Jews in Dzhurin and, therefore, their number must be diminished. The praetor reassured them that the order does not

175 "The slayer slew, the blossom burst, and it was sunny weather!" H. N. Bialik, "The City of Slaughter," in *Complete Poetic Works of Hayyim Nahman Bialik*, ed. by Israel Efros (New York: The Histradut Ivrit of America, 1948), vol. 1, pp. 129–143.

176 The Hebrew month of Shevat is in January–February.

apply only to Dzhurin but to all the camps in Transnistria. We see clearly the evil intentions of those whose hate for us is in their blood: to assist the Angel of Death, who has shown very little efficiency in annihilating the Yids in Transnistria. Of the 250,000 persons who were uprooted from their homes in Romania, almost half continue to gasp for air, which was not the aim of the deportation.

We still do not know when the terrible decree will be implemented, but the fateful document has already been signed. Another detail was also revealed to our emissaries: the *kapporres* chickens will be first and foremost the Ukrainian Jews, and the deportees from Bessarabia and Northern Bukovina, who were granted the pleasure of enjoying Stalin's paradise for more than a year, will be honored in the second *hakofe*.

The "lords" of Shargorod, Dr. Teich and Dr. Shapiro, secretly transmitted Rashi's interpretation of the order of the praetor. They acted with devotion to the great overlord so that some of the Ukrainian Jews would have the option of paying a ransom to rescue themselves from the disaster. A local family must pay a pittance of 1,000 marks to save themselves. That's not bad. The Jews should not be alarmed: the high-level officials will not refuse gold coins, or even American dollars, even though America is an enemy, from anyone who does not have any marks ... As for jewelry, the question will be raised. The righteous of Shargorod concluded by saying that this *Aktia* has already been fully implemented with fanfare in Shargorod and in Murafa. They hope that Dzhurin will not be left behind, as is fitting for a "model colony" ...

Well, obviously, when hundreds of lives are at stake, such an important secret must not remain hidden, and the abscess must be cut open as quickly as possible. It was opened on Monday at dawn and the stench spread throughout the entire camp. The elderly rabbi of Dzhurin, Rabbi Herşel Karalnic, the spiritual leader of the local Ukrainian Jews, was the first to be invited to the community building. Under Soviet rule, people simply called him Herşel Shoyhet—to ward off the evil eye—and he is still angry that people attach the R [for Rabbi] to his name ... Should I live to the age of Methuselah, I will never forget the fearful image that unfolded before my eyes when the doctor conveyed to Rabbi Herşel the news of the danger threatening his people. All the council members gathered at the community building, where it was as silent as a cemetery.

Only the whispering voice of the doctor, who made the effort to speak a broken Yiddish so that the rabbi would understand him, could be heard. The doctor always speaks only in German. Yiddish is as foreign to him as Judaism in general. German culture is rooted deep in his heart, as someone who was educated according to the imperial way of life in old Austria. In his old age, he was destined to be a Jewish leader, alas, a real pain in the stomach …

An amiable, elderly man, *Mara D'atra*—a tall, thin old man with a short, white goatee, a hat on his head, and Dzhurin-style boots on his feet, and with no sign of slick rabbinical scholarship—is clearly a reincarnation of the lofty Rabbi Yozefl from Sholem Aleichem's "A Tale of A Thousand and One Nights."[177] He does not cease to demonstrate through his actions his greatness and readiness to sacrifice himself for every Jew. I hope that I will have another opportunity to render, at least in broad strokes, a portrait of this truly righteous man and lover of Israel.

As Rabbi Herşel listened to the doctor's speech with closed eyes and remained seated on his bench of honor for a few long minutes, we clearly saw an ancient figure from a tragedy by Sophocles rise high above his small surroundings, petrified in an unworldly mist. However, the rabbi promptly regained his composure, opened his wise, penetrating eyes wide, and cried out with a wail, "Jews, why are you standing around and not acting quickly when every moment is like gold! Tell me what I should do to help save [lives]. Indeed, gentlemen, there is one thing you must know: I will go with the Dzhurin Jews, with everyone who is doomed to exile. Take all that is still in my possession in my house as quickly as possible in order to save lives!"

Well, indeed, they immediately gave Rabbi Herşel [Karalnic] the honor of organizing a committee of Dzhurin Jews to impose a ransom of sorts on every family to save at least part of the community. Regarding the Jews from Northern Bukovina and Bessarabia, the council pledged to

177 The Rabbi Reb Yoyzefl is identified with Kasrilivke, the town of the "small people." He is known as a peacemaker who is always ready to listen, help, and support the members of his community. See Sholem Aleichem, "Alt nay kasrilivke," in Aleichem, *Ale verk*, vol 5:4 (Yiddish) (New York: Forverts, 1944); see also Aleichem, "Kleyne mentshelekh mit kleyne hasoges," in ibid., vol 7:1.

pay a ransom for 200 families, and the community immediately launched a wide-scale operation in Dzhurin unlike any other ever before.

A dozen militiamen were deployed to bring the wealthy persons and anyone suspected of possessing a hidden nest egg to the community building, with no excuses. The "lords" were confident that in the heat of the moment it would be possible to extort decent sums, which would possibly also suffice to save the soup kitchen for a while.

While the rabbi [Herşel Karalnic] was sitting in the community building, it was besieged by hundreds of people, because the secret had already become widely known. The rabbi came out pale and even though he tried to walk with steady steps, one did not have to be a prophet to understand from the look on his face the danger hovering over everyone. Once again it was suddenly *Tisha B'Av* in all the houses and living quarters—not only among the local Dzhurin residents but also among the non-kosher Bessarabian and Northern Bukovina Jews. Even the "kosher" Jews from Southern Bukovina and Moldavia, the well-connected people, alas, were stunned. Such decrees are like a flood, and no one knows how to reach the shore. It brought to mind the dark days of 1941 when the catastrophe of the expulsion of the Jews from the villages began, ending with the deportation of all the Jews from Bukovina, Bessarabia, and part of northern Moldavia. The local residents of Dzhurin, who had never before had a taste of exile and were still sitting within their own four corners, although crowded together with the exiles in wretched, narrow, small rooms, are more dejected than we are. Having been deported from our homes long ago, we have long since forgotten that we once possessed our own houses.

On Tuesday, the council began to work with fervor. Although the rabbi of Dzhurin attended the meeting and contributed to the prestige of the operation, he did not lead the council alone but with Iohanan Darman, a young Torah scholar who was highly motivated and enthusiastic. He was not mobilized in the Red Army, because he had already long before paid his debt to the Soviets when he lost an eye during the civil war.

The council set a ransom of 150 marks per person—an amount that most Dzhurin Jews cannot pay. The locals are no less impoverished than the deportees. Among the few Ukrainian Jews, there are women, children, disabled persons, and elderly people. There are quite a few children among the Dzhurin Jews, *ke'naynehore*. In these districts, more than anywhere else, they have allowed themselves to worry about the duration of the world and not to fret too much about the English pessimist Malthus and his morose prophecy.[178] This backward and remote shtetl has always been immersed in poverty, even when it was possible to work somewhere—in the sugar factory or in the surrounding kolkhozes.

The main livelihood of some of the Dzhurin women is baking bread and buckwheat knishes, which they then sell clandestinely at the market. Only one bakery is allowed to sell bread—its owners are wealthy deportees who received "kosher certification" from the community and who pay a monthly fee. A group of Jewish militiamen ensure that no one, God forbid, cut into the fat profits of the bakers, who have purchased the monopoly on bread for a certain price.

Some residents of Dzhurin make a living by selling household goods or by engaging in all kinds of small trading, God forbid. Others settle for a few marks from renting out a small room or a bunk bed, and the rest stretch out their hands for a donation and count on a bowl of soup from the soup kitchen once a day. The lucky ones even get half a loaf of bread from the "Aid to the Poor Society," a kind of small rival of the soup kitchen that relies on private charity—without help from the community—and is run by the rabbi of Dzhurin himself.

And suddenly a certain Iohanan Darman comes and stridently demands a fortune in cash from a gang of beggars and paupers that even a city that has a few powerful, wealthy residents would not be able to provide! It seems that there are a number of hidden Jews among the people in Dzhurin who have "hiding places"—buried treasures, bowls filled with gold coins from the time of the tsar, and even "soft money" (green banknotes from Columbus' country). So the evil tongues whisper, but go persuade those "*lamedvovnikim*,"[179] who curse, deny everything, and shed crocodile tears,

178 Thomas Robert Malthus (1766–1834) was an English priest, demographer, and political economist. He was most famous for his gloomy forecasts regarding the disparity between natural population growth and the capacity to ensure adequate food supplies for the entire population.

179 According to Jewish legend, there are thirty-six incognito *tzaddikim* (righteous and saintly persons by Jewish standards) in every generation, and thanks to them the world exists; see B.T Sukkah, 45b. In Yiddish, *lamedvovnikim* also refers to a modest and poor man, among other things. Kunstadt occasionally uses this phrase ironically.

asking why their enemies have invented such lies and false charges against them to ingratiate themselves with the council.

There is little time left to complete the ransom *Aktia* and therefore the Jews of Dzhurin are hustling and struggling, alas, to procure money from everyone who has any. The peasants from the surrounding areas have discovered that really good deals are to be had literally in the streets, and many non-Jewish women are going up the hill to snatch up Jewish property at bargain prices. Clothes, shoes, bedding, tables, chairs, and all kinds of household goods are being discarded all around the hovels. Sometimes you see a goat tied to a post—the breadwinner of the family from the "good old days." The cunning peasants immediately see that the Jews are desperate for cash and bargain over every item ten times before they show them a whit of a mark and milk them dry. Jews peel the tin roofs off their homes and exchange the panels for a pittance, drag out the last wooden bunk bed from their cubbyholes, and give up their *Shabbes* clothes and their only pair of boots. The women pull off their wedding rings from their fingers and the gold earrings from their ears. Some people unexpectedly pull out "Napoleon" and "Nikolai" coins, gold coins that they had buried in hiding places and saved for hard times, the times that have now arrived ...

To describe the tragic scenes that have unfolded and continue to unfold before the council, a gifted but unimaginative writer is required, because true evil surpasses the most prolific imagination. I must stop now, because a community messenger has just arrived to summon me to the community building immediately.

July 18, 1942, 6 A.M.

The three fateful days that were allocated to the Jews of Dzhurin to collect the ransom money (100,000 marks) came to an end yesterday evening, and the required treasure had not yet been amassed, not even half of it. The doctor saw that it was impossible to meet the deadline and approached the district doctor Shapiro in Shargorod—the main advocate in this matter—to ask him to try to persuade the praetor to extend the deadline by a few days. The reply arrived yesterday evening. It's not a terrible problem if the small fortune arrives a little late, as long as it arrives. So, all is well again and people can continue to peel off their roofs and stuff the Ukrainians with kosher bargains.

The messenger from Shargorod who conveyed the good news also mentioned in passing that they are preparing an impressive reception there in honor of the governor, General Alexianu. The colony chief, Dr. Teich, with the help of his friend, the praetor, will request an audience [with the governor]. When our doctor heard this news, he suddenly rose from his chair and told the council members that he must, for goodness' sake, leave immediately for Shargorod, and indeed he disappeared right away.

It is clear to everyone that the "old man" is desperate for a smidgeon of honor from the overlords, and intends to push his way in there and thereby be present at the meeting, not to have the decree revoked, God forbid, or to beg for mercy for the deported people. He will grovel in the dirt before the most minor Romanian overlord, clutching the briefcase in his hands and agreeing with everything that the overlord demands. Indeed, when conversing with the overlords, he does not watch his tongue and says things that are liable to cause great harm to the entire population. Alas, the members of his community have had enough of all his show of "valor" before them …

The council does not at all approve of the doctor's sudden journey to Shargorod or his involvement in the matter of the ransom. People are worried that he might talk when he shouldn't, and say too much, and make promises at their expense. The entire matter of the ransom is not kosher and has stirred up all kinds of whispering and suspicions. Why are they registering the Jews specifically in the Shargorod district and allowing them to ransom themselves with great treasures, whereas in Moghilev, they actually drove out the Ukrainian Jews without any talk of ransom there? Is it possible—people are murmuring—that the whole matter of the heinous threat by the praetor is the advice whispered in the praetor's ear by various members of his inner circle? Some evil tongues have even mentioned names. This is unacceptable to me. If we are dealing with fraud, is it possible that a Jew would give such despicable advice? The Romanian overlords are capable of managing their town on their own when it comes to methods for uprooting the Yids.

Once again, there is something in the air that does not smell like heaven, precisely surrounding this whole mysterious affair, both here and in Shargorod itself. Although the ancient Romans established the principle "money has no odor,"[180] for some reason, there is too much whispering about the question of who will deliver the treasure to Shargorod. The doctor himself very much wants to be the good emissary, but the council members stubbornly insist that one of them accompany him because ... it is dangerous to transport such a large fortune alone. They decided that the person would be the council member Bobi Rosenrauch, a deportee from Siret (Bukovina), once a powerful, wealthy man, and even today he is no pauper. In praise of him: he deals no blows and is adamant about keeping secrets. Whoever considers him a fool is one himself ...

July 19, [1942] 6 A.M.

An intriguing guest appeared yesterday afternoon at the community building and introduced himself as Kveller, the colony chief of the Krasnoye "colony" in the Moghilev district.[181] Covered in dust and sweat, he came to see his "colleague," the colony chief, to learn from him how to work for the common good. His entire appearance was

---

180 Kunstadt writes in Yiddish "*non ales*," referring to the saying coined by Emperor Vespasian Pecunia *non olet*—money has no odor.

181 Krasnoye is a small town in the Moghilev region near the train station of Yaroshenka. Of the town's population, 96 percent were Jews. In 1926, 2,002 Jews lived in the town. In 1941, when the Romanians entered Krasnoye, they established workshops and employed the local Jews, who at that time numbered 200. In the summer of 1942, around 300 Jews who had been deported from the Shargorod ghetto were taken to Krasnoye from Dorohoi. These deportees lived in the destroyed homes of the local Jews, in conditions of terrible overcrowding. With the annihilation of the Skazinets camp, a ghetto was established in Krasnoye, surrounded by a fence. In September 1942, another 700 deportees from Bukovina were brought to Krasnoye. At that time, there were a total of 1,300 Jews in Krasnoye. The Jews worked at forced labor, performing various tasks for the authorities and in the local forests. German units were posted to the region, and their soldiers would visit the ghetto from time to time, shooting the Jews on various pretexts. Six workshops were active in Krasnoye: tin, carpentry, mechanics, sewing, shoemaking, and a barbershop, all run by the Romanian authorities. The Jews who worked for them received food as their wages. See Lavi, *Pinkas Hakehilot*: *Rumania*, p. 507; Carp, *Cartea neagră*, vol. 3, pp. 383, 358, 441.

very different from the presumptuous attire of the colony chiefs in the Moghilev district—a Jew dressed in a threadbare, patched, cloth suit, wearing worn-out shoes with holes and a crushed cap from the days of grandmother Yenta on his head.

He had just arrived from Krasnoye by foot, a distance of around 50 kilometers. He told us that tomorrow at dawn, God willing, he would set out on foot for Moghilev to attend a Central Council meeting of all the colony chiefs. The appearance of this exhausted and wretched public servant who represents about 1,000 prisoners in the camps in Krasnoye, begged comparison with the colony chiefs in our district: one after the other, they boast about their doctorate degrees and only grind out "highfalutin German," live like overlords, travel by car to Moghilev, and spare no community money, both when it is necessary and when it is not. Our doctor, who left on Friday for Shargorod to mingle at the governor's gathering, must have heard about the meeting in Moghilev, but he will probably not make his way there on foot like his "colleague" from Krasnoye ...

Kveller also said that he intends to take care of another community matter in Moghilev. He will collect some more of the small amount of cash sent by the central council of the Jewish communities in Romania[182]

182 The Comisia Autonomã De Ajutorare (Autonomous Aid Commission), headed by Arnold Schwefelberg, was established at the end of January 1941 by members of the Federatia Uniunilor De Comunitati Evreesti (Federation of Communities in Romania) to help Jews in Romania who were suffering under Ion Antonescu. The members of the Comisia Autonomã De Ajutorare included Dr. Wilhelm Filderman, Fred Şaraga, and Emil Kostiner; representatives of the Zionist movement: Mişu Benvenisti and Dr. Kornel Iancu; businessmen; and a group of women who had previously been involved in helping the afflicted Jews. Dr. Filderman, the head of the Federatia Uniunilor, had headed the Uniunea Evreilor Romani (Union of Romanian Jews), UER, that was dissolved in 1938. In December 1941, the Federatia Uniunilor was disbanded by the Romanian authorities and replaced with the Centrala Evreilor Din Romania (Jewish Center in Romania), headed by Dr. Nandor Gingold, but it was not allowed to provide aid to Jews deported to Transnistria. Only in the years 1942–1944 did the Comisia Autonomã De Ajutorare, operating alongside the Centrala Evreilor, manage to send aid to Transnistria, including money, clothes, food, etc., thus saving many deportees' lives. In January 1943, the authorities allowed a delegation, headed by Fred Şaraga, to visit a few ghettos in Transnistria. This visit and others helped to ease the lives of the deportees and finally brought about the return of the orphans and later of the deportees to Romania. The Comisia Autonomã De Ajutorare also collected money and supplies for those affected by riots in Bucharest in January 1944, and thereafter more actively tried to improve the lives of the 40,000 Jews deported from villages and towns and transferred to detention camps throughout Romania.

from Bucharest to support the Krasnoye *Lagernikes*. To prove his credibility, the colony chief of Krasnoye pulled out a typed letter in Romanian from his pocket, saying: "We do not forget our brothers in need and send them assistance—103 marks." The letter bears two ornate signatures and a round, dignified seal. This amount is enough to buy 3 poods of flour—it doesn't matter—the Bucharest Jews who are still at home indeed remember, and rightly so, their brothers and sisters who are in some godforsaken place! …

Allow me to point out to the credit of our "lords" that they did not allow the head of the Krasnoye community to drag himself on foot to Moghilev (more than 50 kilometers). The community rented a suitable wagon from a non-Jew the next day. This good deed cost more than 103 marks…

It is worth immortalizing some of the details that Kveller related regarding the horrific expulsion from Krasnoye. On *Shabbes*, June 27, 1942, the local praetor ordered the immediate deportation of the 1,200 Jews in the shtetl—900 local residents and 300 from Bukovina—to the village of Tyvrov [183] by the Bug. The gendarmes immediately carried out the decree without delay that same day. They [Jews] were allowed to take as much of their belongings as they could carry and set out on foot. The praetor showed some "generosity" by providing a number of Ukrainian carts for the children, the elderly, and the weak. All the council members and the rabbi were among the deportees.

In Tyvrov, the Jews found and moved into the empty but damaged houses of the Ukrainians who had fled at the time of the deportation. Although they had a roof over their heads, they nevertheless lived in dread, because Tyvrov, which is divided into two parts by the river Bug, has a terrible reputation. The Romanians rule the western part, while the non-kosher flag of the SS executioners waves on the other side—and the region has been "*Judenrein*" for some time already. Before *Peysech*, the neighbors from the other side[184] came to visit Romanian Tyvrov and

183 Tyvrov is a town in the Moghilev region, in the Krasnoye district, near the Bug River, 25 kilometers south of Vinnitsa. See Lavi, *Pinkas Hakehilot*: *Rumania*, vol. 2, pp. 444–445.

184 This refers to the SS forces incursion beyond the eastern side of the Bug. Every so often, the Germans would cross the river in search of women and alcohol in Tyvrov.

slaughtered 350 local Ukrainian Jews with German precision. They did not tarry long and completed this “formidable task” within half an hour. The fortunate ones were killed by a bullet on the spot, but not everyone was granted this, and the SS men took the 350 bodies, including several wounded, and threw them into a mass grave.

The peasants from the surrounding areas welcomed the new guests from Krasnoye with an account of this act and even added that they had seen with their own eyes the ground of the mass grave continue to heave for some time after the slaughter.

Do not believe in miracles, Kveller says, and do not delude yourself that the praetor sent gendarmes to Tyvrov three days later to bring the Bukovina Jews back to Krasnoye for no reason, because they need them to work in the fields. When they returned to Krasnoye, the praetor ordered that all 300 persons be crammed into a narrow road and fenced inside the “ghetto” with a barbed-wire fence. Still, this is better than continuing to be the neighbors of the SS, as was decreed against the 900 residents of Krasnoye who have been left behind in Tyvrov for the time being …

July 21, 1942 (7th of Av, 5702), 6:30 A.M.

This year my two birthdays fall one after the other. Today is my birthday according to the Hebrew calendar and tomorrow according to the non-Jewish calendar. I never celebrated this date, because even in the “good years,” I thought that the 7th of Av, 5661, had not brought me much happiness, so there was no reason to celebrate. In Transnistria, this Kohelet-like attitude has certainly not changed …[185]

Nevertheless, I would like to know what surprises the new year has in store for me. I admit that since childhood, a spark of mystical superstition glimmers within me, and I am convinced that whatever happens on a birthday somewhat hints to the future. One year ago, on this day, it seemed to me that my forty-first year would shine brightly. I

185 Kohelet (Ecclesiastes) 7:1–3: “A good name is better than precious oil; and the day of death than the day of one’s birth.”

had a clear sign: the previous evening, the electric lamp suddenly turned on again in my home, after not functioning for more than a month. I was still living with my family in my own beautiful and comfortable apartment, but a sense of disaster and dread was hovering all around. Ever since the war with Russia had broken out, it had been forbidden to allow any light to filter through the windows at night because of the danger of Russian air raids. The Romanians found a solution and covered the windows with blue cardboard, but the Jews did not dare to follow suit for fear of being falsely accused of sending signals to the enemy through the windows. There already had been enough calamities in the wake of this false accusation against the Jews and, for this reason, Jewish blood had flowed in Dorohoi, Iași, and Cernăuţi, as well as in other places.

It was exactly on the eve of my birthday, one year ago, that the blackout decree was canceled, since the Germans had already occupied vast territories deep within the Soviet Union, and the danger of Russian air raids in Southern Bukovina, more than 600 kilometers from the front, had obviously passed. Well, if there was light among the Jews, it was reminiscent of *Purim*, "The Jews had light ..."[186]

As full of light as this year has been for me, for my relatives, and for the entire Jewish population of Bukovina, may it be so bright for all the enemies of Israel! Still, let's not complain! We have indeed passed through seven levels of hell and to this day remain riddled with anxiety, abandoned like leprous dogs, yet still alive. Whoever lives can also survive ...

A bright, golden July day shines outside, brimming with the joy of summer. What signs will this summer day bring me? I will certainly not have to wait long for an answer. I have no idea what appearance my birthday will assume next year. Our sages were right: "Seek not things concealed from you, nor search those hidden from you."[187]

186 Esther 8:16.

187 B. Chagigah 13a.

[July 21, 1942] 6 P.M.

Today was a lucky day for me: no calamities have befallen me, and those who provide me with my bread have not harassed me. I interpret this as a good sign and anticipate that my forty-second year of life will bring at the very least deliverance …

(**Added a year later**: What a year of deliverance! That year, my righteous mother and also my father-in-law passed away in bitter agony—both in the same week …)

July 27, 1942, 6 A.M.

The magical summer days are going by quickly, and it feels like we will soon miss them. A second winter in Dzhurin—I do not want to think about such a disaster at all. It is, by the way, foolish to worry about what will happen in the coming months when at any moment history is liable to turn on its head. She, history, has been struggling to give birth for three years. The travail has reached its peak, and something must emerge—either a stillborn or a living child …

[July 27, 1942] 2 P.M.

Yesterday morning in the community building, the curtain came down on the drama known as the "ransom." At around 9 A.M., the rabbi of Dzhurin, Rabbi Herşel, accompanied by Iohanan Darman, the president of the ransom committee appeared. Yohanan (the local Jews call everyone by their Jewish names) did not arrive empty-handed, God forbid. Under his arm, he carried a fine *talis* bag embroidered with gold thread and with a Star of David in the center. The two were escorted to the door of the community building by a Jewish militiaman—a husky fellow with whom it is not worth getting involved.

We welcomed the distinguished guests, and all the council members, led by the colony chief, rose from their benches and stood in honor of the venerable *Mara D'atra*. As soon as the two emissaries appeared, they cleared the building of everyone and told me that I could go home to rest for an hour. They usually send me to the front room, however, there are secrets and then there are secrets. They stationed two militiamen outside the building to ensure that no one approach it.

There, in the true holy of holies, the last act of the ransom drama unfolded. The *talis* bag did not contain a prayer shawl, two pairs of *tefilln*, and a prayer book but rather ransom money from the Dzhurin residents—blood-drenched bank notes and some gold coins. Although the "colony office" in Dzhurin is organized as required, with a bookkeeper, a cashier, and all kinds of receipts and forms, on this occasion they permitted themselves not to write down the sum anywhere. They imposed a gag order regarding the value of the treasure and they firmly ordered the rabbi and the Dzhurin functionaries to keep it a secret. One hour later, the colony chief, Moshe Katz, and Bobi Rosenrauch were already escorting the treasure to Shargorod. The three principal movers and shakers spent the night in Shargorod and the next day they returned to the camp with two good tidings: first, the overlords demonstrated immeasurable goodwill and did us the great favor of accepting the money, even though it was well below what they expected (100,000 marks); second, the native residents of Dzhurin, at least most of them, may allow themselves to prepare a fat kugel for *Shabbes*, because it seems that they will not be deported soon, unless a new decree is issued ...[188] They hope to fulfill their duty by dooming only 5 percent, because a general exemption is impossible ...

188 This case of bribery, of ransom money paid to prevent the deportation of Jews from the ghettos, is one of many instances that illustrate the unique nature of the case of Transnistria—the general disorder that prevailed among the Romanian government officials, bureaucrats, and soldiers, together with the appetite for bribes and payments that were the accepted norm among Romanian officials, military personnel, and all elements of the authorities. These two factors, which proved more dominant than the Romanian antisemitic ideology, created "cracks" in the regulations and instructions established by the government in the framework of the policy toward the Jews. These "cracks" had implications for the daily lives of the Jews in the ghettos, because the Jewish leaders were able to maneuver between them in their efforts to improve the living conditions in the ghettos and to consolidate aid and rescue strategies for the deported Jews. It should be noted that individuals and families who arrived in the ghettos who had the means could also maneuver within this narrow space and obtain a permit to remain in the ghettos or, alternatively, to avoid misfortunes, such as deportation, punishment, or any other caprice of the Romanian rulers.

And another honey cake was presented to the "lords" of Dzhurin: they alone will decide who will be deported. Particularly regarding the Jews who come from the non-kosher areas—Bessarabia and Northern Bukovina—if only for now, they will be exempt from deportation. As for the future, God is the Father and the praetor is a Tatar [fortune teller] …

This bundle of good news illuminated the gloom in the camp, as though we heard the *shofar*[189] blows heralding the messiah's arrival. Everyone is sure that he will not be included in the unfortunate 5 percent who will be designated for the new deportation. It is strange how the deeper you are in the ground, the stronger your faith becomes. It does not occur to anyone to fling the *get*[190] at the feet of the Master of the Universe and renounce this small plot of the beautiful world …

[July 27, 1942] 10 P.M.

Even though I was once closely associated with the press, it was never in my nature to eavesdrop to discover the secrets of strangers. In Transnistria, where the less you know the better, this tendency of mine has certainly not changed. However, I just happened to find out about the sum of the ransom, even though I did not strain my ears to learn this secret. A certain resident of Dzhurin, my best friend and a functionary himself on the ransom committee, came to visit me an hour ago to sniff out if the council members are telling the whole truth regarding the rescinded decree. He assumes, he informed me, that even though I do not have the great honor of belonging to the seven lords of the town (his own words …),[191] I nevertheless may catch a word in the community building that is not intended for an outsider's ears, and he added in these words: "Is it conceivable that our last bone marrow has been sucked dry, and we will be left beaten and discarded? A trifle: 47,000 marks in cash, about three

189 A horn of an animal, usually a ram, used in modern Judaism during Rosh Hashana and at the end of Yom Kippur.

190 Jewish divorce papers.

191 B. Megillah 27. The expression "seven nobles of the town" refers to the officials who were managing the city for the benefit of the residents.

dozen gold coins, three pocket-watch chains of pure gold, and a gold, antique goblet ..."

In truth, I could not swear by my *talis* and *kitel*[192] that the committee members have not deceived [the community], God forbid, and, therefore, I could only offer words of comfort. Well, someone else in Dzhurin already knows how much our bone marrow amounted to. It remains concealed from me and those like me who choked on the bloody Jewish possessions, and what diabolical mind thought up this *Purim* game, which was so profitable for him. There is no secret that will not at some point surface like oil on water, but who will live to see that! ...

July 28, 1942, 6 A.M

Today is the eleventh birthday of my only son Bertl. Today is also a Tuesday, just like the day when early that radiant morning he slipped into God's beautiful little world. How different then and now are! It seems to me that my life then was someone else's, and that I, Roza, Iza, Bertl, Mother, and Rivka have always been roaming around among the ruins of Ukraine, wearing rags, chopping wood, dragging pails of water from the rusty pump to the top of the hill, and sleeping on hard boards without a mattress. Did we really once use a fork and a napkin and, as opposed to now, a toilet like ordinary people, instead of a latrine with masses of tormented and mortified men and women?[193]

What once was is becoming increasingly vague from day to day, and even in dreams, the old country rarely visits. Can the past ever be revived?

---

192 A white cotton or linen robe worn by some Orthodox Jews on Rosh Hashana, Yom Kippur, and at the Passover Seder, that is also used as a burial shroud.

193 The deportees came mostly from places in which the living conditions were adequate, with running water and toilets in their homes. However, the inhabitants of Transnistria, including the Jews, lived in shtetls and mainly in villages where the conditions were very poor. The houses had no running water and therefore no toilets, and the residents used to relieve themselves by the river, or even in the streets. The matter of relieving themselves and public toilets comes up in the diary and in most of the survivors' testimonies and memoirs. This demonstrates the cultural and mental gap between the local Jews and the deportees.

[July 28, 1942] 3 P.M.

Today before noon, it was extremely dark even though the July sun demonstrated what it could do, burning at 30 degrees [Celsius].[194] The darkness did not come from the outside but rather was invoked by one of the sources of evil from Moghilev, Prefect [Constantin] Năsturaş[195] himself. This oppressor, who causes the Jews to shudder with fear, suddenly appeared in the camp, accompanied by a band of minions, including the gendarmerie commander from Dzhurin, Floreanu. Of course, he did not [come] to pay homage to the Yids, God forbid, and he did not enter the community building but remained outside and began shouting, why are the houses and ruined hovels not freshly whitewashed, why are there no paved sidewalks, why isn't there a single corner that gleams and sparkles as in a pharmacy, and why doesn't the camp look like a clinic.

Enraged like Esau, he decreed that "order" must be imposed in the camp within ten days, otherwise he would drive out all 4,000 Jews from the paradise of Dzhurin. He topped it off by issuing an additional decree: the Jewish typhus hospital for typhus patients, which is located in a state building (that once housed a Ukrainian school), must be evacuated and moved to the ghetto.

The decree of evacuating the hospital is completely impractical, because there is no place in the camp to insert a pin. Today, twenty

---

194 Eighty-six degrees Fahrenheit.

195 Colonel Constantin Năsturaş, a radical antisemite and poet who wrote under the pen name Poiană Volbura, was the second prefect of the district of Moghilev from May 1942 to April 1943. Năsturaş was active in expelling the Jewish workers from the factories and replacing them with Ukrainians from other locations. In a memorandum that he sent to the authorities of the districts and towns, as well as to the gendarmerie legion, he claimed that while at the outset of the industrial development there was a need for Jewish professionals, now it no longer made any sense to employ more to hold on to them, emphasizing that implementing his instructions was a matter of "national honor." In another document, he claimed that "we will remain here with the Ukrainians and not with the Jews." Presumably these words hint at his ambition to "purify" Moghilev of Jews. However, it was not possible to dispose of the Jewish professionals and experts, who remained until the arrival of the Soviets. The two large deportations to Skazinets and Pechora took place during Năsturaş' tenure. See Carp, *Cartea neagră,* vol. 3, pp. 355, 361; CNSAS, I-329788.

patients are hospitalized, all of them ill with typhus. The plague, which raged from winter to spring, has not yet completely subsided. Doctors think that it will flare up again in the autumn. Typhus is spread by lice and, therefore, the lethal Rickettsia bacteria thrive in cold and wet conditions, when the people wrap themselves up in rags, allowing the lice to settle in.

If Dzhurin earned the title "model colony," which the non-Jewish overlords in Shargorod and Moghilev awarded it in appreciation for the community's efforts, it is, after all, thanks to the hospital, which they set up with their bare hands, literally out of nothing. The hospital, however, possesses a treasure that is worth more than money: doctors, student-orderlies, and nurses who work with devotion day and night for no payment other than a loaf of bread. They endanger their lives constantly and fight a stubborn war against invisible bacteria. Whenever a sick person is discovered, he is taken directly to the hospital, and his home and possessions are disinfected. A primitive disinfecting apparatus was brought from Moghilev, and its tin-plated chimney continuously emits black smoke. Its boiling pot is always filled with clothes, underwear, and rags. If only the same could be said of the pot in the soup kitchen but full of beans and millet, of course! …

Thanks to the dedicated staff of the hospital, headed by the zealous and wise Dr. Moshe Greiff, the plague has not spread in Dzhurin as much as it has, for example, in Shargorod (more than 1,500 victims to date) or in Moghilev (6,000 victims). The council has offered its assistance to enable the hospital's lifesaving activities, despite the chronic conflict with Dr. Greiff, due to the personal ambitions of a number of the "lords," which overshadow the relations between the council and the hospital.

Some of the medicines come from the central [council] of Jewish communities in Romania, which sends them to the Central Council of Jews in Moghilev for the various camps in this region. The Central Council distributes the medicines as it sees fit, according to its sense of justice; some receive more and some less, and this allocation is completely inadequate. Therefore, whatever is lacking must be purchased in cash in Moghilev, mainly injections to strengthen the heart and to fortify the patients' resilience. At present, there is no medicine that cures typhus, and we must content ourselves with strengthening the ailing body, and whoever is blessed to live many years overcomes the threatening disease. The Rickettsia bacteria usually cause impairment for life: damage to the heart, kidneys, gastric problems, nerves …

Allow me to point out that the local Dzhurin Jews are immune to typhus for this reason: the plague has always been like a member of the household in these areas, and every resident of Dzhurin has already had chicken pox, measles, and … typhus. The Rickettsia bacteria never return to a previous dwelling. Therefore, the deportees from Romania have indeed borne the brunt of it—a punishment for maintaining cleanliness in the old country …

The prefect and his gang departed directly, and the bewildered council members began to rack their brains regarding what to do now. Less than a quarter of an hour had passed when screams and wails were suddenly heard through the open windows. A Jewish militiaman entered the community building, confused and stammering that the gendarmerie commander Floreanu had just reappeared in the camp with a whip in his hand and had burst into the apartments of the Jews, cruelly beating anyone he found, even the elderly and the children. He intends to settle accounts with the negligent Yids, he bellows, as his eyes dart around in murderous rage.

Indeed, the murderer immediately entered the community building like a storm, obviously without saying good morning, and roared, foaming at the mouth, that he will show the pack of Yids what he knows how to do. He will shoot them all someday, or at least chase all of them over the Bug to the SS men. He announced two decrees on the spot and threatened a death sentence for anyone who does not obey them. First, all men, including boys, ages fifteen and up, must gather at the square opposite the gendarmerie every morning, escorted by militiamen. There he [Floreanu] himself will select the men he needs to work here or outside [the camp]. And second, he absolutely prohibits anyone from standing by the door or looking out the window. Whoever dares to defy the order can expect a bullet. Apart from this, he will limit the time that the cursed Yids may leave their homes and he will teach them some manners. In his rage, spittle dribbled from his mouth, and not one of the "lords" dared say a word.

It is clear that the oppressor [Floreanu] decided to take advantage of the prefect's order by striking fear into the council members in the heat of the moment in order to extort a large bribe. His scheme was successful, and it will be to the detriment of the soup kitchen and the hospital. Even if the decrees will be rescinded, we have all been reminded where we are and that we were not sent to Dzhurin to enjoy ourselves …

July 29, 1942, 7 A.M.

And so it was. Yesterday afternoon, someone from the council approached the post chief [commander of the gendarmerie] Floreanu with a request and then asked in passing how many men he would require to work the following day. We usually ask this every afternoon in order to prepare the requisite number of workers for the following morning. Floreanu muttered under his breath, "fifty" and did not mention again assembling near the gendarmerie [post]. Well, the camp rejoiced in this miracle that cost a fortune. We have learned to savor the moment without considering the price.

The black cloud hanging over our camp has not yet dissipated. We have been forewarned that on Thursday, July 30 [1942], no Jew should dare appear in the streets, because a group of Romanian officers will arrive at the gendarmerie [post] for some kind of gathering. Although the danger of deportation has been deferred for the time being by means of the ransom money, there is a danger of evicting [the Jews] from the factory quarter[196] and of further overcrowding the already crammed, suffocating camp. There is a sheaf of unknown dangers that have not yet been named but that appear unexpectedly in all sorts of forms. The pleasant summer that prevails outside pours salt on the painful wounds. Gloomy surroundings might have eased the heaviness of the darkness within.

196 This refers to the people of means from Southern Bukovina who were allowed to live in the houses of Ukrainians.

July 30, 1942, 7 P.M.

In the camp, people were gripped with dreadful fear about this Thursday but, as they say: nothing is as black as we fear, or as white as we hope. The color gray is somewhere in-between as, for example, is also true of today's gray Thursday.

The *Lagernikes* got a taste of prison today, but no one was hurt within the confines of their 4 cubits. As of last night and until this evening, no Jew was permitted to set foot in the streets, and it was also strictly forbidden to stand by the door, or to look out the window. We have already mentioned the prohibition of going to one of the three public latrines. The alleys looked like a cemetery, but the odors notably reminded us that the huts were inhabited by living creatures with vital needs …

The officers met at the gendarmerie building where the guests, together with the gendarmes, celebrated with a feast fit for a king—with Jewish foods, Jewish tableware, Jewish pastries, and … Jewish money. The council was relieved, because yesterday the [gendarmerie] commander Floreanu had ordered the community to make the preparations for this revelry. They considered this a good indication that the fateful Thursday would pass without tribulations. It was not a waste of money …

The *Lagernikes* fully complied with the order and did not stick even the tip of their noses outside, although the sun was blazing and we were really suffocating in the gloomy mouseholes. Everyone remembered all that had happened on Tuesday when Floreanu conducted a pogrom in the Jews' apartments. We know that he injured exactly thirty-two Jews. Some of them are so traumatized and broken that they are lying with fever on their wooden bunks or on the floor. The murderer thrashed the skull of a two-year-old infant with a whip, and the doctors fear that he will not survive the concussion. His mother—Gitel Sapasnik—a deportee from Hotin,[197] was holding the baby in her arms when Floreanu whipped her and "unwillingly" struck the infant.

---

197 The Jews of Hotin, a town in Bessarabia, were expelled from their homes as early as the summer of 1941, following a pogrom conducted by the peasants from the surrounding areas and the Romanian gendarmes who had invaded Bessarabia at the outbreak of Operation Barbarossa, and the retreat of the Soviet army. The Soviets ruled Bessarabia for only one year, 1940–1941, in the framework of the Ribbentrop–Molotov

The chickens were released from their cages an hour ago and, in a flash, the alleys immediately became black with a throng of people. Shouting to one another, they related the miracles and wonders, and how they had managed to get through that Thursday unscathed, confined to their cages. The clamor of the crowd, which was as noisy as in the women's section on *Yom Kipper* when the Torah scroll is taken out, mingled with the grating cries of Dzhurin's "merchants," youngsters who tried to make at least a small profit in the course of an hour—"matches," "cigarettes," "candy," "almonds." Before the people managed to relate the wonders, the Jewish militia drove them back to the hovels, because the hands of the clock mercilessly pointed to the fateful hour of the curfew—7 P.M.

Today, the council functionaries, including me, had the privilege of going out in the streets—to work and back. As I passed through the vacant alleys, I was struck with fear and I ran the short distance to the community building, like an arrow shot from a bow. The council itself was peaceful and calm today. There was no one to deport and, of course, no one to beat. This respite backfired on me: as a result of their idleness, my bosses picked on me and I became the chicken for *kapporres* for the entire holy community.

At about 3 P.M., a guest of our own arrived at the community building, Poldi Knobler,[198] one of the big shots in Moghilev. He is a member of the Moghilev Central Council and a good friend of the Romanian overlords. He handles all kinds of small business transactions for them. One of "his" overlords indeed brought him along to the party at the gendarmerie [post] in Dzhurin today. The news that Knobler conveyed—and if one can believe him—was not very cheering.

First, he informed us that 3,000 people will be deported from Moghilev to the camps next to the Bug. There are too many Jews in the holy city of Moghilev and too few in the death camps of Pechora, Tulchin, Vapnyarka, etc.

---

pact that divided Europe into spheres of influence under Nazi Germany and Russia. After the massacre of the Jews of Hotin, the remnants were deported from their homes and wandered on the roads for many weeks. Some survivors of these convoys managed to reach Dzhurin, among other places.

198 Poldi Knobler was one of the directors of Orphanage No. 1 in the Moghilev ghetto.

Second, the 3,000 deported Jews who are suffering in the camp of Kopaygorod, about 50 kilometers from Moghilev, have been afflicted by severe hardships and their lives are hanging by a thread. A few days ago, on July 21 [1942], all of them, children and adults, were driven from their wretched, crowded dwellings to a nearby forest, where they are roaming under the open skies, dying of hunger and thirst, dropping like flies. The forest is surrounded by Romanian soldiers and Ukrainian militiamen, and a machine gun is positioned every 100 meters. Five Jews who tried to slip out of the forest to obtain some food have already been shot. When the autumn rains will begin to fall, no refugee and no trace of the Jews will remain in the forest.[199]

The third of the good tidings: they will soon begin to implement the order to establish ghettos surrounded by barbed-wire fences throughout Transnistria. In places where it is not possible to create a ghetto, for whatever reason, the Jews will be sent to the Bug.

In general, in the "lucky" region of Moghilev, it is increasingly cheerful …

August 1, 1942, 7 A.M.

The delightful summer is going by and the second winter in Dzhurin is approaching slowly. We can already imagine what this means, because we

---

199 On July 5, 1942, Orăsanu, the commander of the gendarme legion of Moghilev, ordered the expulsion of all the Jews of Kopaygorod, who were taken to a transitional camp of sorts in the nearby forest. Only the heads of the Jewish committee, Jewish policemen, and their families remained in the town. The camp was surrounded by a double barbed-wire fence, and Jews who were caught outside it without permission were executed. Hundreds of Jews died in the camp due to the terrible conditions and the food shortages. The German officer Hans Meitert brutally commanded the camp during the first few days, although he had no official authority to do so. Not long after their deportation to the camp, young people, skilled workers, and doctors were returned to the ghetto of Kopaygorod. Using bribes, they succeeded in providing food to the people in the camp. In September 1942, those who survived the camp were returned to the ghetto. See Lavi, *Pinkas Hakehilot*: *Rumania*, vol. 1, pp. 501–502; David Keisch testimony, YVA, O.3/13166. After the war, Orăsanu was sentenced to twenty-five years of penal servitude; see CNSAS, P-7795, file 1; Alexander Spiegelblatt, *Miba'ad Le'enit Hasha'an* (Hebrew) (Jerusalem: Carmel, 2017), pp. 146–193. For more details, see the entry of August 8, 1942, 8 P.M.

ourselves experienced the first winter in these wretched living quarters, in hovels without windowpanes and often without a stove and without a splinter of wood. Most people do not have blankets, and their limbs freeze in the endless winter nights as the howling snowstorms and the biting cold rage outside.

The coming winter is likely to be even more dreadful, because the miserable rags with which the people have wrapped themselves are already falling apart, or have been exchanged for a loaf of bread or 1 pood of potatoes. Deprivation has significantly weakened the body and diminished its ability to endure the cold and hunger. When deliverance comes, who knows if a living Jew will be found to rescue between the Dniester and the Bug after a second winter!

[August 1, 1942] 8 P.M.

Tomorrow is Sunday, the weekly market day. Will the peasants dare to show up with their goods at the market, where they are subject to pogroms by the gendarmes?[200]

I still have some money in my pocket and the few marks must suffice for 1 pood of potatoes, a bunch of onions and, if it is really cheap, also for a cup of cheese. The rest of the goods are not meant for me and those like me.[201] My wages barely suffice for half a month, and I dare not ask for a raise, even though I toil from dawn until late at night, am subjected to humiliation, and often find myself in danger. The community couriers receive the same salary that I receive. A raise in my salary by only 50 measly marks would amount to smoking a cigarette for the community

---

200 The local rural peasants brought their goods to the market in Dzhurin, exchanging them for the possessions of the Jews that they had brought with them from Romania. At a later stage, when the Jews no longer had anything left to trade, it was possible to buy the produce for rubles or marks used in the occupied territories. The Romanian regime harassed the local Ukrainians, stole their produce, and did not hesitate to overturn their stalls, expelling them from the market with batons and blows, and preventing them from making a living.

201 Most of the deportees had hardly any money or goods to purchase or to trade for the products that the Ukrainian peasants brought to the market. However, as noted in other places, there were enough people with means to buy the goods.

treasury. They throw money around like mud, often where it is not needed, and yet there is nothing to grope for in my pockets. The doctor would enjoy throwing me out. He does not like me for a number of reasons: I am not from Suceava. I do not lick his boots and sing songs of praise about him, and he, the German assimilationist, does not like my Jewish behavior, or that I speak only Yiddish. He has often made it clear to me that he would like to replace me. There is no shortage of volunteers, especially among his close associates from Suceava …

August 2, 1942, 6 A.M.

Since Friday, July 31 [1942], everyone is concerned with issue of the ghetto, which has caused a terrible commotion in the shtetl. The commander of the gendarmerie *Feldwebel* Floreanu suddenly appeared at the community building with some news: At the gathering of the officers the other day, he was ordered to set up a ghetto in Dzhurin without delay. He is thinking of carrying out the order today and, in a shrill voice, he suddenly roared: "The Yids have lived a pleasant life here long enough, and this must come to an end. I will reduce the present ghetto on the hill by half and, what's more, I will also move the 200 families from the factory quarter there."

The "lords" began to implore the commander to postpone the implementation of the order for a few days and not to reduce the area of the ghetto. They pleaded with him to grant someone from the council an "audience," and he, may his name be blotted out, understood what that means … his anger eventually subsided and they managed to persuade him that for the time being all the deportees could stay on the hill as they have until now. However, the 200 families in the factory quarter must move to the ghetto today. Another Dzhurin miracle! …

Only an hour later, a respectable delegation led by the second-in-command, Moshe Katz, went to the gendarmerie, obviously with "the rewards of divination in their hand" (not empty-handed).[202] Of course,

202 Numbers 22:7: "And the elders of Moab and the elders of Midian departed with the rewards of divination in their hand."

this was the main intention of the corrupt Floreanu. The deal did in fact cost a fortune, but the delegates got their way. The ghetto will indeed be set up, but only in ten days, when the commander returns from his vacation. Until then, no one will move from his spot, not even those in the "factory quarter." Well, in the course of ten days, something might happen—either the dog will die, or the overlord ... In the meantime, those in the factory quarter will try to look for "apartments" on the hill, where there is no place to insert a pin.

At the community building, they began to diligently register apartments. The people from the factory quarter stormed the community building, straining to grab the best dwellings—for the most part they are well-connected people with respectable [sums in their] pockets, because otherwise they would not have been able to settle in the Ukrainian quarter on the other side of the river. Pleading, quarreling, and shouting have ensued, women with babies in their arms are pleading that no new tenants be placed in their crowded apartments, and a gang of wheeler-dealers who have close ties with the inner circle of the "lords" are whispering in their ears to try to broker good apartments. In the "Housing Office," they came up with a plan to uproot families, to tear them from their poor cubbyholes and squeeze them into mass quarters to make room for the aristocrats from the factory quarter. It is sad that the poorest of the poor will bear the brunt of the bitter fate of wandering, if it comes to this. There are no secrets in Dzhurin, and the camp is in complete turmoil.

Yesterday, *Shabbes*, the deputy commander of the local gendarmerie (Floreanu has gone on holiday; if only he were already on his way back ...) notified the council that the inhabitants of the factory quarter must evacuate by Wednesday, even before Floreanu returns. The meaning is clear: This non-Jew also wants to make a profit. The community will also have to feed this leech with Jewish property. In the meanwhile, the ghetto has been seized by panic that only continues to escalate.

August 8, 1942, 6 A.M.

The crowd of the factory quarter began to move out before being driven out in panic any day now. The Housing Office settled them in "kosher" apartments on the hill. They housed the new tenants in the mouseholes, regardless of whether or not there is room for them to lay their heads. Yet, because it is summer, the pampered ones have the choice of sleeping outside.

They evacuated around 2,000 persons from Shargorod to villages in the surroundings this morning, and we fear that Dzhurin will also be included in this round of deportations. The council in Shargorod compiled a list of the 2,000 candidates for deportation and even informed them that they may begin preparing to depart. The panic that has seized Shargorod is incredible, and there are militiamen stationed around the community building to prevent anyone from approaching and to protect the "lords" from the onslaught.

[August 8, 1942] 2 P.M.

From the day that the oppressor Floreanu went on vacation, there is a prevailing sense of relief in the camp. People dare to appear in the streets beyond the permitted hours. Some young people even sneak out to take a brief dip in the creek that borders the factory quarter. Not even a turkey could drown in the creek but, nevertheless, it has a little cool water.

[August 8, 1942] 8 P.M.

Moghilev council member Poldi Knobler, who previously had brought the news about the mass catastrophe in Kopaygorod, did not exaggerate. Today a young man who slipped out of the forest arrived from there, and he related details that made our hair stand on end. At the beginning of July, almost 3,000 Jews, mainly deportees from Bukovina, were living in wretched conditions in Kopaygorod. This is the number of the remaining remnant out of 6,000 people, because half of them died last winter from hunger, cold, typhus, and neglect. There is in fact a council, just like there is among respectable people, headed by a lawyer Ricu Kupferberg.[203] However, the local leaders did not at all concern themselves with the deported Jews, did not set up a soup kitchen or hospital, and did not extend assistance to anyone but only looked out for themselves and for their relatives.

A few weeks ago, a German officer suddenly arrived unexpectedly, having been appointed to some government function here. This German undertook to evacuate the shtetl and make it "*Judenrein*," with the approval of the local praetor. He carried out this diabolical plan on July 21 [1942]. That day, the oppressor walked past a synagogue and heard the voices of Jews who were praying fervently. The officer burst into the holy place, brandishing a whip, and began whipping the worshipers. You have the gall, he roared, to hold a Bolshevik meeting to plan an attack on the German army! I will tell the prefect in Moghilev immediately what the Jewish bandits are planning in Kopaygorod … you will hear from me in three hours.

The council allowed the fateful three hours to pass without doing anything. In fact, the colony chief, Ricu Kupferberg, did not sit idly by for those 180 minutes. On the contrary, he tried to persuade the praetor that he and his family, and some of those close to him and the wealthy should remain, if the prefect orders an expulsion. The praetor did him a favor because, of course, there is more than enough community money … (**Added in 1947**: Ricu Kupferberg, the uncrowned king of the Kopaygorod camp, was put on trial for war crimes for his good deeds by a Romanian tribunal after the liberation).[204]

---

203 At the beginning of 1942, the local gendarmes in the town established a Jewish council, headed by Kupferberg, and the Jewish police. The council was to provide the gendarmes with manpower for forced labor. Many Jews were sent outside the town to pave roads and to work in agriculture. Those who managed to survive in the camp returned to the town in September 1942. A ghetto was established in the former Jewish quarter of the town, surrounded by a barbed-wire fence, and all the remaining Jews, about 2,500 people, were gathered there in terrible overcrowding. The new council included regional representatives who were chosen by the Jews according to their place of origin. Fabius Ornstein from Vijnița was chosen as head of the council.

204 Baruch Rostwecker testimony, YVA, O.3/1732.

Three hours had elapsed when major [Colonel Năsturaş] of the gendarmes in Moghilev appeared in the shtetl with a gang of armed soldiers to carry out the expulsion. Like wild beasts, the gendarmes ran from apartment to apartment and drove all the people into the market square. In some cases, the persecuted were not allowed to take anything at all with them. Only the colony chief, the council members, and their relatives were allowed to do so. When the entire population was gathered, everyone was driven into the forest, about 5 kilometers from the shtetl. Empty barracks from the time of the tsar are still standing there, and 500 persons were crammed into them, even though there is not room for even half of that number. The majority, however, is roaming around outside and lying on the damp ground.

No one offers the people even a slice of bread, and their only source of sustenance is what the peasants in the area secretly bring—a potato or a loaf of bread—for the price of gold, passing the food through the barbed wire that encloses the forest prison. Whoever has a mark survives somehow, and the rest become swollen from hunger. Every day, they dig a mass grave for the victims. The camp is surrounded by armed Ukrainian militiamen, who shoot anyone who dares set foot outside to bring a cup of water from a spring that is 3 kilometers away. Thirst is even more unbearable than hunger, and not a few miserable persons endangered their lives trying to bring water for a thirsty baby or an exhausted, elderly mother. Those who ran the risk did not return.[205]

August 26, 1942, 2 P.M.

Almost three weeks have passed since the last entry, and they have been very hot, in both senses of the term. A ghetto already has been set up in Dzhurin, right down to the last detail, *in a guter sho*! More than 600 persons have moved from the non-Jewish quarter and settled in the kosher alleys on the hill. Anyone who was able to manage to snatch a hovel for

---

205 For a description of the deportation of the Jews of Kopaygorod to the death camp in the nearby village, see Lavi, *Pinkas Hakehilot*: *Rumania*, vol. 1, pp. 501–502; David Keisch testimony, YVA, O.3/13166.

rent remained there. Those who relied on the evenhandedness of the Housing Office and without connections have been lodged in ruins and cowsheds, or in mass housing where dozens of people had been crammed in already.

Mother and Rivka had the privilege of living in an alley close to the factory quarter, which was actually within the area of the camp but which, nevertheless, was declared off-limits by the post chief, Floreanu. Despite my urgent efforts, I was not able to find a small room that was suitable for them on the hill and we were forced to move into a hovel without doors and windows. However, I was then miraculously able to find a tiny room in the home of a non-Jew at the edge of the ghetto—in a neutral neighborhood, neither kosher nor non-kosher. The small house, really a kitchenette, is in good condition, with doors and windows, and clean surroundings. Until the war, the house had belonged to a Jew, who evacuated with the Red Army a year ago. A peasant immediately grabbed the house and became the landlord. He has two Jewish tenants who are charged rent.

In order to rub salt into the wounds, the post chief, Floreanu, has just now announced that he is allowing those evicted from the factory quarter to resettle in three alleys in that quarter. He offers this like sweets to a corpse after ritual cleansing, since the factory quarter is already completely "*Judenrein*." None of the [evicted] inhabitants from the factory quarter intends to move out of his new mousehole and to rely on Floreanu's sense of decency. People fear that, as a result of the overcrowding in the ghetto, typhus will flare up this year even more sharply than it did last year. What good is fear at this point! … The plague has stopped completely since the beginning of August, thanks to the summer, which allows people to keep their bodies clean.

As for the danger of expulsion, it is very quiet in Dzhurin, and no one knows whether the decree has indeed been rescinded as a result of the ransom payments. They expelled several hundred persons from Shargorod, mainly from the northern Moldavian city of Dorohoi—the poorest of the poor. Some families escaped and managed to sneak into the Dzhurin paradise. Until they were registered in the list of the "fortunate ones" of Dzhurin, it was not so easy for them. Of course, no places were prepared for them—so they crammed into overcrowded cowsheds and cellars.

There have also been thin rays of light in the past three weeks. For example, the doors of the soup kitchen reopened after being shut for some time. They even set up a second boiling pot that would suffice to make 800 portions of soup. A few dozen needy individuals—children and the ill—receive a fourth of a loaf of bread to supplement the soup. As the French say: sometimes something good results from a sorrow.[206] During the panic triggered by the expulsion, the wealthy loosened their purse strings a little more—some willing, some indignantly—and the community coffers were restored a bit.[207] However, what is the value of these fortunate instances when the lion's share of the community funds disappears, because "I will appease him with the present,"[208] and the lust [for riches] of the leeches only continues to grow. They have become much too accustomed to bribery, these Romanian bloodsuckers, and now we have no choice. All day long, messengers from the gendarmes run around with lists [of goods] at the expense of the community—ranging from delicacies to expensive clothes and furs for the Ukrainian prostitutes of the officers.

[August 26, 1942] 8 P.M.

Allow me to explain why I abandoned these pages for three weeks. One night, when I could not close my eyes, I read through my previous entries and fell into a deep depression because of the paucity of my memories. I realized that my pen was feeble and my brain had dried out, because

---

206 The expression that is closest in meaning to this in English is: "Every cloud has a silver lining."

207 Yehudit Nir interview by Sarah Rosen, February 15, 2011, Ramat Gan; Shlomo Shteinmetz interview by Sarah Rosen, January 17, 2010, Ramat Gan. Some of the deportees from Southern Bukovina who arrived in Dzhurin managed to bring some money and valuables with them. They were considered people of means and were required to pay taxes. Shteinmetz was one of the Jews to whom they turned for taxes and contributions.

208 Genesis 32:21; Jacob sought to appease Esau's anger with an offering. So too, the council funds were used as bribes and payments to appease the anger of the Romanian authorities and to annul decrees, such as the closure of the market on a whim, or the deportation of workers for forced labor.

otherwise I would have rendered a portrait of Transnistrian life as it really is, and not only vague impressions.

At first it seemed to me that this diary would write itself, because sensations literally roll around underfoot here, begging for mercy, just to be lifted up and preserved for future generations. Every Jew in this region has his own story, and he is the hero of a poignant tragedy that surpasses the imagination of Sophocles. However, it seems that every moment in Transnistria is so charged that it requires so much time and such a broad perspective that does not allow squeezing it into a few meager lines of a diary, recorded hastily, standing tensely on one foot. It may even be a sin to break the bloody chronicle of Transnistria into small change. The brutal and devastating material requires a different approach.

Therefore, I decided to stop writing the diary and to destroy the pages that I had written, which make me angry and resentful. I eventually overcame my despair and listened to the counterargument within me that claimed: a miracle may occur and your fragmentary writings may be the only remaining memory of Transnistria, and when it falls into the hands of someone who is more talented than you, that person will make it more digestible, as is fitting.

Hence the pages will continue to breathe with difficulty for now, but no one can guarantee their long life …

August 28, 1942, 7 P.M.

My friend, the *hazen* from Rădăuţi, Moshe Solomon, who noticed that the hearts of the people had been eased a little by the stream of miracles in Dzhurin, took advantage of this propitious moment. In short, yesterday he staged an artistic event in quite a respectable hall actually. The tenants of a spacious room in the former public school—a total of thirty-one persons—agreed to clear out their apartment for the duration of two hours, either for the sake of art, or for the sake of the [free] tickets.

I did not openly take part in the program to avoid provoking the doctor, who is irritated by Jewish performances in general (What will the non-Jews say! he argues), but I did indeed contribute to it. First, I lent my volume of children's stories by Sholem Aleichem[209]—the only Yiddish book in the camp. Second, I contributed a satirical poem, inspired by Bialik's "*Tomar Ehyeh Rav*" [Say I Will Be a Rabbi],[210] which in contrast offers a grotesque reflection of the cornerstones of Dzhurin. A young man from Vijniţa, Moshe Shneider, who also performed in Yiddish theater in the old country and who has artistic talent, recited the tale *Di Fon* [The Flag][211] and sang the poem in a familiar melody. I made sure that Shneider would not, God forbid, cite my name as the author, since this could be detrimental to me.

This time the fee was the usual one among respectable people, and not a potato or a splinter of wood, as it was during *Hanuke*: a half mark for grownups and half of this for children. I declined taking any part of the earnings, because I am, *ke'naynehore*, already a wealthy Jew with a monthly income of 100 marks. In contrast, Solomon doesn't come close to me in terms of wealth, even though he is occupied doing more jobs than I do. He prepares tombstones (how he came to this craft, I don't know? …) and he also sells old rags at the market. He is a rabbi (of young children …); a *hazen* (when he manages to get on a *bima*!):[212] an impresario; the Caruso of Dzhurin;[213] and the father of Arnold, who is also a budding Caruso.

The council members and their associates attended the performance, but not the colony chief. If I'm lucky, he will not know who wrote the song, which is far from a hymn to him.

Now here is the text of the poem, which merely presents documentation of the times with scant literary pretentions. I agree with the critics who want to make ash and dust of this "poetic masterpiece."[214]

---

209 Sholem Aleichem, *Kinder* (Yiddish) (Warsaw: n.p., 1951.)

210 Hayim Nahman Bialik, "Tomar Ehiye Rav," in Bialik, *Hashirim* (Or Yehudah: Dvir, 2005), pp. 400–402.

211 Sholem Aleichem, *Di fon* (Yiddish) (Vinipeg: Y. L. Perets shul, 1900); Aleichem, *Arba'a Siporim Leyladim*: *Ha'olar, Hasha'on, Hadegel, Ha'etrog* (Hebrew) (Tel Aviv: Sifri'at Po'alim, 1983).

212 In Ashkenazi synagogues, the bima, the raised platform where the prayer leader stands, is located at the front of the synagogue, close to the ark.

213 Enrico Caruso (1873–1921) is one of the most famous tenors in the history of opera.

214 This performance is also mentioned in the Shlomo Shteinmetz interview by Sarah Rosen, January 17, 2010, Ramat Gan. Shteinmetz relates that the school hall in which the

What Will Become of Me?

I'm trying to be a doctor
But no patients have I;
Perhaps a pharmacist,
After all, I'm a clever guy.

Refrain:
Oy, what trouble, oy, how black,
My trousers are made of sack
And no shirt covers my torso,
A wife I certainly have though,
A dozen children, not a few,
And a mother-in-law too.

I want to be a broker,
But I'm not cut out for stealing;
Here in the shtetl of Dzhurin,
Nature is really grueling.

(Refrain)

I run to be a matchmaker,
Everyone laughs at me;
Today brides and grooms
Matchmakers themselves they can be.

(Refrain)

---

performance took place was packed with Jews, and that it was a moment of joy in their bitter daily lives. See also the Fritzi Salner testimony, YVA, O.3/VT/8790.

I'm considering a butcher's shop,
A butcher I wish to be.
A group of young butchers lament nonstop,
Their condition is quite gloomy.

(Refrain)

There is no way to earn a living,
People cry and complain.
So then can a butcher too
The truth not proclaim?

(Refrain)

I apply myself to commerce,
But there are no buyers with whom to trade;
Perhaps I'll become a thief?
Of that, I am too afraid.

(Refrain)

If I want to cook some soap,
The militia does not allow it;
The community has a cartel;
Under orders, it must be guarded.

(Refrain)

I ask for alms;
Come back tomorrow! they say.
I ask for a loan,
But empty-handed I'm sent away.

(Refrain)

I rush to the soup kitchen
For some bean soup to take.
Our kitchen's dishes throughout the world
A name for themselves they did make.

(Refrain)

Without a note,
No soup can I get,
Because I am wealthy,
And my livelihood is set.

(Refrain)

It is possible to get a note,
But entails too great a trial;
Hunger sorely torments me,
My stomach is dry for quite a while.

(Refrain)

The colony chief I became,
For I had no other choice,
To guard the people of Israel
Against transgression and vice.

(Refrain)

Still it's better than nothing,
Although it doesn't pay well;
Just a bit of respect,
As far as I can tell …

(Refrain)

But only in my dreams
Is this respect mine.
When awake, I am nothing;
For deliverance, I pine.

(Refrain)

What will become of me?
I ask myself, wondering,
And my desperate heart
Is almost exploding …

(Refrain)

August 30, 1942, 2 P.M.

Today a survivor from the Kopaygorod forest arrived in the ghetto. He is from my hometown and a good friend, and he is not just anybody: he was the district rabbi from my hometown, Rădăuţi, Rabbi Israel Hornik.[215] His relatives from Moghilev managed to bribe a Ukrainian militiaman, one of the forest guards, and to save the rabbi and his wife. Immediately following their arrival, I ran to welcome them in the small hovel where the guests were housed, together with the three persons who were already living there.

Although we had parted only eight months before, I did not recognize the rabbi. Not only had the hair on his head and beard turned completely white (a year ago, he barely had any gray), but his whole mien and his morbid appearance really shocked me. Standing before me was a shriveled skeleton, skin and bones, without the strength to pronounce two words. He strained to whisper to me that he weighs a total of 35 kilos, having left

215 Rabbi Israel Hornik (1878–1948) was born in Zaleszczyki. He served as the rabbi of Vicov from 1900 and published many works on religious topics. Rabbi Hornik was a member of the rabbinate in Rădăuți from 1920. When the remnants of the Jews of Rădăuți returned to the city from Transnistria, he served as rabbi of the town. See Margalit-Postilnik, *Radauts*: *Kehila Yehudit Betzemihata Uvisheki'ata*, p. 38.

30 kilos behind in the forest as a memento. He added that if he recovers a little, he will not stop telling and retelling accounts about the death forest that are not at all fictitious.

The rabbi of Rădăuţi, a renowned genius and Torah scholar whose knowledge is encyclopedic, is an expert storyteller who also wrote a history of the Jewish community of my hometown of Rădăuţi, which was not printed due to the war. He brought this invaluable manuscript with him, carrying it with him and safeguarding it during the most dangerous of times.

I almost forgot: When I shook his hand to greet him, he asked me in a broken voice: You are a bit familiar to me, but what is your name? Before the deportation, we would meet and converse almost daily. Apart from that, the rabbi was gifted with a perfect memory (he could recall every tractate in the Talmud, the rulings in all kinds of books, citing not only the page but also the place on the page ...). So, if he did not recognize me, clearly ten months in Transnistria have indeed left their mark on my face ...

The greatest tribulation lies in the fact that Transnistria not only destroys the body but unmercifully corrupts the soul. The most refined sentiments wither, the little spirituality that remains vanishes, and a "reverse development" occurs, a regression to the level of a monkey that is aware of only his physiological needs. The main concern for everyone is a small loaf of bread, 1 pood of potatoes, a corner in mass living quarters, and the fear of expulsion, gendarmes, and the militia.

However, some of the deportees have even lost the will to live. They neglect themselves, sinking in filth, and they refuse to bother to go to the soup kitchen for a bowl of soup. They toss and turn for a while, flung down on a handful of rotten and stinking straw in some cowshed, until they release their tormented soul. They are then dragged to the cemetery without shrouds and without coffins, but this already, at the very least, does not bother them.[216]

---

216 These deportees were mostly those who had survived the decimation of the Jews of Bessarabia and Northern Bukovina, who were massacred in summer 1941, before the deportation. They arrived in Dzhurin destitute after endless wandering and marches on the roads. They constituted the weakest group in the new demographic system that was created in the ghetto by the arrival of the deportees. Having no money or means, they

By the way, funerals are nothing new in Dzhurin, and no one pauses when the members of the *Hevra Kadishe* pass by, carrying a corpse on a stretcher covered with a black covering from which stick-like feet protrude. The community decided some time ago to provide a longer covering that would cover the feet of the dead, but there is no cash available. Gendarmes cost less, alas, than the honor of a dead person …

Hundreds of abandoned persons are starving in the hallway of the large *bes medresh*, which people call the "synagogue poorhouse," waiting indifferently for the Angel of Death. Their number does not decline, even though not one day passes that the members of the *Hevra Kadishe* do not drag out "clients" on a burial stretcher, most of whom are from Hotin (Bessarabia), the poorest of the poor. So why does their number not decline? To this question you will get a clear answer from the Housing Office—the poorhouse is the last stop for the unfortunate people who refuse to maintain cleanliness and thus endanger the lives of those who live in close proximity to them. Therefore, the community conferred about this and decided to send them to the hallway of the *bes medresh*, where they can do no harm to anyone, because they are among people like themselves.

The truth is that the candidates for death in the poorhouse do not suffer from hunger. The soup kitchen provides them with soup and a portion of bread and, in addition to this, the distinguished rabbi of Dzhurin, Rabbi Herşel Karalnic, rivals traditional *tzdoke*:[217] with the help of some of the elders in Dzhurin, he collects food and clothes for the living dead, and lugs the loaded baskets himself. It is not enough for this legendary righteous man to feed these skeletons from Hotin, but he also sits with them in the filth and stench, conversing with them and striving to hearten these lost souls.

A strange fact: typhus does not have the upper hand in the poorhouse, and the Angel of Death uses other agents to trap victims in his claws. Doctors believe that the murderous Rickettsia bacteria is transmitted by

---

were unable to rent a place to live among the local Jews and therefore crowded into the local synagogue under terrible conditions. The description of these Jews recalls that of a *Muselman*—a German term widely used among concentration camp inmates to refer to prisoners who were near death due to exhaustion, starvation, or hopelessness.

217 Charity.

only one single louse, while millions of lice, which crawl all over the people and in every corner of the poorhouse, can do nothing, because the body gets accustomed to the disgusting, crawling vermin. The filth becomes an armor against typhus. Go fathom the secrets of nature! …

September 1, 1942

Three entire years have passed since that black Friday, September 1, 1939, when the radio broadcasts announced to the world that the catastrophe that all humanity feared, in particular the Jewish people, had begun. Everyone was notified then that early that morning, Hitler, may his name be blotted out, had ignited the fire of hell in Poland. Crushed and frightened, we, the Jews in Romania, and probably throughout Europe, sat crowded around the radio, straining to listen to the threatening news, which flowed like streams of glowing lava—news of destroyed cities, villages engulfed in flames, hordes of uprooted refugees, destruction, and annihilation.

The younger generation, who until then had not yet known the taste of war, did not understand the meaning of the menace now upon us as did we, the war veterans, who had lived through World War I in 1914–1918. It was clear to us, the veterans of war, that in the beginning it is greeted with cheerful cries and hopeful prophecies that foretell that within a few weeks the dove of peace will return and hover over God's beautiful little world, but gradually the Angel of Death settles in and establishes himself as landlord for many years. Sinking deeper and deeper into swamps of blood and tears, they count weeks at first, then months, and finally years that last forever. Finally, the Angel of Death becomes tired of brandishing his sword and fed up with the irritating labor. He then takes a vacation for a while, both in order to rest from the hard work and to allow the people to generate fresh live goods for his sword.

Thus, it pleased God to establish world order, ever since He created Cain and Abel and, apparently, thus it will continue to proceed as long as His beautiful little world exists. There has never been a lack of justifications for mass slaughters: whether carried out in honor of God, or in honor of God's appointed kings and counts, or to defend the sanctity of the fatherland, or to uphold the sublime teachings of Karl Marx, or to save the world from those teachings—the Angel of Death is always just …

This bloodthirsty madness has been raging for three full years, and millions of human beings have already been slaughtered, first and foremost the Jews. The demon who rules over the non-kosher people, the "writers and thinkers," has undertaken to annihilate all the Jews, old and young, as far as his *Stukas*[218] and armored vehicles can reach. He has already managed to capture most of Europe, where the majority of Jewry resides, and he has kept his word. At present, we do not know how many Jews have been murdered by the cruel oppressor so far, but one thing is certain: if some extraordinary miracle does not occur quickly, of the 7 million Jews in Europe, no remnant whatsoever will remain.

The madness of World War II will certainly come to an end as well. They will sign peace treaties and delude themselves, whoever survives until then, that there must be no more war—there will not be. Diplomats will lay out plans for eternal peace. Writers will flood the bookshop windows with pacifist musings and will brandish Isaiah's empty prophecy, "and they will beat their swords into plowshares."[219] They will show films with real images of massacres in the movie theaters, and everyone will be revolted by the heinous, mutual slaughter of human beings. At the same time, the seeds of the next war will slowly ripen in the depths of the depraved human soul once more. Both sides will find an excuse at the opportune time, and the wedding will begin once again from the beginning, with more guests and more abundant fare …

Nevertheless, there is some consolation, so to speak: one day people in this world will get along without the admonishments of a few persons—indeed we live in a period of rapid progress—and then there will be no more war …

However, for now, we are far from the conclusion. The fire rages from one end of the earth to the other. Millions are going up in flames like bales of hay, cities and countries are being destroyed overnight, and no one is trying to throw a bucket of water on the fire. During the first year

218 The Stuka—Sturzkampfflugzeug (dive-bomber) was used by the Luftwaffe (German air force) during World War II.

219 Isaiah 2:4.

of the war, Pope Pious XII stammered out a few words to quench the conflagration, but now silence prevails in every corner. Only the sounds of the explosions of all the bombs, the crashing of the weapons, the roaring of the murderers, and the death cries of their victims are heard. The goblet of tribulations is still far from full, and Jews still continue to gasp for air in Europe.

September 9, 1942

I can clearly see how this diary is dying—the intervals between one entry and the next are too long, like the breaths of a dangerously ill patient. I simply lack the desire to pick up the pen, and every incident seems to be trivial and not worth recording. People gradually get used to the situation, and the worm begins to become accustomed to his home in the horseradish. That's just how it must be and not otherwise, and it is a shoddy illusion that we were once people with names, with papers, with our own four walls, with the right to look a non-Jewish official in the eye and not flee from him as from the devil.

The Jews in the camp are now feverishly busy with the High Holy Days, the *minyonim*, the prayer leaders, and preparing delicacies, alas, for the holiday. This certainly allows us to forget for a moment where we are, where we were a year ago, and, especially, how we can vanish in the blink of an eye. Blessed be Pura,[220] the minister of oblivion—the only good angel who anoints the wounds of the Jews with a little balm!

As a result of the holiday gathering and because the peoples' senses have been dulled, news that arrived yesterday from Moghilev barely resonated. It concerns the shtetl Bar near the Bug.[221] Only Jews from

---

220 Pura is the angel responsible for forgetting; see S. [Semen Akimovich] An-ski (Shloyme Rapoport), "Hayei Adam," Ben Yehuda Project, https://benyehuda.org/ (accessed June 16, 2022). Shloyme Rapoport was also known by the pseudonyms S. Vid'bin, Z. Sinanni, and S. Sinani.

221 Bar, a small town in the Moghilev region, is around 60 kilometers southwest of Vinnitsa. In the fall of 1941, Jewish deportees from Bukovina who had been evicted from Moghilev were taken to Bar. These were mainly craftsmen. Jews in Bar were marked with a yellow badge and performed forced labor, clearing debris left by the bombings. In August 1942, the Germans carried out the first *Aktion*. Jews were shot to death with vicious cruelty, and

Bessarabia, about 500 persons, were sent there, where they were settled in the shabby huts of the Ukrainian Jews. They did not lack livelihoods—they worked in the fields for the farmers. There is no gendarmerie post in that place, however, there is a small problem: on the other side of the Bug, the area of the German occupation, camps of SS men are in full view.

So what, they [the Jews] thought: who is forcing us to look across the Bug! Today, there is no longer anyone in Bar to consider. A week ago, on *Shabbes*, the SS murderers decided to sail across the Bug in order to establish "German order" in neighboring Bar, which pertains to the Romanian area. On *Shabbes*, the non-kosher people knew that they would find the entire community at home, which would make it easier for them to carry out their plan. And so it was. Whoever was praying in the *bes medresh* and whoever was resting at home from the week of toil—no one was missing.

It took no more than an hour to drive the few Jews out of town, to order them to dig two long graves in a little forest, to line them up facing the open graves, and to shoot everyone with automatic weapons. The Ukrainian militia who showed up unexpectedly hauled the perforated bodies (not all of them were already [text missing][222]

They scattered withered leaves and dried twigs. The SS men sailed back over the Bug, and Bar was once again "*Judenrein*."

September 11, 1942

A day rarely goes by without someone arriving in Dzhurin after fleeing from the death camps near the Bug—Pechora, Tulchin, Vapnyarka, Cariera de Piatră,[223] and so on—mostly children from the ages of six to fourteen or fifteen, who set out relying on Divine Providence, even though they know very well that the Ukrainian militia ruthlessly

---

their bodies were cast into pits that had been dug in advance. See Lavi, *Pinkas Hakehilot: Rumania*, vol. 1, pp. 403–404.

222 The rest of the sentence is missing in the typed copy of the diary in our possession.

223 Cariera de Piatră (Stone Quarry) is the site of the stone quarries in the Tulchin region. See ibid., pp. 496–497.

shoot every Jew roaming along the dirt roads. Children manage better than adults, hiding in small forests or in meadows by day and wandering in the dark of night. An adult rarely dares to set foot outside surreptitiously.

The fortunate ones who manage to get out alive and come to Dzhurin arrive exhausted and tattered, without a shirt on their body, barefoot, and most with a sack around their loins instead of trousers. They first turn to the council, of course, where they beg to be registered as inhabitants of Dzhurin. They are rarely successful, however, because the "lords," especially the doctor, fear the danger of the gendarmes finding a non-kosher person on whom to prey in the camp. The truth is that they give the wanderers a shirt, a pair of trousers, sometimes a pair of old shoes, and equip them with provisions for the journey, but on one condition: that they continue their wanderings in the evening.[224]

Who can and who is permitted to determine the limit for saving a life? There is a discussion in the Talmud about this very question: A person is wandering in the desert and he has a small flask of water. Another wanderer who is dying of thirst approaches him. However, the dilemma is that the flask barely suffices for one person for one day. If they divide it, both wanderers will die of thirst. One sage believes, nevertheless, that they should divide it, and a second rules that it is preferable to save oneself, at the cost [in life] of the other. In Dzhurin, the "lords" believe that the second sage is right ...[225]

---

224 Throughout the entire period of the existence of the ghettos, many Jews sneaked into them, seeking refuge, including Jews fleeing from labor camps on the eastern bank of the Bug, such as Trikhaty, or from other camps such as Vapnyarka or Pechora. Moreover, many Jews also fled from villages, where they were concentrated in cowsheds or pigsties, and tried to find refuge in the ghettos where the conditions, in spite of everything, were less horrific. Some tried to reach the ghettos in order to be reunited with their nuclear or extended families. The Jewish councils were forbidden to shelter them, and thus the issue of the refugees became another difficulty with which the councils had to contend. Rosenstrauch, who feared the gendarmes, preferred to rescue the residents of the ghetto rather than to hide the refugees. And yet the ghettos were not hermetically sealed, and on many occasions the councils ignored this order, enabling significant numbers of refugees to integrate into the ghetto population. See Rosen, "Tzibur Veyahid," pp. 181–184.

225 B. Bava Metzia 62a: "If two are traveling on a journey, and one has a pitcher of water, if both drink they will die, but if only one drinks, he can reach civilization. The son of Patura taught: 'It is better that both of them drink and die, rather than that one should

By the way, it was possible to hide children somewhere in an attic, and no rooster would have crowed. Indeed, it has happened already more than once that those who fled from the camps, who unfortunately could not find the way to the community building, found refuge among warmhearted people and remained in Dzhurin. The gendarmes do not have a list of the people in the camp, and the partial lists in the community card catalog were not given at Sinai and thus may be completed—yes, if only they would ...

I often happen to have the opportunity to talk with these refugees who relate terrible details about "life" in the death camps to me. I cannot believe my own ears upon hearing what a human being is able to endure. And yet, they add, no one in that hell takes his own life and, even there, people continue to hope for that vague notion called "deliverance."

Are we not all a reincarnation of the biblical generation in the desert who endured forty years of wandering to pave the way for the generation of redemption? Who then will be the generation of redemption if the destroyer's sword does not spare even a child in a cradle? At least there is one consolation: We will not suffer for forty years until we reach the edge of the eternal end. Indeed, we live in the period of "the greatest progress" ...

September 14, 1942 (Fast of Gedaliah)

The first *Rosheshone*[226] in exile is over. The holiday was strongly felt in the camp. The Jews celebrated the Day of Judgement down to the last detail in seven *minyonim*, blew the *shofar*, sold *aliyes*[227] (one mark

behold his companion's death.' Until Rabbi Akiva came and taught: 'that your brother may live with you: your life takes precedence over his life.'"

226 Jewish New Year (Rosh Hashana in Hebrew) .

227 In many synagogues, Jews may offer a donation to the synagogue for the honor of reading one of the sections of the Torah portion, which are called *aliyot* (literally, ascent) during a service. The maftir is the portion of the verses of Torah read by the last person called up on a Sabbath or festival. This last *aliya* is considered the most significant honor, and it is often given to a prominent member of the synagogue, or to someone who is celebrating a special event.

for the *maftir*, a real bargain like those found among thieves ...), sang "*Melech Elyon*"[228] resoundingly, and sobbed during "*Uneytane Toykef.*" The only inconvenience was having to begin praying at dawn and to get to "*Aleynu*"[229] no later than 10 A.M.

On *Eyrev Rosheshone*, the praetor from Shargorod telephoned the gendarmes and ordered them not to allow the Yids to gather, supposedly to pray but in fact to hold Bolshevik meetings in their synagogues. It seems that the Master of the Universe will have to do without the complements of His servants in Dzhurin this *Rosheshone.* We have recourse of sorts to miracles, and a miracle occurred on *Eyrev Rosheshone*: the post chief, Floreanu, graciously received a delegation from the council, who presented him with a respectable note [with a bribe], and he promised that no gendarme would set foot in the camp until 10 A.M. in the morning unless, he added, there would be an unexpected inspection "from above," and then it would indeed not be so good. The community made the arrangements accordingly, and the matter was successfully settled.

Whoever still had a nice suit wore it on *Shabbes*, the first day of *Rosheshone.* We met people with polished shoes, and the sorrow on their faces lost some of its sharpness. We shook hands and expressed our wishes, first of all, for the defeat of our enemies and then for deliverance for the Jews, because as long as the enemy brandishes his sword, it [deliverance] is afraid to show its face.[230] The holiday atmosphere vanished around noon, when the living dead appeared in the streets with

---

228 The piyut "*Melech Elyon*" (Supreme King) is recited during the High Holidays.

229 The *Aleinu* (which means, it is our duty to praise) prayer is said at the end of each of the three prayer services, morning, afternoon, and evening, every day.

230 This description of the festival in the ghetto reveals how important it was to make an effort to observe the yearly events and their meaning, to preserve the memory of the past, their Jewish culture, and, of course, their faith. For comparison, see the description of Yom Kippur that Oscar Rozenfeld wrote in October 1943 in the Łódź ghetto. He provides a detailed description of the preparations for the day, the appearance of the people and their dress, the gathering of families, and also refers to the meaning of the day. Toward the end of the description he writes: "In order to summarize the atmosphere at home and in the streets, it is possible to say: Yom Kippur 1943 turned the ghetto into a "shtetl" in every meaning of the word." See Aryeh ben Menachem and Yosef Rav, eds., *Kronika Shel Geto Łódź*, vol. 3 (Hebrew) (Jerusalem: Yad Vashem, 1989), p. 598.

their bowls in their hands, dragging themselves to the soup kitchen to receive their holiday meal: a fourth of a loaf of bread and a boiled egg, in addition to the traditional bean soup. *Rosheshone* comes once a year, so the community made an effort and added an egg. On the second day of *Rosheshone*, people did not enjoy such luxuries …

In the afternoon, a few women and only two men went to the stream to cast off their sins.[231] The women were old and withered, and their transgressions had long since expired.

The second day of *Rosheshone* already looked completely different. It fell on a Sunday, the weekly market day, as though just to spite us. The truth is that also on this day people celebrated in the *minyonim*, blowing the *shofar*, singing and sobbing, although the crowds were sparser, because the Day of Judgement faced tough competition from the market. Indeed, no one schlepped any valuables and household objects to trade at the market, and there were no cries of "*spitshke*" (matches), "*bubelitshki*" (potato knishes), and "cigarettes"—the calls of young people who feed their families while their fathers perform forced labor from dawn to dusk. Nevertheless, more *minyonim* showed up in the market than in the *bote midroshim*. The camp draws all its subsistence from the weekly market, and whoever fails to make sure to get a bit of food then will starve the entire week.

And yet again, as though to spite us, groups of peasants arrived with wagons filled with the goods. When they saw that there were fewer buyers than usual, the peasants began selling the goods dirt cheap. This news quickly spread through all the *minyonim*, and the *bote midroshim* were soon almost completely empty. It is indeed a serious transgression to desecrate the holiday, but it is even a worse sin to pass up such amazing bargains that come once in a *Rosheshone* …

231 Kunstadt refers to the tradition of tashlich—the casting off of one's sins—as it was practiced in the Dzhurin ghetto. On the first day of Rosh Hashana, in the afternoon, observant Jews would go to the seashore or the bank of a river in which there are fish and recite special penitential prayers and Micah 7:19, which asks that one's sins be cast into the depths of the sea: "You will cast all their sins into the depths of the sea." It is also customary to shake out one's garments as a symbol of shaking off one's sins.

[September 14, 1942] 2 P.M.

Here is some good news, which was just reached the community building in honor of the new year:

A young man, a survivor of the massacre in Bar turned up in the community building and asked to be registered as one of the fortunate inhabitants of Dzhurin. He related, incidentally, that the SS men from the other side of the Bug appeared unexpectedly on August 20, 1942, in the shtetl of Kirilovich, which is on the Romanian side, and slaughtered all the Jews—approximately 1,000 Ukrainian Jews. The system they used was tried and tested: those sentenced to death dug the graves themselves; the Germans then fired into the crowd; and the Ukrainian militia threw the bodies in, both the dead and the wounded. The young man himself spoke with peasants who were at the scene.[232]

More news concerning the death camp of Pechora came from Moghilev, and there are two versions—one horrific and one has a "happy ending"... Let us begin with the first version: on the first day of *Slihes* the gendarmes drove out 500 people from Pechora to an open field and lined them up to shoot them. However, at exactly that time, a Romanian major happened to drive by in his car and stopped to see what was going on. As soon as he learned the truth, he ordered them to take the Yids back to the camp, where they will be allowed to die slowly, since it is a sin to waste the bullets. This is how the wedding was called off ... according to the second version, the whole story about the major never happened. The murderers accomplished their formidable task as planned, and 500

---

232 This apparently refers to the decimation of the Jews of Odessa, who were deported to the region of Berezovca from January 31, 1942, to June 1942. The Germans and Romanians collaborated in the murder of the Jews in the villages of Dvorianca, Criniski, Cuznea, Maitovca, Cotonea, and Ripiaki. The Romanians were responsible for bringing the Jews to the region of Berezovca, to transfer them from place to place, and to prevent their escape. The Jews were murdered by local gendarmes at the order of colonel Emil Broşteanu. The gendarmes ensured that the Jews were always concentrated in places that made it easier for the German killing units to act efficiently and swiftly. The murderers took the Jews' belongings. The Germans, as opposed to the Romanians, made sure to burn the corpses immediately in order to prevent the spread of plagues. See Ancel, *Toledot Hashoah*: *Romania*, vol. 2, pp. 977–978; Ancel, *The History of the Holocaust in Romania*, pp. 384–387; Carp, *Cartea neagră*, vol. 3, p. 226.

living dead were promoted to the level of the really dead. So, isn't this a "happy ending," Transnistrian style? …

And for once, Odessa is on the table. A week ago, 300 Jewish workers who had been sent there to perform forced labor were shot. Since the occupation, no Jews at all live in Odessa. It is difficult to verify to what extent this information is true—it comes from the Ukrainians—but slaughters are carried out wherever the Germans set foot, and why would Odessa be an exception!

Notebook Two

My Mother's Death

September 15, 1942, Dzhurin

With this entry, I begin the second volume of my diary, whose first page saw the light of an oil lamp on April 11, 1942, as a trifle, and eventually the 180 pages of the notebook were filled from cover to cover. Today, I begin a second volume, not because a period of my life has ended, but because there is no more space to add a letter in the previous notebook. The subtitle of the first volume "A Summer in the World of Chaos"[1] is also applicable to this one, according to the calendar, because autumn will arrive in just a few days.

Yet, bidding goodbye to summer today, even though it will reign until September 23, for eight more days, has its risks. Vey, vey, what else can happen this week, both in the world at large and in Transnistria! Not a day goes by without fateful tragedies, today in this camp and tomorrow in another—deportations occur unexpectedly, like lightning on a bright, summer day. Jewish life has no value, less than an animal's life, and it is truly a miracle that Jews today continue to gasp for air on this side of the Dniester—Jews without a name and without [the protection of] any laws. There is only one law that applies to them: the ordinance called "*Ordonanta*" (Order) No. 23 from the governor, General Alexianu, with its dozen and a half prohibitions, all ending with a promise: the "death penalty."[2]

---

1 This subtitle was apparently omitted in the typed copy of the diary in our possession.

2 Order No. 23 was issued on November 11, 1941, by Alexianu, the governor of Transnistria. This was in fact the legal basis for the existence of the Jews in Transnistria. An examination of the dozens of paragraphs in the order reveals that it mainly concerned the living conditions of the Jews in the ghettos, their organizations, their housing, and their obligation to work for their subsistence and for the benefit of the Romanian authorities. The first clauses of the order concern the requirement to settle the Jews in places designated by the Romanian authorities, in the same villages and small towns where local or Russian Jews had previously lived. As was noted, the movement of the Jews was restricted and they were required to choose a representative from among themselves who would then have to be approved by the praetor, the commander of the local gendarmerie. The order then discusses the organization of the Jewish community's internal structure. Another clause of the order deals with the obligations of the head of the ghetto, who was personally responsible for providing workers for forced labor in accordance with the demands of the authorities, whether these were Romanian, German, or civilian. The remainder of the clauses relate to the obligation of forced labor, and the wages that the forced laborers received for their work—1 mark per day for simple workers; 2 marks per day for skilled workers. The salaries of experts were paid in food allowances as determined by the authorities.

The deportees who have not lost their minds completely have rid themselves of the illusion that the enemy will send them back home at some point—whether the well-connected people or the entire holy community. By the way, most of the deportees have had enough of the old country and have no desire to return there but rather to flee somewhere far away, far from Europe—to America, to *Eretz Yisroel*, to Australia, even to the other side of the Sambatyon.[3] They claim that they are even ashamed to look their former neighbors in the face—the hypocritical Romanians—after the great humiliation inflicted on them, when they were driven out barefoot and naked to the desert of doom, like mangy dogs. The Romanians—not all of them—joined the lament of the Jews at the time, wished us luck in our "new lives," and could hardly wait to seize the beautiful Jewish apartments and to inherit the property left behind. However, they avidly did us one favor: they took the valuable objects from the Jews for safekeeping until they would return at some time. The Romanians were convinced that "some time" will come after the messiah and, so far, they have been right.

Meanwhile, news arrived from Romania (it is possible to correspond through the "Red Cross," and Jews are experts at reading between the lines …) that the Jews also live there in fear of deportation. In Bucharest itself, rumors are circulating that they will deport 40,000 Jews, if not the entire honorable community, from the capital city to Transnistria in October. There are more than 100,000 Jews there—most lack a residence permit.[4] The news from Romania oppresses the despondent people in the camps even more, in particular those who receive assistance from there—whether from relatives, or from Zionist organizations or other institutions.[5] The impressive aid from the federation of the [Jewish] Romanian communities to assist the camps in Transnistria—cash,

---

3 According to rabbinic literature, the Assyrian king Shalmaneser exiled part of ten of the tribes of Israel across the legendary river Sambatyon (also Sanbatyon and Sabbatyon).

4 Antonescu intended to purge the Regat of Jews. See Ancel, *Toledot Hashoah*: *Romania*, vol. 2, pp. 1223–1229, 1231–1234.

5 In February 1942, aid for the Jews in Transnistria began to arrive from the Jewish communities in Romania, sent by families who had not been deported and by the Comisia Autonomã De Ajutorare in Bucharest. See Lavi, *Pinkas Hakehilot*: *Rumania*, vol. 1, p. 515.

shipments of clothing, shoes, food, and medicines—are also in jeopardy. In any case, some of the donations reach the afflicted.

From letters and from the mouths of the "couriers" (non-kosher messengers), we have learned that the Jews in Romania have enough troubles. They are dragged away for forced labor and are fleeced, yet they would not change places even with the fortunate people in the "model colony" of Dzhurin ...

[September 15, 1942] 8 P.M.

The shtetl of Nemirov on the other side of the Bug is a stronghold of slaughter dating from the time of Chmielnicki. When Bialik wrote his elegy about the Kishinev pogrom in 1903, he decided to title it "Nemirov Burden," supposedly referring to the distant past to deceive the Russian censor.[6] These lines relate to the credible, desolate news that we learned today.

In Nemirov, about 40 kilometers from Dzhurin, the SS murderers chose to conduct an *Aktia* in their usual style, to make the shtetl "*Judenrein*" on *Eyrev Rosheshone* (September 11 [1942]). The local Jewish residents had long since disappeared—they evacuated together with the Red Army in July 1941, or were slaughtered immediately following the occupation. However, approximately 300 Jews arrived in Nemirov during the year of 1942—they had been sent there with their families from Romania for forced labor. On *Eyrev Rosheshone*, SS men seized thirty healthy, respectable men and allowed them to continue the travail of forced labor. Those who did not find favor in the eyes of the SS beasts—the elderly, the weak, women, and children—were taken out of the shtetl, where the Germans shot them in a mass grave that the victims themselves were forced to dig.[7]

---

6 The poem by Bialik, "In the City of Slaughter," was written in 1903, following his visit to Kishinev. It was first published under the title "Masa Nemirov," in order to receive the censor's permission to publish the poem. For the English translation, see H. N. Bialik, "City of the Killings" in Bialik, *Songs from Bialik: Selected Poems of Hayim Nahman Bialik*, ed. and tr. by Atar Hadari (Syracuse: Syracuse University, 2000), pp. 1–9.

7 Alexianu authorized the dispatch of 5,000 Jews from the Tulchin region to the headquarters of the SS units from Gaysin to be used to pave the strategic road of Nemirov–Bretslav–

The savage cruelty of the German executioners toward children has led to a macabre phenomenon: small children leave their mothers—they already lost their fathers long ago—and flee from the camps by the Bug, barefoot and naked, relying on Divine Providence. Most die on the way, but some manage to reach the "good" camps of Shargorod, Dzhurin, Murafa, and some even make it to the holy of holies, Moghilev. These [barely] living orphans—sometimes they are no older than about five—with their small mouths of children relate such shocking details that the ears cannot comprehend their stammering and broken speech. It seems that standing before us are not toddlers but instead exhausted skeletons of old people about to die, bearing a mountain of the sorrow of the world, of endless wandering on their shriveled shoulders. The only clothing they have is a sack around their loins. God, God, how is it possible that You exist, if you see this and mercifully remain silent before everyone, offering the banal claim that Your ways are hidden and a person is not allowed to ask any questions? …

September 16, 1942, 7 A.M.

The summer is taking leave of us. Last night, a wild storm raged, portending the impending wet, cold, and muddy Dzhurin autumn. The sun is still shining for the time being, but like a stepmother, and whoever has warm clothing or an overcoat is glad to wear it. I have not gotten rid of the sandals that I have been wearing without socks since the beginning of summer, even though their time has already passed, and the time has come for socks and shoes. However, when I think of my ruined shoes with the rotten and patched leather uppers and the worn-out soles, which will certainly not survive the Dzhurin autumn and the endless snow, I am willing to let my feet shiver as long as it is still dry outside. So I will

---

Seminca–Gaysin. About 3,000 Jews, most of whom had been deported from Cernăuţi in June 1942, were taken in the first transport by the SS units on August 18, 1942. The children and the elderly were killed first and, by the end of 1943, most of them had been murdered in various selections, including whoever was still able to work. See Ancel, *Toledot Hashoah*: *Romania*, vol. 2, p. 984.

extend the vacation from my shoes, which will soon reach the end of their journey …

In Dzhurin—and where not?—it is natural for compassionate Jews to do a person a favor by giving advice. So people often tell me that it would be better to put on shoes and socks like everyone else, because there is a time for everything. I offer all kinds of excuses and keep the simple truth to myself, because I would rather swallow a frog than explain myself to strangers.

By the way, it's useless to try to justify yourself, not even to your own family. Children do not want to know anything about their mother and father, all the more so, brothers about their brothers—not to mention distant relatives. There are, of course, exceptions, but they are few and far between. Whoever has a better meal goes off to a corner, like a dog with a bone—to ward off the evil eye. There have been wealthy people, loaded with cash and valuable objects, who solicited the community for notes for the soup kitchen and lined up with the living dead to receive a bowl of broth. Neighbors informed us that these beggars in disguise poured the soup into a bucket of slop at home, where another meal was waiting for them … when the secret was revealed, the council fined them large sums and crossed them off the list of recipients.

Distinguished and wealthy Jews, respectable men from the old country, are stocking up on produce, flour, wood, and whatever they can get to prepare for the winter, and are not at all bothered by the fact that people are starving to death all around them. The council must take drastic measures to squeeze a donation out of these people, and shouting can be heard as far as the heart of the heavens until they manage to see a whit of a mark. It is possible to count the good people on the fingers of one hand.

September 17, 1942

After about two months of ostensible calm, today again black darkness has overcome the camp, like in the good old days. The truth is that even during the "calm" two months, we lived anxiously and trembled at the slightest rustle, and heard "happy" news daily from every direction, but we nevertheless got a bit of a chance to breathe a little. The oppressor Floreanu loosened his tight grip on the ghetto and even turned a blind eye when the prisoners snuck out through a small opening in the cage, although this is absolutely forbidden. They did not, God forbid, sneak out of the area of the camp but rather went to the market, where there is a small fair every day until 9 A.M. and, on Sundays, when the weekly market is held. Jews even began to inhabit [dwellings] among the Ukrainians in the side alleys of the ghetto on the hill, which was prohibited. Farmers brought food to the market, although this is strictly forbidden. Women went down to the stream to wash. Some *Lagernikes* removed the Star of David from their clothes, and some of the well-connected people, those with connections and money, even received from the gendarmes permission to work for the farmers in the villages and return to the camp at night.

While the small fair was well underway this morning, Floreanu unexpectedly showed up, accompanied by a group of gendarmes, and gave a performance as he had done in the past. Whips cracked on skulls, goods rolled under feet as during a pogrom, and the square was emptied immediately. The post chief [Floreanu] then burst into the council [community] building, fuming like a forest robber, and roared—why have the Jews forgotten where they are and for what purpose they were deported here. From now on, he announced to the colony chief and to the "lords," he himself would see to it that the following decrees would be fulfilled:

— The bazaar [market] will be held only once a week, every Sunday from 6 A.M. to 9 A.M. The farmers will be prohibited from bringing any flour, fresh produce, potatoes, and beans to the market.

— Every Jew, without exception, including small children, must wear the Star of David on his lapel.

— All certificates to go out to work in the surroundings are null and void.

— The punishment for these transgressions is the death penalty—[offenders will be] shot on the spot.

It is difficult to describe the panic that these decrees spawned throughout the camp. A delegation of community advocates promptly set out for the gendarmerie [post], and not with empty hands, to try to revoke the decrees. They were there for a short time and returned stunned and dumbstruck, their faces downcast. It was obvious that they failed to accomplish anything. I must stop now, because a messenger is calling me to go immediately to the community [building].

[September 17, 1942] 9 P.M.

Allow me to ask the Master of the Universe for forgiveness for suspecting Him of giving Floreanu the idea of striking the camp with darkness Himself. There are human beings, indeed some of our own, who brought about the trouble through their good deeds.

It was a brief episode that was not at all pretty. Already in the first months of this exile, a gang of people with cash in their pockets and shoulders twice as broad as mine would turn up among the exiles after secretly undertaking a trip to Moghilev to bring from there all kinds of merchandise, kosher and non-kosher. They would sell the goods at an excessive profit. Along the way, they would load the wagons with food—flour, honey, grape juice, and the like, which they and their agents would buy at the market for any price and would make large profits. The gendarmes apparently have known about this trade and have turned a blind eye. Otherwise, it is not clear how their risky business has succeeded until today, while starving refugees who dare to go out of the camp in search of a pood of potatoes pay for this daring with their lives.

The council, starting with the colony chief, have known about this trade and have not interfered with the profiteers' business. On the contrary, they have befriended them. And when the time comes to pay for all sorts of community needs, they deal cautiously with these people and settle for a few hundred marks to fulfill the minimal obligation. They, the speculators from Moghilev, are not thrown into the basement nor threatened with being sent to forced labor, and they are certainly not honored with any blows. The "lords" claim that it is better to be on good terms with those profiteers, because they have very close ties with the gendarmes—and not, God forbid, for the sake of the world to come ... They sometimes use their connections to advocate on behalf of individuals or the general public in times of trouble. As we say: when a thief is required, they will even bring him down from the gallows ...

However, when problems arise, it doesn't help to put out the whispering coals. And so it happened that another band of young men, also with fat wallets, began to envy the abundance enjoyed by the travelers from Moghilev and they too tried to do the same thing. However, they banged on closed doors, because the stakeholders did not allow the "foreign nuisances" to join the business. Nevertheless, Jews are indeed stubborn and those who were left out resorted to old-time measures: snitching. As long as the information reached the council and the local [gendarmerie] commander, it was tolerable. As a matter of fact, the leech Floreanu enjoys this, because the other side that rules the roost spares no bribes, which are fit for a king, in order to put out the fire before it flares up.

So the thwarted competitors came up with a new idea: change the address and confound the overlords in Shargorod. Yesterday, the commander of the district gendarmerie in Shargorod himself, *Oberleutnant* Garama, appeared in Dzhurin with a stack of sharp denunciations against the Dzhurin profiteers in his briefcase, and immediately conducted a manhunt for the snitchers. Those people found out about the danger in time—they have their footmen among the gendarmes—and the commander found nothing in the search. Floreanu was not here during this pandemonium, because he was in Moghilev.

Floreanu returned and discovered what had happened only in the evening. He found the denunciations on his desk, where *Oberleutnant* Garama had left them to remind him to discover the identity of the informers. The envious people had thought it best not to sign their denunciations with their own names but had written names drawn from the—*Haftoreh*.[8] As Floreanu read through the papers, he was blindsided by the explicit mention of his name in one of them. They do not say,

8 A section from the Books of the Prophets that is read after the parashah in the synagogue.

God forbid, that this "fur-clad saint"[9] is the traffickers' partner, but only that he sees and is silent ... The leech in Shargorod does not require a detailed explanation ...

Floreanu burst into a fit of murderous rage. I have already described what happened next. He then informed the community advocates that even though not all the *Lagernikes* were responsible for blackening his name but only a certain charlatan, the entire public would pay for this. He is not the first to do this, and because of the dangerous saying, "All Israel are responsible for each other," catastrophes have always befallen innocent Jews on account of the real or invented transgressions of individuals.

September 18, 1942, 7 A.M.

Floreanu did not make idle threats. Today at dawn, Ukrainian militia encircled the ghetto and did not allow the farmers to bring produce or come to buy all kinds of goods at the market, as is the custom every morning. Women and children wandered around the market with nothing to do, bearing their wretched wares on their shoulders, as did hundreds of buyers with bottles, pots, and small baskets, who were prepared to purchase food. The Ukrainian militia then raided the market and drove out the people in the market, because all trade is prohibited.

Floreanu's wrath is so great that last night he even refused to authorize the council's messenger to take 300 portions of bread to the forced laborers who are cutting stone near Murafa, in spite of the fact that the council is obligated to provide bread for them. The hearts of even the inner circle and the wealthy people are pounding, because no one knows what tomorrow, or even today, will bring.

9 Rabbi Mendel of Kotzk once said of one tzaddik that he was a "*tzaddik in peltz*" (a righteous man in fur), and this is how his disciples interpreted the words: there are those who warm only their own body, and there are those who warm the entire house. And what is the difference between them? He who warms his body is warm, but he does not help others. He who heats up the house does so for the benefit of others as well.

September 19, 1942, 3 P.M.

Today too the market remains empty. Apparently, the weekly market will not take place tomorrow. Advocates from the council are bursting through Floreanu's door, offering him everything they can, but to no avail.

I wandered around the market today for more than an hour with a bottle in my hand to obtain a sip of milk for Roza, who has been bedridden with a high fever since Monday and cannot eat anything. I returned with an empty bottle. Dr. Greiff, who makes house calls every day, does not even know what is wrong with her and says that only in two days' time will he know if it is typhus. She lies in a rancid hovel on a rickety bed from the days of Methuselah, where I and the children sleep crosswise and cover ourselves with the same blanket and eat from the same flatware. If Roza got the nice package [typhus], they will take her to the hospital. Who knows if I and the children are already carrying the Rickettsia bacteria, which typically only shows signs of itself after about three weeks. We all keep clean, as much as possible, but the trouble is that I come into contact all day long with neglected, lice-infested people because of my work at the community building. It could well be that I brought Roza the gift …

I could ask why my mother is suffering such dreadful poverty, without a bed, without a potato to sate [her hunger], with no shoes on her feet and no intact [not tattered] clothing on her body? What good were the fast days that she observed her entire life—she fasted every Monday and Thursday, *Eyrev Roysh Hoydesh*,[10] and the day after having a bad dream, not to mention the required fast days? What have her daily prayers, her tears that accompanied her prayers, her good deeds of righteousness from time immemorial accomplished? Such questions roll around underfoot in Transnistria, but who can we ask and who can give an answer, which is not the meaningless pilpul of "*Mipney Hata'eynu*"![11] …

10 The first day of a month.

11 Literally, "because of our sins," the reason for all suffering, as derived from the Musaf prayers for the three pilgrimage festivals: "And because of our sins we have been exiled from our land."

September 20, 1942 (*Eyrev Yom Kipper*, 5703), 2 P.M.

The oppressor Constantin Floreanu kept his word and did not allow the weekly market to take place today, Sunday. Ukrainian militia and gendarmes were posted along all the streets and alleys that lead to the ghetto, where they drove away the peasants who gravitated toward the market. The armed guards redirected the wagons and pedestrians to alleys near the Ukrainian cloister outside the ghetto, where Jews are forbidden to set foot. The market took place there, and the people in the camp looked down from the mountain with covetous eyes and aching hearts at the abundance, seeing how the Ukrainians from the factory quarter raked in bargains for almost nothing.

At dawn, Moshe Katz hurried to Floreanu with a large bribe in hand to revoke the evil decree. Only at around 8 A.M. did the oppressor have mercy and allow the farmers to bring goods to the market for a period of two hours. This favor had the taste of a spoiled dish, because most of the merchandise had already been sold and only a few farmers kept their promise, bringing meager leftover food to the market. The crowd literally tore the foodstuff from their hands, and the cunning, rich Ukrainians raised the prices sky-high, so that only the well-to-do could purchase anything from them. No one wanted to buy the goods, and the market people and peddlers were left holding all their wares.

Although Floreanu had explicitly set a limit of only two hours, the Jewish militia did not hurry to expel the sparse crowd from the market, and the hands of the clock reached the hour of 12 P.M. Floreanu then suddenly appeared in a fit of rage with a whip in hand. People immediately ran away like poisoned mice, and once again the foodstuff rolled on the ground and all kinds of items were scattered under foot. This time Floreanu did not use his whip just to crack skulls but turned on the Jewish militia and beat them cruelly for not emptying the square at 11 A.M. Thus, *Eyrev Yom Kipper* got off to a nice start.

I managed to buy 1 pood of potatoes and a bag of beans. Because of the astonishingly high prices, my wallet refused to bow before the wealthy and [it was difficult] to pay the high price.

Dr. Greiff has concluded that Roza does not have typhus but is simply ill. Well, that is still comforting.

[September 20, 1942] 5 P.M.

(**Added in Israel in 1967**: I erased the names of two of the "heroes" of the drama that unfolds in the following entries, because they have already received their punishment in this world. One of them, referred to further as A.—no indication of his real name—was killed following the liberation, in the summer of 1944, by Ukrainian "Benders" (underground fascist bands). His murdered body was found in a river. The second, B.—this too does not allude to his real name—actually immigrated to *Eretz Yisroel*, where he worked until an old age and even died there).

The Jews are now sitting with the aura of an additional soul at the meal before the fast—some at a table with roasted meat and stew, and some (most) with a thin bean soup and a slice of bread—preparing to transcend the physical for twenty-four hours. Because of our many iniquities, I am now drawn into hard, weekly labor that places me and other *Lagernikes*, if not the entire camp, in mortal danger. I just returned from the gendarmerie, where I had the privilege of becoming acquainted with the commander, Constantin Floreanu, although I have often seen him in the community building and he has seen me. But let us begin with the best part.[12]

Even though it had been decided that the community building would be closed on the afternoon of *Eyrev Yom Kipper* and that I could enjoy a Dzhurin-style vacation, so to speak, it turned out that my supervisor was of a different mind. At around 2 P.M., I had just lay down for a nap on my wooden bunk when a militiaman appeared panting at my hovel and asked me to report directly to the colony chief at the community building. Roza and the children turned pale as a sheet, not to mention myself, since this meant trouble. Having no choice, I went to where I had been summoned.

The boss, Dr. Rosenstrauch, sat in the community building, and to his right was the second-in-command, Moshe Katz. Without any introduction, the colony chief addressed me in German in these words: "Go home quickly and shave, and from there go without delay to the post chief,

---

12 Meaning, to start from the beginning. Indeed, the Shaharit prayers, the daily morning prayers, begin with the blessing of Bilam cited in the verses Numbers 24:5–8: "How goodly are your tents, Oh Jacob, your dwellings, Oh Israel!"

Floreanu, who has ordered you to go to him. A Jewish militiaman will escort you there." This announcement left me speechless—what do I have to do with the scoundrel Floreanu all of a sudden? It occurred to me that apparently someone had lied to him about me and had made false accusations against me, perhaps a superfluous word of mine, or who knows what fabrication. If it was defamation, who knows if I would return alive from the lion's den? Allow me to mention to Moshe Katz's credit that he noticed the anxious expression on my face and added: "You have nothing to fear; if you are clever, no harm will come to you." The doctor cast an angry look at Katz for expressing these simple words of solace. In short, only one hour later, I stood in the holy of holies of the gendarmerie in the factory quarter, where I had never set foot. I was taken into the office, where Floreanu sat at his desk and was writing something. I greeted him in Romanian with the customary greeting to rulers: "*Să trăiţi*" (may you live) and thought to myself the second half of the verse: "for only one more moment!" I was alarmed and astounded when Floreanu answered me respectably, "*Bună ziua*" (Good day!), and motioned to me with his hand to sit opposite him.

He stopped writing, opened a drawer in his desk, and removed a file containing various types of documents. A postcard lay at the top, which he handed to me saying, not necessarily out loud, and even with a slight hint of courtesy:

> I am imposing a duty on you, which is for the good of your brothers in faith in the camp and also for your own benefit. If you fulfill the duty completely, you will prevent a great catastrophe in the camp, and I will know how to show my appreciation. However, if not, the fate of you and the others will be bitter. In short: this postcard was written most audaciously by one of your people, but he did not sign his name. This scoundrel denounced me to my superiors, saying that I turn a blind eye and allow speculators to pile up barrels of gold, because undoubtedly I am also in partnership with the loathsome profiteers.
>
> Since I heard that you engaged in graphology in your home [country] before the deportation and were even a reliable expert

in the court of justice, you will certainly be able to discover who the vile snitch is. I demand a clear answer from you by tomorrow, without Jewish artifice, do you understand?"

I immediately understood that a fellow member of the council had apparently done me a favor. In the old country, I had indeed engaged in graphology as a hobby and had become an expert in identifying the authors of forged documents. My name was often cited in newspapers in connection with prominent trials against all kinds of people who had committed acts of fraud and deception with the help of forged documents or declarations and anonymous denunciations. The indictment was often based on my opinion and, on more than one occasion, prominent experts in Bucharest agreed with my conclusions, when a second opinion was requested from them. My strange and dramatic experiences as a court graphologist would be enough to fill a respectable book, but this is not the right time, and Dzhurin is not the appropriate place …

It was clear to me that it was useless to try to deny my knowledge of graphology and, not only that, that it would bring on a renewed flare-up of the murderous rage of the post chief. At the time of the incident, I had the fleeting thought that it might be possible to save the camp by seeking help elsewhere, perhaps even in Moghilev. I did not refuse but I did ask for a week to compare the writing on the back of the postcard with [that in] other manuscripts. After all, there are about 4,000 people in the camp, I added, and a job involving such responsibility cannot be taken lightly.

The mask of ostensible good heartedness on Floreanu's face was stripped away in the blink of an eye, and he glared at me with murderous eyes and bellowed: What nonsense are you talking about (he was already speaking to me using the familiar form, "*tu*")—4,000 *Lagernikes*! This was surely written by one of the speculators' competitors, so how many of them are there! Listen Kunstadt! (without adding "Mr." …) You have until the day after tomorrow at noon to reveal to me who wrote this card. It is no problem for you to work day and night, since people like you are cutting stones on the roads and digging peat in Tulchin, while you walk around like the master of the house with your Yid [wife]. You can leave." He did not respond to my second greeting, "*Să trăiţi*."

I rushed back to the community building, panting, to begin working on finding the anonymous informant. Never in my long career as a graphologist—around twenty years—had I found myself in such a dangerous predicament. The objects of suspicion were always one or a few individuals, and I would compare their handwritings. Only once did it happen that I had to look through seventy documents to discover an anonymous writer, which I managed to do after working for six hours. This time it meant checking hundreds of handwriting samples, because the informant could have used a woman or a child to cover up the act. Well, it is definitely impossible to complete such an enormous job in two days.

I turned the card around in my hand and focused my gaze on the ten lines of neat handwriting that were clearly written by someone with a good education. This was how I would always proceed in order to "photograph" the writing in my mind and to enable myself to identify it by comparing it with other handwriting samples.

Unfortunately, the handwriting was not distinguished by any clear and striking characteristics, which is a real disadvantage in this type of work, because most handwriting is of an ordinary nature, and it is really difficult to find common indications that would ensure a reliable opinion. I would have to check at least 500 handwriting samples that lack any conspicuous signs, so how will I be able to finish this?

And then something happened, which religious Jews call divine inspiration. Six words from the anonymous card suddenly stood out before my eyes and I recalled that I had recently come across this phrase. According to the sacrosanct rules of graphology, a graphologist is not supposed to base his opinion on the content of the text but only on the basis of its graphic qualities—there are more than forty graphic characteristics in an infinite range of combinations. Indeed, the experienced graphologist refrains from reading the manuscript to avoid being influenced by the content. In practice, I had always behaved in this manner, but this time I made an allowance, trying to grasp at straws like someone who is drowning. Fortunately, this inanity was successful.

Allow me to describe how this matter was conducted to avoid making a mistake. The Jewish regime in Dzhurin includes a range of institutions, so to speak, which exist among people outside [the camp], [living] in freedom, as though we were human beings, nevertheless, and not a crushed worm without a name and without the protection of the law. Among these many institutions, there is a "court" and there are judges, lawyers, a registrar, and … litigants. This court deliberates mostly financial matters and issues verdicts that the *Lagernikes* must respect. The Jewish militia supervise the defendants so that they do not, God forbid, get away. Most of the "litigation" concern trivialities—claims of a mark or two, disputes between householders and tenants about rent, a borrowed bed, etc., and other serious matters such as these. However, there are sometimes cases of a broader scope concerning business in the old country, or illegal speculation on the roads, or even in Dzhurin itself. Whoever intends to turn to the court must submit a petition in writing. Since the court is in a small building near the community building, I sometimes go there to pry into the records out of curiosity, even though everything is completely confidential. However, they consider me one of their own and the secretary is not wary of me.

I will now come to the point. I recently saw a statement of a claim in the court by a fellow townsman of mine, A., against one of the wealthy men in Dzhurin for a respectable sum of 10,000 marks. The claim dealt with some kind of non-kosher trade that was only alluded to—to avert the evil eye. Although the defendant is known everywhere by his nickname "Bobi," for cautionary reasons, A. wrote in the statement of claim that he is suing "Bobi, who is also called Adolf and Abraham." He had checked somewhere and discovered that in the certificates, Bobi was called (in other words, he was once called …) Adolf, and he is called to the Torah on the day of a *Yortsayt* by the name Abraham. He mentioned all three names, so that the accused could not come up with a pretext claiming that this does not refer to him. The informant clearly had the same thing in mind when he wrote in that fateful card that "Bobi, also called Adolf and Abraham," holds a place of honor among the speculators. The combination of these same three names in both documents suddenly opened my eyes and showed me a trail.

My fellow townsman, A., was a prominent merchant in the old country and was known to be a very wealthy man. He never concerned himself with community matters, and getting a coin out of him for public needs was like drawing blood from a stone. In the final months before the deportation, A.'s behavior suddenly changed, and he began to get involved in the community and to show his enthusiasm for the wider action of collecting sums for the groups of deportees from Northern Bukovina, mainly from the Seletin region. The Romanian authorities had driven these first victims of the deportation into the camp of Edineţi (Bessarabia) already in July 1941—immediately after the "liberation"—and endless convoys passed through the neighboring city of Rădăuţi. An emergency aid committee was immediately formed and, in no time, it collected a few hundred thousand lei to rent wagons for the deportees to Edineţi, and to equip them with supplies and clothing for the journey. The sword of deportation was already hanging over the head of the Jewish community of Rădăuţi—10,000 people—and no one shirked from making a generous donation to this lifesaving fund. A. joined the council and became a big shot there, the head trustee and cashier. Everything was conducted on the basis of trust, because they did not dare record expenses and income.

On the unfortunate train that dragged the third transport of Rădăuţi Jews to Transnistria on that *Simches Toyre*, 5702 [1941], A. once again got involved in community matters—he was one of a group of people who collected a large fortune in the cattle cars in order to "bribe the overlords and ensure good places in the new home." You may read about the outcome of this fraud in one of the earlier entries.[13] A. also disappeared in Atachi, and only two weeks later did he show up in Dzhurin. If people went to him with claims about the sums that they had given him, he argued that all the money had gone into the pockets of the overlords, and indeed, as a result, the people were now in "lucky" Dzhurin ... A. is one of the wealthy and well-connected people here, living a good life, and his name has been omitted from the [forced] labor lists.

As I was sitting in the community building, wondering what had led A. to write this denunciation—I was still a little doubtful about the matter—the colony chief entered and asked hypocritically what Floreanu wanted from me. I gave him a brief account of the matter but did not mention even the slightest hint of my suspicion. The boss wanted to know when I would begin doing the work and collect writing samples from all the suspects (he did not mention A.'s name). I answered that I was completely exhausted today and would start the job tomorrow at dawn.

---

13 See the entries of April 29, 1942 and May 20, 1942.

The doctor went on his way and I immediately turned to the secretary of the court of justice, Herman Guttman, and asked him for the file of A.'s lawsuit, "on behalf of the doctor." As soon as I got hold of the file, it became clear to me that my suspicion was not unfounded. The prominent graphic characteristics were similar in both handwriting samples—the statement of claim and the card.

The file is now in my hovel, on the old, damaged dresser that serves as a table, so to speak, and I find myself in a difficult predicament. What should I do? I will now sit down immediately and, before *Kol Nidrey*,[14] I will begin to study the material according to all the laws of graphology to discover the whole truth. I must not be influenced by the initial glance. A serious graphologist does not give his final opinion based on the first impression.

I have no doubt that the science of graphology would concur with the first impression that the handwriting samples made on me. Handing over A.'s name means condemning him to death, because Floreanu has his finger on the trigger, and shooting a Jew is like smoking a cigarette for him. However, not delivering on this and keeping silent can bring a tremendous disaster on the entire camp, not to mention on me and all my family. Even the Gemara rules: "informers … may be cast in and need not be brought up" (it is a *mitzve* to hand over an informer).[15] This dilemma is like an ancient tragedy; how can I disentangle myself from it? For now, no one but me knows the secret, and I lied to Roza, saying that I am working on the register of a very irresponsible individual.

September 21, 1942, 8 P.M. (*Motzei Yom Kipper)*[16]

My first *Yom Kipper* in the Transnistrian exile has just ended, a day charged with dramatic tension that surpasses a gripping crime novel.

---

14 This is to the first communal prayer service of Yom Kippur that is recited immediately at sunset on the evening of Yom Kippur.

15 B. Avodah Zara 26b.

16 Nightfall, which marks the end of Yom Kippur.

I sat down before *Kol Nidrey* to delve into the secret of both handwriting samples and to find out the whole truth. By the dim light of the oil lamp, I racked my brain, straining my eyes for four hours, and Roza begged me to put out the lamp, because she cannot sleep with the light on. I finally reached the unequivocal conclusion that A. had written the denunciation in his own hand, which can bring destruction on who knows how many Jews. Whether out of desire to take revenge on his enemies, or out of jealousy, he has endangered the lives of the entire community.

Alarmed and exhausted from this work and from the dramatic result, I was not able to write my opinion on the spot. I feverishly tossed and turned on the bed of boards with my eyes open, and one single question clutched at my heart like red-hot tongs: Am I permitted to sacrifice one sinful individual to save the entire population of thousands of persons?

When I saw the first quivering rays of the hazy autumn sun penetrate my hovel, I immediately threw on my clothes and sat down to write the opinion. First of all, I listed the established evidence, each one with a number, as graphologists do and, at the end of the fourth page, I wrote the fateful conclusion: "In light of these arguments, I believe that A. is the writer of this anonymous card." Obviously, I had to add my signature, and it seemed to me that I was signing a death sentence.

Even before the ink had dried on the paper, a militiaman came running and called me to go immediately to the home of the second-in-command, Moshe Katz. In any case, I had planned to go to him to ask for advice. He has a valuable quality: he is no fool and it is possible to talk to him. When I entered Moshe Katz's apartment—he lives in a nice house, wealthy by Dzhurin standards, and there is even a large electric lamp on the table—he received me with the words: "So, how are you?" I answered, "Either good in the full sense of the word, or 9 cubits deep in the ground." I added, "The fate of the camp is in your hands, and I trust your judgement." Then I handed him my opinion and pointed to the last two lines.

Moshe Katz, who is no milksop—on the contrary, he often shows hard-heartedness and spares no …[17] at that moment—turned white as snow and was unable to utter a word. He had not expected his old friend from the old country and the trustee of the emergency aid committee in

17 The rest of the sentence is missing in the typed copy of the diary in our possession.

Rădăuţi to engage in intrigue that reeks of death. It took a while for Katz to regain his composure and to say to me: "I am speaking to you now not as a boss to a subordinate but rather man to man in times of trouble. First of all, I kindly request that you not relate, God forbid, what you have discovered. If the doctor pesters you, you must claim stubbornly that you have still not completed the work. Miracles may yet occur by noon tomorrow. I am rushing immediately to ask the rabbi of Siret, Rabbi Baruch Hager, for advice so that he assume responsibility for this."

Just before they began praying *Musef* in the *minyan* of the rabbi of Siret, the fateful discussion took place between Moshe Katz and the rabbi—a wise and brilliant Jew, the son of the famous *tzaddik* of Vijniţa, Rabbi Israel Hager, of blessed memory, who is worldly and has diplomatic skills. I was not present, but Moshe Katz told me that the rabbi listened to the whole story with his eyes closed, gave it some thought, and then said in a firm voice: "Today is a holy day and it is not the time for secular concerns. Tomorrow, God willing, we will consider the matter, if the oppressor has not met his downfall by then."

The ominous secret got out and not, God forbid, from my mouth. Katz apparently told the doctor everything, and there was no need for more. The camp seethed and split in two. One side contended that A. should be handed over to the post chief the next day, while others claimed that we should not do this. In the meanwhile, A. disappeared.

The "lords" will try tomorrow to put out the fire with a large sum of money, and there is a rare window of opportunity here: tomorrow the oppressor Floreanu celebrates his birthday (may it be his last! …) and we already informed him that the council would be very happy if he would allow us to organize a feast at the community's expense. He did not refuse and even invited the colony chief and Katz to the banquet.

Apart from the drama concerning the sad "hero" A., *Yom Kipper* went well. The *minyonim* were full; people beat their chest, reciting the *Al Het*,[18] mainly for the sins of the others; people sobbed and wailed during the *Uneytane Toykef*; and just like that, for no reason, people complained that the sun was traversing the blue heavens slowly, as if no one's heart was weak from the fast. As soon as they heard the long blow of the shofar

18 The confession of sins that is recited ten times in the course of the Yom Kippur services.

after the *Ne'ila*,[19] they ran to break the fast—some with roasted meat and *tzimmes*—and others—the majority—with a bowl of bean soup. The real day of judgment, however, will take place tomorrow …

September 22, 1942, 2 P.M.

This entry deserves a title inspired by Sholem Aleichem: "The Miracle of *Motzei Yom Kipper*." However, there is a difference here: In Sholem Aleichem's "The Miracle of *Hoshayne Rabbe*,"[20] danger hovered over the head of one single, innocent, tormented Jew and a boorish priest, while today's miracle saved who knows how many people from annihilation. In a nutshell: the telephone at the gendarmerie rang unexpectedly last night at 10 P.M. The caller, the commander of gendarmerie of the Shargorod district, *Oberleutnant* Garama, ordered that the post chief, Floreanu, be sent to him immediately. At that moment, Floreanu was in the vicinity with a Ukrainian woman, and he came running in his pajamas to the telephone, where his superior imparted some tidings: the commander of the Moghilev gendarmes, who is in charge of the entire region, had dismissed Floreanu from his post and he should be so kind as to turn his seat over to his successor, someone named *Feldwebel* Georgescu, as early as the next morning. Floreanu held his tongue and, by the way, no one asks any questions in the military …

No one in the camp knew about this miracle and, this morning at dawn, Jewish militiamen hastened to the gendarmerie, bringing two baskets packed with wine, cakes, roasted ducks, and all the best in honor of the oppressor's birthday. Less than an hour later, the militiamen returned empty-handed and related that all hell had broken lose among the gendarmes. Floreanu is running around like a poisoned mouse—his face is green. They did not dare to ask what the matter was. When

19 The closing prayer of Yom Kippur, when a man's fate is sealed.

20 Sholom Aleichem, *Der Nes fun Heshayne-Rabe* (Yiddish) (Warsaw: Boimritter Publishers, 1910). For the English translation, see Aleichem, *Tevye the Dairyman and The Railroad Stories* (New York: Schocken Books, 1987), pp. 186–194, https://shron1.chtyvo.org.ua/Sholom_Aleikhem/Tevye_the_Dairyman_and_the_Railroad_Stories_anhl.pdf?PHPSESSID=6tq8363odj4071h2nc7sfqv756 (accessed June 16, 2022).

they presented the gift to him, he roared: "Inform the council members that the banquet will take place exactly at 12 P.M." Within half an hour, everything exploded. One gendarme disclosed the secret to a Jewish militiaman, and everyone immediately knew about the miracle of *Motzei Yom Kipper*. The rabbi of Siret was right when he said that it was better to wait until the following day …

The community delegation—the colony chief, Moshe Katz, and his brother-in-law Leon Neuman—went to Haman's last meal dressed in holiday clothes.[21] Katz told me to wait in the community building until they returned. At around 3 P.M., the "lords" returned, slightly inebriated and with beaming faces. Moshe Katz told me: "Oy, you have the luck of an apostate! Floreanu now has other things to worry about apart from your opinion." There is no need to describe what I felt at that moment. Fate has already granted to me quite a few miracles, but today's miracle surpasses all of them. Oy, when will we be granted times without troubles and without miracles! …

[September 22, 1942] 8 P.M.

I no longer had to go to Floreanu and, of course, he did not ask for my opinion. He already ceded his seat to his successor, and it seems that he will leave Dzhurin tonight already. I will not hand my opinion over to anyone, even if my bosses demand it. I have an excuse ready: I ripped up the dangerous piece of paper.

The "lords" who joined the party cannot say enough about how good natured and affable Floreanu was to them. It went as far as kissing after gulping more than four glasses. The oppressor even made excuses for his "agitation" (as he called the cracking of the whip on skulls) and explicitly said that he will ask his successor to treat the inhabitants of the camp well, exactly as he did. During the meeting in the afternoon meeting, the doctor even said: "It's such a shame to lose Floreanu, just now, precisely when he so respectably reconciled with us!" And there was a tear in his

21 Haman, the chief minister of King Ahasuerus who attempted to annihilate the Jews and whose downfall is recounted in the Book of Esther, which is read on the holiday of Purim.

eye … By the way, this reconciliation cost a great fortune. Perhaps the community is right, but it seems to me that we bend over backwards too much for the non-Jews, and it is unnecessary to ingratiate ourselves so much …

September 23, 1942, 3 P.M.

This matter of the denunciation has entered a new phase—although it is no longer dangerous and charged with dramatic tensions. The new commander of the gendarmerie knows nothing of what happened and is occupied with more important matters, such as the partisans who have overrun the surrounding forests. By contrast, the council began to vigorously investigate whether A. had made the denunciation on his own account or had partners. Following the investigation, the community will impose harsh punishments on the informers, who endanger the general public. People are even saying that they apparently intend to approach the Moghilev Central Council in order to have the speculators transferred to a different camp.

The accused speculators—the wealthy and well-connected people and their cronies—are pressuring the community to take harsh action against the informers. Otherwise—they argue—they themselves will go to the high-level officials, and not necessarily the Jewish ones. This means basically the same thing in a different guise—endless denunciations that are likely to lead to a terrible calamity.

This morning, following much debate, the council members finally reached a decision regarding this sordid issue. During the deliberation, I waited in the back room, because of the grave secrets … Thereafter, they called me in and informed me of the decision, because they honored me with the "*maftir*."[22] And this is the verdict: the investigation will entrust two trustworthy people—the rabbi of Siret, Rabbi Baruch Hager, and a lawyer from Vijniţa Dr. Yosef Diamant. As fate would have it, I will have

22 Kunstadt refers to the maftir, hinting at the expression "*kana lo maftir*" (literally, bought himself a maftir), to what happens when a person offers more than he can afford to buy a maftir, to indicate that he was embroiled in this matter.

the "honor" of proving to the council, in A.'s presence, that he wrote the denunciation. The bosses have dragged me into this mess, and I must not protest in order not to lose my meager livelihood.

Immediately following this decision, they invited the two investigators to the community building. At the same time, they sent a Jewish militiaman to immediately fetch A., who went out in the streets that morning. It took half an hour to bring A. to the community building, where the two investigators were already seated, as I was. The rabbi spoke to A. in a gentle voice, urging him to admit his guilt and to accept a fine for the serious crime that he had committed against the general public. A. pretended to know nothing and absolutely denied the entire story. He did so with such sangfroid that the investigators began to think that we were accusing an innocent man.

After a short time, the rabbi understood that his restrained moral reproofs were in vain and he turned to me with these words: "You are an expert in handwriting. What do you think of this?" Even though I was sure of my opinion, I asked A. to write an entire page of paper while I dictated some text. He began writing and obviously tried hard to write slowly and to disguise his original handwriting. However, the trick did not work, because he managed to alter his graphic style only slightly in the first lines and then fell back to his old style. This phenomenon is well known in graphology and, therefore, the graphologist focuses his attention mainly on the last section of a text.

I briefly examined what A. had written and then said to his face: "Do not hold it against me, but you wrote the anonymous card and I will prove it to you." I began checking the common characteristics of the handwriting samples, and A. understood me well, because he is an educated man—he completed high school—and he is a crafty schemer. He tried to deny it at first, but the color of his face changed at once. He nervously wiped the perspiration from his brow and finally asked the rabbi to grant him a few hours to consider the matter. This time the rabbi demonstrated his authority and would not allow any break, telling him that the truth always remains the same, however much or little one considers it, and that he must answer with only one single word: yes or no—said the rabbi.

The council sent me out, because I had already carried out my function, after all, and I left as one flees from a fire. Two hours later, the rabbi came into the second room, where the entire council was assembled, and announced with a shaking voice that A. had admitted everything. I felt like the blood drained from my face, because I had been the emissary, however unwilling, who had led to the present troubles of a Jewish refugee, albeit one who had put the entire community in danger because of his ambition and envy.

The second act of the drama began: investigating who had been A.'s partners. There was no doubt that there were partners, because the Romanian style of the card clearly indicated this. A. knows very little Romanian and could not write such a text on his own without mistakes. This investigation was conducted in the presence of all the council members. Although dejected and drowning in perspiration, A. once again completely denied having any partners.

Once more, the council closed itself off in a separate room with the person in question. The clock already showed 2 P.M. when the rabbi opened the door and called everyone in. He addressed the "lords" and said: "Gentlemen, I am no longer an investigator but a Jew who begs for mercy for a repentant man. Yes, A. has admitted this and he will tell you himself who convinced him to make the denunciation and even dictated to him word for word the text of the card." The rabbi looked at A., who with a quiet voice, choking back tears, pronounced the words, which fell like a bomb: "I admit that B. persuaded me to commit the act and dictated the text in Romanian."

No one had expected this sensation and it even seemed that A. had invented a plot against an enemy. Until the deportation, B. had played a prominent role in Jewish life in Bukovina. He was renowned among the Jewish functionaries, honorable in the eyes of God and men, an eminent man who was very friendly with the Romanian overlords, who showered him with honors, a brilliant speaker, and a wise Jew. People would entreat him to arbitrate important matters. Right up until the deportation, he continued to lobby for the good of the general public in dangerous situations. In Dzhurin, where he ended up in October 1941, he lost his drive and did not engage in community affairs, even though he could have done so. He leads a modest life in the camp, although he is one of the "wealthy," so to speak, and subsists on cash or the sale of his belongings. So how could it be that he could fall from this high level and commit such an act, which could have wreaked destruction were it not for the miracle that occurred?

By the way, during the investigation, A. was told that if he would hand over his partner, he would only be punished with a fine. Now the suspicion has arisen that A. threw out just any name to avoid a harsher punishment. A. was allowed to go home and the rest of the trial was postponed until today, when they will decide to summon B. to the community building to confront A. face-to-face.

I am shocked by this sequel, because I have been closely acquainted with B. for some years and have often seen how he ventures to challenge a decree against the community in order to have it revoked. In truth, I am aware of his faults, but his virtues greatly outweighed them. When I agreed to help discover the snitch in order to save the entire Jewish community of Dzhurin, I never imagined that this speck of dust would become an avalanche of snow that would sweep away an honorable Jew such as B.

September 24, 1942, 9 P.M.

Yesterday at 10 P.M., the order to bring A. to the community building was suddenly issued again, and the "lords" sharply demanded that he reveal his real accomplices. A. stubbornly claimed that, other than B., he had no partners whatsoever. B. had given him the idea of writing the denunciation letter in order to blacken the name of the butcher Floreanu in the eyes of his superiors and cause his downfall. And A. added cynically: On *Motzei Yom Kipper*, everyone clearly discovered that the scheme had worked …

This investigation was conducted because the council endeavored to avoid the shame of drawing the honorable functionary B. into the sordid affair. Now the community has no choice and they decided to summon B. to the community building today and make him swear [to tell the truth]. They thought that B. would deny the claims and would spit in A.'s face, because there is no evidence other than A.'s testimony.

The council sent the militia to summon B. and the messenger returned immediately, reporting that B. is lying in his bed with a high fever since yesterday afternoon. They also discovered that A. had gone to visit B. yesterday afternoon and had spent more than an hour with him. A. obviously told him that he had divulged the secret, which triggered the sudden outbreak of the illness.

It was clear to everyone that something here stank, and it was no longer possible to hide the scandal. Everyone in the camp found out that A. had confessed, and people demanded his destruction. However, no one knew that B. was also involved in this.

Sharp disagreements erupted within the council. Some argued that the council should go immediately to B. and to interrogate him there and then. However, the doctor and Moshe Katz argued that they should wait another day, and so it was decided. This drama will further unfold tomorrow morning.

September 25, 1942, 7 P.M.

Oy, the drama has played out to such an extent that my head is still spinning, and I can find no rest. The drama began already at about 9 A.M. All the council members were seated around the table and the colony chief, who presided over the board instead of the rabbi of Siret, sat at the head. The rabbi [Hager] had informed them that he could not be present today, because of his wife's sudden illness. Although it was clear to everyone that the illness was brought on by diplomatic bacteria, no one dared to push the venerable rabbi up against the wall. Indeed, the second investigator, Dr. Yosef Diamant, arrived. The colony chief ordered me to write an invitation to B., requesting that he be so kind as to take the trouble to come to the community building. The messenger returned promptly with a note from B. in which it was written that due to exhaustion, he would come only in the afternoon. The colony chief wanted to postpone the matter to the following day, but Moshe Katz and other council members opposed this.

In the end, the decision was made that the hospital director, Dr. Moshe Greiff, would go directly to B.'s home to see whether he really lacked the strength to walk the short distance to the community building. If he really could not walk, the council would make the effort to go to his home. Dr. Greiff delivered his opinion: if only he himself, the doctor, were that weak.

Upon hearing this news, the colony chief himself wrote an invitation and, in his own words, explicitly threatened to send militiamen to fetch him. This note was effective, and we soon saw B. through the window, slowly approaching the community building, leaning on a stick, even though he never uses a support. At the same moment, they also sent for A. and snuck him into a neighboring house.

B. entered the community building, pale as a sheet and with his right hand clutching at his chest. The colony chief instructed him to sit and allowed him to regain his composure. He then conducted this conversation with him:

> **The doctor:** You probably know why you have been summoned here?
>
> **B.:** How would I know?
>
> **The doctor**: Do you not know that A. has admitted his crime and has accused you of advising him to write [the card] and even dictating the content of the denunciation?
>
> **B.** (Astonished but composed) Really? This is the first time that I am hearing those lies.
>
> **The doctor:** Well, what if A. tells you to your face what you just heard. Will you admit it?
>
> **B.** (Calm and with a straight face) I have nothing to admit, and A. cannot dare to drag me into his mess.

Following a signal from Moshe Katz, the door of the next room opened at that moment, and a militiaman led in A., his eyes downcast and without looking at anyone in the face. B. was startled for a moment, as though he had seen the devil, but quickly recovered and stared at A. with a penetrating gaze, like a hypnotist gazes at his medium. The doctor turned to A. and asked him to repeat his words of the day before, when he had admitted his actions. A. looked down and remained silent. This was sufficient for the doctor and he quoted in Latin (as is his nature ...) the saying: Silence means admission. Moshe Katz, however, was not happy with this statement and spoke harshly and loudly: "You can either repeat what you said yesterday or be flung somewhere in the Moghilev gendarmerie." This was followed by a short conversation:

> **Katz:** State clearly who persuaded you to make the denunciation and dictated the wording of the card!
>
> **A.:** (In a broken voice, whispering and pointing at B.) Him!
>
> **Katz:** What do you mean by "Him"! Say clearly the name of your accomplice!
>
> **A.:** (In a barely audible voice) So, B.

B. listened to the accusation stone-faced and did not reply at all. They did not continue to press B., and that's how the investigation concluded today. I was tasked with writing down a protocol of the conversation, and all those present signed, including A. and B. I too had to sign my signature by order of the doctor, although I tried to avoid doing so at first. The doctor placed the protocol in his briefcase, although I usually hold on to the protocols of meetings.

Meanwhile the council has still not decided what will happen next. The doctor wants to dismiss the entire matter and claims that the investigation can endanger the entire camp. It may be that he is not entirely wrong because, under the present circumstances, it is better not to blow up the stinking mess. In contrast, Moshe Katz is dangerously agitated and seeks to tear the culprits apart, limb by limb, along with the speculators who brought on the danger. He demands that they be banished from Dzhurin, or at the very least, that all their possessions be confiscated for the public good. Expulsion, however, is dangerous, because it begins with the speculators but may end up with the entire holy community. Who is capable of approaching our enemies to ask them to drive out Jews! ...

September 26, 1942, First Day of *Sukkes*

Today is a holiday. A considerable number of men went to the *minyonim* and enjoyed reciting *Hallel*, *Hoyshanes*,[23] and other holiday delights. An *esreg* with a *lulev*, which were smuggled by a Romanian courier from Bucharest, even found their way to the rabbi of Siret. I seize a free moment and sit bent over my notebook, which has been reflecting the troubles and the miracles, so to speak, that have happened in Transnistria for half a year already.

The first stanza of an old Yiddish song that I remember from my childhood has stuck in my head like a pesky fly.

> When the first day of *Sukkes* comes,
> A story from the time of childhood
> Comes to mind.
> Our *Sukkeh*[24] was declared unfit
> By someone who has already departed,
> Rabbi Shlomele, the judge …

However, this stanza needs to be slightly adapted. The incident that comes to mind did not take place long ago during my childhood but only a year ago on the first day of *Sukkes*. And it was not a *Sukkeh* that was declared unfit but rather the homes of the Jewish community, which numbered tens of thousands of persons,[25] in my hometown of Rădăuţi, including my beautiful home. And it was not Rabbi Shlomele, the judge, who was guilty but rather, in contrast, the entire world—both the Nazi demons and the supposed civilized and democratic nations, who look on in silence while the Jewish people are being murdered.

---

23 *Hallel* is the prayer of praise, composed of Psalms 113–118, that is recited on holidays. *Hoshanot*, from the Hebrew words *hoshana* (please bring us salvation), are special prayers recited every day of Sukkot while holding the lulav (palm branch) and the etrog (citron), which symbolize the intrinsic unity of the Jewish people.

24 A hut that serves as temporary dwelling during the holiday of Sukkot.

25 The community of Rădăuţi numbered 5,600 people on the eve of the war. Kunstadt included the refugees who arrived in the Rădăuţi in the summer of 1940 in the figure that he noted.

Then, on the first day of *Sukkes*, 5702 [1941], the menacing lightning struck and ignited the fire, which was extinguished only on *Simches Toyre*, when the last transport of Jews rolled out of the holy land of Bukovina on the way to the desolate land between the Dniester and the Bug. I still see that dark first day of *Sukkes* before my eyes—dark and yet bright—the mild autumn sun was shining and the air was permeated with autumn gold, with wonderful scents of ripeness, with autumnal yearning and in an autumnal mood.

I was then seated at a place of honor at the eastern wall of the synagogue in the *vatikin minyen*[26]—then I was still a kind of notable, so to speak … and I listened to the prayer leader sing "*Umipney Hata'eynu*." Suddenly the community *parnas*[27] appeared and handed me a telegram, which the postman had just delivered. I was the community secretary and therefore the community mail was brought to me. As soon as I opened the telegram, my eyes saw black. The central council of the Jewish communities in Romania had sent the following telegram from Bucharest: "Send two delegates to Bucharest immediately regarding an important matter." I surmised straightaway that this was related to the threat of expulsion that had been hanging like a sword over our necks since the war with the USSR had begun.

In order not to cause any panic among the crowd of people who were looking at me in surprise, I put the telegraph into my pocket as though it were nothing and remained in my place for a while. I left discreetly only after the *Birkes Kehanim*[28] and went to the head of the community, Aizic Presner,[29] with the good tidings. The community administration was immediately summoned, they chose delegates to [send to] Bucharest and … did nothing. At that time, a Jew could travel to Bucharest only with authorization from the prefect, and the prefect of Rădăuţi, Ionescu, an oppressor of the Jews, who was a member of the "Iron Guard," did not agree under any circumstances to grant an authorization. He answered

26 The shaharit minyan at sunrise.

27 The chief administrative officer of a Jewish congregation.

28 The priestly blessing.

29 Aizic Presner was deported to the Moghilev ghetto and served as a member of the local Jewish council. See CNSAS, I-329796, vol. 2.

cynically: "Why the urgency? Save your money and send a letter instead of delegates!" The evil man knew what was going on and sought to prevent the Jews from rescinding the decree.

Well, the delegates did not travel then but only three days later, secretly with the help of God. At any rate, they did not manage to do anything, because the expulsion decree against all the Jews of Bukovina and Bessarabia had already been signed by Marshal Antonescu in August 1941. Antonescu, Hitler's puppet, had met with German officers and the ambassador Baron Killinger in the Bessarabian city of Tighina where they clinched the deal.[30]

And today is the first anniversary of that first day of *Sukkes*! I sit and write down my memories, but for whom, for what, and for when! …

September 27, 1942, Second Day of *Sukkes*, 5703, 2 P.M.

Today, I have had for once a happy holiday, a true day of our rejoicing! At 10 A.M. today, my sister, Rivka, was taken on a stretcher to the hospital, because she got the nice package—typhoid fever. There is something worse—typhus—but then the patient does not suffer for long: either way, it is over after only a few days. By contrast, typhoid fever shows more "mercy," and it is sometimes possible to be cured of it, mainly young people, but they are racked with pain for quite some time, sometimes even for months, and it sucks the life out of them. However, the problem is that all the patients in the hospital lie mixed together in overcrowded conditions, and they are often actually infected there with the dangerous Rickettsia bacteria. It is precisely that tragedy that struck her. She lives

30 The Tighina Agreement was signed in the town of Tighina, Bessarabia, on August 30, 1941, by the representative of the Romanian Chief of Staff, General Nicolae Tătăranu, and a representative of the Wehrmacht, General Arthur Hauffe, with the participation of the German ambassador Manfred von Killinger. According to the Tighina Agreement, the area between the Bug River and the Dniester River was turned over to the Romanian administration that would serve as a concentration area to which the Romanians would transfer the Jews of Bessarabia and Bukovina. Hitler called this geographical area Transnistria—beyond the Dniester.

with Mother and is her entire support, because I live far away and am very busy at work until late at night. Today, I really did not recognize Mother—she is skin and bones but her faith cannot be not broken. Mother accepts everything with love, observes the fasts as she has done all her life, prays, argues with the Master of the Universe, and interprets her nighttime dreams positively. She clearly sees the birth pangs of the messiah, she says, and the deliverance will certainly arrive this year. My mind is not on my work, and the new calamity has completely stunned me.

September 28, 1942

The hospital director, Dr. Greiff, is doing his best to save Rivka. She is lying with a high fever in isolation in a "good" room (with few patients). Apart from lemonade, she is not allowed to put anything in her mouth, and she is being treated with injections to fortify her resilience. For now, there is no cure for typhus, and the body must fight it alone. Dr. Greiff, a good friend of mine and a frequent visitor to my home, reassures me that everything will yet be well, and not to be in a hurry but to wait …

Mother drags herself, supported by a cane, a few times a day to the hospital, which is not far from her "apartment," to keep abreast of Rivka's condition. The doctor and the student–orderlies assure her that everything is fine, but allowing Mother to enter is neither spoken of nor is it even a consideration.[31] I visit Mother twice a day, early in the morning and in the evening. She bears her sorrow with strength and demonstrates once again her tenacious character.

Allow me to note the names of the students who volunteer as orderlies in the hospital for infectious diseases and risk their lives every day: Dov Katz, Bertl Hart, Burcshi Braun, Carl Rosenblatt, Sami Shapira, Poldi Ungariş, and Bertl Neuman. They studied medicine in Romania. Apart from Dr. Greiff, Dr. Gabriel Shtir, Dr. Julius Frenckel, Dr. Efroim Şabat, Dr. Rosenstrauch, and Dr. Klipper work in the hospital—according to a system of rotational shiftwork. All have devoted their lives to the patients

31 Jeremiah 3:16: "Neither will it come to mind; neither will they make mention of it."

and, for this reason, Dzhurin is known in Transnistria as the camp where the Rickettsia bacteria has claimed the least number of victims.

September 30, 1942

Rivka's condition has worsened. She can no longer drag herself to the window to allow Mother and me to see her through the windows. She is confused and her delirium, which was brought on by fever, does not cease. Some of the injections—of grape sugar, camphor, caffeine, and so on—are not available in the hospital and must be obtained on the "black market" for a lot of money in Dzhurin terms. Let me note explicitly that the council is considerately providing the money for Rivka's medicines.

October 2, 1942

There is no change in Rivka's condition—intense fever, confusion, and weakness. Dr. Greiff claims that she will overcome the dreadful disease, because her heart is strong and resilient. It torments me to see Mother shrinking more and more each day, barely able to stand on her feet, as a result of running to the hospital daily and standing for hours in front of the closed window.

October 3, 1942, *Shminatzeres* 5703

An entire year has passed since we were cruelly torn from our lives and chased out like hunted dogs, without the right to live and without the courage to die. All the good signs that we interpreted as signaling the coming deliverance have dissipated like mist on a spring morning, and a second winter in Transnistria will soon be upon us. The fire continues to rage evermore all over the world, and only yesterday the leading bigwig on the opposing side **(added in 1945: Churchill)** announced to the world that we can expect another two or three years of this bloodshed and suffering before the evil snake will be destroyed. Will there still be any Jews left in Europe then?

A year ago today, on *Shminatzeres*! Like a day in an insane asylum—no, like in one of the seven levels of hell, as they are described in the old *Muser* books.[32] A third of the Jewish residents were already on the road, having departed with the first transport on the night of *Hoshayne Rabbe.* All the roads and alleys were filled with the wagons of non-Jews, which transported the meager belongings of the Jews to the train station. Non-Jewish peasants and local townsmen went freely into the homes of the Jews and took whatever their hearts desired. No one opposed them, because it did not matter who would be the heir, Vassily or Pietre.

While people everywhere were packing the odds and ends of their poverty in their homes and preparing for the far-flung journey into the world of chaos, I left my home and set out for the community building to save the community books (that date back to the year 1857)[33] and to take them to city hall. I had been the community registrar for many years, and those approximately thirty books—the chronicle of a major Jewish community that was destroyed—listed the three most important events in a person's life (birth, marriage, death). I abandoned my family and went to save the records, because of their great significance for the remaining remnant, who may return to the city one day. I managed to persuade the Romanian commissioner of the municipal registrar at city hall, Simata, to take the books to his department, but I had to carry the books from the community building to city hall, because there was no one to help, and I almost ruptured my bowels.

---

32 Jewish *Sifrut Musar* (ethical literature) was written from the Middle Ages onwards. It sought to strengthen the readers' faith in God, encourage them to keep the commandments, and give meaning to life, in particular the lives of the Jews in the sufferings of exile. *Musar* literature includes various types and genres of works, especially philosophical. In the eighteenth century, *Musar* literature developed in Poland a "clear social trend" that included harsh criticism of the rich and the ruling classes, injustices committed by the community leaders, and the difficult situation that the masses of the people endured, demanding that the situation be rectified. See https://en.wikipedia.org/wiki/Musar_literature (accessed June 16, 2022).

33 The registries were the books in which the population records were recorded: births, deaths, marriages etc. Rabbis usually managed the community record books.

I waited until Simata placed the last volume in the cabinet and went home to pack my scanty poverty. I do not know if a remnant of those records remains, and whether anyone will take an interest in them and will make use of them, but I do not regret my actions.

(Added in 1945, after the liberation, in Rădăuţi)

The books were preserved at city hall and Simata himself brought them to the community building immediately following the return of the few survivors. He is a Romanian who deserves to be awarded the title Righteous Among the Nations.[34] These books were of great benefit to the survivors who immigrated to *Eretz Yisroel*, or who immigrated to other countries, because it was not possible to obtain a passport in Romania without documents.

Dzhurin, the Continuation of the Entry of *Shminatzeres*

In the *minyen*, it is customary to recite the *Yizkor* now—Vey, vey, what a long page of *Yizkor* has been drawn up since last year! Let me be no different myself from the public, and I will make this entry my memorial to the home and the community.

October 4, 1942, *Simches Toyre*, 5703, 7 A.M.

A year ago, at this very moment, the third, the last, transport of Jews—about 3,000 persons—left the train station of Rădăuţi for Transnistria.

---

34 The term "Righteous Among the Nations"—*Chasidei Umot HaOlam*—was drawn from Jewish tradition. It appears in the literature of the sages to describe non-Jews who come to the aid of the Jewish people in times of need, or non-Jews who respect the basic tenets set down in the Bible, including the prohibition of bloodshed. The Yad Vashem Law took the existing term and added new meaning to it, characterizing the Righteous Among the Nations as those who not only saved Jews, but risked their lives in doing so. This is the basic criterion for awarding the title.

My family and I had the privilege of joining this *Simches Toyre hakofe*. This has been the most terrible year in my life so far and, nevertheless, the pen desires to write the old Yiddish saying of comfort, "just not worse."

In the meanwhile, it is *Simches Toyre*, and the Jews sang and danced at the *hakofes* last night. Some *minyonim* even enjoyed a glass of *samagonka*—a kind of alcoholic drink made from plums, which the peasants distill in casks. The *minyen* of the rabbi of Siret had a great celebration until 11 P.M., and one young man L. H. experienced such spiritual transcendence that he fell into a hole and broke his leg while walking home in the dark. The doctors treated him the entire night and thought that he had to be taken to the hospital in Moghilev early in the morning. The problem is that the journey to Moghilev for a Jew is like the parting of the Red Sea, because it is necessary to first obtain authorization from the district commander of the gendarmerie in Shargorod. Advocates are literally breaking down the door of the local gendarmes, asking them to obtain the authorization by telephone. No problem—scoff people in the camp—when such a thing happens to one of the speculators, the gendarmes present him with the authorization on a silver tray. However, no such luck this time …

I'm in a hurry so as, God forbid, not to miss the bargains at the weekly market. After all, the autumn is cold and wet, and we must stock up on 1 or even 2 poods of potatoes … my wallet is almost empty, and a new problem has arisen: they have stopped paying my meager wages on time, and it is extremely difficult to obtain a whit of a mark. The bosses claim that the community coffer is empty. There is certainly not enough for both the overlords and their whores, as well as for me and for others like me …

October 4, 1942, 3 P.M.

In honor of *Simches Toyre*, the district commander of the Shargorod gendarmes honored the camp of Dzhurin with a special *hakofe* this morning: we must provide 100 men for work in a forest near Kryzhopol, in the Balta district, no later than the day after tomorrow. This decree is different from the previous one,[35] because the site is almost 100 kilometers away from here, and there are no more Jews in the area. Furthermore, it will be necessary to register the disabled, the *heder*[36] children, and the elderly, unless they begin to get their hands on the well-connected people as well.

The head of the Labor Office, David Buksbaum, and his subordinates, have already sat down to register the names behind closed doors. A militiaman stands guard outside and does not allow anyone to enter. There are doors that are not locked with a lock and key, but they are not for the general public.

October 5, 1942

There is a big commotion in the community building. The list of 100 names already looks like a mended garment, covered with patches. There has been a succession of erasures and additions, of whispering in ears and of slipping notes, of cries and wailing and curses and threats. Militiamen are storming homes, announcing the good news, and warning that anyone who tries to escape[37] endangers his family and is liable to be deported. The council members deny any responsibility and claim that the commander of the Shargorod gendarmes compiled the list based on the records of the people in the Dzhurin camp, which he has had for some time. Whoever does not believe them may ask Buksbaum himself. People race to Buksbaum, he gawks at them with innocent eyes and replies: Would a council member lie! No one dares approach the colony chief. He thinks that everyone will soon be sent away to work, even babies in cribs.

---

35 The conscription of Jews for forced labor paving roads near Dzhurin.

36 Jewish elementary school where children learn to read the Torah and other books in Hebrew.

37 When it became known that Jewish policemen accompanied by gendarmes were rounding up men to perform forced labor, the men would hide in order to avoid being caught. See Yaakov (Jacky) Pistiner interview by Sarah Rosen, January 17, 2008, Haifa; Shlomo Shteinmetz interview by Sarah Rosen, January 17, 2010, Ramat Gan.

October 6, 1942, 6 P.M.

Already at dawn today, the Jewish militia raided the roads and alleys in order to round up the people who were sentenced to work in the Kryzhopol forest.[38] The list included quite a few of the well-connected people and those close to them, but when the militia entered the hovels, they found only common people. The prophet Elijah did not appear to these emaciated skeletons during the night and did not reveal the secret to them …

In the meanwhile, the hands of the clock continued to move, and it was already 8 A.M., and the militia had only managed to gather about sixty broken skeletons and undernourished children. Five armed gendarmes then burst into the community building and their leader bellowed: Where are the 100 workers whom we must escort to Kryzhopol? The doctor immediately sent for the head of the Jewish militia, Iosef Stein,[39] and whispered a secret in his ear. The doctor then turned to the gendarmes and said: Before you set out on your long journey, it is only right that you have a bite to eat. The gendarmes did not refuse and sat down in a special room to celebrate with a meal fit for a king—liquor, sausage, and a cake, which the militia swiftly brought them.

The secret that the doctor had imparted quickly ceased to be a secret. The militia raided every corner and seized whomever they happened upon: the elderly, the disabled, children, and even one of the speculators who was caught off guard. They reached the quota of 100 within an hour, but what merchandise! Most of the people belonged in an old age home or an orphanage, and all of them were worn and ragged, lacking a warm piece of outerwear. Many wore old galoshes instead of shoes, and others simply wrapped their bare feet with a sack. A few of them limped and some of the old people leaned on sticks. The militia lined up these

---

38 On October 2, 1942, 700 Jews were rounded up in the Moghilev region: 100 from the Shargorod ghetto, 100 from the Dzhurin ghetto, and the rest from the Moghilev ghetto itself and the surrounding area. These Jews were taken to the forest of Kryzhopol to cut down trees. They were housed under deplorable conditions, without food and with almost no clothing. Due to the terrible conditions, many became ill, and others froze to death. See Carp, *Cartea neagră*, vol. 3 p. 284.

39 Iosef Stein served as head of the Jewish police in Dzhurin.

human shards in the square by the community building. The families of those sentenced ran toward them, women wailed and threw themselves to the ground. Young orphans without mothers sobbed and tried to reach their fathers in the line, and even people without any relatives among the macabre group could not stop their tears. The community provided each one with a loaf of bread, and the commander of the gendarmerie roared: "*Ininte mars*!" (forward march!) The line moved out of the square and left for the gendarmerie post from where the crowd would be taken on foot to the nearest train station, Rakhny, and from there by train to Kryzhopol. That's what the commander of the gendarmerie promised and, if it is true, it will not be a lie …[40]

After the men set out, poor things, the frantic people in the camp, including the women and children, raised such a commotion, cursing and even trying to burst into the community building. The militia forcibly dispersed the "rebels." None of the "lords" showed their faces in the streets. When I returned from work at around 2 P.M., I was really ashamed to cross the street, even though I have nothing to do with labor issues. No one asks for my opinion, and my word carries no weight. On the contrary, it would only be detrimental to those sentenced.

I was ordered to announce in the soup kitchen that, as of today, portions of soup will be distributed to the wives and children of the laborers in Kryzhopol. I presented the list to the director of the soup kitchen, Bubi Met, and he read it over and said: these are my regular guests in any case. As a matter of fact, I will have portions to spare.

October 8, 1942

Rivka is still burning with fever and does not recognize anyone. I have not been able to persuade Mother to limit her trips to the hospital and to stop standing for hours in front of the shuttered windows. I am ready to send the children a few times a day to provide some refreshments—in any case, the sick should not eat—but Mother is stubborn and is not willing

---

40 It later became clear that the people were forced to march to the camp in Kryzhopol—a distance of 200 kilometers.

even to listen. She drags herself with a walking stick to the hospital and is really wearing herself out. If this continues, it will not end up well for her, perish the thought. Dr. Greiff did not stop warning Mother that she should not push herself too hard but to no avail.

October 10, 1942, 1 P.M.

Because of the holidays and mainly because of the Kryzhopol drama, no one at the community building managed to continue the investigation of the denunciation that agitated the camp two weeks ago; as it says in the Gemara: "later troubles make them forget the earlier ones."[41] Yesterday evening the "lords" resumed dealing with the dirty laundry not in order to punish the culprit but to impose a respectable fine. The people involved are wealthy, and there will be something to extort. Besides, the speculators demand that a verdict be reached as soon as possible. They have convinced themselves that the council will award them a considerable sum as compensation for the anxiety that they have endured. If not, these people threaten that they know where a door opens in Moghilev, not to mention Shargorod. This can lead to a great disaster, because the denunciations mention that butcher shops are in operation in the camp, when the governor has strictly forbidden the slaughter of animals in Transnistria, unless the beast is dying.[42]

Although the colony chief kept the file under lock and key with the intention of suppressing the matter, the council members, led by Moshe Katz, pressed him to proceed with the trial and even threatened to hand in their resignations. The trial began yesterday at around 7 P.M. The colony chief conducted the procedures. He honored me with the *maftir*: reading the dangerous denunciation out loud. While I was in the middle of reading, Moshe Katz suddenly rose from his seat, lashed out in anger against A.,

---

41 B. Berachot 13a.

42 The Romanian government regarded Transnistria as a resource for economic exploitation to fill the state treasury. The Romanian authorities transferred entire herds of cattle to Romania. See Alexander Dallin, *Odessa, 1941–1944: A Case Study of Soviet Territory Under Foreign Rule* (Iași, Oxford, and Portland: The Center for Romanian Studies, 1998), p. 178.

who was standing with B. in front of the table, and punched him under his chin. He then shouted at him, "You scoundrel, why did you seek to bring misfortune on thousands of Jews?" A. wiped his face and whispered: "B. egged me on. I beg for mercy for three reasons: my parents, my past, and … my mental condition. Everything is not right in my head …"

Moshe Katz delivered a searing accusatory speech against A. and B., arguing that even if they would confiscate everything they possess, it would not outweigh the severity of the transgression. The doctor changed his position and frightened the culprits with his harsh words. The council members deliberated briefly, and the doctor finally declared the verdict: A. and B. will jointly pay the community a fine of 3,400 marks. Even though this is a considerable sum, the two guilty parties were not shocked. On the contrary, it seemed that they had expected a much harsher punishment. Both were careful not to show any gratification and they tried to negotiate the amount. However, they immediately agreed and requested that they be allowed to pay the fine the next morning. B. also added that he would pay half of his share of the fine and would leave his *streimel*[43] as a pledge in lieu of the second half. The doctor whispered something in Moshe Katz's ear, but the "second-in-command" answered aloud: "We do not understand the business of robbery but rather matters of denunciation. The entire sum must be paid by noon tomorrow." The whole trial took half an hour and then both sides parted, obviously satisfied.

I have my doubts, especially regarding the obligations of A. and B. Tomorrow will show if I am not mistaken.

October 11, 1942, 3 P.M.

In the meantime, I was not wrong. Neither A. nor B. have yet shown a whit of a mark. In contrast, today at dawn, B. suddenly appeared in my hovel and begged me to put in a good word for him with my bosses, so that they would not push him up against the wall. Of course, I brushed him off. I have no say with the "lords" and I do not want to get involved

43 A sable fur hat worn by the Hasidim on the Sabbath and on holidays.

in this dirty business. This guest was very disagreeable to me. My hovel is close to the community building, and the streets have eyes. If a rumor of the visit reaches the ears of my bread givers, it could backfire on me, unjustifiably and for no reason.

October 15, 1942, 8 P.M.

A Ukrainian peasant brought a note from Kryzhopol to the community building today, which was written to the family of one of the 100 deported men. The news is not good. The gendarmerie commander's promise that the workers would be taken to Kryzhopol by train was a ruse. The people were dragged on foot from one gendarmerie post to the next, and they slept under the open sky, hungry and exhausted. As long as the Dzhurin gendarmes accompanied the convoy, it was only half as bad, but then the guards changed, and the new wardens of hell treated them [the Jews] like criminals.

The note shocked the families of the deported men, and groups of wailing women and children immediately burst into the community building and threw themselves on the ground; some fainted and had to be revived. The "lords" made every effort to calm the distraught relatives and promised that they would send a wagon with food to Kryzhopol today. Nothing more can be done. To reassure them, the council members added false comfort: the work in the forest would last only two weeks.[44] The shocked families finally dispersed, richer in empty promises.

October 17, 1942, 2 P.M.

Here's a new Dzhurin miracle: the "forest Jews" from Kryzhopol returned today,[45] everyone, but don't ask in what condition. Ragged and exhausted.

---

44 This was a false promise. The council had no influence on the decisions of the Romanian authorities.

45 Although the promise had no basis, the deportees who were deported on October 6, 1942, returned to their homes less than two weeks later, on October 17, 1942.

Most of them were barefoot, covered in dirt and mud, their beards tangled and overgrown, their eyes sunken in their yellow faces, hungry and beaten—this is how they strode into the camp after wandering for eleven days. They say that, on the way there, they were forced to run a distance of about 200 kilometers alongside roads, even though the distance on the main road is only 100 kilometers. The escorts beat their guts out, not sparing any blows with the butts of their rifles and torturing them every step of the way. They would have collapsed from hunger had it not been for the Ukrainian peasants from a few villages, who took pity on the deportees and gave them food.[46]

Only after six days of wandering did the convoy reach the Kryzhopol gendarmerie post. There they let the Jews wait under the open sky for half a day as a cold rain fell. An official finally appeared and announced that the number of men required to work in the forest had already been filled, and the Dzhurin Jews would shortly return to the place from where they had come. The way home was easier, because everyone felt a great sense of relief.

Immediately after the return of the men from Kryzhopol, they were taken to the hospital yard, where the orderlies took their filthy clothes and burned some of them, while others were thrown into the disinfection boiler, depending on the condition of the article of clothing, since all the returnees were infested with lice. Relatives of some people brought a change of clothes, but the majority had nothing to change into and they had to wait naked until the disinfection process was concluded. There were also some compassionate people who brought a shirt, underwear, trousers, or a pair of old shoes from their own meager belongings—the rabbi of Dzhurin, Rabbi Herşel Karalnic, literally moved heaven

---

46 Two groups can be distinguished among the local Ukrainians: Nationalist Ukrainians and rural peasants. The Ukrainian nationalists included members of the Ukrainian militias, who collaborated with the occupying power. The peasants were simple people, who worked hard to make a meager living from agriculture. They too suffered at the hands of the German occupiers and later the Romanian rulers, who treated them cruelly. This incited their hatred for the occupiers, and some of them even began to identify with the affliction of the Jews and to feel a sense of shared suffering. This led some of them to provide food and sometimes hideouts to the Jews, and occasionally to pass on information about what was happening outside the ghettos. See Dalia Ofer, "Life in the Ghettos of Transnistria," *Yad Vashem Studies*, 25 (1996), pp. 229–274.

and earth to clothe and shoe in every way possible those coming from Kryzhopol—the "forest Jews."

[October 17, 1942] 8 P.M.

Although those guilty of writing the card were fined and were supposed to pay their fine a week ago, they have shirked paying and have delayed payment, using all sorts of excuses. However, the pitcher shattered today—Moshe Katz broke it. He is filling in today for the doctor, who is in Shargorod, so he seized the opportunity, while holding the reins. He sent for both "heroes" and informed them that, God willing, they will spend the night in the militia cellar, and also the following nights, if they do not pay the fine immediately. Seeing that no subterfuge would help them anymore, they begged to be allowed to go home in order to bring the cash. To this Katz responded: "With great pleasure and indeed to honor you, militiamen will escort you there and back …" In short, it took no more than half an hour for the two churls to place thirty-four 100 [denomination] notes on the table in the community building. In any case, they made a good deal, because whole 100 [mark] notes have less value, and speculators pay only seventy 1 [mark] notes or thirty-five 2 [mark] notes for a 100 [mark] note. Moshe Katz had no choice, because the verdict failed to mention that the sum had to be paid in "small" denominations …

October 18, 1942

A cabinet crisis has broken out in the "Jewish state." For a long time already, the council members have been quarreling with the colony chief, Dr. Max Rosenstrauch. He sees himself as a kind of governor of Dzhurin and often does foolish things that cause trouble and pain. He cannot hold his tongue and says unwarranted things to the Romanian overlords and justifies them without being required to do so, and he is afraid to speak up when it is necessary to rescind a decree. He is constantly afraid that he will be ousted. The council, he argues, may engage only in matters of charity and must not express any opinions about work or about the relations with the occupying authorities. He is particularly harsh and rigorous in carrying out all kinds of orders.

His behavior drives the council members crazy, especially Moshe Katz, who aspires to be a dictator himself, but not in the same fashion as the doctor. He is indeed very stubborn and riles the whole world against him, but he is nevertheless a Jew with a Jewish heart and with a great sense of responsibility for the general good. His virtues outweigh his faults, and he receives both blessings and curses. The disputes between the doctor and the "second-in-command" have actually come to blows, but they have fought and then have apologized.

Today, once again, an argument broke out over a trivial matter—something about a dispute between a tenant and his Dzhurin landlord—and suddenly Moshe Katz's zeal flared up and he abruptly rose from his seat, grabbed his iron stick in his hand, and shouted in the doctor's face—"I will no longer set foot over this threshold!" He slammed the door shut and disappeared. At that moment, the councilman Bobi Rosenrauch, a devoted adjunct of Katz and a decent fellow, went too far: he immediately drafted his resignation, presented the paper to the doctor, and left without saying goodbye. Only four council members remained at the table—Ungariş, Valdman, Eltes, and Neuman—who stepped in and will make it easier for the doctor to preside over "his kingdom" in his own way. Nevertheless, I am also convinced that the current ire will last from the Fast of Esther until *Purim*, and the indignant movers and shakers will quickly return to their seats.[47]

---

47 Relations between the members of the council in Dzhurin were tense and stormy. Numerous arguments, disagreements, and dramas erupted between the head of the council Max Rosenstrauch and his deputy, Moshe Katz. Yehudit Nir, Katz's daughter, described the two as being like "two cats in a bag"; Yehudit Nir interview by Sarah Rosen, February 15, 2011, Ramat Gan. The source of their arguments and disagreements was their difference of opinions regarding how the ghetto should be managed and, particularly, Rosenstrauch's behavior toward the local Romanian authorities. Katz claimed that Rosenstrauch punctiliously fulfilled the orders of the Romanian authorities, sometimes going too far in his efforts to please them. In other cases, Katz argued that Rosenstrauch ingratiated himself with the Romanian authorities. Due to these disagreements, Katz resigned from his position. However, after many efforts were made to persuade him to return, he relented, as the author of the diary notes. Despite the disagreements between Rosenstrauch and Katz, Rosenstrauch needed Katz and his help. It is also apparent from

As for me, if I must rely on the doctor's sense of justice, my meager slice of barley bread is precarious. He has it in for me, as I have written on more than one occasion, and if it weren't for Moshe Katz, who has my back, I would have been left out in the cold a long time ago. One should not ask for a new king.

[October 18, 1942] 8 P.M.

The cabinet crisis in the community building has not, God forbid, driven anyone to despair, because the camp is not very attached to its leaders, even to the best of them who sit in the holy of holies. On the contrary, people are occupied with the news, products of the "IPA" mill, which spread today—no one knows from where or when. Here is a short list from the rumor mill, which are actually good tidings: Italy is apparently thinking of abandoning the wedding [alliance] and signing a separate peace agreement; Jews from Romania will no longer be sent to Transnistria, only the Roma [will be sent]; they will soon provide the deportees between the Dniester and the Bug [Jews of Bessarabia and Northern Bukovina] with papers, they will be granted land, and they will once again be human beings, and will even be sent home in the autumn; the well-connected people from the kosher regions (Southern Bukovina and northern Moldavia [Dorohoi]) will be completely free [to return] from the exile.

When in deep water up to one's neck, a person will even grasp at the straw of the "IPA" and will even fashion a straw for himself…

Kunstadt's words that the conflicts between the two created two camps in the council: supporters of Katz, including Kunstadt himself, the council member Bobi Rosenrauch, and apparently also Katz's brother in law, Leon Neuman, whom Katz appointed to manage the council's accounts and put him in charge of sanitation and the cleaning of the ghetto. Council members Ungariş, Valdman, Eltes, and Neuman apparently supported Rosenstrauch. Moshe Katz received substantial support from the Jewish public in the ghetto. Every time that he resigned from his post—this happened on several occasions—"goodwill delegations" arrived at his door to try to convince him to return.

October 19, 1942 (8th of *Heshvan*, 5703), 6 A.M.

It is important to note the Jewish date because, according to our calendar, a year has passed to the day since our entry through the "gates" of Dzhurin. The worm has gotten used to the horseradish and fears that he will be ordered to leave. What has this first year in the world of chaos taught me? To fear the Angel of Death less, and that there is nothing better than barley bread to satisfy the stomach.

By the way, let me not commit a sin against posterity. What am I, a Rothschild who can afford to eat pure barely bread! The truth is that this bread is only half barely flour and the other half potato …

[October 19, 1942] 3 P.M.

Mazel tov! The delegation that ran back and forth between the colony chief and Moshe Katz finally succeeded in the matchmaking. Moshe Katz, accompanied by members of his inner circle, strode firmly into the community building this morning and sat down in his empty chair. The doctor began the "historic" meeting with a lofty proclamation that henceforth he will completely renounce his dictatorial practices, but … nevertheless, he will not allow thugs to push him around. These additional words caused Moshe Katz to suddenly rise up from his seat in an attempt to leave again, but the matchmakers did not allow him to depart, and the doctor made it clear that his remark about bullies were not intended, God forbid, to allude to the council members. The doctor extended his hand to the second-in-command and *Sholem al Yisruel*.[48]

They immediately sent for the council member Bobi Rosenrauch, Moshe Katz's right-hand man, who demonstrated more piety than his own rabbi himself and even submitted his resignation. Bobi immediately appeared, and the doctor showered him with compliments and even said that no one could take Bobi's place, and the camp could not do without him, as he is one of a kind in his generation. Only when Moshe Katz

48 An expression that means that nothing can be done.

indicated with a wink that he could sit down, did Bobi take his seat and once again began to sacrifice himself for the sake of our brothers, the children of Israel.

A constant, far more serious problem than that is the task of repairing the ruined apartments. When the post chief, Floreanu, drove the Jews out of the factory quarter during the summer, the Housing Office and the Labor Office pushed hundreds of people into dilapidated hovels, vestibules, cellars, and barns, as long as they would have a roof over their heads, even one with holes in it. The well-to-do immediately moved into Ukrainian houses at the edge of the ghetto. In contrast, the poor—the great majority—remained in the ruins, taking comfort in the community's promise to repair the apartments promptly. However, the fact is that no one has lifted a finger and now, when the frosty nights are beginning to afflict us, they are crying out, and the inhabitants are besieging the community building. The "lords" have set about doing something about this matter. There can be no talk of repairing the ruins, because this will cost a fortune and besides, we cannot obtain the necessary materials. So, they have begun to take easy "housing measures": throw out the tenants who live too comfortably, squeeze more people into hovels, and … spare the well-connected people. It's a big scandal, blows are flaring up like mushrooms after the rain, and the militia are flooded with work. The doctor has imposed the honor of dealing with the apartments on the head of the Labor Office, David Buksbaum—a decent fellow with an "iron hand"—and he rules the roost high-handedly.

[October 19, 1942] An Hour Later

I just got back from the hospital. Rivka is still weak and the typhus has not broken, although her fever has dropped considerably. She has developed a complication in her lungs—this is the appalling nature of typhus, to be associated with all kinds of afflictions. Dr. Greiff fears that she will not leave the hospital soon, and then she will need very expensive treatment to recover. Mother can barely drag herself on her feet; she has sprained her knee and looks like a living corpse. Furthermore, she is stubborn and she refuses to be examined by a doctor—apparently because she is afraid that he will order her to lie down. She is still dragging herself to the hospital several times a day, hobbling and leaning on a stick, and I cannot persuade her to sit at home in her hovel and allow the children to take the food to the hospital.

When I see Mother, dejected and sick—a dried out skeleton—who is clearly dying slowly, my heart breaks, and my brain is confounded, and I do not know in what kind of a world I am wandering. I must not show my distress and I must do my work perfectly in order not to lose my meager livelihood. Of course, I would have brought Mother here with me were this not likely to lead swiftly to her death. The four of us—Roza, the children, and I—are suffocating in a dark hovel, 2 meters long and 3 meters wide, and there is really nowhere to insert a pin. We eat, cook, sleep, and … write literature for the future generations in this hole! I do not know what to do in this difficult situation. Mother reassures me that I should not cause myself any anguish because of her, because she has only one single request for God: that Rivka will come home healthy soon. Precious words of comfort from a loving mother intensify the pain of my sore wounds.

[October 19, 1942] 10 P.M.

I had the opportunity to prepare 10 poods of wood for the winter, whole trunks that have to be sawed and split. When a peasant brought me this treasure, more than a dozen Jewish woodchoppers came running to earn a few marks. I saw a fellow townsman among them, Mendel Asher, wearing rags and with a saw and an axe in hand. In the old country, this Jew also engaged in sawing wood, but in a different manner. In Marginea, near Rădăuţi, he owned a large board saw, measuring 10 meters, which cost millions.

Mendel Asher did not speak to me but looked at me with such sad eyes that I had to turn my face away. I asked him if he was serious, and he answered me: "If you want to have mercy on me, forget the past and let me cut your bit of wood. What do you prefer? Two or three pieces? Thin or thick ones?" I settled on three, thick …

October 24, 1942

The flight from the death camps by the Bug to the "fortunate" Moghilev district continues to increase. Almost every day, living dead—those who are able to complete a journey of approximately 60 kilometers and not die of hunger or cold, or from the gendarmes' bullets along the way—arrive here, fleeing from Pechora, Vapnyarka, and other hells. The journey takes about two weeks and even more, because they hide during the day. Not knowing the way, they ask the Ukrainian villagers. It often happens that non-Jewish women take pity on the wanderers and give them a piece of bread, while their husbands slip away to hand the "criminals" over to the gendarmes. There are also cases of kindheartedness among a few Ukrainians, and they provide food and clothes, and even hide someone in an attic for a while.

The people who arrive from "there" look like corpses pulled out of graves, like some kind of unreal creatures. Without a shirt, their bodies are covered with dirty rags; barefoot, their hands and feet are covered with suppurating wounds; and their faces have the pallor of mummies—thus they appear in Dzhurin, in Shargorod, in Murafa, and even in holy Moghilev. When we look at these living dead, Jews uprooted from their homes like all of us, we are ashamed that we sometimes complain about the apartment being too small, the barley bread causing stomach problems, or being dispatched to work. We ourselves are not protected from being sent to the Pechora camp—who is forcing us to anticipate troubles! ...

When the fugitives manage to set foot in the community building, they are not received as welcome guests and, of course, no one invites them to settle in the "model colony" of Dzhurin. The colony chief particularly enjoys addressing the new arrivals in high German and in his shrieking voice: "Who summoned you here? What is Dzhurin? A city of refuge? You will not spend even one night here." The sobs and wails of the exhausted babies and women (men only rarely escape) would move boulders, but not hard hearts or the locked [gates of] heavens. The doctor's assistants are already making sure that Dzhurin will not become a city of refuge. They take the "fugitives" to the soup kitchen, where they receive a double portion of soup and a loaf of bread, and send them out of the ghetto at night, entrusting them to God's mercy.

There are also crafty "fugitives," children with the wisdom of an old man, who are wary of the community's charity and steal into the ghetto at night, when no one sees them. They often come upon *Lagernikes* who have warm Jewish hearts and who hide them somewhere in a cellar or an attic for a while, until they can mix in with the rest of the crowd and lose the "look of Pechora." They are not registered with the council as residents, and there is no question of receiving soup in the soup kitchen. The Jewish administration does not want to know about them, unless they contract typhus. Then they are entitled to a corner in the hospital, and usually their own 4 cubits in the cemetery. Their emaciated bodies are not treasure troves of strength that can overcome the Rickettsia bacteria.

Let me explicitly note that Dzhurin is far from being a Sodom in Transnistria. On the contrary, it is much more humane than Shargorod or Moghilev, for example. According to lists drawn up by the council by order of the Romanian overlords, thousands of Ukrainian Jews, as well as deportees from Romania, have been driven out of these places, and we have not heard about anyone sacrificing himself in order to rescind the decrees. Not a single person has been sent away from Dzhurin so far,[49] which really calls for saying, "*ke'naynehore*." And, nevertheless, in my eyes, it is a disgrace and a serious offense to treat the "fugitives" so harshly, supposedly for the common good. Never mind, when it suits him, the colony chief is not so strict, and his people turn a blind eye ...

49 The Romanian authorities did not "thin out" the population of the Dzhurin ghetto as they did the populations of the Moghilev and Kopaygorod ghettos. Jews were expelled from Moghilev to Skazinets and to Pechora, among other destinations, and Jews from Kopaygorod were sent to the camp in the nearby forest, all of which were death camps for all intents and purposes; 4,000 Jews were sent to Skazinets, 2,400 Jews from Romania and 600 local Ukrainian Jews were deported to Pechora; see Carp, *Cartea neagră*, pp. 271, 272, 279, and 280; Shachan, *Burning Ice*, pp. 137–138.

October 26, 1942

The delegates who recently traveled to Moghilev (Dr. Rosenstrauch and Leon Neuman), to exchange the now old Romanian lei banknotes returned today. They brought new banknotes that are worth a quarter of the former value. In Moghilev, there are now people who are making a livelihood by competing with the Romanian National Bank. The truth is that it is still possible to exchange the currency at its full worth in Romania, but where is Romania and where is Moghilev! The Sambatyon, known as the Dniester, which no Jew can cross, flows between them. In contrast, cunning Romanians continue to trade with Transnistria and rake in barrels of gold from the troubles of the Jews. They indeed are the sort who buy the old banknotes in Moghilev and take them to Romania.

In addition, the delegates brought a little cash for the *Lagernikes*—assistance from their relatives in Romania—and also letters. The federation of the Jewish communities in Romania succeeded in enabling relatives to send support and letters to Transnistria via the Moghilev Central Council.[50] Of course, the Romanian censorship first checks every written line. The Romanian occupation authorities in Moghilev exchange the lei for marks at a quarter of their real value—1 mark for 60 lei. The Romanian nobles choke on the other three-quarters. Both the Moghilev Central Council and the Dzhurin council deduct a percentage in professional service fees but, nevertheless, the meager balance ends up in the hands of the fortunate *Lagernikes*. No one has sent me any cash

---

50 There was a change in Romanian policy at the end of 1942 and the beginning of 1943. Due to pressure exerted by the Comisia Autonomã De Ajutorare, the Romanian government agreed to allow families in Romania to send money and packages to their relatives in the ghettos via couriers—military officers or civilian officials returning from a vacation in Romania—which first arrived at the council in Moghilev and were transferred from there to their destinations in the other ghettos in the region. Beginning in 1943, the couriers delivered the packages and money directly to the families themselves in the ghettos. These couriers charged their pound of flesh, sometimes without even delivering anything to the addressees. See Jill Kremer testimony, YVA, O.3/VT/11435; Yitzhak Yalon testimony, YVA, O.3/VT/1238; Iehuda Tenenhaus testimony, YVA, O.3/VT/7748; Naftali Avneri testimony, YVA, O.3/VT/607.

or any letter, as it says in the biblical verse: "I am forgotten, like a dead man, out of mind."[51]

Nevertheless, the delegates did bring me something: news that the Moghilev Central Council will stop contributing 60 marks to my salary every month. The new boss of the Central Council, Dr. Danilov[52] (from Dorohoi) revoked the meager supplement in order … to spare the community coffers!

One year ago, in November 1941, I made the difficult journey to Moghilev to persuade the engineer Jagendorf to employ me in any capacity in the foundry and thereby allow me to move from remotely located Dzhurin to the big city. The engineer dismissed me with an excuse and promised that he would help me through the Central Council, which he ran. He indeed kept his promise, as long as he headed the Central Council. It is possible that if I had moved to Moghilev at the time, against the engineer's wishes, he would have had no choice but to place me in the foundry. Who knows, if this was meant to be fortuitous, because to date 7,000 people have died of typhus and another 500 have been chased to the Bug. Today I remain bound to the Dzhurin camp until the end of time. It is foolish to "split hairs" concerning the delusive word "if"…

The delegates informed us that the Romanian authorities have severely forbidden any correspondence with Romania. Only very brief letters are permitted to be sent to the address of the Central Council.[53] This

---

51 Psalms 31:13.

52 Michael Danilov, born on August 26, 1910, in Dărăbani in the Dorohoi district, was a lawyer who served as the head of the Jewish community of Dărăbani. Before the war, Danilov was a member of the Partidul Ţărănesc (Peasants' Party), PŢ, and a close associate of former prime minister Iuliu Maniu; therefore, he also was close to the Romanian authorities. He served in the Romanian army until 1932. In 1940, he was expelled from the bar association, as were all Jewish lawyers in Romania. In 1941, he was accused of betraying the fatherland and deported to the camp for political prisoners in Tărgu Jiu in southern Romania. Danilov and other Jews in the camp were then deported to Transnistria. Danilov was the head of the community of Jews deported from Dorohoi, a member of the Jewish council, and the head of the Jewish police in the Moghilev ghetto. An entrepreneur, he initiated the rebuilding of the ruins of the sugar plant in Moghilev. See Shelomo David, ed., *Dorohoi: Dorot Shel Yahadut Vetzionut* (Hebrew), vol. 4 (Kiryat Bialik: Irgun Yotzei Dorohoi Vehaseviva Be'Yisrael, 1992), p. 174; CNSAS, p-045109, pp. 1–2.

53 Concerning the order of Radu Lecca, April 17, 1943, which forbade direct correspondence between the deportees and their relatives in Romania that was not via the gendarmerie headquarters, see Lavi, *Pinkas Hakehilot: Rumania*, vol. 1, pp. 364–365.

decree does not concern me. At first, I actually did send postcards to my erstwhile "good brothers" in Romania, but it was a shame to pay the postage. They believe the Romanian saying there: "a dead man does not come back from the grave"—so why correspond with the dead! …

October 27, 1942

There are rumors in Moghilev —the delegates related it today in secret—the Germans demanded another 1,000 Jews for work on the other side of the Bug from the governor but he did not comply with the demand. On the other side, the accursed flag of the swastika waves, and there are immense concentration sites there, where Russian prisoners of war, Ukrainians, and sometimes also Jews are forced to perform hard labor. The Nazi labor Organization "Todt" oversees the work,[54] but in every labor camp, SS men are on a rampage with one aim: to crush the Jews. From time to time, an "*Aktia*" is carried out—they gather those who no longer have the strength to work as required and liquidate them in the usual way in some forest or ditch. The last job that they did for the Germans was to dig their own graves. One person who was miraculously saved from such an *Aktia* recently made his way to Dzhurin from Nemirov—where he had worked—and related terrible stories, which are really unbelievable. His name is Yehoshua Mentsher and he comes from Vijniţa (Northern Bukovina). This survivor was permitted to hide in Dzhurin, because the doctor was in Moghilev at the time.

I believe that the enemy will not be able to annihilate the entire Jewish people, and that the Jews overseas will yet see the defeat of Ashmedai, but this will help the European martyrs like cupping helps a corpse. It is

54 Organization Todt was established in 1933 by Fritz Todt, the general supervisor of road construction and the minister of armaments and munitions in Nazi Germany. The organization planned, managed, and constructed large construction projects of strategic importance, for example, bridges, roads, etc. It used forced laborers, prisoners from concentration camps, and POWs from occupied countries for these purposes. In 1941 and during Operation Barbarossa, mobile units of the organization were created to accompany the fighting forces. See Robert Rozett and Shmuel Spector, eds., *Encyclopedia of the Holocaust* (Jerusalem: Yad Vashem, 2009), p. 350; Ancel, *Toledot Hashoah*: *Romania*, vol 1, p. 351; https://en.wikipedia.org/wiki/Organisation_Todt (accessed June 16, 2022).

indeed true that "in every generation they attempt to destroy us," but the only one who is happy is one who merits sitting on a seat of pillows and singing [on the night of the *Seder*] "and the Holy One, Blessed be He, saves us from their hands …"[55] It is very likely that only a few, lone Jewish communities and individuals in Europe will be saved from destruction. Even during the destruction of the First and Second Temples, there was a very small remaining remnant—but that was bitter consolation. In reality, no one wants to be the exception who recounts his own great miracles …

October 28, 1942, 3 P.M.

That's it, I will no longer be envious of the fortunate people who receive letters from the other side of the Sambatyon. Today at the camp post office—this too exists in the Jewish state—I received the first letter since the first day that I arrived here, and it was sent from Tel Aviv, from my cousin Chaya, through the Red Cross. My cousin wishes me a good year and wants to know how we are. It is dated September 12, 1941, and is addressed to Rădăuţi, my hometown. This letter circulated for thirteen months until it made its way to my palace in the "new home."

[October 28, 1942] 10 P.M.

A very unwelcome guest arrived in the camp today: the first new case of typhus of the new "season." One does not need to be a prophet to say that soon the Rickettsia bacteria will once again spread its arms wide and will help to solve the "Jewish problem." In most homes, people are squeezed in, head to head, and their rags are permeated with lice—the agents of this dangerous plague. Many deportees do not have even a shirt on their bodies, and most possess only one. The severe lack of water contributes to complete self-neglect by a great many people. People worry about every drop of water and do not allow themselves to empty the bucket that

55 Kunstadt quotes from the *Maggid* section, the heart of the Haggadah, which recounts the Exodus from Egypt.

they dragged up the mountain with their last strength for such nonsense as washing their bodies or their laundry. In addition, the suffering has severely weakened the people and decreased their stamina.

Oddly enough, the person who has been harmed by the Rickettsia bacteria today is actually one of the few "wealthy" people who lives in a Ukrainian apartment, possesses enough clothes, and does not come in contact with those who are covered with louse and neglected. Apparently, however, one of them touched him—perhaps in a *minyen*, because he likes the *bima* ...

October 29, 1942, 9 P.M.

My bosses raised my monthly wages to 100 marks. I couldn't take it anymore and I convinced them to submit a petition to the council. I am happy as a poor man who finds a lost item, because the Moghilev Central Council refused to supplement my salary with the 60 marks per month and I will continue to receive the same wages as before.

I need at least 250 marks a month just for the minimum amount of food, without even considering clothing and shoes. My only suit, which I gladly wear on both *Simches Toyre* and *Tisha B'Av*, is already ragged and worn, and "decorated" with fringes and patches. One of my bosses already made sure to inform me that it is a disgrace to sit, wearing such clothes, in the council, where "human beings" come and go. Roza and the children are ashamed to go out in the streets, because they are dressed in rags just like me. I have more trouble with my shoes that have a gaping hole, like a mouth, and will not withstand the mud and snow.

I think that tomorrow I will take Rivka out of the hospital, where she has been lying for thirty-four days. She has overcome the typhus, but her body is very weak, and she is all skin and bones. Dr. Greiff warns me that we must provide her with good care for a long time, so that her lungs will not remain frail. Definitely good advice, but how will we be able to follow it!

Mother is getting weaker day by day; she is wasting away and can barely stand on her feet. Since Rivka's illness, she has aged at least ten years. She was always strong and healthy, and she was resilient, having endured cold and heat during her sad life of kindness and faith. Before she was even forty-one years old, she was widowed and was left to care for two small children, endeavoring to raise her babies and get through difficult times, struggling with poverty and all kinds of troubles. I remember her being ill only once, in 1932, when she contracted pneumonia and the doctors were sure she was lost. Only her iron will and infinite faith in God's mercy helped her to prevail over the Angel of Death. Until Rivka's illness, she was hale, but now I am very worried about her.

[October 29, 1942] One Hour Later

Yesterday afternoon, an order arrived from the gendarmerie to send 100 workers to harvest the ripe sunflowers in the fields in Aleksandrovka, a village around 15 kilometers from Dzhurin. The work is certainly easy, even pleasant, but nevertheless it sparked panic and whoever was able to escape—fled. This was not because of a simple fear of work but rather of a ruse. The people still remember the incident in the Kryzhopol forest, when they were assured that they would be taken by train and would be given food, which were false promises. Therefore, the people are frightened—they indeed promise Aleksandrovka and sunflowers, but in the end it will be a German labor camp on the other side of the Bug.

The gendarmes threatened that if we do not provide the 100 men by dawn this morning, they will come to select the workers themselves. It was once again a *Leyl Shimurim* [night of vigil], with wailing and shrieking and cries, as in the three terrifying nights before the deportation from home. The militia, although they too are deportees, did not handle them with kid gloves and wreaked havoc. By the way, the militia do not have an easy livelihood—far be it from me to speak positively about this gang—and the gendarmes give free rein to their emotions, I mean their whips, first of all, on these young men with a band around their arm, if something does not go exactly as ordered. This recalls Eliezer Steinbarg's parable about the whip and the horse—a painful story of suffering that has no beginning or end.[56]

---

56 Eliezer Steinbarg (March 22, 1880–March 27, 1932) was born in Cernăuţi. He was a

The head of the militia, Iosef Stein, was a respectable merchant in the old country—a wealthy Jew—and he certainly never dreamed that he would become the head of the police. Because of his military past in World War I, when he served as an officer in the Austrian army, he was ordered to organize and head the Jewish militia in Dzhurin. He is what is called "fair"—he does not deal any blows and he does not insult anyone. However, he does carry out his mission in full compliance with the orders of the colony chief. He does not interfere in the conduct of the militia, as long as they bring in people when necessary. He is afraid of losing his post, because it protects him from being sent away to forced labor. It is clear that someone else in his place would certainly not be better and, as for worse, there are no limits …

The "lords' accompanied the militia on their searches of the homes in order to persuade the people that they should not be wary nor afraid. They did not seize the people who were registered for work at night, but told them that they should arrive at the militia yard at dawn, and that the convoy would then depart for the gendarmerie post.

People who had fled during the night were missing in the morning. The quota had to be completed by seizing children, the disabled, and the elderly. The group finally left the camp, accompanied by Jewish militia. Two hours later the militia caught two "*lamedvovnikim*" [righteous people] who had hidden. The doctor himself wrote a note to the gendarmerie, stating that he was sending two men who had disappeared at night. The militia accompanied the two fugitives to the gendarmerie [post], where armed officers carried out the decision according to the law. The two young men now lie in their hovels beaten and swollen, but they managed to obtain what they wanted and did not go to Aleksandrovka. The council members did not oppose the doctor when he wrote the note and claimed that because of such people, the camp is in danger, and that the overlords are capable of sending all 4,000 persons to the Bug.

---

teacher, Yiddish writer, poet, and author of fables. Many of his works were written for children. Presumably Kunstadt is referring here to Steinbarg's poem, "Der hamr un dos stik ayzn." See Eliezer Steinbarg, "Der hamr un dos stik ayzn" (Yiddish), https://benyehuda.org/read/16248 (accessed June 16, 2022); for an English translation, see Steinbarg, *Jewish Book of Fables* (Syracuse: Syracuse University Press, 2003).

This argument is certainly not a hollow claim and, nevertheless, in my eyes, it is a serious offense to hand Jews over to the violent hands of the gendarmes. If it is necessary to mete out punishment, our militia are not innocent and they are capable of carrying this out. It is not necessary to fawn over the pig … The other people who went into hiding did not turn up, because they have now realized that this is not a joke.

October 31, 1942, 9 P.M.

This afternoon, I brought Rivka home from the hospital, where she had lain for five weeks. She is not able to stand on her feet, which have become as thin as a stick, and she had to be brought home on a stretcher. The orderlies who carried the stretcher did not have to exert themselves too much, because she has wasted away to the bone, her cheeks sunken and her ribs sticking out. She does not have the strength to say a word and requires expensive care to recover.

Rivka was brought to Mother in this condition, but Mother beamed with happiness and began to cry like a child. Our beloved mother is no longer very strong, her feet are swollen, and she can barely drag herself around the house with a [walking] stick. She cannot hear—until recently she had the ear of a musician—and her other senses are also not sound, but she is as smart and as sharp as ever. Her face has dried like parchment, and we can see clearly that her strength is waning.

November 1, 1942

Not a day goes by, and in particular not one night, without people slipping into the camp, fleeing from the hell of Pechora. They arrive naked and barefoot, literally wrapped with torn sacks and covered in lice. It is really impossible to stand in the same four corners of these wretched people whose bodies have not tasted a drop of water for months. The trek to Dzhurin from Pechora takes a few weeks, and the "fugitives" dragged themselves through fields and forests and swampy meadows during dark nights, as if they were hunted, mangy dogs with guns pointing at them from all sides.

Most of these guests belong to the groups of Ukrainian Jews from Moghilev who were deported only a few months ago. In Pechora, there are no elderly residents, because none of them survives for more than three or four months. During the first weeks, they still have strength to move their legs and they try to flee. Later, they become physically weak from hunger, filth, and suffering, and remain lying like a pile of muck in a stable, until the Angel of Death takes pity on them and brings deliverance.

The former residents of Moghilev relate details of the manhunt in Moghilev that make the hair stand on end. When the Romanian occupation authorities demanded 4,000 people for Pechora, the council composed a list of names—principally local [Ukrainian] Jews but also a considerable number of Romanian Jews, the poorest of the poor. At night, the militia burst into their homes and seized people like dogs, separating husbands from their wives, tearing mothers from their babies.

Gendarmes chased the captured victims to the train station and shoved them into cattle cars, seventy or eighty in each. In Pechora, they piled the "guests" into empty, crumbling barracks in an open field that were enclosed by a barbed-wire fence. Peasants from the surrounding area risk their lives to bring a loaf of bread or a few potatoes to the fence as a gift, because no one has a single mark. The people eat the grass that grows around the barracks, like animals, until they become swollen. They then suffer for a few days until "deliverance" comes. The Ukrainian militia collect the night's "harvest"—stiff bodies that have already had their full dose of suffering—and throw them in a mass grave every morning. The militia scatter soil on the grave only once a week in order to spare themselves the work. No one registers the names of the deceased, as though they were dead animals. The Ukrainian militia cruelly shoot anyone they see outside the barbed-wire fence.[57]

I just now learned that I too have kin among the victims of Pechora. My father-in-law's sister, Sheindel Stein from Lujeni (near Cernăuţi), barely fifty years old, and her ten-year-old son, Hersh, fell into the hands

57 There is no record of the deaths in the Pechora camp.

of the man hunters in Moghilev and ended up in the hell of Pechora. Aunt Sheindel, a wise, astute, and beautiful woman, threw on her expensive fur coat as they were driven out of their apartment, which she wore when they traveled to Pechora, where she had the opportunity to bribe a militiaman with the coat and flee with her son. She had been wandering around in a forest with two other women all night when she suddenly experienced a coronary spasm and had to sit down on the frozen ground. She tried to entrust her son to the other two fugitive women, but the boy would not agree to leave his mother under any circumstances. The two women continued their wanderings and a short time later, a few shots were heard in the forest.

Thus, the curtain came down on a terrible tragedy of a Jewish family, one of thousands like them. The first act of this tragedy began in June 1940, when the Russians "liberated" Northern Bukovina and seized it from the Romanians, as agreed upon by Stalin and Hitler. The Red "liberators" then entered Cernăuţi and sent several hundred wealthy Jews to Siberia for no reason. The black wagon traveled to the houses in the middle of the night, and whosever fate was sealed was thrown into it.

The Red man hunters also entered the alcohol factory in Lujeni, which belonged to the wealthy man Yaakov Peretz, to give him what he deserved. Peretz smelled the smoke in time and fled. In order not to return with an empty wagon, the "liberators" settled for my uncle Yosel Stein, Aunt Sheindl's husband, who worked as a bookkeeper in the factory and even lived there. No one has heard from him since, and he probably already took leave of all the troubles in "White Bears" [Siberia]. Aunt Sheindel's heart was broken and her health began to fail.

A year later, in July 1941, the tables were turned and the Romanians "liberated" Cernăuţi. Upon liberation, a new calamity befell the few [remaining] Jews: Transnistria. Aunt Sheindel was deported to Transnistria with her two children—a six-year-old girl, Betti, and a nine-year-old boy, Hershele. My aunt managed to remain in "lucky" Moghilev "illegally," and as for what happened next—see above! By the way, little Betti escaped from Pechora—she died in Moghilev of typhus …

On the one hand, the Red liberators, on the other hand, the black liberators—everyone did their best to solve the "Jewish question." Therefore, may these lines be a modest memorial page for the annihilated Stein family and for who knows how many others like them.

November 5, 1942, 8 P.M.

Jews have never been known for their ability to hold their tongues, and in Transnistria this trait has been greatly enhanced. What people know and what they don't know, they make sure to spread around, and not necessarily among their own crowd. Oh well, so the "common people" occupy themselves with gossip—one could argue that they, poor things, do not know what harm their loose tongues can do, but who can pardon the "lords," whose words carry weight and who are indeed aware of the consequences of superfluous words!

These lines can serve as an introduction to a shocking episode that I witnessed today. My hands are still shaking after what I saw and heard this morning at the community building. Only two council members remained with me while the others took off perhaps because of the shame. Allow me to add another brief introduction to clarify the background of the event, which stunned the camp. Ever since the incident about the denunciations against the post chief, Floreanu, the relations between the council on one side and the speculators on the other have worsened. The opposition in the camp has spread more and more, and includes a very large crowd of oppressed and unhappy people. Who is not oppressed in this hell! There are people who have tried to bring down the leaders from their seats, obviously with the help of the lords in Shargorod.

In short, one morning a delegation from the council left for Shargorod, led by Dr. Rosenstrauch himself, to ask Praetor Dindilegan to take the trouble to visit Dzhurin to reprimand the critics who harass the Jewish leadership. Of course, they gave him a note containing the names of the "rebels" and, in addition, a respectable gift. The praetor indicated a willingness to visit the "model colony" of Dzhurin and promised to come.

The oppressor kept his word and appeared at the community building this morning, furious as a forest robber. I saw the face of this scoundrel for the first time and did not dare to move from my desk, even though I understood that something was brewing. In the meanwhile, by order of the praetor, militiamen directly brought in five camp residents as a warning to all the rebels. And here are their names: Dovid Wasserman, former head of the Rădăuţi community; the brothers Matia and Gershon Sonntag from Siret, "non-kosher" merchants; and Gershon Sego and Natan Cohen, two young men from Hotin, who at times secretly slaughter a lamb or a calf to "trade," without a note from the community, and whose main crime was escaping during the roundup for work in Aleksandrovka.

When the crowd had gathered, the praetor began to deliver a moral sermon using his fists. First, he took care of the Sonntag brothers, and I got tired of counting the murderous blows to their faces that he dealt them. Blood flowed from their faces, and the murderer continued to hit them. Then he took to task the two "criminals" from Hotin, and they too came away beaten and bloody.

I thought that the praetor would allow his hands to rest from the beatings and the blood when he got to Dovid Wasserman, a Jew who is an imposing figure with a tough appearance, but I was mistaken. Dovid Wasserman also received his share, two proper blows to his cheeks. I literally felt physical pain, as though I myself had received the blows, because I know Dovid Wasserman's past in the old country and the important role that he played in Jewish life in those days. To be honest, he does have his flaws, but his virtues certainly outweigh them, and indeed who has such an accurate scale that will indicate which side is heavier. My face burned no less from the blows with which the foe honored the other "rebels"—displaced and battered Jews who have been suffering in the world of chaos for more than a year and whose lives depend on restraint.

At the time that this incident took place, the colony chief, Dr. Rosenstrauch waited in the front room, together with Moshe Katz, their teeth chattering. They themselves did not think that the moral preaching would take such a form. At last, the praetor's hands became weary from the blows, and he called in the two dignitaries from the front room. He ordered them to have the militia mete out twenty-five lashes to each of the rebels on their naked bodies for dessert. Moshe Katz managed to persuade him to impose a heavy fine on the accused instead of flogging.

The camp is in turmoil as a result of this incident, and people fear that it will whet the praetor's appetite for beating Jews and that he will become a frequent visitor to Dzhurin. The "lords" claim that the praetor is a seer, and he himself will decide who will stir up trouble in the Jewish state of the "model colony" of Dzhurin ...[58]

November 6, 1942

A woman who had escaped from the death camp of Pechora made her way to Dzhurin today and reported that a Romanian officer had showed up there and had dispersed the entire camp, allowing each one to go wherever his eyes led him. I suspect that this is a made-up story. If the camp has been dispersed, surely this cunning woman probably thinks that she will be allowed to stay in Dzhurin, because then she is not a "fugitive."

A second "duck" [piece of gossip] floats on the mud in the camp: the decree concerning direct correspondence with relatives in Romania has been canceled. It is already permitted to write to whomever we want, whenever we want—but not, God forbid, whatever we want ...

Jewish minds think that there is a close connection between these two reports and have concluded that surely there is a light at the end of the tunnel, and the high-level officials are trying to appease the remaining remnant. Other prophets even maintain that all the Jews will soon be sent home, or at least the kosher, well-connected people from Southern Bukovina and northern Moldavia.

---

58 One year after the deportation, after recovering from the shock of the expulsion, some of the wealthy functionaries in the Dzhurin ghetto sought to replace the head of the council in the ghetto. To maintain the existing order intact, Rosenstrauch and Katz turned to Dindilegan for assistance. They usually did not tend to involve the hostile authorities in such affairs, because this could harm the population, but rather settled arguments and fights internally. In this case, Rosenstrauch and Katz presumably feared a takeover by this group and so they involved the Romanian authorities to ensure their status and position. This case was mentioned in the Shlomo Shteinmetz interview by Sarah Rosen, January 17, 2010, Ramat Gan, and in the Menachem Bernstein interview by Sarah Rosen, April 14, 2010, Haifa.

In the meanwhile, we are lying 9 cubits deep in the mud, in both senses of the term. The true autumn has finally arrived, and the Dzhurin mud has once again appeared with all its charm.

(**Added** a month later: the two good tidings proved to be false …).

November 7, 1942, 3 P.M.

As I was sitting yesterday afternoon in the community building focused on writing, Moshe Katz suddenly called to me, [I have] "good news for you! Praetor Dindilegan is considering moving you to Shargorod, because he needs a graphologist." The doctor added, "It will be better for you there than in Dzhurin, where they are shortchanging your wages." I felt like the blood had drained from my face and did not reply. The doctor, who has a big mouth and babbles on, saying superfluous things to the overlords to flatter them, must have told the Haman of Shargorod about my involvement in finding the writer of the anonymous denunciation. The praetor must have then said that such a person would be useful to him. In my opinion, the praetor has already forgotten the whole matter, and the danger lies in the fact that the doctor can blunder and mention me in favorable terms …

Uprooting me from my "home" in Dzhurin, God forbid, will certainly expose me and my household to danger. In any case, I have already gotten used to my poor hovel, and we eat a slice of bread and are sometimes even satiated. In Shargorod, I will lose my "livelihood" and will be left abandoned. Furthermore, I am terribly afraid of the praetor, who is capable of forcing me to render detrimental opinions concerning the Jews. More than half of the deportees in Dzhurin are from my hometown and, as they say: chop me into pieces but cast me among my own. Nearly half of the Jews suffering in Shargorod are deportees from Suceava, where they lie 9 cubits in the ground—typhus, persecution, and deportation are the daily fare. The local council there boasts of its good deeds, and people quiver before the benefactors as before the devil. And I almost forgot the main thing: I would be separated from my elderly, sick mother and from Rivka, who cannot yet stand on her feet after [having] typhus. I must not uproot these dear persons from Dzhurin, leaving them to God's mercy.

I did not close my eyes the entire night because of my anguish, but I have now been able to calm down a little and hope to be spared. I must not ask for any mercy from my bosses, and it is better to let bad luck slumber. It seems that we will soon be saved from the praetor, because he is about to rise to greatness and move to Moghilev. Good riddance, although his successor will certainly not be a reincarnation of Rabbi Levi Itzhak of Berditchev …

[November 7, 1942] 8 P.M.

A storm is howling outside, the roofs are covered with snow, and the mud has not frozen yet and is knee-deep. It is clearly a sin to set foot outdoors. *Vey, vey,* some Jews who fled from the camps are now roaming the muddy roads and ditches, naked and barefoot, and gripped with mortal fear. When I think about those living dead—and they are constantly before my eyes—I consider myself a prince and reconcile myself to my fate. It is indeed true that there are people in Dzhurin who do not live four people in a small, dilapidated room, 4 cubits by 4 cubits, who do not cover themselves with a worn, patched blanket during cold winter nights, and who do not even know the taste of barley bread but, God forbid, I must not be jealous of them. Better has no limit, and jealousy does not make the borscht fat …

November 8, 1942, 7 A.M.

Welcome to the guest! The winter has indeed arrived, fully equipped: a blizzard, a sea of snow, biting cold. People run across the street hunched over—those who sell something at the empty market, those who try to get hold of a potato, and those who receive alms. There are some fortunate ones who have a sheepskin coat and a fur cap, but they are very few. The "sack people" have not changed their clothes and have no choice but to rub their hands, hop on their rag-swaddled feet, and clench their teeth so that they do not chatter.

There is one consolation: Let me die with the Philistines.[59] Perhaps the same fate that Napoleon's "Great Army" met in 1812 awaits the myriad of murderers who invaded the heart of Russia, almost reaching Leningrad and Stalingrad, and will bring an end to the Jewish catastrophe, if anyone survives through the winter. A whole series of "perhaps" …

The pelts for the shoes that the community bought already in late autumn continue to "dry out" and are becoming increasingly drenched day by day. They will obviously be dry by *Shavues*, God willing …[60]

[November 8, 1942] 8 P.M.

The first day of winter also brought a dark decree that could mean a death sentence for several hundreds of unfortunate and tormented individuals, the most miserable of all—the "*lamedvovnikim*" of Pechora. I will not utter any unfounded assumptions regarding how the gendarmes discovered that people are hiding illegally in the camp, fugitives from Pechora. In any case, the new post chief, Georgescu, burst into the camp today around noon, accompanied by a squad of gendarmes to track down those in hiding. The angels of destruction searched one apartment after another, but they caught only one mouse—a thirteen-year-old boy.

The man hunters set their sights on fatter prey. The commander stormed into the community building in a murderous rage and demanded that a list of all the persons who had entered the camp during the last months be handed over to him within the hour. Instead of telling him that there is no such list and that the council knows nothing about anyone in hiding, the colony chief bowed before the overlord and said: "There is no need for an hour. I will give you what you want immediately." The doctor promptly opened his drawer, pulled out a scrap of paper containing

59 Kunstadt refers to the story of Samson in Judges 16:30 to convey that just as he was suffering during the very severe winter, the enemy was also suffering and dying in the snow.

60 The holiday of Shavuot occurs before the summer begins and, therefore, it was no longer of any help that the pelts for winter shoes would be dry by early summer.

103 names of people in hiding, and presented it to the commander. This means a death sentence for the living dead, most of whom are dying in the *bes midresh* poorhouse, among the "pariahs" of the camp, who are for the most part deportees from Hotin.

The hallway of the *bes medresh* looks like a pigsty and its inhabitants, who have already lost the image of God, wallow on the bare floor with only a bit of rotting straw under their heads. Whoever approaches the *bes medresh* smells the unbearable stench reeking from there, and it does not help to cover your nose with a handkerchief.

When Georgescu received the list, he did not praise the doctor as would have been fitting for such a patriotic act but instead, in a terrifying tone, barked the order to round up the 103 non-kosher persons and to deliver them to the gendarmerie post the next day by 8 A.M. The doctor immediately issued a strict order to the Jewish militia to lock up all the *lamedvovnikim* in the poorhouse at the great synagogue, under guard, so that no one will be able to flee at night, God forbid.

November 10, 1942, 7 A.M.

The militia engaged in a roundup throughout the night and finally managed to gather seventy-seven people at the poorhouse—almost all of them women and children. Twenty-six persons whose names were included in the fateful list gradually disappeared. Advocates and even council members are running to the doctor to request that he erase one name or another from the list, but he claims that the list has been sealed and, after the *Ne'ila*, it is too late and nothing can be done to help. As it is, the camp is in despair, but even the council members are enraged at the doctor for his ruse. Let me note that Moshe Katz, Iehoşua Ungariş, and other community wheeler-dealers, as well as Iankel Katz, the second-in-command's brother, are moving heaven and earth to ease the fate of the condemned and to surreptitiously save people. They will rent wagons and distribute clothes and food, but what good will this do if the way leads directly to Pechora. A fierce storm is raging outside, and who knows how many of the deported persons will reach Pechora. One of them, Mania Roth, a woman of about fifty years of age from

Shpikov (Ukraine), played a trick and already died during the night, immediately after they had brought her to the poorhouse. She left behind a five-year-old boy, and the doctor permitted the child to be taken to a distant relative of the deceased mother in Dzhurin, even though the child's name appears in black and white on the list.

The seventy-seven, actually only seventy-five persons now, are being held at the poorhouse and are "preparing themselves for the journey." The gendarmes informed them that they were waiting for a transport of the same kind of "criminals" from the Shargorod camp and, therefore, they would have to wait until they could form a joint convoy to Pechora. Is it possible that a miracle will occur?

[November 10, 1942] 8 P.M.

For the time being, none of the seventy-five "illegals" detained in the poorhouse have been moved. Two of the infirm people are dying and will be spared the pilgrimage to Pechora.

The colony chief is preparing to travel to Shargorod tomorrow morning. He will take a gift to the praetor—twenty wool blankets and forty sheets—a donation to a Ukrainian school in Moghilev. The praetor recently told him, so the doctor claims, that he is expecting a handsome contribution from the "model colony" of Dzhurin. The doctor therefore sent the militia out to collect blankets and sheets. The militia brought more than they were ordered to fetch, because wherever a door was opened to them, they were given the last blanket, just so as not to turn the militia into enemies. Those who did not have blankets and sheets paid the community their ransom in cash. The community has so many blankets, sheets, and cash left over from this collection, which will certainly come in handy. Immoral? Who still uses this old word, which has long been defunct! ...

And since I have already mentioned the term "hush money," let's talk about another episode that reeks of thousands rather than a few rags. The commander of the legion of the gendarmes of the Moghilev district appeared at the gendarmerie post this afternoon. Suddenly a gendarme showed up at the community building and summoned the colony chief to go to the gendarmerie immediately. The doctor turned white as snow and whispered to Katz: "If I do not return by evening, find out what happened to me."

An hour later the doctor returned, beaming with gratification, like someone who just won a great victory. "It is good, excellent—the old man gushed as he swallowed his words—imagine the scene: the major [praetor] shook my hand and even instructed me to sit down, and then asked me how things are going in the model colony of Dzhurin." The doctor became silent and got a lump in his throat. Moshe Katz asked him curiously, "So that's why you were summoned so suddenly?"

In a choked voice, the doctor answered, "Well, in the course of our friendly conversation, the major mentioned that he would like to buy himself a fur coat at a good price and, while he's at it, also a sheepskin coat for his companion. He even said explicitly that Romanian Jews are known for their beautiful clothes, and such merchandise will surely be found among them, provided that it will be of excellent quality. Since the major is such a noble person, who even said that the model colony will continue to run properly and all will be well, I, of course, promised him that all will also be well concerning the two fur coats ..."

The "lords" promptly decided not to embarrass the colony chief and to honor his commitment. The transaction will cost a bargain price of 2,000 marks—three weeks of food for the soup kitchen. You may consider me a skeptic, but I do not think that the major made any promises, since he is a known oppressor. Who knows whether the doctor himself did not offer the gift! And he could have tried to save the people from Pechora who are hiding here! ...

November 11, 1942, 7 P.M.

The miracle did not occur. At noon today, seventy-three living dead were sent on their way to Moghilev [*sic*][61] from the gendarmerie post after having been detained in the poorhouse since the day before yesterday. Last night, they still numbered seventy-five, and not one of them fled,

61 They were sent to Pechora.

God forbid. However, since dying is free for everyone, two persons died and were taken out on stretchers during the night. The guards barely looked, because they were told not to allow any living soul to leave, but the dead [could depart]—with great respect. This was a trick that was cleverly undertaken to save two people. The dead were immediately resurrected in some cellar, where they were hidden. A case of Jewish self-sacrifice that shines like a sun in the local darkness …

Because of the snow-covered roads, the community did not bother to hire any wagons for the "fugitives," and they will be taken by foot from here to there. The tragedy further unfolded as a storm struck their faces with piercing snow needles and burning frost. Everyone came running as the funeral of the living, the "sack people," came out of the *bes medresh*, and even though the tormented people have no relatives and no redeemers here, wails rose and tears flowed from everyone's eyes. Non-Jewish passersby stopped and crossed themselves. People accompanied the convoy until the ghetto border and followed it with their eyes as long as it was possible to see something, like at a funeral.

The local Dzhurin Jews, with Rabbi Herşel Karalnic at their head, did not rest for two days and collected food, clothes, and shoes for the unfortunate and, thanks to this, the living dead did not leave naked and barefoot, even though they were not dressed adequately to survive the long journey on foot. The council also gave each one 10 marks in cash, a loaf of bread, and a pair of shoes (of wet leather …).[62]

I was not there for the last act of the tragedy because, in any case, I could not help, and my heart began giving me trouble a while ago …

And now a terrible epilogue, which occurred after the curtain fell on the fifth act of the tragedy. A few hours after the convoy had left for Pechora, it became known that the decree only concerned the fugitives from Pechora, not those from other camps. That means that we could have saved at least forty people, and even more. After all, it is not written on anyone's forehead from where a person fled, and the Jews in Transnistria have no name and no papers. We learned this shocking secret from his excellency himself, the honorable commander of the Shargorod

62 Rabbi Herşel Karalnic's public activity, which focused on helping those who had nothing, is evident in this case. Rabbi Karalnic worked together with Rabbi Hager of Siret.

district gendarmes, *Oberleutnant* Garama. This overlord appeared at the gendarmerie post after dinner, and the community organized an honorable reception for him. The colony chief and Moshe Katz asked all the overlords to attend it.

When the heart of the king was merry with wine,[63] Garama told the colony chief: "It is indeed amazing that all of Pechora came to you!" To this, the colony chief replied: "A mistake, my honorable lord. More than half were just "strangers" who were not registered here." The overlord was even more surprised and said: "What a shame that they were all sent away in such a blizzard! The order applied only to the fugitives from Pechora itself." Upon hearing these words, Moshe Katz dared to beg the overlord to save the innocent victims. Garama indeed promised that as soon as he would return to Shargorod, he would send a rider to return the convoy to Dzhurin and to single out whoever is a fugitive from Pechora. But it was already too late, and Garama made an empty promise. The commander of the gendarmerie from Dzhurin, Major Georgescu, knew full well that the decree was directed only at those who had fled from Pechora, but he deliberately ordered the roundup of all the "strangers." He is a zealous enemy exactly like his predecessor, Floreanu. Righteous gendarmes are only found in the cemetery …

November 12, 1942, 7 A.M.

As I look at the empty pages of my notebook, I am struck with fear because of the lines that are liable to spread out over the white paper. I had never before fully understood the curse of the reproach: "In the morning you will say, 'would it was evening!'"[64] Rashi explains: You will miss the previous evening, because the new day will be worse than the day before. In Dzhurin, in general, we long for darkness for cover,

63 Esther 1:10.

64 Rashi on Deut. 28:67: "In the morning you will say: 'Would it was evening,' and at evening you will say: 'Would it was morning!' for the fear of your heart that you will fear and for the sight of your eyes that you will see."

and fear the light, when the enemy sees you more clearly and aims his poisoned arrows at you.

[November 12, 1942] 3 P.M.

The Ukrainian militia who escorted the convoy of seventy-three "fugitives" to Pechora, have just returned. They accompanied the convoy to Rakhny, about 15 kilometers from Dzhurin—the first phase. Other guards will escort the convoy from there. Nothing happened on the way to Rakhny, apart from an insignificant matter: two people died and fell in the snow, a Jewish woman and a child. They left the dead lying there and continued on their way.

[November 12, 1942], Evening

For the first time since I have been in Dzhurin, I have obtained books to read—three completely different works, which have nothing to do with this world of chaos: an old volume of *Hashiloah*,"[65] the German translation of Dr. Josef Klausner's book about the life of Jesus, and a Russian translation of a book of poems by Heinrich Heine. A strange combination: Klausner in German and Heine in Russian! I am hungry for the printed word and strain my eyes in the light of the oil lamp.

November 13, 1942, 7 A.M.

I have just now begun to use the last razor blade of the twenty that I brought from home. In the first months of exile, when I would take out a new blade, I would think that one of two things would happen: either the blades would outlive me, or I would use some of them in freedom. Now I see again that apart from the colors black and white, there is another

---

65 *Hashiloah* was a leading Hebrew-language literary journal, which was founded by the Aḥi'asaf Publishing House in Warsaw and published from 1896 to 1926.

color—gray. Such is our life between the Dniester and the Bug: gray despair, neither alive nor dead.

[November 13, 1942] 3 P.M.

The storm continues to rage, as though the gendarmes are standing over it with whips in their hands. The snow is already almost knee-high and it seeps through even good, durable shoes, and all the more so through old, worn-out shoes. This morning, the gendarmes demanded from the council a number of people to clear the snow from the factory quarter. People hid, both out of fear and because most of them do not have any shoes on their feet. The militia managed to seize thirty people and led them away to work.

The shoes are, in the meanwhile, still wet and are drying in the council storeroom. They remembered to dry the furs in late October, just in time … The winter is paying interest for the beautiful, dry summer. The streets and alleys are buried in snow, and making your way to a community outhouse is like crossing the Red Sea. No peasant has been seen at the market for three days because of the blizzard. If a brave Ukrainian nevertheless shows up with a sack of potatoes or 1 pood of flour, he asks for a ridiculous price that only the wealthy can afford. Oil and salt have completely disappeared and, if you are lucky, it is possible to exchange 2 kilos of granulated sugar for 1 kilo of salt. One cannot acquire these goods with cash.

[November 13, 1942] 7 P.M.

Today for the first time, Rivka rose from her wooden bunk, barely standing on her emaciated legs and taking a step only with the support of a stick. She requires expensive care in a bright and warm house, and in a convalescent home—these dreams are not for us. Mother is clearly very weak, and only her iron will and unwavering faith in God's mercies continue as before, in defiance of all the calamities. Her dreams—she claims—tell her that deliverance is near. Obviously, I do not try to contradict her but rather interpret her dreams positively—the only comfort that I can offer her …

November 15, 1942, 7 P.M.

A thin ray of hope from some distant place in Africa has illuminated for a moment the thick darkness that surrounds us. The English have begun to strike the black continent with heavy blows, and the Nazi army is fleeing like poisoned mice.[66] These reports come from the Romanian newspapers,[67] although they do not call the defeat by its real name but rather use the term "strategic defensive" … The fervent fantasy of the *Lagernikes* is rising like leavened dough, and they consider this to be *Athalta Degeula.*[68] Even sworn heretics believe that perhaps the miracle will occur now—that is, since here we are in the month of *Kislev,* it is conceivable—I wish—the *Hanuke* candles, latkes, and card games remind us of the defeat of the Greeks and the victory of Yehudah Maccabee and its heroes. Is it possible that the Nazi Marshal Rommel is a grandson of the non-kosher Greeks, and perhaps his Angel of Death,

---

66 The Second Battle of Al Alamein, which took place between October 23–November 4, 1942, was a decisive point in the North Africa campaign. During the battle, which lasted for twelve days, the 8th Army of the British Empire, commanded by General Bernard Montgomery, defeated the Panzer Army Africa, which included German and Italian forces under the command of Field Marshal Erwin Rommel. This forced the Axis powers to begin a long retreat westward along the coast of North Africa, a retreat that concluded with the surrender of the German and Italian forces in Tunisia at the beginning of May 1943. The defeat of the Axis powers in the battle of Al Alamein and the defeat of the German army in Stalingrad, which occurred in parallel, signaled the beginning of a turning point in favor of the Allies in the war against Nazi Germany and its satellite states. See Stephen Bungey, *Alamein* (London: Aurum, 2003).

67 Romanian newspapers arrived with military personnel, gendarmes, and members of the civil administration when they returned from vacation in Romania. Jews who worked in the offices of the Romanian authorities had access to the papers. The news spread quickly, as was characteristic of rumors among the Jewish public, raising their hopes for liberation.

68 In classical Jewish texts, this term in Aramaic, which literally means the beginning of the redemption, refers to the process of the redemption and the arrival of the messiah, who will redeem the Jewish people, gather the exiled in the land of Israel, and rule over a prosperous nation.

Marshal Montgomery, is a grandson of Yehudah Maccabee, since, after all, the English claim descent from the Ten Tribes? …

November 19, 1942, 8 P.M.

The calamity that I mortally feared did not spare me. Mother has become dangerously ill. During Rivka's illness, she completely neglected herself; she did not eat or sleep, and exhausted her meager strength. Already then, her feet were swollen—a sign that her heart was betraying her—but I was not able to persuade her to agree to see a doctor. She insisted that there was nothing to talk about until Rivka would leave the hospital fully recovered. Mother has always been stubborn and has always had an iron will, and this quality has persisted. I did not try to persuade her otherwise, so as not to cause her any grief.

Only when they brought Rivka home on a stretcher, supposedly healthy, did Mother feel her ruined body and weak limbs. Dragging herself around in her hovel with a stick was as difficult as parting the Red Sea. Although her legs were like reeds, she would not agree to see a doctor. She was simply afraid that the doctor would prescribe bed rest. Her sharp mind warned her that once she would get into bed, she would not get up again.

However, her condition has deteriorated so much that she has agreed to allow me to call a doctor today. I immediately went to see my good friend, Dr. Julius Frenckel from Cernăuţi—a fine young man, who is "proficient in medicine" and is dedicated to treating the rich and poor alike—the poor even more. Therefore his devotees—most of them common people and the poorest of the poor—will not exchange him for the old doctors, who are puffed up with self-importance and whose gaze is too riveted on the hand [for payment] …

Dr. Frenckel did indeed immediately examine my mother with the help of all the medical means at his disposal and announced that he could not find anything wrong, but that if she wants to recover completely, she must stay in bed for a few days. Outside, the doctor informed me that Mother's condition is very serious. Her heart is completely damaged, her blood pressure has dropped to rock bottom—at almost 105—and, for dessert, a rose [skin infection] has appeared on her leg, and she has a stomach infection. All in all, a nice package for a weak woman who has been suffering in the hell of Dzhurin for more than a year already and who celebrated her seventy-fourth birthday last summer—may she live to be 120.

Poor Rivka—who has still not fully recovered herself, is exhausted from typhus, and has swollen legs—is now getting the real rest that the doctor has prescribed for her. She is taking care of our mother, constantly putting compresses on her legs, and serving her medicines and delicacies. As long as our mother was healthy, Rivka slept with her in the single wooden bunk. Rivka must now sleep on the floor, because Mother must keep her feet raised due to the infection and takes up all the space in the narrow wooden bed.

I run to visit Mother several times a day. I help her by going shopping, providing the medicines, and chopping a few pieces of wood. I slip out of the community building, risking a bleak end. Roza herself has a heart condition and does not leave the house. As for "bedclothes," we cover ourselves with my worn-out coat, which does the trick during the day and at night. By day, it is my royal garment and, by night, I spread it over four people …

[November 19, 1942] 9 P.M.

Dr. Julius Frenckel just came out of my hovel; he came himself to announce the "good news": Mother's rose [skin infection] has begun to turn into an abscess. In his opinion, they must operate on the plague tomorrow to prevent a tragedy. It will really take a miracle for Mother to overcome the dangerous illnesses that have assailed her. And precisely now, when a thin ray of hope has broken forth and our troubles may be approaching a happy end, we so desperately do not want anyone of us to be absent when the long-hoped-for moment arrives, and certainly not our beloved mother. She has suffered enough during her long, difficult life, and if someone up above is keeping the books, as she has believed all her life, she deserves to witness deliverance.

November 21, 1942, 7 A.M.

Mother's condition is bitter and bleak. Yesterday morning, Dr. Frenckel revealed that they were compelled to operate on the abscess that same day, and she did not anticipate this at all. I began to search everywhere for an anesthetic, because this operation, although not dangerous, must not be performed on the elderly without local anesthetic. I ran around for hours and was unable to find anything, even though I knew that the drug merchants, who trade in medicines sent from Romanian relatives, had some. I offered the last mark that I had, but the merchants hedged, making excuses. They know that I am the community secretary and are afraid lest I say a superfluous word to the lords.

I returned to Mother in despair, and she suddenly told me in a weak voice that she regretted having agreed to the operation. She has faith in God's mercies, she says. I tried to convince her that it is a simple operation, but I finally desisted, so as not to cause her any grief, or because I did not want to assume responsibility.

The abscess is causing Mother severe pain; her foot is swollen with pus and cannot be touched even lightly. Her face is contorted with pain, and she sobs like a small child, even though her nature has always been to bite her lip in times of trouble. This has severely affected Rivka, and her feet are swollen again. Mother has agreed to have a young girl spend a few hours each day with the two patients to assist them.

When Dr. Frenckel learned that Mother had changed her mind, he threatened to stop making house calls, because her life is hanging by a thread, and only the knife can save her. I am in a difficult predicament and see no way out.

[November 21, 1942] 3 P.M.

The delegates—the colony chief and Bobi Rosenrauch—returned from Moghilev and brought significant donations for the *Lagernikes*, sums from relations in Romania.[69] This does not pertain to me, even though I desperately need a little cash in this difficult time in order to save Mother.

They report the news that couriers have brought from Romania: it is believed that the Romanian state will soon appoint a delegation to investigate why the Jews from Southern Bukovina and northern Moldavia were also deported to Transnistria, although the decree was supposed to apply only to the "liberated" provinces of Bessarabia and Northern Bukovina. If this is not a false tale, as I think it is, the Romanian rulers are probably trying to throw dust in the eyes of the world. No deliverance will come out of this.

The real reason for the journey to Moghilev was not, God forbid, to bring aid to relatives but for a much more important one: to take two expensive fur coats to the major of the gendarmes of Moghilev.

As soon as the council decided not to humiliate the doctor and to keep his promise to the major, those in the community building began to search for suitable fur coats. Wealthy people displayed expensive furs, furriers eagerly flaunted their expertise, and the matter of the fur coats was not omitted from the agenda of the council meetings for two entire weeks. All other problems were set aside for the time being: with God's help, they found exactly what they were looking for, emptied the community coffers completely, and prepared to send them.

Of course, the doctor himself had to take the gifts, and they barely managed to convince him that Bobi Rosenrauch should travel with him, but the old man set a condition: he alone would take the gifts to the overlord, without a guard. The council members also laid down a condition: when he would present the bribe, it would be a good opportunity for the colony chief to request relief for the Dzhurin camp. The doctor promised that he would work miracles.

And now the wonder of wonders: after returning from the journey, the doctor reported to the council. He began the story by describing at length

69 Toward the end of 1942 and at the beginning of 1943, the lives of the deportees began to stabilize to a certain degree, mainly thanks to the aid packages from Romania and the change in Romanian policy regarding the Jewish deportees. The Romanian authorities allowed shipments of aid from Jewish communities in Romania whose member had not been deported to Transnistria. This aid included money, tools, clothes, salt, etc.

the kind of ruses that he employed to slip into the major's home, which is under watch by a Romanian guard post. Jews do not dare set foot in that area, but he entered the holy of holies without fear. As he approached the overlord with the package under his arm, the major eyed him with a strange look and said: "Good, but do not think that I am demanding anything for free. I am even willing to pay 300 marks, provided that the experts say that the merchandise is worth it" (the community paid 3,000 marks in cash for the two fur coats ...). The doctor clearly trusted the noble major and gave him the goods to evaluate.

"And imagine his magnanimity," the doctor boasted, "the major shook my hand warmly and said: 'Come back tomorrow at the same time. I will order the guard to let you in.' Of course, I arrived exactly on time. This time, the major instructed me to sit down and apologized, saying that his wife was not at home, and he had nothing to offer me. As for the furs, experts said that they are not bad, although there are better. When we parted, the major once again shook my hand and even praised the leadership of the 'model colony' of Dzhurin."

The doctor became silent and it was obvious that he had finished his account. Councilman Iehoşua Ungariş, the council's cashier, who is always carrying a stuffed briefcase under his arm—a symbol of his importance ... —asked a strange question: "Can you return the 300 marks to me now that the coffers are completely empty?"

"It's gone," the doctor whispered with downcast eyes—"the major did not reach for his pockets, and I did not dare make any demand so as not to bungle the deal. After all, he could have changed his mind and rejected the coats."

Moshe Katz wanted to know what relief and favors the doctor had procured for Dzhurin in exchange for the inflated bribe. Stuttering, the doctor haltingly muttered that he actually asked the overlord to allow the farmers to bring foods to the market. "But even before I had finished the sentence"—reported the doctor—"the major impatiently waved his hand and bellowed: 'Well, I will see what can be done. Goodbye!'" Thus, the discussion in the community concluded.

Unfortunately, the situation is no better in other camps and often even worse, especially in holy Moghilev. Whoever does not like it can hold his tongue and keep quiet. It is dangerous and of no benefit to anyone to voice criticism. On the contrary, the general population will suffer even more as a result of manifestations of rebellion.

[November 21, 1942] 9 P.M.

I have already often mentioned the series of beatings that have become a daily occurrence in the community building. Whoever has God in his heart and a small whip in his hand delivers blows. The battered victims contort their faces and remain silent. It's always the same: resistance will bring disaster to both the "rebel" and to his relatives. This afternoon I was destined to witness two scenes of beatings once again, not the first time and certainly not the last. Even though I have already had time to get used to this, my face burns in shame and sorrow seeing Jews beating Jews. The verse, "and he said to him who did the wrong: 'Why do you smite your fellow man?'"[70] has remained unanswered since the days of Moses …

November 25, 1942, 2 P.M.

Mother is in grave condition. The abscess actually burst open, but she is experiencing heart palpitations, and her pulse can barely be detected since yesterday. She is lying down, with no strength and no appetite, but her mind is as lucid as ever, and she understands what is happening to her. Both the doctors—Dr. Frenckel and Dr. Greiff—who visit her every day, encourage me with the words, "God is almighty"… Were it not for Rivka's typhus, such a misfortune would not have come about. Grandmother Serl, my mother's mother, lived until the age of ninety-two, and my mother, with her strong body, would certainly have taken after her. Can a miracle still occur? The answer will come soon and I fear it.

---

70 Exod. 2:13.

[November 25, 1942] 9 P.M.

The community is already beginning to settle firmly in Dzhurin, as if we are doomed to live out our lives here. The community cooperative was opened here today—a kind of general store,[71] run by the engineer Fitzio Sharfstein, a deportee from Gura Humorului (Bukovina). The *Lagernikes* will be required to buy everything at the cooperative, and the militia will oversee that the "small merchants" and the owners of stalls at the market will not compete with it. The profits will go into the community coffers. This has ruined a considerable number of meager livelihoods, and the number of candidates for a bowl of bean soup in the soup kitchen has increased.

One hour after the cooperative opened its doors, the first "shoppers in fox furs" had already appeared—two gendarmes with a note from the commander with a list of the many products that the gendarmerie lacks. Of course, the welcome guests were not allowed to leave with empty baskets, and instead of cash they paid with "*Mulţumiri*" ("thanks") ...

December 8, 1942 (Fifth Day of *Hanuke* 5703)

I have not touched these pages for quite some time. I am overcome with despair and consequently I view everything as foolish child's play. For what and for whom do I write? We are sinking deeper into the black abyss and the thin rays of light from the distant world (**1945:** the English victories in Africa and the Russian victories in Stalingrad) do not reach as far as Dzhurin to banish the thick darkness.

In Dzhurin itself, life drags gloomily on with no earthshaking news. The poor are starving and shivering from cold, and the wise ones among them will flee to the place where all sorrows cease ... small merchants and speculators secretly trade, brokers negotiate, and whoever still possesses a rag sells it for a bargain price or exchanges it at the market for 1 pood of

---

71 The council established the cooperative to prevent a black market and to enable the Jews to purchase goods at subsidized prices. The goods and products for the cooperative were purchased with the money it collected in taxes from the well-to-do and also from packages from Romania.

potatoes or a little wood. The Jewish regime goes on, as among respectable people, with its own militia and its own criminals, where a non-Jew has no claim, with a high court and all its paraphernalia. The fire under the pots in the soup kitchen blazes every day and, in the hospital, the doctors and orderlies and nurses do not sit around with nothing to do, God forbid. The Rickettsia bacteria is already making sure that they do not get bored …

As for me and my relatives, things certainly could be better. Mother is still lying in bed weak and ill, and her strength is failing from day to day. Rivka has yet to overcome the aftermath of typhus; her feet are swollen, and she can barely drag herself around. Nevertheless, she cares for Mother with devotion and does everything possible to alleviate her bitter fate. The few hundred marks that my mother had saved for Rivka's new overcoat are running out like a tallow candle, and what will happen when the last mark is spent?

I cannot sleep and I tire my shortsighted eyes during the long winter nights, reading *Anna Karenina* in Russian until after midnight. [May] My troubles [be] on the heads of the "heroes" who, being wealthy, find no other solution than to throw themselves under a speeding train! … In Dzhurin, those people would have had other worries already.

So why have I suddenly become reconciled with my pen? Because of a new delusion that comes from nearby, indeed from Shargorod itself. That city is agitated and seething with the news that the entire world has begun to take an interest in the remaining remnant in Transnistria, and there is a strong belief—listen to this—that they plan to transport the entire community to *Eretz Yisroel*! This strange and unbelievable news comes from a letter that Jews from Bucharest smuggled to relatives in Moghilev and, in the meanwhile, the Dzhurin camp is in a state of upheaval, and Jews are debating where it is better to settle: in Tel Aviv or in a kibbutz.

Religious Jews are excited and claim that they will not budge from Jerusalem and will recite *Tiken Hatzos*[72] every night at the Western Wall …[73]

72 *Tikun Hatzot* in Hebrew (literally, midnight rectification) are prayers, which are recited beginning at midnight, that consist primarily of Psalms and verses from the Torah that refer to the destruction of the Holy Temple and the longing for the redemption.

73 In November 1942, an unofficial emissary sent by Radu Lecca, the Commissioner for Jewish Affairs in Romania, arrived with a proposal to send 70,000 Jews from Transnistria to emigrate from Romania in return for a payment of 200 lei per person to the Romanian

December 9, 1942 (1st of *Tevet*, 5703), 9 P.M.

Already at dawn, a sad and unfortunate day began and ended tragically. When I arrived at dawn to see my mother—I can barely wait for the morning—I found her in the exact same condition as the day before: exhausted and slowly wasting away. I began chopping a few pieces of wood with a blunt pickaxe, since the Ukrainian landlord has refused to lend me his axe, because it has become blunt. I therefore struggled to chop the pieces of wood as thinly as possible, and a piece of honed wood flew off, striking my left hand and breaking the watch on my wrist.

Never mind my body, but I'm very sorry about the watch, because it did not belong to me but rather to my son, Bertl, who received it back home as a gift, when he was … secretary of the deported community of Siret, and he was just a ten-year-old scamp!

This was possible in the crazy, dark summer of 1941, when the 2,000 Jewish people from Siret (Bukovina) who had been uprooted from their homes already in June 1941 were sent back from the Regat camps in Craiova and Calafat to Rădăuţi and settled there temporarily.[74] The Siret

---

treasury. This bribe would cost a total of 3.5 million dollars. Chaim Berles, the senior representative of the Jewish Agency in Constantinople arrived in Mandatory Palestine specifically for this purpose. The plan raised many doubts and questions about the feasibility of the operation among the management of the Jewish Agency. Dov Yosef, who was the secretary of the Jewish Agency's Political Department, feared that the Allies would not allow the transfer of such a large sum to the enemy, and that it would be impossible to conduct negotiations without the knowledge of Britain and the Allies. Doubts also arose regarding the possibility of transporting such a large number of people during the war. Eventually the "Transnistria Plan" was not implemented, because of the opposition of the Germans. See Chava Wagman-Eskholi, "Tohnit Transnistriya: Hizdamnut Hatzala Vehona'a" (Hebrew), *Yalkut Moreshet,* 26 (1979), pp. 155–171; and Dalia Ofer, *Escaping from the Holocaust*: *Illegal Immigration to the Land of Israel, 1939–1944* (New York and Oxford: Oxford University Press, 1990), pp. 187–188.

74 All the Jews of Siret were expulsed by order of the Romanian army in June 1941. The elderly and sick who were unable to walk were shot, and their bodies were cast into the Siret River. The rest of the inhabitants were deported on foot to Dorneşti and from there they were transported by train to Craiova and Calafat in southern Romania. Around two months later, the Jews were returned to Rădăuţi in Bukovina and sent to work in labor camps. They were later deported once again, this time over the Dniester to Transnistria. Two of the trains carrying these deportees arrived in Yampol, and then they were taken to the ghetto in Bershad; two other trains arrived in Atachi, and from there the deportees continued on an exhausting march to Moghilev and to other ghettos in the region,

Jews organized their own community in Rădăuţi, and Bertl became their secretary for a number of reasons: first, because he types well, and because I was among the few, rare persons who was still permitted to own a typewriter at that time. The Romanians had confiscated typewriters from the Jews to prevent them from corresponding with … Stalin! However, the second main reason was different. What supposedly was the primary aim of the "community of Siret," so to speak, other than submitting petitions to the authorities to request relief for the uprooted! The fascist "Iron Guard" ruled the roost in Romania at that time, and its angels of destruction, wearing green shirts and girded with a leather belt with a revolver attached to it, stood guarding the doors of city hall, the prefecture, and other government offices. Jews feared them like the devil and avoided contact with them. Bertl, a shrewd little fellow, who does not have particularly Jewish facial features, would go fearlessly into their offices, sporting a green hunting cap on his head, and would present the requests wherever necessary, even to the prefect Ionescu himself.

Bertl demanded no pay for his trouble and did not receive any, but the people from Siret would shower him with gifts, and one day they even presented him with a wristwatch. This watch, which today met its end, possessed an important quality: its numbers were permeated with phosphorous and glowed in the dark. Oy, oy, for so many hours during sleepless winter nights, I did not take my eyes off the glimmering numbers.

Upon returning home from [visiting] Mother, I told Bertl what had happened to me. At first, he turned pale, but when he saw my bandaged hand he said: "Don't fret, Father, what matters is that the watch bore the brunt of the blow. No problem, it can be fixed." I indeed went straight to an expert watchmaker, a fellow townsman of mine, and he promised me that he would revive the watch.

And now the second, tragic part of today, which has nothing to do with the cheap watch, the tragedy of a young man, a mensch, and a

---

including the Dzhurin ghetto. See Lavi, *Pinkas Hakehilot*: *Rumania*, vol. 1, p. 483; Itzhak Artzi, Feibish Herman, and David Sha'ari, eds., *Siret (Seret) Shelanu* (Hebrew) (Tel Aviv: Irgun Yotzei Siret Be'Yisrael, 2003), pp. 136–163, 184, 194–195.

relative—a tragedy that behooved me to note the Jewish date alongside the non-Jewish one (1st of *Tevet*, 5703).[75] This marks the *Yortsayt* (who will commemorate it in future generations! ...) of my brother-in-law, Moşe Sonenschein, a young man of around thirty-eight years of age who died in Dzhurin and was buried in the local cemetery today. He was married to Elke, Roza's older sister, and the father of a little boy Herş, today three and a half years old. This tore the first link from our family chain of eleven persons who together were cast violently into the hell of Dzhurin.

As soon as I sat down at my desk in the community building, a messenger rushed in to inform me that Moşe Sonenschein had just died and had to be given a proper burial. Even though I had foreseen his death for weeks, the news of his passing stunned me. He is clearly a victim of the exile in Transnistria. Back home, Moşe was a trusted foreman at my father-in-law's mill in the village of Milişăuţi (near Rădăuţi) and had no financial worries. When he arrived in Dzhurin, he had to secure a livelihood at the very least for himself. My father-in-law—a very wealthy man until the deportation—and Rachel arrived in Dzhurin, literally naked and barefoot, with small bundles under their arms and without a penny. Rachel—a doctor of chemistry, who in Rădăuţi owned her own cosmetics factory—took charge of Elka and the child, and they are now living in a small house together with a hatmaker, Biniamin Tzirolnik, in addition to the landlord, his wife, and four young children who also "live" there! Rachel supports the four of them by furtively peddling pieces of soap and a little powder at the market, and if she brings home a revenue of 2, not to mention 3, marks per day, it is considered a good day. There was no room for Moşe in this large apartment, and the landlord would not agree to allow him to stay there. So, Rachel then rented a place for him, so that he would have somewhere to lay his head.

The only livelihood that Moşe found was working as a water carrier. He dragged two jugs of water on the slippery road to the top of the mountain several times each day during the entire winter, literally working himself to death, to earn a few marks. He was not accustomed

75 December 9, 1942.

to doing such grueling work, and he became emaciated, nothing but skin and bones. During *Peysech*, I managed to persuade the head of the Labor Office, David Buksbaum, to add him to the list of "substitutes," who hired themselves out to work for the gendarmes instead of the wealthy *Lagernikes* for 3 marks a day. It isn't a piece of cake but it is still better than carrying water.

Moşe made a living working as a substitute for a few months, but his weakened body could not carry on, and he was left lying in bed, with no strength left. The tragedy was that he had completely lost the will to live, and he let himself go, falling into that state of apathy that led to the destruction of countless persons in the Balta district, as well as several in Moghilev and Shargorod. He did not suffer from hunger, and a doctor examined him from time to time, but he already bore the stamp of the Angel of Death on his face. Rachel brought him enough food, but he did not touch the meals. The doctors call this terminal exhaustion "Transnistriatis."[76]

Poor Moşe, forgive me if I ever offended you. I could not help you. Too many sorrows befell me in the past year, and I don't know in what world I am wandering. You will already sleep, without worries tonight, and who knows whether we should not envy you.

There was barely a *minyen* for the funeral at the cemetery. A *shoyhet* from Bessarabia, who lost his entire family and now wallows in the poorhouse of the great synagogue, recited *Eyl Moleh Rahmim*[77] and the first *Kaddish*, which will probably also be the last. The muffled knocking of the shovels was then heard as the members of the *Hevra Kadishe* hurriedly cast dirt into the grave. They, the members of the *Hevra Kadishe*, have no time, because their livelihood is abundantly blessed: another two funerals are awaiting them.

---

76 The Transnistria syndrome was characterized by depression and apathy that led to self-neglect to the extent of suicide, similar to the condition of the *Muselman*. Israel Margalit (Postilnik) writes about the "Transnistriatis" disease, which spread in the Bershad ghetto and other Transnistrian ghettos, because of the unbearable conditions and severe hunger. The person suffering from this disease "loses the will to live. He is overcome with deep apathy and indifference, and nothing interests him anymore: not food, not relatives, not he himself." See Margalit-Postilnik, *Radauts: Kehila Yehudit Betzemihata Uvisheki'ata*, pp. 156–156.

77 *El Maleh Rahamim* (God full of compassion) is a prayer recited for the departed.

The wind howled in anguish, a cold rain mixed with snow from the clouded sky above whipped our faces, and it began to get dark. Our feet sank into a thick, sticky mud, and it was as difficult to pull our shoes out of it as the parting of the Red Sea. My family and I returned from the cemetery in order to continue "life" in Dzhurin ...

December 15, 1942

The *shiva*[78] for Moşe Sonenschein has ended. Because of this tragedy, I have not been in the mood to take up my pen until today, even though there is more than enough to write about. For example, the curse of the "good tidings" that are conveyed every day but that come to nothing. One of these rumors persisted for an entire week—international talks are underway to take us all to *Eretz Yisroel*, and Romania agrees. There is just one obstacle: England, the "people of the Bible" who trace close ties to us through the Ten Tribes,[79] will not allow them to save the meager remaining remnant at the eleventh hour. Their warships guard the coasts of *Eretz Yisroel* so that, God forbid, not a single Jewish survivor will sneak in from the grave of the living of Europe. It seems that this tall tale was invented by a quintessential enemy of Israel to exacerbate the suffering of the deportees by dashing their hopes. It is reminiscent of the salty foods that the Babylonians compelled the Jewish exiles who were banished from *Eretz Yisroel* to eat following the destruction of the First Temple, so that the Jews would die of thirst, because they did not give them water ...[80]

Another report is perhaps not a fabrication, but neither will it bring any meaningful assistance. A state delegation will arrive soon in Transnistria to investigate how the deportees have managed in their "new home."

78 The traditional seven-day period of mourning following the death of a family member.

79 Kunstadt refers to the ten lost tribes that had constituted the Northern Kingdom of Israel.

80 Eicha (Lamentations) Rabbah b. This legend is also mentioned in Louis Ginzburg, *The Legends of the Jews*: *Vol. 4*, *Bible Times and Characters from Joshua to Esther* (The Project Gutenberg eBook, 2001), http://gutenberg.readingroo.ms/2/8/8/2882/2882-h/2882-h.htm#chap82 (accessed June 20, 2022).

In order to provide the delegation with a semblance of fairness, it will include two Jewish delegates: a former lawyer from Cernăuţi and a current functionary in Bucharest, Dr. Zitter, and the wealthy man from Bucharest Natan Klipper, who himself was once a resident of Vatra Dornei (Bukovina) and who left for the capital on the eve of the deportation with all his property.[81] They will also include a well-respected Romanian woman and senior official of the "Red Cross" in order to throw as much dust as possible in the eyes of the world. The Romanian authorities are clearly doing this to blow smoke in the eyes of the "world at large" and to show that the Jews in Transnistria live in accordance with the law. It is sad and a disgrace that Jews, and not just anybody, will allow themselves to be dragged into such a hypocritical delegation and thereby help—even if inadvertently—our sworn enemies to annihilate the meager remnant between the Dniester and the Bug.

The masses are convinced that this delegation will bring the longed-for deliverance. Indeed, they seized the empty Jewish houses immediately following the deportation and stole all the abandoned property. Will the fascist Romanian authorities now begin to throw out the new tenants and resettle the wearied and oppressed Yids? Will the German executioners, who are in complete control in Romania, allow it? If deliverance comes, it will only come from elsewhere and not from this preposterous delegation …

December 25, 1942, 2 P.M.

The gaps between the entries are getting longer and longer. My spirits have sunk since Mother became so ill, and I see clearly that her strength

---

81 Natan Klipper, a rich businessman from Vatra Dornei in Southern Bukovina, managed to escape with the rest of his family to Bucharest and to save his many possessions, using his connections with senior figures in the Romanian authorities. Klipper was charismatic and daring, and he had a strong sense of public duty, which helped him greatly in making connections and successful contacts with members of the regime when he was called upon to assist the Jews in distress. In order to soften the hearts of the authorities who held the fate of the Jews in their hands, generous payments were necessary. Klipper funded more than one bribe with his private funds. See Yalon, *Sefer Hazikaron Shel Yehudei Vatra Dornei*, vols. 1–2, pp. 13, 26, 34, 74, 109, 509, 530, 607ff.

is fading away from day to day, even though Rivka and I are trying very hard to keep the light, which is the shining sun in our dark life, from extinguishing. I have no desire to write, my thoughts are incoherent, and my mind is blank.

Today Mother's face appeared to light up, apparently in an effort to lift our spirits, and she succeeded. An indication [of this]: these lines ...

The story about the investigative delegation seems to be as true as the dream about being taken to *Eretz Yisroel.* No one is talking about these delusions anymore, and the Creator of the Universe has provided fresh news, which is passed on by word of mouth: the laments of the "guests" who fled from Pechora and from the rest of the nether hells near the Bug, or from the Bershad and Balta districts. They continue to roam on dirt roads and through forests, which the winds have covered with snow while blizzards rage, persisting and even intensifying. Indeed, the deportees claim that precisely because of the threatening conditions outside, it has become easier to avoid the gendarmes and the Ukrainian militia, who lie in wait on the roads for Jewish "fugitives." The angels of destruction recoil from the menacing conditions outdoors, which denotes "Jewish luck"...

We have heard terrible stories concerning the mass tragedies in the camps of the Bershad and Balta districts, where today about 10 percent of the people who ended up there in the autumn of 1941 are still alive. Approximately 14,000 Jews died of cold, starvation, typhus, and neglect last winter at the kolkhoz Tsibulevka near Bershad.[82] There is not a single Jewish family in these regions who has not rendered some victims. Many families have been completely annihilated, everyone. In fact, there are Jewish councils called "Obshchina"[83] in those districts, but I do not want

---

82 Tsibulevka *vece* (old) and Tsibulevka *noua* (new) were two neighboring villages that were occupied by the German army in July 1941. Some of the local Jews left with the Soviet army, and thousands of those remaining were murdered by the Germans during the first days of the occupation and buried in a mass grave. In November 1941, 1,270 Jews from Bukovina were taken through the border crossing in Yampol to Tsibulevka *vece*, and another 1,200 Jews were taken to Tsibulevka *noua*, most from Bukovina and the rest from Bessarabia. The deportees were concentrated in two cowsheds that were fenced in, which were declared a ghetto. See Lavi, *Pinkas Hakehilot*: *Rumania*, vol. 1, pp. 491–492; Ancel, *Toledot Hashoah*: *Romania*, vol. 2, p. 786.

83 This representative body included a few local Jews and served as a Jewish council in this region of Ukraine. Councils usually dealt with matters of burial, marriages, and kashrut.

even to repeat what the refugees are saying, and I believe that the truth is beyond imagination.

January 1, 1943, 7 A.M.

Another sad and gloomy week has passed in a similarly agonizing manner as the previous week. Mother is ill, Rivka and Roza can barely stand up; outside, it is cloudy; in the house, there is poverty and darkness; in the community building, they quarrel and they flatter the non-Jews. The terrible year of 1942 has come to an end and, *in a guter sho*, we are already writing the date January 1, 1943!

It is still dark outside, and I am writing by the light of a tallow candle. A lantern is a luxury here that is reserved for wealthy men, and not so much the lantern as much as the oil: 1 liter of oil costs more than half a pood of potatoes, and my occupation does not afford me such an expense. Therefore, I am destroying my shortsighted eyes for hours by the light of the tallow candle that flickers doggedly in the wind—my window, which is covered with cardboard instead of windowpanes, displays a degree of hospitality and allows the wind to enter through the cracks in the rotten frames. The hovel is permeated with soot and smoke. Roza complains that I am filling the "salon" with smoke, but I am not afraid that she will divorce me and I carry on.

As I sit in front of the tallow candle, the sad memories of my childhood days, when I would wake up at 3 A.M. and would sit down to memorize *Yoyreh De'ah*[84] in my mother's house, rise and float. As soon as the day would dawn, I would go the "Vijniţa *shul* [synagogue]" and would continue to study there until late in the evening, as is the custom

---

Sometimes they mediated between the Jewish communities and the *satrosta* (head of the city or village). See Rosen, "Tzibur Veyahid," p. 132.

84 Yoreh De'ah, or Yod, as it is also known, is the second part of the compilation of halacha (Jewish law) by Rabbi Yaakov ben Asher, entitled *Arba'a Turim*. There is a parallel part to it in Yosef Karo's *Shulhan Aruch*. The laws included in the Yoreh De'ah concern a wide range of topics, including Torah study, charity, circumcision, conversion, excommunication, mourning, and more. They are considered secondary in importance only to the halachot in *Orah Hayim*, the first part of *Arba'a Turim*, which deals with laws about daily matters.

of an assiduous Torah scholar. Then I used to swallow the fine print with enthusiastic fervor, hoping, with the perseverance of Bialik, that it would not be so terrible, that the difficult period would one day pass away forevermore, and yet, thirty years later, more or less, I am starting over again as before, except that now a desolate desert of immeasurable distress and suffering has taken the place of the enthusiasm of the golden dreams of youth.

Well, we have now entered the fifth year of the war, according to the dictum that "one day of the year is as important as the [entire] year." The year 1942 was a terrible year, and who can fathom the thousands of victims among our people who have been sacrificed over the past twelve months wherever our sworn enemy rules. It is a grievous error to assess the victims, who did not have a Jewish burial, only on the basis of the mass graves or the piles of bodies in the trenches and on the bottom of lakes and rivers. No, we must also take into account the thousands of living dead who are still languishing, dragging themselves around, wrapped in sacks or rags and longing for the Angel of Death; we must also reckon the masses of orphans who have lost their parents either on the dirt roads or in the camps, who are drifting from place to place like withered leaves in autumn storms in fallow fields or plains, or are dying in mass hovels; we must count the wandering "fugitives," who escaped from the death camps and are dragging themselves with their last bit of strength to the "fortunate" camps, where they find the doors locked; we must take into account the hundreds of thousands who were uprooted from their homes, who have been suffocating for more than a year in ruins and barns, feeding on food for animals, who do not take off the dirty, stinking rags from their bodies, who shake at the slightest rustle, and who do not possess a single healthy limb; we must estimate the myriads of heart conditions, lung conditions, digestive disorders, skin abscesses, and other kinds of diseases, which the year 1942 bestowed as a gift on our brothers, the children of Israel, in all the exiles and all the camps, to prepare them for the passage of the Angel of Death; we must gauge the seas that were filled with the tears of the far-flung Jews, the dashed hopes, the sighs of despair, and the sleepless nights that befell 1942. When we finish this reckoning, we will be able to begin to sum up 1942. But what will come out of this! …

January 4, 1943, 7 A.M.

The few Jews in Dzhurin are being recounted. The colony chief, who was summoned to Moghilev by phone a few days ago, sent a letter by special courier with an order to immediately conduct a census of all the *Lagernikes* from Romania. The lists must be taken to the local gendarmerie headquarters by January 6. Orphans are to be registered in separate lists, divided into three categories: orphans who lack both parents, orphans without a father, and orphans without a mother. The person's name, age, profession, and place of origin must be included in the lists.

This is already the seventh count, *in a guter sho*, even though no good came of its six predecessors. No, on the contrary, despite the fact that the results of the count led to bad outcomes, such as manhunts, Jewish minds have once again begun to run wild and interpret everything positively. The secret of our existence lies in this unshakeable Jewish faith, as the knife hovers over our necks …

Since the doctor is in Moghilev, this is a good opportunity to legalize at least the "non-kosher fugitives" who are not registered. Many of them are hiding in cellars and barns, and they are literally starving to death. They do not receive any soup from the soup kitchen, because as far as the "colony" is concerned, they do not exist. No one wants to know about these "pariahs" and they chase them away with sticks. Although there are a few dignitaries who treat these "non-kosher [people]" with a warm Jewish heart, what can they do about the doctor who goes crazy at the mention of the name "Pechora." He is on high alert to ensure that no *Shatnez*[85] sneaks into his model colony.

---

85 In Judaism, *shatnez,* which is derived from Leviticus 19:19 and Deuteronomy 22:5, 22:9–11, refers to a forbidden mixture, such as wearing a fabric containing both wool and linen, the interbreeding of different species of animals, and the planting together of different kinds of seeds.

Among the people in hiding, quite a few are the non-kosher of the non-kosher. They are not Romanian Jews, in general, but the few remaining remnants of the decimated Jewish communities in Ukraine, where German and Romanian murderers have slaughtered almost all the Jews. It will not be possible to slip these *lamedvovnikim* into the registration lists and prepare cards [in the card catalog] for them, because they do not know a word of Romanian. In the event of an inspection by the gendarmes, the secret will be exposed and the entire camp is liable to suffer a terrible disaster.

January 5, 1943, 7 A.M.

Mother is no longer sick with a specific illness, but she is so weak that she is unable to move any of her limbs and she certainly cannot get out of bed. She is nothing but skin and bones, and only her heart continues to beat somehow, and her iron will is still struggling with death. Rivka, who is still not healthy herself, is completely devoted to Mother, and her eyes are always red from crying. I visit a few times each day to lend a hand as much as possible and, every time that I visit her on her sickbed is devastating to me. The doctors believe that the hardening of her arteries is advancing swiftly, and there is no cure.

From the day that Rivka was infected with typhus around *Sukkes*, she has not set foot in the streets. She used to earn a small sum of money peddling used clothes, and now the meager "livelihood" has been spent. They are subsisting on the 600 marks that Mother saved for Rivka's overcoat, and the amount is running out. Rivka still has a pair of gold earrings, a present from Mother, and even if she finds a trader now, the revenue will scarcely suffice for two more months.

I draw my livelihood to support four people from my wages of 100 marks and, apart from that, I am once again receiving the supplement from the Moghilev Central Council, because the engineer Jagendorf again sits in the president's chair.[86] Sometimes I earn 1 or 2 marks for

86 Throughout the period that the Jews of Bukovina were in the Moghilev ghetto, there were several councils. Siegfried Jagendorf served as head of the council for two periods: November 18, 1941–June 15, 1942; and December 15, 1942–May 10, 1943.

writing a letter or a request, but these resources do not reach the sum of 200 marks. In order to appreciate the value of 200 marks, here are some of the prices that people paid at the market on Sunday: 1 pood of barley flour, 55 marks; 1 pood of potatoes, 18 marks; 1 pood of wood, 3 marks; one egg, 1 mark; two onions, 1 mark; half a kilo of butter, 15 marks; 1 kilo of salt, 9 marks; one pair of shoes, 600 marks; one suit, 2,000 marks! This is not to mention luxuries, such as meat, honey, cream, and the like—because they cost me and others like me triple the price …

However, if I may, I do not want only to complain! In the autumn, I was able to obtain a few beans, some poods of wood, some unfermented wine, and grains, and in the meantime, I am living off these supplies like a wealthy man. The wood will suffice until February, because Roza cooks on a small kerosene burner, which does its job with a few strips of wood; the stove is completely antiquated and I am not supposed to light it at all. The wall of my hovel borders the wall of the landlord's stove in the other room, and when we touch it, it feels warm. Why should I be greedy! …

As long as God provides barley bread and potatoes, no member of my family goes hungry. Alas, these foods constantly cut like a knife below my heart, but we ignore the knife and continue chewing. Where is it written that my stomach specifically should be privileged and should leave Transnistria unscathed, if indeed it is destined to live a long life!

Roza has developed a heart condition and, of course, it plagues her. She complains that she occasionally feels a stab in her heart, like that of a needle, and gets dizzy and wakes up several times a night due to a shortness of breath and must sit up. Never mind, who pays attention to such nonsense! I too have begun to suffer from dizzy spells and, as for the nights, I do not shut an eye.

The children are actually holding up well, eating whatever there is, sleeping whenever and wherever they can, and they feel good, unless a manhunt is underway, or the gendarmes are killing Jews. On the other hand, their intellectual decline pains me greatly. For more than a year, they have not studied, have not opened a book, and have associated with ill-mannered children. I am fettered to my meager livelihood, and everything at home—except for the cooking—weighs on my shoulders. Roza does not go out of the hovel and thinks that passive resistance against our bleak fate will have some effect and, therefore, I have no time left to educate the children. Indeed, one way or another, this exile will not last forever, and if we are granted deliverance, I will rectify their education somehow and will fill in the gaps.

[January 5, 1943] 3 P.M.

If I thought that everything was going so well for me, today I received a new gift: my father-in-law, Şmuel Merling, suddenly came down with a high fever. The doctors do not know what he has and tell us to wait and see. He is not yet a very old man—in November 1942, he turned seventy—but his heart is weak, especially since the deportation. Who knows if he was not granted a nice package, because typhus has once again spread its arms wide, and it is lively and merry in the hospital ...[87]

January 7, 1943, 7 A.M.

My father-in-law has been lying with a high fever, has taken nothing into his mouth, and has been feeling unusually weak for almost two days now. We will know only tomorrow whether the Rickettsia bacteria has come to visit him. The hospital only admits patients who have been conclusively diagnosed with typhus so that they do not contract it in the hospital. It is not at all possible to isolate suspected cases, and there is really no place there to insert a pin. Rachel is constantly taking his temperature, but the quicksilver is so merciless and climbs up the smooth walls. I have only visited my father-in-law once since he fell ill. I cannot help him, but I could bring home the gift to my family.

---

87 There was an outbreak of typhus once again in the winter of 1943, but this time it did not strike as severely as in the previous winter of 1941–1942. This may have been due to the vaccinations against the disease and also because some people developed a natural immunity after recovering from it during the first winter.

January 8, 1943, 3 P.M.

My father-in-law's diagnosis is as clear as oil on water: typhus. His entire body, skin and bones, is covered with red spots—the heralds of the cruel guest. They took my father-in-law on a stretcher to the hospital an hour ago. Rachel insisted on accompanying her father and to care for him in the dangerous environment, even though Dr. Greiff warned her against it; due to the shortage of nurses, the director allows relatives to take care of their loved ones, if they are willing to endanger their lives.

Before going off on her fateful path, Rachel bid me farewell as one who is leaving for war. By the way, she made it clear that if anything happens to her father, she will take her own life. I reminded her that she must not even consider this, because she is responsible for her recently widowed sister, Elke, whose husband, Moşe Sonenschein, just died, as well as because of their son, Herş. This argument made a strong impression on her, and I am convinced that she will keep a stiff upper lip and will not do that.

[January 8, 1943] 9 P.M.

While one is still speaking, another arrives.[88] Today at noon they took my father-in-law to the hospital, and Rachel went with him to the *Akedah*,[89] and an hour later a messenger came running to me to tell me that Mother feels extremely ill. I immediately went to see Dr. Julius Frenckel and took him to Mother. He examined her and said: "It will be all right. I will give her a nice injection immediately." These, however, were only empty [words of] comfort for the patient and for Rivka. The doctor told me the truth outside: her heart is beating with its last bit of strength, her pulse is weaker than that of a chick that just hatched from an egg, and the situation is beyond desperate. He promised to return in the evening and give her

88 Job 1:18: "While he was yet speaking, there came also another." This passage in Job refers to four messengers who brought news of catastrophes, one after the other, before the previous one had finished speaking.

89 Gen. 22:1–18 recounts the *Akedah*—the binding of Isaac by Abraham—that concludes with God sparing Isaac's life.

an injection, and he kept his word. Mother does not stop groaning, her entire body hurts, and I bend down to approach my ear to her mouth in order to hear what her lips whisper. Not a word of despair comes out of her mouth, and she hopes for miracles, as she has hoped throughout her entire, sad life. I see clearly the approach of what I do not want my lips to utter and I am left stunned in the face of the cruelty of fate.

And now let us to turn to the general public. When compiling the lists of the people in the camp, it was possible to make kosher [permit] all the "fugitives" from the camps in Romania and even a few "non-kosher" Ukrainian Jews, with the help of a ruse: changing their Russian names to proper ones, like those of the Romanian Jews. So "Svetlana Sapashnik" was changed to Sheindl Karbonari, "Sasha Tziolnik" to Martshel Matshelaro, and you would have to be a prophet to discover who is hiding behind the brand new, kosher names! It was opportune that the colony chief had spent some time in Moghilev. He returned only yesterday evening, but the lists had already been in the hands of the post chief, Georgescu, for an hour. The doctor's first question upon crossing the threshold of the council [community] building was: "So, did you compile the lists honestly and register only kosher *Lagernikes*? I will look over the copies tomorrow."

However, a Dzhurin miracle occurred, and the doctor was not able to check the copies and stir up who knows what kind of trouble. He unexpectedly received a phone call and was summoned to Moghilev, because the investigative delegation had shown up there.[90] The

90 This refers to the investigative delegation that was headed by Iuliu Mumuianu, the representative of the Romanian regime, and by Fred Şaraga the Jewish representative appointed by the Comisia Autonomă De Ajutorare. This delegation left Bucharest on December 31, 1942, and reached Odessa on the evening of January 1, 1943. The members of the delegation were welcomed by Prof. Alexianu, ruler of Transnistria, in the presence of Colonel Mihail Iliescu, supervisor of the gendarmes in Transnistria; Rumanescu, the financial supervisor of the government; Rădulescu, supervisor of labor, and other senior government officials. The delegation visited the ghettos of Moghilev, Balta, Bershad, and Zhmerinka between December 31, 1942, and January 13, 1943. The delegation discussed the amounts of money that the Jews received as aid in each of the various ghettos and demanded that these sums be used for orphans, hospitals, and nursing homes for the elderly who were unable to work. Following the visit of this delegation, a report was published, known as the Şaraga Report, detailing the situation in the ghettos in terms of internal life, including hospitals, orphanages, soup kitchens, and more. Likewise,

Central Council explicitly demanded that Moshe Katz accompany the doctor. There they know full well what a competent fellow the colony chief is and that he is capable of blurting out council matters that can be detrimental. Both the delegates, wearing holiday clothes and beaming, left for Moghilev. Therefore the kosher *lamedvovnikim* will continue to be "lucky" residents of Dzhurin, until the next round of troubles …

The concern of the delegation is evidently an illusion and deliverance will certainly not come from this.

The prices are rising like yeast. The farmers bring a few products to the market, and the wealthy snatch up the goods and throw around bills of tens like stuffed cabbage. Whatever the rich do not snatch up falls into the hands of the buyers–speculators, who do not haggle but thrust bundles of banknotes into the peasants' hands. They do not lose money in the deal and fleece those who fall into their clutches throughout the week. The council has actually tried to stop the disgusting speculation, but here they lack the true zeal that they show, for example, when bribing the overlords. The militia, whom they dispatched, has not put too much effort into it, and only they know why …

There are two obvious reasons for the lack of goods at the market. First, the Romanian occupation authorities steal fresh produce, livestock, dairy products, and all kinds of foods from the farmers, leaving them only what is necessary to survive, unless a farmer hides part of his harvest at the risk of his life. Second, the peasants have begun to lose faith in the mark for the umpteenth time, apparently as a result of the Russian victories on the front, and they are unwilling to accept this currency.

---

recommendations were made for the continued funding of each of the ghettos that they visited in accordance with their needs. The heads of the ghettos gathered in Moghilev to discuss the aid and its distribution, according to the needs of each individual ghetto. Moshe Katz and Max Rosenstrauch were invited to attend the meeting. See the Şaraga Report, YVA, M.20/104; see also YVA, M.29/104.

January 9, 1943, 3 P.M.

Whenever I see a messenger approaching me at the office, my heart plummets, because no good news awaits me. This morning I was entitled to receive a dispatch delivered by a messenger that I should go immediately to my father-in-law's apartment, because they had begun to disinfect the clothes and household items, as is done in cases of typhus. I went there immediately. What my father-in-law had left behind on the day of the deportation could have been enough to support the entire Dzhurin camp for several years …

They took two new patients to the hospital today, and the plague continues to spread its arms wide. Who knows how many people are already carrying the Rickettsia bacteria, which makes its presence known only after about three weeks! It is possible that Roza, one of the children, or I are already carriers of the dangerous guest, because, until he succumbed to the disease, my father-in-law would spend a few hours every day at my hovel to skim through a book. Rachel also used to come by often, at least once a day. By the way, I myself can bring home that bargain, because I am around many people, especially the neglected poor who come to beg for a portion of soup or medicine. I am actually not too alarmed, because there is not much to miss …

January 10, 1943 1 P.M.

My father-in-law's condition is very serious. His heart is failing, and Dr. Greiff informed us today that if the patient was thirty years younger, the danger would certainly be less serious. My father-in-law is conscious but has no strength, and is unable to utter a word. Rachel talks to me through the window. Her eyes are red and swollen from crying, and she has not slept for three days and is constantly checking on her father to see if he is still breathing. She told me that yesterday she found a louse on her dress, but she does not even care.

Mother's situation is as bitter as wormwood.[91] Since yesterday, her arms—two thin sticks—are also swollen, a sign that her heart is quitting. The doctors fill her with all kinds of medicines and do not spare any injections, and Rivka continues to feed her to fortify her, but this only helps temporarily. My bosses—the doctor is in Moghilev, may he stay there for a long time! … —are being considerate with me and are not pestering me about absenting myself from work for hours. I rush around the entire day between the patients as in a world of chaos. I really have nerves of steel, and their only retaliation is to not allow me to close my eyes during the endless nights. So that I do not get bored on my wooden bunk, Roza wails in bed, choking back her tears during the night in order not to wake up the children, and whispers, "Oy, Father! Oy, his heart!" Such nice turmoil within me and around me …

January 12, 1942 [*sic*] [1943], Tuesday, 6th of Shevat 5703, 6 P.M.

My father-in-law surrendered his soul.

At dawn this morning, Roza instructed me to get fetch 100 grams of sugar and take it to the hospital, so that Rachel can make some coffee for my father-in-law. As soon as it was light outside, at around 8 A.M., I went to look for sugar. The wretched "restaurant," whose owner had already done me a favor a few times and sold me a bit of sugar for a fortune—3 marks for 100 grams—was still closed. So, in the meanwhile, I ran empty-handed to the hospital to find out what was happening. I cracked the door open where my father-in-law lay and called out Rachel's name.

She came out immediately, wearing a fur overcoat, and her face was strangely red, but not so tearstained that I would be alarmed. I asked her, as always: "So, how is Father [father-in-law]?" To this I received a calm reply: "Fine, very well." This answer surprised and confused me, and I asked further: "How high is his fever?" Rachel replied, stuttering more than enunciating: "He no longer has any fever at all." Her strange

91 Kunstadt's description of his mother's condition recalls the words in Proverbs 5:4: "But her end is as bitter as wormwood, as sharp as a two-edged sword."

response dumbfounded me and I stammered: "Tell me immediately how he is doing." Rachel then burst into wails of despair and whispered: "Why are you pretending that you don't understand? Father is dead!"

That is how I found out that my father-in-law had concluded his journey of human torment and was "granted" "deliverance"—not the kind that he, the stubborn believer and optimist, was sure he would experience but rather the Transnistrian version.

This black news hit me hard, as if I had been struck by thunder. Although Dr. Greiff had prepared the family from the outset for the final end, because the illness had begun with a heart attack, I nevertheless did not expect that the end would be so near. I was grief-stricken, knowing what a dear, close friend I had lost. He loved me almost more than his own children, even though we often bickered, mainly about politics. His infinite optimism was the complete opposite of my melancholy, which has tormented me since my childhood—from the day that I was orphaned, when I was not yet eight years old.

My father-in-law wholly believed that true deliverance would come and that all his stolen property—the estates, the mill, the sumptuous house, and the expensive household goods—would be returned to him on a silver platter, and, in addition, gifts and bonuses for the hardships that he had endured. Until the last moment, he believed that Hitler and all the enemies of Israel would soon be defeated, and the Jewish people would rise to greatness as in the messianic days. This faith did not stem from a denial of the truth—he was a wise Jew, a learned man with a sharp mind. It also had nothing to do with zealous piety—he was far from being a *tzaddik*, although he observed the laws of Judaism. His optimism was innate, ingrained in his iron will to live and to live to see the fall of his enemies.

I refrained from arguing with him during the last months, because of his failing health. He became increasingly emaciated from day to day, and the dignified and energetic Jew became a thin stick. He absolutely hated Dzhurin, and yet Dzhurin will remain his only and final estate, forever ...

Rachel told me that he passed away before dawn this morning at 4.30 A.M. Before death began to approach, red spots appeared for a second time on his body, after having already disappeared the first time. This phenomenon is the visiting card of the Angel of Death. His death took only a few minutes, and he did not struggle long against the one with a thousand eyes. He always wanted to die suddenly, when the time would come.

I had to recover quickly from the terrible blow in order to organize the funeral: prepare the ground, a bed sheet for a shroud, boards for a coffin—it takes a great deal of effort to obtain all this in the camp, especially when the purse is empty. In the end, I provided "all the goods" for my father-in-law—[may] such a year befall all our oppressors who brought on his end!—and the funeral [procession] left the hospital at 2 P.M. Many gathered to escort him, and tears flowed from many eyes, although people in Transnistria are accustomed to not weeping for the dead, especially one who is seventy years old. However, the deceased is nevertheless Şmuel Merling, one of the most important dignitaries in the great city of Rădăuţi, and everyone knew him. The tears certainly also flowed, because the people saw before their eyes the gloomy destiny that awaits them …

It was a clear, sunny winter day, the frost burned but the wind did not strike our faces. The snow crunched underfoot, and the fresh air shimmered thin and transparent like a pale veil—it was the first clear day in a few weeks.

The rabbi of Rădăuţi, Rabbi Israel Hornik—who was saved from the horror of the forest of Kopaygorod[92] and is a good, longtime friend of mine—gave a warm eulogy at the cemetery and did not spare any words. When the bride is an orphan, the wedding jester's job is easy … The *hazen* of Rădăuţi Moshe Solomon—also a good and trustworthy friend of mine—recited *Eyl Moleh* [*Rahmim*] from the depths of his heart and soul, the last shot[93] for the benefit of the deceased. At three o'clock, the shovels of dirt were flung on the fresh grave. Good friends tossed a handful of dirt—a last "farewell," alas—but I stood at a distance,

---

92 Kunstadt described the massacre of the Jews in the forest about 5 kilometers from Kopaygorod in the entries of July 30, 1942 and August 8, 1942. See also "Kopaygorod," in Guy Miron and Shlomit Shulhani, eds., *Entziklopediya Shel Hageta'ot* (Jerusalem: Yad Vashem, 2009), http://www.yadvashem.org/yv/he/research/ghettos_encyclopedia/ghetto_details.asp?cid=916 (accessed June 20, 2022); Carp, *Cartea neagră*, vol. 3, p. 279; Lavi, *Pinkas Hakehilot*: *Rumania*, vol. 1, pp. 501–504.

93 Injection.

clasping my hands. I don't believe in such gifts and do not throw mud on someone who was near and dear to me. Thus, another Transnistrian tragedy ended. Şmuel Merling is no more!

Let me note a few details here regarding the location of the grave. My father-in-law was buried near the grave of Yaakov Bernstein from Rădăuţi (on the left side) in the same row as the grave of Berl Rath from Rădăuţi, where an iron tombstone stands. (Dr. Immanuel Schertzer from Suceava was buried on the right side a few months later).

My father-in-law was born on November 22, 1872, in the village of Ludi Homorului in the Suceava district (Bukovina), to his parents, Hersh and Beila Merling, in a wealthy home of millers. As a child, he went to Rădăuţi, where he studied in a *heder* and later in the *bes medresh*, as was customary then. At the age of twenty-one, he married Basya Klang, the only daughter of the wealthy man Chaim Klang. By the way, she died at a young age in 1921, and my father-in-law did not remarry.

A shrewd merchant with a sharp mind, my father-in-law soon prospered and worked hard to become one of the wealthiest men in the city, owning 40 acres of arable land, a forest, a mill, and all kinds of other businesses. Although he was occupied with his business, every day he would drop into the Vijniţa *kloyz* [94] and study a page of Talmud, or at least a few pages of *Ein Yankv*[95] or the *Midrash*, and take part in the students' "discussions and learning."

After the untimely death of my mother-in-law, Rachel began to fill two different roles: managing her cosmetic factory and running the not-so-simple home—her father and four unmarried orphans. She did all this with love on condition that no stepmother would take the place of her departed mother.

When the fascist "Iron Guard" seized power in Romania in 1940, they confiscated all the property of the Jews, especially in the villages. My father-in-law was obviously not treated with great respect, and they robbed him of all his property and the mill in Milişăuţi (near Rădăuţi)—a

94 Small house of prayer.

95 An essay by Yaakov Ben Habib from the sixteenth century that comprises a collection and an interpretation of most of the legends found in the Babylonian Talmud and the Jerusalem Talmud. See Jacob Ibn Chabib, *En Jacob*: *Agadat of the Babylonian Talmud* (New York: Hebrew Publishing Co., 1970).

treasure worth millions of lei. Only the large house in the center of Rădăuţi and his expensive household goods remained in his possession until the day of the deportation. My father-in-law and his family left literally with only one shirt, because the remainder of their possessions were left abandoned at the train station.

A distant relative, Mendel Laufer, said the first *Kaddish* by the grave and he assumed the obligation of reciting *Kaddish* for the entire year. As a token of appreciation, he was given the shoes of the deceased.

(**Added later**: I avoided saying the *Kaddish* as long as my mother was alive so as not to tempt the devil …)

And now I must go visit Mother, to see what is happening there. Of course, I will not mention today's tragedy.

[January 12, 1943] 10 P.M.

I just now visited Mother again. The doctor cannot feel her pulse, but her heart is functioning all the same with its last bit of strength. She cannot take even a sip of pale tea, and if she takes anything in her mouth, she immediately vomits. We can barely hear her voice when we bend down to approach an ear to her mouth, but her mind is as clear as ever. She looks at me and Rivka with compassionate eyes, because she sees our bitter sorrow, and this tears my soul apart. According to the doctors, the tragic blow may happen soon, but they surmise that her stubborn heart is still capable of resisting for a while. Miracles? It is their nature to appear at the twelfth hour …

January 13, 1943, 8 P.M.

I visited Mother several times today. She clearly recognizes me, and my arrival sparks a pale glimmer of joy in her bleary eyes that goes out quickly. She is suffering bitterly, groaning intensely, and breathing with difficulty, and she has no strength to whisper a word. We can see that it is as difficult for her to move her tongue as it is for a healthy person to lift a heavy weight. Since this morning, her mind is no longer lucid, and at times she hallucinates, her words are cut off, and she is unable to say anything. She perhaps is not delirious, but she tries hard to say something and does not succeed. She is fasting completely, because her body can no longer digest even a spoonful of tea. Dr. Greiff has stopped giving her injections, because the serum remains in her veins and is no longer of any benefit and only prolongs her suffering. Neither I nor Rivka have the courage to demand that the doctor actually draw out her dying as long as possible, which will cause our mother terrible suffering. There is even a [Jewish] law that one should guard against making any noise near a dying person so as not to delay death. This is a harsh ruling for relatives but not for the person sentenced to a long passing. Even strangers who come to the house cannot bear to see the suffering of this righteous woman. For this too, a person has to be fortunate not to have to watch helplessly as his parents struggle with death and expire. Here we are—Rivka and I—who have always been lucky and precisely now this fate has befallen us …

[January 13, 1943] 11 P.M.

Who can close his eyes [to sleep] when his mother is dying? So, allow me to try to put aside my load of sorrows for a while and write about matters concerning the general public. The two delegates—the colony chief and Moshe Katz—returned today from Moghilev, where they met with the Romanian investigative delegation. The delegation includes: the former representative of the [National Christian] party of Goga–Cuza, Prof. [Iuliu] Mumuianu from Iași (one of the leaders of the fascist party, who thirsts for Jewish blood); a captain and *Feldwebel* in the Romanian army; the general secretary of the federation of the Jewish communities in Romania, Fred Șaraga,[96] and three ordinary Jews from

96 Fred (Efraim) Șaraga was born on October 16, 1891, in the city of Iași in Romania. Șaraga was a merchant and activist. He and his brother Josef established a small textile factory in the interwar period. In the 1930s, he and others established a loan bank for Jewish merchants and small craftsmen who were refused loans by other banks. Fred Șaraga was the general secretary of the Comisia Autonomã De Ajutorare and the head of the delegation of Jews that visited Transnistria, first, to find out what exactly was the

Romania whose names we had never heard: Dr. Marcovici, Eber Kahn, and Shechter.[97]

These three delegates have relatives in Transnistria and they succeeded in persuading the high-level officials that they should accept them into the delegation to enable a meeting with their families.

The delegation is intended to deal with certain matters: ascertain the number of the remaining remnant; whether the Jews work for the state; whether there are hospitals; whether they are making use of the aid sent by the Romanian Jews through the federation; whether there are craftsmen in the camps, and what their trades are.

At the meetings, they were not sparing in the obsequious style of the protocol that they wrote, and thus the high delegation fulfilled its mission. Obviously, these protocols did not at all allude to a number of trivialities, for example: that of the 250,000 persons who were sentenced to deportation, less than half linger on, gasping for air, and their number is declining daily; that the living dead, "the fugitives" from the death camps, wander around the dirt roads and wherever they appear they are beaten with sticks; that hunger, plagues, cold, neglect, the whips of the gendarmes rage in the "new home," and the number of graves of the masses is increasing rapidly; that all kinds of officials and lords flay the seventh [layer of] skin off the deportees, and most of the gains are used to bribe the occupiers and their lackies; that everyone lives in sheer terror of losing his life, and that the life of a Jew is worth less than an onion peel.

The delegation did not want and was not allowed to see such nonsense. The high-level officials had already made sure that the guests would not see anything superfluous, which, God forbid, could ruin the good name and success of the "colonies" in blessed Transnistria. The delegates

---

precise situation there and, subsequently, to help the Jews deported to Transnistria to return to Romania, in particular the orphans to Romania. Şaraga, also known as the father of the orphan children, eventually managed to return approximately 2,000 orphans—boys and girls, young men and women—to Romania. Most of these children were able to reach Mandatory Palestine in boats that had places reserved for the orphan children from Transnistria. Şaraga immigrated to Israel in 1944 and died in October 1961.

97 This delegation headed by Iuliu Mumuianu is first mentioned in the entry of January 8, 1943.

from the province were permitted to speak with the council only in the presence of Major [Colonel] Năsturaş, the commander of the legion of gendarmes [*sic*].[98] Who then would dare to disclose secrets when he knows that the guest is indeed about to leave, but the landlord remains …

98 Constantin Năsturaş was the prefect of the Moghilev region with the rank of colonel and not the commander of the gendarmerie legion, as previously mentioned. In the heat of writing, Kunstadt seems to have erred several times in describing Năsturaş' role and rank. See Carp, *Cartea neagră*, vol. 3, pp. 355, 361; Lavi, *Pinkas Hakehilot*: *Rumania*, vol. 1, p. 485; Rosen, "Tzibur Yeyahid," p. 87.

Siegfried Jagendorf, head of the Moghilev Central Council. Photo Collection, YVA, 99FO9.

Dr. Max Rosenstrauch, head of the Dzhurin ghetto. CNSAS, file I-0049412, Pisa Personala.

Moshe Katz, deputy head of the Dzhurin ghetto. Katz Family Collection, courtesy of Yehudit Nir.

Rabbi Baruch Hager. Photo Collection, YVA, 5027/748.

Notebook Three

[From the Depths][1]

1 Unlike the other parts of the diary, Kunstadt began writing the third notebook on January 16, 1943, without giving it a title and a title page. Only when this notebook was almost finished did Kunstadt entitle it, as he noted in the last entry of this notebook, dated November 17, 1943.

January 16, 1943, *Motzei Shabbes*, 8 P.M.

I write the first lines of the third notebook of memoirs while my mother spends her first night under a stone. When she was torn from me forever, yesterday afternoon, the first and most beautiful period of my life came to an end, and a period of emptiness in my soul ensued, a period of eternal sorrow over a loss that will never be recovered. Even if a miracle occurs and I live to see deliverance, what good is it without my mother! These are not bitter, black thoughts of a faithful son in the second day of the mourning period, but rather the absolute and extremely bitter truth.

Mother's death has shaken me like a catastrophic earthquake, and the most refined and the purest chord in my soul has broken—one that cannot ever be replaced. I have felt more than enough sorrow in my life, but the current pain is unlike anything I have ever known. Until yesterday, I was still a child—really an old child with a lot of silver strands in my hair—and when I would visit Mother, the decades that had passed since she had sent me off to *heder* with some food disappeared like magic. It seemed to both of us that it was 8 A.M., and that she handed me a little paper bag with two pieces of bread smothered with shmaltz and an apple, stroking my head and saying with a beaming face: "So, go on your way safely, it's already late ..."

Until yesterday morning, someone loved me with that divine love that only a mother can feel. Until yesterday, I was a boy, who had someone to indulge him. Yesterday, at 8:30 A.M., as Mother's left eye closed slowly for the last time—the right had already fulfilled its mission earlier—I really and truly became an orphan—no longer a child, no longer a beloved only son, no longer the last comfort of a good and devoted mother, I have to pause for a moment ...

[January 16, 1943] An Hour Later

I have recovered a little and will continue. I returned from the funeral yesterday evening, sat down next to Rivka to sit *shiva* for half an hour to include *Eyrev Shabbes*, and walked home, not recognizing the street that I was wandering along. Because of the strange circumstances in which I find myself, I will not be able to observe the *shiva*. I bear on my shoulders the obligation of taking care of everything, both for my household and for Rivka, because both Roza and Rivka are ill and cannot leave the house. Apart from this, I cannot be absent from the office for a week, because then I will not have a job to which to return. The colony chief is waiting for the opportune moment to dismiss me and to replace me with someone from his hometown. How can I afford to take such a risk! Mother herself would have forbidden it.

I also have refrained from rending my clothes as a sign of mourning, and not necessarily because I believe that there is no need to adorn an immense and genuine sorrow with the fringes of a torn garment, but because no one would notice another tear. However, I will recite *Kaddish*, if our sworn enemies do not interfere ... both in honor of Mother and because I am not 100 percent sure that a person is completely extinguished like a burnt-out match as soon as the body dies. Spiritual life is replete with hidden secrets and complex mysteries, and I have certainly not fathomed the full truth. Who knows if we will ever discover the secrets of life and death, and perhaps it is better that they remain an enigma.

Last night was a terrible night for me, and I will never forget the nightmare. Perhaps a person feels this way on the first night that he discovers that he has had a limb amputated. I don't tend to cry, and tears get caught in my throat, and I get all choked up. Out of pain, I dug my nails into my flesh but refrained from making a sound, because the four of us were lying sideways on the wooden bunk. It seems to me that the torment of the grave, which is discussed at length in *Muser* [ethical] literature really means the suffering of the living on the first night, following the burial of a person who was near and dear to them.[2] The dead no longer feel any pain, but the anguish of the mourners is just beginning. Time will surely alleviate their intense sorrow, although they have no desire at all to hope for such comfort.

---

2 "Torment of the grave," a concept of the Kabbalah that is mentioned in *Sefer Hatanya*, refers to a punishment intended to shake the sins off a person that clung to him and covered him like a "*klipa*" (shell), which means spiritual impurity in Jewish mysticism. After a person is buried, four angels descend to the grave and shake the body of the sinful person in his grave until he sheds the *klipa;* Rabbi Shneur Zalman, *Iggeret HaKodesh—Sefer HaTanya* (Cernăuţi: n.p., c. 1860).

January 18, 1943, 3 P.M.

The epidemic rages and new patients stream into the hospital every day. The beds are already almost all full and there is no choice but to make plans to lay patients on the floor. Yesterday the engineer Chaim Ostfeld from Gura Humorului fell victim to the Rickettsia bacteria at the age of forty-five. He altruistically served as the manager of the soup kitchen in Dzhurin: not for any personal gain. Although I am not writing down a list of the camp victims in these notebooks—that is what the community register that I manage is for—I will nevertheless write a few lines about Chaim Ostfeld, because his death was the reward for his nobility and his love for his fellow man. A few weeks ago, he noticed a line of naked and barefoot "sack people" waiting by the soup kitchen under the open sky to receive a bowl of soup, while the wind blew against them unmercifully. The living skeletons shivered from the cold and hopped from one foot to the other in the snow. He ordered the guard to let in a few dozen old and sick people who were about to collapse. The guard carried out the command, even though for sanitary reasons no one was allowed to cross the threshold of the kitchen, and those waiting in line received the bowl of soup through a small window. One of these guests—all of them were infested with lice—unintentionally transmitted the crawling camp vermin to Ostfeld, which paid him back for his good deed …

January 27, 1942 [*sic*][1943], 7 A.M.

My mother has been lying under a stone for twelve days and the Master of the Universe's beautiful world goes on as if nothing has happened, even for me, as the intense grief of the first days following the catastrophe slowly begins to subside. It often occurs to me, like an irksome fly at the end of summer, that perhaps Mother is in a better place, because she has been relieved of today's worries and the fear of tomorrow's troubles.

The horizon is black as soot and even when a thin ray of light shines faraway, it goes out quickly and the darkness becomes thicker. Not one day goes by without funerals, mainly of old and sick people but, of course, also of many young people. The main supplier of the members of the *Hevra Kadishe* is the poorhouse of the great synagogue, the waiting room for the cemetery. The dead often remain lying there in the filth on the floor for a day or two until the members of the *Hevra Kadishe* mercifully come for them. The living dead walk over their "real" counterparts in the severe overcrowding, encountering stiff bodies, falling down, and getting up with their last strength. Someone will trip over their bodies tomorrow. It is a shame and a disgrace (two words that are also defunct ...) that the community does not prepare a small chamber for the dead in the building of the great synagogue until their burial. The high-level officials claim that there are other more important expenses. Yes, if only these expenses were for the soup kitchen, the hospital, and so on, this would be a very strong argument ...

Entire families have been wiped out in the poorhouse and, nevertheless, the number of those dwelling in the *bes medresh* does not decrease because the vacancies are quickly filled. New tenants are brought to this last stop on earth every day—creatures who have reached a state of complete neglect, who have stopped eating, washing, and even covering themselves with rags. They have no choice but to send them to the poorhouse—for a brief period ...

[January 27, 1943] 3 P.M.

For the first time since I have been in exile in Transnistria, they remembered me in Romania and sent me aid—2,500 lei in cash. This amount is enough for 2 poods of cornflour, if I happen to get a bargain at the market—this means food for almost a month, and that is certainly not something to turn one's nose up at. In Bucharest, there is an organization of people from Rădăuţi, which is headed by a wealthy man and activist Shammai Hart, and these former fellow townsmen of mine collect money and occasionally send some to Transnistria, [where is it distributed] according to a list. So, they have also included me in this charity list, thanks to who knows which *meyletz yoysher*. A large portion of the recipients are not needy and live quite well in terms of Dzhurin, but they are good at begging and crying out to Romania. On the other hand, a large number of deportees are dying of hunger and cold, and no one remembers to help them, because they do not know to whom to turn.

The same occurs with the so-called "Zionist money," which arrives secretly and at mortal risk through couriers at the address of the rabbi of Siret, Rabbi Baruch Hager, based on lists that someone here has prepared and sent to Romania. One of those involved in preparing these lists is the head of the Labor Office and the "iron fist" of the camp, David Buksbaum of Siret. He claims that, were it not for him, the Basel Program would not have made its way to Bukovina. Heretics claim that his "Zionism" only began in Dzhurin. In fact, both he and other "Zionists" of his kind, who took control of the Zionist aid here, were surely righteous Zionists in the old country, where no one had heard of them or had ever mentioned them. As a result of the credibility of the lists, the majority of the aid goes to people who never took part in the national movement, did not contribute to Zionist funds, and even fiercely opposed Herzl's great vision. In contrast, very few true, veteran Zionists appear on the list, and they cannot bear seeing this. Obviously, my name does not appear in the list of the "Neo-Zionists," because of my somewhat Zionist past during my childhood …

Regarding the extensive promises made by the investigative delegation, as yet we have not seen any significant results. No clothes, no shoes, no wooden boards, no glass, no tools for the craftsmen. It is precisely now, during the harsh winter, that we need this aid.

January 30, 1943, 7 A.M.

Today is a very dark anniversary: a full ten years since the demon Hitler seized power in Germany. He will certainly lose the war against the entire world, but he has already won the war against the Jews. To whom will deliverance still come in the Jewish streets of Europe! …

[January 30, 1943] 7 P.M.

In the soup kitchen, 1,000 servings of hot soup [a day] are already being distributed for dinner, and the number of recipients continues to grow.

This year the need is even more severe than it was last winter. The people have nothing left to sell, and their bodies are already spent from the long suffering.

A day does not go by without several deaths. I am the registrar who records in Romanian the names of the dead and all the details that can be obtained. I often only know the name and nothing more when a person who dies has no family, or is the last remnant of a family whose members have been annihilated—mainly "fugitives" from the camps. The camp doctor (currently, Dr. Greiff) is required to sign his name in one of the columns [in the registry], and it is necessary to enter the cause of death. The disease that fells the young and old in Transnistria does not yet have a scientific name, although the doctors have facetiously dubbed it the Latin horror "Transnistriatis." Dr. Greiff almost always writes down the neutral diagnosis "myocarditis" (heart disease), even for the victims of typhus and other plagues, by order of the colony chief so that, God forbid, the model camp's reputation not be tarnished should the Romanian overlords glance at the population registry. For it is possible that people will die of hunger, cold, plagues, and neglect even in the Dzhurin paradise! …

February 3, 1943, 2 P.M.

This evening, they began to distribute an additional serving of soup in the soup kitchen. As long as a storm is not raging outside, some of those who seek the delights of the soup kitchen will somehow hang on by stretching out their hands. On good days, they even manage to obtain a mark in cash from begging, as well as old bread, meals that have been left standing for too long, an onion or some dried barley, and the like. Such miracles do not occur when a storm is raging and the snow is knee-high. Late, but nevertheless not too late, the community saw that they have no option but to dig into their pockets.

On days when it is freezing cold but there is no blizzard, one encounters creatures in the market who seem to have just left the stage of some kind of wild fantasy production or horror drama. One comes across young people who are literally half naked, some are partially dressed, wearing one pant leg or one leg of long underwear, and some wear dirty rages, tied with strings, exposing their naked body. Others walk around in dirty, torn underwear, which recall the faded shrouds of a corpse that has lain for a long time. There are some who, instead of a coat, wrap their bones with a patched sack or a filthy rag, which in its first incarnation was a jacket and, in its second incarnation, became a kind of belt with fringes, without shoulders or sleeves. One also sees fortunate people who actually have trousers made of sacks for both legs and jackets of sorts with shoulders and sleeves—patched with overlapping multicolored patches—not bad. However, even among them there is usually a flaw: they wear these regal garments directly on their lice-infested bodies, because a shirt and underwear are only for the wealthy …

A shadow from another world, which reeks of death, hovers over their yellow shriveled faces and greasy hair that has not seen the semblance of a comb or a pair of scissors since who knows when. They have a blank and impenetrable stare, their hands and feet shiver from the cold, but sitting alone in your "apartment" is not permitted. As for a livelihood—to go begging for a coin or a piece of bread—it is irrelevant …

In the Russian rag *Odesskiye Novosti*, which is printed by the Germans in Odessa, I read part of the speech given by Hitler, may his name be blotted out, on the tenth anniversary of his seizure of power. The demon decreed that Jews have always been the dregs of humanity, and that true good will come to the world for the first time when the nations will join forces to burn the *hametz*[3] known as Jews. One thing is certainly true: today we look like the worst of the dregs.

While I am writing these lines, my fingers are frozen from the cold, because a piercing wind is constantly blowing through the broken window of my hovel. For two days the storm has been raging—a guest from the endless Russian steppes. For this reason, I must take a break, even though I want to continue and go back and discuss in detail the terrible annihilation of the Jews. By repeating this, I risk boring someone who may read these pages someday. Never mind, I did not commit to providing "scoops" and to avoid boring anyone …

---

3 Leavened food that is forbidden during Passover. It is customary to burn any remaining leavened products in your possession the morning before Passover.

February 4, 1943, 2 P.M.

The council member Iehoşua Ungariş—the community "finance minister"—collapsed a few days ago and has not been seen in the community building since. Today we know the reason: typhus. He was taken to the hospital. The Rickettsia bacteria is a capricious fellow: sometimes he makes his presence known only three weeks after settling in with a new landlord, and in rare cases he sends his greetings even earlier. The sooner you identify the killer, the greater the chances of saving others from becoming infected.

Just last *Shabbes*, January 30, Ungariş sat at a council meeting, and I [sat] near him. In the suffocating crowdedness of Dzhurin, it is not possible to take precautions. If there are still some healthy people wandering around who have not been infected, they are apparently immune to the Rickettsia bacteria. The doctors laugh at this explanation and cite their holy books, where it is written explicitly that only someone who has overcome typhus remains immune. If someone asks the simple question of why there are almost no cases of typhus in the poorhouse of the great synagogue, where the tenants are covered with lice from head to toe, Dr. Greiff, the skilled expert on "lice-ology" also comes up with an answer—the books do not say that lice cannot be immune [to the Rickettsia bacteria] …

On more than one occasion, after coming home from work, I found lice on myself and nothing happened. These were apparently some of Dr. Greiff's "immune lice"! …

We heard about the blistering defeat of our sworn enemies near Stalingrad. Perhaps deliverance is beginning to emerge after all. "If their fall has begun …"[4]

February 9, 1943, 3 P.M.

Shabbes, February 6, I found a louse on my jacket, and today my head hurts, and I feel ill. Is it possible—don't open your mouth to the devil?

4 Esther 6:13: "If Mordechai, before whom you have begun to fall, is of the seed of the Jews, you will not prevail against him, but you will surely fall before him."

Having no other choice, I must continue to toss and turn at night on the wooden bunk next to Roza and the children, and cover all four of us with my coat. In the meantime, I say nothing, to avoid causing a panic in the house.

In the ghetto there are rumors of a new trend, which has nothing to do with dreams of returning to the homeland (repatriation), or with nightmares of being driven to the Bug. First, you look around to see who is standing behind you and then you whisper a remarkable secret very quietly: in the surrounding forests, there are quite a few partisans—both Ukrainian and Jews—who are not sitting around doing nothing.[5] People even mention with utmost secrecy the names of Jewish inhabitants of Dzhurin who are involved in partisan activities in the area. We do not know what the source of this information is, but there are indications that something is not right. The Jewish militia who are posted at the gendarmerie post report that the "armed guards" are agitated, and they dare not set foot outside the barracks after sunset and are always armed. They have also doubled the watch around the barracks. There is more to write about, but one must not push one's luck …

5 Two main partisan groups were active in Transnistria: one was made up of local nationalist Ukrainians, under the leadership of Stephan Bandera. This group supported Nazi policy, believing that in doing so they would gain Hitler's support to establish an independent Ukrainian state. Its members, former Ukrainian policemen, were organized into armed military and paramilitary units, who served as a supporting arm of the German army in Transnistria. Their collaboration with the occupation forces in Transnistria also took the form of harassment, pogroms, and atrocities that targeted the Jews. The second group of partisans was that of Soviet partisans, who began their activities with the turning point on the Eastern Front at the end of 1942, and against the background of the opposition to the occupying powers in Transnistria. As the partisan units consolidated, their commanders understood that they could use the ghettos as rest stops and hiding places for their members, and that the ghetto inhabitants would even supply them with medicine, food, clothes, and more. For further discussion of partisan activity and collaboration with the ghettos, see the group testimonies of the ghettos of Shargorod, Moghilev, and Dzhurin, YVA, O.3/VT/10547; the group testimonies of the ghettos of Murafa and Bershad, YVA, O.3/VT/10552; Shachan, *Bakefor Halohet*, p. 295; Rosen, "Tzibur Veyahid," pp. 164–168.

February 16, 1943, 6 A.M.

The hospital is already full and, as of tomorrow, they will have to lay patients on the floor. They have already prepared bundles of straw to spread out on the floor. Some of the patients were taken to the hospital when their disease was already at an advanced stage, because the doctors said nothing concerning patients from the wealthy strata. No one has wanted to enter the living grave when the diagnosis is not absolutely certain, and not even afterwards. Therefore, people try to avert this, provided that they live alone in an apartment, and there is money in their pockets …

For the time being, the plague is showing some mercy, and the number of dead is not too high. Most of the victims are people over fifty and who are sickly. However, the trouble is that the Rickettsia bacteria sneaks in discreetly, so to speak, and by the time the plague has spread its virulent arms, it has already reached its peak. The plague also began mildly last year, and then people fell like flies later.

[February 16, 1943] 2 P.M.

The stalwart director of the hospital, Dr. Moshe Greiff, had been waging a war against typhus for almost a year and had won many victories, until he was defeated in his own war. He himself has been lying in "his" hospital with typhus for a few days, and his condition is not at all good. He is a good friend of mine, a frequent visitor to our home, and, nevertheless, I do not dare to pay a visit to the sick and set foot in the hospital. The council has appointed a replacement, Dr. Gabriel Shtir, from Vijniţa. Since the day that the plague intensified, a doctor has remained in the hospital even at night, whereas prior to that, students had sufficed.

[February 16, 1943] 3 P.M.

Just this week, when half of the winter had already gone by, did the clothes sent by the Jewish central council in Romania for the inhabitants of the camp in the Moghilev district arrive in Moghilev. It turned out that only a smattering of the most necessary clothes—suits, overgarments, underwear, and blankets—arrived. In contrast, they were not sparing and generously honored us with hats, soft collars, neckties, velvet gloves, and a few hundred pairs of … swimming trunks! It is doubtful whether everything that was sent from Bucharest actually made it to Moghilev, because more than enough greedy Romanian hands intervened along the way. Obviously, the Moghilev Central Council will take a substantial portion for the ragged and poor locals, but will nevertheless not completely dishonor the "model colony" of Dzhurin. They prepared a storage room for the gifts here, and the custodian of all the treasures will be Iankel Katz, the brother of the "second-in-command"—actually a decent fellow with a Jewish heart, but a fervent *cohen*[6] who believes that he has the monopoly on justice and truth in the camp. So, now he will have the opportunity to demonstrate this …

Roza, Rivka, the children, and I are all in need as is everyone else. I will just have to swallow my pride in order to get underwear, a suit, and a shoe. Who knows whether this will have an effect … I do not feel well, I have a headache, and it is difficult for me to work. What does this mean? …

[February 16, 1943] 9 P.M.

Major [Colonel] Năsturaş, the commander of the gendarmerie legion in Moghilev [*sic*] [prefect of Moghilev], demanded by telephone today that the gendarmerie submit to him a list of all the Ukrainian Jews in Dzhurin without delay. The colony chief hurried to comply in the blink of an eye and brought the list to the gendarmerie already this evening—obviously not omitting a single person. Such lists do not smell like roses. They already drove out all the Jewish population from Yaroshenka, in

6 Katz, which is the acronym for *Cohen Tzedek*, is a name that indicates a connection to the dynasty of priests. In the literature of the Talmud and the Mishna, the priests were portrayed as being irascible.

the Moghilev district, to Pechora, a few days ago. The peasants say that the Jews have been banished from other places as well.

February 20, 1943, 7 P.M.

I still do not feel too bad—a sign that the louse on my jacket was a decent fellow, with no evil intentions …

From time to time, high-ranking Romanian officers appear in the camp to find bargains among the Jews, mainly jewelry. A Jewish broker usually accompanies them, so that the people will trust them and not be afraid. One of them suddenly arrived today—the major of the gendarmes in Tomashpol,[7] and commended himself with strange news: soon all the deportees from the "kosher" provinces (Southern Bukovina and northern Moldavia) will be returned to Romania. The most reliable sources have informed him of this, and if he is telling a lie—the overlord claimed—may they decapitate him when he comes back again. Never mind, news of this kind is not new in Transnistria, but when an important functionary puts his head on the line, perhaps for the first time, there is something to this …

Fear of dire defeat in the wake of the events on the fronts stands out between the lines of the Romanian newspaper that secretly falls into our hands. The blank spaces right in the middle of the military expositions speak much louder than the printed lies, and sometimes the censor overlooks something, and words of great significance sneak in. In the midst of our dejection, this is the only drop of balsam.

---

7 Tomashpol is a city in southwest Ukraine in the Vinnitsa region. Following the Nazi invasion of the Soviet Union in June 1941, most of the Jewish men in the area were drafted into the Red Army. The Germans occupied the city on July 20, 1941. Shortly afterwards, the Germans, together with Ukrainian collaborators, carried out a pogrom against the Jews of the town, in which 150–240 people were murdered. In December 1941, Tomashpol was transferred to Romanian control—it was included in the occupied area of Transnistria. The Romanians established a ghetto there in which the Jews of the town, as well as from surrounding villages and even Bessarabia, were concentrated. The Jews were sent to perform forced labor and many died from diseases. The Jews who survived were liberated by the Red Army on March 16, 1944. See Miron and Shulhani, *Entziklopediya Shel Hageta'ot*.

And always the same old question—will there be anyone left when deliverance comes? …

February 26, 1943, 6 A.M.

Dr. Moshe Greiff, the director of the hospital, is no longer with us. On Wednesday evening, February 24, he fell like a hero—a victim of his dedication and idealism. The Rickettsia bacteria was unforgiving and won a gloomy victory over its number one enemy. By the way, Dr. Greiff's replacement, Dr. Gabriel Shtir, has been lying in bed with a fever for three days now, and it is believed that he too has been infected with the nice package.

Dr. Greiff's end came unexpectedly. Until Wednesday, the doctors believed that his condition was not life threatening, mainly thanks to his strong heart and iron will. However, a toxic pneumonia suddenly appeared that brought on the tragedy with lightning speed. All at once, his body again turned blue and was covered with red spots, and it was over!

People whisper that Dr. Greiff did not receive the necessary, warm sympathy from his colleagues who treated him during his illness, which I think is a hideous suspicion. In truth, because of his tempestuous temperament, the deceased sometimes had sharp arguments with the other doctors, and he dealt with most of his colleagues like a cat with a mouse. Now people are lodging complaints—why did they treat him with luminal[8]—a medicine that the deceased did not believe in and also did not use; why didn't they inject him in time with medicines to prevent pneumonia (pulmaseft [?] and the like). Obviously, the doctors offer all kinds of excuses, but it is not necessary to reply. When the devastating Rickettsia bacteria ensnares someone, there is no magic remedy that can help …

In any case, his stubbornness was mixed with nobility, and he was ready to sacrifice himself for everyone, for anyone in need. He warmly and lovingly received the poor, needy patients—about 95 percent more

---

8 The most common antiepileptic medicine in the world and the oldest medicine still in use, this medicine was used for patients suffering from typhus.

than the wealthy. His quarrel with the council stemmed from his desire to ease the fate of the poor.

His death struck me and my household like thunder. We have lost a beloved and dedicated friend—both me and the entire camp.

Everyone attended the funeral yesterday afternoon. The colony chief, Rabbi Herşel Karalnic, and others spared no warm eulogies—and they lavished praise on the deceased until the seventh heaven. There was a downpour of *Eyl Moleh Rahmim*.

The masses loved the deceased very much, and he was dear to their hearts. Many of the *Lagernikes* trudged with tattered shoes and galoshes riddled with holes (some with their feet wrapped in rags) to the cemetery to escort their defender to his grave.

[February 26, 1943] 9 P.M.

Today a peasant brought news from the nearby ghetto of Derebchin[9] that the local gendarmes had ordered all the Jews to gather outside the gendarmerie at 8 P.M. There are about 200 Jews there—all local Ukrainian Jews. The council promised the peasant a handsome sum if he would go to Derebchin the next morning and bring news of what was happening there.

February 27, 1943, 2 P.M.

The good news from Derebchin spread through the camp at night, and it became *Tisha B'Av* everywhere. At dawn, a dense crowd laid siege to the community building to keep watch for the peasant, who was to bring a resolution. The peasant finally appeared at about 11 A.M., bringing a note from a Jew from Derebchin, saying:

---

9 Derebchin, a village in the Moghilev region, in the district of Shargorod, 8 kilometers from Dzhurin, was one of the centers of sugar production in the region. The sugar plant was destroyed by the bombings during the German invasion of Transnistria, and the deported Jews, led by Moritz Katz from Moghilev, rebuilt it. See Lavi, *Pinkas Hakehilot: Rumania*, vol. 1, pp. 425–426.

> A Transnistria version of a miracle has occurred. They indeed summoned everyone and no one failed to appear at the appointed hour. We waited until 9 P.M. and only then did the commander of the gendarmerie appear—a Romanian *Feldwebel*—with the Ukrainian village elder acting as translator by his side. The commander burst out laughing and said: "So, Yids, have you been duly frightened? It was not worth your while, because I only wanted to meet you face-to-face, since I'm 'new' here. Go home, and if I need you, I will let you know. However, I will tell you one thing: do not take even one step outside the ghetto, if you value your lives! …"

Moshe Katz immediately came out and announced the good news. Had we heard the *shofar* of the messiah, the joy would not have been greater. What a surprise! As a result of such gatherings of the entire holy community, there is no longer a single Jew left to be found on the other side of the Bug up to the Volga. The non-kosher Germans call their slaughters "*Aktzyes*," and they are conducted in the same manner. The guests dig their own graves and remain inside them forever. Well, what happened in Derebchin is indeed a miracle …

[February 27, 1943] 8 P.M.

The delegates who traveled to Moghilev to bring the gifts from the federation of the Jewish communities in Romania returned today, sitting in the driver's cabin of a truck that was loaded to the brim. The portion intended for Dzhurin arrived separately—an entire wagon of goods of all kinds, such as planks, glass, medicines, clothes, underwear, and shoes. A second truck will bring the rest tomorrow. I suspected the kosher [people], when I wrote that the Moghilev [Central] Council would take a percentage for its own needy. Yet they brought an abundance from Moghilev.[10]

10 From October 1942, with the establishment of the Jewish communities in Transnistria and as their situation somewhat improved, aid sent by the Comisia Autonomă De Ajutorare in Bucharest, as well as from private individuals in Romania to relatives in the region, began to arrive through the council of the Moghilev ghetto. Consequently, the

According to the shipment list, there are a few [pairs of] shoes, about twenty suits; however, in contrast, a haul of vain fripperies: suspenders, brimmed hats, garters, bathing trunks, silk underwear for profligacy, umbrellas, collars, ties, corsets, and so on. They sent whatever they could get their hands on, without understanding the strange local conditions and needs. It was vital to obtain many, many simple shirts, underwear, cloth trousers, jackets, even used [clothing], woolen blankets, and especially shoes. The few shoes that they sent are mainly light ankle boots, women's pumps with low heels that are suitable for the boulevards of Bucharest, and even slippers for the salons of the wealthy. However, in Dzhurin, there is a need for sturdy, cowhide boots with double soles that are suitable for mud and snow.

There is not much that we can do with these fripperies and they will only bring jealousy and hatred, scandals and shouting, and … the council has appointed a committee of eight people who will decide who will enjoy these good items and how much will be distributed. Since the items were sent explicitly for the deportees from Romania, the committee will certainly pass over the Ukrainian Jews. And it is precisely those who fled the camps by the Bug, almost all of them Ukrainian Jews, who are walking around in rags, without a shirt on their body and with their feet wrapped in rags. Such behavior will not endear us, the Romanian "*bishenitzes*," to the local Jewish residents. The local residents welcomed us as important guests at first, but over time there has been a turnabout, and perhaps both sides are at fault. They, the veteran residents of Dzhurin, feel wronged by the "*bishenitzes*" and the Jewish regime, although they live by virtue of these uninvited guests. From the places throughout Transnistria, where there were no deportees from Romania, the Romanian occupation authorities have driven out all the Ukrainian Jews and have sent them to camps near the Bug, where most of them have already died.

---

connection between the ghettos and the leaders of the large communities in Moghilev became stronger, and their assistance was extended to the small ghettos in their region. See Lavi, *Pinkas Hakehilot*: *Rumania*, vol. 1, p. 361; Yeshurun, "Hahitargenut Ha'atzmit Shel Yehudei Bukovina Begeto Moghilev," p. 96; see also the group testimonies of the ghettos of Shargorod, Moghilev, and Dzhurin, YVA, O.3/VT/10547, and the group testimonies of the ghettos of Murafa and Bershad, YVA, O.3/VT/10552.

March 1, 1943, 3 P.M.

About 600 *Lagernikes* have submitted requests to the council for clothes and shoes. There is no demand for suspenders and brimmed hats. The [number of] requests are rising like yeast, and the council will begin to distribute items only when it knows who and what. I also submitted a request. If you just live long enough, you get to become a beggar who doesn't even have a shirt ...[11]

March 3, 1943, 2 P.M.

The council has not yet completed the preparations regarding checking and sifting through the 1,000 requests for clothing and shoes. The council threw quite a few of the applications into the trash from the outset, because these ostensibly naked and barefoot people who are known to be wealthy took advantage of the requests to avoid paying and so on.

Nevertheless, more than 500 "kosher" requests that everyone agrees on remain and, in most of the cases, they will surely give something, just to fulfill the minimal obligation, and not what is needed nor as much as required, because there will not be enough for everyone.

Among the clothes, there are a few dozen really elegant items: suits and coats made from the finest material, beautifully tailored. The "lords" are thinking of selling these things and using the money to buy underwear and cloth trousers. The community will also allow the well-to-do inhabitants of the camp to exchange used clothes for expensive articles, according to their real value. Certainly, a nice idea in theory, but when it will be carried out, it is likely to entail all kinds of preferential treatment and dirty tricks at the expense of the poor. The owners of all kinds of precious items have already begun to whisper wherever it is necessary ...[12]

---

11 Although the Dzhurin ghetto was considered a "better ghetto" in the eyes of the deportees, living conditions there were still unbearably harsh, particularly for the destitute deportees, who accounted for most of the inhabitants of the ghetto. The relatively wealthy people in the ghetto were mainly from Southern Bukovina.

12 There were serious allegations of discrimination and differential treatment among the various groups of deportees. See Kurt Shternshus testimony, YVA, O.3/VT/9370. In the

It is very important to distribute the articles quickly before the leeches among the gendarmes discover that all kinds of fine items are to be found among the Jews. These blood suckers are likely to skim off the cream for their Ukrainian prostitutes, and the "lords" will offer them the booty on a silver platter.[13]

Such an incident occurred yesterday involving candy—a happy portent. Among the gifts from Bucharest, there were twenty boxes of fine candy, which were probably intended to be given to the children or to the ill. The council, however, thought that the children and the ill can do quite well without the candy and they handed the boxes over to the cooperative. The revenue, the council ruled, would go into the community coffers. However, in order for there to be a demand for the candy—the community leaders innocently claimed—they set a much lower price. So, of course, they soon found people who were willing to acquire the sweets—at bargain prices, even before anyone in the camp knew about the bargain, and the goods fell into the hands of the leaders for next to nothing … However, it was not meant to be that all the boxes would fall into Jewish albeit not so clean hands. Someone at the gendarmerie post whispered—certainly not a Japanese[14] … —the secret that in the cooperative, in a secluded corner, on the bottom shelf, there is some candy. A gendarme immediately appeared with a note from the commander Georgescu requesting to "purchase" five boxes of candy. He would soon send the cash, at the latest within a month … However, since there were only four boxes on the shelf, hidden away for the well-

---

Bershad ghetto, the Jews complained about the unfair distribution of clothes that came from Romania. They also complained that instead of distributing the clothes among the needy in the ghettos, the council sold them at the market to put money in its coffers. See Avraham Korn testimony, YVA, O.3/VT/12272. The phenomenon of selling clothes that came from Romania to the Ukrainians was one of the ways for the ghetto leaders to raise money to fund welfare institutions and to bribe officials among the Romanian authorities. Moshe Katz from the Dzhurin ghetto testified that the clothes were sold at a high price to local Ukrainians, and the proceeds were used to fund the social institutions in the ghetto. See Ancel, *Documents Concerning the Fate of Romanian Jewry*, vol. 8, pp. 527–534.

13 Romanian gendarmes as well as other officials among the Romanian authorities plundered the parcels from Romania.

14 In other words, not a foreigner.

connected people, they had to commit to sending the fifth box as soon as a new shipment would arrive from Romania …

It would not have happened had they delivered all the candy to the hospital for the ill from the beginning, because the gendarmes stay a mile away from the infectious hospital—these "heroes" with their bayonets. But what difference does it make now! …

[March 3, 1943] 9 P.M.

Patients are already lying on the floor in the hospital, and who knows whether the floor will suffice. The new director of the hospital, Dr. Gabriel Shtir, is also now lying in "his" hospital in critical condition, but he is fortunate: he was lucky enough to get a bed. The young physician, Dr. Julius Frenckel, is now managing the hospital. The Rickettsia bacteria has no power over him, because he himself fell ill in the first round of typhus a year ago and remains immune.

As people feared, the plague has become more virulent. Today typhus is progressing in a different way: it invites other guests—complications of the heart, lungs, internal organs, and brain. The most dreadful complication is the collapse of the nervous system. The patients lose their minds, have horrible convulsions similar to epileptic fits, scream heartrending cries day and night, and suffer terrible pain and spasms until the Angel of Death takes pity on them. Most cases of complications end in "who will die."[15] There is no shortage of medicines now, especially injections, because a few packages arrived from the federation with all kinds of medicines. The council member Leon Neuman,[16] the second-in-command's brother-in-law—a Jew with a very small hand, even though he is almost 2 meters tall—is in charge of the medicines. It is not easy to get him to unlock the holy ark and hand over the vial of life, but

15 "Who will live and who will die," from the piyut "*Unetane Tokef*."

16 Leon Neuman and Moshe Katz were accused and tried after the war for, among other things, trafficking medicinal drugs that the community in Romania had sent to other ghettos in Transnistria. Kunstadt's use of the expression "with a very small hand" to indicate Neuman's unwillingness to distribute the medicine. This allegation was not proven. See CNSAS, P-50679, vol. 1, pp. 27, 42, 46.

nevertheless [the situation now is] better than a year ago, when the holy ark was completely empty.

March 4, 7 P.M.

A German military airplane crashed near Dzhurin and went up in flames this afternoon. The pilot was killed on the spot, while three officers, severely wounded and burned, were brought to the Jewish hospital on a sled. As they were being transported, one of them died. All the Jewish doctors from the camp rushed to the hospital and tried to save the wounded. This time Leon Neuman promptly opened the holy ark and provided plenty of medicines, bandages, injections, and whatever was necessary. As the saying goes: what they don't give to Yaakov, they give to Esau. They actually enjoyed these gifts in the camp …

High-ranking Romanian officers and the praetor himself immediately came running from Shargorod and saw with their own eyes the Jews' treatment of their accursed murderers. It seems that already tomorrow they will transfer the wounded to another hospital, because they are in too close proximity to the Rickettsia bacteria …

This incident has caused quite a commotion in the camp. People are terrified and they don't even know why. And while the Jews certainly did not cause the plane to crash and, not only that, they even saved the wounded pilots, you can never know with the Germans. Everyone has a kind of "and Jethro rejoiced" [attitude]:[17] whether because the "catastrophe" has brought on very little suffering in its wake, or because people think that the whole thing could certainly have occurred far from Dzhurin. In any event, this sensational event has not caused any harm to the Jews, and if only it will continue like this! …

---

17 Rashi on Exodus 18:9. Rashi offers two interpretations of this expression: the first literally means, "and Jethro rejoiced," while according to the second, Jethro's flesh was covered in goosebumps, meaning, that he was afraid. Thus Kunstadt describes having mixed feelings.

March 6, 1942 [*sic*] [1943], 8 P.M.

The matter ended smoothly and the camp was spared after two somewhat fearful days. Nine German officers were reported to have been killed in the plane crash, and only two wounded [officers] are still alive. This morning, the nine dead were evacuated from the factory quarter to Vinnitsa, where they were buried in a military cemetery. The two wounded were already taken out of the Jewish hospital yesterday evening. People were afraid that the funeral of the dead would take place in Dzhurin. Yesterday, the Jews were forbidden to go out in the streets, which were teeming with German military officials, who came to take care of their "friends" and principally to investigate the cause of the crash. Only when the Jews learned that the dead had vanished in hell was a stone lifted from their hearts and they came out of their mouseholes.

March 16, 1943, 3 P.M.

Ten days have passed since the last entry—days without shocking events, and nevertheless riddled with sorrow and hardship. The winter here has many disadvantages and only one single advantage: they do not send us to work in the snow-covered fields. However, we just now found out from Moghilev that as soon as the winter is over, the real wedding will begin. The Romanian occupying authority decided to generously "lend" deported Jews to the German labor camps on the other side of the Bug, and this means something completely different from cutting stone on the main road in the Moghilev district. In the meantime, let me not take on sorrows on credit, because the present troubles suffice.

The clothes, shoes, and other items that the federation sent for the needy in this camp are getting moldy in the storerooms. Already more than five weeks have passed since they were delivered and we are still at the beginning, even though we should already have forgotten about them. The council is fooling around with committees and subcommittees, inventories, tables, and other nonsense, and the main thing is not to reach the end. If a poor man's request manages to make it safely through all seven levels of hell and all the decision makers rule that he should be granted a pair of trousers or shoes, then another problem begins: the storeroom. It is not so easy to obtain anything from there. In truth, the boss, Iankel Katz,[18] does not sit idly by, God forbid, in the storeroom: He is busy moving the items from one shelf to another and arranging them all day long; one clearly perceives how he takes pleasure in seeing the full shelves and does not allow himself to empty them. There are people with notes in their hands, who refuse to be dismissed with any excuses and demand what has been granted to them. This results in scandals, indignities, and shouting. Only a few lucky ones have had the privilege of leaving the holy of holies carrying a package.

My request is still lying in a torpor somewhere in the possession of some subcommittee, and all my efforts to intervene in the meanwhile are like a voice crying in the wilderness. The second-in-command, who is also a fellow townsman of mine and was once a good kinsman, offered me the sage advice: "What's the hurry? The later you get it, the longer you can wear it …" Indeed, a wise statement from someone who has no inkling of what it feels like to have nothing but a torn jacket and tattered shoes that let in more water than they keep out …

March 22, 1943, *Shushan Purim*, 2 P.M.

According to the non-Jewish calendar, a second winter in Transnistria has passed. This winter was much easier than last year's grim winter. The month of March this year looks like the eve of spring; the snow has completely disappeared, and even the irksome mud has lost its charm. Because the winter has been mild, wood is cheap and is not lacking, if a person has a mark in his pocket. Whoever has the strength and courage to steal into the nearby forest—about 4 kilometers outside the kosher confines—dragged home as many hewn branches as possible, for himself or for so-called "trading" purposes.

All the clothes and shoes are lying safely in the storeroom, and those on the committees continue to erase and to reregister in order to

18 Kunstadt refers to Moshe Katz here using the name Yankel, which is Moshe in Yiddish.

reach a just, true, and pure distribution—in time for *Shavues*[19] [almost summer] …

Typhus is raging and dangerous complications often appear unexpectedly, and yet the percentage of "who will die" is lower than it was a year ago for two reasons: first, because there is no shortage of injections that strengthen the body's resilience; second, because most of the patients now are from the wealthy strata—people who know no hunger and, therefore, their bodies are able to fight the murderous bacteria—the poor died a year ago already.

March 24, 1943, 2 P.M.

I finally managed to persuade Moshe Katz to reach a decision regarding my request for clothes. Although my petition did not evince any greed on my part, they only granted me a small portion of the necessities: a suit, a pair of underwear, and a pair of socks for me; for Roza, Rivka, and the children, all kinds of rags. No shoes for anyone. However, I unexpectedly received a pillow and will no longer have to sleep with my hands under my head.

Now more tribulations await me: obtaining the articles from the storeroom. Perhaps Iankel Katz, my fellow townsman and also my partner in weighing meat at the butcher shops, will be willing to do me a favor and will stretch out his hand to the holy shelves.[20]

The third terrible difficulty—donning for the first time in my life rags that I requested and wearing them in public—at this point, I care

19 The Jewish holiday, which commemorates the giving of the Torah and celebrates the completion of the seven-week Omer counting period between Passover and Shavuot, takes place toward the end of spring.

20 In Dzhurin, as in the ghettos of Moghilev and Shargorod, the councils maintained a monopoly on shohetim. Taxes were imposed on the shohetim and on the butcher shops, and it was prohibited to open a butcher's shop or to slaughter without the council's permission. According to the claims of the heads of the councils, the income from the taxes on the sale of meat was intended for the good of the general public in the ghettos and was collected to aid the community, but it also was part of the mechanism of control used by the council. As a result, the price of meat, already high, rose even further.

about this like I care about last year's snow. If you lose everything, why not shame as well! …

March 25, 1942 [*sic*] [1943], 9 P.M.

I would like to write briefly about the topic of "how Jews earn a living in Transnistria?" I do not want to embark upon economic discussions but simply to record what our eyes see and our ears hear in the Dzhurin camp, where the situation is no different than the situation that prevails in other camps in the Moghilev district in which most of the remaining remnant is to be found. I will not discuss the camps by the Bug and in the Bershad district, because there "living" means: waiting for the Angel of Death.

The truth is, as it turns out, that had Y. L. Peretz lived in Transnistria today, instead of writing the tale "What Are the Multiple Needs of a Jewish Woman?"[21] he would have written a different kind of story entitled "What Are the Multiple Needs of a *Bishenitz*?" It has become clear that everything that we believed was of utmost importance in those days, without which it would really be impossible to survive, has the value of a hollow egg—barley bread and even a soup of potato peels are foods fit for a king; it is possible to live in a stable that has a roof like a sieve; shoes are really an unnecessary burden, as long as there are rags to wrap around your feet.

Nevertheless, this [topic] cannot be dismissed without an explanation and, thank God, there are indeed Transnistrian livelihoods. Some people engage in "trade" and carry all their goods on their shoulders. This is no easy livelihood, because trade must be conducted in secret, while guarding against both the militia and, as distinct, the gendarmes, and the community wheeler-dealers. The councils do not prohibit trade but they impose such high taxes—to protect the cooperatives—that the small traders have to pay out of their own pockets. However, there are not that many merchants in the camps, at least there are fewer than there are brokers. Brokering is an ancient Jewish livelihood, from the times

21 Y. L. Peretz, "Vos darf a yidene? " in Peretz, *Ale verk*, vol. 2 (Yiddish) (New York: Cyco, 1947), pp. 125–127.

of Kasrilevke,[22] and is once again flourishing in Transnistria. This profession is closely related to a third Jewish "livelihood": selling one's last shirt. The brokers are therefore good emissaries.

There are a handful of craftsmen in the camps who manage to earn a meager living from the awl, razor, or scissors—other crafts do not suit our conditions. The vast majority, however, eagerly awaits a stipend: from organizations in their towns in Romania, or from underground Zionist sources in Romania—and more than a third wait for their two portions of soup from the soup kitchen, for lunch and dinner. The devotees of the soup kitchen do not usually sit empty-handed but rather stretch out their hands for a piece of bread, a potato, a handful of flour.

In the summer, there was another source of livelihood, which actually brought in a respectable 3 marks per day, provided that Buksbaum, the director of the Labor Office, liked you: working for the gendarmes as a substitute for a wealthy person. However, this is a summertime livelihood, just like the earnings of a few dozen girls and women who would sneak out of the camp and work in the fields for farmers in the area.[23]

Of course, people do not starve to death, if they have relatives or good kinsmen in Romania who are in with the high-level officials and obtain respectable sums from aid organizations for their "unfortunate brothers and sisters in Transnistria." Such a relative makes it possible not only to eat wheat bread with butter but even to play a game of poker every night until midnight ...[24]

---

22 The literary name of Sholem Aleichem's hometown.

23 The Jews did seasonal work in order to support themselves. Young men and women worked in agriculture in the surrounding villages during the summer. In her diary, Miriam Korber Bercovici relates that she and other young men and women found work in agriculture. See Miriam Korber Bercovici, *Jurnal de Ghetou: Dzhurin Transnistria, 1941–1943* (Bucharest: Kriterion, 1995), pp. 87–88. In the ghetto of Murafa, young men and women, as well as older women, were taken in the summers of 1942 and 1943 to work in tobacco fields. The testimonies relate that many children, ages ten to fourteen, "volunteered" to work in the tobacco fields, because they received a bowl of soup and could collect for themselves any tobacco leaves left on the ground, dry them, and sell them in the market to Ukrainians in the surrounding area. Shulamit Meiner testimony, YVA, O.3/9926; Kurt Shternshus testimony, YVA, O.3/VT/9370.

24 As aid began to arrive from Romania, in particular private help from families in Romania who had not been deported, the situation of the recipients of the aid improved and, in the words of Kunstadt, not only were they no longer hungry for bread but they could allow

A sum recently arrived from the Rădăuţi association of townsmen in Bucharest with a list of 150 Rădăuţi deportees who depend on this gift for their livelihood. However, the money first fell into the hands of the council, and the lords decided that in the meantime no one would receive not even one groschen.[25] They had an excuse ready and waiting: since the money sent was in lei, they should wait a little while until the exchange rate for the mark would fall so that the lei could be exchanged at a good rate to the benefit of the recipients. The treasure lay at the council for over a month, and they are paying the meager stipends only now … at a severe loss for the recipients. The exchange rate for the mark is now 30 percent higher than it was one month ago, and each recipient of 150 marks—according to the calculation—has lost 20 marks, that is 1.5 poods of potatoes, as a result of the twisted financial dealings! The second-in-command changed the money in Moghilev. Neither I nor anyone else, God forbid, suspects any wrongdoing, and yet this seems like the secrets of the Torah that a simple mind cannot grasp …

So, let us end as I began: "How do Jews make a living in Transnistria?"—Through miracles and wonders, if I am not mistaken … "

March 26, 1943, 7 A.M.

Spring has sprung with all its might, and the radiant and fragrant surroundings only serve to darken the mood even more. In the camps in Transnistria, spring does not herald revival and renewal but rather all kinds of calamities, labor camps, expulsion to the Bug, visits from enemies, longing for the lost past, for a different spring. People yearn for last year's stormy winter that lingered until *Shavues* and protected us from the summer hardships.

---

themselves to play cards in the evening. Fritzi Salner recalls that many young people played cards in the evening to relieve the boredom and pass the difficult hours with nothing to do; see Fritzi Salner testimony, YVA, O.3/VT/8790.

25 A groschen had very little value; meaning, no money would be distributed.

Praetor Dindilegan recently informed the colony chief that Dzhurin will be required to provide 600 men for work "far away" and, apart from this, a designated number, according to the need, for work in the fields in the surrounding area. He informed us that if we do not provide the workers in a timely fashion, he himself will come to select them.

Last year Dzhurin provided 300 workers, who toiled at hard labor until late in the autumn without any pay. They drew their strength for the hard labor from half a loaf of barley bread and a thin bean soup, which they received twice a day. Many of them returned with their health impaired, suffering from tuberculosis, rheumatism, and stomach conditions. During the winter, more than a dozen of these patients died as a result of the gifts that they had brought home from the hard labor. Others lay ill with typhus for some time and are still unable to stand up on their own two feet. I dread the new work season, may it come upon us for [our] good! …

March 31, 1943, 2 P.M.

Lucky for me, I got through the torments entailed in obtaining the clothes that had been granted to me. The custodian of the treasure, Iankel Katz, displayed great consideration and selected befitting articles for me: a suit for me, although already worn and slightly stained but nevertheless immeasurably more respectable than my dirty, torn jacket, which I have been wearing since the day that we were deported. Apart from that, I was entitled to a pair of underwear, actually new. Roza, Rivka, and the children were given dresses, pants, and shirts. Bertl was even granted a pair of galoshes. For dessert: a fluffy pillow. Everyone will be envious of the treasure …

April 2, 1943, 2 P.M.

Dr. Schiber, an elderly ophthalmologist from Suceava, lives modestly in the camp. All day long, people who are suffering from problems with their eyes visit his small room, where there is no place to insert a pin. The elderly man has no medical tools, but he has something more valuable than instruments: a noble soul and a kind heart—qualities that are rare in this place.

Today, for the first time, Dr. Schiber appeared in the community building. He came specifically to see the colony chief, his fellow townsman, and presented him with a gift: a sheet of paper covered on both sides with his fine handwriting. The colony chief tried to put it in his drawer, but Dr. Shiver requested that he read it on the spot. The colony chief ordered me to read it out loud and here is a summary:

The text began with a line in bold script in red ink: "Save hundreds of people from blindness before it is too late!" This was followed by details written in black ink. A strange phenomenon has been occurring in the camp for a few months—the ophthalmologist announces thus—a phenomenon that portends a mass tragedy. Increasing numbers of people are complaining to him that their eyesight has suddenly deteriorated—by day, they see as though they are looking through a cloud and at night they become completely blind. Upon examining the patients' eyes, the doctor found that this is not simply an eye disorder but rather a dangerous result of malnourishment. When the body lacks the necessary vitamins, the retina of the eye shrinks. All the patients are among those who receive soup from the soup kitchen, and their only nutrition comes from pea soup, or bean soup, and a quarter of a loaf of barley bread. There is only one treatment: improving the diet provided by the soup kitchen. In truth, he does not dare to demand milk, honey, butter, eggs, or wheat bread for the soup kitchen people, because he is not that senile, but rather he proposes that, only three times a week, the soup be changed for a soup made from dried fruits in order to try to save their deteriorating eyes from eternal night.

I had barely finished reading the last line when the colony chief sprang up from his bench and told the doctor in these words, in German, of course:

"What you are saying, Herr Colleague, is out of the question! Where will we find the money? Do not forget where we are living."

The elderly ophthalmologist shrugged his shoulders and left without saying another word. The colony chief took the manuscript from me and put it in his drawer under a pile of other requests, which do not concern the eyesight of hundreds of people.

The colony chief's claim that they lack the means to save the deteriorating eyes is an empty excuse. The state of the community coffers has actually improved significantly now with money coming in from all sides: subsidies from Romania, taxes from merchants, and the handsome profits of the cooperative. However, the problem is that a grave curse rests on this blessing of good fortune: they squander the cash both where they should and where they should not. More than half the money vanishes on bribes, and we have sated the throats of the leeches that all the water in the ocean could not quench. Messengers from the gendarmes run back and forth all day long with notes requesting all kinds of goods from the cooperative—gifts that the gendarmes give to their whores and to the Ukrainian families in whose homes they get drunk at night. If we do not "supply" something exactly as requested, because there is none to be found, the next day the gendarmes appear in the market with whips, beating both the peasants and the Jews mercilessly and chasing them out. Then the advocates hurry to beg forgiveness from the overlord and the affair costs a fortune ... much of the blame for this lies on the shoulders of the speculators who throw around hundreds [in cash] to hide their non-kosher trade and to stuff the throats of the gendarmes. The leeches believe that there is plenty to milk from the Yids ...

April 4, 1943, 2 P.M.

The investigative delegation that blessed Transnistria with its presence two months ago will once again visit these regions in the month of April. We have learned with certainty the aim of this new visit: to prepare the transfer of about 5,000 orphans to *Eretz Yisroel.* The Moghilev Central Council is uncharacteristically busy for the sake of the greater good, and it seems that a few well-connected people will manage to accompany the orphans and thus be able to sneak out of the cage. For some reason, the story of the orphans seems too good to be true. On the other hand, the scheme about the escorts actually makes sense ...[26]

---

26 The investigative delegation that blessed Transnistria with its presence two months before would once again visit these regions in the month of April. Although the councils and

April 5, 1943, 7 A.M.

The typhus epidemic is waning, because of the early arrival of spring. For ten days, there have been no new known cases, and a few patients are still lying in the hospital, out of danger. The poor have thrown off their lice-ridden rags, and the people have begun cleaning their apartments as much as possible. The council has distributed lime to whiten the walls free of charge—a gift from the Romanian Jews.

The plague was less destructive this year than it was last year, even though the sanitary measures were poor as a result of the strange conditions. The old disinfection machine was dragged to the apartment of the patient, sometimes only a few days after a new case was discovered,

---

their leaders recognized that they were responsible for finding a solution to the problem of saving the orphans, financial difficulties prevented them from tackling this issue until mid-1942. Until this period, the very meager resources of the councils were divided among three main areas in parallel: the issue of hunger was addressed by establishing soup kitchens; the plague of typhus and other diseases by establishing hospitals, isolation rooms, and disinfection facilities; and, finally, the issue of the orphans. The situation of the orphans in Moghilev was the worst, as is borne out in the report written on May 21, 1942, by Dr. Meir Weinstein, one of the senior members of the investigative commission appointed by Jagendorf, who was the head of the Moghilev ghetto at the time. Dr. Weinstein reported that children were suffering from terrible illnesses, were in a pre-tuberculosis condition, and were malnourished. Due to the lack of heating and of soap, it was impossible to wash the children. See YVA, P.9/29, p.10; Rosen, "Tzibur Veyahid," p.186. The question of the orphan children in Transnistria also concerned the leadership of the Comisia Autonomă De Ajutorare in Bucharest. Following the visit of the delegation from the Comisia Autonomă De Ajutorare, headed by Fred Şaraga in January 1943, a more solid assistance for the orphans was established. The Şaraga Report of the delegation and its conclusions moved the Comisia Autonomă De Ajutorare to allocate considerable sums of money designated specifically for this purpose. They demanded a separate accounting for the orphans, and indeed, specific aid money from Bucharest was allocated for this purpose. The data in the report by the Comisia Autonomă De Ajutorare reveals that in January 1943, there were 373 children in Orphanage No. 1 in Moghilev; 214 children in Orphanage No. 2; and 174 children in Orphanage No. 3. The orphanage in Shargorod housed 186 children and that in Bershad, 122. In Dzhurin, there were fifty-one children without either a father or a mother. See Shmuel Ben-Tsiyon, *Yeladim Yehudim BiTransnistriya Bitekufat Hashoah* (Hebrew) (Haifa: University of Haifa, Mahon Leheker Hashoah, 1989), p. 144, 199; Rosen, "Tzibur Veyahid," pp. 184–186. At the end of 1943, after the Jewish community exerted pressure on the Romanian authorities and upon the publication of the Transnistria Plan, which provoked public debate in the Allied states, the Romanian government was prepared to negotiate with the Jewish community regarding the return of the orphans from Transnistria. This indeed began to happen only at the beginning of 1944. See Ofer, *Escaping from the Holocaust*, pp. 187–188.

because it was impossible to take the machine up the mountain through the sea of mud (there were no horses to haul it …). When smoke eventually began to come out of the chimney, the lice were not afraid and only warmed their limbs. Apart from this, the people hid whatever was possible, because the objects that underwent this process came out broken for the most part and covered with soot. Even in the hospital itself, the sanitary conditions were poor. Some of the patients were rolling around on the floor, and the straw under them was swarming with lice. They were crawling on the walls, on the ceiling, on the blankets, and even on the white coats of the doctors and nurses. There were patients who lay in their own clothes, which had not been disinfected, because they had no shirt to change into, and there is no laundry in the hospital.

The community remembered only two weeks ago that something had to be done. Indeed, all the rooms in the hospital were whitewashed and cleaned, and they even took out shirts, sheets, and blankets from the holy storeroom for the patients who do not have their own underwear.

Let us be fair to the Moghilev prefect, who has begun to show an interest in the health of the Jews in the camps in his area. The prefect ordered the local post chief to make sure that Jews do not walk around the camp with beards and side curls, because the lice that spread the plague hide in the tangled beards and side curls. The gendarmes did not need to be asked twice, and yesterday a few angels of destruction raided the camp with scissors in hand, grabbed the Jews with beards, and shaved them all at once, as was the custom in Poland on the eve of the war. They did not find anyone with side curls, because no one here has adopted that style, apart from a few rabbis. The barbers made a handsome income in the camp today—whoever had any sign of a beard rushed to get rid of it, even though the gendarmes did the work for free …

April 6, 1943, 6 A.M.

I have "renewed" the old suit that the community granted to me. I really feel like a new man in this outfit. Now my bosses will not badger me because I am not dressed respectably. Anyway, they will have to find other transgressions …

[April 6, 1943] 3 P.M.

I decided on a tombstone for my mother, and it will be ready in the course of the week. In Dzhurin, in addition to his other occupation, the *hazen* from Rădăuţi, Moshe Solomon, also makes tombstones (he never had engaged in this craft …) and he does an excellent job. There is no lack of buyers in Dzhurin, where people die [“]with gusto.[”] It will be a small stone, a pauper's poor offering, and Mother will surely forgive me.

For the time being, I have not missed a single day of *Kaddish*, even though this entails difficulties and sometimes also risks. As a result of the plague, the council has closed all *minyonim* except for one, where everyone who is saying *Kaddish* comes together—quite a large crowd that continues to grow. One is liable to bring home a crawling gift from there … While I say *Kaddish*, it seems to me that I am talking to Mother, and she listens to me and looks at me with profound sadness, exactly as she did when I visited her for the last time. *Oy vey*, such a conversation …

April 7, 1943, 2 P.M.

As of yesterday, I began reviewing and editing the pages of this book of memories, which will, God willing, celebrate its first anniversary next week on April 11. I am erasing superfluous words, or those that are too sharp, leaving what I deem suitable, as though the typesetter is standing behind me, looking over my shoulder, waiting for the manuscript. As I pour over a year of Transnistrian memories, I see on every page to what extent the hopes and illusions, as well as worries and fears, have been insignificant and empty. It has all been a gloomy dream that dissipates like a cloud, and yet the dream continues. The written pages attest that there is only one truth that never lies: death. The descriptions of my mother's demise are momentously tangible, and I would not write them any differently today.

By the way, today I went to my mother's grave for the first time since the funeral. The muddy pile of earth could not have made me any sadder than I already was, obviously.

April 8, 1943, 6 A.M.

In times of mass misery and general affliction, a person's imagination tends to divert itself and sprout all kind of legends and tales, like mushrooms after the rain. One such wonderful, new tale is circulating in the Moghilev district word of mouth among both the Jews and the Ukrainian peasants. This terrible story is being passed on mainly by women, each one according to her own version, while the men are ashamed to admit that they too, the wise and the knowledgeable, are very eager to believe it. So, listen to the story:

Not far from Shargorod, there is a small shtetl named Borivka, where a few hundred Jews lived, until the occupation. In July 1941, when the Romanian soldiers occupied Podolia [Transnistria], they killed all the Jews in the shtetl, every one of them. The Jews' homes remained vacant and soon became ruins, because the peasants did not stop tearing off parts of the houses, stealing doors and windows, ripping up floors, peeling off the roofs, and uprooting the fences.

For some time now, the peasants have noticed a light shining at night from the *shoyhet's* slaughterhouse, but whoever approached the shattered window saw that it was dark and empty inside. One neighbor wanted to get to the bottom of this secret and decided to spend the night in the ruins, together with his wife. He made a bed for himself on the floor, next to the peasant woman, and dozed off. His wife was unable to close her eyes.

At around midnight, the hovel was suddenly filled with light, as in the middle of a sunny day, and the frightened peasant woman saw that all the local Jews had gathered there, the pious ones, dressed in prayer shawls, praying. Terrified, her hands became paralyzed and she lost her tongue, and thus she lay for an hour, until the prayers came to an end. The group of Jews disappeared in the blink of an eye, and only one single Jew remained; in fact he was the peasant's neighbor, who was practically a member of his household. The Jew whispered to the peasant woman: "Know that your husband, who dared to disturb our rest, will die in three days' time. Nothing will happen to you, because you are innocent. And now I will reveal a secret to you: the suffering of the Jews will end on April 20." Once again, the hovel became dark, and the Jew disappeared. The peasant woman woke up her husband and told him the story. His teeth began to chatter and he struggled to drag himself home. He came down with a high fever and died on the third day …

This means that we must wait until April 20, when this tale will blow over, and a new one will replace it. By the way, this year the first day of *Peysech* falls on April 20, which is the birthday of the demon Hitler, may his name be blotted out. It is highly doubtful that the first anniversary of his death will also fall on that day, regardless of the prophecy from Borivka …

April 9, 1943, 7 P.M.

The tombstone has been standing over my mother's grave since this morning, but only on Monday, the 7th of *Nisan* (April 12) will the unveiling ceremony take place. It is a modest stone, and I had to struggle to meet this expense. What difference does it make, large or small, as long as it is a solid stone …

On the front of the stone is engraved:

> Here lies [R.I.P.]
> A modest and pious woman
> *Rebbetzin Marat* Chana
> Daughter of Rabbi Mordechai Efraim,
> [Who] Died on the 9th of Sh'vat [January 15]
> 5703 [1943]—May her soul be bound up in the bond of life.

On the other side of the tombstone in Latin letters is written:

> Kunstadt Chana, Rădăuţi

On the same day, we will have a double "celebration"—we will also place my father-in-law's tombstone. Today I managed to write a poem entitled "At My Mother's Grave," and I intend to read it during the tombstone unveiling ceremony, instead of giving a eulogy. It is doubtful whether this poem has any literary value, and I did not set out to find favor in the eyes of the literary critics. Not one single letter in this eulogy that is written in rhyme was composed to glorify lyrical beauty, but rather it is a hot tear on this cruel pile of earth. (This poem appears on the title page of this volume of memories).[27]

April 11, 1943, 6 A.M.

Today, this diary celebrates a milestone: it is one year old. Its pages describe memories and events as experienced around me and within me—not all of them, and not always in full detail. For the most part, I have found myself in a state of despair, observing everything with contempt, and mostly distracting myself with the chronicle while the roof burns over my head. It is possible that the few memories that I have saved from oblivion are of no real value due to their thoroughly subjective nature. I have devoted too much space to myself, as if I were more than a meaningless grain of sand in a desert. The fact that I have not refrained from judging people and situations according to their behavior toward me, for better or for worse, is also certainly a serious flaw. However, I have a bit of an excuse: this diary clearly bears an explicitly personal imprint, and I do not pretend to produce an academic chronicle. I do not intend to enter the realm of a future historian, were he to appear, and to demonstrate a measure of objectivity about the disaster of Transnistria.

Will these pages be fated to celebrate a second birthday? I adhere to the discerning saying of the sages [of the Mishna and the Talmud] of blessed memory: "Seek not things concealed!" ...[28]

---

27 The poem was apparently omitted from the title page in the typed copy of the diary in our possession.

28 B. Hagiga 13b: "Seek not things concealed from you, nor search those hidden from you."

[April 11, 1943] 7 P.M.

It is perhaps a good sign that the first entry in the second year bears a hint of hope, at least for the most unfortunate in the camps—the lonely orphans. By order of the Moghilev Central Council, they began registering all the orphans in the camps today. This is related to the investigative delegation that will soon come to Moghilev.[29] Perhaps these abandoned babies, who wander around like withering leaves in an autumn storm, will be rescued.

And now a second entry, which may be interpreted for better or for worse. The praetor from Shargorod, Dindilegan, has been transferred to Romania and has already ceded his throne. The heir is a Romanian overlord from Focşani, Rusu. The verse "So perish [all your enemies]"[30] is fitting for Dindilegan, because he has caused great distress for all the Jews in the entire Shargorod district, including Dzhurin. His despicable name is mentioned often in these pages, and what I have written is just a drop in the ocean of his good deeds. His hands are smeared with Jewish blood—literally—and no one will miss this murderer, apart from a handful of good kinsmen who receive benefits from Shargorod (read the chapter about the "ransom" crime! …).

The heir will certainly not be a reincarnation of Rabbi Levi Yitzhak of Berdichev, but there is no one worse than Dindilegan. The day before yesterday the colony chief and Moshe Katz went to Shargorod to bid farewell to the evil one and make the acquaintance of his heir. Dindilegan introduced the delegates to Rusu and even grumbled that the "model colony" of Dzhurin is doing well. Rusu, the delegates relate, appears to be a levelheaded man and does not give the impression of being a scoundrel like his predecessor. Rusu even kindly promised to ease the conditions, within the limit of the law. For this reason, he will soon come to visit Dzhurin. It will not be long until we discover whether they are the same thing in a different guise …

---

29 The delegation headed by Fred Şaraga, which visited Transnistria in January 1943 to investigate the situation of the ghettos, especially that of the orphan children, planned to conduct another visit in April 1943.

30 From the song of Deborah, Judges 5:31.

It is a week until *Peysech.* The community leased the right to bake *matzos* to a gang of merchants. These are the same people who leased the bread monopoly and are not giving up their fathers' inheritance ... they will take flour to the bakers and receive ready-made *matzos*. This transaction is only for the wealthy, because the *matzos* are of good lineage, and one must not dupe them with barley or potato flour. Wheat flour appeared unexpectedly at the market but at the price of gold. Poor people will fulfill their duty with potato, corn cakes, and a fine portion of *maror.*[31] I count myself among these, and if only this was the last of my worries. The rabbis have permitted the cooking of bean soup in the soup kitchen during the days of *Peysech.*

April 14 [*sic*],[32] 1943, Monday, the 7th of *Nisan*, 5703, 7 A.M.

So far, eighty-six orphans who have lost both parents have been registered, and today they will draw up another list, and the number will reach 250. These lists include all orphans, including the descendants of Ukrainian Jews, although their origin has been noted. A flimsy virtue ...

On the other hand, the "lords" have forbidden composing a list of "living orphans,"[33] that is, children whose fathers were drafted into the Red Army when the war broke out. Unless a miracle occurs, these babies will never see their fathers again.

There is no shortage of orphans in Transnistria, and their number continues to rise thanks to the mercies that the Master of the Universe shows His chosen people. The only orphanage in the Moghilev district is in Moghilev, and they accept only orphans registered with the local council. The caregivers there have divided the children into two classes:

31 *Maror* (bitter herb), one of the six foods on the Seder plate that each serve to tell the story of the Exodus during the Passover Seder, symbolizes the bitterness of slavery in Egypt. Most Ashkenazi Jews use horseradish, as did Kunstadt, while most Sephardic Jews use lettuce or celery.

32 Monday, April 12, 1943, coincided with the Hebrew date of the 7th of Nisan, 5703.

33 Orphans who had one parent.

those who are still among the living and the doomed. The second group includes those children upon which the hell in Transnistria has stamped its seal with tuberculosis, rickets, anemia, and other dangerous diseases. They are left abandoned, because it is "a shame to waste oil" on them, and the door to the orphanage remains closed to them. This is how they think that they have successfully "solved" half of the orphan problem ...

The lucky group of "living" orphans are granted entry into the holy of holies of the orphanage, provided that they have no relatives in the place. In truth, they are saved from hunger but they continue to wander around in rags, and the rooms are filthy and neglected. Nevertheless, they are still far better off than those in the camps in the area, where orphans are left abandoned, even though there are enough projects ... on paper.

In Dzhurin and everywhere in the camps, one encounters them at every step, the naked and barefoot, the gaunt and shrunken children with the yellow faces of the elderly who are dying, with legs like sticks and vacant eyes, who stretch out a hand and beg for a piece of bread or a potato. The council has often thought about establishing an orphanage, but it remains just a thought. Now the "lords" offer a new excuse: we must wait for the delegation to arrive. Perhaps it will send the orphans to *Eretz Yisroel* after all.[34]

---

34 As previously stated, the issue of the orphans was only one of the many difficult problems confronting the Jewish councils in the ghettos. In April 1942, the Moghilev ghetto council began to deal with the tragedy of the orphan children and established three orphanages. Despite beginning to grapple with this problem at the end of 1942, the orphanage opened in Shargorod only on June 8, 1943, after the council was able to raise the necessary funds and find a suitable building. The orphanage in Dzhurin opened on October 24, 1943, with great pomp and splendor under the direction of the Rădăuţi lawyer Bigo (Bernhard) Hart. About fifty orphans were gathered in a hall in Murafa, which was a very small ghetto. This was not an orphanage that offered all the usual activities for the children as did those in Moghilev, Shargorod, or Dzhurin, but at least the children were provided with food, clothing, and protection. The conditions in Bershad were among the most severe compared with all the other ghettos. During the first winter of 1941–1942, half its population died of typhus. The orphanage in this ghetto opened in the spring–summer of 1943. For a list of orphans in several orphanages, see YVA, P.9/7; Ben-Tsiyon, *Yeladim Yehudim BiTransnistriya*, p. 187; Şaraga Report, YVA, M.20/104; YVA, O.11/44; Rosen, "Tzibur Veyahid," pp. 184–194.

[April 12, 1943] 3 P.M.

Today at 10 A.M., the "*Hanukes Habayis*"[35] of my mother's tombstone took place. Outside it was a beautiful and dry day, the sun shone like on the eve of *Peysech*, but my eyes saw black. A large crowd gathered, even though I had informed only a few people. The rabbi of Siret, Rabbi Baruch Hager, was also there, as well as the rabbi of Rădăuţi, Rabbi Israel Hornik, and the rabbi of Gura Humorului, Rabbi Moshe, the head of the rabbinical court. I read my poem "At My Mother's Grave" at the beginning, and many people wiped their eyes with handkerchiefs. The *hazen* from Rădăuţi Moshe Salomon recited *Eyl Moleh Rahmim* and that was it. Rivka saw our mother's grave for the first time, since she was not at the funeral because of her swollen legs. None of the "lords" came, and I did not invite them. Whoever wanted to be there could have known about it easily.

We all walked to my father-in-law's grave from my mother's grave, and there too we flooded the cold stone with *Eyl Moleh Rahmim*. We then placed a tombstone on the grave of the hospital director Dr. Moshe Greiff. I celebrated three happy events all at one time …

April 15, 1943, 3 P.M.

Only a few days remain until *Peysech*, and I still do not have any *matzos*. Groups of bakers have already begun to bake *matzos* at their own expense and are charging 9.5 marks per kilo, exactly three times the price of last year. The *matzos* do not matter at all to me, but the children keep asking me when I will bring *matzos*. So I must go to the community—in the old country, this was known by the name of *Ma'es Hitin*[36]—in order not to

35 Kunstadt ironically refers to the unveiling of his mother's tombstone as a housewarming party.

36 Flour for the holiday of Passover, *Kimha dePisha* in Aramaic, is first mentioned in the Jerusalem Talmud by this name. This refers to an ancient tradition of giving money or food products to the poor for the holiday of Passover. It was traditional to conduct special fundraising in the month between Purim and Passover for this purpose, and the funds collected were distributed to the poor as money or food for the festival.

destroy the *matzos* dream of the children, who are missing out on their childhood games because of deprivation and fear.

The concern of "how will I provide for *Peysech*?" troubles me less than the worry of "how will I provide for after *Peysech*?" Soon I will have to part with my *Shabbes* fur and the silver watch that I inherited, if the brokers will arrange a volunteer to buy them. And then? There are plenty of other questions that have no answer …

April 18, 1943, 6 A.M.

The list of orphans has already been completed and is ready for the delegation. The council has registered all orphans up to the age of twenty. The colony chief insisted that the age limit should be fourteen, but to no avail. In the end, he had to be satisfied with the assurance that he will be able to add and erase names when the time comes.

I took a chance and managed to enter Rivka among the orphans who have lost both parents, even though she was born a little too early. I did this with the consent of a council member, who promised me that he would lend a hand to help the "trick" succeed, in light of her lamentable situation. At times, it is good to clutch at straws.

Yesterday, I clutched at an even thinner straw. I discovered that they are preparing a list of former Zionist activists in utmost secrecy in order to persuade the delegation to allow them to accompany the Dzhurin orphans to *Eretz Yisroel*. I was able to sneak into this list, even though I do not belong to the "Dzhurin-style neo-Zionists."[37] The fact that I sold shekels when I was a young ten-year-old boy could be to my detriment.

For the time being, the delegation has not arrived in Moghilev. Tomorrow evening, we will celebrate the first *Seyder* and immediately after *Peysech* there is the non-Jewish Passover [Easter]—clear obstacles that will delay the delegation's arrival. It really is a matter of life and death to take the orphans to *Eretz Yisroel* without delay, before it is too late. According to what we read in the Romanian newspapers, Turkey will

37 See the entry of January 27, 1943, 3 P.M.

soon be obliged to get involved in the world madness, and then the sea passage at the Bosporus will be closed for who knows how long.

[April 18, 1943] 3 P.M.

I swallowed my pride and managed to receive a few *Ma'es Hitin* marks from the community to acquire the necessities for *Peysech*. This bit of cash was enough for 3 kilos of *matzos*, a flask of oil, and a dozen eggs. The children were overjoyed when I appeared with the package of *matzos* under my arm.

[April 18, 1943] 9 P.M.

In Moghilev, the ruler has changed—a new prefect has arrived, [Constantin] Login.[38] He had ruled in Tulchin until now, and his reputation as a Jew-hater precedes him. He sent thousands of Ukrainian Jews over the Bug to German camps and he cruelly tortured the remaining remnant who nevertheless remained in the Tulchin district. He forced all males—even the elderly, the ill, and fourteen-year-old boys—to dig peat for twelve hours every day. The forced laborers stood in water up to their knees and received as wages half a loaf of barley bread and an onion every morning.

In Moghilev, they fear the decrees of this overlord. There are approximately 12,000 Jews in the holy city today; most are "non-kosher" who have nothing to do with the "kosher" foundry under engineer Jagendor's rule.

---

38 Colonel Constantin Login, the third prefect of the Moghilev region, was considered the cruelest prefect in the region. He had served in his previous role in the Tulchin region. Login forbade any contact between officials of the various authorities and the Jews. During his term, it was even forbidden for Jews to enter the prefecture building. See Yeshurun, *Hahitargenut Ha'atzmit Shel Yehudei Bukovina*, p. 22; Carp, *Cartea neagră*, pp. 281–282.

April 19, 1943, *Eyrev Peysech*, 1 P.M.

Outside, *Erev Peysech* of *Shir Hashirim*[39] is upon us, bright and pleasant—a real contrast to the bustle of Dzhurin. *Eyrev Peysech* is manifest in the camp, and even the yellow faces of the human skeletons reflect the holiday glow. There is no one to be seen in the market but, in contrast, there is such a commotion at the crowded butcher shops that it is literally life-threatening. The butchers made sure to stock up on enough meat and have exploited the opportunity to drive up the prices as much as possible. The council does not get involved in the prices of meat and does not pick a quarrel with the butchers, because they constantly threaten to strike.

The people try hard to forget where they are, at least during the holidays, and that we are already celebrating the second *Peysech* in a world of chaos. Many also want to dupe the Master of the Universe, while reclining during the *Seyder* and singing "*Avoydim Hayeynu*" (we were slaves), even though the present slavery has nothing to be ashamed of in comparison with [slavery in] the time of Pharoah …

[April 19, 1943] 6 P.M.

The high holiday mood in which the *Lagernikes* had immersed themselves in spite of the hardships was suddenly ripped to shreds a few hours ago by a Transnistrian-style misfortune that struck mainly ten families, but spoiled everyone's holiday. The post chief, Georgescu, unexpectedly appeared in the community building and ordered the colony chief to send all the shoemakers in the camp to the gendarmerie post, escorted by a militiaman. Since no one had anticipated such troubles, the militia managed to gather all sixteen shoemakers within a half hour and to take them to the gendarmerie.

---

39 The saying "the Eve of Passover of Shir Hashirim (Song of Songs)" reflects the custom of reading the scroll of Shir Hashirim during the week of Passover, in part because of the profuse descriptions of the blossoming of spring.

The post chief, Georgescu, selected ten tradesmen from among them and announced that they would be taken to Moghilev already today, because shoemakers are needed there. All ten of them are indigent, the sole providers for their large families. Heartrending scenes took place in the community building, women and children threw themselves to the ground and begged that their breadwinners at least be allowed to observe *Peysech* at home, but it was a lost cause. An order from "above," indeed from the new prefect, Login himself. The only thing that the community managed to do was to register the families in the list of soup kitchen recipients. The *Seyder* that everyone was preparing to celebrate is already of such good cheer …

April 22, 1943, First Day of *Holemoyed*, 6 A.M.

The new praetor from Shargorod, Rusu, arrived in Dzhurin on the first day of *Peysech* for his first inspection and actually brought good news—if only it really is true: this summer the state will not demand any workers from the Dzhurin camp to build roads, because there is currently no need for such work. On the other hand, the camp will have to provide some people to work in the fields in the surrounding areas.

This information has wiped away the gloom that spread as a result of what had happened to the shoemakers. The people prefer to work in fields, and many *Lagernikes* stood in line at the Labor Office to ask for preferential treatment: to be registered for such work, together with their families, and to be permitted to move to a village.[40] The atmosphere became festive once again.

As for the shoemakers, the advocates managed to bail out one of them, because his wife is lying ill, and their three babies wander round the house neglected. The other nine, whose families were less fortunate, were sent to Moghilev on the night of the *Seyder*.

---

40 Agricultural work in the fields was considered preferable for a number of reasons: first, the workers returned home at the end of the working day. Second, it was possible to collect produce that was left on the ground after the harvest. Sometimes the Ukrainian farmers took pity on the Jews and gave the Jewish workers some food. See Kurt Shternshus testimony, YVA, O.3/VT/9370.

April 28, 1943, 6 A.M.

Today is *Isre Hag*. Long ago, *Isre Hag* in general and particularly *Isre Hag Peysech* would evoke a bitter taste of longing in my heart for the holiday that had passed and that would only come again to visit a year later. It was a strange feeling of longing, and people had little desire to embark upon a new summer, or a new winter, when the weekday issues and difficulties resumed. The truth is that those times were indeed ordinary, and yet that did not mean real calm for the Jews in Romania. Not a day went by without taunting us about being only Jews who should not compare ourselves to the others, the real owners of the country … That is what I mean about the prewar period, before the fascist enemies of Israel seized power in Romania and adopted the Nazi attitude toward the Jews.

This *Isre Hag* does not evoke any longing in me, none at all. After such a *Peysech*, there is nothing that I miss. I left all the *matzos* for the children and only tasted them, while I enjoyed the luxury of the mamaliga [cornmeal polenta] and potatoes, until I was satiated. The *Peysech* dishes, a few clay shards, were like those that we use all year round. Go ahead and yearn only for [the prayers] *Ya'alehy Veyayvo*[41] and *Mipney Hata'eynu*! …[42]

The devout inhabitants of the camp convinced themselves that *Peysech* would bring deliverance—whether because of the Borivka prophecy or because of this holiday's tradition of miracles from time immemorial. Well, once again they were disappointed, not for the first time and probably not for the last time either … during the days of the holiday, all kinds of dreadful rumors spread that proved to be unfounded. There are people who are evidently sadistic by nature who invent malevolent lies to cast fear on the depressed spirits, just as others do the opposite and scatter false hopes that dissipate immediately and intensify the sorrow.

41 A blessing recited on holidays asking that the prayers rise on high and be answered by God.

42 Additional prayers and blessings said on the three pilgrimage festivals and other holidays.

Regardless of the external and the internal conditions, some nice youth from the aristocracy, whose hearts crave luxuries, arranged a party in a hall on the seventh day of *Peysech*, ostensibly for the benefit of all the poor. The head of the initiative was a lawyer from Cernăuţi, Dr. Berger, who lacks no money, does not work, and behaves here as though he were at a resort. Although the council in fact tried to prevent holding the party, which is like a slap in the face to most of the people in the camp, it did not help. The members of the clique are cronies of the officials, and the post chief, Georgescu,[43] gave them permission, in black and white, to the council's chagrin. The party went on until midnight, music resounded, couples frolicked, and the camp seethed. Militiamen stood guard at the entrance so that no one would sneak in to ruin the party. The people view this as a danger to the general public. The high-level officials will deem that the Yids are not lying deep enough in the ground, if they desire to hold such parties, and the indigent will suffer the consequences.

[April 28, 1943] 7 P.M.

The incident of the nine shoemakers has concluded with a "happy ending." All of them returned to Dzhurin today, dusty and tired. They were not taken to Moghilev but rather to Odessa. They wandered around in Odessa throughout *Peysech*, until they were told that the quota had already been filled, and they should return to Dzhurin. Nine families were condemned to having their *Peysech* ruined!

May 4, 1943, 7 P.M.

When I came to work at my office today, a surprise was waiting for me. I no longer needed to bother going to the holy of holies in the council [community] building, because my desk had already been placed in the

43 Georgescu was also responsible for issuing permits, among other things, for all ghetto activities.

front room. The colony chief played a trick, as he has threatened to do on more than one occasion. Now only the "lords" alone will be privy to the secrets, and there will no longer be a chicken for *kapporres* on whom to cast suspicion. There is no secret that will not be known within a few hours. The colony chief is a champion at divulging secrets, even to the Romanian overlords, and this often leads to many tribulations.

May 6, 1943, 1 P.M.

This morning at 4 A.M., the gendarmes and the militia surrounded the home of the dentist Leon Hirschorn, a deportee from Vijniţa (Bukovina), and ordered him to load his meager possessions, as well as the members of his household, onto a Ukrainian wagon, which was waiting outside the house, without delay. The wagon set out before sunrise, led by two gendarmes. This took place while the alleys were still empty to avoid causing any panic. The destination of the unexpected journey was the camp of Krasnoye,[44] about 30 kilometers from Dzhurin. The Moghilev prefect, Login, ordered the post chief by telephone to dispatch the dentist today, because he desperately needs a change of air …

The prefect did not make the diagnosis about the change of air himself, but in fact the council did. For some months, Hirschorn has been a sharp critic of the "lords," has refused to pay the high sums[45] demanded of him, and has dared to openly and aggressively oppose the camp bosses. Above all, he declared war against the second-in-command, and sparks flew.

In the old country, the dentist was the mayor of Vijniţa and was in a position of authority for a long time. He is by nature a man who does not allow himself to be pushed around, and especially when people take too much interest in his pockets. He misjudged Transnistria and took risks that were strictly forbidden. One day, someone reported him as required and, as for the conclusion: see above! People in the camp are very upset about this matter and are angry at those who took advantage of the overlords' power to drive out an uprooted Jewish family somewhere

44 Lavi, *Pinkas Hakehilot: Rumania*, p. 507; Carp, *Cartea neagră*, vol. 3, pp. 383, 358, 441.

45 This refers to the taxes that he was required to pay to the council treasury.

into the Ukrainian wilderness. We will not probe whether and to what extent Hirschorn deserved a punishment, because it certainly should not have been expulsion. So, this is the first time that the gendarmes drive out a registered "kosher" Jewish family from the camp. It is only difficult at first …

May 11, 1943, 3 P.M.

If there are breaks of a few days between the entries, it does not mean that there is no raw material for the pen. Each day in these regions would suffice for a dozen scrolls of lamentations, which would not be ashamed before the prophet Jeremiah's song of woe. However, it is precisely this abundance of tragedies that leads one to fall into despair, fettering one's hands and drying up one's mind. I try to take up my pen and … suddenly I put it back in the ink. I sit down by the open window and look out at the sleepy [scene], where a group of barefoot and half-naked boys with pale faces and thin hands are playing excitedly "*Zukre-Folke*"—a kind of Ukrainian sport, which requires only two sticks and half a dozen small stones.

In particular, when I am lucky and I happen to get hold of a small book, it obviously overshadows the evil inclination of ruining paper myself. Apart from that, such a small book has the virtue of carrying me far away to other times and other surroundings, far from Transnistria in 1943.

I have just finished reading—no, devouring—Shalom Aleichem's novel *Blondzendike Shtern*,[46] which I had previously only heard about. However, I was not fated to fully rejoice, because the stars did not speak to me in S. A.'s [Shalom Aleichem's] iridescent language but rather in Russian. The truth is that the translation is quite good, a kind of Yiddishized Russian, which suits it but, nevertheless, lacks homey, Jewish charm. The name of the translator is unknown to me, because the title page is missing. The greatest misfortune is that some pages from the middle of the book are also annoyingly missing from the most engrossing

---

46 For an English translation, see Shalom Aleichem, *Wandering Stars: A Novel* (New York: Viking, 2009).

chapters. It is a custom in Dzhurin to tear out pages of borrowed books on the advice of God for a designated purpose that requires a blessing … never mind, also regarding literature, we cannot be spoiled here. In the entire camp, there are only a few dozen books, which pass from hand to hand and become leaner and thinner from day to day …

In the thick darkness of the Transnistrian exile, these wandering stars shone for a week like a ray of sunlight from a distant, beautiful world of which we too were once a part.

May 13, 1943, 5 A.M.

What I have just learned from reliable people who came back from Moghilev some time ago is really unbelievable. The story has been embellished but contains a kernel of truth. In short, the high Romanian overlords have turned on the real cream in Moghilev, the recipients of all the benefits, the playboys who have connections and who squander the community funds, who live it up while all around them people fall like flies from hunger and plagues and simply having no strength left. They rebuked this group in particular, because they are allowing the poor people to vanish even though the community coffers could save many of them from death.

Our "lords" categorically deny the entire matter and threaten to punish those who spread such ugly rumors concerning their "dear colleagues" from Moghilev. How could anyone stir up such evil thoughts in the "model colony"! …

Allow me to note that the exiles in Transnistria are fated to have many bosses on their heads. The prefect, the commander of the gendarmerie legion, and the central Jewish council are in charge in Moghilev, the center of the district. There is a fourth scourge in the province's camps: the regional praetor. The prefect and the praetor pass themselves off as the civil administration, while the gendarmes rule as the occupation authorities and the executors of the dangerous Order No. 23.

And now to the heart of the matter: the previous prefect of Moghilev, Iliescu,[47] has also just been replaced along with the commander of the

---

47 Colonel Iliescu was the commander of the Romanian gendarmerie in Transnistria, which

Moghilev gendarmerie legion, Năsturaş. [Constantin] Login sits on the prefect's throne today, and the gendarmerie legion is led by a new commander, Major [Gheorghe] Botoroagă.[48] Jews tremble before the new major, because a rumor has spread that he is an evil overlord and yet also incorruptible. It soon became clear that he is no gem, but he will not suffer any injustices, even when they harm only deported Yids.

While walking down the street, Major Botoroagă came across groups of people—skeletons with yellow faces and dull eyes, draped in torn sacks, including miserable little orphans begging for a piece of bread. At first the overlord was dumbfounded, because they had told him in Tiraspol, in the palace of Governor General Alexianu, that Jews live in Transnistria like a god in Odessa and have no desire whatsoever to go home. It suddenly occurred to him to stroll through the town and visit the homes of the Jews, both those of the wealthy and those of the simple people.

Already the next day, the major appeared, accompanied by a Jewish militiaman, in a number of mass housing quarters where the poor are crammed together, suffocating in pain and filth. The major covered his nose with a perfumed handkerchief, but he did not run away. On the contrary, he got even closer to the cauldrons, where the emaciated women were preparing lunch: a potato peel soup—and glanced at the clay shards used as dishes. Over the course of a few hours, the overlord wandered around the dark alleys of the poor people of Moghilev and visited the stinking ruins. He turned toward another area, where the wealthy people live, the leaders and wheeler-dealers. He did not need a handkerchief to block the odor there. Rather, he enjoyed breathing the aroma of the delicious stews and pastries that were cooking and baking in the fragrant and bright kitchens. He saw no cauldrons and no clay shards containing potato peel soup there. He simply noted something down in a little notebook without saying a word.

---

was based in Odessa. Năsturaş was the prefect. See Carp, *Cartea neagră*, vol. 3, pp. 355, 361; Lavi, *Pinkas Hakehilot: Rumania*, vol. 1, p. 485; Rosen, "Tzibur Yeyahid," p. 87.

48 Major Gheorghe Botoroagă served as the commander of the gendarmerie in Moghilev from April 1943 until March 1944 and was known for his cruelty toward the Jews. See Yeshurun, *Hahitargenut Ha'atzmit Shel Yehudei Bukovina*, p. 25. Botoroagă was tried in 1945 and sentenced to life imprisonment and punitive labor; see CNSAS, P-7795, file 1.

The next day the major began an investigation, demanding to know why most of the deportees suffer in terrible conditions, and a small portion live ostentatiously. People in the camp learned that the overlord had decided to accept the complaints of the "simple people," and there are brave inhabitants in the camp who began writing to the major, detailing everything that is wrong in the camp.

One day the major appeared unexpectedly at the [Moghilev] Central Council building, accompanied by two Romanian bookkeepers, and confiscated the books from the bookkeeper in order to examine the tabulations. This resulted in the immediate arrest of two of the prominent wheeler-dealers, Dr. Danilov[49] and Aizic Presner, who were taken to Tiraspol, where they were imprisoned and are awaiting trial in a military tribunal. Today the sword is hanging over the heads of some of the other wheeler-dealers in Moghilev.

They suddenly opened the locked storerooms and began to distribute clothes and shoes, articles that were covered with mold, due to the prolonged storage. They even accepted into the orphanage a number of children from the "doomed" category," who roam around abandoned like withered leaves and beg for alms.

May 14, 1943, 6 A.M.

Pope Pius XII has sent emissaries to look around Transnistria and learn how the deported Jews live there. The leader of the delegation is the Pope's ambassador to Bucharest, the nuncio [Andrea] Cassulo, who is accompanied by some priests and a Romanian noblewoman.[50] The

---

49 Michael Danilov was accused of collaborating in the deportation of thousands of Jews to Skazinets and Pechora, where many of them died of starvation. See CNSAS, p-045109, pp. 1–2.

50 This refers to the visit of a delegation appointed by Pope Pius XII to Moghilev. The delegation, headed by the nuncio Andrea Cassulo, the papal ambassador in Bucharest, toured Transnistria to see the conditions in which the Jewish deportees were living. The Romanian authorities took the members of the delegation to the foundry, Turnatoria, to show them how the work was carried out and how the welfare of the Jewish workers was being attended to. However, the delegates were unable to ignore the poverty and neglect that they saw on the way to the foundry. See Itzhak Yalon testimony, YVA, O.3/1238.

delegation appeared in Moghilev a few days ago. The Romanian overlords endeavored to show them what was expedient, for example the foundry and so on, in order to dupe them into believing that the deported Jews had struck it rich.

Nevertheless, the delegates were able to get a glimpse of the terrible sight of the other Moghilev through a narrow opening in the black curtain that blocked their view. What their eyes saw shook the priests up quite a bit, and as they left they offered the Catholic Church's tried-and-true comforting remedy: they promised the people that they would pray as much as possible, begging God to bring peace to the entire world. Upon parting, the nuncio presented the Pope's gift to the "colonies" in the Moghilev district: a half million Italian lira in cash.

On the other hand, with respect to saving the orphans, we neither see nor hear the Romanian delegation, for whom we are waiting like the messiah. Yesterday the council members Moshe Katz and Leon Neuman—the card players in the camp ironically call them the "good pair"—went to Moghilev … in order to find out what is going on with this delegation. This is not just about orphans but also … about their escorts to *Eretz Yisroel*!

May 17, 1943, 5 A.M.

Yesterday a special messenger brought a letter from Shargorod, signed by the praetor, Rusu, which said: since we are preparing to build a highway near Sosnovka (22 kilometers from Dzhurin) and workers are needed, the council is required to provide a list of all men who are capable of working, without exception, within forty-eight hours.

Concerning the more fundamental issue of the pope's attitude to the fate of the Jews of Europe in general, his relations with Nazi Germany, and his silence on its anti-Jewish policy, see Itzhak Minerbi, "Demuto Ufo'olo Shel Pius Ha-XII" (Hebrew), *Bishevil Hazikaron*, 35 (2000), pp. 4–11; Aryeh Leon Kubovy, "Bishulei Shtikato Shel Pius Ha-XII Vereshito Shel 'Hamismah Hayehudi,'" (Hebrew) *Yad Vashem Studies*, 6 (1967), pp. 7–22; Gutman, *Entziklopediya Shel Hashoah*, vol. 4, s.v. "Pius Ha-12," pp. 967–970; David Bankier, Dan Michman, and Iael Nidam-Orvieto, eds., *Pius XII and the Holocaust: Current State of Research* (Jerusalem: Yad Vashem, 2012).

Although according to the Romanian labor decree, the obligation for forced labor applies only to men between the ages of eighteen and fifty, the colony chief ordered the registration of men between the ages of sixteen and sixty. This led to a heated argument with the council member Iehoşua Ungariş, which almost came to blows, however, the old man [Rosenstrauch] won. The Labor Office, that is, David Buksbaum, has already prepared the list, and the colony chief himself will take the treasure to Shargorod tomorrow. He actually promised that he would try to persuade the praetor to lower the age limit to eighteen to thirty, but he is more inclined to propose that they actually dig up the dead and send them off to hard labor. That's how the boss of Dzhurin is …

[May 17, 1943] 3 P.M.

The head of the Central Council in Moghilev has again been replaced. Moritz Katz, a deportee from Iţcani, has been appointed to take the place of the engineer Jagendorf, and he has begun to preside as president.[51] Once again, the monthly supplement of 60 marks to my meager salary that the engineer Jagendorf granted is at risk. As if I don't have enough troubles here, I am doomed to join the circle dance in Moghilev …

People report that the new prefect in Moghilev, Login, has already demonstrated his first "noble" gesture toward our brothers, the children of Israel: he deported the remnant of Ukrainian Jews from Moghilev to some camp in the Ananiev district.[52] A year ago, 4,000 of these "non-

51 In the period of November 18, 1941–March 6, 1944, and until the liberation of Transnistria by the Soviets, four council heads served in Moghilev. Jagendorf was the head of the council for most of this period. Moritz (Moshe) Katz served as head of the fourth council in the Moghilev ghetto from April 11, 1943–March 6, 1944. It should be noted that Moritz Katz was a member of the Jewish council in Moghilev from its establishment. For more, see Yeshurun, *Hahitargenut Ha'atzmit Shel Yehudei Bukovina*, pp. 50–51.

52 One of the thirteen districts in Transnistria. The city of Ananiev, which was also the administrative center of the Odessa region in Ukraine is located in this region. The city lies on the bank of the Tylihul River. On the eve of the German invasion of the Soviet Union, around 1,800 Jews lived in Ananiev. The German army conquered Ananiev in August 1941, during Operation Barbarossa, at which time the Germans murdered about 300 Jews. In September 1941, the city passed to Romanian control, and the remaining

kosher" people were sent to Tulchin, Pechora, and other places by the Bug. Some of the deportees managed to escape at great risk from their new "homes" and to return furtively to Moghilev. Login has now found a solution for them.

It appears that both of the detained wheeler-dealers from Moghilev, Dr. Danilov and Aizic Presner,[53] have been judged by the Tiraspol tribunal. No one knows for sure.

May 18, 1943, 5 A.M.

Why do I often write [at] "5 A.M."? Is a summer day not long enough to write memoirs? This question is really inane, but not in Dzhurin, which has, *ke'naynehore*, many virtues, apart from one single deficiency: not a single home here has a toilet. The "*bishenitzes*" from Bukovina tried to rectify this shortcoming and have placed latrines in three places at the very edge of the ghetto.

So, the people are quite pleased with these latrines that were joined together with broken boards and one long beam from one end to the other, and they crowd into them "head to head" (the opposite could be said …) all day long. Well, I came up with a clever idea, like a few such wise men, and often rise at the crack of dawn to visit there when there is no need to wait in line for a long time. The wait is as waiting always is, but the trouble really begins only once inside, when one finally grabs a seat on the beam—men and women together … then voices rise from the outside, for example: "Uncle, Aunt, are you learning the whole Torah in there?" or "Excuse me, mister, should I get you a newspaper?" or "For heavens' sake, Jews, leave some for the others! …" and such wisecracks, which I

Jews, numbering approximately 300, were concentrated in a ghetto and murdered in October–November 1941.

53 Michael Danilov and Aizic (Isidor) Presner, both members of the Moghilev council, were also involved in bribing Ţugui, the deputy director of the Ministry of Finance in Transnistria. The two were tried in Tiraspol on May 11, 1943, and sent to prison in a camp for political prisoners in Vapnyarka. See Yeshurun, *Hahitargenut Ha'atzmit Shel Yehudei Bukovina*, pp. 49–50. Danilov and Presner were released from Vapnyarka following Jagendorf's intervention. See Jagendorf, *Jagendorf's Foundry*, pp. 145–147.

will not note, so that the page does not blush … I must stop now, because a messenger has just summoned me to a butcher's shop.

[May 18, 1943] 7 P.M.

Even though the lists of men who are fit for work are already in the doctor's drawer, he delayed taking them to Shargorod until tomorrow, so that in the meanwhile a committee of doctors will sort the people. The doctors examined everyone in the blink of an eye and wrote down their evaluations. It is strange that almost all the beggars and paupers are found to be completely healthy, according to the committee, while precisely the wealthy people and the playboys have come down with all kinds of illnesses and must guard against them! The rich men's diseases are subtle—mild rheumatism, stomach ulcers, gallstones, and the like—which cannot be seen and one must take their word for it. These dangerously ill people swear with all kinds of oaths and vows that they are not allowed to bend over, not to mention lift a stone, and go try not to believe them …

The colony chief himself wrote the diagnosis in red ink next to each name on the list, and the papers are locked in his drawer.

May 20, 1943, 6 A.M.

The colony chief himself took the lists of the men who are fit for work to Shargorod and has returned. Quite an intervention—they will take only men between the ages of eighteen and fifty! The old man announced the news, and we must thank and praise His Beloved Name, if this will fulfill our obligation to Sosnovka. The Germans have demanded from Prefect Login 1,500 Jews to build a bridge over the Bug, and the prefect certainly did not refuse. The Moghilev Central Council, which is in possession of lists from all the camps in the district since last year, has already compiled a list of 1,500 men, simply registering names without knowing whether these people are disabled, ill, or even still alive today. According to the account, Dzhurin will be required to provide a group of around 100 men. The lot can fall on anyone, even on the well-connected people, or the members of the inner circle.

The doctor asked the "lords" to keep quiet in order to prevent a panic, and in the course of a single hour the good news resonated throughout the entire camp!

May 21, 1943, 1 P.M.

Here they come! The "good pair" has now returned from Moghilev and has brought news, good and bad. Let me begin with the good news:[54]

It is not true that all the Ukrainian Jews from Moghilev were sent to a camp in the Ananiev district. In the meantime, only 600 people have been driven out, because the militia was not able to gather a greater number during the nighttime manhunts. Those who hid—evil tongues say that they paid a bribe … —are still in Moghilev after all.

On the other hand, it is true that Prefect Login invited all the new council members, headed by the president, Moritz Katz, to visit him and informed them that the Jewish council's obligation does not consist of hastening the death of the deportees. Therefore, he demands that the new functionaries, which he appointed, not allow people to die of hunger in Moghilev. The community must provide every hungry person with at least one meal per day. It appears that this mitigating spirit is related to the visit of the papal delegation.

The council members also brought news that I had feared: the new functionaries of the Central Council have decided to reduce unnecessary expenses and revealed that if they eliminate the 60 mark supplement to my salary, the Moghilev community coffers will truly benefit. Therefore, they indeed did away with this superfluous expense. This means that my salary, God willing, will be exactly 100 marks per month. To struggle with great shortages, perhaps 300 marks would suffice.

---

54 This refers to Moshe Katz and Leon Neuman's trip to the Moghilev ghetto regarding the delegation from Romania. See the entry of May 14, 1943.

May 26, 1943, 7 P.M.

Let me present a few local chronicles, as editors call them, and describe briefly three events that occurred in the last twenty-four hours and did not shake the foundations of the world:

Event No. 1: Yesterday afternoon the council was informed by telephone that the two Moghilev big wheeler-dealers, Dr. Danilov and Aizic Presner, who were recently taken to Tiraspol for trial, were released on Thursday, May 20. This is a big day for the Jews and the "lords" quickly organized a lavish feast together with a bunch of their cronies. The post chief, Georgescu, and another officer even did them the honor of attending. It was a real celebration for Jews and non-Jews alike that lasted until midnight. The money that they squandered could have sufficed for a week of food at the soup kitchen.

Event No. 2: That same night, as they were celebrating the "miracle" of Tiraspol, in the attic of a decrepit hovel, G. G., a young man from Rădăuţi, hanged himself. Fortunately, the neighbors saw what was happening in time and cut the cord a moment before it was too late. He did not commit the act because of unrequited love, or a Hamlet-like complex, but because his wife had pestered him for a few days to buy a flask of milk for a sick baby at the market for half a mark. However, the trouble is that G. had long since forgotten what half a mark looks like, not to mention 1 mark. G. thought that the rope would release him from all his sorrows, but this is not the case when one is unlucky …

Event No. 3: That night, while the celebration was in full swing in the community building and while G. forgot that he is unlucky, a bunch of thieves could no longer bear the anguish of the packed shelves in the storeroom where clothes, shoes, and items sent from Romania for the needy in the camp have been gathering mold for a number of months. So the thieves lightened the load of the shelves, out of pity, and took forty coats (there were simply no more than that …), fifty sweaters, a pile of underwear, along with other items. The loss is worth at least 30,000 marks. Strange: the storeroom is located on the main street, directly opposite the militia.

Today the militia is on a rampage and is searching in vain. It is all lost. Dzhurin's gossipmongers are spreading a vulgar lie that the entire matter concerning the theft is nothing more than somewhat of a pretense. They [the thieves] will certainly receive the verdict that they deserve, because there are lies and then there are lies …

Certainly, it would have been futile for the thieves to take pity on the shelves had the gifts from Bucharest been distributed in a timely manner rather than playing with the rags and clasping them like valuable jewels.

May 27, 1943, 3 P.M.

Some time ago, the community received a sum of 5,000 marks for Zionists from an underground Zionist organization in Romania. In the meantime, the matter remains cloaked in utmost secrecy. No one has seen a whit of a single mark.

May 31, 1943, 5 P.M.

The Zionist money has finally been dealt with properly. Around eighty people have been lucky enough to receive a contribution, ranging from 45–150 marks, and all are complaining. Those who received nothing obviously are making an even greater commotion. Dzhurin today has more Zionists than Jews, and all have been fervent supporters of Dr. Herzl, already from the cradle, and the right hand of the Bukovina Zionist leader Dr. Meir Ebner.[55]

They did me a favor with 70 marks in spite of my defect: my Zionist and Hebraist past ever since my childhood. I am surprised that I found favor with the Dzhurin-style neo-Zionists. What, 45 marks will not be enough for the assimilationist that I have always been! …

---

55 Dr. Meir Ebner was born on September 19, 1872, in Cernăuţi, the capital of Bukovina. A jurist by training, Ebner engaged in journalism and politics. Among the leaders of the Zionist movement in Bukovina and in Romania, he served three times as a member of the Romanian parliament. He immigrated to Mandatory Palestine in 1940. See David Tidhar, ed., *Entziklopedia Lehalutzei Hayishuv Uvonav*: *Demuyot Utemunot*, vol. 4, s.v. "Dr. Meir Ebner" (Hebrew) (Tel Aviv: Sifriat Rishonim, 1952), p. 1648.

June 2, 1943, 2 P.M.

My eyes are closing and I would like to shut them for a moment on my wooden bunk, because I came home from work last night at 2 A.M., after a hot, gloomy day that continued today until around lunchtime. I will strike the iron while it is hot and will record a summary of this drama, which reminded everyone where we are living.

The trouble began yesterday at 9 A.M., when the post chief informed the council that the camp must provide 130 workers within twelve hours, which we are required to send to build a bridge over the Bug. Let me note that the council members Moshe Katz and Leon Neuman received information about this matter while they were in Moghilev recently. They even managed to take a look at the list that the Moghilev Central Council had drawn up for Dzhurin on the basis of an old list from a year ago. The providers [functionaries] in Moghilev, who do not know anyone in Dzhurin, wrote down names as in a lottery any which way just to fill the lines: the deceased; women whose names they exchanged for men's names, Chone replaced Chana, Perel became Berl, Zisel became Zisiya, and so on; the frail; the ill; and mainly a group of members of the inner circle and the well-connected people, as well as a few community functionaries. Upon seeing this mess, their eyes darkened—so the delegates now report—and they persuaded the great overlord himself, Major Botoroagă, that the Labor Office in Dzhurin will provide the list when the time comes.

The truth is that the Labor Office prepared such a list in utmost secrecy and sent it to Moghilev, and the matter appeared to be resolved. When the gendarmes yesterday demanded the 130 men, the council had no doubt that this meant the persons chosen by the Labor Office.[56] Therefore, Jewish militia went through the streets and alleys with papers in hand to gather the people on the list. Some of them got wind of this in time and understood that this meant them, and they fled to the fields or to neighboring villages.

56 The lists prepared by the council members appointed by the Labor Office in Dzhurin were sent to the Moghilev ghetto for approval. The inhabitants of the ghettos were left in a state of complete uncertainty regarding the names on these lists.

The militia was able to catch only fifty-six men by 3 P.M. By order of the colony chief, the militia arrested the wives of the fugitives as a guarantee. Cries and wails were heard all around the community building throughout the day—the militia guarded the entrance to the holy of holies.

Suddenly, at about 4 P.M., the Moghilev legion telephoned the commander of the local station and ordered them to bring the 130 men registered by the [Moghilev] Central Council, according to a copy of the list found in the gendarmerie headquarters in Dzhurin. And they added that Governor General Alexianu ordered the shooting of anyone who tried to dodge working. This news struck the community building like lightening. How can the deceased, women with men's names, the blind and the lame—not to mention the members of the inner circle—be summoned!

However, there was no alternative, so the militia was dispatched to conduct a manhunt once again, while two gendarmes with loaded rifles settled into the community building to supervise the *Aktzia*. However, the militia was unable to hunt down the people in hiding and returned empty-handed.

Around 8 P.M., the post chief, Georgescu, burst into the community building and announced, actually in a quiet voice, that ten of the detained wives would soon be shot and then those in hiding would come out of their mouseholes. My poor pen will tire of describing the panic that this fearful announcement caused. The "lords" fell at the feet of the murderer until they succeeded in persuading him to delay the terrible slaughter. Yet they did not manage to persuade him that he should settle for other people instead of members of the inner circle and community functionaries. Haman agreed to concede only regarding women with men's names. It was really a miracle that my name did not appear on the Moghilev list.

The militia brought the sick with fever on stretchers, [and] dragged the disabled and tuberculosis patients, and arranged them in the "march convoy." Council members themselves were running around the hovels until 2 A.M. to warn people that if they hide they would endanger the lives of everyone and Jewish blood would flow. It was a *Leyl Shimurim* in Dzhurin, permeated with wails and cries reaching up to the heavens. The gendarmes shot into the air from time to time to frighten the crowd.

I did not consider going home, because the safest place was nevertheless the community building, even though it was swarming with gendarmes.

Finally, at around 3 A.M., the quota was filled, apart from a few people in hiding. A convoy was arranged in marching formation—what a company it was. As though out of spite, rain poured down, and you could literally touch the darkness with your hands. Among those caught, it was possible to see by the light of the lanterns many human skeletons who were barely able to stand on their feet, disabled and hunched over, having just been released from the hospital after being severely ill with typhus, collapsing from disease, many barefoot and dressed in rags. Fathers were torn from motherless orphans, men from paralyzed wives. There were frenzied scenes of separation, horrifying images from a hellish nightmare. The council distributed bread and a few marks to each man [to be deported], and the company left the square, escorted by gendarmes.

This morning the militia caught a few *lamedvovnikim* who had hidden during the manhunt yesterday. They were sent to the gendarmerie post escorted by guards. They were not welcomed there with honey cake and brandy. The post chief is threatening to send these creatures to Tiraspol to be tried for sabotage. If he carries out his threat, this means the death sentence, according to Order No. 23. Advocates rushed at once to the post chief, and not empty-handed, to prevent the disaster.

Who can judge whether the council had the right to deliver those who were hiding into the hands of our sworn enemies? The "lords" justify this, saying that the lives of who knows how many persons were hanging by a thread because of these fugitives, and they handed them over to the gendarmes not as punishment but rather as a warning for the future. The problem is as old as mankind itself, and already in the Bible an analogous incident occurs in connection with the scoundrels from Sodom who demand that Lot hand over his foreign guests. The Bible deals with this and solves the problem using angels, who strike the evil Sodomites with blindness.[57] In Dzhurin, no angels appeared, apart from angels of destruction. There is a wise saying: "Do not judge your neighbor until you have stood in his place." According to Rashi, whoever has not been

57 This is a reference to the story of Lot in Gen. 19.

at death's door in the hell of Transnistria should not pass judgement on this question …[58]

[June 2, 1943] 8 P.M.

The remaining men who had hidden yesterday voluntarily turned themselves over to the militia this afternoon. They were taken to the gendarmerie post and the post chief, Georgescu, showed some consideration (may his throat be struck with as many plagues as the numerous hundreds that this consideration cost! …) and reconsidered his dangerous intentions. In order to reach the number of 130, he will send them to Moghilev as latecomers who were delayed for important reasons. The panic has subsided, and whoever fell into their hands in the manhunt got a really bad deal.

June 6, 1943, 6 A.M.

Yesterday sixteen of the 130 men who were dispatched to Moghilev in dramatic circumstances on June 1 returned to Dzhurin. The majority of the liberated are severely disabled and hunched over, but there are also a few healthy people who found favor with a *Feldwebel* who declared the "goods" unfit. No doctor examined anyone, and quite a few living skeletons remained in the group of captives.

All those whom the *Feldwebel* declared fit for work were sent to a German labor camp on the other side of the Bug, to Trikhaty,[59] in the Ochakov region, not far from Odessa—where they are building a bridge over the Bug. The Germans have promised that they will detain the people for only thirty days and then exchange them for a second set. The German officers came to take the people to Organization Todt, which

58 Kunstadt ironically comments on the reality in Transnistria by referring to Rashi's commentary on Genesis 19.

59 The camp of Trikhaty, which was under German control, was located on the eastern side of the Bug River. The workers constructed a bridge over the Bug, and workers who had no strength left were often shot dead. Few returned from this camp.

only engages in building roads and bridges. They reassured them that the SS has no authority over them whatsoever and that they will not harm a hair on anyone's head as long as they work diligently.

The fortunate ones who were released informed us that there is a terrible panic in Moghilev. They shudder in fear of their own shadows and are jealous of the Dzhurin paradise ...

[June 6, 1943] 8 P.M.

Distinguished guests arrived a few days ago from Moghilev, escorted by two armed soldiers: Dr. Wilhelm Filderman and his wife from Bucharest.[60] The new resident of Transnistria is not just anyone but rather the president of the federation of the Jewish communities in Romania who, until the war, was the leader of the Jews in the Regat for a quarter of a century. The organization that he led with wisdom and authority was the Uniunea Evreilor Romani (UER), which constituted the center of Jewish public life in Romania for generations, until the end of World War I. At this time Romania inherited the new provinces of Bukovina and Transylvania from the fallen Austria, as well as Russian Bessarabia. The Jews from these provinces, who had a much higher social and cultural standing than the mostly backward Jews in the Regat, where they had no rights, had established national organizations, most of them Zionist. A sharp and bitter conflict arose there between the assimilationists of the UER,[61] led by Dr. Wilhelm Filderman, and the national organizations, led

60 On May 22, 1943, Dr. Filderman learned that the ruler of Romania, Ion Antonescu, intended to deport him to Transnistria. However, Antonescu changed his mind and decided to send him to the labor camp at Târgu Jiu in southeast Romania. This camp, which was for both political prisoners and Jews, was known for its terrible conditions. The pretext for Filderman's arrest was a letter that he had written criticizing the antisemitic policy of Antonescu's regime. In order to avoid deportation, Filderman fled and hid under the guise of poor health. Filderman eventually was arrested on June 1, 1943, and was deported to the Moghilev ghetto in Transnistria. See Jean Ancel, ed., *Filderman Wilhelm*: *Memoirs and Diaries,* 1950–1952, vol. 2 (Jerusalem and Tel Aviv: Yad Vashem and Goldstein-Goren, 2011), pp. 438–450

61 The Uniunea Evreilor Romani (Union of Romanian Jews), UER, was the oldest and most renown Jewish political organization in Romania until its dissolution in 1938. The association called for the emancipation of Jews and the participation of all Romanian

by Dr. Meir Ebner (Bukovina), Rabbi Iehuda Leib Tsirelson (Bessarabia),[62] and Dr. [Yosef] Fisher (Transylvania).[63] The "UER" had strong ties with the Romanian ruling party, the "liberals" (really common reactionaries and inveterate Jew-haters), led by the Brătianu brothers, and vigorously supported the liberal candidates in different types of elections. The Romanian overlords generously rewarded the sycophants with favors.

Dr. Filderman himself demonstrated remarkable organizational talent, courage, and a warm Jewish heart, but he was zealously opposed to the Jewish renaissance movement and held firmly to his assimilationist theory. Thanks to his colossal influence in the Regat, he persuaded the masses that they should not leave the country and not let themselves be deluded by the Zionist dreams. When the roof was already burning over their heads, it was too late …

His close relationship with the authorities were disrupted when World War II broke out, but he nevertheless secretly maintained good relations with the high-level officials and sought to alleviate first and foremost the plight of "his people," the Jews of the Regat. It is widely believed that as a result of his intervention with the dictator Marshal Antonescu, with whom he has been friendly for many years, the Jews of the Regat were spared deportation in autumn 1941, while the Jews of Bukovina and Bessarabia paid the price.

People say that the German ambassador in Bucharest, Baron Killinger, ordered Marshal Antonescu to deport the Jewish activist Dr. Filderman to Transnistria as soon as possible. Since his life was in danger, Dr. Filderman did not try to rescind the decree. There is another rumor: Marshal Antonescu punished Dr. Filderman, because he was not

---

Jews in the political life of the country, and refused to cooperate with the organizations that sought to establish a national Jewish party. See Shachan, *Bakefor Halohet*, pp. 13–14.

62 Rabbi Iehuda Leib Tsirelson (December 24, 1859–July 6, 1941) served as the chief rabbi of Bessarabia and the city of Kishinev. Rabbi Tsirelson was also a member of the Council of Torah Sages of Agudath Yisrael and a member of the Romanian parliament in the years 1920–1926. See Mordechai Slipoi, *Hagaon Rabi Yehuda Leib Tzirlton: Hayav Ufe'ulotav* (Hebrew) (Tel Aviv: Netzah, 1948).

63 Dr. József Fisher was a member of the Romanian parliament and chair of the Zionist movement in Transylvania.

able to arrange the ransom of the [Romanian] Jews in Transnistria for an immense fortune that the American Jews were supposed to pay.[64]

The prefect Login received Dr. Filderman as an important guest and provided him with a comfortable home outside the ghetto. No one is allowed to approach him, and a Ukrainian militia stands guard outside his apartment. Dr. Filderman will have plenty of time in Moghilev to ponder his harsh error of many years ago in retrospect.

June 8, 1943, 4 P.M.

A series of deportations to the Vapnyarka camp is underway, but the victims are not a bunch of beggars, as usual. The Prefect Login has set his sights on the community wheeler-dealers, the real cream of the crop, and is sending them away as payment for their good deeds. In the meantime, the previous president of the Central Council, Dr. Danilov, and his secretary Dr. Yonah Kessler, have been sent there. The sword of Vapnyarka also hangs over Aizic Presner and [Poldi] Knobler, and people are moving heaven and earth to ensure that they will be spared. It is believed that they will extricate themselves from the decree.

For the time being, no one is laying a finger on the former president of the Central Council and "uncrowned king of Moghilev," the engineer Sami Jagendorf, and he continues to run the large foundry, where thousands of deported Jews work. In truth, no one for now pins any dishonest acts on him, and they only complain that he runs it like a dictator with an iron fist. He argues that he would otherwise not be able to maintain discipline, and the foundry would close. The existence of the large Jewish community in Moghilev depends on this foundry.[65]

---

64 This refers to the Transnistria Plan, which was never implemented, because of the opposition of the Germans. On the Transnistria Plan, see Wagman-Eskholi, "Tohnit Transnistriya," pp. 155–171; Dalia Ofer, *Escaping from the Holocaust,* pp. 187–188.

65 Regarding this claim and other testimonies concerning the foundry, see Yitzhak Yalon testimony, YVA, O.3/1238.

June 11, 1943, 7 P.M.

Yesterday twelve more of the 130 men who were sent to work in Trikhaty returned. These fortunate ones, young and healthy each and every one of them, and none of whom are counted among the group of "sack people," were declared unfit in the camp of Trikhaty itself and sent back to Dzhurin—they report—because … they are not suitable. The rest, mostly ailing, destitute beggars are left to do harsh labor, because they are indeed suitable …

June 13, 1943, 7 A.M.

Someone did the twelve unsuitable young people a fitting favor. The gendarmes unexpectedly burst into their homes and took them to the post chief. The post chief informed the dozen "unfit" ones that he had just received a telephone call from Moghilev instructing him to send the freed men to Tulchin without delay, because they need more hands to dig peat there. In less than an hour, the twelve "fortunate ones" were crowded together on a truck bound for Tulchin, escorted by armed guards. People whisper that one of the big shots in Shargorod—not, God forbid, a Japanese … —did this good deed to take revenge on one of his enemies. I am not writing down any names, because I cannot believe that such a terrible suspicion could indeed be true …

[June 13, 1943] 3 P.M.

Digging peat in Tulchin means standing for twelve hours a day in knee-deep water and doing hard labor under the supervision of the Ukrainian militia, who spur the workers on with whips. A half loaf of barley bread and a portion of thin potato soup twice a day provides them with the strength to perform this hard labor. The laborers roll around in stables at night on rancid hay that is swarming with lice.

Approximately 300 people were sent from Moghilev to Tulchin a few days ago—entire families, including young children, and the elderly. It is very likely that all the "colonies" in the Moghilev district will have to provide slaves for Tulchin, and the "model colony" of Dzhurin will in all likelihood also have to join the circle. The peat-*Aktzia* is a bottomless pit, because there is a vast amount of peat, and also great loss: people fall like flies there, and the holes must be filled with fresh "merchandise" …

June 17, 1943, 8 P.M.

If only in the last entry I had prophesied the coming of the messiah rather than that Dzhurin would receive the honor of joining the peat *hakofe* in Tulchin! The great *hakofe* already took place today! To be honest, in the meantime, they needed only 100 men, but the problem is that the peat spreads its stench here and in all the camps. Even though the Labor Office kept the order absolutely secret, many people smelled the fumes and fled. Those to whom Elijah the prophet did not appear in time and did not reveal the secret to them fell into the trap, as always …

Once again there were shocking images of a manhunt, of cries and wails, of women throwing themselves at the feet of those in power and fainting, of whispering and pleading, and finally the company set out for the gendarmerie just before sunset, each man with a loaf of barley bread under his arm and 5 marks in his pocket, which had been distributed to them.

June 22, 1943, 7 A.M.

Two entire years to the day have passed since the war with Russia began. The madness and savagery rages, the fire burns furiously in every corner of God's beautiful world, and there is still no sign of the end of the war. When will deliverance come and to whom? …

July 12, 1943, 8 P.M.

I have had no desire to take up the pen for about three weeks. No "great" events have occurred, and I have already written in these pages from time to time about the "minor" dramas of the bleak, daily routine of Dzhurin and about those of the other camps in the Moghilev district. People are starving, people are wallowing in the mass housing quarters, people are dying in the poorhouse of the great synagogue, and people are living in luxury and sitting around at night playing poker—these are no longer sensational enough to deserve being recorded for posterity.

So I need an extraordinary shot of sensation in order to pull myself out of my lethargy and nevertheless impel myself to [resume] this notebook of memories. And we just got such a shot of vigor—an event that took place here and stirred up everyone. A trivial matter: they dethroned the princes of the Jewish regime, the holy council? For the time being, they still rule, but with great apprehension, until the lords in Moghilev appoint their successors.

The struggle for leadership nevertheless reached its peak unexpectedly. The affair of the dentist Leon Hirschorn, who was sent with his household to the Krasnoye camp as punishment for opposing the powers of the Jewish regime (I have already written about this)[66] was the last straw that broke the camel's back and led to the "catastrophe." Hirschorn, a sharp Jew who does not let himself be pushed around, did not accept the harsh sentence and began to move heaven and earth. He went as far as the commander of the gendarmerie legion in Moghilev, Major Botoroagă, and related strange details regarding the behavior of the "lords" in the model colony of Dzhurin. The major, who meddled in the affairs of the big shots in Moghilev, as I previously wrote, sent his trusted servant, council member Sami Rachmut of the new [Moghilev] Central Council, to Dzhurin to investigate what is going on. The major will issue a verdict on the basis of Rachmut's report.

The investigator appeared in Dzhurin on Wednesday, July 7, and the purpose of his visit was an open secret. The underground opposition mustered courage and surfaced. People jostled to testify around the

---

66 See the entry of May 6, 1943, 1 P.M.

apartment in which Rachmut was dwelling and poured out sacks of complaints before the special envoy regarding the council and the Labor Office. The "lords" too did not sit idly by and managed to persuade the investigator (well, the lies that slanderers will tell!) that he should not come down too hard on them but only suggest to the major that he replace the council. The leaders in Moghilev who were punished paid a heavy price: the Vapnyarka labor camp …

This morning Rachmut returned to Moghilev with his briefcase stuffed with protocols, testimonies, accounts, and other papers. One of the papers contains a list of the "new" rulers, who must rise to greatness with the major's consent, but this is really a true secret. The opposition is now freely raining tar and sulfur on the "lord," who have lost favor, and is making plans regarding which of the functionaries and militiamen should be dismissed and who will take their places.

As for my meager income, the leaders of the opposition secretly assured me that they will not touch me, because I am not on the "blacklist." Toward the end, on July 5, the council raised my salary to 200 marks, probably because they sense that their end is near.

The community building is in chaos, and everything appears to be a reflection in a distorted mirror. The "elders" are stunned and are doing the poor many favors, treating them like an expensive jewel, [which is] like putting a bandage on a wound. No more contempt, no more slaps in the face! If only this will last …[67]

Although life is not a bowl of cherries under my bosses, in particular the colony chief, who hounds me unmercifully, I do not pray for a new king. By the way, what good do prayers do already …

---

67 At this stage, in July 1943, life in the Dzhurin ghetto had settled down, and there were those among the Jews, mainly the wealthy, who opposed the council and voiced their criticism of it, while the heads of the ghetto tried with all their might to hold onto their power and their ability to determine how the ghetto would be run. As the internal tensions between the various groups in the ghetto intensified, the opponents approached the Romanian authorities to request assistance to overthrow the council. The Romanian authorities presumably did not wish to "upset" the existing order in the ghetto and therefore did not collaborate. To maintain order, the opposition leader Leon Hirschorn was sent to the Vapnyarka work camp.

July 18, 1943, 9 P.M.

The camp has been in chaos for more than a week, and wherever you go you hear the same refrain: the fall of those in power. The Jews have racked their brains to figure out who would be the "new" leaders and whether this would be good for the Jews. The presumed "new ones" are rushing to distribute honors, threatening to dismiss people from their posts, and not making any promises to "their people."

The elders have already recited the *Videh* and even bid farewell to the crowd at a gathering, during which Moshe Katz delivered a sad sermon that could have melted a heart of stone. People responded with subdued applause in order not to lose favor with the successors.

And then on Friday, July 16, the curtain fell, not on a drama but rather on a tragicomedy. The old council will continue to rule! On that Sabbath eve, the president of the Central Council, Moritz Katz, who is Major Botoroagă's right-hand man, unexpectedly appeared in Dzhurin, followed by his groveling subordinates to investigate again whether there is anything to the accusations against the council. No one knows why the major had to send someone to investigate for a second time—apart from the "lords" ... the elders were able to prove to the great man from the [Moghilev] Central Council that they, poor things, are innocent. The truth is that, particularly with regard to financial matters, the council members are not considered thieves, as happens in other camps in the Moghilev district. The cooperative in the camp has goods worth around 100,000 marks, and all the institutions are running properly today, according to Transnistrian supervision [standards], in any case better than in Moghilev and in Shargorod. The transgressions relate more to criminal matters, mainly in the context of the grievous labor.

President Moritz Katz sent for the leaders of the opposition and discussed their claims with them for a few hours. In the end, he reached the decision that it is better for matters to remain as they stand. There was only one single victim: the director of the Labor Office, David Buksbaum; the president did not, God forbid, dismiss him from his position but punished him with a bit of a vacation, until he repents ...

The camp has resumed dealing with its usual concerns. I myself am not happy about the victory of the "elders" and I also am not suffering from it either. A patient is in pain regardless of which side he lies on …

July 19, 1943, 7 P.M.

Bad news arrived from Tulchin regarding the situation of the people in the camp who had been sent to the peat pits. Hunger, filth, and the cruel blows at the hands of the Ukrainians is driving people to risk their lives and to flee every day. For the most part, the fugitives do not get far, because the Ukrainian militia guard the camp on all sides and shoot without mercy those who flee. People are whispering in the camp that soon they will once again demand people for Tulchin, and whoever is able no longer sleeps at home. The local council has turned to the [Moghilev] Central Council with a request that they not demand from Dzhurin any more workers for Tulchin.

July 22, 1943, 7 A.M.

Today is my birthday. My forty-second year has terminated. There is nothing to miss.

July 27, 1943, 7 A.M.

This year the summer is rainy and sad, unlike last summer. People wallow in deep, thick mud, as though it were autumn. Because of the rain, they cannot begin reaping the harvest. The farmers claim that if it will not clear up soon, the crops will rot.

[July 27, 1943] 8 P.M.

The community building has the feeling of *bein hazmanim*.[68] The "lords," apart from the colony chief and Leon Neuman, are staying away and not showing up. They are having a fit about the brazen ones who took their place. The lethargic condition has neutralized every community initiative, even though they should have and could have done a lot for the general good. The colony chief himself granted additional bread (250 grams) for 105 needy persons who rely on the soup kitchen—all of them elderly and orphans. Yet more than 300 people in this category remain deprived. They are breaking down the doors of the community building, requesting that they too be a granted a little bread. The doctor honored me with the *maftir*: taking care of these complainants, that means comforting them with false promises for the future. I choke on every lie.

People are saying that the former Moghilev council member Aizic Presner was nevertheless sent to the Vapnyarka camp.[69] I cannot guarantee that this information is true.

July 28, 1943, 3 P.M.

Today is Bertl's twelfth birthday. He will soon be a *Bar Mitzve*, if deliverance hastens to arrive. I received a gift today, apparently for this celebration: my friend Avraham Friedman from Bucharest sent me 5,000 lei. He just became aware of where I am and promised me that he would continue to help me. I am in desperate need of help.

These are fateful days on the fronts and our fate lies in the balance. The camp is in turmoil and seething, the imagination is working at full force, and people are restless. The people cry out for deliverance but are gripped by mortal fear. History will proceed and the Dzhurin camp has no say in the matter …

---

68 The term refers to the vacation periods of yeshiva students during the weeklong festivals and from Tisha B'Av until the beginning of the month of Elul.

69 Indeed, Aizic Presner was sent to the Vapnyarka work camp.

We have learned from Moghilev that the Jewish leader from Romania, Dr. Wilhelm Filderman, has been released from his Transnistrian exile and sent home. Jewish minds interpret this positively: the government apparently intends to send all the deportees home and, therefore, needs Dr. Filderman to prepare for their return. Go dally with Jewish faith! …

July 29, 1943, 7 P.M.

Blank spaces of censors now cover the front page of the Romanian newspapers on which the news from the fronts and the military commentary are printed. From what the censor allows—there is no point in a newspaper without words—one gets a sense of what is happening on the Eastern Front. The "Reds" are chasing the Germans as one hunts down mad dogs, and the journalists have coined a new expression for this: "defensive-offensive." If this expression continues a little longer, the front will come close to Transnistria. Who knows what this means!

People are running around the camp in confusion, pricking up their ears to catch a bit of news, even if only from the "IPA" mill, and "Let me die with the Philistines"[70] can be heard from all sides. There is no lack of prophets. Some believe that precisely because of the events on the front we will soon be sent home and not left abandoned, while others draw the opposite conclusion from the same information. Who knows who will be the prophet of truth! …

The harvest has been delayed by an entire month because of the rain. Today is the first sunny day after a deluge of four weeks. The yield is extraordinary, and the peasants do not recall such abundance. And yet the price of food has not come down at all.

August 2, 1943, *Roysh Hoydesh Av*

Another soup kitchen was opened today for the deportees from Cernăuţi, Vijniţa, and Vatra Dornei. Fellow townsmen who are residing in Bucharest

70 Judges 16:30.

have pledged to send 100,000 marks every month for this institution. The council actually tried to thwart this unwelcome rival (what, others have also mastered this trick? …) but were unsuccessful. Everyone receives tasty soup and half a loaf of bread in the new soup kitchen. The new soup kitchen is run by its own committee and, of course, the wheeler-dealers who have had a firm grip on the public good for three and a half years do not like this.[71]

Last night I had a strange dream. I saw Dr. Herzl before my eyes, I greeted him and kissed his hand. He shook his head in surprise and said: The Jews do not kiss a person's hand when they greet each other. I woke up with heart palpitations and could not close my eyes again. Do you have to be Dr. Sigmund Freud to interpret this dream and get to the bottom of its source? …

News is pouring in from the fronts, truly earthshaking. The situation of stalemate has clearly passed, and the film rushes ahead at full speed. Oh, if only we were onlookers somewhere across the sea, or at least on the other side of the Dniester, and not actors in the gigantic drama that is coming closer and closer all the time! …

August 10, 1943, *Tisha B'Av*, 3 P.M.

Moghilev demanded a list of 135 able-bodied men—the announcement of a wedding to take place soon in Dzhurin. Most of the people in the camp sleep in the fields at night out of fear. The people dread the peat in Tulchin more than the bridge that the Germans are building in Trikhaty.

August 17, 1943, 2 P.M.

Deliverance is crawling along slowly and who knows when it will reach these regions. The Romanian occupying authorities suddenly ceded the

71 The establishment of new soup kitchens for the deportees from Cernăuţi, Vatra Dornei, and Vijniţa affected the class hierarchy within the ghetto and the preferential treatment given to the deportees from Southern Bukovina, because of their financial means and their proximity to the center of power in the ghetto.

new crop. From the day that the seeds began to ripen, armed guards had watched the fields like a jewel, so that the peasants would not, God forbid, steal a handful of the produce, because everything belongs to the nation, apart from a tiny portion for the meager subsistence of the peasants. Just now, when the harvest is at its peak, the guards suddenly disappeared and left it to the trusteeship of the Ukrainians. They, the cunning peasants understand the matter and they know what to do. Well, the price of flour indeed fell by half (1 pood of wheat flour costs 40 marks, and 1 pood of barley flour costs 20 marks), and it seems that there will be even greater bargains later.

There is a strange sense of turmoil at the gendarmerie post; the armed guards are afraid of their own shadows and do not dare set foot outside the barracks at night. The partisans in the fields have begun to operate. People whisper about all kinds of miracles and wonders regarding their activities, and certainly some of these are not tall tales.

[August 17, 1943] 9 P.M.

We found out that more than thirty forced laborers had fled from the peat-pits in Tulchin, and apparently the gendarmes or the Ukrainian militia killed all of them. There were four persons from Dzhurin among the victims. One of them was a young student from Siret, Izidor Kamil, a talented poet and author who worked for the local underground newspaper *Curierul*.[72] By the way, I will write specifically about this newspaper at some point.

---

72 *Curierul* (Messenger) was an underground newspaper published in the Dzhurin ghetto. In the months of April–September 1943, it appeared every week. The newspaper was made up of three handwritten pages containing articles written by Albert Hart, Dov Katz, Şimşon Şapira, and Carl Rosenblatt, medical students from Bukovina whose studies were interrupted by the deportation. The main problem they faced was how to obtain paper, a rare commodity in the ghetto. Kunstadt, the author of this diary, came to their aid. Members of the editorial staff, including Carl Rosenblatt, copied by hand the first six copies of the manuscript in the isolation ward of the hospital, which the police did not dare enter for fear of infection. In order to avoid identification, the authors signed the articles with their initials. Kunstadt himself also contributed articles for the paper, signing them with his pen name "the wanderer." The paper included articles and reports concerning the lives of the Jews in the ghetto and frequently criticized those "at the

As a result of a disagreement with the "second-in-command," Moshe Katz, the council member Ungariş resigned. The council members Eltes and Valdman have also not been seen in the community building for weeks. The Jewish administration is run by the colony chief with the "good pair"—Moshe Katz and Leon Neuman—at his side. The colony chief and Katz traveled to Moghilev yesterday, leaving Neuman solely in charge. Just so nothing will happen when the boss is away! ... The small council has completely fallen from grace. There are no initiatives whatsoever, they do not demand any special fees from the rich. It seems like the end is near ...

August 19, 1943, 8 P.M.

Here is some reliable news from near and far:

— It is now certain that the four people from the camp of Dzhurin who recently fled from digging peat at Tulchin were indeed shot, along with other fugitives.

— Yesterday thirteen people returned legally to Dzhurin from Tulchin. They were released by a doctor. As for their appearance, the dead look

---

helm," meaning the Jewish leaders, and their conduct. The caricatures in the paper were drawn by Eliezer Hager, the son of Rabbi Baruch Hager, who was blessed with artistic talent. On June 26, 1943, a six-page celebratory issue was published, dedicated to Dr. Filderman, the head of the Jewish communities in Romania, who arrived in Moghilev on June 1, 1943. Following the great success of the first edition, which was passed from hand to hand in the ghetto, many texts that expressed the plight of the deportees were submitted for following editions. When the head of the council, Max Rosenstrauch, discovered the existence of the paper, he summoned Carl Rosenblatt to his office and demanded that he discontinue the publication of the paper at once. At this point, the publication had already moved from the isolation ward of the hospital to an attic in the ghetto. At the end of September 1943, the publication of the newspaper ceased after a copy fell into the hands of Floreanu, the commander of the gendarmerie in Dzhurin. Only a substantial bribe quelled his anger and prevented a disaster from striking the inhabitants of the ghetto. Moshe Katz was one of the staunchest opponents of the paper. His daughter, Yehudit Nir, commented on this matter in an interview that Sara Rosen conducted with her: "My father completely forbade any such activity. In this regard, he was extremely afraid of the Romanian authorities, because he feared that it could harm the entire population of Dzhurin, and the Jews...would be harmed." See Rosen, "Tzibur veyahid," pp. 220–224.

better. They also brought news about the slaughter of the fugitives, in addition to other reports that make your hair stand on end.

— Sunday, August 15, in Shargorod the young and only son of the local colony chief, Dr. Meir Teich, died from renal tuberculosis. His mother could not bear the calamity and poisoned herself that same day. Both victims were buried in a common grave. This is another link in the chain of Transnistrian tragedies.

— And here is a tragedy of a different kind in Dzhurin itself: A young woman, twenty-nine years of age, wanted to hide the shame of bringing a "non-kosher" child into the world, and a doctor took pity on her for 50 marks. The result: a fresh grave in the cemetery …

— Last week sanitary inspections really rained down on the camp. Romanian doctors from Moghilev visited the mass housing quarters, inspected the three community latrines, the hospital, and even the pump. While they were at it, they instituted all sorts of regulations to improve the health conditions of the Yids. May it only be for the better! …[73]

— This year we eradicated typhus quickly, already in the spring, but its little brother—typhoid fever—has spread its arms wide. Once again, all the beds in the hospital are full and many patients from the wealthy class are hiding in their homes with the protection of doctors. The illness progresses mercifully, so to speak, and only exhausts the patients over the course of a few weeks, until they are left without any strength. Some of the patients are blessed with infirmity for the rest of their lives—heart, kidneys, and so on. Nevertheless, some fresh graves in the cemetery show that the "good-hearted" typhoid fever is not completely estranged from the Angel of Death …

73 The Romanian doctors feared another outbreak of typhus, as had occurred in the winter of 1941–1942. They were concerned that the plague would spread beyond the borders of the ghettos.

August 20, 1943, 3 P.M.

The gates of the ghetto have been flung wide open unexpectedly. The post chief informed us that because typhus spreads mainly because of overcrowding in the mass housing quarters, he has agreed to allow the Jews to live also on the other side of the bridge in the factory quarter. It seems that this benevolence is not his own idea, but rather he received an intimation from "above." Jewish minds are sparing no interpretations, each one more rose-colored than the other ...

August 27, 1943, 5 A.M.

Rumor has it that the high-level officials are really considering putting an end to the exile in Transnistria. The good tidings have come from Moghilev, Shargorod, and, by implication, also from Bucharest.

August 29, 1943, 5 A.M.

Activity has resumed in the community building. The indignant functionaries have returned to their seats and once again show signs of energy. Regardless of the golden dreams of returning home, they have begun to install themselves and to establish new institutions. They will set up a public bathhouse next week—although quite primitive and rather small—but nevertheless a significant step in the battle against plagues. They are planning to force all the persons suffering from self-neglect to use the bath at least once every week.

It seems that the project of establishing an orphanage is almost complete. For more than a year now, the "lords" have been discussing this matter, but only talking. The main obstacle was: the question of finding a suitable building for this institution, when there is no place in the ghetto, not even to insert a pin. Since the post chief has allowed us to settle in the Ukrainian part of Dzhurin—in the factory quarter—many wealthy persons in the camp who have the means began to move there and [there is more space] on the mountain. Therefore, the council cleared out the large Ukrainian school on the top of the mountain and gave the people other apartments in order to make room for the orphanage.

People are preparing beds, tables and chairs, straw mattresses, and the like, and if no unexpected obstacles arise, or unless deliverance comes, the orphanage will open in September or October. The institution will be run by the lawyer from Rădăuţi Bigo Hart,[74] a young man and a true idealist, who is not enjoying any hot springs in Dzhurin. He earns a livelihood for himself and for his household through "trading in wood": he sneaks into the forest every morning, collects branches, drags them a distance of 4 kilometers to his home, chops them himself, and is thus a merchant among the all others … this trade suffices for a potato and a loaf of bread. Now the Dzhurin wood magnates will lose a rival.

September 1, 1943, 5 A.M.

Four years ago, Hitler, may his name be blotted out, set the world on fire, and the fire rages even more savagely than it did in the beginning. But let us talk about happier things.

Typhoid fever has made itself at home in Dzhurin. All the beds in the hospital are full, and they are laying new patients on the floor. Injections have been sent from Moghilev, which ostensibly prevent the disease before the bacteria sneaks into the body. Many *Lagernikes* have received the injections—no one is forced—but nevertheless people have fallen ill after taking precautions, perhaps because the serum was produced from dead bacteria. My family and I rely on Divine Providence …

---

74 Dov Bernard (Bigo) Hart, born in Jacobeni, Southern Bukovina, was a lawyer from Rădăuți who began practicing law before World War II. In the summer of 1940, the facist-Nazi regime forbade Jewish lawyers from working in their profession. This prohibition remained in effect until the deportation of the Jews of Rădăuţi to Transnistria. Following the deportation, Hart arrived in the ghetto of Dzhurin, where he was appointed director of the orphanage that was established there. Bigo Hart immigrated to Israel, where he resumed his work as a lawyer. See Dov Bernard (Bigo) Hart testimony, YVA, O.33/4009; R. (Hart) Bernis testimony, YVA, O.3/VT/9003; Margalit-Postilnik, *Radauts*: *Kehila Yehudit Betzemihata Uvisheki'ata,* p. 132. In her self-published memoirs, Yehudit Nir relates that Hart "did his work with noteworthy dedication and cared for the children as though they were his own"; Yehudit Nir, *Mishoah Letekuma* (n.p.: self-published, 2012), p. 53.

The council has begun to wage war against typhoid fever in earnest. They are building new latrines and moving people from the filthy mass housing quarters to the factory quarter; doctors escorted by the militia are inspecting the apartments for cleanliness, but it is no use. The crops of fruits and vegetables also contribute to the spread of the plague, because the starving people are devouring cheap, raw food without washing it. The communal latrines also contribute their share along with the masses of flies and all kinds of repulsive crawling creatures that swarm over the market like clouds, crowd into the hovels, and spread the dangerous bacteria. Doctors are surprised that a healthy person is still to be seen in the streets.

September 6, 1943, 5 A.M.

Forty patients are lying ill with typhoid fever in the hospital, and the number of patients hiding in their homes is much greater.[75] Some of the patients in the hospital are lying on a little straw on the floor, without a sheet, a pillow, or a blanket. It is really a crime that beds were not prepared in time. The Jewish Central Council in Bucharest sent wooden boards a few months ago, but they have been placed in storage, along with glass and with the clothing for the orphans, and they will probably remain there until the messiah arrives. Only yesterday people began to build beds, but not, God forbid, from the Romanian wood, but rather from the dilapidated, rotten boards that the militia confiscated from the attics of the Ukrainian Jews. People also managed to get their hands on a small amount of sackcloth for sackcloth mattresses. The authorities have declared the "model colony" was infected with typhoid fever, and no one may enter or leave it. Now we have a new concern: if they nevertheless release the deportees, Dzhurin will remain battered by the plague. This seems like a futile concern! …

---

75 Many families refused to hospitalize their sick relatives because of the terrible conditions that prevailed in the hospitals—in Dzhurin and in other ghettos. The families preferred to care for them at home with the help of doctors who conducted home visits.

Incidentally, rumors of approaching liberation by the Romanian regime are once again circulating throughout Romania and Transnistria. High-ranking Romanian officials spare no allusions, and the letters from Romania vow that the news is well-founded. There are different versions, particularly regarding "when" and "how," but nevertheless something is brewing among the high-level authorities. Letters from Bucharest report that the regime has already prepared ghettos in Bukovina to "welcome guests." They will remain there in quarantine for three weeks and will then be released.

The camp is in turmoil and seething as a result of this news. People are preparing their suitcases, sacks, and rope; they are patching their shoes and mending their clothes. People are not thinking about purchasing food in time for the winter, when the prices are very low, and the wealthy even baked honey cakes last week for the journey. Now they, poor things, must finish eating the honey cakes in Dzhurin before they—I mean the honey cakes—get moldy!

The excitement of returning home is so strong in Shargorod and in Murafa recently that the wealthy people have purchased nags and wagons for the long trip home. This drove the government officials crazy, and the gendarmes announced that the punishment for spreading rumors about returning home would be the death penalty. The people were indeed alarmed and ... were quiet for twenty-four hours. I dare not prophesy regarding this matter. Perhaps you must indeed go to sleep when the world cries out, "you are drunk" ...[76]

[September 6, 1943] 9 P.M.

A foreign gentleman with ribbons [military decorations] appeared in the camp yesterday evening, and as usual the "lords" ingratiated themselves and even had a drink with him. The post chief found out about this—God forbid, the prophet Elijah did not come to him in a dream and reveal the secret ... —and appeared unexpectedly this morning in the camp,

76 According to this folkloristic saying, if someone says that you are drunk, you should ignore him. However, if more than one person says that you are drunk, you should go to bed.

where he visited various apartments to find out with whom the Romanian officer had met yesterday. The post chief is suspicious that the guest is a "courier"—a non-kosher messenger who smuggles money from Romania, half for me and half for you.

The post chief did not find what he was looking for and nevertheless a kosher bargain fell into his hands. The post chief came across an immense treasure in the home of an old bachelor A. (**Added in Israel**: it is not worth giving his name, because he is already dwelling in the ground), who has connections among the esteemed inner circle: a sock full of all kinds of good things, that is 1,500 dollars, four gold rings set with diamonds, four golden watches, and lots of pure gold.[77] The overlord got his hands on the treasure and took the guy with him. The advocates moved heaven and earth to persuade the post chief to return the possessions, or at least not to punish the owner of the wealth, but the overlord was adamant and would not listen to anything. He will send A. under escort to the gendarmerie in Moghilev tonight.

September 7, 1943, 3 P.M.

Neither ancestral privilege nor the connections of wealth shielded the guy with the treasure, and he was taken to Moghilev, escorted by two armed guards, and with chain handcuffs, not exactly of pure gold ... At the same time, an influential, special messenger set out for Moghilev with cash in his pockets to try to save A. and perhaps also the treasure.

Less cheerful news has arrived from the neighboring camp. The local council was informed by Moghilev that in the coming days the camp must supply 300 men to Tulchin, ostensibly to work on the train tracks and not to dig peat. From another nearby camp, Derebchin, we have learned that the gendarmes took eighty men and boys from their homes and sent them to work somewhere. These reports are depressing and are dampening the joy of the fairy tales about returning home. The "lords"

77 Another routine case of a smuggler who brought money and valuables to the deportees from families in Romania. Usually the couriers took a percentage, a fee for bringing the money. In many cases, the funds did not reach their destinations, because the couriers stole them.

themselves deny the rumors about repatriation, but they themselves are preparing for the journey, buying suitcases, boiling butter, and baking honey cakes …

September 8, 1943, 3 P.M.

We received an unexpected blow to the head tonight, which made us forget in the blink of an eye the empty dreams of returning home and the preparations for the journey! Suddenly around midnight, there were grating sounds of wails, shrieks of women and children, bellowing screams in Romanian in the camp—which recalled the dreadful night of panic in Atachi in the autumn of 1941, on the eve of the crossing of the Dniester. People came out of their hovels and of the mass-housing quarters in terror, dressed as they were, to find out what was happening. However, the people soon returned to their dwellings and chained the doors, even though this was as useful as cupping a corpse.

This is a brief narrative: Moghilev demanded 100 men for work in the German labor camp Trikhaty on the other side of the Bug. The gendarmes decided to do without the Jewish militia and rounded up the people themselves, using their whips. The angels of destruction have a list of names that the Labor Office prepared in utmost secrecy. Since no one knew about it, almost all the birds were found in their cages. The gendarmes burst into the apartments and dragged out the people who were registered. If it occurred to anyone to flee, he was caught by Ukrainian militia who were stationed around the camp. Since about 300 people are already engaged in labor, fate befell the "dregs"—elderly men and women, people just released from the hospital, and boys.

Once again, the shocking image of farewells was repeated, of women fainting, of toddlers sobbing and clutching at the legs of their fathers and brothers, of the distribution of loaves of bread and a few marks from the community, of the registration of families to receive portions of food from the soup kitchen. The battered group of human skeletons finally set out, escorted by gendarmes who bellowed at them, prodding them to hurry. The people in the camp have one single concern: to where can one disappear tonight? People believe that we may expect to prepare for another round tonight, because they have not reached the required number of 100 people.

September 9, 1943, Thursday, 7 A.M.

The people were right. The fury of the previous night repeated itself, but [it was] far more terrible, because the birds had already flown away. Screams and wails reached the heart of the heavens, they dragged out children, women, and girls from the hovels, and if it seemed to them that someone was trying to flee, the gendarmes struck them on the head with their whips. All around the militia [post], where the living harvest was imprisoned, terrible scenes played out until 6 A.M., when the transport left for the gendarmerie.

We found out that they required only ten men and twenty-five women (this is the first time that they also seize women) today, but the roundup was achieved with much more difficulty than on the first night. As for the men, only a few dejected, disabled men were caught in the net, those who did not have the strength to flee to the fields or the cemetery. However, the women and girls were caught at home, because they did not think that this also applied to females.

The day before yesterday, the authorities in Moghilev demanded 1,000 people for labor. The Labor Office did not bother to prepare a list but rather dispatched the militia to seize anyone in the streets. The militia caught whomever they encountered, and "kosher" workers from the foundry also fell into their hands. The authorities dispatched the transport in the blink of an eye, before engineer Jagendorf could move heaven and earth, demanding to know why they had seized his workers.

[September 9, 1943] The Same Day, the 9th of *Elul*, 5703, *Parshat Kiteze*, 10 P.M.

It is worthwhile also to record the Hebrew date in order to remember the *Yortsayt*. Last night, the in-law Etele surrendered her soul. She had struggled with death since July 25. Her demise has had a severe impact, although it is not possible to praise her after her death. Uncle Yekel will take the calamity badly and will take it to heart. Apart from this, he is plagued by all kinds of ailments and already reeks of the grave himself. It seems that he will soon meet his other half. (**Added after the liberation, April 1944**: A cryptic allusion to the capitulation of Italy "Etele" and the Germans, "Yekel").

September 12, 1943, 4 P.M.

The autumn is making itself known in earnest. The rain is lashing down, people are shivering with cold outside, and they are no longer wearing their summer sandals. My family and I are almost barefoot, there is not a splinter of wood in the pantry, and I am relying on God's mercy.

The second transport of slaves—ten men and twenty-five women—returned from Moghilev yesterday. What happened? They were late for the collection in Moghilev by about three hours, so they were left, poor things, with a slap in the face, and sent back to Dzhurin. This resurrection of the dead lifted their gloomy spirits a little.

September 24, 1943 (the 24th of *Elul*, 5703) 4 P.M.

Have the last twelve days passed completely empty, without any "material"? A short answer to this: "An ox has a long tongue, yet cannot blow the shofar ..."[78] (**Added after the liberation, April 1944**: I did not dare to write anything about the deathly fear in the camp. Partisans ambushed a gendarmerie patrol about 3 kilometers from the camp and shot at the patrol but did not hit anyone. People were living in mortal fear, anything could happen! The place was swarming with senior officers, who came to investigate the incident, and the atmosphere was charged with

78 Kunstadt quotes a Yiddish proverb. This and other proverbs are cited in Joseph L. Baron, *A Treasury of Jewish Quotations* (Lanham: Rowman & Littlefield, 2004).

terror. Everyone's life was hanging by a thread, but a miracle occurred in Dzhurin ...)

The weather is beautiful again, "September Gold" in Izik Manger's words.[79] I am still keeping [in reserve] my worn-out shoes and cannot part with my sandals, without socks, even though I am shivering. Bertl no longer has anything to keep, because the shoes [that he brought with him] from home have become, over the course of two years, too small for him, and he can no longer wear them.

October 3, 1943, the 4th of *Tishrei*, 5704, 6 A.M.

Well, it seems that we have slipped into the new Jewish year of 5704. It will become clear on this page whether it will be a good year, *in a guter sho*. The two days of *Rosheshone* passed without incident, and no one prohibited the Yids from wailing in their synagogues to their hearts desire. The *minyonim* were indeed full, and *hazonim* and prayer leaders trilled the *piyut Meylech Elyon*, rabbis gave sermons and demanded that people repent, women shed floods of tears during *Uneytane Toykef*, and even during *Hayom Te'amzeynu*,[80] men (as many, alas, as are still here! ...) delighted in the *hazonim*'s stunts and the surfeit of *aliyes*. While walking home, we were not sparing in our greetings for a Happy New Year and good wishes on the Creator's account. Even sworn heretics pondered whether or not the new year would, nevertheless, bring deliverance.

I must stop now, because a messenger is summoning me to my mundane work.

---

79 Itzik Manger, "September Gold," in Manger, *Demerung in shpigl*: *Lid un balade* (Yiddish) (Warsaw: Bibliotek fun yidishn pen-klub, 1937).

80 "*Hayom Te'amzeinu*" (today You will strengthen us) is a prayer that is recited on the High Holidays.

[October 3, 1943] 9 P.M.

Yes, regarding the question of whether the new year began well in Dzhurin, we received a clear answer already on the first day after *Rosheshone*, *Shabbes Teshuve*. The sun shone in a clear, autumn sky, the air was pleasant and saturated with the yearnings of bidding the summer farewell, people strolled through the alleys that had the scent of *Shabbes* rest—no militia was to be seen in the area, and the market was vacant and abandoned.

And then five gendarmes suddenly appeared in the camp, led by Sergeant Chuchanu, a murderer who boasts that, in the summer of 1941, he shot with his own hands ten Jews in the camp of Yedinetz (Bessarabia) on the eve of the deportation to Transnistria. The armed soldiers went straight to the building of the Jewish militia. Within minutes, we discovered that the gendarmes had not come to hear the sermon of the rabbi in the great *bes medresh* but rather to convey a new order that had just arrived from Shargorod. Because the governor has reinforced the decree regarding setting foot outside the ghetto, all men, starting with boys from the age of ten, must gather in the market within half an hour. There each one must sign a pledge not to set foot outside the kosher boundaries. Jewish militia raided the streets to round up the people without delay and promised everyone that the gendarmes intended only to gather the signatures.

There were in fact a few clever people who considered the entire matter unusual. Why do they require ten-year-old babies for such signatures, and why all of a sudden will the gendarmes stand and watch the Jews transgress the Sabbath and write? However, there was no time to investigate this, and indeed the market was immediately black with groups of people—all kinds of men—old and young, disabled and lame: every variety of male to be found in Dzhurin.

Bertl quickly called me from the creek, where I had gone to bathe, and the two of us immediately went to the assembly so as not to miss, God forbid, the holy *mitzve*. Upon arriving at the market, I saw a pretty dense crowd there, including quite a few women, who had come to sign in the name of their husbands. There were smart men, who preferred to endanger their wives while they hid in an attic or in an open field …

I looked around and did not like what I saw. Armed gendarmes were positioned around the market, while Sergeant Chuchanu bellowed out commands, brandishing a revolver. He ordered the people to stand in line and not move from the spot, otherwise he would shoot. He separated the men from the boys, and ordered the women to leave immediately. I winked at Bertl that he should disappear and he cleverly, discreetly sneaked out of the line and disappeared.

I myself stood in the line next to the "lords," even though they were trembling from head to toe. If they were only pretending to do so, then they are amazing actors. Anyway, I thought it was better to stand next to the "big shots" who are friendly with the gendarmes.

When the entire crowd stood in orderly lines, the sergeant began rejecting people and sending all the boys, the elderly, and the disabled home. He approved around 200 adults, and ordered them to go to the yard of the militia building. Then all hell broke loose. The gendarmes had to send seventy people to Moghilev to work, and they came up with a new idea to replace the old system of roundups at night: dupe the wise men of Chelm to get them into the net by resorting to trickery.

The wives and children of the husbands and fathers who had fallen into the trap began to wail and shriek, because they feared that the enemies had who knows what kind of evil intentions. The sergeant ordered his servants, "fire," and shots from five rifles resounded in the air in order to calm down the terrified people in the camp …

After about an hour, the group of 200 men marched out to where they would choose "who are they that shall go."[81] The "lords" also marched in the line in order to try to save whomever they could during the march. I also went with them, and I was able to rescue two sick persons from the wolves' teeth. The operation lasted until the middle of the night, and the sergeant assembled a company of seventy men. He freed the rest of the men and even ordered two militiamen to escort them back to the camp. Whoever fell into the net was a matter of luck, unrelated to any intervention. No ancestral privilege was of any use to any person on whom the sergeant's eyes fell. There were quite a few ill person, elderly,

81 Exod. 10:8–9: "And Moses and Aaron were brought again unto Pharaoh; and he said unto them: 'Go, serve the Lord your God; but who are they that shall go?'"

and even fifteen-year-old boys among the seventy people. Each one of the deportees is a tragedy in and of himself.

Due to the three continuous days of "rest"—*Rosheshone* and *Shabbes Teshuve*—there was no bread to ration and so the community distributed 20 marks to each person.

Today, Sunday, the demonic director of the Transnistrian tragedy produced a new play on the Dzhurin stage, which made people forget the calamity of yesterday. I will relate this tomorrow, because my nerves are nevertheless not made of steel …

October 4, 1943, 7 P.M.

The Sunday drama that I promised to write about received a continuation this afternoon—a second part of sorts. The story requires a kind of "flashback" (a look backward) as the cinema directors call it. I already wrote that at the end of the summer, sanitation committees poured down on Dzhurin seeking to discover to what extent we abide by the *Shulhan Aruch* [laws] of hygiene in the "model colony." There were decent inspectors, who did their minimal duty, minimally ethically, and with a royal feast for lunch at the community's expense. Others scolded and threatened but nevertheless did no harm.

However, on September 10, it happened that the regional military doctor from Moghilev, Lieutenant Ionescu himself,[82] in all his glory came down on us—he is an enemy of Israel, and in Moghilev they tremble at his gaze. The evil one, may his name be blotted out, gathered all the doctors, castigated them with terrible curses, and promised them that he would teach them a harsh lesson, because the camp is not hygienic enough. One doctor who responded received a slap in the face. The misfortune continued: when the lieutenant turned to return to the gendarmerie, something not very fragrant was discovered behind the

82 Lieutenant Ionescu, a regional doctor in the Moghilev district terrified the deportees. On January 10, 1943, Ionescu declared, "We sent you here to die, but we demand from you that there not be any plagues here." See Carp, *Cartea neagră*, vol. 3, p. 270; Lya Benjamin, ed., *Comisia Internationale Pentru Studierea Holocaustului in Romania*: *Raport Final* (Iași: Poliron, 2005), p. 309.

fence, which one encounters where there are no toilets near the hovels. He then became murderously enraged like Esau and went to the militia, where he demanded a list of all the doctors, orderlies, and group leaders in the camp. A Dzhurin militiaman, not a foolish young man, provided a list that included only ten group leaders (out of twenty-four), three doctors, and two orderlies. Fortunately, the [Romanian] doctor did not read the list at the time (he was speaking with many more doctors at that exact moment …) but rather put it in a file and left.

The regional doctor returned to Moghilev and delivered a report full of venomous hate to the prefect Login. He informed the prefect that he had found a dreadful epidemic in Dzhurin and, because of the Yids, in the Dzhurin camp, all the Romanian officers, soldiers, and functionaries of Transnistria would die of the plagues. He therefore suggested that all the doctors, orderlies, and group leaders be sent somewhere on the other side of the Bug, because they are to blame and bear full responsibility.

The Moghilev "lords," who are all friendly with the prefect Login, learned of the false and dangerous accusation and acted to mitigate the decree: only five group leaders and one doctor will be sent away, but only if the doctor conducts another inspection in Dzhurin and finds that the sanitary conditions have not improved. This news was transmitted a few weeks ago by Moshe Katz and a stone was lifted from the hearts of the accused. So far, the "flashback."

Gendarmes suddenly appeared in the camp yesterday afternoon and went to the militia. Panic erupted because everyone was still stunned by the incident of the "signatures" of *Shabbes Teshuve*. It eventually became clear that this time the armed gendarmes were only looking for five group chiefs and a doctor. The panic only lessened slightly, because the enemies cast the net on admirable people who had helped everyone as much as possible given their limited means.

At the top of the list of the accused group leaders was Bobi Guttman, a young man from the wealthy class, a sharp and decent man who was on good terms with the gendarmes, and a man with a wide-open hand and a warm Jewish heart. If the water came up to the neck and all the advocates failed, Bobi would rush to the rescue, and not for the sake of a reward. He is a great risk-taker and will be sorely missed in the camp.

The condemned group leader Armin Goldenberg of Suceava, an idealist with a noble soul, who sacrifices himself for the orphans and all the "pariahs" of the camp, is a totally different kind of man. With his own hands, he bathes their filthy bodies and washes the tangled and lice-infested hair of the skeletons who are lodged in the poorhouse, sees to it that they remain clean as far as possible, and offers comfort and encouragement to the desperate souls.

The other three group leaders also managed to make good friends among the poor, even though the obligations of a group leader are actually replete with pricks and spears. If they sometimes had to eat pig, at least they did not suck out its bones.

As for the condemned doctor Breznitz, he is the best of doctors in the highest sense of the term, a Jew who helps and comforts, and demonstrates devotion to and love of Israel.

No ancestral privilege helped and, even though the community was willing to pay money openhandedly, the five group leaders and Dr. Breznitz were taken away to Moghilev. That it could have been much worse offered small comfort to the people in the camp. Indeed, there were three doctors, ten group leaders, and three orderlies on the list of the regional military doctor Ionescu.

This consolation soon proved to be false comfort. The other five group leaders were sent away this morning, as well as Lipa Hercsher, the secretary of the Labor Office, a very fine young man, who has been working more than two years in this position and endeavors to do good and set right the injustices committed by his boss, the "labor minister," even though by so doing he jeopardizes his meager income. Well, he has received a reward for his good deeds …

In the meantime, it is impossible to find out where the seventy people who got caught in the trouble of the "signatures"—the *Purim Shpil* [a Purim play] of *Shabbes Teshuve*—are. It seems that they are in Tulchin. The families are breaking down the doors of the community building trying to learn what has happened to these seventy people. Almost no man sleeps in his apartment anymore, because people fear that one night all the people in the camp will be sent away somewhere.

October 6, 1943, 7 P.M.

Bobi Guttman and Dr. Breznitz, two of the five group leaders who were taken to Moghilev on Sunday, returned today. We discovered that this "miracle" occurred at the expense of the second group of group leaders, the five people who were sent on Monday. It was an exchange of sorts: two out of the cage, five in! The colony chief had rushed to Moghilev …

We now have clear information concerning the seventy persons who were caught and sent away on *Shabbes Teshuve*, during the *Purim Shpil* "signatures." They were taken to Nikolayev, next to the Dniester [*sic*] [Bug], about 400 kilometers from Moghilev, where they are working for Organization Todt, building a bridge.

Psychotic fear of a manhunt rages in the camp, both among men and among women, and upon going out in the streets or to the market in the morning, hearty greetings are exchanged, like someone had returned from afar.

October 7, 1943, 3 P.M.

This morning, at 9 A.M., the second-in-command, Moshe Katz, called a meeting of chosen people, the "prominent people," and informed them that he and his brother-in-law, Leon Neuman, were resigning. A series of debates ensued, and all the orators actually begged the "good pair" not to abandon the camp. In the end, Moshe Katz relented and withdrew his resignation.

It may very well be that the two functionaries were serious about planning to resign from power in the current, crazy times when one does not know what today will bring, let alone what tomorrow will bring. However, the question remains: why did Katz invite only our people to this "historic meeting" and not the critics? Go, discover the truth! …

[October 7, 1943] 9 P.M.

A new decree: the post chief, Georgescu, has ordered that as of tomorrow, *Eyrev Yom Kipper*, the weekly market will not be held at the marketplace but rather in a square in the Ukrainian quarter, near the cloister, 3 kilometers from the ghetto. Even if the gendarmes and the Ukrainian militia will allow the Jews to go there, it will certainly not be to engage in actual "trading" and to sell anything, because trade is strictly forbidden. Hundreds of *Lagernikes* earn their meager livelihood from selling a bit of soap, a cigarette, a sweet, or just an old rag at the market. If the decree is not repealed, they will have to put a third pot in the soup kitchen.

Exactly one year ago on *Eyrev Yom Kipper*, the former post chief, Floreanu, forbade holding the weekly fair at the marketplace. Then the "miracle of *Motzei Yom Kipper*" occurred (who still remembers that entry? …).[83] We have already had our fill of miracles. The nations of the world somehow manage on their own without miracles and wonders, if only that could be said about us! …

October 8, 1943, *Eyrev Yom Kipper*, 2 P.M.

The market was empty and desolate today. Moshe Katz left today for Shargorod and will try to rescind the decree. He did not travel empty-handed …[84]

A courier smuggled in a large sum from Romania to support the underground Zionist organization of 300 "Zionists," according to a list. Each fortunate person received 4,000 lei. My name does not appear on the list, which includes only "Dzhurin-style neo-Zionists," and even quite a few members of Agudas [Yisroel] and haters of Zion, who in the old country persecuted Zionists and poured fire and brimstone on Herzl's dreams. The most distinguished of the organizers of the "Zionist" list is "labor minister" David Buksbaum without whose help the Balfour

83 See the entry of September 22, 1942, 2 P.M.

84 The closure of the markets and the prohibition against bringing food to the inhabitants of the ghetto were routine occurrences and a proven method for wresting bribes.

Declaration would not have come about. In his eyes, I am completely disqualified, because I dared to take a stand against him.

My situation is so bad that I am no longer afraid of being sent to a labor camp. There is nothing left for me to do. Winter is at the doorstep, we are all naked and barefoot, without a potato or a piece of wood. How will this end? ...[85]

Tomorrow is *Yom Kipper*, but the mood is like on the eve of *Tisha B'Av*. This new year has begun well! ...

October 10, 1943, 6 A.M.

Eyrev Yom Kipper had its sensational incident, a continuation of the lucky first week of the new year. Someone informed the gendarmes that a courier had smuggled a great treasure into the camp—the "Zionist" aid. When the people were going to *Kol Nidrey*, the adjutant of the gendarmes, a murderous non-Jew, suddenly appeared in the camp with a revolver in his hand and burst into a few homes (according to a note...) to look for the courier. He found nothing, but we were scared to death. The advocates cleaned up the matter with the help of a substantial bribe.

[October 10, 1943] 3 P.M.

The market was empty also today, and the Ukrainian militia did not allow any farmer to arrive there with food, and not even empty-handed. Moshe Katz did not manage to achieve anything in Shargorod. The occupation authorities have decreed that markets can only be held in the regional centers and only once a week: they are expressly trying to prevent the rural masses from convening too frequently at this time, on days when the situation on the front is so bad. Speculators take risks smuggling food in from the surrounding areas, but they fleece anyone who falls into their

85 In 1943, the deportees who managed to bring valuable items, clothes, etc., with them, exchanged them for food, heating materials, means of sanitization, such as oil, clothing, medicine, etc. Many of them were left with nothing and subsequently had to find creative ways to survive. Many deportees risked their lives by leaving the ghetto.

hands, God forbid. And there is a difficult problem: how will produce be acquired for both soup kitchens?

October 24, 1943, the 25th *Tishrei*, 5704, 7 P.M.

After a long pregnancy and difficult labor for more than a year, the orphanage finally opened today, *mazal tov*! About sixty poor orphans, boys and girls—most who have lost both their father and mother—from Bukovina, Bessarabia, northern Moldova, and Ukraine—they all have a roof over their heads, *in a guter sho*, their own 50 centimeters on a shared straw sack, and four full meals a day. The rooms are clean and bright, whitewashed and renovated, sparkling with cleanliness and order, not at all in the style of Dzhurin. There is also a classroom, a shower, a kitchen, a large garden, and the most important: a toilet, as there are among people.

The Jewish Community Center in Bucharest sent a great deal of clothes and shoes for the orphans but this is not sufficient. There are not enough blankets for the cold nights. Some of the children are not entitled to shoes, because there is a lack of shoes in large sizes. The feet of the orphans, who have wandered around barefoot for two years, have grown substantially—this has not occurred to anyone in Bucharest …

As a result of the overcrowding and the lack of beds only the most in need have been admitted to the orphanage, mostly those who lack both a father and a mother, and who have no relatives. The orphanage is, without a doubt, an extremely important initiative, even though they thought of it a bit too late, just before the end. Without the extensive help of the Romanian Jews, the plan would not have been realized.

The dedication ceremony took place this afternoon at 2 P.M. in the garden of the orphanage. Everyone gathered together, and the post chief assured us that we need not fear any manhunt. The orphans, lined up on both sides of a primitive stage, bathed and dressed in the new clothes, with shining faces, brought tears to everyone's eyes. These were very different children, not the emaciated skeletons, who only recently were begging in the streets and stealing a beet from a peasant's wagon to stay alive. A festive meal was prepared for the children and then the program began.

The Rădăuţi *hazen*, Moshe Solomon, sang "*Mizmor Shir Hanukes Habayis*,"[86] accompanied by an accordion ([played by] Grafer) and a fiddle ([played by] M. Farizer). The colony chief delivered a sermon in German, followed by the rabbi of Dzhurin, Rabbi Herşel Karalnic, the rabbi of Siret, Rabbi Baruch Hager, and the second-in-command, Moshe Katz, who spoke in Yiddish. People wiped their eyes with handkerchiefs during the speeches. When the bride is an orphan, it is irrelevant ... obviously the speakers demanded that the people lend a hand as much as possible for the benefit of the institution. I too took part in the program and read a poem that I had written in honor of the gala. I will include the text later, not, God forbid, because of it "literary value" (by no means! ...) but rather as a historical document.

An orphan—Marta Kilshtok—recited a Yiddish poem, and at the end, the colony chief gave another speech, because he enjoys hearing himself speak. Following the artistic program, they took the people through the rooms and showed them where the children will live. The children began to dance in a circle, like real children and not like faded leaves.

The "lords" and their inner circle then gathered in a club to make a toast and enjoy themselves. Although I was also invited, I refused. I do not participate in any parties at the public's expense, even for the sake of a *mitzve*, and especially at such a fateful time as this, when the roof is burning overhead.

Orphans

Tears flow from our eyes,
Although today it's not fitting to cry.
Hot tears pour out of everyone's eyes,
One might think us sad and sigh.

Today is a holiday for orphans.
We must not whimper or complain!
How beautiful, how spic-and-span
Is the home that they did gain!

86 "A Housewarming Song."

Rooms so spacious, warm, and light,
And on beds with a straw mattress they sleep,
With no worries for food and drink at night,
The community will provide for their keep.

From the tender children's bodies, they doffed
All the rags, so old and worn;
In royal clothing, they are now dressed,
No need for patches, for they are not torn.

Shirts, jackets, and also trousers,
Shoes, socks, and dresses so new,
Envelop the thin, little bodies
Of the boys and girls too.

Yesterday barefoot, naked, and miserable,
Their clothes were tattered rags,
Where they spent the day, at night they were unable,
Without a roof, without food in their bags.

These neglected shadows
Have changed overnight;
Like all children, they've now become,
As if they had never endured such blight.

Thus, it is good and also fine,
So why are there suddenly tears in our eyes?
Yes, this is a remarkable question
That merits the Jews' consideration.

One thought chases another,
And the images that emerge the most
Are of their fathers and mothers
In a grave under the frost.

Like animals, some lie without cover
Somewhere in a trench or a meadow,
At the bottom of the Dniester are others,
Lying drowned in the depths below.

Before our eyes, we see hovering
Groups of bloody martyrs so dear,
Fathers and mothers of the children,
The sorrowful impression is searingly clear.

Happiness is silenced, clouded over,
With sadness the heart is incised,
Why are the Jews over and over
The victims who are sacrificed.

No, the time of revival is upon us,
Our courage we must reclaim!
Wipe the tears from our eyes, we must,
Hope will lead us to our aim!

October 26, 1943, 3 P.M.

A new manhunt has just begun, only by the Jewish militia, in the meanwhile. The familiar panic that accompanies such *Aktzyes* has erupted in the camp. Most of the men have disappeared. People are saying that the gendarmes just shot two Jews who tried to run away to the nearby forest. We indeed heard loud shots coming from that direction. For the first time, I am using the ribbon on my sleeve as an amulet: I wrote in large print "Secretary of the Colony." I do not know whether the gendarmes will be frightened by this *mezuzah*. I am not sure whether I should set foot in the streets today. Although perhaps the community building is a safer place of refuge, alongside the "big shots." Go be a prophet!

A year ago at this time, we had already forgotten about this matter, but this year the Master of the Universe has bestowed us with a long, dry, and sunny autumn—really great for catching Jews.

[October 26, 1943] 6 P.M.

I, nevertheless, went to my office, mainly to find out what the shooting meant. A Dzhurin-style miracle took place: they shot and missed! Three young men were returning from a funeral at the cemetery and when they saw a gendarme from a distance, they ran off in the direction of the forest. The gendarme fired at them but did not hit them.

October 27, 1943, 3 P.M.

It was a night of shouting, wailing, and fears, not the first and probably not the last. In the evening, a gang of gendarmes appeared in the camp and a real manhunt began. The good pair—a gendarme and a Jewish militiaman—burst into the apartments and seized whomever they encountered—almost all of them sick, the elderly, and young boys. Whoever still had the strength, fled to the fields in time.

It later turned out that they demanded a total of only twenty craftsmen for Moghilev, but they did not inform the council of this in advance. The Labor Office would have provided the twenty craftsmen within half an hour, without panic and without a manhunt. The gendarmes, however, have discovered that catching Jews and freeing them later for a handsome bribe is a very fine business. Why then bother the council! …

Among the captured are persons who had suffered the torment of the sinner in the grave in Tulchin or in Trikhaty in the summer, and the doctors there declared them unfit and freed them. For this reason, they thought that they were safe and did not flee.

Once again my heart is pounding with regard to Bertl, even though he only turned twelve in the summer. He is a strong, tall fellow, so go argue with the Angel of Death—may it not come to that—who is not even a *Bar Mitzve* yet! I warned him to go out in the streets as little as possible during these dangerous times.

October 29, 1943, 6 A.M.

Today it is two years since my family and I saw the Dzhurin paradise for the first time. Will I celebrate the third anniversary here as well? All signs point to "No" ...

During these two years, I contributed to the local cemetery three persons: my mother, my father-in-law, and my brother-in-law. Not to mention "health" issues, such as Rivka's typhus and Roza's heart disease.

Rumors are circulating that we will soon be transferred, because of the situation on the front. Some say to camps in Bessarabia, and others believe it will be Dobruja,[87] and I don't believe any of these tales. The high-levels officials have other concerns...

[October 29, 1943] 8 P.M.

I am beginning to establish myself in Dzhurin like a dignified householder, precisely in defiance of all the rumors. For more than two years, we have been eating, if there is anything to eat, from clay shards, but since this morning Roza has become prosperous. I brought home a real treasure from the cooperative for her: four plates, four bowls, and four spoons—all from aluminum, a comb (not to tear one's hair), and a tin bucket. Not, God

---

87 A region in southeast Romania, between the Black Sea and the Danube. Upon the outbreak of World War I, Bulgaria joined the Germans and Austro–Hungarians, and thus was a partner in the defeat. The Treaty of Neuilly turned the region of Dobruja over to Romania. In September 1940, the Treaty of Craiova returned the area of southern Dobruja to Bulgaria, following German pressure. This step, initiated by Hitler, strengthened Bulgaria's alignment with Germany. After the war, the area was again divided between the countries in the framework of the Paris Peace Treaties in 1947.

forbid, free of charge, even though the federation of Jewish communities in Romania sent all the gifts on the explicit condition that they would be distributed for free to the *Lagernikes*. However, the "lords" ignore these conditions and took all these goods to the cooperative, where they sell them for a high price to Jews and Ukrainians alike.

My foot had not yet crossed the threshold of the cooperative as a buyer until today, because my wallet would not allow it. However, it seems that someone suddenly appeared to the council members in a dream and ordered them to distribute some of the articles to the community workers at lower prices. They allocated exactly what everyone would receive, and thus my household was established.

Salt, for example, the community does not sell salt at all. They are keeping the half wagon that the federation sent locked up with seven bolts in the storeroom until … the spirit moves them. I begged the colony chief to allow me to buy 1 kilo of salt for cash but to no avail. Today at the market I bought a glass of salt—200 grams—for 3 marks.

Allow me to say a good word about the Dzhurin wheeler-dealers: in Moghilev, in Shargorod, in Bershad, and wherever else, they do not administer the gifts from Bucharest any better, and worse has no limit …[88]

October 31, 1943, 7 P.M.

After another break of four weeks, the weekly market was resumed today in the ghetto. The decree was cancelled by itself. As a result of the abundant crops, we somehow managed to carry on this month, because the peasants smuggled in products [to sell] for next to nothing, in fact.

Today too they literally gave away the goods very cheaply, and the farmers even took back many products because there was a lack of buyers.

---

88 All the goods and commodities sent by the Comisia Autonomã De Ajutorare in Bucharest that were intended for the deportees in fact were not divided among the inhabitants but rather sold in the cooperatives in order to fill the council's coffers. These funds were to be used to buy food for the soup kitchens, as well as to bribe the Romanian authorities. See, Ancel, *Documents Concerning the Fate of Romanian Jewry*, vol. 8, pp. 527–534; Rosen, "Tzibur Veyahid," p. 236.

No one is storing goods for the winter as they did a year ago, because people believe that they will not spend the winter in Dzhurin, for better or, God forbid, for the opposite. Wood, on the other hand, is worth the price of gold—5 marks for 1 pood. This summer it was possible to obtain wood for 1.30 marks per pood, but when the wallet is empty, even an ox can cost a groschen …

November 2, 1943, 3 P.M.

The new typhus season has begun. They took the first typhus patient to the hospital today. There are more than twenty-five patients with typhoid fever there, and the number continues to grow. This means that they are also in danger of being infected with the Rickettsia bacteria.

The doctors think that the new guest is not a local but rather was brought here by the forced laborers from Tulchin or from Trikhaty.[89]

November 4, 1943, 5 P.M.

It appears to be a snowy evening outside. It seems to everyone that we are facing significant events that will change our fate, one way or the other. There are many signs and more than enough interpretations.

The mark continues to fall and has reached its lowest point: 85 marks for 1,000 lei. The peasants have not yet discovered the secret and are still trading in the mark as before.

---

89 The threat of typhus had not passed completely. Indeed, there was a danger that Jews arriving from work camps would bring the disease with them. Although there were some typhus patients in the ghetto, the percentage was much lower than that in the winter of 1941–1942, due to the preventative measures implemented by the councils and the medicines that began to arrive from Romania.

[November 4, 1943] 10 P.M.

The people who were sent from the camp to dig peat in Tulchin at the beginning of the summer have now been allowed to return home after five months of forced labor. They were sent from Tulchin to Moghilev, to the assembly point, and from there they were sent on foot to Dzhurin. We expect the guests this evening. A few were lucky enough to catch a ride on a Ukrainian wagon and arrived an hour ago in Dzhurin. They are neglected and unshaven, their faces like those of patients just released from the hospital, and their gait is frightening. Their clothes are torn and filthy, their shoes ruined and without soles, and a few are completely barefoot. Only when all the people return will we know who paid with his life in the Tulchin manhunt.

Already for more than two months, we have not received any sign of life from the approximately 200 *Lagernikes* who were sent to work for the Germans in Trikhaty. Their families are despondent, and pious wives have consulted the Rabbis regarding whether they should sit *shiva*.[90]

November 5, 1943, 7 P.M.

The guests from Tulchin arrived, *in a guter sho*—seventy yesterday, and the rest, those who lagged behind, today. The council rented wagons from Ukrainians and sent them to fetch those still on the way. Because Tulchin is famous for its plagues, the entire throng was taken to a hall in the hospital, where they will remain in quarantine for three weeks. A person shudders at the sight of these broken vessels, who have lost human semblance—barefoot and naked, neglected and unkempt. They have tossed and turned in stables for five months, and have not removed their clothes at night. Only tatters remain of their clothes, most go barefoot, and some have bound their feet with rags. Their faces are sunburned and they are emaciated, only skin and bones, their eyes are blank, their backs hunched over, their hands and their entire bodies are covered with

90 The Jewish deportees in the ghettos knew that those taken to the German camp in Trikhaty were doomed to die.

festering wounds. All are limping and groaning from sharp pain in their knees and thighs—a result of standing in water for twelve hours every day. The murderous peat has given them lifelong gifts: heart problems, ruined lungs, kidney diseases, rheumatism, and joint ailments.

When all the Tulchin people had been assembled and counted, we discovered a terrible thing: Dzhurin had contributed more than thirty persons to the Tulchin disaster. My poor pen is unable to describe the horrifying scenes that played out when the wives, children, parents, and brothers of the dead discovered that they had to sit *shiva*. The orphanage will accept a large number of new charges …

As for the victims from Trikhaty, Nikolayev, and Varvarovka,[91] the bitter truth will soon be known, because the work must be completed by the beginning of the winter.

November 7, 1943, 7 P.M.

As of today, there are already eight new typhus patients lying in the hospital—not a bad start at the beginning of November. The people brought the plague with them from Tulchin. Their clothes and rags were burned, and the "lords," poor things, were forced to take underwear and clothes from the holy shelves of the storeroom to give to those confined in quarantine. Instead of shoes, they received sandals—still better than going barefoot.

The perils of typhus today hover not only over the patients but over the entire camp. In the summer, the Romanian inspectors warned that if

---

91 Varvarovka was a labor camp in Ochakov district. In this camp, Jews worked on the construction of a new bridge over the Bug, linking southern Transnistria with Reichskommissariat Ukraine. The Romanian segment of the bridge connected Trikhaty and the town of Ochakov, and its construction was entrusted to German firms from the Reich. The work began in the spring of 1943 and concluded that December. Four thousand Jews, mostly deportees from Romania, were turned over to SS squads and held in three camps on the Romanian side of the Bug (Trikhaty, Varvarovka, and Kolosovka), and two on the German side (Kurievka and Matievka). See Tuvia Friling, Radu Ioanid, and Mihail E. Ionescu, eds., *International Commission on the Holocaust in Romania: Final Report*, http://www.inshr-ew.ro/ro/files/Raport%20Final/Final_Report.pdf., p. 167 (accessed June 20, 2022).

an epidemic broke out, all the Jews in Dzhurin would be sent somewhere over the Bug, because the Yids alone are entirely responsible for this.

November 8, 1943, 7 P.M.

The autumn has begun in earnest. The thick, deep mud resurrected and set on the moribund shoes of those lucky ones who still possess such a treasure. Not a few of the *Lagernikes* trudge in the sticky muck with their feet bound in rags, and some walk around barefoot in the cold damp. Rumors are rife throughout Transnistria that we will soon be driven out. Anyone who possesses heavy items is getting rid of them at bargain prices. People are mending backpacks, buying suitcases, and, in Moghilev, the rich are acquiring horses and wagons. If the disaster occurs, this means the end for everyone, even for those with horses and wagons …

November 9, 1943, 7 P.M.

The mark is dangerously ill and is about to expire. On Sunday, in Moghilev, 150 marks were received in exchange for 1,000 lei (instead of 25, according to the official exchange rate …). Speculators from Moghilev then descended upon Dzhurin with trucks and cleared out all the food from the weekly market, throwing around marks like stuffed cabbage. On Monday, the peasants discovered the secret, and no one saw even half an ounce of flour or a potato at the market. Whoever had a mark in his pocket bought whatever he saw, just to get rid of the paper cadavers. A panic erupted in the cooperative, and the shelves were emptied. Today it is possible to buy only nails, ink, and shoe laces there.

The peasants were actually seen at the market today, but when they saw the empty shelves at the cooperative, they demanded insane prices for the produce—1 mark for an egg, 5 marks for a bottle of milk, and so on. Most of the peasants absolutely refused to accept marks and demanded goods for food. The ruble, in contrast, was revived and has risen to the rate of 1 ruble for 1 mark. Only recently, we received 20 rubles for 1 mark. Why is this surprising when we hear about the achievements of the ruble-bosses [the Soviet advance] …

In the meantime, I do not pay attention to the mark. In my cubbyhole, there is enough food for at least two weeks—potatoes, beans, and onions—and in the shared pantry is 5 poods of my own wood, which mercifully will suffice for about a month in the winter. I will not worry about what will happen after that, because it will not help in any case. By the way, it is inconceivable that the occupation authorities would allow the mark to fall unless deliverance is already at the door.

[November 9, 1943] 10 P.M.

The gendarmes have confiscated almost all the livestock and wagons from the kolkhozes and have taken them to Romania. The Romanians are clearly preparing to depart and do not want to leave anything behind for the new landlords, who are moving ever closer. The officers and subofficers in Moghilev and Shargorod have sent their households to Romania. These are indeed good signs that revive the heart and instill fear.[92]

Typhus is spreading out its arms and new cases are discovered every day. The doctors claim that the plague had not really weakened in the summer as they had thought. They simply misdiagnosed it—typhoid fever—because in the summer the Rickettsia bacteria causes the emergence of tiny microscopic dots that cannot be seen with the naked eye.

November 10, 1943, 7 P.M.

Yesterday the mark was completely rejected in Shargorod. Only a few peasant women appeared in the market with bottles of milk—a food that

---

92 The Romanian authorities anticipated that the Soviets would regain control of the area and therefore endeavored to fully implement their policy of the economic exploitation of Transnistria during the entire period of the occupation.

must be sold before it goes bad. People paid whatever the peasant women demanded for the milk.

Only one butcher today opened a butcher shop and ostensibly sold meat of a carcass. Militia had to be posted by the door in order to prevent a disaster. No one was sold more than one pound.[93] The boys who run through the alleys and in the market with boxes of sweets, mondelech (a kind of cookie made from sunflower seeds cooked in honey), razors, and matches did not show up today.

The first snow fell today, but it immediately melted in the thick mud. The third winter in Dzhurin is, without a doubt, the last.

November 11, 1943, 6 P.M.

There are already reliable statistics on the victims from Tulchin. At the beginning of the summer, 240 persons were sent from Dzhurin to dig peat and a total of 209 persons returned. Thirty-one men died of typhus and of other plagues, neglect, exhaustion, starvation, and hard labor, and some were killed while escaping from the camp.

November 13, 1943, *Motzei Shabbes*

The mark–ruble exchange rate has now fallen to its lowest level—1 ruble for 120 marks. They squandered all the merchandise in the cooperative, and the simple people did not have the privilege of enjoying all the good things. The big shots and members of the inner circle continued to take out more and more packages, and thus rid themselves of the marks. Today the shelves are bare.

On Thursday morning, the butchers announced that they would sell 215 kilos of meat at the butcher shops. To prevent a rush, the colony chief decreed that they should only sell 100 grams per person on the basis of notes from the council. The group leaders sat down to write the notes quickly and took them to the militia, where they were distributed. In the

93 About half a kilo.

meantime, the hands of the clock approached 3 P.M., and when the people went to the butcher shop with the notes, they found the door locked. The butchers hurried to give a piece of meat to anyone who did not require a note before the group leaders had finished their work. The colony chief was very angry, but there was nothing to be done.

In the bakeries, they baked a smattering of bread and sold the loaves only to the well-connected people, as many as they wanted to buy. The masses who waited in line for a few hours went away empty-handed.

Yesterday, Friday, the situation improved a little. Peasants appeared in the market with milk, cream, cheese, chickens, and even potatoes and flour. They accepted marks, but the prices were insane. These are a few of today's prices compared to the prices before the devaluation of the mark: 1 liter of milk for 12 marks ([previously] 2 marks); 1 pood of butter, 50 (10); 1 pood of potatoes, 25 (4); 1 pood of wood, 10 (3.50); 1 pood of wheat flour, 140 (40); and so on. Farmers also came to the market today with produce, and one farmer even sold 1 pood of potatoes for 10 marks.

The psychosis about returning to the homeland has again flared up to such an extent that the "lords" convened an assembly at which time they chose fifty people—a certain number from each town—to organize the journey when the longed-for moment would arrive. The main thing is that the functionaries will ensure that the women, children, the elderly, and the ill will not drag themselves on foot. I observe these gatherings as child's play, but I bite my tongue, because the crowd would literally stone me for such heresy.

Nonetheless, I received a few hundred marks of aid from a "Zionist" list, and it has the flavor of food that had stood for too long. A month ago, I could have acquired food and wood for the winter in exchange for these expired pieces of paper, and today I can only look at their defiled form …

November 14, 1943, Sunday, 7 P.M.

At today's weekly fair at the marketplace, many peasants arrived unexpectedly with wagons loaded with all the best. They had no choice but to reconcile themselves to the mark, yet the prices were very expensive, although a little lower than the week before. It seems that the mark has recovered slightly. We have found out that in the neighboring camp of Murafa, they did not squander all the produce during the panic and did not put all their eggs in one basket, as they did in our "model colony." Today, the cooperative there is selling all the goods to everyone, without exception. The psychosis about returning home continues to subside slowly and, in the homes of the wealthy, they pamper themselves with exodus-from-Dzhurin honey cakes instead of bread.

November 16, 1943, 7 A.M.

Dr. Efroim Şabat (from Siret), the director of the hospital, passed away an hour ago—a victim of the Rickettsia bacteria. His demise was clearly an act of mercy, because the cruel demon took revenge on its number one enemy in an exceptionally cruel manner: it stole into the chambers of his brain. The patient convulsed horribly for a week, cried and wailed incessantly for an entire day, and tore out of bed in an attempt to escape. Apart from his family, strangers guarded his bed and did not allow him to flee. His agony was unfathomably excruciating, and even those closest to him whispered a prayer that this strong young man (barely fifty years old) would be released from his torment. The doctor did not lie in the hospital but rather in his home, which is on the ground floor of Iankel Axelrod's "palace," where my family and I have a small apartment on the upper story. For a week, the cries of the doctor could be heard in my cubbyhole, and it was truly unbearable, also because the doctor was our good neighbor and a good friend.

A strange fact: the highest percentage of death from typhus occurs precisely among intellectuals, and the illness advances more virulently among them. The doctors can find no explanation for this.

Dr. Şabat had directed the hospital since May 1943, not for the sake of receiving a reward, and literally sacrificed himself through his dedication to his dangerous work. The first director, Dr. Moshe Greiff, paid with his life last winter for his tenacity and willingness to sacrifice himself. His successor, Dr. Gabriel Shtir, also came down with typhus already in the first days of his directorship and survived only after being ill for a month. The third director was Dr. Julius Frenckel. The Rickettsia bacteria had no power over him, because he had already overcome the illness in the past, but he had another woe: he had a sharp tongue and could not tolerate any injustice. Well, he picked a quarrel with the "lords," especially the "good pair," and spoke his mind. The rulers tried to convince another doctor to become the director of the hospital to replace the rebellious Dr. Frenckel. However, no one wanted to risk his life, apart from Dr. Şabat, a quintessential idealist and a noble soul. It was a crime to hoodwink a person who is not immune, and all for the sake of ambition and victory.

The funeral of this martyr will take place this afternoon. His death has caused sadness and pain among everyone in the camp.[94] Dr. Gabriel Shtir is once again the director of the hospital.

If anyone ever writes a chronicle of the Transnistrian exile, he will have to dedicate a chapter at the very beginning to the Jewish doctors who fell like scythed hay in the battle against the dangerous bacteria. The fate of their dead colleagues did not deter them in the least from their dedicated work for the general good. Even though they were versed in the severe danger, more than simple people were, they fought barehanded against the cruel, invisible enemies, armed only with the iron will to save and to aid. Honor and glory to the Jewish heroes in white coats—doctors, orderlies, and nurses!

[November 16, 1943] 9 P.M.

The funeral has already ended. Everyone accompanied the deceased to his last resting place, and tears flowed from everyone's eyes. Four warm eulogies offered a reflection of the deceased's good deeds. They did not spare any *Eyl Moleh Rahmim*, but Dr. Şabat's soul will find his way to the Garden of Eden[95]—if such a place exists—even without these prayers. Once again, a poor boat sunk in the stormy sea, and the waves honored the victim for a moment, forming a circle around him. And immediately, no sign or trace of the circle remained, and the sea continued to rage.

---

94 Dr. Efroim Şabat, who had been deported from Rădăuţi, treated patients with great devotion. He was infected with typhus and died from the disease. See Margalit-Postilnik, *Radauts: Kehila Yehudit Betzemihata Uvisheki'ata*, p. 169.

95 Judaism is vague about the afterlife. Some Jews refer to it as *Olam Haba* (world to come) and some to *Gan Eden* (Garden of Eden).

November 17, 1943, 6 A.M.

This notebook is nearly finished and has not yet received a title. Today I am ready to summarize it and adorn the third notebook of memoirs with the title: "*Min Hama'amakim*" [From the Depths]—"*Mima'amakim*" is the shorter form in Psalms,[96] I began writing in the third notebook quite close to my mother's fresh grave, on the first day of the *shiva*, when the acute grief was unbearable.

Slowly the pages have been covered with cheerless, desolate lines, with a concise chronicle of calamities, and tragedies, and deathly terror, of disappointed hopes and vanished dreams, of many black clouds and very few tiny rays of light. In the end, we are still lying 9 cubits deep in the ground. In fact, we are sinking constantly deeper into the abyssal depths and who knows how far we will descend!

I know that the brilliant English writer Oscar Wilde also entitled his memoirs from prison *From the Depths*, although in Latin, *De Profundis*.[97] I do not begrudge him …

[November 17, 1943] 10 P.M.

The mark has almost recovered, although the prices of food are still 50 percent higher than before the devaluation of the currency. The peasants bring all sorts of goods but there are few interested buyers, and people only buy the absolute necessities. The people squandered their marks on trifles and now they regret it.

Three wagons arrived in Moghilev with presents from the federation of Jewish communities in Romania, a portion for Dzhurin. It seems that separate packages arrived for the deportees from Bessarabia—the poorest of the poor—bearing the names of the families. The colony chief and Neuman left for Moghilev to bring the treasure.

---

96 Psalms 130:1: "Out of the depths have I called You, oh Lord."

97 Oscar Wilde, *De Profundis* (New York: Dover Publications, 2013). This long letter, which was written while Wilde was imprisoned for homosexuality, was first published in 1905.

Moshe Katz summoned the dignitaries of Bessarabia, and they discussed an arrangement: the separate packages will not be distributed to the designated recipients themselves, but rather a kind of general stockpile of these gifts will be created and then distributed equally among the neediest. At present, those invited to have a say in this have not given any answer. They hesitate to refuse, because they fear that the leaders will decide to do "justice" themselves.

The thought of a stockpile is really fitting and fine, but why suddenly of the packages that were sent to specifically named persons from Bessarabia, who are all poor, hungry, barefoot, and naked? Are the Bukovina "*bishenitzes*" Cossacks who are exempt from the half-shekel contribution? There are many wealthy, well-connected people and "upper crust" people among them, whose relatives and good friends shower them with very valuable items, medicines, and all the best, and the source of the gifts is embarrassing? However, there is an excuse: no one whips himself, apart from a lunatic …

* * *

This third volume is nearing its end, the final lines. It is not because of any change, here or there, that I will begin a fourth volume of memoirs, but rather the caprice of the [book]binder. Will the fourth volume be destined to be bright? We should not try to look behind the curtain of the future, because as it is written, "he that increases knowledge increases sorrow" (the less one knows, the healthier …)[98]

---

98 Eccles. 1:18: "For in much wisdom is much vexation; and he that increases knowledge increases sorrow."

The Iron Foundry of Siegfried Jagendorf, Moghilev.
Photo Collection, YVA, 3363/22.

The Iron Foundry of Siegfried Jagendorf, Moghilev.
Photo Collection, YVA, 3363/2.

Laborers at the Iron Foundry of Siegfried Jagendorf, Moghilev.
Photo Collection, YVA, 3363/9.

Notebook Four

The Birth Pangs of Deliverance

The son of David will not come until they despair of redemption.
(Talmud [B. Sanhedrin 97a])

November 23, 1943, Tuesday, the 25th of *Heshvan*, 5704, 7 P.M.

I persuaded myself that it will be a *sgule* to record on the first page of the fourth notebook of memoirs something happy, a good sign for the empty pages. So, I waited and yearned for a week for a piece of news not seeped in gloom. Only today did I find this boon, but it is not really good news.

The laborers from Dzhurin who were rounded up in a manhunt and sent to the German labor camps in the summer returned today. Not all of them, God forbid, have returned to the Dzhurin paradise! In the month of May, they were sent all at once, but one can only get out of Trikhaty through a small, narrow slit in the barbed-wire fence. Therefore, they are returning alone or in small groups, according to luck, their brains, and … something else!

About half of the people have returned to date. Whoever sees them, these "fortunate ones," does not need much imagination to imagine the jagged woes that they suffered in Trikhaty. Not one of them has a shirt on his body, a few have wrapped their body with a sack instead of trousers, most are completely barefoot, and the rest have wrapped rags around their feet. Their flesh has been eaten away by lice and bedbugs, and they are covered with festering wounds, and their faces, *oy*, their faces! The expression, living dead, does not do the reality justice, but where will I find a suitable word! Six months of hard labor under the heels of the German executioners, hunger, murderous beatings, neglect, mortal fear, and persecution—all these tribulations have turned young people into broken skeletons, desperate and beaten, bereft of the strength to rejoice at their release from hell. Never mind that the German and Romanian two-legged animals treated them with their usual abandon, indeed this is no surprise. They have a strong tradition of this for generations and generations. We committed minor sins against them: we killed their god, poisoned their wells, drank a cup of Christian blood on *Seyder* night, defiled their sacramental bread, took over the entire world, have a long nose, came up with up the Red Torah, and what sins did we not [commit]!

However, we are mortified to hear from the mouth of the returnees about a few hyenas who showed up in Trikhaty, our own flesh and blood, who themselves had been deported and uprooted from their homes, and who sold themselves to the devil and rose to greatness among the Nazis as "labor supervisors." These scoundrels, in truth only a few creatures, bloodsuckers who were caught during a manhunt, denounced them, and led to the slaughterer whoever did not give them the last of their last funds. These despicable creatures advised the Germans regarding who should be destroyed and thus bear responsibility for spilling Jewish blood. They also whispered in the ears of the Nazi beasts, urging them to demand as many more slaves as possible from the camps, even though they did not need them, with the intention of: new people—new treasures. The forced laborers dreaded the afflictions endured at the hands of their own people more than those inflicted by the German thieves.

This depraved gang sprouted up like poisonous mushrooms not only in Trikhaty, but wherever the inhabitants of the camps were driven like sheep: in Varvarovka, in Tulchin, in Kurievka,[1] in Nikolayev, in Cariera de Piatră,[2] in Odessa, and so on.[3] The camp hyenas raked up treasures soaked with Jewish blood and rivers of tears. So as not to remain silent, [I will mention] such accursed names as Anshel Gruber and Adolf Borg from Trikhaty, and Katsher from Varvarovka, who were among the most contemptible informers.[4]

---

1 Kurievka is a village in the Nikolayev district, on the eastern bank of the Bug River. In the summer of 1943, the Germans set up a labor camp in Kurievka. The Jewish workers were put at the disposal of Organization Todt, which built bridges and paved roads in the southern light of the Bug River. The camp was subordinate to the work center in Varvarovka and was guarded by Ukrainian police. The workers were employed in erecting a wooden bridge, and were housed in two open stables, without doors and windows, in harsh living conditions. See Lavi, *Pinkas Hakehilot*: *Rumania*, vol. 1, p. 505.

2 Cariera de Piatră (stone quarry) is in the Tulchin district, 8 kilometers from Ladejin. Before World War II, there was a Russian penal camp on the rocky west bank of the Bug River that was quarried, thus the name Cariera de Piatră as well as a cemetery. Following the Nazi occupation, a transit camp for deportees was set up on the site through which thousands of Jews from Bukovina, Bessarabia, and the Regat passed. Upon arrival at the camp, the prisoners were held for several days in outdoor quarantine. During this time, they were tortured and robbed, and only then they were allowed to enter the camp buildings; see Camp Cariera de Piatră, YVA, Carp Archive, vol. 7, p. viii.

3 The conditions that prevailed in the labor camps in all these places were horrific.

4 Kunstadt refers here to the painful problem of the collaboration of some Jews with the Nazis. He judges them harshly and does not offer any mitigating circumstances. This phenomenon occurred, of course, in other ghettos and camps throughout occupied Europe.

Added after Liberation in April 1944

The dates at the beginning of the following entries are not written in numbers but in words. I feared that the notebooks would fall into non-Jewish hands and therefore sought to efface the appearance of a diary. Not an act of naivete!

Twenty-Fourth of November, [Nineteen] Forty-Three, Three in the Morning

Transnistria comprises Tulchin, Pechora, the other side of the Bug, where Jews are tortured to death and long for the Angel of Death, but there is also the "other Transnistria"—recreation rooms where wealthy gangs of people sit by day and by night, playing poker and "ours and yours," and not for beans. This has been going on for a long time in Moghilev and in Shargorod, and also for some time now in Murafa and in Dzhurin. The "master colony" will indeed not lag behind. What do they care, the young hedonists—they too are floating on a plank in a wild sea, just like everyone else! What do they care that two women from the Hasidic *kloyz* in Dzhurin just tried to poison themselves but did not succeed! There are often serious scandals—women come down on their "caretakers" in the meeting places, and the screams reach up to the heavens. The roof is burning overhead but the game goes on ...

[Twenty-Fourth of November, Nineteen Forty-Three] 9 P.M.

Two Dzhurin laborers returned from the German labor camp of Varvarovka, freed by a miracle. The guards in Varvarovka were armed Cossacks. Their cruelty is far worse than the bestiality of the German murderers. They inflict cruel whippings for no reason and sometimes they also use their loaded rifles and shoot Jewish laborers.

An exhausted laborer in one of the "Jewish blocks"—underground caverns—recently was startled during his sleep and cried out. The Cossacks immediately shot into the cavern. The bullet did not hit the man who screamed but rather a tinsmith from Rădăuţi, Adolf Hart, a father of two children. Hart was wounded in the thigh and was left lying in a pool of blood. The Cossacks immediately entered the cavern and seeing the bloody Jew dragged him out and buried him alive. He begged the murderers to shoot him in the head but in vain.

The Jewish camp manager, Katsher, strips those people who have the rare luck of being released almost completely naked. He divides the plunder with the German officers with whom he gets drunk and plays cards.

We have discovered that the camp hyenas from Trikhaty, Anshel Gruber and Adolf Borg, recently traveled to Bucharest with an authorization from the German officers and fraudulently obtained forty suits, shoes, underwear, dishes, and food for the Jewish laborers from the community federation. In order to fulfill their minimal duty in case of an inspection, they threw a few articles at the residents, like a bone to a dog. Then they sold all the goods to peasants from the surroundings for a vast amount of cash and distributed it among the German officers.

Those returning from Trikhaty relate that there they used to take the ill and wounded to a German "hospital" for treatment. They never found out what became of their remains. Nevertheless, the Jews prayed—in the utmost secrecy—on *Rosheshone* and *Yom Kipper* in a prayer quorum after work, and some even fasted on *Yom Kipper*, go dally in figuring out our stiff-necked people! …

The people were sent back to Dzhurin from Trikhaty in locked cattle cars without any food. One died of starvation during the journey—Iaakov Tshatshkes from Cernăuţi. Only one single time did they get something to eat during the journey, at the train station in Zhmerinka,[5] where a

---

5 Zhmerinka, a district administrative center in the Moghilev region, 32 kilometers southwest of Vinnitsa, was an important railway crossroads. See Lavi, *Pinkas Hakehilot*: *Rumania*, vol. 1, p. 440; Vadim Altskan, "On the Other Side of the River: Dr. Adolph Herschman and the Zhmerinka Ghetto, 1941–1944," *Holocaust and Genocide Studies*, 26:1 (April 2012), pp. 2–28.

messenger brought fourteen loaves of bread from the Jewish council for … 160 persons, as well as a pot of bean soup.

November 25, 1943, 7 A.M.[6]

The delegates Dr. Rosenstrauch and Leon Neuman have been in Moghilev for two weeks and have just returned with sacks of news.

First, the matter of repatriation has come up again for the umpteenth time. The state inspector for the "colonization" of the Jews in Transnistria, Paraskivesku, has just taken the trouble to travel from Bucharest to Moghilev, where he spent a few days, and related that the state has already signed a swift order to send the deported Jews back to Romania. According to him, the delegates from all the Jewish communities in Romania at a state conference pledged to support the liberated Jews at their own expense. However, nothing was said about returning to their old homes in Bukovina and Bessarabia. It seems that they will divide the guests among the ghettos of Cernăuţi, Botoşani,[7] and in the Banat province.[8] Only about 50,000 of the 250,000 people who endured the decree of expulsion are alive today, perhaps even less. They also summoned the regional doctor Ionescu to Bucharest for instructions concerning the disinfection of those going home.

And second, the delegates did indeed bring something substantial, and not just gossip: boxes of clothes, underwear, shoes, dishes, food, and the like—a gift from the UER. They sent gift packages marked with the names of the families for the deportees from Bessarabia—clothes and underwear, but no shoes.

The colony chief promised that now they will hasten to distribute the gifts as quickly as possible. First, of all they will bestow them on the

---

6 Despite what Kunstadt wrote above in the entry of November 23, 1943, in a note that he added after liberation in April 1944 about writing the dates at the beginning of the following entries in words and not in numbers, he resumed writing the dates with numbers in this entry.

7 Botoşani is the capital of the Botoşani region in Moldavia, located in the northeast of the Regat in Romania.

8 This province in southwest Romania was part of the Regat.

returnees from Trikhaty, Varvarovka, Tulchin, and the like, and then on the rest of the people. The old man says that it is possible that any day now an order will arrive, commanding us to take our packages on our shoulders. I intend to submit a petition and ask for clothes. I will only be ashamed if they refuse me …

[November 25, 1943] 8 P.M.

They have not brought any new typhus patients to the hospital. There is a total of four patients still in the hospital.

November 28, 1943, Morning

The mark has regained its value, and it is possible to get products dirt cheap, at the same prices as on the eve of the currency panic. Only wood is expensive—8 marks for 1 pood, six times more than a year ago. The peasants brought all kinds of good things to the weekly market and literally dragged the buyers by the sleeve, but the people buy food only for one week. Sugar is suddenly being sold for "almost nothing"—18 marks per kilo, while one pays 26 marks for [a kilo of] salt! A strange phenomenon that can only occur in Transnistria …

[November 28, 1943] 3 P.M.

Typhus is still raging out of view. Yesterday and today they brought another three patients to the hospital, forced laborers who brought the gift with them from Tulchin. They recently released from quarantine too soon more than twenty people, who were ostensibly "clean" and in fact carried the dangerous bacteria into their homes.

In the community building, they are working feverishly to compose lists for the distribution of clothes to the needy. It is a serious problem that they did not send any shoes, which are needed no less than clothes and perhaps even more so. One encounters many people who are completely barefoot in the streets, trudging through the cold mud. Others do not go outside, because their bare feet cannot bear the damp and cold.

November 29, 1943, 6 A.M.

Here is a reliable list of the victims, who had been deported from Dzhurin in June as part of a transport of 220 people from Dzhurin, and who died digging peat in the Tulchin labor camp:

Four people died of "natural" causes (that is, hunger, plagues, exhaustion): 1) Avraham Berzner from Rădăuţi; 2) Meir Fund-Bartfeld from Cernăuţi; 3) Fishl Soldinger from Suceava; 4) Moshe Gesman, a resident of Dzhurin.

The following were killed by gendarmes and Ukrainian militiamen while escaping and did not get a Jewish burial:

1) Iudl Blechman, a resident of Dzhurin; 2) Moshe Beznos, from Hotin; 3) Feiviş Broiner, a dentist from Cernăuţi; 4) David Halinger, from Rădăuţi; 5) Avraham Henig, a barber from Cernăuţi; 6) Adolf Hebel-Katz, from Cernăuţi; 7) Carl Vagner, from Siret; 8) Edi Wolf, from Rădăuţi; 9) Şalom Sontag, and 10) Şmuel Sontag, two brothers from Vijniţa, the only children of an old, sick widow; 11) Lerner Haim, a tailor from Hotin; 12) Shlomo Neiberger, a student from Rădăuţi; 13) Immanuel Solner, from Gura Humorului; 14) Leizer Meiketman, a resident of Dzhurin; 15) Izidor Kamil, a student from Siret—a delightful young man, a writer and a poet; 16) Herman Kastinger, from Gura Humorului; 17) Israel Kilimnik, a hatmaker from Hotin; 18) Itzi Kishner, from Hotin; 19) Iankev Kishner, the elder, from Hotin; 20) Iankev Kishner, the younger, from Hotin; 21) Iasha Roif, from Hotin; 22) Orel Stolier, from Siret.

My pen bows in silent pain before these names—each one a symbol of a destroyed world—and for the groups of martyrs from Tulchin whose names are not recorded in these pages, because I do not know about them.

[November 29, 1943] 9 P.M.

I present here a poem that I composed, moved by the impression made by the lamentations of the laborers returning from Tulchin, Trikhaty, and Varvarovka.

The stanzas reflect but a hint of the tragedies and deaths that occurred in the hell known as labor camps.

It is clear to me that the poem has little literary value; perhaps only the poetic value of an onion peel. Nevertheless, I will preserve this modest memory of the catastrophes, because of the documentary spark that burns therein. Perhaps I am making a small contribution to the construction of the chronicle of Transnistria, which will be published sooner or later, provided that there will still be Jews left to assume this task.

May the critics forgive me then for daring to encroach on the field of poets, and I will forgive them today for ridiculing these lines and the bard who wrote them.

By the way, allow me to note an important fact here. In Transnistria, poets are as prevalent as mushrooms after the rain. Even children carry around a pencil and a notebook and write poems, mostly in Yiddish. According to the old axiom, the muses are silent when the cannons thunder, but in the mad times in which we live, everything is upside down, so why should the muses hold their tongues?

March of the Transnistrian Slaves

With shovels on our shoulders,
We stride to our work site;
Work is a blessing from God, our Father,
Idleness is a bitter blight.

Worn out and ragged,
No trousers or shoes have we,
To hard labor we are pushed,
Run, they shout, run quickly.

Roads await us, peat and bridges,
Yearning for Jewish work and sweat;
We must break stones and dig,
Be the days sweltering hot or soaking wet.

Food they do not give us,
No bread and no money do we merit;
The work of the Jews has been strenuous
The next world we will surely inherit!

Who sleeps on soft cushions?
With straw we are content;
One hundred huddled in a cowshed
For entire weeks on end.

The smell here isn't a heavenly scent.
But our noses, they are indifferent;
And when small creatures bite,
So what? We just scratch day and night.

No exile can last forever,
Especially a summer night,
Eagerly awaiting a new morning,
No one closes an eye out of fright.

Sighing and groaning, pining in pain,
Of our wives and children, we are bereft;
Alas, abandoned they remain,
Who provides for them there, who is left?

Too many other thoughts
Burn holes in our brain,
Images from a time long ago,
Gone like smoke, none remain.

About a time when Jews
Lacked no home and no bread;
When life had meaning too,
And there was logic in death.

Hey, day has come, get up quickly!
We are not nobles who can sleep late!
Put your shovels on your shoulders swiftly!
Go straight to work! Do not wait!

November 30, 1943, 7 P.M.

When I went out in the streets this morning to say a quick *Kaddish* in a *minyan*, I saw that the entire camp was in an uproar. Whomever I asked about this gazed at me in astonishment like at an old good-for-nothing and, rushing by, blurted out in my face: "What world are you living in? They are sending all of us home today, to Romania."

For the first time since I have been reciting the *Kaddish* for my mother, I dared to forfeit the *minyen* and turned abruptly to the community building to find out the real truth. I immediately found out from the "lords" and the wheeler-dealers that the news did not come out of thin air. A trifle! This morning at dawn the post chief, Georgescu, appeared at the militia building accompanied by two sergeants and ordered them to summon the colony chief and Moshe Katz immediately. The two fathers of the "model colony" came straightaway, and the overlord told them the news: today all the exiled Jews will return to Romania. About 200 wagons of Ukrainians from the neighboring kolkhozes will come to the camp at around noon to load the chattel, mainly women, children, the elderly, and the ill. To ensure that everything will run smoothly, the post chief ordered us to immediately assemble 200 men at the militia post, who will each be responsible for a wagon.

The "lords" indeed immediately set to work. First, they sent the Jewish militia to bring without delay the 200 men who will have the privilege of supervising the exodus from Transnistria. Second, they ordered the storeroom managers to distribute everything on the shelves—clothes, underwear, utensils, food—without notes and without any formalities—equally to everyone.

The news spread through the camp in the blink of an eye and the streets became a madhouse. People ran around with suitcases, with sacks, with packs, while congratulating and kissing each other as they ran. In short, for the Jews there was [light and joy]. The truth is that apart from me there were a few other skeptics who did not really like the unexpected deliverance, to the extent that quite a few men hid in an attic, a cellar, or in a field. No problem, they thought, when the wagons start moving, we will come out of the mouseholes. In the great synagogue, where I slipped in to recite the *Kaddish*, a *minyen* had barely gathered—some elderly men from Dzhurin, people who are not considered for repatriation or for manhunts …

Because of the skeptics, the militia indeed did not a find trace of any men during the manhunt. And only then did the matter explode. The gendarmes intended to hoodwink the mouse into a cage, using the wisdom of Greece, repeating the lucky *Purim Shpil* of *Shabbes Teshuve*. The same thing in a different guise: then it was "signatures," today it is "repatriation."[9]

When the post chief saw that the mice had realized what was happening, he ordered the militia to resume their old mode of conduct: dragging people from attics and cellars, rummaging through the fields and the cemetery for those hiding there until they assembled a company of 200 persons. In fact, we later found out that only 60 men were needed. Since the younger and somewhat healthier people had disappeared, the ill, the disabled, the elderly, the children, and even the community functionaries, the nurses, and the orderlies paid the price. The militia brought in more and more "goods" to the militia post, but the gendarmes sent away the young children, the hunchbacks, the blind, and the lame.

Now, at 7 P.M., another twenty-eight people are needed to meet the quota. It will be a night of merrymaking.

---

9 See the entry for October 3, 1943, concerning the use of deception to carry out deportation for forced labor.

December 1, 1943, 3 P.M.

The gendarmes, accompanied by the militia, searched the apartments and the hideouts throughout the night, arresting women as guarantees for husbands in hiding, and the wails reached the heart of the heavens. At dawn the post chief demanded that he be presented with a list of all colony employees, and he himself sifted through the names and decided who would be the lucky ones. This is the first time that such a thing has happened, because until now the gendarmes have spared the community apparatus so as not to slaughter the hen that lays the golden eggs.[10] I do not know to whose credit the post chief skipped over my name, because I myself have never had any contact with him. Perhaps nevertheless an honest *meyletz yoysher* showed up unexpectedly in a time of danger …

With this list in hand, the militia did not need any use of force, because not one single community worker had hidden. They took all the teachers from the orphanage—Dov Katz, Iankev Kamil, and Iosef Fishkovitsh—altruistic workers. They only spared the orphanage director, Bigo Hart. The post chief burst into the cooperative and seized the entire staff and a few close associates. That is how they filled the quota, and the 60 people marched to the gendarmerie post. From there they took them to Moghilev, the assembly point. The final destination is Varvarovka. The camp is like a cemetery, nobody is to be seen in the streets. Those in hiding do not stick their noses out.

December 2, 1943, 7 P.M.

Eighteen people from the company that fell into the trap yesterday returned from Moghilev this afternoon. The committee of doctors released them, and this was a matter of luck. There are a few community functionaries, as well as some elderly and sick people, among the fortunate ones. On

10 Until this point, the members of the council had provided the Romanians with lists of names of people designated for forced labor. In order to release the people, they would bribe the Romanian commanders. The Romanians exploited the Jewish public as much as possible through their leaders.

the other hand, many cripples, even some who had already suffered all summer in Tulchin, Trikhaty, or Varvarovka, remain in the cage. They sent the throng by train to some place in the Odessa region, where they will dismantle a factory. The Germans apparently are preparing to leave and intend to take as much as possible with them.

The winter has slipped in, and there is a proper snowstorm. The *lamedvovnikim* have begun to appear, but they remain at the periphery, and avoid the area of the militia post.

December 5, 1943, Sunday, the 8th of *Kislev*, 5704, 8 P.M.

Today at the afternoon prayer, I finished saying *Kaddish* for my mother. I have not missed a single day of *Kaddish* in the course of eleven months, even though this was at times very difficult for me and sometimes even fraught with mortal danger. I am pleased that I was able to do this.

Instead of drinking a toast in the synagogue on the *Yortsayt*,[11] I took five loaves of wheat bread to the rabbi of Dzhurin for him to distribute to whomever he saw fit. The rabbi continues to insist that the main thing is not to use one's lips to mumble the prayer *Al Het*[12] and strike one's chest but rather to open one's pockets to save the neediest from hunger and cold. Indeed, the God-fearing "*bishenitzes*," literally risking their lives, have lashed out at him with claims that he is a heretic and a sinner who leads the masses astray. The six rabbis, who celebrate the exile here, keep far away from him, because of his ways. I personally have great respect for this *tzaddik* of yore and Mother would have agreed with me.

---

11 The Yiddish term *Trinkan Tiken* refers to the custom of drinking a toast of liquor on the anniversary of a person's death.

12 A confessional prayer of repentance for transgressions.

December 6, 1943, 7 P.M.

The council is once again dangerously ill and they brought in a medical expert from Moghilev—the president of the Central Council, Moritz Katz—to save the dying from extinction. The same factors that often have led to "cabinet crises" in the Jewish administration, as I have frequently mentioned, still exist. In fact, there is one cause: the council's [power] struggle, mainly between the second-in-command, Moshe Katz, and the colony chief, Dr. Rosenstrauch. The old man claims that he bears the entire responsibility before the occupying authorities for everything related to labor and discipline in the "model colony," and that no one should interfere, not even the council. In truth, the council has only the character of a charity, a branch of the Moghilev Central Council. Well then, the old man bends the law like a dictator, according to his wisdom (of which he does not have much …) and seeks first and foremost to execute by force all the overlords' orders and decrees in exchange for a pat on the back.

The council does not agree with this course, and this is also the opinion of the *Lagernikes*. Moshe Katz, who aspires to be a dictator himself but has other intentions, has been waging a sharp struggle with the old man ever since the council was established. He, Moshe Katz, is a clever and a decent fellow, who is close to the lords, but he will not sell the birthright to Esau for a pot of lentils, and he knows his way around.[13]

---

13 The character and acts of Moshe Katz were a subject of dispute, as is expressed in Kunstadt's diary. On the one hand, he was a man of principles and courage, who bravely and stubbornly negotiated with the Romanians. Through bribery and brazen argumentativeness, he exerted great efforts to minimize the number of deportees to labor camps, and succeeded more than once in preventing the implementation of a decree ordering the closure of the market. Some testimonies indicate that he saved Jews caught outside the ghetto from being shot to death, and allowed people who fled from camps, such as Krasnoye, and who were to be sent to forced labor camps to remain in the ghetto. He was popular among the residents of the ghetto, who preferred to approach him rather than Rosenstrauch. On the other hand, Moshe Katz collaborated with many of the injustices committed by the members of the Moghilev Central Council, who held Katz in great esteem, and on more than one occasion invited him to meetings there, together with Rosenstrauch. See Avigdor Shachan, *Bakefor Halohet*, p. 198; Ancel, *Documents Concerning the Fate of Romanian Jewry During the Holocaust*, vol. 8, pp. 527–534; the group testimony from the Moghilev ghetto, Dzhurin ghetto, and Shargorod ghetto, YVA, O.3/VT/10547; Max Antzer testimony, YVA, O.3/1237. See also the comments by Menashe Miller, a student of Rabbi Baruch Hager

Following the severe cabinet crisis in July, only two council members still participated in the work at the community building—the little brothers-in-law Moshe Katz and Leon Neuman—while the others were stewing in anger. Neuman also recently resigned in anger, because of the colony chief's dictatorial practices, and only the old man and Moshe Katz have remained at the helm—the two roosters who peck at each other's eyes. During the last manhunt, November 30, the old man himself ruled the roost and indicated who from among the colony collaborators should be sent away, and he did not even spare Moshe Katz's two brothers—Iankel and Aaron—(they were both saved through ruse ...). Moshe Katz then left the community building in a rage, leaving the management of the community to the old man in charge.

The colony chief soon realized that he could not cope with the challenges of the difficult problems facing the Jewish administration without energetic coworkers, and telephoned the righteous one of the generation Moritz Katz, asking him to come immediately, for God's sake, and to make peace for the second time. Moritz Katz indeed arrived today at noon and has been working diligently with the means at his disposal to restore domestic peace. He summoned the two irate in-laws and the leaders of the opposition, and has strived to establish a council that is capable of accomplishing something.

[December 6, 1943] 7 P.M.

The righteous one of the generation from Moghilev has managed to make the match. He gave the former friends a good scolding, both the widower and the critics from the opposition, indicating that Transnistria is not the appropriate place to continue the fierce quarrels that took place in the Jewish communities in the old country. No one among us, including the

---

of Vijniţa: "the deputy head of the committee, Moshe Katz was a Jew devoted to saving Jews...In the circumstances of those days, there were certainly Jews who in innocence and out of fear for their lives committed various crimes against their fellow Jews. However, Moshe Katz did not allow such crimes and devoted his soul to saving the lives of the Jews in the ghetto"; see Menashe Miller, ed., *Sefer Hai Uvaruch*: *Be'emek Habaha* (Hebrew), vol. 2 (Haifa: Machon "Makor Habraha," 1993), p. 190.

president of the Central Council—he asserted—can swear to it that he will not be thrown out one day to some hell on earth and sent to the place from which one only returns in a dream …

They finally reconciled, cobbled together a new council with the old faces, apart from Ungariş, and added six new council members from the intelligentsia.

December 8, 1943, 7 A.M.

The new council was reconstituted yesterday. They created a tremendous number of departments and committees, and did not spare any honors as in the former times of community politics and the paradise of the office of the synagogue warden. It seems to everyone that the matter is settled in the community house, and they are acting like a young couple …

In the last few days I have written long scrolls with protocols of the endless and redundant meetings—more than in the previous two years. Uplifting speeches have been delivered right and left, and plans for the common good have poured out of a sack riddled with holes. What, alas, will the new rulers be able to accomplish in the chaos of Transnistria!

All the beds in the hospital are already occupied by typhus patients. There are apartments whose tenants have all been infected. Because the Jewish administration is in its death throes and there is panic on all sides, only a very weak war is being waged against the Rickettsia bacteria, unlike last year.

December 9, 1943, 7 P.M.

A relative of Roza, who had been in exile in the camp of Kopaygorod, came to visit us today. I asked him for details about the situation there and will record here a brief summary of his remarks, because he is a serious and trustworthy source.

The first year of exile, 1941–1942, was truly devastating for the 4,000 inhabitants of the camp. By the spring of 1942, almost 2,000 persons had died from hunger, cold, plagues, and exhaustion. The disaster reached its peak in July 1942, when the entire camp was driven into a forest, except for a few well-connected people and "lords." I have already written about this in the past. They kept the people outdoors under the open sky, fenced in with barbed wire, for a month. The forest tragedy annihilated close to 500 people, and most of the survivors suffer from afflictions for their entire life. The council there was led by a lawyer from Bukovina, Ricu Kupferberg, who ruled as colony chief and did not concern himself with the *Lagernikes* at all but only with his own lot in the forest tragedy, and who did not lift a finger for the public to rescind the decree.

Following the release of the remaining remnant from the forest, the Moghilev prefect Login taught this leader a lesson and sent him and his wife to the peat-pit in Tulchin. At the same time, the prefect appointed a new colony chief Fabius Ornstein[14] from Vijniţa, and this young man is the opposite of his predecessor—a Jew with a warm heart, courage, and a readiness to dedicate himself to the public good.

Immediately after the return of the survivors from the forest to Kopaygorod, Ornstein began to work zealously to prevent further catastrophes in the camp. Thanks to his initiative, they established the most important help institutions: a soup kitchen, where they have distributed three meals a day; an orphanage, where they have accepted all the orphans without exception, around 150 children; a hospital with twenty-five beds; and they have organized a strictly supervised administration. They know nothing about manhunts in Kopaygorod. When Moghilev demands workers, the council [in Kopaygorod] chooses only men who are fit for work, mostly young, single men without family obligations, and the colony chief himself checks every case. The colony chief himself also then takes those chosen to Moghilev, and he often even manages to persuade them to reduce the quota and send people back. Ornstein, who is a very important figure in Prefect Login's eyes, because of his serious attitude, frequently manages to persuade him.

For example, while the manhunt for sixty men was underway (see the previous entry about the "repatriation–*Purim Shpil*"),[15] they demanded

14 For more about the management of the ghetto during the tenure of Fabius Ornstein, see Lavi, *Pinkas Hakehilot*: *Rumania*, vol. 1, pp. 501–504.

15 The entry of October 3, 1943.

forty men from Kopaygorod. Ornstein rushed immediately to Moghilev and succeeded in persuading the prefect to waive the workers from Kopaygorod. They were also spared the panic that raged in Moghilev, Shargorod, and Murafa a few weeks ago.

Yes, Kopaygorod has indeed been reformed, and yet there is nothing to envy: 2,500 victims and the forest tragedy are far too great a price for such good fortune …

December 10, 1943, 7 P.M.

Today the commander of the gendarmerie in Skazinets, where the penal camp for Moghilev criminals is located, came to visit the community building. His name is Grigori Popescu, and he came to the "model colony" to see how a respectable camp is run. The colony chief really glowed with satisfaction as he led the guest through the places of which he is proud: the orphanage, the cooperative (where the commander was given special "attention"—a package containing all kinds of the good things, weighing 10 kilos …), the "court" [of justice], the pharmacy, the soup kitchen—when the needy were not there—and the offices. On the other hand, the commander did not get to visit the poorhouse and the mass-housing quarters. The overlord inscribed in the orphanage guest book that everything appeared to be in excellent order, and the colony chief's face glowed, as though he had won the big jackpot …

December 11, 1943, 3 P.M.

The first three days of the "democratic" administration in the community building have in the meantime only brought on meetings of all kinds of committees and subcommittees, day and night, beautiful, poetic sermons, never-ending scrolls of protocols, dozens of decisions and resolutions, which are destined to end up in the wastebasket. I am writing my fingers off, and there is no more room in the cupboard for the mountains of papers. The renovated council plays at "community activism," according to the old version, oblivious to its surroundings.

They have now decided to create a "*Keren Hayesod*" [foundation fund] in simple terms: to bring in a little cash into the community coffers. Toward this end, they invited those of means, the wealthy and the influential, to the community building and tried to persuade them in the name of good and justice to consider the community needs and to contribute for the sake of doing a good deed. The owners of the wallets saw the way the wind was blowing and requested receiving aid [themselves] in their need ... now that absolute democracy rages in the camp, the important guests were allowed to go home without being harassed. To be honest, allow me to note that, after long debates, the "lords" indeed immediately decided to importune the rich further, but they then only tried to win them over in a pleasant manner and with gentle words of *muser*. Will it be possible to fill the pots in the soup kitchen with real democracy? ...

The clothes distribution operation is progressing very slowly, not as is needed during the current, insane times, when we do not know what tomorrow will bring. In the meantime, all those returning from the labor camps have been clothed, but as for the rest of the public, they are too busy with "democracy" and bureaucracy. I am one of the "fortunate ones" and have already received a few articles—underwear and a couple of pieces of cheap clothing. Still, it's better than nothing.

[December 11, 1943] One Hour Later

The post chief today demanded that the council provide him with a list of all *Lagernikes* from the Regat within twenty-four hours. There are only thirteen of these people, who came from the Dorohoi district, in the camp. Only the Jews from the Dorohoi district were deported from the Regat, approximately 5,000 persons. It seems that the well-connected people of the Regat will nevertheless be sent home soon.[16]

---

16 In January 1944, when the return of the Jews of Dorohoi became possible, the heads of the Jewish community in Romania began negotiations with the Romanian authorities

[December 11, 1943] 9 P.M.

The Department of Culture of the Transnistrian General Government intends to publish a book entitled "Monographs about Jews in Transnistria." The high-level officials clearly intend to throw dust in the eyes of the world and present lies, what never was and never happened, to demonstrate that the uprooted Jews immediately struck it rich [in Transnistria].

The prefect of Moghilev, Login, has sent printed questionnaires to all "colonies," including Dzhurin, which we must complete and send back. The overlords are suddenly desperate to know how the expulsion was conducted, what happened at the bank of the Dniester on the eve of the crossing, how we settled into our "new homes," how the people make a living, and even what we think and how our moods fare in the paradise between the Dniester and the Bug.

There are also questions that indicate that they believe that the Yids are foolish and stupid. For example, go tell the whole truth regarding whether Jews trade in "non-kosher" goods in the "colonies," and whether couriers from Romania arrive frequently, smuggling in cash and letters. Order No. 23 decrees no less than the death sentence if the reply is "Yes." And yet our clever colony chief [Dr. Rosenstrauch] murmured under his breath that we must record everything in the questionnaires, as they really are, to demonstrate our loyalty to the state. By the way, he himself will fill in the answers, and who knows what kind of troubles he will bring upon us, unless the council intervenes.

December 12, 1943, 3 P.M.

Yesterday Moshe Katz brought important news from Shargorod. The praetor Rusu announced that in the course of the coming week they

---

regarding the return of orphans from Transnistria. It should be noted that at this time the Soviet army was already about to reconquer the area and seize it from the Germans and the Romanians. The Romanians were willing to return the Jews of Dorohoi, because Dorohoi was part of the Regat until 1938, when it was administratively annexed to Southern Bukovina.

will send home the deportees from the Dorohoi district (the Regat). A Romanian commission came to Moghilev concerning the repatriation, but no one knows to whom this refers. They are waiting there for a second commission in which a Swiss representative from the "Red Cross" will also play a role and will investigate the situation of the "colonists." Therefore, the regime is indeed hurrying to create an optical illusion—the book that I previously mentioned.[17]

[December 12, 1943] 9 P.M.

This afternoon the council held extensive debates regarding the state monograph. They finally appointed a committee of three people—Dr. Iosef Diamant, the lawyer Şmuel Fafliker, and my humble self—to write the chapter about Dzhurin. I have been tasked with painting a picture of Jewish life in Bukovina from the beginning of the war (June 22, 1941) until after the expulsion (October 1941), to describe how the "colony" of Dzhurin organized itself, and what social activities were held here. Certainly, important matters, when the tongue is not fettered. If only I can manage to bear in mind the saying, "Wash my fur, but do not get it wet," because otherwise they will reject my report. I would waive this "honor," but I must not jeopardize my meager livelihood.

December 13, 1943, 3 P.M.

Typhus has permitted itself to spread outside the boundary of the ghetto and also is raging in the villages among the peasants. This is a kind of vicious circle: the peasants now bring the gift to Dzhurin, and people are infected at the market. The illness is serious and causes complications, especially in the inner ear. A few people have already fallen victim, but the mortality rate is not high, thanks to the abundance of injections.[18]

17 See the entry of December 11, 1942.

18 Medicines, including vaccines against typhus, began to arrive from Romania at the beginning of 1943.

[December 13, 1943] 9 P.M.

I have already completed my contribution to the monograph—whether *in a guter sho*, we will know in time … The result is twenty-four pages crammed full with crowded writing, and yet I touched only a very small portion of the broad issues. I mainly touched upon the most painful aspects of the Transnistrian morass. I often had to be content with lines when scrolls were really needed and only hinted at the most essential. The manuscript will go through two censors—the council with the colony chief, first, and the Romanian editors in Tiraspol. They will have enough to erase and change, mostly the veiled allusions.[19]

December 14, 1943, 7 P.M.

Sometimes I tutor my son, Bertl, in the *Humesh*—to learn the *parshe*.[20] Today I taught him the romantic portion "*Vayeshev*"—the story of Yosef and his brothers—thoroughly. Upon discovering that our father Yaakov put on sack [cloth] on his loins as an expression of mourning when his sons imparted the news that a wild animal had torn Yosef to shreds, Bertl asked me: "Well, and did our father Yaakov walk around naked until then?" Certainly, if one is not wearing a sack, one walks around naked, according to Transnistrian concepts! …

December 15, 1943, 8 A.M.

A rumor circulated yesterday evening that there would be a manhunt at night. The men fled from the homes, mainly to open fields, even though the snow is almost half-a-meter deep, and the wind strikes their faces with piercing snow needles. They spent the night hiding outside and have still not returned.

---

19 Despite searches in various archives, we have not been able to find this monograph.

20 The *Humash* is the first five books of the Jewish Bible, which are divided into *parashot* (sections that are read each week in the synagogue on the Sabbath).

December 16, 1943, 3 P.M.

We again had distinguished guests in the camp today, the commission from the Red Cross. The commission's arrival was not unexpected, because last night the praetor Rusu from Shargorod telephoned the post chief to inform him that the camp must take on a festive appearance, and every corner of the camp should shine in honor of the important guests. The people cleaned and scrubbed throughout the night, the militia searched the streets and alleys for signs of anything that does not smell fragrant, and the group leaders inspected the apartments.

Three luxury automobiles with the guests arrived in the ghetto at about 10 A.M. In addition to the dignitary Charles Kolb,[21] the commission also included an important activist at the Red Cross in Geneva, the Romanian noblewoman Lutsia Ioan, delegates from the Romanian "Red Cross," Colonel Rădulescu, the commander of the Moghilev gendarmerie legion, Major Botoroagă, the prefect from Shargorod, Ruso, and a group of their servants.

The commission first went to the orphanage, the pride and joy of the "model colony," which they greatly enjoyed for half an hour. Then they drove to the hospital, where it is tidy and clean, even though the beds are full. The Romanian overlords intended to show the highlights, but Charles Kolb appears to be a person who does not allow himself to be dazzled. He probed and queried and asked basic questions, such as: "Why are the Jews not allowed to go out into the surroundings to work in the kolkhozes?" "Why do they seize people for work, including the ill and the elderly and

---

21 The Red Cross made efforts to act through two channels in order to ease the suffering of the Jews in 1943 by organizing the delivery of aid to the deportees and by attempting to intervene in several countries that were allies of the Reich or satellite states. In November 1943, Charles Kolb, a representative of the Red Cross, was posted in Bucharest, which gave new impetus to the work of the international organization in that city. Kolb, together with the representative of the Red Cross in Romania and the representative of the Red Cross in Geneva, visited the ghettos in the Moghilev district. Despite the measures taken by the authorities, the Jewish representatives were able to provide the delegation with documented information on the real situation. Dr. Meir Teich was able to pass on a detailed report and Charles Kolb forwarded it to the Comisia Autonomă De Ajutorare in Bucharest. See Carp, *Cartea neagră*, vol. 3, p. 304.

those who care for large families?" "Why are the workers not paid for their hard labor?" And so on.

Our "lords," led by the colony chief, listened to the questions and were careful to give answers that have only an iota of truth. They recognized in the faces of the Romanian overlords that they must hold their tongues, so that the festival will pass quickly and the weekdays remain. And then something happened which clearly showed that the camp is not only made up of a group of frightened, dejected creatures who turn a cheek to receive a slap, but rather there is also someone with courage, who is willing to endanger himself for the general good. This man is named Marcel Aronovici, a fellow from Vaslui (from the Regat)[22] who endured a few months of the hellish torment of digging peat in Tulchin a year ago. This young man, together with nine other people who had returned from the camps of Trikhaty, Varvarovka, and Tulchin, were summoned to the commission by the council, at Kolb's request, to relate how they had spent those months of hard labor. The Labor Office intentionally chose simple people, thinking that these men would not dare to tell the terrible truth.

The functionaries at the Labor Office were mistaken. Marcel Aronovici showed that his tongue is not dumb. Well, he spilled out details about Tulchin as from a sack, so that the hair of the delegates from Geneva stood on end. Kolb listened attentively to the words and from time to time shook his head "no," meaning, it cannot be, except perhaps among wild animals. Marcel's courage had an impact on the other nine "witnesses," and they also spoke out about the hell of Trikhaty and Varvarovka, although in simple terms. We clearly saw the color of the faces of the Romanian overlords change and the colony chief hop from one foot to the other in rage, but all was lost. When Marcel returned from the commission, people received him with applause and kisses, and a few tried to raise him up and carry him on their shoulders, but he refused this honor. This is the first case of open revolt in the Dzhurin camp, even though only in words. May Marcel be crowned with blessings!

The council members did not spare any promises that soon all the deportees would be sent home, first of all those from the Regat, and then

22 The capital of the Vaslui region in Moldavia in the Regat.

those from Bukovina and Bessarabia. As for the question of "when," we will know in time …

By the way, I almost forgot: before the commission arrived, the militia had driven everyone from the market and the alleys and, with harsh warnings, forbade anyone to go outside as long as the commission was there. The gendarmerie issued the order, which was intended to prevent a grave danger: the guests must not, God forbid, encounter any naked and barefoot creatures—the living dead who roam the streets in the Transnistrian paradise. How could they be allowed to discover in Geneva that in Transnistria the Jewish "colonists" nevertheless do not live like gods in Odessa …

December 17, 1943, 7 P.M.

I submitted my manuscript regarding the monograph about Dzhurin to the council. I first read the text to people with a literary sense, and the criticism was not bad. This does not mean that the chief censor, the colony chief, will also like my lines and my heretical allusions. So what …

The other two staff members, Dr. Diamant and the lawyer Fafliker, have also completed their chapters. I have read the texts and noticed that they too did not try hard to ingratiate themselves. The high-level officials will not derive much pleasure from the Dzhurin opus, since this was not our aim. Who knows what kind of verdict the authors will receive, because of both what is said and what is not said …

December 18, 1943, 7 P.M.

The day before yesterday, Thursday, the Red Cross commission traveled from Dzhurin to Shargorod and spent the night there. Charles Kolb presented a questionnaire that posed quite strange questions to the council there, for example: "Is the intention in Transnistria to destroy all the deported Jews in various manners?" "Does the remaining remnant have the stamina to endure a third winter under these horrifying conditions?" "Are all the Jews not liable to be annihilated if the Germans retreat from

Ukraine?" And a quite germane question: "Are the Jewish 'colonies' capable of organizing repatriation to Romania, if the Romanian state will agree to it?"

It is conceivable that the entire matter of repatriation is nothing more than wishful thinking, especially at this time, and yet the despondency has been eased slightly.

[December 18, 1943] 12 A.M.

This time I am not sitting down to write my memoirs at night because of the bedbugs or my agitated nerves. I just now returned from the community building after having been suddenly summoned there by a messenger three hours ago for an urgent assignment. An order had just arrived from Moghilev to repatriate the deportees from Dorohoi (the Regat) already tonight, so I had to immediately assemble a list of the seventeen fortunate people and take care of the paperwork.

The shtetl is in an uproar and is seething, and until things become clear, the men have fled to the fields. We have already been disappointed enough by good news like this that ends in a manhunt. However, there was no reason to fear this time, because the Jews from Dorohoi really did hit the jackpot. According to the order, the Dorohoi Jews had to put their baggage on their shoulders and advance toward Moghilev, where the assembly point for the repatriation is located. Negotiators persuaded the post chief (not for the sake of the next world, God forbid …) that he should requisition wagons in the kolkhozes (where some still remain in readiness …) so that the crowd not journey by foot in the middle of the winter. The repatriates will be kept in quarantine briefly, before being loaded into wagons at the Volcineţ station.

The people of Dorohoi assembled with their bundles in the community building and waited for the wagons. Of the twenty-four persons who arrived in Dzhurin in the autumn of 1941, seventeen remain. Seven will not be repatriated, because they have already established permanent residence in the Dzhurin cemetery. Those who are returning home are elated, but they also continue to ask whether the authorities intend to send them to Pechora …

December Nineteenth, 1943, 8 A.M.

The gendarmes sent sleds for the people of Dorohoi instead of wagons, because the roads are covered with snow. Those returning home were seated on four sleds with all their belongings, while the two escorts sat on the fifth sled like lords: the colony chief and a delegate, an Adolf Leibovici, a member of the inner circle. Hundreds of people were there when the sleds moved off at 3 A.M., and even a fiddle was heard. This is the *Leyl Shimurim* in Dzhurin, which does not reek of a manhunt.

December 20, 1943, 9 P.M.

Six hundred persons from Dorohoi set out from Shargorod on peasant sleds that the community rented for them. The state actually promised to send trucks for those to be repatriated, but the vehicles deliberately arrived a day late.

All the people of Dorohoi from the Moghilev district gathered at an assembly point in Moghilev, where they spent two days under the open sky—that is, in a kind of quarantine. At the same time, their belongings were disinfected in a very vicious manner. Clothes and underwear were maliciously damaged in the disinfection apparatus, and the "liberated" were treated very roughly. All kinds of angels of destruction snatched and plundered whatever they could from their meager belongings. The crowd, which had been made kosher, was taken from Moghilev to the train station at Valtshinetz.

As for the repatriation of other groups, we know for certain that all the orphans without both mother and father, around 5,000 children, will be taken to Romania, perhaps by the end of the month. The Romanian state has refused to accept Jewish orphans of Ukrainian Jewish origin. The federation of the Jewish communities in Romania has pledged to support all the orphans at its own expense, including those without either a father or a mother.

On the other hand, the chances of sending all the deportees back to their old homes have decreased. The magistrates of Bukovina and Bessarabia are moving heaven and earth to ensure that their Yids are not sent back, and they will surely succeed. I really do not want them to send us away from here, exposed to the cruelty of winter. Such a journey will undoubtedly claim many victims. It is so cold in my cubbyhole that a dog would flee for his life. I have obtained a small stove that can barely hold splinters. As long as we feed it with thin slivers of wood, it gives off a small amount of heat. My left foot has been afflicted with terrible rheumatic pain, which really bothers me.

December 21, 1943, 8 P.M.

(Written in Hebrew, as a *sgule* …)[23] Two young men who had been sent from Dzhurin to the German labor camp in Kurievka returned today.[24] They recount a horrific incident that occurred there a few days ago. The officers demanded that a company of Jewish slaves complete part of the bridge in a week. Although the laborers worked strenuously, they nevertheless did not meet the deadline. The SS Einsatzgruppe immediately conducted a just trial. The executioners cast lots, and whoever had the bad luck—eleven Jews—were hanged, while all the laborers stood in a circle around the gallows and were forced to witness the dark destruction. By the way, not a single day went by there without the SS men or the Ukrainian militia shooting Jews. A middle-aged Jew, a fellow townsman of mine—Izik Singer—was shot a week ago by a Ukrainian militiaman when he sat down on the ground to gulp down some potato peel soup—according to the order, they are required to eat standing up.

More than 500 men from Dzhurin have been sent to work since June 1943 and, so far, less than 350 have returned. We know for a fact that at least fifty have died, and this is not the last word.

---

23 Although Kunstadt states that this entry was written in Hebrew, in the typed copy of the diary in our possession, it is written in Yiddish.

24 A village on the eastern bank of the Bug River. The Germans established a labor camp there. The deportees were forced to construct a wooden bridge over the Dniester River under terrible working and living conditions. See Lavi, *Pinkas Hakehilot*: *Rumania*, vol. 1, p. 505.

December 23, 1943, 8 P.M., Third Candle of *Hanuke*

Let us at least note in the date that it is *Hanuke*, the holiday of miracles and courage.

The colony chief, who accompanied to Moghilev the Jews of Dorohoi, who were returning home, came back today. Even though he tends to praise the Romanian overlords and kowtow to them, he nevertheless relates details of the cruel treatment of the "liberated" Jews of Dorohoi by the occupying authorities. More than 3,000 repatriating Jews roamed around for a week among stables and ruins before being sent onward. The disinfection of their belongings entailed vicious treatment. They shaved the people from head to toe, and in the first two days, the Romanian orderlies shaved the women's bodies. Only then did they allow Jewish women to do the shaving. The operator of the disinfection machine intentionally raised the pressure of the steam in order to scorch the belongings. The repatriating Jews had to undress and change underwear and clothes under the open sky in the freezing cold.

Fred Şaraga, the general secretary of the Romanian communities, has been in Moghilev for a week to relieve the fate of the repatriating Jews. The federation has sent a tremendous amount of clothes, underwear, and food for the Jews of Dorohoi who are on their way home—a fine expression of Jewish unity. Fred Şaraga claims that they will send all the deportees home, but when and where, he does not know. He asserts that they are making every effort regarding this matter.

I am writing these lines by the light of a real lamp—for the first time in two years—which I borrowed in honor of *Hanuke.*

A separate committee has been set up in Moghilev to organize the repatriation from all the camps in the region, if it comes to this. The committee comprises three people: Moritz Katz, the president of the Moghilev Central Council; the Shargorod colony chief, Dr. Meir Teich; and the Dzhurin colony chief, Dr. Max Rosenstrauch. Perhaps it will do something after all! …

December 25, 1943, 8 P.M.

The rumors of an imminent repatriation of the Romanian "*bishenitzes*" have rattled the Jews in Dzhurin who no longer had hope of being saved. They have convened a meeting and have chosen their own committee, even if it will not be needed, headed by the activist Iohanan Darman, to look after the local Ukrainian Jews. After our repatriation, they will remain "at sea," poor things, subject to all kinds of misfortunes, because they have no contact with the occupying authorities, do not understand Romanian, are considered by the occupiers to be Bolsheviks and enemies, and will not be capable of satisfying the leeches, according to the firmly established tradition.

The local Jews, all beggars and paupers, are in a great danger of being sent to the Bug and even further, if the Romanian Jews will no longer be here. The Ukrainian Jews have already been deported from Moghilev and other places in Transnistria to Pechora and other hells long ago. Only for their sake would it be worthwhile to delay repatriation until the great deliverance, which is already not far from the door …

There are still three patients sick with typhus, without fever, in the hospital. However, this does not mean that the plague has completely subsided. The Rickettsia bacteria does not take leave just like that, especially in the middle of the winter. But let us not take on any worries on credit …

December 30, 1943, 10 P.M.

It has been a week of non-Jewish holidays, parties, golden dreams, and many sorrows. Here is a brief day-to-day rundown of the week:

Shabbes, the First Day of the Time of Our Rejoicing, "_Nitel_" [Christmas]

The Ukrainian doctor from the factory quarter organized a banquet fit for a king and invited the "lords" to the celebration. The "lords" did not decline the invitation, surely for the sake of good relations. That day we found out the names of more people from the Dzhurin camp who had perished in the labor camps of Trikhaty, Kurievka, and Varvarovka under the Germans.

Sunday, the Second Non-Jewish Holiday

A young Ukrainian woman who has a very good relationship with the post chief—they are probably engaging in a kosher task together—invited the "lords" to a party in honor of the holiday. Who would refuse to do such a good deed, for the benefit of all! ...

Monday, the Third Holiday of the Exiled Communities

Today was the really big celebration in the barracks of the gendarmes, paid for by the council. The "lords" are already collapsing from exhaustion, poor things. It is not a trivial matter not to close an eye for three nights, although everything, you understand, is done for the sake of heaven. As if prompted by the devil, exactly at 2 A.M., when the party was reaching its peak, the telephone rang and the colony chief and Moshe Katz were summoned immediately to Moghilev. The poor things had to leave when it was just beginning to get interesting ...

In the soup kitchen today, they poured out a pot of bean soup that went bad, poor thing, into the trash. What is the matter? Some of the recipients have not appeared in the kitchen for a few days, because of the heavy snowfall, and they have no shoes. It is believed that their names will be erased from the list, because the community is not to be mocked ...

Tuesday

The council of Shargorod issued an order: we must prepare two lists here immediately: first, one of all the orphans and, second, one of all the local Dzhurin Jews. May this be for our good ...

Wednesday

Our big shots were dragged out of the party on Monday night, as I described above, and today we know the reason for this. They were reprimanded in Moghilev, because, together with the Dorohoi Jews, a few refugees who were not originally from the fortunate region also snuck out. They are waiting in Moghilev for the activist Fred Şaraga like the messiah, because he has promised to bring news of a general repatriation soon.

The authorities have disbanded the neighboring "colony" of Kantakovitz,[25] because most of the people in the camp there were originally from Dorohoi and have gone home. About twenty people who were not from Dorohoi remained, and the regime transferred them to Dzhurin and ordered them to be registered as kosher residents of the "model colony." The new guests established their homes in the empty homes of the Dorohoi Jews and have begun a new life here, close to *Nei'la* [near the end].

Today, Thursday

Both the king and the second-in-command returned from Dzhurin [*sic*] [Moghilev]. It turned out that only kosher Dorohoi Jews from Dzhurin were repatriated, and that the denunciation concerned other camps. By the way, news has already come from Dorohoi that they have arrived safely in their hometown.

The delegates report that the general repatriation is considered a sure thing in Moghilev, in the bag, and it seems that the miracle will occur as early as January.

January 1, 1944, Evening

A new year in the world. This marks the sixth year since the bloody madness began, and the fire is raging on all the continents more intensely and with greater cruelty. The Angel of Death is collapsing from exhaustion, but the Master of the Universe is spurring him on with a fiery whip to continue his work unrelentingly.

This year in Dzhurin is like last year, that is, like yesterday. A branch of the Moghilev Repatriation Committee has been established here, and it has assembled groups of forty people who will travel home together. The Moghilev Central Council is working vigorously, and has appointed a vast range of functionaries and emissaries and just plain bums, and continues to prepare for the exodus from Transnistria even before the ruler has opened the cage.

---

25 It is unclear what this is.

The colony chief left today for Moghilev, and the rest of the "lords" went to the gendarmerie for the big celebration in honor of the non-Jewish new year. The council flaunted its wealth: six militiamen marched out with *shlach mones*,[26] each with two splendid cakes in his hands. Who can decree whether this behavior is crooked or straight. It is written in the *Humesh* that Grandfather Yaakov also behaved in this manner toward the Esau of his day! The difference is only that the grandfather paid for the gifts out of his own pocket ...

January 2, 1944, 9 P.M.

A grotesque coup has taken place while people are busy with packing their bags to go home. The prefect of Moghilev, Login, telephoned the post chief today, instructing him that the council must be replaced without delay. Apart from the colony chief, only the council members Moshe Katz, Leon Neuman, Bobi Rosenrauch, Dr. Sheierman, and B. Valdman will remain in their positions, while all the others can sit at home. Only one victim from the old guard fell: Eltes. "Democracy," sections, and subsections are over; no more scrolls of protocol or sticking one's nose in forbidden places. So, the two big shots, the colony chief and the second-in-command, have in the meanwhile made a mess of things to take over the regime! ...

I too have registered with one of those groups of forty [who will travel together], so as not to appear too clever and separate myself from the public.

January 5, 1944, 7 A.M.

Yesterday, the Shargorod colony chief, Dr. Meir Teich, appeared in the community house, surrounded by "his people": the labor minister, Zand; the administrative director of the orphanage, Brecher;[27] and other small

---

26 Gifts consisting typically of cakes, confections, fruit, wine, or money that are given on the holiday of Purim.

27 Friedrich Brecher, who was deported from Câmpulung, worked in a sawmill and was

fish. They looked around here and there to examine how the "model colony" of Dzhurin is run, and Dr. Teich did not spare any advice. In other words, we need advice for the future, while we are already standing with one foot on the other side of the Dniester! …

The almighty ruler of Shargorod wrote in a protocol that Dzhurin is indeed an exceptional place and, as a parting gift, he left instructions in the name of the praetor: all men without exception must shave their heads. The praetor apparently has respect for beards and side curls but never mind, the Dzhurin barbers will also have a good day! …

[January 5, 1944] 3 P.M.

The colony chief has returned from Moghilev empty-handed. They are expecting Fred Şaraga in Moghilev like the messiah, because he is supposed to bring deliverance. Regarding Şaraga's arrival, there are different dates: the 8th, the 20th, and pessimists even refer to the first stanza as documentary memory:

> Do not fret, / Şaraga will come at *Purim*, / and if not *Purim*, / then *Peysech* / or even *Sukkes*, what do I know …

As for the Dorohoi Jews: they had an easy journey, apart from a rigorous inspection at the train station at Cernăuţi. An inspection was conducted there to ensure that they were not carrying any "piglets" (Russian currency), "*lokhsen*" (dollars), leather, new fabrics, and written or printed writings. This means that, in the case of repatriation, these memoirs will not remain in my possession.

---

known as an expert in the treatment of wood. Brecher was active in the Shargorod ghetto council and was the driving force behind the establishment of this orphanage. He would gather orphan children in the streets and take them to the orphanage. See Tzvi Brecher, "Beit Hayetomim BeShargorod: Mifalo Hanehedar Shel Friedrich Brecher, *z"l*," in Avni, *Sefer Zikaron Lekehilat Yehudei Câmpulung –Bukovina Vehaseviva*, vol. 1, pp. 336–338.

[January 5, 1944] Evening

There are rumors that the mark is once again dangerously ill. All the goods in the market disappeared in the blink of an eye, and the crowd burst into the cooperative and grabbed salt, soap, shoelaces, and other bargains in a panic. They sold to everyone whatever they demanded and as much as they wanted, and did not raise the prices. They are also in a panic about the mark in Shargorod today.

The people are very rattled by the sensational news from the fronts. They are frightened and do not know why; they are hopeful and do know not what to hope for; they want [something] and do not know what. Three new cases of typhus have been discovered.

January 6, 1944, 3 P.M. (written in Hebrew)

The colony chief has resorted to a vicious ploy that is liable to bring on trouble to hundreds of families. He inspected the cards [in the card catalog] of all the people in the Southern Bukovina camp and erased all those who at first lived in Northern Bukovina and only moved to the southern part in 1941. After the bloody liberation, many Jews from Northern Bukovina were saved by moving to the kosher Southern Bukovina, which had not been under Soviet rule for a year. These refugees were registered in Transnistria as coming from Southern Bukovina in order to wipe their Red stain off their faces. They are convinced that in the case of repatriation, they will first liberate the "kosher" Jews of Southern Bukovina. The colony chief could not bear that a few hundred families had deluded themselves into believing that they too belong among the fortunate ones and erased them, even though no one demanded it of him. He will probably boast about his patriotic act before the Romanian overlords, as he is accustomed to doing.

January 10, 1944, 3 P.M.

Difficult, fatal days. For three days we have been seeing from the top of the mountain in the camp how masses of Ukrainian refugees are being dragged along the road in the factory quarter from Vinnitsa to Moghilev. There are numerous military vehicles loaded with soldiers, cannons, and all kinds of gear on this road to Moghilev. All are coming from the East, where the Russians won a great victory near Uman and breached the front.

This morning we heard muted cannon shots from a distance. Rumors are springing up like mushrooms after the rain, one more bizarre than the next, and are immediately dissipating. It seems that the activist from Bucharest Fred Şaraga is already in Moghilev. The colony chief traveled there on Friday, January 7.

January 12, 1944, 9 P.M. (*Lashon Hakodesh*)[28]

The front is apparently not far away. We frequently hear muted shots, German vehicles rushing along the road, roaring and buzzing, and German airplanes racing past them on high like lightning, singly or in fleets.[29] The peasants are afraid to go to the market, and the few who do go demand a fortune for a potato or a bottle of milk.

People snatch up the goods from their hands. Flour, wood, and oil have completely disappeared. There are speculators who steal into the villages, smuggling in produce to trade. They fleece whoever falls into their hands. These people do not only risk their own lives but those of the entire camp. The forests are teeming with partisans, and the gendarmes have warned us not to set foot outside of the ghetto. Neither the militia nor the council has the power to restrain the greedy speculators. The

---

28 Although Kunstadt indicated that this entry and others that follow were in *Lashon Hakodesh*, that is, Hebrew, all the entries in the typed copy of the diary in our possession are in Yiddish.

29 On the reports of the defeat of the Germans and their retreat, see Carp, *Cartea neagră*, vol. 3, p. 305.

entrenched discipline has completely broken down, and it has become as in the verse, "every man did that which was right in his own eyes."[30]

January 13, 1944, 9 P.M. (*Lashon Hakodesh*)

The tension heightens from hour to hour. Inflation has reached its peak. One kilo of salt costs 90 marks; 1 liter of oil, 30 marks. There is no wood available, because the forest is swarming with soldiers, who are lying in wait for the partisans. Who knows how long this interim situation will last and how it will end!

Letters have arrived from Bucharest, declaring that the state no longer plans to continue the repatriation of the deportees to Transnistria and has done its duty by repatriating the Jews from Dorohoi who are "their own."

Since before noon today, German vehicles have also been racing on the road through the ghetto, past the "palace" where I celebrate the exile. My heart rejoices at the sight of this stampede, although, at the same time, it is pounding like a hammer. The deadlock has come to an end.

January 15, 1944, *Motzei Shabbes*, the 20th of *Tevet* (*Lashon Hakodesh*)

German vehicles continue to race by nonstop, day and night, on the main road from Vinnitsa to Moghilev, which crosses the factory quarter. German soldiers have settled in the area of the camp—the good apartments have been vacated for them—and there is a regular turnover, one comes and another goes. Until today, they have not bothered anyone, but Jews avoid walking down the street to avoid seeing the demon and testing the "Graciousness [of the Lord]."[31] Six Germans are living next door to my apartment.

30 Judges 21:25.

31 Psalm 90:17, "And let the graciousness of the Lord our God be upon us; establish You also upon us the work of our hands; yes, the work of our hands, establish You it." This verse was recited to guard against evil forces.

The German soldiers cook their food in the soup kitchen, use the hospital's disinfection machine, and bring in trucks loaded with wood from the forest. They distribute the wood for free, especially if someone helps them with something. The soldiers consider the Jews from Bukovina, who speak German well, as important, but they [the Bukovinians] are careful not to argue with them. They [the Germans] invite people to listen to the radio with them, but everyone comes up with an excuse. Regardless of their good behavior, everyone heeds the admonishment, "And your life will hang in doubt before thee."[32]

Surprisingly, just yesterday in the neighboring settlement of Derebchin, they shot eleven Jewish residents and wounded four. People find it comforting that an SS murderer committed the deed on his own initiative and not in the course of an "*Aktzia*."[33] However, there are rumors that following the intervention of the Red Cross, the Romanian occupying authorities persuaded the Germans not to bother the Jews in Transnistria. What about the incident in Derebchin? It is indeed a complex question …

I still have a few pieces of wood in my dwelling that will scarcely suffice for three days. Let us not worry about the fourth day, when we do not know what the fourth minute is liable to bring. Cannon shots can still be heard, more frequently and louder than before. The birth pangs of the deliverance are severe, and if only the newborn will not be malformed! …

January 19, 1944, 7 P.M.

We no longer hear the thunder of cannon fire. German military vehicles are still speeding by on the main road, but much less frequently than before. The German soldiers have already left the ghetto, and the fear has lessened. The peasants are appearing in the market with their goods, and there is wood once again. The prices suit the pockets of the wealthy.

Three people from Dzhurin returned from the German labor camp of Varvarovka today—ragged and worn out, their feet wrapped in rags,

32 Deut. 28:66: "And your life will hang in doubt before you; and you will fear night and day, and will have no assurance of your life."

33 See the report in Carp, *Cartea neagră*, vol. 3, p. 305.

covered in lice, their faces like the faces of the dead after thirty days. They say that they were hauled for more than a week in cattle cars with a transport of "liberated" [Jews] to Moghilev, and that thirty-one persons died from cold and starvation on the way.

January 24, 1944, 7 A.M.

The messiah has finally appeared in Moghilev, I mean Fred Şaraga. He came to organize a repatriation—not of the entire holy community but only of the orphans. Orphans up to the age of fifteen will be sent back to Romania. The orphans will find a restful place in the regions of Iaşi, Botoşani, and Dorohoi, some in orphanages, and some with Jewish families.[34]

January 30, 1944, 9 P.M.

Fred Şaraga came to Shargorod yesterday regarding the repatriation of the orphans. The Shargorod council demanded from our council a list of all orphans who lack both parents, up to the age of sixteen [*sic*],[35] even though the state has imposed the age limit of fifteen. Şaraga hopes that it will be possible to persuade them regarding the three additional years.

The council tasked me with the duty of compiling the list according to the card catalog and a straightforward questionnaire at the orphanage. Since the colony chief has been in Moghilev for a while, I have dared to "kill" more than one father and mother in the card catalog in order to create fully orphaned children from those who only lack either a father or a mother. I also lowered the age of many orphans so that their ages do not exceed eighteen. On the other hand, I did not dare to register orphans originating from Ukrainian Jewry, because this could lead

34 About 2,000 orphans, who did not have a father or a mother, left on trains from Moghilev to Romania. They were taken in by Jewish families in Iaşi, Botoşani, and Buzău.

35 Kunstadt refers to an additional three years in this paragraph, which corresponds with the age of eighteen that appears in the following paragraph.

to the disqualification of the entire list at the border. My heart truly bled when I registered the "kosher" children in the orphanage, while all around they wailed and requested that the infants originating from Ukrainian Jewry not be left behind. The most valuable of gems are among them, the single remaining remnant of refugee children from the devastated Jewish communities (Vinnitsa, Proskurov, Tomashpol, Nemirov, and so on). Allow me to note that the "lords" did not interfere with my work and even hinted that I should not be rigorous. I have composed a list of ninety-one orphans and pushed the limit as much as possible. The list is now in Shargorod. May this cholent that I have concocted succeed! …

February 3, 1944, the 9th of *Shevat*, 5704, 3 P.M.

Today is my mother's first *Yortsayt*. After coming home from [reciting the] *Kaddish* this morning, I went to the cemetery to take a look at the pile of mud. While trudging through the sticky mud with my ruined shoes, the sole of my left shoe decided to peel off completely. I had to turn around and go to a shoemaker, who patched up the broken vessel as best he could. Only at about 10 A.M. did I again go back to the cemetery. Where will I mark next year's *Yortsayt*, and will I make it to that? …

February 9, 1944, 8 P.M.

The situation is like *bein hazmanim*. The gendarmes are preoccupied with their own problems and do not bother us, the peasants bring an abundance of goods to the market and drag buyers by the sleeve, rumors arise and dissipate, and the orphans are still here. They are waiting in Moghilev for the final order from Romania.

[February 9, 1944] One Hour Later

The colony chief has already returned from Moghilev. The gendarmes received an order from Moghilev that they should make a list of all former state officials, war orphans (from World War I, regardless of their ages), and the disabled. It seems that those included in these categories will return home together with the orphans. With great difficulty, I too was registered among these well-connected people, thanks to a scrap of paper that Roza managed to smuggle over the Dniester by resorting to a ruse. This paper states that I worked for the state as a translator and as a certified graphologist at the tribunal. The colony chief objected to my registration, but this time I was lucky: the council member, the lawyer Fafliker, also registered as a translator, and the old man had no choice. Perhaps I will merit a miracle after all.

February 15, 1944, 7 P.M. (*Lashon Hakodesh*)

Transnistria is finished—on paper! The entire region between the Dniester and the Bug that has born the name Transnistria since 1941 is henceforth called the "the vanquished region between the Dniester and the Bug." This decision was made by the Romanian state. The area will no longer be divided into Romanian-style regions and districts but rather into military zones, under the command of General Potopeanu. No one knows the reason for this, but there are numerous interpretations. My heart is heavy, even though we are no longer in Transnistria …

[February 15, 1944] 10 P.M.

Today, the 21st of *Shevat*, a late *Tu B'Shevat* celebration was held at the orphanage, which was to serve as a farewell party at the same time, because we are waiting for the repatriation order of the orphans at any moment. The celebration took place in a large hall, and more than 300 people gathered, even though the entrance fee was 2 marks. The program included Yiddish folk songs, sung by a children's choir (directed by the *hazen* from Rădăuţi, Moshe Solomon); dance and rhythmic gymnastics; a dramatization of David Frishman's novel *Tithadesh*.[36] I contributed a prologue, and apart from that a charming orphan (Marta Kilshtok) recited a poem, while standing high on a gymnastic pyramid of children.

We had to be tougher than iron to swallow the tears of joy upon seeing the miracle that had befallen the sixty children, who had been abandoned on the Ukrainian plains. They now look like other children, clothed and shod, their cheeks have the color of the living, and their eyes beam with happiness and childish mischievousness.

The tremendous accomplishments of the orphanage during the barely four months of its existence have been achieved, for the most part, thanks to the devotion of the director, Bigo Hart, but let me also note the devoted help of the entire staff—teachers, educators, cooks, and workers—who have fully performed their duty, enthusiastically following in the footsteps of the director. When Bigo Hart bade farewell to his children on the stage, everyone dabbed their eyes with pocket handkerchiefs, even though he strived with all his power to avoid unnecessary pathos. The success of the celebration was enormous—both morally and materially. Since only some of the people in the camp had obtained tickets, the entire program will be repeated tomorrow.

I present the text of my prologue below, only as documentation, because the verses reflect aspects of life in Transnistria, and it is important to preserve them for future generations. I preempt my critics so that they will not feel the need to frown: the prologue has no poetic literary value.

1. Indulge me, dear guests, / these lines so few, /
   Before today's show / of finery before you, /
2. You know, a real production, / proper and respectable, /
   Must begin with a prologue, / full of foolish babble … /

36 David Frishman, *Shelosha She'ahalnu*: *Tithadesh* (Hebrew), https://benyehuda.org/read/4078 (accessed June 14, 2022). The novel tells the story of the son of a poor tailor. He never wears a new garment, so no one ever congratulates him and wishes him enjoyment of his new clothes and renewal. He dreams of hearing this blessing of renewal. His life falls apart until, as he lies on his deathbed, he sees a vision of angels going up and down and wishing him well on his new clothing. After his death, he is buried in new, white clothes, but he does not hear the blessing, "Wear it well!"

3. A prologue means / for the entire audience a greeting, /
Welcoming with a sweet smile / all those at the meeting, /
4. Each and every one, old and young, / Jews of all classes, /
Whether from a good family, pure silk, / or the masses; /
5. Whether from Dzhurin, the beautiful city, / with streets so dry, /
Where on a wet day / no need for galoshes to get by; /
6. Outside every house, there is a well / and the windows are intact; /
Straight into your mouth, / roasted doves fly in flocks; /
7. Where wood is almost free, / and bread is cheap as well, /
Where honey flows, milk too, / as from a dry well … /
8. You are strangers, foreigners, / driven from your home, /
Of your belongings nothing remains, / not even a comb; /
9. Whether you come only from Hotin, / or from Bukovina, /
Or from Romanian lands / in this local area, /
10. Whether you are poor and naked, / hungry all day long, /
Or always happy, satiated, / ready for dance and song; /
11. If you trade in matches, / thread, sweets, apples, /
Rubles, marks, or "piglets" / needles, or even buttons, /
12. Cries of "flour," "almonds," "soap," / "chopped straw," "yellow sugar," /
Weighing fairly, salt and millet, / money is rare; /
13. If you've lost, *oy vey*, / your inheritance from your grandmother, /
Be it buying salt, or playing cards, / there is no shame, do not bother … /
14. Whether you exchange it for flour and oil, / shirts, rags, underwear, /
Because need torments you, / and the cold is hard to bear; /
15. Whether you are a knave, / waiting for messengers to arrive, /
Have uncles with lots of gold, / know no tears, and continue to thrive; /
16. Perhaps you are greater than God, / I mean a council member, /
Telling everyone to donate money, / working fervently from January to December; /
17. Trudging in the mud, / digging peat, and not demanding clothes, please, /
Or medicines, or soup, / remaining stoically silent as you freeze, /
18. Or hoping hungrily, / waiting for salvation, /
A really fine remedy / for the pain and starvation; /
19. All of you, I greet you here, / your presence is an elation /
At the little orphans' / *Tu B'Shevat* celebration; /

20. And I heartily wish / that for an hour you will forget /
How sick you are / of the exile, pain, and sweat, /
21. May music, dance, and song / chase away the depression /
And grant you fresh courage / to bear the oppression; /
22. Now you, beloved children / let us hear and see /
Dance and sing, laugh and jump, / a holiday I hereby decree!

February 16, 1944, 3 P.M.

My shoes—which no longer deserve the honor of this name—will expire very soon. The shoemaker has asked me explicitly not to appear before him with these cadavers but to bury them in the cemetery. Some advice! …

February 17, 1944, 3 P.M. (*Lashon Hakodesh*)

We have learned that the police in Bucharest have laid their hands on a few activists from the underground Zionist organization involved in sending support to Transnistria through Romanian couriers.[37] This means that this source of saving lives will dry up. Hundreds of families await the few marks every month as they do the messiah, so as not to die of hunger, including me.

I am carrying in my pocket a petition to the council to approve my request to receive a loaf of bread every day in addition to my wages, just as they have granted to the militia. Moshe Katz told me that in principle

37 At the beginning of 1943, modest financial aid arrived from the Zionist movement in Romania through the leadership of the veteran Zionists in the ghetto, led by Israel Biber from Vatra Dornei. Toward the end of 1943, when the victory of Nazi Germany was no longer certain, the Romanian policy softened slightly. Deportees began to receive aid from relatives in Romania, and this assistance improved their situation somewhat. So too, the Jewish community in Romania rallied to help, and the special Comisia Autonomã De Ajutorare (Autonomous Aid Commission), now operating alongside the Centrala Evreilor Din Romania, began to transfer aid from the communities to the ghetto councils. There was no other aid program of this kind in Europe, and it constitutes an important part of the history of the Jews of Romania. See Lavi, *Pinkas Hakehilot*: *Rumania*, vol. 1, p. 515.

he agrees, but that it will not be possible to help me, because then other community workers will follow with the same request. That's a fine but unacceptable excuse.

February 18, 1944

Fred Şaraga returned to Bucharest already a few weeks ago and promised that within a few days he would return to Moghilev to take the orphans.[38] He seems to have dropped out of sight. Has something gone wrong?

The Moghilev Central Council hastened to congregate the orphans from small locations in the centers of Moghilev, Shargorod, Dzhurin, Murafa, and Kopaygorod. Eleven orphans from Derebchin were brought to Dzhurin—more than half are new orphans as a result of the slaughter that an SS executioner carried out there recently. They lodged the "foreign" orphans in a house outside the orphanage in Dzhurin, because they are not clean, and they have no other clothes for them. A blizzard is raging outside, apparently in honor of the infants who will have to make their way on the roads to the central assembly point.[39]

February 19, 1944, *Motzei Shabbes*

I was summoned to the gendarmerie yesterday afternoon. The post chief informed me that by Sunday, February 20, all the orphans who are waiting to be repatriated must be taken to Moghilev. They said nothing

38 On January 26, 1944, Fred Şaraga left for Moghilev to arrange the return of orphans from Transnistria to Romania. See Ben-Tsiyon, *Yeladim Yehudim BiTransnistriya*, pp. 230–232.

39 On February 15, 1944, after receiving the official order authorizing the return of the orphans to Romania, two delegations left Bucharest to arrange the return of the first group of orphans. One was led by Fred Şaraga, who was responsible for the return of the orphans from the northern regions of Transnistria, and the other one was led by Dado Rozenkrantz, who was responsible for orphans from the southern regions of Transnistria. The orphans were concentrated in two central locations: Moghilev and Balta. See Carp Collection, YVA, O.11/98, p. 348; and Ben-Tsiyon, *Yeladim Yehudim BiTransnistriya,* pp. 230–232.

to me about the age. The wind has blown snow all over the roads, which continues to fall without mercy, and vehicles will not be able to get to Moghilev, only sleds. But where will they find enough sleds and horses after the gendarmes have taken almost all the cattle and horses from the kolkhozes? Apart from this, the peasants are afraid to make long journeys, because partisans often steal their horses and their fur coats along the way.

After I returned from the gendarmerie post, the council made a call to the Shargorod council and asked about the ages and the transport. There they are as informed as we are in Dzhurin, and they cannot give any advice.[40] They have begun preparing food here for the children's journey and sacks to wrap their feet, but by no means will they dispatch the children while the blizzard is raging. Nevertheless, they have realized in Moghilev that the children's lives will be endangered if they set out in such a storm, and an order was issued from there by telephone today that the children should only be sent on Friday, February 25.

The distress in the camp has reached unusual proportions. It has been two months since we have not seen a courier step foot here with support. It seems that even the reckless Romanians are afraid to deliver money to Transnistria at this time and are giving up the profits of half for you and half for me.

February 21 [1944], 7 P.M. (*Lashon Hakodesh*)

The transfer of the orphans has hit a snag, as if a vicious demon is obstructing the way. Five gendarmes set out on horseback this morning in order to patrol the surroundings. They were shot at as soon as they left the factory quarter. One of them, Levau—actually a decent gendarme who

40 According to the decision of Antonescu, only orphans who were bereft of both their father and mother, and who were under the age of fifteen would be returned to Romania. In order to organize their return to Romania, lists of the orphans in every location were drawn up according to three categories: 1) orphans under twelve years of age; 2) orphans under fifteen years of age; and 3) orphans under eighteen years of age. See the Carp Collection, YVA, O.11/98, pp. 345–357; Ben-Tsiyon, *Yeladim Yehudim BiTransnistriya*, pp. 230–232.

was not a murderer—was killed on the spot. An old Ukrainian was also killed—the village elder's father—and his son were seriously injured. The two Ukrainians had only just arrived on a sled. The gendarmerie is seething, and many new gendarmes from Shargorod have been brought in, and a Jew cannot go near the gendarmerie post. Advocates have asked the post chief to requisition sleds for the orphans, and he replied that the community must solve the problem itself, because he has more important concerns at present.

February 22, 1944, 9 P.M.

A miracle has occurred, and they will transfer the orphans to Moghilev after all. The colony chief returned from Moghilev today and brought some good news: two trucks are already on the way to Dzhurin in order to take the children. Because of the mounds of snow on the main road, some vehicles will arrive a few hours later.

The old man then began to go over the list of the orphans that I had assembled in his absence and compared each entry with the cards in the card catalog. That's how he discovered a few of my "transgressions" and wanted to tear me apart for daring to register orphans of up to eighteen years of age and also including a few "half" orphans. Fortunately, he did not see that I had killed many fathers and mothers to create "whole" orphans. The old man promised to settle accounts with me some other time, and crossed out twenty names on the list with a red pencil. He ordered me to write up the list again immediately while he kept his eyes on my fingers to make sure that I would not stumble again and commit a "minor theft." Nevertheless, around thirty "non-kosher" [orphans], whose ages were not discovered, remained on the new list. The number of kosher children is about eighty-four.[41] Shouting was heard in the community building and people argued that they must stick to the principle of "It will be neither mine nor yours"[42]—if it is not possible to rescue all the

41 Concerning the number of orphans in the Dzhurin ghetto, and the number of girls and boys, see the Şaraga Report, YVA, M.20/104; see also the entry of April 4, 1943.

42 I Kings 3:26.

orphans, then they should all remain here. However, King Solomon ruled otherwise in ancient times.

The children have been sentenced to suffer for who knows how long until Şaraga arrives to take them home.

February 23, 1943, Evening

The orphans left for Moghilev, *in a guter sho*. For a technical reason, fourteen orphans have remained here; they will be taken tomorrow morning, because they were only barely able to fit seventy children in the two open back trucks. Twenty-one children, originating from Ukrainian Jewry, remain in the orphanage. The transport includes orphans from Dzhurin and from the neighboring places of Derebchin and Politanki. Most of the children are not dressed suitably for such a journey and are exposed to frostbite at minus 15 degrees [Celsius].[43] Some of them do not have any shoes.

February 25, 1944, Friday, 4 P.M.

They did not send a truck from Shargorod for the rest of the orphans, and the community rented sleds for a very large sum. Although only fourteen children were to travel, according to the list, thirty children set out on the sleds. Those who were not registered traveled at their own risk and will try to sneak into Moghilev with the "kosher" orphans. "Non-kosher" orphans also departed from Shargorod and Murafa, relying on Divine providence. The community building is besieged by mothers and fathers who are begging [the council] to rent sleds for their children, even though they are not orphans, because a miracle could happen, and the children could mix in with the orphans in Moghilev and could be saved. Of course, the colony chief shows them the door.

43 Five degrees Fahrenheit.

February 26, 1944, *Motzei Shabbes*

The day before yesterday, the gendarmerie received an order by telephone that the Rabbi of Siret, Rabbi Baruch Hager, along with his household, should travel to Moghilev, because the state granted his repatriation. Rabbi Baruch Hager is a son of the old Vijniţa *tzaddik* Rabbi Israel Hager of blessed memory and is impressive in his own right. In the course of the two and a half years of exile, I often met him and even worked with him under dangerous conditions, as I already recorded at the time on these pages. In the meanwhile, I must remain silent about quite a few events for various reasons. Rabbi Baruch Hager is among the outstanding individuals who are extremely rare in today's chaotic world. He withstood the trial of Transnistria like a truly righteous man, providing assistance and encouragement, and not just with words.

The news of his repatriation elicited joy and sadness and intense longing all at once among everyone. He has been an unflinching activist and managed through his underground connections in Romania to ensure that heavy sums were sent regularly to support the general public. The funds reached him at mortal risk to many lives. He would send his youngest son, Eliezerle (a gifted young man of many virtues, intelligence, and courage) to the Ukrainian quarter, where the courier was hiding, and Eliezerle would bring the fortune. He was once caught in the act, and his life hung by a thread. He was saved through a miracle and a bribe. The gendarmes also led the rabbi himself to Moghilev once, where he was in grave danger. Everyone came to bid him farewell yesterday. The rabbi comforted the crowd and said that he would accomplish more for Dzhurin there than he could here. I personally will greatly miss this dear, noble righteous man.

February 27, 1944, Evening

The commander of the gendarmerie informed the committee that tomorrow at dawn all the men must gather at the square near the gendarmerie post with shovels to clear the snow from the main road. Many men are now roaming around in the fields, because more than once people have been burned by the gendarmes' lies. Clearing snow could mean German labor camps …

The "lords" issued an order that everyone must report for labor tomorrow, including the community functionaries. They themselves, the "lords," will also go with the crowd. My bosses released me from this, because I must prepare a list of the orphans without mothers and send it to Moghilev tomorrow morning.

People are coming and going to ask me for advice regarding whether to go to the gendarmes tomorrow or not. I refrain from giving advice because, if indeed it is only a question of clearing snow, it will be a disgrace to hide. As a result of my silence, I have acquired unmerited enemies.

We received a telephone call from Moghilev to apprise us of some important information regarding the orphans:

1) The long-awaited emissary Fred Şaraga has arrived in Moghilev and will lead the transport of the children to Romania.
2) The orphans from Dzhurin have arrived safely in Moghilev. They have been ushered to a hall and are receiving plenty of food.
3) A date for the transfer of the children across the Dniester has not yet been determined.
4) The colony chief and Moshe Katz were suddenly called to Moghilev. However, the two big shots have postponed the journey until tomorrow, until after the "snow squall."
5) The eight children from Dorohoi who remained in Dzhurin in December must arrive in Moghilev immediately, and from there they will be sent together with the other orphans.
6) We must send the list of orphans without mothers to Moghilev immediately.

February 28, 1944, 2 P.M.

The snow-clearing incident was indeed not a fabrication. Although many men went into hiding, 165 men with shovels on their shoulders nevertheless showed up. The community functionaries and the members of the council were the first to march out. It troubled me to have to remain in the community building, because my bosses ordered me not to move from my place and to watch over the community building, lest anything unexpected happen. They shoveled the snow for three hours to clear the main road, and the gendarmes were satisfied.

The fourth volume is destined to end with a "happy ending." The poor man's joy: when he recovers what he had lost …

The End of Volume Four: "The Birth Pangs of Deliverance"

Notebook Five

Escaping the Lion's Den

You, who has made me to see many and sore troubles,
will quicken me again, and bring me up again from the depths of the earth.

(Psalms 71:20)

Dzhurin, February 29,1944, the 5th of *Adar*, 5704

The fifth book of these memoirs is fated to begin on a strange day that comes to visit only once every four years, when it is a leap year according to the non-Jewish calendar. Will this book that begins on a capricious date reflect the same sadness and the same torments as its four older brothers,[1] who did not dream of getting the youngest at an advanced age? And who knows whether this fifth volume is indeed the youngest!

So, enough with the introductions, and let us get down to the daily work, may we get to a good start: it seems that we have survived a third winter in exile. This year the winter was merciful, less snow, the frost was not too bad, but once again there is mud. The snow has almost completely melted, but its traces torment the ruined shoes. Barefoot people, on the other hand, have no reason to complain …

We have learned from Moghilev that Fred Şaraga, the messiah from Bucharest, will lead the orphans to Romania through the parting of the Dniester today. It is believed that the *Eyrev Rav*[2] who attached themselves to the transports from all the camps will return in shame and humiliation, because the inspection in Moghilev was rigorous, and they disqualified even people on the kosher lists. A dozen "lords" and functionaries from Dzhurin have been in Moghilev now for a week at the expense of the community, clinging to the big shots.

Today we sent a list of the orphans without mothers, a total of thirty-three names, to Moghilev. I also prepared this list, but I did not dare to sneak in a single non-kosher person, because Leon Neuman, the stand-in for the colony chief sat next to me and watched my fingers. We discovered that in the camps of Murafa, Kopaygorod, and Luchinets, the councils registered all the orphans, made "whole" orphans out of "half" orphans, and paid no attention at all to their ages. Only here and in Shargorod did they demonstrate such patriotism and deferred to the Romanian overlords.

---

1 Meaning the four previous notebooks written by Kunstadt.

2 Kunstadt applies the Biblical term that refers to the mixed multitude that joined the Israelites during the Exodus from Egypt to the persons who were not authorized to join the transports.

March 1, 1944, Evening

News has come from Moghilev that the whole orphans departed this morning. The state inspectors did not allow the unregistered to join the transport.[3]

March 3, 1944, 3 P.M.

The *minyen* of community providers is still celebrating in Moghilev, and so we still do not know which of the Dzhurin orphans were disqualified during the inspection. We discovered from a reliable source in Moghilev, who was present in Tiraspol when the orphans were sent from there to Moghilev, that the local commander of the gendarmerie legion, Petrescu, explicitly authorized the council to register in the list all children up to the age of eighteen and to make them whole orphans, even if their parents are still alive. During the inspection, the Romanian overlords relied completely on the lists from the councils regarding the status of the orphans. They only rejected grown children, who apparently had long since forgotten when they had celebrated their eighteenth birthday … We could have saved all the children in Dzhurin and Shargorod, even those born of local parents, had the colony chiefs possessed a glimmer of Jewish compassion and self-sacrifice and less desire to ingratiate themselves with the overlords, like the obsequious Jews of the old days. We have lost a golden opportunity that will not come again! …

March 5, 1944, 3 P.M.

Today some of the most well-connected people who managed to obtain authorization to repatriate will return to Romania from Moghilev:

3 Strict inspections were conducted at the train station and at the crossing of the Dniester in Moghilev. Anyone not of the required age or who was found not to be orphaned of both parents was removed from the train. Crying, pleading, and begging were of no use. See Ben-Tsiyon, *Yeladim Yehudim BiTransnistriya*, p. 232; Yitzhak Yalon testimony, YVA, O.3/1238.

the engineer Sami Jagendorf; the president of the Moghilev Central Council Moritz Katz; Dr. Bobi Bodik. The Dzhurin colony chief, Dr. Max Rosenstrauch, has risen to greatness and will take the place of the president of the Moghilev Central Council. It is such a shame that Dzhurin has lost this jewel only now, near the end. Moghilev has once again acquired a bargain! …

Our "lords" are still in Moghilev and are rubbing shoulders with Şaraga, probably in order to arrange their own repatriation. This will not include me, and I am waiting for the great miracle that Şaraga will not bring …

March 8, 1944, Evening, *Purim*, after the Reading of the *Megillah*

Guests in the ghetto! About fifty children and young people have returned: those who risked their lives trying to join the transport of the orphans. They have wandered around for two weeks in Moghilev and most of them even managed to squeeze into the wagons and reached the station of Volcineţi,[4] on the other side of the Dniester. However, a rigorous inspection was conducted there, and only the children who had a repatriation ticket, stamped by the Moghilev prefect on the basis of the lists from the councils, were allowed to remain in the wagons. The remaining "non-kosher" crowd—a total of 473 boys, girls, and even a few women … —the gendarmes took them back to Moghilev in wagons.

The "non-kosher" were imprisoned in Moghilev, and the prefect informed them that they would be sent to the other side of the Bug, together with the council members who allowed such a crime. Advocates finally succeeded in persuading him to release the "non-kosher," but

---

4 The trains of the deportees from Southern Bukovina (Cernăuţi, Suceava, Rădăuţi, Vatra Dornei, etc.) arrived at the train station of Volcineţi. From this station, located in a fallow field, the deportees reached the crossing of the Dniester in Atachi and from there continued in rafts to the city of Moghilev. See Jetti Elenbogen testimony, YVA, O.3/VT/9539; Batsheva Akerman testimony, YVA, O.3/VT/11356; Yosef Wischnizer testimony, YVA, O.3/VT/7038; Fritzi Salner testimony, O.3/VT/8790; Meir Kostiner testimony, O.3/VT/8316.

before doing so, they had to sign a declaration, admitting to their crime. The entire Dzhurin list passed through safely, and all my "transgressions" are already in Romania. The "non-kosher" had left Dzhurin for Moghilev at their own risk; no one had sent them.

Together with the "non-kosher," the ten "lords" and their inner circle, who had spent two weeks in Moghilev at the community's expense to obtain repatriation for themselves, returned to Dzhurin. They came out only with promises, and the community paid dearly for these promises … Only the colony chief, Dr. Max Rosenstrauch, did not return, because he now reigns in Moghilev as the president of the Central Council. It is unnecessary to recall his merits, because these pages have often related details regarding his behavior. By the way, I was not in the know about everything and, for various reasons, I did not record everything. It is likely that at times I pushed the limit too far and did not fulfill the commandment, "Do not judge your fellow man until you have stood in his place."[5] However, allow me to note one thing: there is not a single person in the camp who misses him.

In the meantime, in Moghilev, they have not yet appointed a replacement for the [Dzhurin] colony chief. Moshe Katz heads the office only temporarily and refuses to accept the honor. Moshe Katz has honored me with a rebuke that I deserve. While preparing the list of orphans, I mistakenly omitted a little girl from the orphanage, and they almost sent her back to Dzhurin. However, they managed to add her to the list in Moghilev, and she left Transnistria safely.

(In *Lashon Hakodesh*) At this moment, we heard a faint explosion from far away. Something has started to happen once again in our region in the last few days.

March 11, 1944, *Motzei Shabbes* (in *Lashon Hakodesh*)

The situation has once again become tense. On the Vinnitsa–Moghilev road that runs through the factory quarter, convoys of crowded German military vehicles race from the East, laden with soldiers and weapons of

5 Pirkei Avot 2:4.

destruction, exactly as in the beginning of January. We are constantly hearing the shooting of cannons and the humming of airplanes in the sky, although we cannot see them. At night, the airplanes drop flare bombs in various colors, which remain in the air for a while. These illuminate the way for the rushing cart owners …[6]

Although I cannot guarantee whether it is true, people say that during the inspection of the orphans at the Volcineţi station, they stole the repatriation tickets from forty-three kosher orphans and replaced them with forty-three well-connected non-orphans. The children who were robbed could not defend themselves, and they were sent back to Moghilev. It seems that the delegates who accompanied the transport had a part in this. I have already been weaned from using the term, "impossible" …[7]

March Twelfth, 1944, the 12th of *Adar*, 5704, 1:30 P.M.

A Soviet airplane dropped bombs on the ghetto a few minutes ago, wounding and killing several people. My hands are shaking from the shock. The unstable "palace" where I work shook like a *lulev.* Today—Sunday—the weekly market is taking place, and there are a lot of people at the marketplace. Blessed is He Who performs miracles for us!

[March 12, 1944] 3 P.M. (in *Lashon Hakodesh*)

The Russian plane dropped a total of nine bombs [on Dzhurin]. Two fell near the Jewish hospital and made deep pits. All the hospital windows were shattered. There were doctors, orderlies, nurses, and ten patients

---

6 By this time, the Soviet forces had already advanced considerably on the Eastern Front into Transnistria, and the thunder of the approaching Soviet cannons could be heard in the ghetto.

7 Hannah Meller related that she and her sister were among the orphans who were designated to return to Romania. However, at the last moment their names were taken off the list and replaced with the names of those who had connections to the Jewish leadership; Hannah Meller interview by Sarah Rosen, March 12, 2010, Haifa. See also Hannah Meller-Faust, *Me'ever Lanahar*, pp. 217–233.

in the hospital at the time, but no one was injured. One bomb fell on a Ukrainian house, where Motel Ber from Rădăuţi lives. His younger son, Iosl—a fine, twenty-year old, young man—was severely wounded and was taken to the hospital. A woman was injured lightly.

We are constantly hearing cannon shots, each time closer and closer. The people are hiding their few possessions in the cellars, because the danger of a bomb falling underground is supposedly lesser. I have nothing to hide, and it is really foolish to save a rag when your life itself is at risk.

March 13, 1944, 1 P.M. (in *Lashon Hakodesh*)

A gang of German soldiers who had gotten drunk in a Ukrainian inn in the factory quarter suddenly appeared in the ghetto yesterday afternoon. They raised a ruckus and demanded that the militia provide them with drinks and women. At exactly that time, a few council members were on their way home from the community building, and the German soldiers encircled them and confined them in an empty hall. One of the drunken soldiers brandished his revolver and threatened to shoot if they would not find within an hour a soldier who had just disappeared. He ordered all the detained council members to stand facing the wall. Suddenly the deputy commander of the Jewish militia, Herman Schaffer, appeared—an intelligent and brave fellow—and managed to calm the raging soldiers, promising that he would immediately find the missing soldier. The militia searched every corner and soon found the guy. The Germans immediately released the arrested council members. Schaffer then took the soldiers to a Jewish family, where they reveled until midnight and left the ghetto.

A young community employee, the community messenger Goldshmidt, and I just happened to stay late in the community house. We saw the wedding through the window, chained the door, and did not go home. We were frightened to death and waited for the "guests." No living soul was to be seen in the streets, apart from the German soldiers with rifles on their shoulders, who bellowed and chortled, and enjoyed tormenting the Jews. Night fell slowly, and we remained sitting in the dark. No one approached the community building and, at around 9 P.M., we ventured to set foot outside. I did not encounter a living soul on the way home. Roza and the children rejoiced when I entered the house, as though I had come back from that world.

However, we were not destined to have a calm night, because the family to whom Schaffer had taken the German soldiers lives near to my home, separated only by a small strip of garden. There, at the neighbors' house, the revelry went on until midnight. My family and I, and my landlord, Iankel Axelrod, and his household did not get undressed until the Germans had left, and the light at the neighbors' home was extinguished. We finally lay down to sleep, dressed in our clothes, but no one closed their eyes until the morning.

Today no German is seen in the ghetto, no shots are heard, but fleets of planes are racing across the sky. We do not know to whom they belong and we shudder at the thought of more bombings. The market is empty, and no one accepts the mark any longer. The *bein hazmanim* cannot last for long; one way or another! …

(Yiddish) Today the colony chief was summoned urgently to Moghilev, but no one has set out. In the current situation, making a journey expressly means martyrdom. The community building is empty, the council members are keeping their distance, and no one is seen there. I alone must watch over the building until the last moment. Spring is shining bright outside, it appears to be a delightful *Eyrev Peysech*, like in the good old days, but my heart is very heavy …

March 14, 1944, 2 P.M. (*Lashon Hakodesh*)

The young man Iosl Ber, who was wounded in the bombing the day before yesterday, passed away today. It is strange: for the first time since the deportation, Jewish blood has been spilled in the camp of Dzhurin precisely by those who are supposed to bring deliverance …

Dense and endless convoys of crowded military vehicles are pulling out day and night along the main road to Moghilev. Real miracles take place at every moment, as long as a community of 4,000 Jews still exists in the grave of the living. All contact with the gendarmes has been cut off. The gendarmerie [post] is completely dark, they are packing papers, sealing boxes, and preparing to leave. German platoons have settled in the factory quarter, and it is swarming with German soldiers.

The market is empty, and if a peasant appears with a basket of potatoes or a little milk, he asks for salt instead of money.

March 15, 1944, 2 P.M. (*Lashon Hakodesh*)

There were many German and Romanian soldiers in the ghetto last night. A miracle occurred and torrential rain poured until midnight; consequently, the soldiers did not wander in the streets. There have been some cases of robbery, but no one has been beaten. People are sitting in their homes behind closed doors that are locked with chains and are terrified by the slightest noise. I rarely go to the office, since there is no work. The most important community institutions—soup kitchen, hospital, police, pharmacy, and orphanage—are functioning but the cooperative is closed. Police roam the streets but they avoid the German soldiers. The columns of vehicles on the main road continue without end.

March 16, 1944, 11 A.M.

The ghetto is full of Germans. Everyone sleeps fully dressed, if we sleep at all, and our hearts pound at the thought that a German might burst in. Last night passed peacefully. The Germans do not bother the Jews whom they encounter. The gendarmes have already fled from the gendarmerie, and Dzhurin is, *in a guter sho*, under German command. They maintain contact with the Jewish militia.

We cleared out the orphanage and the community building today, and transferred the buildings to the German command for their soldiers. I gathered together a large portion of the archive and took it to my cubbyhole. The records that I have kept the entire time since the end of 1941 have great documentary value. I locked the files in the pharmacy, because there is no place to fit a pin in my cubbyhole.[8]

---

8 All these materials were confiscated by the Soviets when they entered the ghettos.

The children from the orphanage were taken to the court hall—fortunately most of them were rescued toward the end—and they also brought their meager possessions with them. There is a great danger that the Germans will evacuate the ghetto, or at least the main street (where my cubbyhole is located ...), to make room for their soldiers who continue to pour into the ghetto. The ghetto has assumed the appearance of a military camp. It is swarming with soldiers, officers, motorcycles. They are moving telephone lines to the command quarters. However, we cannot confine ourselves in our homes, because there are only three latrines. The Germans have taken advantage of Jewish hands to dig a line of latrines for themselves. Jews who work for them receive generous amounts of food and bring home packs containing all kinds of good things. However, it is impossible to appreciate these tidbits when one sees the Angel of Death before his eyes.

Friday, March 17, 1944, the 22nd of *Adar*, 5704, 1:30 P.M. (*Lashon Hakodesh*)

German soldiers have been lodged in almost every house, but so far they have not caused any harm to anyone. Some of them chat with the people from Bukovina, who speak German well, and there are some who say clearly that they have lost the war. They relate that the front is now very close, and that their army will withdraw from the entire area, as far as Lemberg [Lvov]. We no longer hear any cannon shots.

Twenty-seven Jews were brought from the camp of Pechora, and the local German commander freed them all. We are shocked by this unexpected grace coming from the Germans.

Chaos prevails in the camp. The council no longer functions, and only the soup kitchen and the militia continue to operate. There are a few thousand kilos of wheat and potatoes, as well as other food products in the storeroom. There is an urgent need to open the storeroom and distribute the food to everyone before it will be too late. People are saying that a group of underworld elements are planning to break down the doors of the storeroom and rob it. In the meantime, Jewish militia are guarding it. The sugar factory in the factory quarter, which was bombed to pieces, contains a great deal of wood and, by the grace of God, people in the camp take wood from there, because there is no longer any owner. People lie down in bed fully clothed in the camp, and there is no question of closing one's eyes.

There was pounding on my landlord's door last night at around 2 A.M. Since he does not understand German, I went out and asked what the matter was. A soldier called out that he wanted to know if any soldiers were quartered in the house. I said no, and the group left.

Today it seems quieter than yesterday, a kind of "and after the fire a still small voice,"[9] or perhaps this is the quiet before the great fire? …

The Great Miracle Has Occurred!!!

Dzhurin, Soviet Union, Monday, March 20, 1944, the 25th of *Adar*, 5704, 1 P.M.

The three most horrible days of my life are over, and we are all in the Soviet Union, since *Motzei Shabbes Parshat Vayikra* [*sic*], March 10 [*sic*] [18], 1944, at 9 P.M. In order to describe the experiences of these three days of darkness, a person requires, apart from talent, nerves of steel. I am still in a state of shock, which does not allow me to concentrate and find the appropriate words. Every nerve in my body is rattling, and it seems unbelievable that we have indeed endured the ordeal, as if a dream, and come out of it safely. We have been showered with miracles, more than we had ever hoped for, and yet we tremble, lest the wheel turn back, God forbid, because in war, anything is possible.

While I was writing the previous entry, on Friday, March 17, endless vehicles, troops, cannons, and wagons continued to pass by on the main road, yet we felt that the crisis was very close. The Germans in the ghetto did not bother anyone and reassured us that we need not fear them, only

9 I Kings 19:12.

the SS soldiers, if they show up. A high-ranking German officer who was lodged with a Jewish family even promised that the Jews would be spared in the region between the Dniester and the Bug, because it is a Romanian-occupied territory. Fearing for their lives, the people have clung on to this piece of straw, hoping that for once this would not be a false hope.

On Friday, around 2 P.M., a terrible explosion was heard in the camp, and bits of iron flew through the air. The Germans blew up a broken truck in the middle of the ghetto. Without considering the danger, abandoned children crowded around the destroyed machine and took whatever they could from it, as if there was nothing else to worry about here.

At around 5 P.M.—candle-lighting time—the real "*Lecha Dodi*"[10] began. Following a 24-hour pause, cannons began to thunder nearby. The shabby, rickety houses in the ghetto shook, and the windowpanes that are patched with cardboard played the accompanying music (a 5-minute break: an air-raid siren. My family and I fled to a field in the blink of an eye. We heard muted humming in the air and explosions from the direction of Shargorod).

There was nowhere to hide, and people began to flee like poisoned mice, each one to a different house, as if looking for protection under a stranger's *mezuzah*. We who live on an upper floor went down to the neighbor, Perel, actually the landlord's daughter, who lives with five babies in a 4 by 4-cubit cubbyhole in the same palace underneath us. Every shot pierced a hole in our hearts, setting our nerves on edge, which in any case were about to explode. A German soldier informed us that these were German cannons. Is it possible that the Germans will decide to halt near Dzhurin, and the place will become the actual front line? ...

In the evening, we saw how two German platoons, with all their equipment, marched away from the front, straight through the ghetto street. On Friday, Jews dug trenches for them and in exchange received entire packages of bread, sausages, and jam. The Jewish men returned safely from work yesterday.

---

10 *Lecha Dodi* (Come, my Beloved), is the prayer that is sung during Friday night service to welcome the Sabbath.

Thunder resounded every five minutes until 9 P.M., and then the concert was silenced. My family and I went back to our floor, while other neighbors stayed in Perel's "bunker." Of course, no one lay down to sleep. Cannon shots were heard around 3 A.M. Although the night was dreadful, we were more afraid of the morning, because the new day would surely bring all kinds of good things with it. The day finally began to dawn, and a laughing, eve of spring sun immediately shone in the ominously quiet surroundings.

By noon, the shtetl looked like a cemetery. German soldiers were no longer to be seen, and the Jews did not stick their noses outside. A group of abandoned young boys gathered around the storeroom and sought to rob it, but the militia and a few brave people, actually from among the "simple people," succeeded in foiling this attempt amicably. As a matter of fact, people from the underworld themselves even helped to empty the food from the storeroom and took it to the soup kitchen, where they distributed soup and bread that *Shabbes* as always, as if nothing was happening.

The real contractions then began at 2 P.M. The fifth act of the drama "Dzhurin Exile" unfolded with lightning speed, with blood and fire and pillars of smoke, as is described in the *Hagaddah*.

The Germans began distributing whatever there was in their warehouses in the factory quarter: flour, shoes, boots, blankets, and other valuable objects. They gave them to the Ukrainians and to the Jews. There are enough people in the camp who scurry for kosher bargains, even while the roof is burning overhead. Mainly young people swarmed the factory quarter seeking treasures. Hundreds of people, mostly Ukrainians, gathered around the warehouses, and each one wanted to snatch up the bargains before the other and to scrounge up as much as possible. In this ruckus, the first Jewish victim fell at the hands of a German murderer. A German shot three bullets from a pistol into the head of a young man from Cernăuţi, Şalom Iwanir, and killed him on the spot. A terrible panic broke out, and the entire crowd fled in the blink of an eye wherever their eyes led them. Everyone in the ghetto was frightened to death, because they feared that the shedding of Jewish blood would whet the murderer's appetite for more.

Clouds of black smoke, mixed with fearful tongues of fire, suddenly rose from the building that housed the German warehouse with the treasures. The Germans themselves had made *Havdala*[11] over the treasure. The evening approached and from the mountain where Jewish Dzhurin is located, we saw how the fires spread in various neighborhoods at the foot of the factory quarter. (A 5-minute break: a "bird" zoomed in the air, and we all fled to a field). No one had any doubt that the Germans would soon set the ghetto on fire.

The wind blew the thick, black clouds of smoke from the factory quarter to the ghetto and enveloped the shtetl like a sheet of soot. Our vision was completely obstructed, and we could not breathe because of the smoke. No one knew what to do: to stay where we were or to flee. Where could we run in such a panic, while terrified Germans were swarming all around, scurrying like poisoned mice. People swiftly put on as much clothing as possible and prepared packages of food, as though getting ready for a long journey. Things became even livelier at around 5 P.M., when the Germans began to blow up trucks loaded with ammunition. There was a terrible racket of explosions, and pieces of red-hot iron and slivers of grenades flew through the air in the ghetto for a whole hour. The factory quarter was enveloped in black smoke, and blue, yellow, red, and green rocket fire flashed among the dark clouds. The fire thundered and exploded, a pungent smell of burning sulfur filled the air, and we saw the true description of the doors of hell flinging wide open on *Motzei Shabbes* as written in a *Musar* book.[12] It was indeed the last scene of the drama, yet the most dangerous.

At nightfall, the German technical units began to cut the telephone lines in the ghetto, and great numbers of German soldiers immediately began to stream onto the main road of the ghetto, fleeing from the trenches. They ran, panting, frightened, and exhausted, their faces gray, their uniforms covered in mud, and their boots caked with mire. They did not have any intention of committing any wild misdeeds but only of

---

11 Kunstadt indicates that the Germans set the warehouse on fire by referring to the Havdalah, a ceremony performed on Saturday night, which involves lighting a multi-wick candle to mark the end of the Sabbath and the beginning of the secular week.

12 According to the Kabbalah, every Sabbath, the gates of hell open, and the wicked are allowed to go to the outer gates, where they meet other souls who linger there after being purified in hell but cannot yet ascend to heaven. After the Sabbath is over, the wicked must return to hell. See https://www.hidabroot.org (accessed June 15, 2022).

fleeing as quickly as possible. A few actually hid in the fields and then surrendered to the Red Army.

These were the last armed Germans that we saw in Dzhurin. Immediately after *Motzei Shabbes*, Dzhurin became a "no-man's-land"—the most forsaken of the forsaken. No landlord, no living soul in the streets, no glimmer of a light in a window. The Jewish militia fulfilled their duty right up to the last moment and roamed the streets with lanterns in hand. Shots were heard in the distance but, at the same time, they were weaker than yesterday. We sat in the dark in the camp, dressed and ready for the journey, our teeth chattering.

And as soon as the week began, after two hours of "no-man's-land" the good news spread: they [Red Army] are already here! People gathered near the hovels, announcing the news of deliverance to relatives, brothers, and simply to everyone. Yet, no one dared to light a candle in a house. The first to see the longed-for rescuers were indeed the Jewish militia. In the meantime, no regular Red Army personnel have entered the shtetl yet but rather only small groups of partisans, who had fought in the surrounding forests.

Everyone felt the miracles that had befallen all of us. The enemies clearly had no power to do any real evil, just as the bits of fire and red-hot iron from the factory quarter had no power over the skimpy shingle roofs of the ghetto. So, now we will go home without the assistance of Fred Şaraga and the colony chiefs …

No one lay down to sleep but not due to fear. There was noise outside during the night, and the police lit up every corner, searching for hidden Germans.

At around 1 A.M., someone knocked on my door and shouted in Yiddish: "It's me, from the militia, open up." I unchained the door, and two fellows with rifles entered, without any uniform, only with the Red star on their cap. They were accompanied by a Jewish militiaman. I greeted them warmly in my poor Russian, and one of them did not even allow me to finish the sentence before shouting angrily at me: "*Davay seychas pomagay*" (give me paper immediately)! I was left dumbfounded, and the militiaman intervened: "Do you not understand? The comrades need paper to write on, and you certainly have papers from the council. That is why I brought them to you." There was a whole package of paper from the council, around 100 sheets, on my table. I handed the paper to the partisan. Instead of thanking me, he said angrily: "*Eto malo. Mne nuzhno tysyachi*" (These are too few. I need a thousand). The militiaman barely managed to calm him, and the two liberators left without a farewell. Apparently, this is their style but, nevertheless, I like them more than the "good" Germans.

Sunday morning, the first day of deliverance and liberation.[13] By dawn all the streets were already black, because there were so many people, and no child remained in the crib at home. Everyone wanted to see the liberators with their own eyes, to be convinced that it is not a dream. They now have come in masses, on foot, on horseback, in small cars—real Red Army soldiers. They [Red Army] had no time to linger in the shtetl, because they had to chase the enemy westwards as fast as possible, to smite him, and not allow him to recover. The shtetl had the air of a holiday, of revival and renewal.

And the director [of the orphanage] Bigo Hart has just now taken the orphans back to their homes from the court hall. However, the rooms had already been occupied by new tenants who did not want to move out and threatened to settle accounts with the former functionaries. In order to avoid fighting and to calm the atmosphere, Hart lodged the twenty-one children in a storeroom and in the kitchen in the orphanage for the time being.

Time passed slowly until 8 A.M., and no had any desire to go home when there was such a celebration outside. A humming sound suddenly began in the sky, and twenty-seven airplanes appeared. Everyone was sure that these were "ours," because they flew right over our heads, slowly and sedately. Black smoke suddenly began to spill out from the planes, and the surroundings immediately were shaken by horrific explosions. The sky was veiled with a black cloud of smoke, and it seemed that the world

---

13 The Dzhurin ghetto was liberated by the Soviets on March 19, 1944. According to reports of the Comisia Autonomă De Ajutorare in Bucharest, in January–March 1943, there were 4,050 Jews in Dzhurin—3,053 deportees and 997 local Jews. According to the lists from the headquarters of the gendarmes of September 1943, there were 2,871 deported Jews in Dzhurin—2,490 Jews from Bukovina, 381 from Bessarabia, and a few dozen from the Dorohoi district. See Lavi, *Pinkas Hakehikot*: *Rumania*, vol. 1, p. 425.

had vanished now.[14] The terrified people rushed to cellars, to the fields, and others simply threw themselves on the ground. Shouts and wails mixed with the thunder of the explosions, windowpanes shattered and shards flew through the air, pieces of red-hot iron and a flood of sparks darted overhead. I was in my room, together with my family, when the "wedding" began. Iza and I went down to the cellar of the "palace"—at a depth of half a meter … —where the danger was even greater, if the house would come down on us. Roza was lying in bed with a fever, and Rachel was here visiting her. They both insisted on staying in the room at first, entrusting themselves to Divine providence. However, a minute later Roza dragged herself out of bed and joined us after all, while Rachel supported her [clasping her] under her arms. Bertl, in contrast, fled and disappeared somewhere in the fields.

All the occupants of the house fled to this "hideout," with a few dozen small children and hysterical wives. A madhouse is a weak image of what happened during the five minutes that we spent in the cellar. These were the five most dreadful minutes of my life. The people around me let out screams of terror, tore out their hair, threw themselves on the ground, shrieked accusations at the Master of the Universe. Roza and Rachel stood next to a wall, stunned and petrified, and Iza held on to me tight and continually asked: When will it be over? A young woman of Dzhurin fell to my feet and cried: "You are a righteous man (what a righteous man! …), ask God to save us!" The bombs seemed to be falling hard on the heart of the ghetto and, at any moment, the ruined houses would fall and bury everyone, if a red-hot shard would not penetrate our bodies before that. Once again it became quiet but another ten minutes passed before we dared to leave our "hideout."

When we went out, we could not breathe, because we were choking on the smoke, mixed with the smell of something burning. It was as dark as night, even though the sun shone with all its might. There were shrieks and wails from all sides, and it seemed that who knows how many victims had fallen in the ghetto. In fact, these were not the cries of pain of the wounded but of people who had been separated from their loved ones in

14 On March 20, 1944, German planes bombed Dzhurin, killing thirty-two Jews; ibid.

the panic and did not know where they were. I too screamed in a voice that did not sound at all like my own, "Bertl, Bertl," but the child did not appear. One neighbor told me that he had seen him with other Jews somewhere in the fields in the vicinity of the cloister. Bertl returned an hour later, his little face pale and his body shaking. He told me that he did not think that our hiding place was safe enough, and that he had thrown himself to the ground, face down, in the field until the explosions went silent. I thought that he was right.

The smoke dissipated quickly, and only then did it become clear that the ghetto had experienced a miracle of miracles. Not one bomb had fallen on the ghetto, as if an invisible hand had prevented this. The Germans had carried out this murderous operation precisely on the Ukrainian part of Dzhurin, the factory quarter, which is at the foot of the Jewish section of the mountain. Almost no Jews live there. The pilots had blundered. They had intended to destroy the highway between Vinnitsa and Moghilev and the bridge over the river to impede the advance of the Red Army. The highway and the bridge were not at all damaged. In contrast, the bombs turned the twenty-six Ukrainian houses into dust and ashes, and killed about thirty people who lived in these houses. There were also four Jewish victims from the Dzhurin ghetto, people whose feet had carried them to their deaths. Since dawn, a race to the factory quarter had begun to take possession of the food and items from the warehouses that the Germans had not managed to set on fire in time. The victims died near a warehouse. These are their names: Loti Heitner, the wife of Rădăuţi tailor Itzhak Heitner; the two sisters-in-law Scharf, from Vijniţa; the mother-in-law of the tailor Katzapu from Hotin. Two Jews were severely wounded, another three were slightly injured. All the wounded—both Jews and Ukrainians—were taken to the Jewish hospital.

This disaster extinguished the joy over the longed-for deliverance. When we hear the humming of a vehicle, we flee to the fields or dive into ditches, we lie down to sleep fully clothed and prepare ourselves for another bombardment at any moment. In truth, the front is moving further and further westward, the shooting already sounds distant, Dzhurin has no strategic value, and yet we are still in great danger. Even now, more than twenty-four hours after the calamity, my hands are shaking as I write. Roza's heart disease is grievous, and it is difficult for her to breathe, the children are restless, and we continue to listen for the humming from above.

In the shtetl itself (I will no longer use the painful names "ghetto" or "camp"), moving scenes occur that are encouraging and revitalizing. Red Army soldiers stream in from all sides, and there are many Jews among them. There is also no lack of our brothers, the children of Israel, among the senior officers. The local Dzhurin Jews receive greetings from their relatives who were mobilized in the Red Army. There are even lucky ones who have the good fortune of meeting their husbands, children, or brothers with the Red stars on their caps, face to face. The joyful sounds and merriment of a sumptuous wedding are everywhere.

The Red Army soldiers cannot grasp that about 4,000 Jews in Dzhurin were entitled to live to see deliverance. They did not encounter a single Jew until they reached the western side of the Bug. Wherever the Germans trod, they annihilated all the Jews, all of them. They, the Red Army soldiers, do not believe in miracles and claim that the defeat of the Germans did not leave them enough time to put an end to all the Jews in their own manner in these areas as well. I myself, and most of the Dzhurin Jews, do not agree with this explanation. The Germans had plenty of time to destroy the remaining remnant in Transnistria, and miracles were actually occurring beneath the surface.

We are completely cut off from Moghilev and from places that are even closer, and we do not know where deliverance has already arrived, and where the miracle has occurred. The Jewish regime has been abolished, and no new boss has assumed leadership. I am no longer doing anything and I am also not keeping any records since the day before yesterday, because I lack reports regarding cases of death. For the time being, they are distributing soup in the soup kitchen every day, as long as there is food in the storeroom. The hospital also continues to function with its reserves. The pharmacy is closed and so is the cooperative, and the Jewish police have ripped the badges from their sleeves. Everything seems raw, new, and something will probably happen, as long as they allow us to live, and the front continues to move further and further westward. Although everything has changed, one institution remains as before, and as a matter of fact works with even greater resourcefulness: the "IPA" rumor mill. Now it is really spreading its arms and lacks no material: induction into the Red Army, repatriation of the deportees, the fate of the mark, and, of course, the global events and some prophecies.

So, let us come to the end of this entry, the really most important and fateful of all the memories until now. I certainly have not said all there is to say about the events, but at least endeavored to provide a taste …

March 21, 1944, 11 A.M.

"A Shtetl Looks Skyward" is a fitting title for this entry. No one takes off his clothes and shoes at night. By day, people sit dressed in a coat or fur, ready and waiting to run to the fields at any moment. People continue to look skyward to see whether some demon is not approaching. We hear buzzing in the skies more than enough but from a distance. We often hear dull explosions from afar. Yesterday, at 10:30 P.M., many German demons flew by, and we immediately heard powerful explosions from a distance. The people fled in the darkness everywhere, looking for shelter in the fields and in the cemetery. My family and I remained in my cubbyhole, because it was already after the fact. The children slept well and did not hear anything.

People again ran to the fields a few times today, and I also fled, mainly because of the children. Bertl goes his own way and flees alone, because he has no faith in my cities of refuge. Panic and fear of bombardments hover over everyone since Sunday like a heavy burden and destroy the joy of deliverance.

Murafa, 10 kilometers from Dzhurin, was liberated only on Sunday, March 20 at noon. No Jews were hurt there, and no bombs fell. In contrast, a street battle raged between the German and Red Army for three hours, and everyone there recited the *Vidui*. Deliverance does not come very easily … Shargorod was freed on *Motzei Shabbes*, at the same time as Dzhurin. It seems that the Germans killed some Jews there. However, there were no bombardments.

Officers report that Moghilev has also been liberated, but there were bitter fights, because it has a crossing over the Dniester. The Germans blew up the largest bridge over the Dniester at the last moment. The remaining remnant there numbers approximately 15,000.

No regime has been set up in Dzhurin yet. The local Jews are whispering, seizing the benches, and threatening to settle accounts with the former leaders. The colony chief is lucky to have left for Moghilev in time, because he was liable to be the first to bear the brunt of their anger. There is no sign of the council members in the streets, even though their good deeds tilt the scale in their favor, outweighing their transgressions that were for the most part done under duress due to the difficult circumstances. The Jewish regime in Dzhurin acted with compassion as much as possible, especially compared with Moghilev, Shargorod, Bershad, Kopaygorod (in the first year), and so on.

[March 21, 1944] Half an Hour Later

The brief break was violated by a barrage of automatic fire (the Red Army calls it "*Zakuska*" [appetizer]) from close range. First of all, the four of us stretched out on the floor with our faces toward the ground. I immediately went outside and discovered that there was no reason to fall on the floor. A Jewish lieutenant had fired shots of joy in honor of his parents, whom he had come to visit at that moment. He greeted them so that the whole world would hear. We are living through exciting, singular days—holidays and days of awe at the same time.

[March 21, 1944] 5 P.M.

In the next few days, there will be a mobilization of men to serve in the Red Army. No one knows whether this means only former Soviet citizens or also the Jews deported from Romania.[15]

15 Immediately upon entering, the Red Army drafted all men aged nineteen to fifty into the military.

March 22, 1944, 2 P.M.

Yesterday evening, the general staff with officers from the regional "Voenkomat" (Soviet Recruitment Bureau) from Shargorod appeared in the shtetl to organize recruitment. They contacted the provisional leaders of the Jews of Dzhurin (Finger, Kabilansky, Traktirshok) and ordered them to provide a list of all men between the ages of nineteen and fifty by midnight, because they would have to appear before the Recruitment Commission the next day. The new bosses sent for me and tasked me with the duty of preparing the material from the "colony's" previous card catalog and of supervising the writers of the list in Russian. They provided me with ten young men who are proficient in Russian, who immediately sat down to write with fervor in the former community building. I willingly took on the job, both for idealistic reasons and to come up with a small livelihood until our journey home. With the consent of the new bosses, we drew up four separate lists: 1) Ukrainian Jews; 2) Jews from Bessarabia; 3) Jews from Northern Bukovina; 4) Jews from Southern Bukovina. This morning the Recruitment Commission began its work in Dzhurin. For now, only Ukrainian Jews have been summoned. The fate of the rest is not yet clear.

The beautiful spring that marked the week of liberation has vanished. It is cold, wet, muddy, and cloudy. A fine snow mixed with rain has poured down from above. We no longer hear any shots, a sign that the front is far away. There is nothing to buy in the market, and the peasants reject every currency except the ruble. As for me, 93 marks and 3,000 lei have been invalidated—not a fortune but for me it's a treasure. My house is empty, and I must not think about what the future will bring. The most important thing is that we have been saved from the Germans, and things will continue to get better.

March 24, 1944, Friday, *Eyrev Roysh Hoydesh Nisan*, 12 P.M.

The Recruitment Commission is working diligently. Dzhurin serves as the center for the entire surrounding area. Thousands of Ukrainian men have besieged the building where the commission is doing the sorting. The doctors are very rigorous and are adhering to the rule "*Nado voyevat*" (We must fight). Few Jews enlist, and those who do are also not "*Perve sort*" (prime merchandise …) The commission will examine them later. The men whom the doctors deem fit—99 percent!—are taken immediately to the army units to which they have been assigned. As for the deported Jews, the commission is waiting for instructions from "above."

[March 24, 1944] An Hour Later

In the meantime, it is not possible to buy anything with cash. The peasants are demanding oil, or salt, instead of money.[16] Yesterday, for the first time since the liberation, the butchers slaughtered a beast and sold the meat for 1 ruble per kilo on a "stand-in-line" basis. I stood in line for two hours for nothing. The protection of connections prevails, as before, and only the well-connected people have changed. The same thing in a different guise …

[March 24, 1944] 6 P.M.

Yesterday afternoon, a meeting was held in the court hall, may heaven protect us, in order to choose a "Natzrod" (Executive Council of Jewish Dzhurin). They "unanimously," obviously, chose, a Ukrainian Jew, Finger, which the Shargorod "Ispalkom" (Regional Executive Council) sent especially for this purpose. His deputy is a Dzhurin Jew, the agronomist Kabilanksy, who fought with the partisans. There is also another Jew from Dzhurin in the Natzrod, Akiva Traktirshok, and a representative of the deported Jews, Meir Motes from Rădăuţi. They also appointed as secretary a young woman from Dzhurin, Bronia Blechman.

16 In the first days immediately following the liberation and the change of regime, the peasants mainly traded agricultural products for other goods, because of the great uncertainty regarding the value of the local currency.

This afternoon the Natzrod set to work in the former council building. I gave the old archives from the "colony" to my successor, apart from the card catalog and the monograph about Dzhurin, which have nothing to do with the local Jews. I wander around with nothing to do, with no source of income. There is no work for me in Dzhurin, and I hope that I will not grow old here. In the meantime, I still do not know how and when.

All the Ukrainian Jews among the former camp residents are returning to their homes—Shpikov, Tulchin, Tomashpol, Yampol, Nemirov, Vinnitsa, and so on. They have ended up in Dzhurin as "non-kosher"—fleeing from the death camps by the Bug. No one stops them and the roads are clear for everyone to walk and travel on. The Red Army soldiers are kindhearted and do not refuse to take anyone on a military vehicle, or even a tank, without payment.

This is already the second night that we have slept in our clothes. We tossed and turned wearing clothes and shoes for six nights, ready to flee wherever our eyes led us. The fear of the greetings from above has completely disappeared, even though we still hear humming in the sky at night. The front is far away.

March 26, 1944, 10 A.M.

The front newspapers, which the Red Army provides in abundance announce good news: the Red Army has liberated almost all of Bessarabia and is getting close to Cernăuţi, the capital city of Bukovina. In Eastern Galicia, the army assaults Lemberg [Lvov] from the Ukrainian front.

Today, for the first time, a real weekly fair took place at the market. Most of the peasants insisted on bartering—food in exchange for oil, salt, soap, and the like. A few agree to accept the ruble but for very high prices. Here are some of the prices: 1 pood of potatoes—10 rubles; 1 pood of cornflour—60 rubles; 1 pood of butter—20 rubles; 1 liter of milk or one egg—1 ruble, and so on. Rachel gave me a small amount of rubles—an inheritance from my father-in-law, who had hidden them. The banknotes, however, are in large denominations (hundreds) and cannot be exchanged. The peasants only accept 1 or 2 ruble banknotes.

For now, we are still living on what we had prepared, and the reserves will suffice for about two weeks. After that—we'll worry about it then. The new rulers reassure us that they will send the deportees back to Romania as soon as Bukovina has been cleared of Germans. *Peysech* is coming soon, and I have nothing for the holiday, just as I have nothing for after the holiday.

Some of the former leaders in Shargorod have been arrested, but they have not concerned themselves with any of them here. Nevertheless the "fallen gods" are terrified and are planning to flee as quickly as possible before the people turn against them.

March 28, 1944, 4 P.M.

Today the Recruitment Commission summoned all Jewish men of Ukrainian origin between the ages of nineteen and fifty. Except for the disabled, all the rest—about forty people—were sent to Shargorod, where doctors will examine them. The departure of the men looked very different from their parting following the manhunts conducted by the gendarmes for two and a half years. The truth is that their relatives cried and their hearts were heavy, but the young men strode off cheerfully and confidently.

The peasants have become reconciled to the ruble but they are fleecing us. There is no flour to be found. Today a dear brother brought me a half kilo of meat for 5 rubles, and there was rejoicing in my home. For almost a month, the dishes in my home have been *parve*.[17] For 1 liter of milk, if you can get any, one pays 4 rubles. Who can afford such terribly high prices, apart from a few rich people. They should have transferred us to a large city where there is work, until they send us home. There is no one to turn to; it is as if we were living on an island in the middle of a stormy sea.

17 Neither meat nor dairy.

[March 28, 1944] 8 P.M.

Today, for the first time a Jew from Moghilev appeared, a woman who came to look for relatives. The birth pangs in Moghilev were very severe. During the last days before their defeat, the German soldiers wantonly robbed and murdered, but the grievous troubles began with the liberation. There was a series of bombings day and night, and dozens of Jews have been killed in their homes and in their wretched hiding places. Today they still lie down to sleep in their clothes, so that they can flee in the blink of an eye when the sirens begin to wail and the anti-aircraft artillery begins to thunder.

Some brave Jews risked their lives and crossed the Dniester to Bessarabia, just not to be in Transnistria. One jumps on a truck or a tank and pins one's hopes on God, traveling as far away as possible.

April 2, 1944, 10 A.M.

Since yesterday a snowstorm has been raging mercilessly as in January, and it is impossible to set foot outside. I sit holed up in my cubbyhole, because my "shoes" are completely ruined and they absorb more water than they can drain out. The shoemaker absolutely refuses to fix them anymore. New shoes cost several hundred rubles, which is beyond my means. I sit with my arms folded and think and think. There is no work here for anyone in this godforsaken place.

People are saying that Bessarabia and Bukovina are already almost completely liberated. Most deportees think that they should set out on the way at their own expense, on foot or on a Russian vehicle, to try to make their way home. The problem for me is that Roza suffers from a serious heart condition; Rivka is very weak, since she came down with typhus; the children are young; and we are all naked and barefoot. How can we set off on foot with such a group? Otherwise I would take the risk like the others in order to get home. It is doubtful that I will find any of my property there and that my home has not been destroyed, but anything is better than [being in] a strange place, lonely as a stone, and with no livelihood. I will somehow earn a livelihood at home, and I will no longer be fastidious about work.

[April 2, 1944] 4 P.M.

The plight of the deported Jews from Romania, both here and in other "colonies," has become absolutely appalling. The local Jews manifest hatred toward the "*bishenitzes*" and are retaliating against them for the sorrows that they once endured under the Jewish regime. They do not remember that the "*bishenitzes*" lie deep in the ground, perhaps even more than the locals, and have filled the Dzhurin cemetery, apart from those who died in the labor camps. They have forgotten that Dzhurin is the only place in Transnistria where the Romanian occupying authorities did not drive the Ukrainian Jews to the Bug, precisely because of the "*bishenitzes*" from Romania and their negotiators. And even if a few leaders committed transgressions against a Ukrainian Jew once—exactly as they did against their "own" brothers … —why is the general public guilty? But go argue with those who turn a deaf ear. Whoever among the Dzhurin inhabitants has God in his heart reviled and cursed and threatened the "*bishenitzes*," threw them out of the apartments, grabbed the borrowed household items, and even said things that were uncalled-for and that should not be said …[18]

At a meeting held the day before yesterday, they poured fire and sulfur on the leadership of the former "lords" and decided to establish an aid committee that will deal with the remaining inherited institutions (soup kitchen, hospital, pharmacy) under the supervision of the Natzrod. However, what will the new functionaries do [without] the contributions

18 It is important to note that the local Jews in Transnistria in general, and in Dzhurin in particular, initially welcomed the deportees, brought them into their small, crowded homes, and crammed in together with them. Over time, the local Jews became the minority in their homes. The leadership in the ghetto was made up of deported Jews from Southern Bukovina, and they instituted a new order in the ghetto. Therefore, the local Jews were the first to be dispatched from the ghetto and the last to receive aid from Romania. As life in the ghetto became more difficult, relations between the deportees and the local Jews deteriorated; the local Jews blamed the deportees for their troubles and the calamities that fell upon them.

from outside that poured in from Romania? The wealthy Jewish Americans will now be able to help the remaining remnant and save them from misery until they return home, but in the meantime we do not see or hear of any sign of aid.

April 3, 1944, 9 A.M.

A blizzard has been raging wildly for three days now. The streets are covered with mounds of snow. Our liberators have apparently brought us a gift from Siberia. The plans to walk to Moghilev have for the moment been frozen, until the real spring arrives.

April 4, 1944, the 11th of *Nisan*, 5704, 9 A.M.

Only today did the snowstorm subside. As a result of the storm on Sunday, the weekly market did not take place, and no one has acquired food for the approaching holiday. This year we will have to do without *matzos* and will have to fulfill the duty with a potato. A considerable number of people say that they will not refrain from eating bread, if they can get it. Others are planning to bake *matzos* on stoves. Apart from potatoes, I have not prepared anything for *Peysech*. In the meantime, I exchange a 50 and another 50 from the "inheritance" of my father-in-law, but the pocket has been emptied out. I approached one of the new big shots to ask for some kind of work, and he spared no promises that he would act as a *meyletz yoysher* on my behalf. That promise has the value of a hollow egg.

The hatred toward the former leaders is growing from day to day, but no one bothers them. After the liberation, they searched the home of the former council member Leon Neuman and found a great deal of medicines, which they confiscated for the Red Army. Neuman claims that he received these medicines as a gift from relatives in Romania. So they also raided the homes of other "big shots" and found salt and various products. They claim to have purchased these goods for honest money.

The front is now far away, but German planes still appear at the important centers of Podolia (Transnistria), where they drop bombs. The strategic Zhmerinka train station experiences this almost every night.

[April 4, 1944] 4 P.M.

Since idleness enervates my soul, I have begun to draft a German–Russian dictionary, [writing] from time to time with the help of my landlord's daughter, Henia, a qualified teacher. I need a dictionary like that, because I sometimes have to write a petition to the authorities, or a letter searching for relatives, for which I receive a ruble in payment. Apart from this, I am reviewing my memories, erasing, and writing about things that I had not mentioned.

April 11, 1944—the Second day of *Hol Hamo'ed Peysech,* 7 A.M.

Half of *Peysech* has passed already. Most people have no *matzos*. Some have baked flat crackers on their stoves just to fulfill the duty. They are distributing bread at the soup kitchen just as they do during the rest of the year. The local rabbi, Rabbi Herşel Karalnic, raised a loud outcry and persuaded the new bosses that beginning from today they will give out mamaliga[19] instead of bread. The rabbi himself gathered the cornmeal from the people and took it to the soup kitchen. Roza baked a few "*matza*" crackers at the home of the landlord for the sake of the children—alas, so much for a kosher *Peysech*! We are celebrating the holiday with mamaliga, potatoes, and without eggs. On the first day, we even saw a smidgen of meat in the bowl.

On the first *Seyder* night, a strange, happy occasion took place in the hall of the Ukrainian school, where about twenty families live. A Soviet major made it known that he wanted to celebrate the night of the *Seyder*

19 A Romanian porridge made from cornmeal and thus not hametz.

with the Jews, because he himself is the son of a rabbi, and his family was annihilated by the Germans. At the same time, he sent a messenger with two baskets full of eggs, sugar, oil, and live chickens. People found out about this *Seyder* in the shtetl, and more than 100 people attended the happy occasion. The major was truly the most important guest at the event. He sang Yiddish songs, told Yiddish jokes, kissed everyone, and even organized some dancing. Thus they enjoyed themselves until the morning light. I sat at home, because my heart is not inclined to celebrating in my current situation.

[April 11, 1944] 10 A.M.

Let us not forget: today is the second birthday of this diary. My memoirs will soon come to an end, as soon as we are liberated from the exile of Transnistria and return home. The five notebooks only offer a pale reflection of these strange years but, nevertheless, are better than nothing. Perhaps they will one day contribute to the chronicle of the decrees of Hitler, may his name be blotted out, regarding the calamity of the deported Romanian Jews, and for this reason it was worth recording, at mortal risk, the episodes, images, and impressions. Whomever I may have forgotten will forgive me, because I have strived to do my duty to the best of my abililty.

[April 11, 1944] 5 P.M.

A birthday present for the diary: According to what the officers say, the entire area of Bukovina has been liberated since April 8 and so has my hometown of Rădăuţi. I do not know how much Rădăuţi suffered in the battles. It means that we will immediately be able to set out on the journey home.

April 12, 1944, 11 A.M.

It is beautiful outside, really pleasant, and spring has returned. The shtetl is vibrant, and people are traveling from one place to another to see relatives, in search of a little income, to find ways of getting home. Approximately 25,000 Jews from all of Transnistria have flowed into Moghilev, and their suffering has not been a mere charade. Everyone there is hoping to be granted the parting of the Dniester.

The Voenkomat [Soviet Recruitment Bureau] in Moghilev has mobilized all Jews between the ages of eighteen and fifty from among both the locals and the deportees from Romania. Those between the ages of fifty and fifty-six years only had to register but were not mobilized. Those whom the doctors declared fit have already gone off somewhere out there and were ordered to take ten days' worth of food with them. It is not known whether they have been taken for labor or to the front.

I had no choice and had to empty my pockets almost completely in order to "repair" my shoes, because we are surely about to take a long journey.

April 16, 1944, *Isre Hag Peysech*

Well, somehow *Peysech* is over, and now there is a series of serious post-*Peysech* concerns: mobilization, repatriation, livelihood. Regarding mobilization, each region has a different system. In Moghilev, Kopaygorod, and Luchinets, the deportees were conscripted. In contrast, in the district of Shargorod to which Dzhurin and Murafa belong, for now, they are leaving the "*bishenitzes*" in peace. In the regions of Bershad, Balta, and Yampol, this is not at all a problem, because the handful of the remaining remnant left in time and crossed the Dniester near Yampol. At any rate, not many Jews there were granted deliverance, because 90 percent of the deportees died of hunger, cold, plagues, unusual deaths, and deprivation.[20]

---

20 Upon the liberation by the Red Army, most of the deportees set out to return to Romania. Many made their way to the crossing of the Dniester on foot and spent many weeks

For the time being, the regime is not allowing anyone to cross the Dniester in Moghilev, and the reason is not clear. The Jews are impatient and sitting on pins and needles, and want to return from exile already.

Yesterday a Soviet captain in Dzhurin related that he had been in my hometown of Rădăuţi a few days ago. The city did not suffer from the battles, but there are no people there, because all the inhabitants were evacuated to the neighboring shtetl of Siret.

The Red Army has already occupied a large part of northern Moldavia[21]—the cities of Botoşani, Dorohoi and Fălticeni[22]—where tens of thousands of Jews live. The Romanian residents mostly have fled from these places deep into Romania, and almost only the Jews remain there. German planes bombarded the center of Botoşani last week, and there were many Jewish casualties. The large city of Botoşani, which had 100,000 inhabitants, has become like Tel Aviv[23] and a young lawyer from Rădăuţi, Max Veber, sits on the mayor's throne. Those repatriated from Transnistria who are trying to make their way home, in the meantime, have gathered in Botoşani and settled in the beautiful, empty homes of the Romanians who fled. For once, the opposite happens …

In most parts of Romania where the Germans are still in control, the Jews are suffering severe distress. They are in danger of being rounded up and sent somewhere. Two weeks ago, the Jews were deported from Hungary to a death camp in Poland. The miracle experienced by the remaining remnant of Transnistria is becoming even more striking.[24]

---

walking home. Others went on wagons and made their way to Romania, while others traveled on Soviet trains from the crossing of the Dniester in Moghilev. Most of the deportees dreamed of returning to their homes, but many feared the attitudes of their neighbors and, therefore, returned to the homes of relatives who remained in Cernăuţi instead. See Fuchs, *Sefer Yehudei Sutsheva*, vol. 1, pp. 131–132.

21 The north of the Regat, the Dorohoi district.

22 The cities in the north of the Regat.

23 It is not clear what Kunstadt had in mind when citing Tel Aviv. Perhaps he was referring to the bombing of Tel Aviv by the Italians in 1940, or alluding to the fact that the mayor was a Jew and to the repatriation of the Jews who had settled in the city.

24 The deportations to Auschwitz-Birkenau of the Jews of northern Transylvania, which had been annexed to Hungary, continued. This indicates an awareness of the great difference between the unbearable suffering and death rates of the Jews in Transnistria and the fate of the Jews deported by the Germans.

April 18, 1944

A Soviet Post Office has opened in Dzhurin, and it is possible to write to [anyone] anywhere, also to the liberated areas of Romania. The rates are cheap: 20 kopeks for a card and 30 kopeks for a letter. Local Jews have already received letters from relatives in the Soviet Union. People besiege the Post Office all day long and continue to ask if something has arrived for them.

The Recruitment Commission has arrived once again and is sorting men between the ages of eighteen and forty-seven. They are leaving the deported Jews alone, but this is happening only in Dzhurin, and the reason is not clear. The "*bishenitzes*" have been conscripted in other places and sent to barracks, where they are training them to shoot properly.

Quite a few people have already set out for Moghilev from here, mainly youths but also those who are married and those with young children. They easily make their way to Moghilev, because Russian military personnel who travel on the main road in trucks and tanks take those seeking repatriation with them for a pittance, and sometimes even for free. Others travel to Yampol, where it is easy to cross the Dniester. Although the authorities do not allow people to cross the Dniester in Moghilev, young people for the most part have come up with a ploy to get to the other side quickly, in Atachi. The train is still not running and it is necessary to go through Bessarabia on foot, or to resort to the mercy of Soviet trucks and tanks. The throng, for the most part, is making its way to Southern Bukovina, which will probably remain in the hands of Romania, in order to wander from there further into the wider world: to America, *Eretz Yisroel*, Australia, and wherever they can go.

In Moghilev, and all the more so in the provinces, there are pessimists who are in no hurry to leave Transnistria, not until Lemberg [Lvov] is liberated. They have been mockingly nicknamed "The Lembergers." I too deserve this title.

Last night we heard loud humming for nearly an hour, and the eastern sky immediately turned red, like a terrible fire, and the flames continued all night long. It was German planes that destroyed Zhmerinka, 50 kilometers from here.

April 25, 1944

The former "lords" and former militiamen (some of them have already fled to their homes from here) were summoned by the Natzrod to sign a pledge that they will not leave without the Natzrod's permission.

April 26, 1944

On both sides of the main road, at the foot of the mountain, many families camp out by day and by night with their young children and personal belongings, waiting for military trucks to pass to take them to Moghilev or to Yampol. They are no longer taking anyone for free, and drivers are charging increasingly high prices. Some fortunate people were taken in a vehicle that drove them to Botoşani for free. The crowds wait for twenty-four hour periods and sleep under the open sky. Fortunately, the sky is clear, and the spring is warm.

However, many people are not waiting to get lucky and are setting out on foot in order to get home as soon as possible. Some are saying that the regime will soon close the border between Northern Bukovina, which is the Soviet zone, and [Romanian] Southern Bukovina. The wealthy people pay an exorbitant price for the ride and, as a result, the simple people suffer and have to trudge on foot. Whoever has any articles gets rid of them, selling them at bargain prices, and once again the peasants inherit the meager poverty of the Jews. The streets are empty, because most of the young people have already left. I am caught in a bind, because of Roza's condition and the poverty that rages in my empty pockets. I will wait a little longer, until the train will start running from Moghilev to the West. Somehow we will manage to get to Moghilev.

The former colony chief Dr. Max Rosenstrauch left Moghilev in time and is already on his way home. He did not wait for any kind of luck …

April 27, 1944

Both state schools in Jewish Dzhurin have already opened, but only the children of the local Jews have enrolled. Only Jewish teachers work there. There are no schoolbooks and not even notebooks—everything is still raw.

April 28, 1944

Hundreds of families are waiting for an opportunity [to get a ride] by the main road, and others are leaving on foot. We feel that we are a large, excessive burden in the eyes of the local Jews. Everyone is tormented by one single concern: how will we get home safely?

April 30, 1944

Today I happened to receive the Romanian newspaper *Izvestia* that published a report from the front, dated April 10. According to this communication, two cities were liberated: Odessa and … my hometown of Rădăuţi! This is quite an achievement! The same newspaper also reports that the Nazis seized power in Hungary on March 19, 1944, casting a heavy pall over the country. The SS demons have already in the first week arrested 50,000 Jews and the *Aktzia* continues. This information has caused me terrible anguish, indeed because of all the Jews, and especially because of my stepsister, Malka Sapira, who lives in Miskolc, and her children, who live in Budapest.

The soup kitchen has been closed already for two weeks, but no one feels it. The poor have fled—people without the weight of belongings—and one no longer sees anyone stretching out one's hand for alms. Diverse types of trade in all kinds of goods has developed. People are rushing by in cars and by train—the stretch from Moghilev eastward has already been repaired—as far as Kiev, from Moghilev, obviously. People are engaging in feverish speculation, here and back, and that is why the high prices continue to rise. For example: 1 liter of oil costs 80 rubles; 1 kilo of sugar, 50 rubles; 1 kilo of butter, 100 rubles; 1 pound of wheat flour, 140 rubles; 1 pood of barley flour, 70 rubles; 1 kilo of meat, 10 rubles; 1 liter of milk, 3 rubles; and one egg, 1 ruble. Only potatoes are cheap—1 pood for 4 rubles.

The local rabbi, Rabbi Herşel Karalnic, delivered a sermon at the synagogue yesterday and asked the people to donate significant sums as a loan to the regime. The Natzrod is calling upon the wealthy people among the deportees, who have not yet left, and demands their contribution. They dig into their pockets respectably so as not to endanger their journey home. I earned my first 10 rubles since the liberation, translating a document from Romanian into Russian. Two poods of potatoes are good …

May 1, 1944, 10 A.M.

Red flags were hoisted on the militia post and on two other buildings in honor of the workers' holiday, the first Red flags that I have seen in my life. A May Day celebration was held at the local club last night, with speeches and songs. I too was there, but the joy did not touch me, because I am so depressed. We have indeed been liberated but are nevertheless in a daze.

May 2, 1944

Yesterday, in honor of May Day, the first train set out from Moghilev on the new bridge over the Dniester, which the Germans had blown up. This means that it is now possible to travel home by train, if the regime will not object. They are seizing people in the streets in Moghilev to work in the coal mines of Donbass[25]—men, women, and girls alike. They do not ask

25 Donbass is an area in southeast Ukraine that contains one of the largest coal deposits in Europe. The coal deposits in Donbass were vital for the Germans. The area passed to the control of the Ukrainian Soviet Socialist Republic after the Russian Civil War. During World War II, the area endured extreme poverty and scarcity. The area was under Nazi occupation from 1941 to 1942. In 1943, the Soviets regained control of the area. The

who they are or from where they come. Therefore, people are avoiding going out in the streets. People did not expect that after the liberation and on the eve of going home, they would again begin to be afraid of manhunts, as in former days.

There is an uninvited guest in the shtetl: typhus. The hospital had been empty for quite some time, and suddenly new cases have been discovered unexpectedly, cases brought by merchants and peasants from distant regions. A patient was transferred to the hospital today from the house where I lived in exile. The young man would often come to my house and sit on my wooden bunk.

May 3, 1944

Military trucks now appear rarely on the main road. Those who are making their way home with everyone and with all their belongings sometimes spend a full twenty-hours under the open sky until the opportunity presents itself. Because there is a train from Moghilev to Romania, it is more expedient for the army to send transports by train and to spare the vehicles. For the time being, they are not allowing any civilians to board the train cars in Moghilev, and the trains are packed with soldiers.[26]

---

war caused terrible destruction, and many deserted the area. When World War II ended, restoration work began in the Donbass area. Many Russian workers were brought in to work in and to populate the area, including many Jews who were seized and sent to work in the coal mines, as well as in agriculture, industry, and in the rehabilitation of the other industrial enterprises. There were many very young men and women among the Jews who were captured and sent to Donbass. See Meller, *Me'ever Lanahar*, pp. 233–255; Lea Prais, *Be'arefel Hanedudim*, p. 183.

26 The Soviet army did not allow the Jews to travel on the trains, but many jumped onto the train cars and joined the soldiers. Sometimes these were freight cars, flatbeds train cars that were exposed to the wind and rain. Despite this fact, many Jews risked their lives and jumped onto the train cars. See the testimonies of Marcel Biner, Ziva Gutkin (Zelter), and Herta Rosenberg (Pistiner) in Yalon, *Sefer Hazikaron Shel Yehudei Vaṭrah-Dorne Vehaseviva, Buḳovinah–Romanya* (Hebrew) vol. 2, pp. 457, 509, 599; Batsheva Akerman testimony, YVA, O.3/VT/11356.

May 5, 1944, Friday

The speculators are carrying on like thieves in the forest and are taking all the food deep into Russia, to Kiev, where they pay insane prices. The inflation is dreadful. Here are a some of today's prices (tomorrow they will rise even higher …): 1 pood of wheat flour, 200 rubles; 1 pood of cornmeal, 120 rubles; 1 pood of barley flour, 100 rubles; 1 liter of oil, 80 rubles; 1 kilo of meat, 20 rubles; one egg, 1.50 rubles, and so on. People sell their last shirt, and the rubles disappear from their hands. I see this and am dumbfounded at how the Socialist state allows such wild speculation. The high-level officials are very happy that they are taking goods to the big, starving cities. Kiev, Berdichev, Vinnitsa, and the like take precedence over Dzhurin …

Three-quarters of the wanderers have already left Shargorod. People are now traveling frantically from Murafa and Kopaygorod. The Murafa "*bishenitzes*" all come first of all to Dzhurin to try their luck here, by the main road, because they do not see any military vehicles there [in Murafa]. The competition from Murafa makes it more difficult for the wanderers from Dzhurin to seize an opportunity to travel. When a vehicle appears, they besiege it from all sides, and the wealthy people proffer their fat wallets to the drivers, saying: "Take as much as you want, as long as you allow us to get into the vehicle." I sit as if on pins and needles and lack the courage to set out on a dangerous journey with a sick wife and young children. Rachel and Rivka are watching me and waiting, just not to be separated from us.

May 8, 1944, the 15th of *Iyar*, 5704, Tuesday

People are traveling and setting out on foot, wandering around for days with their belongings by the main road, and slowly the shtetl is being emptied of the "*bishenitzes*." Wealthy people are hiring Ukrainian wagons for a huge fortune and setting out at night to avert the evil eye. The former "Labor Minister" David Buksbaum also left very quietly last night, with crates of belongings. They have arrested the "fallen" big shots in Shargorod—the "colony chief," Dr. Teich, the "labor minister," Zand, and the head of the militia, Scharf, and sent them to Vinnitsa for trial.[27]

May 9, 1944

Almost all of the former "lords" have left. Tonight the brothers-in-law, Moshe Katz and Leon Neuman, "the good pair," set out with Ukrainian wagons. The Natzrod is aware of this but does not oppose it. Sometimes one good deed conceals a mountain of transgressions. If the calamity in Dzhurin was less severe than, for example in Moghilev, Shargorod, or Kopaygorod ("only" 25 percent were victims …), it is nevertheless mainly thanks to the council, in which Moshe Katz was "*Mi lanu gadol*" (Who is great for us), [the big shot] who was constantly engaged in "*Ma Yafit*"[28] around the colony chief.

Dzhurin has become a pious, God-fearing shtetl in the past few weeks. We do not see any man who is not growing a respectable beard on his face. The beards are a *sgula* against being seized for Donbass during the journey or in Moghilev itself, because who wants old men? I myself do not believe in this *sgula*, and my good brothers are astonished.

I plan to wait here for another two weeks and then to set out on the road. In the meantime, I am packing up everything in my cubbyhole in order to get a little more money for travel expenses. It is very difficult for me to get rid of our meager belongings.

---

27 Immediately upon the entry of the Soviet forces to the ghettos of Transnistria, the heads of the ghettos and the community leaders were arrested and tried for collaboration with the Nazis. Some of them were tried immediately after the war in Vinnitsa, such as the head of the ghetto of Bershad, Binyamin Korn; others were tried in Bucharest. See the trials of: Max Rosenstrauch, CNSAS, I-94912 and P-50679, 2 vols.; Aizic (Isidor) Presner, CNSAS, I-329796, 2 vols.; Moshe Katz, (şi alţii) CNSAS, P-050679; Danilov Mihail (Mihai), CNSAS, P-45109; and Meir Teich, CNSAS, P-50678, vols. 1–2; see also Avraham Korn interview by Sarah Rosen, January 3, 2012, Haifa.

28 Kunstadt ironically portrays Moshe Katz as a sycophant, referring to a term found in Talmudic and *Musar* literature in connection to Moses, "Who is as great as Moses," which emphasizes Moses' modesty and wisdom. Regarding the term used to describe Rosenstrauch, "How fair and how pleasant art thou, O love, for delights!" from Shir Hashirim (Song of Songs) 7:7, see the entry of May 30, 1942.

May 11, 1944

It is estimated that more than half of the wanderers have already left and people continue to walk along the main road. A few local residents have also set out for Moghilev with the intention of joining those who are repatriating and crossing the Dniester …

May 14, 1944, Sunday

Already more than 60 percent of the local "*bishenitzes*" are gone, and the rest sit on their baggage and are preparing to set out. The crowd postponed the journey until after today's weekly market in order to trade the rest of their meager belongings and gather a few rubles for travel expenses. Well, there was indeed a market today, unlike any that Dzhurin had seen before—mountains of objects, from graters and clay pots to pillows and bedding, expensive leather coats, and silk underwear. There were rags and watches lying around at the market. Peasants rummaged through the possessions of the Jews, turned their noses up, and offered a price that made one feel like spitting in the faces of these buyers. Even though the people were willing to sell everything at bargain prices, nevertheless, they were not able to get rid of the whole pile.

We too—Roza, the children, and I—wandered around the market for a few hours, laden with rags and household goods, but we managed to get rid of only part of our treasures for a pittance.

I am thinking of joining the circle dance at the end of the coming week and to set out on the road with the masses. Good news has arrived concerning my hometown of Rădăuţi. The Romanian residents have returned from the evacuation—from Siret—and a few hundred of the remaining remnant have also returned. The city has not suffered, there is food and also some options to earn a livelihood. Shots are still heard from a distance but the front is constantly moving westward.

May 21, 1944, Sunday

We are still here. We are waiting for today's weekly market and are trying to sell something. Of the 4,000 deportees who suffered in Dzhurin, only 600 persons remain today—people with serious family problems like me, or just "Lembergers" who are afraid of the front.

The news from Bukovina in the last week has not been good. The front has been halted not far from my hometown and, for the time being, there is a stalemate. In Cernăuţi, which is the assembly point for those going home, life is not a bowl of cherries for them. There are no empty homes, and the inflation is intolerable, and they are seizing people in the streets for Donbass—men, women, and girls. Whoever manages to reach Cernăuţi with great difficulty is stopped by the militia in the suburb of Jucica,[29] and they do not allow them to cross the bridge over the Prut to enter the city. Those who are repatriating must remain in the villages in the area. About 15,000 "*bishenitzes*" are waiting in Moghilev for the providential moment of the parting of the Dniester. They are in dire straits. They are vehemently abducting people for Donbass, and long beards do not help.

May 30, 1944

There are reports of a terrible disaster that has befallen a few hundred deported Jews who had been conscripted into the Red Army following the liberation in Moghilev. They were sent by train somewhere in the East and as soon as the train had arrived at the large station of Bryansk, fleets of German planes flew overhead and bombed the railway station and the troops there for two hours. The demons turned everything into fire and ashes, and the number of casualties was very high, because the railroad cars were packed with new recruits. The victims include hundreds of Jews from Bukovina and Bessarabia, who had made preparations in Moghilev to go home. A very large number of seriously wounded is lying in hospitals. The injured from my hometown are: Apel-Stop (lost

29 A small town in Northern Bukovina, where several hundred Jews lived.

a hand and an eye); Max Schulzinger (lost a leg), Muniu David (lost a leg), and perhaps also others whose names I do not know. It was a crime that the Soviet authorities seized foreign citizens who had suffered in camps for three years and were preparing to return home and sent them to the front. There is no international law that justifies forcing foreign citizens to fight, and especially the remaining remnant of emaciated and physically broken Jews, who have already endured more than enough the torment of the grave. Go argue after the *afikomen*.[30]

May 31, 1944, the 9th of *Sivan*, 5704, Wednesday

I decided to go with my family and our belongings to the intersection of the main road on Sunday, June 4, to wait for a passing opportunity. There are only about 300 persons remaining in Dzhurin, most of them ill, elderly, and "Lembergers." It is foolish and even dangerous to continue to enjoy the air of Dzhurin, like a worm that has become accustomed to the horseradish.

They have begun to seize people also in Dzhurin, like in the old days, heaven forbid. Since there are no longer any young people here, they are seizing older people. Yesterday they seized my brother-in-law, Moshe Menaches, a sixty-year-old Jew, and they are holding him hostage because his two daughters, Lola and Medi, had already fled to Moghilev yesterday. Who knows whether they will not send him to the coal mines in Donbass! My sister, Rivka, was seized the day before yesterday, the second day of *Shavues*, and it was extremely difficult to rescue her from detention. She is somewhere in hiding today. Therefore, we must get out of here as quickly as possible, if we value our lives.

This entry is the last in Transnistria—so I hope—and even this notebook is reaching its limit. I am already on the last page and am writing sparingly in small and dense letters. When I will safely live through the miracle of the parting of the Dniester, I will write a few words of farewell.

30 The afikomen is matza, set aside to be eaten toward the end of the Seder meal.

For now, farewell Dzhurin, and I will certainly never forget you, because of the mound of earth in your cemetery that covers the most precious treasure I have ever had: my mother.

Sadagura, near Cernăuţi (Bukovina)

July 2, 1944, Sunday, the 11th of *Tammuz*, 5704

We were not able to leave Dzhurin on June 4 [1944] as planned but rather eleven days later on Thursday, June 15, 1944. Roza's heart [rate] was unstable and any exertion on her part was very dangerous then. When we set out on the road with our few belongings, it was a radiant summer day, a propitious day for deliverance. My landlord, Iankel Axelrod, and his family, accompanied us and bid us farewell with tears in their eyes.

A few people, mainly from other places, were waiting at the station, and we sat down on our baggage. Luck soon shined upon on, and an empty military truck soon arrived and stopped by the road to pick up people. A major, the owner of the vehicle, sat next to the driver, a military man. We could not believe our ears: the officer offered to assume responsibility to take us to Ştefăneşti, next to Botoşani, Romania, for a sum of 3,000 rubles. Another family from my hometown, the Dr. Avraham Hart family, joined us, for the same sum. Rivka, Rachel, and I scraped together our last rubles and crawled into the vehicle with our baggage. We were eleven people when we arrived in Dzhurin at the end of October 1941, but only eight of us sat there: me, Roza, Bertl, Iza, Rivka, Rachel, Elke, and her young son, Herş. My mother, my father-in-law, and my brother-in-law, Moshe, remain in Dzhurin forever.

We saw Dzhurin for the last time at around 12 P.M., and our hearts felt strangely cheerful and light, relying on the mercy of God. After a difficult two-hour journey, we reached the city of Yampol, where we had to cross the Dniester on a ferry. The major got out of the vehicle and ordered us not to move from our places until he returned, because he was going to find out where to cross the river. Half an hour later, he returned with a gloomy expression and informed us that there was a strict military guard by the Dniester, and they were not allowing any civilians to cross. And then he said to us: "So, excuse me and get out of the vehicle. You will probably find an opportunity to get to Moghilev from here, because from there you can cross the Dniester by train. And now, pay the 3,000 rubles for each family!"

We were thunderstruck and blindsided. All our arguments and pleading were futile, and we had to hand the rubles to the major. The two devious men threatened that it would be very bad if we would not dig into our pockets, and the driver even pulled out a revolver slowly and began to play with it ...

We all crawled out of the truck [and went] into a side street, which was completely empty, and entered an empty home that must have been inhabited by deported Jews until a few days before. We suffered in Yampol for two days and almost despaired until finally a local Jew saved us and helped us to rent a wagon from a kolkhoz—with our own money—to get to Moghilev. Only on *Shabbes*, June 17, the wagon left at dawn, and in the evening we arrived exhausted and frazzled in Moghilev at around 6 P.M. We went to the apartment where my brother-in-law Moshe Menaches had lived with his household for a few weeks.

New troubles arose in Moghilev. A permit from the district in which we previously had lived was required to cross the Dniester by train. I had to travel under very difficult conditions to Shargorod to receive this authorization. My rain coat was stolen on the way there. The time that we spent in Moghilev was very difficult also because of the danger of being cast into the coal mines in Donbass, since the manhunts in the streets continued daily.

Immediately after I returned from Shargorod, without a raincoat but with the travel permit in my pocket, I immediately began to make preparations for the journey home, without delay. It was possible to rent a cattle car to travel to Cernăuţi. A number of families from my hometown pooled together and rented a cattle car, and we also joined them. Rachel, Elke, and Herşele in the meantime remained in Moghilev with my brother-in-law's family, while Roza, Iza, Bertl, Rivka, and I bade farewell to the holy city of Moghilev. On Sunday, June 25, 1944, we crossed the Dniester in a packed cattle car on our way home, as opposed to the one in that cursed October 1941.

During the journey, we learned that the regime had closed the border between Soviet Northern Bukovina and Romanian Southern Bukovina, so we would have to remain wandering in Cernăuţi for the time being. The trip lasted a day and a half and was dreadful. There were rumors that civilian passengers were being thrown off the railroad cars along the way, and that soldiers were being seated in their place. With every station that we passed safely, another stone was lifted from our hearts.

The train arrived in Cernăuţi on Monday, June 26, at 6 P.M. They stopped us in Jucica and did not allow us to enter the city. Requests and pleas did not help and, having no choice, we settled in the nearby shtetl of Sadagura, about 3 kilometers from Cernăuţi. It was once a famous Jewish town, the center of the Ruzhiner Rebbe, but today no Jews are to be seen. I immediately found a state post as a bookkeeper (even though I had never practiced this profession …) there, and I settled into a sumptuous, respectable home. A new exile has begun, but it is not at all comparable to the Transnistrian exile.

Although I promised to conclude these memoirs once and for all as soon as I reached the other side of the Dniester, I nevertheless have set my mind on adding a page to this notebook and on saying the real *Aleynu* only when I am back in my hometown. There are no prophets who can prophesy when exactly this will happen, we should not try to predict, and no day is like any other. Perhaps I will nevertheless be able to "blacken" [cross illegally] the border and reach Rădăuţi. Those who showed more courage and daring and left Transnistria immediately after the liberation crossed the border without any difficulty, because the border was still open then.

Rădăuţi (Southern Bukovina)

April 13, 1945

Today we finally made it home at long last. We suffered for ten months in Sadagura, although our sufferings did not have the taste of Dzhurin. I did not lack a livelihood, and we did not live too badly, and my director at the Promkombinat (the cooperative of the tradesmen) was completely satisfied with me. This was actually a problem, because he had no desire whatsoever to let me go. I once saw my name on the bulletin board at the institution center in Cernăuţi, where they praised me to the heavens, and I saw black. Such praise could block my way home. Iza and Bertl attended a Ukrainian school, Roza, Rachel, and Rivka traded at the market bits of soap, a pencil, a piece of clothing, and whatever they had. I managed to save a few thousand rubles. I did not try to cross the border illegally again and waited until they allowed us to return home.

Finally on *Hol Hamo'ed Peysech*, 5705, an order was issued allowing anyone from Southern Bukovina to cross the border and go home. My boss tried to prevent me from leaving—he was a Ukrainian enemy of Israel—because he had no replacement for me, but he did not succeed. On the last day of *Peysech*, they came for us, the lucky ones, and sent us to the border point in Herţa[31] in wagons. We wandered around there for a few days, until we crossed the border on April 10, 1945, and arrived at the Romanian border point Pomârla, near Dorohoi. That same day we were taken to Dorohoi, where the Jewish community and the Joint[32] prepared a festive welcome for us. Our transport was the first transport of the remaining remnant that entered Romania with the authorization of the agreement between the Soviet Union and Romania. (**Added later:** Our names were published in the Jewish press in America. A trifle: 250,000 Jews were sent to hell, and 300 returned all at once! …)

Although the Jews of Dorohoi wanted us to remain with them as their esteemed guests for a while, no one allowed himself to be persuaded,

31 A town in the Dorohoi district.

32 American Jewish Joint Distribution Committee (JDC).

and the next morning we went to Rădăuţi in wagons, which the activists in Dorohoi willingly provided us.

We arrived in Rădăuţi last night and went straight to my house. The house is empty, because the Romanian heirs moved out in time and, apart from neglect, the house did not suffer any damage. Rivka's house was also not destroyed. In contrast, my father-in-law's home, a magnificant building in the middle of a park, was burned down to the ground. My position as community secretary was waiting for me, and I was received with joy. The community has been operating for almost a year, and the community bookkeeper, David (Duchia) Shuler, filled in for me, and saved my place for me.

I see many strange faces, because Rădăuţi is a center for all those who are drawn to Romania in order to continue further, mostly to foreign countries. Of my fellow townsmen, 2,500 people are missing and will never return to this city—a bloody contribution to the massive destruction.

Rădăuţi, my hometown, where I was born and raised, has lost its charm without the cherished Rădăuţi Jews, my friends and acquaintances, who were so dear to my heart—without my beloved mother, whom I left in the Dzhurin cemetery, along with my father-in-law, and so many martyrs.

I have decided to leave Rădăuţi and Europe. My great aspiration is the *Eretz Yisroel.*

And thus I conclude my painful memories of the "Deportation of the Jews beyond the Dniester … ," which I have been able to preserve at great risk and to bring to a safe shore. If I merit seeing the publication and distribution of these memoirs in the Diaspora of Israel, it will be the happiest day of my life.

Lipman Kunstadt and his granddaughter, Shuli.
Courtesy of the Kunstadt family.

Kunstadt, his daughter, Iza, his granddaughter, Shuli, his sister-in-law, Rachel, and his son-in-law, Jakob Lakner (left to right). Courtesy of the Kunstadt family.

Index